Historical Dictionaries of Literature and the Arts
Jon Woronoff, Series Editor

1. *Science Fiction Literature*, by Brian Stableford, 2004.
2. *Hong Kong Cinema*, by Lisa Odham Stokes, 2007.
3. *American Radio Soap Operas*, by Jim Cox, 2005.
4. *Japanese Traditional Theatre*, by Samuel L. Leiter, 2006.
5. *Fantasy Literature*, by Brian Stableford, 2005.
6. *Australian and New Zealand Cinema*, by Albert Moran and Errol Vieth, 2006.
7. *African-American Television*, by Kathleen Fearn-Banks, 2006.
8. *Lesbian Literature*, by Meredith Miller, 2006.
9. *Scandinavian Literature and Theater*, by Jan Sjåvik, 2006.
10. *British Radio*, by Seán Street, 2006.
11. *German Theater*, by William Grange, 2006.
12. *African American Cinema*, by S. Torriano Berry and Venise Berry, 2006.
13. *Sacred Music*, by Joseph P. Swain, 2006.
14. *Russian Theater*, by Laurence Senelick, 2007.
15. *French Cinema*, by Dayna Oscherwitz and MaryEllen Higgins, 2007.
16. *Postmodernist Literature and Theater*, by Fran Mason, 2007.
17. *Irish Cinema*, by Roderick Flynn and Pat Brereton, 2007.
18. *Australian Radio and Television*, by Albert Moran and Chris Keating, 2007.
19. *Polish Cinema*, by Marek Haltof, 2007.
20. *Old Time Radio*, by Robert C. Reinehr and Jon D. Swartz, 2008.
21. *Renaissance Art*, by Lilian H. Zirpolo, 2008.
22. *Broadway Musical*, by William A. Everett and Paul R. Laird, 2008.
23. *American Theater: Modernism*, by James Fisher and Felicia Hardison Londré, 2008.
24. *German Cinema*, by Robert C. Reimer and Carol J. Reimer, 2008.
25. *Horror Cinema*, by Peter Hutchings, 2008.
26. *Westerns in Cinema*, by Paul Varner, 2008.
27. *Chinese Theater*, by Tan Ye, 2008.
28. *Italian Cinema*, by Gino Moliterno, 2008.

29. *Architecture*, by Allison Lee Palmer, 2008.
30. *Russian and Soviet Cinema*, by Peter Rollberg, 2008.
31. *African American Theater*, by Anthony D. Hill, 2009.
32. *Postwar German Literature*, by William Grange, 2009.
33. *Modern Japanese Literature and Theater*, by J. Scott Miller, 2009.
34. *Animation and Cartoons*, by Nichola Dobson, 2009.
35. *Modern Chinese Literature*, by Li-hua Ying, 2010.

Historical Dictionary of Modern Chinese Literature

Li-hua Ying

Historical Dictionaries of Literature and the Arts,
No. 35

THE SCARECROW PRESS, INC.
Lanham • Toronto • Plymouth, UK
2010

Published by Scarecrow Press, Inc.
A wholly owned subsidiary of The Rowman & Littlefield Publishing Group, Inc.
4501 Forbes Boulevard, Suite 200, Lanham, Maryland 20706
http://www.scarecrowpress.com

Estover Road, Plymouth PL6 7PY, United Kingdom

British Library Cataloguing in Publication Information Available

Library of Congress Cataloging-in-Publication Data

Ying, Li-hua.
   Historical dictionary of modern Chinese literature / Li-hua Ying.
      p. cm. — (Historical dictionaries of literature and the arts ; no. 35)
   Includes bibliographical references.
   ISBN 978-0-8108-5516-8 (cloth : alk. paper) — ISBN 978-0-8108-7081-9 (ebook)
   1. Chinese literature—20th century—Dictionaries—English. 2. Chinese literature—20th century—Bio-bibliography. 3. Authors, Chinese—20th century—Biography—Dictionaries. I. Title.
PL2303.Y59 2010
895.1'09'00503—dc22   2009027237

Printed in the United States of America

Contents

Editor's Foreword   *Jon Woronoff*   vii

Preface   ix

Reader's Notes   xi

Chronology   xiii

Introduction   xxi

THE DICTIONARY   1

Bibliography   295

About the Author   465

Editor's Foreword

Chinese literature is an amazingly hardy breed. During the modern period, roughly since the beginning of the 20th century, it has had to contend with the most adverse conditions: Confucianism, Buddhism, and imperial rule; invasion and occupation by Japan; the long civil war between the Nationalists and the Communists, and then under communism the dictates of Mao Zedong and other leaders; and the rampant materialism of the present day. Yet, in every period, it has found forms of expression and in some cases flourished, leaving an impressive legacy that is still being enriched at present. Alas, while those who know Chinese can enjoy it, this privilege is only gradually being shared with outsiders as more and more works are translated into English and other languages. This is finally encouraging its spread to new readers and new admirers, who are becoming familiar with a plethora of new authors—novelists, essayists, playwrights, and poets—and masses of intriguing works. Yet, this did not emerge from a vacuum, and Chinese literature is much easier to fathom in the context of its historical and literary trends.

Providing this context, and introducing the authors and their works, is the main task of this *Historical Dictionary of Modern Chinese Literature*. It goes about it in several ways. The chronology traces the evolution, one with many twists and turns and only rare straight stretches, which partially account for the variety and diversity. The introduction provides a useful overview, one in which to insert the authors and their works. The dictionary follows on with hundreds of entries on writers, in all possible genres, of all possible proclivities, with varying styles and subject matter. Other entries present the historical and political events that impacted on this literature and the assorted literary currents and trends that shaped it. Since China is a vast country, with a population of over a billion, it is helpful to remember that it consists of regions, some of which have their own traditions, such as Tibet, and also that Chinese writers not only live and create in the People's Republic of China but also the Republic of China

(Taiwan), Hong Kong, and Southeast Asia and, indeed, at present in the United States and other Western countries. Having once discovered how rich this literature is, there will inevitably be many who will want to read the works either in the original or translation and gain further background, which is facilitated by the bibliography.

Given the extensive period, the geographical spread, and the broad range of writers and works, the author of this volume has done an extraordinary job of bringing all the various strands together and providing a comprehensive picture. Li-hua Ying grew up in the People's Republic of China and studied at Yunnan Normal University, where she received a B.A. in English and also briefly taught. Moving to the United States, and not without maintaining her interest in English literature, she has increasingly specialized in Chinese literature. With a foot in each culture, and attuned to the increasing flows between them, she is an excellent guide to the literature of the world's largest cultural community, the rapidly expanding literary output of which is bound to be known and read increasingly in coming years.

Jon Woronoff
Series Editor

Preface

How to define "modern Chinese literature"? The challenge has to do specifically with the terms *modern* and *Chinese*. First of all, when does the modern period begin and end? Second, by "Chinese," does one mean "of China" or "in the Chinese language"? If the scope is limited to 1918 to 1949, then the issue can be settled without much controversy. If the historical line stretches further down, however, the problem becomes potentially divisive. What about Taiwan? What about prehandover Hong Kong? And the Chinese diaspora?

In the process of sorting through nearly a century of literary production, I have decided to adopt a more inclusive, thus more controversial, definition of "modern Chinese literature" in order to take into consideration the complex and diverse paths of its development. In terms of historical framework, I begin with the May Fourth generation and continue to the present. Acknowledging the defining role of the vernacular language, I have chosen to exclude texts written in classical Chinese during the same period. In terms of geographical boundary, I have also opted for a more inclusive line of demarcation. In addition to writers in the People's Republic of China, Taiwan, and Hong Kong, those who have settled in the West but continue to address the topic of, for the lack of a better word, "Chineseness," are considered as part of the modern Chinese literary enterprise. Treating modern Chinese literature as a continuous and borderless entity, this dictionary of *Modern Chinese Literature* thus adopts a liberal usage of the words *Chinese* and *modern* by selecting from writers publishing since the beginning of the 20th century to the present whose language of expression is Chinese. A more accurate but cumbersome title could be "A Dictionary of Modern Chinese (Language) Literature."

I am certainly aware that the inclusion of Taiwanese writers in this dictionary could be a point of contention. My process of selection, however, is guided by considerations of linguistic as well as cultural and literary traditions instead of political concerns. In that sense, this project subscribes to a growing trend that takes a more general view of a literary institution aptly termed *xiandai zhongwen/huawen wenxue* (modern literature written in Chinese), which includes works from not only the PRC, Taiwan, and Hong Kong but also the Chinese diaspora. Needless to say, the scope is enormous, and in some cases the definition of "Chineseness" is hard to pin down. I have chosen, for the sake of convenience, to leave out many authors in Southeast Asia, which has large Chinese communities still creating and reading literature in the Chinese language. For that and many other reasons, this dictionary is by no means comprehensive or definitive. The criteria for selection are admittedly arbitrary and subjective. The writers whose names are precluded are not necessarily deemed less worthy. These absences could only be attributed, in some cases, to the limited knowledge and lapse of judgment on my part, and in others, to the continuously evolving arena of modern Chinese literature.

I want to thank Professor Tan Ye, who got me started on this project. For the readers interested in Chinese theater, Professor Ye's *Historical Dictionary of Chinese Theater*, also published by the Scarecrow Press, is infinitely more informative than the few entries I have devoted to the genre. Finally, the unfailing love and support my husband, Charles Chao, and son, Kyle Chao, have shown me have sustained me throughout the years. To them I owe a debt of gratitude.

Reader's Notes

The Pinyin system is used to transliterate Chinese terms, except for names that are commonly Romanized, therefore, Taipei instead of Taibei, Chiang Kai-shek instead of Chiang Jieshi, Hong Kong not Xianggang. With regard to writers whose names have more than one transliteration, the Pinyin transliteration is the primary form used with the additional transliteration(s) provided in the dictionary as "a.k.a." (also known as) and in the bibliography in the parenthesis immediately following the Pinyin name. For the sake of consistency, Beijing is used instead of Beiping, the official name adopted during the Republican period (1911–1949).

In the Chinese convention, the surname goes before the given name. When the author's name is mentioned for the first time, the full name is used; subsequently, only the surname is given. In the case of pen names, the conventional use of the full name is adopted. Hence, Lu Xun, instead of Lu, is used throughout the entry.

When a title is mentioned for the first time, the Pinyin title goes before the English translation. Subsequent mentions of the same title are in Pinyin alone. Pinyin titles are not capitalized, except for the first letter of the first word and proper names. English translations of Chinese titles are, however, capitalized. Whenever possible, published English titles, shown in italics within parentheses, are used; in the case when no English publication is available, an English translation, not italicized, is provided by the author. When a term has an entry of its own in the dictionary, the term appears in boldface the first time it is mentioned in an entry other than its own. There are a few acronyms and abbreviations used throughout the dictionary; they are listed below with their full names:

CCP: Chinese Communist Party
DPP: Democratic Progressive Party
KMT: Kuomintang (Nationalist Party)
PRC: People's Republic of China
ROC: Republic of China

Chronology

1891 Su Manshu publishes his translation of Lord Byron's poems, *Bailun shi xuan* (Poems by Byron), the first collection of Western poetry in Chinese.

1898 "Lun baihua wei weixin zhi ben" (The Vernacular Language as the Basis for Reforms) by Qiu Tingliang published.

1902 Liang Qichao creates in Japan the first modern Chinese fiction journal *Xin xiaoshuo* (New Fiction).

1906 Chunliu she (Spring Willow Society) established to perform spoken drama.

1911 Qing dynasty toppled. Republic of China founded.

1914 *Libailiu* (Saturday) created to publish mainly works by authors of the Mandarin Ducks and Butterflies school. *Wan'ou zhi jia*, Chinese translation of Henrik Ibsen's *A Doll's House,* premieres in Shanghai.

1915 *Xin qingnian* (New Youth) founded to promote *xin wenxue* (new literature) and progressive ideas; its first issue is edited by Chen Duxiu, a cofounder of the Chinese Communist Party.

1916 Chinese National Language Research Association founded.

1917 *Xin qingnian* publishes Hu Shi's article "Wenxue gailiang chu yi" (Preliminary Opinion on Literary Reform) and Chen Duxiu's article "Wenxue geming lun" (On Literary Revolution), formally sounding the call for a new, revolutionary literature. Poems written in *bai hua* (vernacular Chinese) by Hu Shi also published.

1918 The first Romanized phonetic system introduced. *Xin qingnian* publishes Lu Xun's short story "Kuangren riji" (*Diary of a Mad Man*), vernacular poems by Hu Shi, Liu Bannong, and others, translations of

Ibsen's plays, and Zhou Zuoren's article "Ren de wenxue" (A Literature for Humanity).

1919 May Fourth Movement erupts.

1920 Hu Shi's poetry collection *Changshi ji* (Experiments) and Guo Moruo's poem "Fenghuang niepan" (The Phoenix Rising from the Ashes) published.

1921 Wenxue yanjiu hui (Literary Society), Chuangzao she (Creation Society), Minzhong xiju she (Society of People's Theater), Shanghai Xiju xie she (Shanghai Theater Association), and the Chinese Communist Party founded. The first issue of *Xiju* (Theater Weekly) published. Yu Dafu's *Chenlun* (Sinking), the first collection of short stories in modern Chinese literature, and Guo Moruo's poems *Shen nü* published.

1922 Hupan shi she (Lakeside Poetry Society) founded.

1923 Xin yue shi she (Crescent Society) and *Xin yue* (Crescent Monthly) founded. Lu Xun's short story collection *Nahan* (Call to Arms) and Wen Yiduo's poetry collection *Hong zhu* (Red Candle) published.

1924 Yu si she (Language Society) and *Yu si* (Language Weekly) founded. Zhu Ziqing's collection of essays and poems *Zongji* (Traces) and Tian Han's collection of plays *Kafei dian zhi yi ye* (One Night at a Café) published.

1925 Cheng Fangwu's article "Cong wenxue geming dao geming wenxue" (From Literary Revolution to Revolutionary Literature) published, triggering the debate between Lu Xun and the Creation Society on the nature and direction of literature. *Zhimo de shi* (Collection of Poems by Zhimo) published.

1926 *Chuangzao yuekan* (Creation Monthly) founded; Lu Xun's short story collection *Panghuang* (Wandering), Lao She's novel *Lao Zhang de zhexue* (Mr. Zhang's Philosophy), and Bing Xin's collection of essays *Ji xiao duzhe* (To Young Readers) published.

1927 Xu Zhimo's poetry collection *Feilengcui de yi ye* (One Night in Florence) published.

1928 *Xiandai xiaoshuo* (Modern Fiction Monthly) created. Ding Ling's short story "Shafei nüshi de riji" (Miss Sophie's Diary), Ye Shengtao's novel *Ni Huanzhi* (Ni Huanzhi the Schoolteacher), Wen Yiduo's poetry collection *Si shui* (Dead Water), and Fei Ming's collection of stories *Tao yuan* (Peach Orchard) published.

1929   Mao Dun's novel *Hong* (Rainbow) and Tian Han's play *Ming you zhi si* (The Death of a Famous Actress) published.

1930   Zhongguo zuoyi zuojia lianmeng (Left-wing Association of Chinese Writers), Zhongguo zuoyi xijujia lianmeng (Left-wing Association of Chinese Dramatists), and Shidai xiju she (Modern Drama Society) founded. Literary journal *Mengya* (Sprouts) created.

1931   Japan invades China's northeast. Xu Zhimo dies in a plane crash.

1932   Fei Ming's *Moxuyou Xiansheng zhuan* (Biography of Mr. Nothing) published.

1933   Mao Dun's novel *Ziye* (Midnight), Ba Jin's novel *Jia* (Family), Shi Zhecun's short story collection *Meiyu zhi xi* (One Rainy Evening) and *Wangshu cao* (Writings of Wangshu) published. George Bernard Shaw visits China.

1934   Taiwan Wenyi Lianmeng (The Literary and Art Alliance of Taiwan) founded. Cao Yu's play *Leiyu* (Thunderstorm) and Shen Congwen's *Biancheng* (Border Town) published.

1935   Xiao Hong's novella "Shengsi chang" (Life and Death), Xiao Jun's novel *Bayue de xiangcun* (Village in August) published.

1936   Lu Xun dies. Left-Wing Association of Chinese Writers disbanded. Lao She's *Luotuo xiangzi* (The Rickshaw Boy), Ai Qing's poetry *Dayanhe—Wode baomu* (Dayan River—My Wet-nurse), and Shi Zhecun's short story collection *Meiyu zhi xi* (One Rainy Evening) published.

1937   Sino-Japanese War breaks out. Li Jieren's novel *Si shui wei lan* (Ripples across a Stagnant Water) published.

1941   Japan occupies Shanghai.

1942   Mao Zedong delivers his speeches at the Yan'an Forum on Literature and Art. Feng Zhi's *Shisi hang ji* (The Sonnets) published.

1943   Zhang Ailing's stories "Qing cheng zhi lian" (Love in a Fallen City) and "Jin suo" (The Golden Cangue), and Zhao Shuli's novella "Li Youcai banhua" (Li Youcai's Rhymed Ballads) published.

1945 Japan surrenders. Civil war breaks out between the Communists and the Nationalists.

1946 Wen Yiduo assassinated.

1947 Chinese Writers' Association founded in Beijing. February 28 Incident takes place in Taiwan, pitting the Nationalist government against the Taiwanese protestors. Qian Zhongshu's *Wei cheng* (*Fortress Besieged*) published.

1949 The Nationalist government withdraws to Taiwan. The People's Republic of China (PRC) established. Liang Shiqiu's collection of essays *Yashe xiaopin* (Sketches from a Refined Cottage) published.

1951 Ding Ling's novel *Taiyang zhao zai Sanggan He shang* (The Sun Shines Over the Sanggan River) and Sun Li's novel *Fengyun jishi* (Stormy Years) published.

1952 Ding Ling's novel *Taiyang zhao zai Sanggan He shang* and Zhou Libo's novel *Baofeng zhouyu* (The Storm) win the Stalin Literature Prize.

1953 *Xiandai shi* (Modern Poetry) founded in Taiwan.

1954 Yuan Guangzhong's *Lanse de yumao* (Blue Feathers) published.

1956 Shu Xiangcheng's novel *Wu Xianggang* (Misty Hong Kong) published.

1957 Anti-Rightist Campaign launched.

1958 Great Leap Forward launched. Lao She's play *Cha guan* (Teahouse) published.

1960 *Xiandai wenxue* (Modern Literature) founded at National Taiwan University. Lin Haiyin's memoir *Cheng nan jiu shi* (Memories of Peking: Southside Stories) published.

1965 Hao Ran's novel *Yanyang tian* (Bright Clouds) published.

1966 Cultural Revolution launched. Lao She commits suicide.

1969 Huang Chunming's *Erzi de da wan'ou* (His Son's Big Doll) published.

1971 Bai Xianyong's short story collection *Taipei ren* (Taipei Characters) published.

1975 Chiang Kai-shek dies.

1976 Mao Zedong dies. Chen Ruoxi's *Yin xianzhang* (The Execution of Mayor Yin) published.

1977 Xiangtu wenxue lunzhan (Debates on Nativist Literature) is held between the nativists and the modernists. Cultural Revolution officially ends. College entrance exams resumed in the PRC.

1978 Lu Xinhua's short story "Shangheng" (Scars) published, launching the trend of "scar literature." Poetry journal *Jintian* (Today), the main platform for *Menglong shi* (Misty poetry), founded. Deng Xiaoping consolidates his power in the Chinese Communist Party and the Deng era begins with economic reforms under way. *Yang Mu shi ji* (Poems by Yang Mu) published in Taiwan and *Lei sheng yu chan ming* (Thunder and Songs of Cicadas: Poems by Liang Bingjun) published in Hong Kong.

1979 Democracy Wall Movement erupts. Wang Wenxing's novel *Jia bian* (Family Catastrophe) published. Liu Xingwu's *Banzhuren* (The Class Counsellor) and Gao Xiaosheng's *Li Shunda zaowu* (Li Shunda Builds a House) published.

1980 Shanghai Literature and Art Press publishes *Waiguo xiandai pai zuopin xuan* (Selected Works of Western Modernism) edited by Yuan Kejia. Yao Xueyin, Gu Hua, and others win the Mao Dun Literature Prize.

1981 Mao Dun dies. Mao Dun Literature Prize established to give awards every four years to novelists. Gao Xingjian's *Xiandai xiaoshuo jiqiao chutan* (A Preliminary Study of Modern Fiction Techniques) published. Wang Wenxing's modernist novel *Bei hai de ren* (Backed against the Sea) published.

1982 *Wang Zengqi duanpian xiaoshuo xuan* (Selected Short Stories by Wang Zengqi) published.

1983 Antispiritual Pollution Campaign launched in the PRC. Bai Xianyong's novel *Niezi* (Crystal Boys), the first novel on the subject of homosexuality by a modern Chinese writer, published. Li Ang's feminist novel *Sha fu: Lucheng gushi* (The Butcher's Wife) published. Gao Xingjian's play *Che zhan* (Bus Stop) premiers in Beijing.

1984 Conference on "cultural root-seeking" held in Hangzhou. Ah Cheng's novella "Qi wang" (The King of Chess), a representative work in the root-seeking movement, and Wang Meng's *Dan huise de yanzhu—zai Yili* (Light Grey Eyes—in Yili) published. Wang Zhenhe's novel *Meigui meigui wo ai ni* (Rose, Rose I Love You) published.

1985 Zhang Jie, Liu Xinwu, and others win the Mao Dun Literature Prize. Han Shaogong's "Wenxue de gen" (The Roots of Literature) and Deng Youmei's *Yanhu* (Snuff Bottles), two important works of the root-seeking movement, and Ma Yuan's "Gangdisi de youhuo" (Under the Spell of the Gangtise Mountains), an influential experimental story based on Tibet, published.

1986 Ding Ling dies. Taiwan's Lianhe wenxue xiaoshuo xin ren jiang (Unitas New Fiction Writers Prize) established. Zhongguo xiandan shi qunti da zhan (The Grand Showcase of Chinese Modern Poetry Movements) is organized by Xu Jingya and Jiang Weiyang, providing a platform to display works of Generation III poets. The official Chinese Writers' Association creates the Lu Xun Literature Prize to award excellence in short story, novella, reportage, poetry, prose, literary theory and criticism, and translation. Gu Cheng's poem collection *Hei yanjin* (Eyes of Darkness) published.

1987 Taiwan's martial law lifted. Liang Shiqiu dies in Taiwan. Ye Weilian's *Sanshi nian shi* (Poems Written in Thirty Years) published.

1988 Chiang Ching-kuo dies. Shen Congwen dies. Lu Yao, Huo Da, and others win the Mao Dun Literature Prize. Chen Yingzhen's *Wo de didi Kangxiong* (My Younger Brother Kangxiong) and Lin Yaode's *E dixing* (The Ugly Land) published. Su Tong's *Yijiusansinian de taowang* (The Escapes in 1934) published.

1989 Tian'anmen Prodemocracy Movement erupts. *Dialogues in Paradise*, a translation of Can Xue's short stories, published.

1990 Gao Xingjian's novel *Ling shan* (Soul Mountain) published.

1991 Eryue He's *Yongzheng Huangdi* (Emperor Yongzheng) published.

1992 Wang Xiaobo's *Huangjin shidai* (The Gold Times) published in Taiwan.

1993 Poet Gu Cheng commits suicide. Jia Pingwa's controversial novel *Fei du* (The Capital City in Ruins) and Chen Zhongshi's *Bai lu yuan* (The White Deer Plain) published. *Red Sorghum*, a translation of Mo Yan's novel *Hong Gaoliang*, and *Backed against the Sea*, a translation of Wang Wenxing's *Bei hai de ren*, published.

1994   Chen Zhongshi and others win the Mao Dun Literature Prize. Zhu Tianwen wins the Shibao Literature One Million (New Taiwan) Dollar Prize with *Huang ren shouji* (Notes of a Desolate Man).

1995   Zhang Ailing dies. Museum of Modern Chinese Literature established in Beijing.

1996   Xi Xi's *Fei zhan* (Flying Carpet: A Tale of Fertilla) published.

1997   Hong Kong handed over to China.

1998   Zhang Guixing wins the Shibao Literature One Million (New Taiwan) Dollar Prize. Chi Zijian, Liu Heng, Xu Xiaobin, Li Guowen, Tie Ning, and others win the Lu Xun Literature Prize.

1999   *Asia Weekly* (Hong Kong) names 100 Best Chinese Fictional Works in the 20th Century, judged by specialists from mainland China, Taiwan, Hong Kong, Malaysia, and the United States. *Mengya* (Sprouts), a literary journal based in Shanghai, establishes New Concept Composition Contest to identify and promote young writers.

2000   Gao Xingjian awarded the Nobel Prize for Literature. Wang Anyi, Wang Xufeng, and Ah Lai win the Mao Dun Literature Prize. Zhang Guixing's *Hou bei* (The Primate Cup) published. *Notes of a Desolate Man*, a translation of Zhu Tianwen's *Huang ren shouji*, published.

2001   Hua zong shijie Huawen wenxue jiang (Flower Trail World Chinese Language Literature Prize), established in Malaysia, names Wang Anyi the recipient of its first prize.

2002   Yang Lian's long poem *YI* [Yi] published. *Red Poppies*, a translation of Ah Lai's 1998 novel *Chen'ai luoding*, published.

2003   Chen Yingzhen wins the Flower Trail World Chinese Language Literature Prize. *A Dictionary of Maqiao*, a translation of Han Shaogong's 1996 *Maqiao cidian*, and *Retribution: The Jiling Chronicles*, a translation of Li Yongping's 1986 novel *Jilin chunqiu*, published.

2004   Fan Wen's novel *Shui ru dadi* (Land of Harmony) and Yu Jian's *Ling dang'an: changshi qi bu yu biantiao ji* (File 0: Seven Long Poems and Notes) published.

2005   Ba Jin dies. Zhang Jie, Zong Pu, and others win the Mao Dun Literature Prize. Bi Feiyu, Wang Anyi, Jia Pingwa, Shi Tiesheng, and others win the Lu Xun Literature Prize. *A Private Life*, a translation of Chen Ran's 1996 novel *Siren shenghuo*, published.

2006   Tie Ning elected president of the Chinese Writers' Association, the first woman to hold that position. *The Chinese Poetry of Bei Dao, 1978–2000: Resistance and Exile* published.

2007   *My South Seas Sleeping Beauty: A Tale of Memory and Longing*, a translation of Zhang Guixing's *Wo sinian de chang mian zhong de nan guo gongzhu*; *The Old Capital: A Novel of Taipei*, a translation of Zhu Tienxin's story collection *Gu Du*; and *Cries in the Drizzle*, a translation of Yu Hua's novel *Zai xiyu zhong huhuan*, published.

2008   Chi Zijian, Yu Jian, Han Shaogong, and others win the Mao Dun Literature Prize. *The Song of Everlasting Sorrow: A Novel of Shanghai*, a translation of Wang Anyi's 1999 novel *Changhen ge*, published.

2009   Liang Yusheng dies. Zhang Ailing's novel *Xiao tuanyuan* (A Small Reunion) published.

Introduction

Modern Chinese literature has been flourishing for over a century, with varying degrees of intensity and energy at different junctures of history and points of locale. It is solidly an integral part of world literature, for from the moment it was born, it has been in dialogue with its counterparts from the rest of the world. As it has been challenged and enriched by external influences, it has contributed to the wealth of literary culture of the world. Gone are the days when a Western reader picked up a book of modern Chinese literature for nonliterary reasons and when Chinese novels or poems were treated as sociopolitical documents. Nowadays, it is more likely that readers appreciate a Chinese novel because it is a great piece of art, not simply because it provides knowledge and information about Chinese society and politics. Indeed, the best literature written in Chinese is on a par with the best literature written in any other language; this has been especially true during the past three decades, which have given us some internationally recognized names, even a Nobel laureate. In terms of themes and styles, modern Chinese literature is rich and varied: from the revolutionary to the pastoral, from romanticism to feminism, from modernism to postmodernism, critical realism, psychological realism, socialist realism, and magic realism, you name it. Indeed, it encompasses a full range of ideological and aesthetic concerns.

In some ways, what gives modern Chinese literature its vibrant diversity is its geographic range. Here the term *Chinese literature* should not be mistaken for "literature of China"—although the People's Republic of China (PRC) itself is already a mind-boggling size—for its creators and readers are widely spread all over the globe. It is not an exaggeration to say that where there are Chinese communities, there is Chinese literature being read and written. Beyond the borders of China, Taiwan, and Hong Kong, there is a whole population of Chinese writers scattered throughout Southeast Asia, Europe, and North America who are connected in their love of the Chinese language as the medium of artistic expression. This is the landscape of Chinese literature today.

In the study of Chinese history, modern China is generally divided into three periods: *jindai* (the recent era), 1840–1911; *xiandai* (the modern era), 1911–1949; and *dangdai* (the present era), 1949 to the present. The curtains of the jindai era were forced open by guns and cannons of Western forces in the mid-19th century. During the next six decades, the Qing dynasty (1644–1911) lost the Opium Wars to Great Britain, its navy was soundly defeated by Japan, and its territories were ceded to the Europeans, Russians, and Japanese. Although the Republican Revolution led by Sun Yat-sen succeeded in overthrowing the feeble and corrupt Qing empire and established the Republic of China in 1911, civil wars put the young republic in grave danger and the country continued to be dominated by foreign powers. Popular discontent reached a boiling point in 1919, when the Versailles Conference transferred the German concessions in Shandong to Japan, instead of returning them to Chinese sovereignty, causing widespread protests that later developed into a full-blown cultural crusade known as the May Fourth Movement. A nationwide soul-searching ensued, led by progressive intellectuals who blamed China's weakened state on its fundamental cultural institutions that in their view had become obsolete and incapable of dealing with the modern world. For the survival of the Chinese nation, they argued, Western ideas and practices, including literature, had to be imported. In this Westward-looking environment, science and democracy became coded terms that represented modernity, progress, and hope for a national salvation.

Prior to the 1980s, most literary scholars tended to adopt the same categories established by historians and saw the May Fourth Movement, which dominated Chinese intellectual discourse in the 20th century, as the force behind the emergence and development of China's literary revolution. The term widely used to describe the literature born out the May Fourth Movement is *xin wenxue* (new literature). Wang Yao in his *Zhongguo xin wenxue shi gao* (A History of Chinese New Literature) emphasized the umbilical relationship between the new literature and the May Fourth Movement and puts "anti-imperialism" and "anti-feudalism" at the forefront of not only the political and cultural but also the literary agenda.[1] Agreeing with Wang, Qian Liqun, Tang Tao, and Yan Jiayan also regarded 1949, when the PRC was established as a watershed, but they preferred the more evocative term *xiandai wenxue* (modern literature).[2] Most scholars in Taiwan, however, do not see 1949 as such a defining moment. Zhou Jin, in his book *Zhongguo xin wenxue jian shi* (A Brief History of Chinese New Literature), which was published in 1980, used the term *xin wenxue* but expanded it to cover works written in the 1970s by writers in Taiwan and Hong Kong.[3] In the mainland, the term *dangdai wenxue* was used widely in the period since 1949. To account for the new trends of literary creativity since the late 1970s made possible by Deng Xiaoping's reform policies, another category *xin shiqi wenxue* (literature of the new era) has also been widely circulated.

Since the 1980s, however, various attempts have been made to bypass these fragmenting periodizations. Huang Xiuji and his colleagues chose a calendarian term that not only expands the historical but also the geographical scope to include literature published outside the mainland.[4] Following a similar model, Chen Liao and Cao Huimin take one step further to argue that the inception of modern Chinese literature should be traced to the end of the 19th century.[5] They consider the publication of an article by Qiu Tingliang (1857–1943) in 1898 a seminal event. Qiu's article, entitled "lun baihua wei weixin zhi ben" (The Vernacular Language as the Basis of the Reform Movement), called for a radical change in the use of language, a proposal echoed by social reform advocates such as Liang Qichao (1873–1929), who promoted the genre of fiction, elevating its status to that of poetry and prose, the privileged forms in classical Chinese literary tradition, and Huang Zunxian (1848–1905), who campaigned for a new kind of poetry that favored *wo shou xie wo kou* (direct expression). Chen and Cao contend that the work of these forerunners who had pushed for a new kind of language and literature eventually led to the full-blown literary revolution resulting in the publications in 1918 of the first significant modern Chinese short story "Kuangren riji" (*Diary of a Mad Man*) by Lu Xun, and vernacular poems by Hu Shi, Liu Bannong, and others, ushering in a new era of cultural and literary reform. Helping to shift the attention from political and social factors to the intrinsic nature of literature are Rene Welleck and Austin Warren, whose work *A Theory of Literature* has influenced the thinking of many Chinese literary historians.[6] As early as 1985, Chen Sihe called for a redirection in the study of the history of modern Chinese literature,[7] setting off a new round of debates in Chinese scholarly circles. Conceptualized in such a framework, the term *xiandai wenxue* has found traction, pushing out *xin wenxue* and *dangdai wenxue*.

Outside the Chinese-speaking world, the term *modern* has been used widely and loosely. C. T. Hsia, in his groundbreaking book published in

1971, *A History of Modern Chinese Fiction*, examines works from 1917 to 1957 and in the epilogue deals with works that were published through the 1970s.[8] The English anthology edited by Joseph S. M. Lau and Howard Goldblatt published in 1995 defines *modern* as 1919 to the end of the 20th century.[9] Relatively removed from the China-centric view held by most literary historians in China, scholars outside the mainland tend to regard the production of Chinese literature as a global affair that resulted from migration and immigration. Recent years have seen major efforts to rewrite the history of modern Chinese literature to take into account authors in the Chinese diaspora beyond the three major regions of China, Taiwan, and Hong Kong. Leading the group that attempts to grapple with the complexity of the field are Dominic Cheung, David Der-wei Wang, and Shu-mei Shih, who have proposed, each with his or her own emphasis, a new conceptualizing framework and terminology: *Huawen wenxue* (Chinese-language literature) or Sinophone literature.[10]

Regardless of the differences in opinion held by literary scholars, all agree that modern Chinese literature emerged in the midst of grave anxieties as a result of China's encounters with the West, whose advanced technology and superior weaponry forced Chinese intellectuals to reflect on their own venerated traditions, both social and literary, and to seek changes that would meet the needs of a new society. In this campaign for comprehensive social transformation, literature was at the forefront. Modern Chinese writers abandoned *wen yan* (literary Chinese), the lingua franca of Chinese writing, and replaced it with *bai hua* (vernacular Chinese) as the language of both prose and poetry. Free verse instead of regulated verse was the preferred form; an interest in critical realism gave modern fiction writing its new style and subject matter that was firmly rooted in the present; and *hua ju* (spoken drama) made its debut, carving an important niche in the Chinese theater traditionally monopolized by the operatic variety.

As educated Chinese wrestled with problems concerning social, political, linguistic, and literary reforms, the introduction of Western literature into the intellectual and popular discourses played a crucial role in fundamentally changing the direction of modern Chinese literary development. Translations of Western writings, including philosophical, scientific, and literary texts, influenced a whole generation of Chinese writers, giving rise to a new literature characterized by its use of the vernacular language as the medium of expression and its humanistic focus on contemporary social issues. Painfully aware of China's reduced status, the May Fourth intellectuals located the roots of their country's plight in the Chinese traditions, particularly Confucianism, which, in their view, had run its course and become a repressive yoke to the nation, preventing it from competing in the modern world. The bankruptcy of traditional values thus created a vacuum, making Western concepts of individualism and personal emancipation a welcome replacement in a culture eager to shed the burdens of its own past. With its devotion to the cause of national salvation, Chinese literature during the first half of the 20th century actively engaged itself with various social and political causes, as China underwent devastating turmoil, including civil wars and the Japanese invasion. While critical realism, which was perceived as best equipped to address contemporary sociopolitical problems, dominated the field, other trends also prevailed. Shen Congwen's pastoral representations of his hometown, a natural society indifferent to moralistic restrictions of Confucian ethics and modern urban materialism, Zhang Ailing's stylized prose that probes the dark side of the human psyche, Shi Zhecun's introspective narratives, Li Jinfa's symbolist poems, and Zhang Henshui's romantic novels coexisted with mainstream writings by Lu Xun, Mao Dun, Ba Jin, and a cohort of socially conscious writers.

In 1949, when the Nationalist government retreated to Taiwan and the mainland was taken over by the Communists, the May Fourth literary tradition branched off in several directions. Although Taiwan under Japanese occupation had seen some Chinese literary activities, it was the arrival of the Nationalist government that turned the island into a bastion and center of Chinese literary creation. With its close ties to the West, the government tolerated a certain degree of creative latitude, provided that writers stayed within the boundary of aesthetics. In this environment, the modernist movement that had flowered on the mainland from the 1920s to the early 1940s was resuscitated in Taiwan. Acting as a link between the two eras were veteran poets such as Ji Xian, a passionate proponent of modern poetry in the mainland, who became a principal player in modernizing the field of poetry making in Taiwan. Pumping new blood into the modernist movement was a younger generation of writers associated with the literary journal *Xiandai wenxue* (Modern Literature), which Bai Xianyong and his friends founded in 1960 on the campus of National Taiwan University. Challenging this Western-inspired trend, the *xiangtu* (nativist) literature, which rose from the south of the island, insisted on local experience and the realist mode of expression.

Hong Kong, with its unique geopolitical position and the sudden influx of talents fleeing Communist China, developed its own brand of literature that reflects the realities of the British colony. Representing the continued experiment with Western modernism was Liu Yichang, who drew on the stream of consciousness technique to bring to life the sense of rootlessness and uncertainty in a city living on borrowed time. At the other end of the spectrum, popular forms of literature thrived; prominent among them were the martial arts novels of Liang Yusheng and Jin Yong, and Ni Kuang's science fiction, which met the needs of readers looking for escape from the pressures of life in a fast-paced modern city. Meanwhile, in the PRC, a monolithic literary establishment pursued its strictly ideological agendas, suppressing creative autonomy in favor of propagandist literature. From 1949 to the end of 1970s, the best of literature written in Chinese came out of Taiwan and Hong Kong, providing a critical link in the chain of modern Chinese literary development since the May Fourth Movement.

As China began its economic reform in the late 1970s, the government's political grip on literature loosened and along with it came the dramatic decline of the influence wielded by Maoist doctrinarians. Closely behind the opening of national borders followed what has been called "the second surge" of importing of Western literature. Chinese writers showed an intense curiosity about authors from the West, as well as those from Latin America, Hong Kong, and Taiwan. A great variety of literary trends, from symbolism to postmodernism, was enthusiastically embraced and appropriated by Chinese writers, resulting in an output impressive both in quantity and quality. A burst of radical experiments with language, narrative techniques, themes, and subject matters were met with great interest. What united this polyphony of voices was a commitment to the sanctity of art, a fundamental departure from the Maoist era. In Taiwan, after the modernist and nativist influences declined in the wake of three decades of remarkable innovation, the literary scene began to diversify in the 1980s. While the more radical faction of the early realist nativist movement turned to a militant nationalist platform, a new generation, well educated and well read, rose to address contemporary Taiwan issues while tapping into the rich resources of Chinese culture. Latin American magic realism, which was received with great enthusiasm in the PRC, was also appropriated by Taiwan and Hong Kong writers. Since the 1990s, a flurry of literary and cultural trends, including postmodernism, neofeminism, and pop culture, have taken root in the postindustrialized societies of Taiwan and Hong Kong. In the PRC, the crackdown on the Tian'anmen Prodemocracy Movement (1989) forced a number of writers abroad as the government tightened its control of literary production. The life in exile, with its attached freedom and anxiety, has provided a new source and venue for their work, and more important, their presence in the West has strengthened a Chinese diasporic literature already star-studded with such prominent names as Bai Xianyong, Yu Lihua, Nie Hualing, and Yang Mu, who had emigrated from Taiwan in the 1970s. As a result, Chinese literary production and readership are more than ever pluralistic and global.

Looking back on the development of nearly a century of literary history, one is struck by the degree of relevancy the past still holds for the present. The critical realist tradition established by writers such as Lu Xun and Mao Dun finds its voice in the works of Han Shaogong, Yu Hua, and others. The spirit of experimentalism in the poems of modernist Li Jinfa is embraced by not only the Misty poets such as Bei Dao and Yang Lian but also the fourth generation poets, including Zhang Zao and Zang Di. The romantic sentimentalism of Xu Zhimo and Dai Wangshu has its followers, such as the tragic poets Gu Cheng and Hai Zi. The rural landscape explored by Shen Congwen is revisited in the nativist movement in Taiwan and the pervasive root-seeking movement in the PRC. Zhang Ailing, who now enjoys the status of a literary icon, has many progenies in Taiwan, Hong Kong, and the PRC, while the Mandarin Ducks and Butterflies school has its reincarnations in popular urban literature. What has come and gone is the brand of revolutionary literature that emphasizes the utilitarian role of literature for ideological purposes.

Like the economy, the literary publishing and marketing industry in the 21st century is increasingly globalized. A book by a Chinese writer residing in London can be simultaneously published in the PRC, Hong Kong, Taiwan, and Canada and marketed worldwide. A politically sensitive work written by a mainlander may not be printed in the PRC but should have no trouble getting the attention of a publisher in Taiwan and eventually finding its way to the shelf of a mainland reader. This fluidity of literary and cultural transmission has given writers an unprecedented opportunity and challenge to be truly innovative, resulting in an impressive and diverse output. What originally grew out of a reaction to Western domination a century ago has proven itself to be capable of holding on to its rich cultural heritage while transcending national and ideological boundaries in search of universal truths about the human condition.

NOTES

1. Wang Yao. *Zhongguo xin wenxue shi gao* (A History of Chinese New Literature). Vol. I: Beijing: Kaiming, 1951; Vol. II: Beijing: Xin wenyi, 1958.
2. Qian Liqun et al. *Zhongguo xiandai wenxue sanshi nian* (Thirty Years of Modern Chinese Literature). Beijing: Beijing daxue, 1998; Tang Tao and Yan Jiayan. *Zhongguo xiandai wenxue shi* (A History of Modern Chinese Literature). 3 vols. Beijing: Renmin wenxue, 1979–1980.
3. Zhou Jin. *Zhongguo xin wenxue jian shi* (A Brief History of Chinese New Literature). Taipei: Chengwen, 1980.
4. Huang Xiuji et al. *Ershi shiji Zhongguo wenxue shi* (A History of Twentieth-Century Chinese Literature). Guangzhou: Zhongshan daxue, 1998.
5. Chen Liao and Cao Huimin, eds. *Bai nian Zhonghua wenxue shi lun* (History of Chinese Literature 1898–1999). Shanghai: Huadong shifan daxue, 1999.
6. Rene Welleck and Austin Warren. *A Theory of Literature.* New York: Harcourt, Brace and Company, 1949; *Wenxue lilun*, trs., Liu Xiangyu et al. Beijing: Sanlian shudian, 1984.
7. Chen Sihe. "Xin wenxue shi yanjiu zhong de zhengti guan" (A Comprehensive View in the Study of the History of New Literature). *Fudan xue bao* (Fudan University Journal) 3 (1985).
8. C. T. Hsia. *History of Modern Chinese Fiction.* New Haven: Yale University Press, 1971.
9. Joseph S. M. Lau and Howard Goldblatt, eds. *The Columbia Anthology of Modern Chinese Literature.* New York: Columbia University Press, 1995.
10. Dominic Cheung, "Lisan yu chonghe: huawen wenxue neihan tansuo—jianlun Chen Yingzhen, Zhu Tianxin de 'lihe' zhuti" (Dispersing and Superposition: the Meaning of Sinophone Literature—A Study of the Theme of "Separation and Reunion" in the Works of Chen Yinzhen and Zhu Tianxin). *Sixiang wenzong* 9: 18–25; David Der-wei Wang, "Huayu yuxi wenxue: bianjie xiangxiang yu yuejie jiangou" (Chinese-Language Literature: Imaginary Border and Cross-Border Construct). *Zhongshan daxue xuebao* 5 (2006); Shu-mei Shih, *Visuality and Identity: Sinophone Articulations across the Pacific.* Berkeley: University of California Press, 2007.

The Dictionary

– A –

AH CHENG, PEN NAME OF ZHONG ACHENG (1949–). Fiction writer, essayist, and painter. Born and raised in Beijing, Ah Cheng worked on farms in Inner Mongolia and Yunnan during the **Cultural Revolution**. Soon after returning to Beijing in the late 1970s, he gained recognition for his paintings and writings. In the mid-1980s, he was a prominent member in the **root-seeking** movement, which represents a concerted effort of young writers to rediscover their cultural roots, which were destroyed in the calamities of the previous two decades.

"Qi wang" (*King of Chess*), his first and best fictional work, is set in the 1970s on a remote farm in Yunnan and based on the life of a group of educated youth. The protagonist is a young man obsessed with food and chess, the former to satisfy his physical needs and the latter to nourish his spirituality. Following the success of "Qi wang," Ah Cheng wrote "Shu wang" (King of Trees) about one man's futile effort during the Cultural Revolution to stop deforestation and "Haizi wang" (King of Children), the story of a devoted and unconventional village teacher. Notable in these stories is Ah Cheng's use of the Chinese language. He appropriates classical Chinese, particularly its terse and compact structure and its elegance, features that are markedly different from the verbiage and political mumbo jumbo of the Mao era. Equally noteworthy is the prevailing presence of traditional values in the stories, particularly those of Daoism and Buddhism.

AH LAI, A.K.A. ALAI (1959–). Poet, fiction and prose writer. "I'm **Tibetan** and I write in Chinese," Ah Lai thus describes himself. He was born in Aba Tibetan and Qiang Autonomous Prefecture in northwestern Sichuan. The Gyarong Tibetans in Aba are a linguistically distinct people who maintain their uniqueness while sharing an ethnic and cultural identity with Tibetans of Kham, Amdo, and U-Tsang. Due to their geographic location and agrarian lifestyle, the Gyarong Tibetans who live in a region situated at the crossroads between the Chinese and Tibetan spheres of influences are arguably the most sinicized Tibetans. Ah Lai learned Chinese at school while speaking the Gyarong dialect in his home village. He graduated from a teachers' training college and taught in a rural school for five years before his publications landed him a job at the Aba Cultural Bureau as an editor for a local literary journal. He later moved to Chengdu, the provincial capital of Sichuan, to edit a science fiction journal.

Ah Lai began his literary career writing poetry, later collected in *Lengmo he* (The Lengmo River), but it is his fiction that earned him his fame. His first and most famous novel, *Chen'ai luoding* (*Red Poppies*), a winner of the prestigious Mao Dun Literature Prize, tells an apocalyptic tale about the final years in the history of the Gyarong-Tibetan chieftain system, covering the period from the end of the 19th century to the mid-20th century. Told by a chieftain's mentally retarded son—a man with supernatural foresights who has witnessed the rise and fall of his family and other chieftains—the novel opens a window to a geographically isolated area whose traditional way of life and sociopolitical system were affected by the outside world as China moved into the turbulent 20th century. The novel unfolds a rich tapestry of conspiracies, shifting loyalty, revenge, and romances.

Following the success of *Chen'ai luoding*, Ah Lai published *Kong shan 1* (The Empty Mountain, Part 1), the first of a trilogy about a small Tibetan village named Jicun. *Kong shan 1* consists of two novellas: "Suifeng piaosan" (Gone with the Wind), a tragic tale about the friendship between two boys, and "Tian huo" (A Natural Fire), which tells how political and human intervention causes an environmental disaster. *Kong shan 2* (The Empty Mountain, Part 2) consists of "Dase yu Dage" (Taser and Tager), a sad story about hunters when hunting ceases to be a way of life, and "Huangwu" (Desolation) focusing on a Chinese peasant living among Tibetans. With the Kong shan series, Ah Lai attempts to break away from the linear storytelling used in his earlier novel and chooses instead to write a trilogy composed of six independent novellas, each with its own protagonists who may appear in the other segments but only as peripheral characters. This decentered, fragmented structure, according to Ah Lai, reflects the realities of village life in modern times. As an offshoot of nearby towns, which are symbols of the state and modernity, the village, in Ah Lai's view, plays no role in choosing its part in the grand national mission. Unlike the countryside in the heroic narratives of **socialist realism** by such writers as **Ding Ling, Zhou Libo,** and **Hao Ran,** the center stage of Ah Lai's Jicun is not occupied by a hero tied with the state in one single ideological vision, but rather by a multitude of small characters, each operating from his or her own center and taking turns to command attention. The realities of such rural life are formed by these little "centers," acting like the small pieces in a jigsaw puzzle. Ah Lai structures his three *Kong shan* novels in such a fashion to reflect the lost or fast disappearing cultures of a mountain village.

Ah Lai's other works include *Aba Ah Lai* (Aba and Ah Lai), a collection of short stories and prose work written in the 1980s and 1990s about his hometown and his own spiritual odyssey, mingling Tibetan folklore with real-life stories, and *Dadi de jieti* (The Earth's Staircase), a travelogue that documents the author's journey across his native land and contemplates the spirit of the people as outside forces intrude upon their lives and ravage their environment.

Ah Lai taps the rich source of Gyarong culture to create poignant and intriguing literary work. His richly detailed narratives about the specific travails of the region in its recent history invoke Tibetan folklore and local legends, generating a sense of timelessness infused by a unique sensibility cultivated from multiple literary and cultural traditions.

AI QING, PEN NAME OF JIANG HAICHENG (1910–1996). Poet. Born to a landed family in Zhejiang, Ai Qing was initially trained to be an artist. In 1929, he went to France to study oil painting and sculpture and was introduced to Marxism and French poetry. The Japanese invasion of China roused his sense of nationalism. Upon his return from Europe, Ai Qing joined a group of leftist artists and was later arrested by the Nationalist government. Unable to paint while in prison, he turned to writing poetry and was soon recognized as an important poetic voice in the nation. In 1941, he went to Yan'an, the Communist base at the time, and became a party member three years later. He moved to Beijing after the Communist victory. In 1957, he was branded a "rightist" and lived in exile on remote farms until 1973 when an eye illness brought him back to Beijing for treatment. In 1979, he was rehabilitated and elected deputy chairman of the Chinese Writers' Association.

Ai Qing earned a reputation in the 1930s as a patriotic poet whose passionate love of the land and its people is expressed in such poems as "Dayanhe—wo de baomu" (Dayan River My Wet-nurse), "Taiyang" (The Sun), "Liming" (Dawn), and "Chun" (The Spring). During the Sino-Japanese War, his poems served as rallying cries for the nation, which eagerly embraced the nationalist spirit sung in poems such as "Beifang" (The North), "Xue luo zai zhongguo de tudi shang" (Snow Falls on the Chinese Land), and "Xiang Taiyang" (To the Sun). Writing in the vernacular language and free style, Ai Qing made a significant contribution to modern Chinese poetry. His technique, defined as simple and straightforward, and his voice, idealistic and sentimental, helped establish a poetic tradition that lasted throughout the Mao era. *See also* MODERNISTS.

AI WU, PEN NAME OF TANG DAOGENG (1904–1992). Fiction writer and essayist. Born into an intellectual family in a small town of southwestern China, Ai Wu spent his formative years in the company of liberal educators and progressive magazines that advocated discarding China's traditional culture in order to transform it into a modern nation. To experience the life of the working class, called for by the leftist movement, Ai Wu left his hometown at the age of 21 and traveled south to Yunnan and Burma, often in the company of small merchants, horse thieves, and other such vagrant personalities. The journey became the source of his most important work, *Nan xingj ji* (Journey to the South), as well as the catalyst for his ideological conversion to communism. In 1929, while stranded in Rangoon, he joined the Burmese branch of the Malaysian Communist Party.

The most memorable characters in *Nan xing ji* are vagrants who live on the fringes of society. Life in the picaresque world of border towns and villages that had attracted Ai Wu proved to be appealing to his readers as well. With the publication of *Nan xing ji*, Ai Wu was established as a serious writer of literature. *Fengrao de yuanye* (Fertile Plains), *Guxiang* (My Native Land), and *Shanye* (Mountain Wilderness), three novels set against the backdrop of the **Sino-Japanese War**, explore the social fabric of the war-torn Chinese countryside and the role morality and tradition play during the national crisis.

After the establishment of the People's Republic of China in 1949, Ai Wu was elected a member of the All-China Federation of Writers and Artists and served as a council member of the Chinese Writers' Association. He published *Bai Lian cheng gang* (The Tempering of Steel), and *Nan xing ji xubian* (Sequel to Journey to the South), which extol ordinary citizens whose sense of collectivism and loyalty to the party are depicted as the driving force behind Communist China's success. During the **Cultural Revolution** (1966–1976), like many other writers of his generation, Ai Wu was forced to abandon his writing and was not allowed to resume it until the end of the turbulent decade. Throughout his literary career, Ai Wu remained committed to the belief that the responsibility of a writer was to champion the working class and to create realist portraits of ordinary men and women.

AN QI (1969–), PEN NAME OF HUANG JIANGPIN. Poet. Born in Zhangzhou, Fujian Province, and graduated from Zhangzhou Teachers' College, An Qi earned her reputation with several collections of poetry, including *Ge: shui shang hong yue* (Songs: Red Moon on Water), *Ben-pao de zhalan* (Running Railings), and *Xiang Dulasi yiyang shenghuo* (Living in the Manner of Duras). Her poems tend to focus on how to tear down the conventional boundaries of poetic language in order to create a sense of freedom without having to make sense of the random fragments contained within the lines. The world in her poems lacks structure, which reflects her perception of reality. The unbridled words and imageries, especially in the poems written since 1998, are a testament to the poet's vivid imagination. An Qi acknowledges her debt in particular to Ezra Pound, to whom she pays homage with the poem "Pound or the Rib of Poetry," and to the Chinese classical novel *Hong lou meng* (*A Dream of Red Mansions*), whose fatalist worldview inspired her to write "Zai Da Guan Yuan li xiangqi de Zhongjian dai" (The Middle Generation Reminded in the Grand View Garden) and "Gei Cao·Xueqin" (To Cao Xueqin). In addition to her own creative work, An Qi is known as a spokesperson for the so-called Zhongjian dai (Middle Generation), a term coined to promote poets neglected by **Generation III** proponents, giving them a distinct identity. She coedited, with Yuan Cun and Huang Lihai, the anthology entitled *Zhongjian dai shi quan ji* (Complete Works by the Middle Generation Poets). An Qi currently lives in Beijing and edits *Poetry Monthly*.

AVANT-GARDE (XIANFENG PAI). Influenced by postmodern literature from Latin America and Europe—particularly works by Italo Calvino, Jorge Luis Borges, and Gabriel García Márquez—the Chinese avant-garde movement began in the 1980s and continues to the present with abated intensity. Deeply invested in narrative form rather than content, the avant-garde writers valorize technique and structure. In a deliberate move away from the realist traditon, they insist that reality as well as history is highly suspect and unreliable and that it is personal experience and individual perception that are essential to narrative art. **Ma Yuan**'s fabrications of Tibetan myths, **Can Xue**'s nightmarish accounts of individuals' inner turmoil, **Su Tong**'s re-creation of local history, **Yu Hua**'s grotesque accounts of violence, **Ge Fei**'s lyrical prose, **Hong Feng**'s deconstructed tragedy, and **Sun Ganlu**'s antifiction all emphasize irony, ambiguity, dreams and fantasies, multiple realities, and a highly individual and creative use of language. As a literary movement, the avant-garde represents one of the two main streams of contemporary Chinese literature, the other being the **root-seeking** movement. There is, however, a tendency found among an increasing number of writers to merge the two approaches in their works. *See also* BEI CUN; CHEN RAN; HAN SHAOGONG; MO YAN; PAN JUN; SEBO; TASHI DAWA; YAN LI; YU JIAN.

– B –

BA JIN, A.K.A. PA CHIN, PEN NAME OF LI FEIGAN (1904–2005). Novelist and essayist. Ba Jin was one of the most celebrated and prolific writers in modern Chinese literature. He grew up in Chengdu, Sichuan Province, in a large wealthy family. Well versed in the classics, he nevertheless became an enthusiastic participant in the **New Culture Movement.** An anarchist in his radical days, Ba Jin acquired his pen name from the Chinese transliterations of Mikhail Bakunin and Peter Kropotkin, two 19th-century Russian anarchists. In the late 1920s, while studying French social history in Paris, he began a literary career that would last for more than six decades. Largely known as a fiction writer, Ba Jin was also a translator, a publisher, and an editor and held many political as well as professional titles, such as president of the Chinese Writers' Association and deputy chairman of the Chinese People's Political Consultative Conference. He was the recipient of the Dante Literature Award (1982) and the Croix de la Légion d'Honneur (1983).

All of Ba Jin's novels were written in the two decades from the late 1920s to 1947, most notable of which are the trilogies: *Jiliu sanbuqu* (Trilogy of Torrent) formed by *Jia (Family), Chun* (Spring), and *Qiu*

(Autumn); *Aiqing sanbuqu* (Trilogy of Love) consisting of *Wu* (Fog), *Yu* (Rain), and *Dian* (Lightning); and *Huo* (Fire), also called *Kangzhan sanbuqu* (Trilogy of the Anti-Japanese War). Other works published during this period include his first novel, *Miewang* (Destruction) about a depressed young anarchist, and its sequel *Xinsheng* (New Life), as well as *Qi yuan* (*Garden of Repose*), *Disi bingshi* (*Ward Four*), and *Hanye* (*Cold Night*). The protagonists of Ba Jin's earlier novels are educated youth caught at the crossroads of tradition and modernity. *Jia*, generally considered his finest piece, best represents his works written during this period. The novel portrays a family in crisis, with the young generation pitted against the old. The Gao clan mirrors Chinese society, in which children are demanded by centuries of Confucian tradition to obey the figure of authority, be it the patriarch or the emperor. Ba Jin points out in *Jia* that such a system does nothing but destroy the lives of the young; the only hope for them is to break free from it.

The Chinese youth at the time readily identified with the passionate heroes Ba Jin created. In contrast with the zealous and optimistic worldview expressed in his early works, Ba Jin in the 1940s took a more somber perspective on history, reality, and human nature. *Qi yuan* and *Hanye* are good examples to illustrate the change. Free of the hot-blooded, idealistic young rebels who populate his earlier novels, these stories focus on the decline of the old family and the tragic consequences when hope is dashed by the reality of war, poverty, and prejudice.

In the 1950s and early 1960s, Ba Jin wrote some short stories and novellas, a few of which were politically motivated and would later be deemed by the author himself as "waste products." He suffered a great deal of physical and psychological abuse during the **Cultural Revolution**. His best-known work in the post-Mao era is the four-volume *Suixiang lu* (*Random Thoughts*), a collection of essays and memoirs expressing regrets about the "false and empty words" he had written in exchange for political protection during the Cultural Revolution.

BAI XIANYONG, A.K.A. PAI HSIEN-YUNG (1937–). Fiction writer. Bai Xianyong came from a prominent military family, one of 10 children of Bai Chongxi (1893–1966), a high-ranking general in the Nationalist army who served briefly as defense minister in the Nationalist government. Bai was born in 1937, in time to experience the **Sino-Japanese War** and the **Civil War** fought between the Nationalists and the Communists. In 1949, while his father was fighting the Communists on the

front, his mother herded the large family first to Hankou, then to Guangzhou, and finally to Hong Kong, where Bai attended primary and middle
schools for three years. In 1952, the family was reunited in Taipei with
the father. Bai entered college as a civil engineering major but promptly
switched to English at the National **Taiwan** University's Foreign Languages Department.

The four undergraduate years he spent at National Taiwan University
marked a crucial milestone for Bai and launched his writing career. In
1959, Bai and some of his classmates, all aspiring writers, founded the
bimonthly literary journal *Xiandai wenxue* (Modern Literature), whose
mission was twofold: to systematically introduce Western modernist
writers including Franz Kafka, James Joyce, Virginia Woolf, William
Faulkner, Jean-Paul Sartre, and Thomas Mann; and to nurture a whole
generation of Taiwan writers. As its editor and frequent contributor,
Bai helped make the journal a trendsetter, leading Taiwan's literature
into an era of innovation and experimentation. The stories he wrote
and published in *Xiandai wenxue* are often reminiscences of childhood
and youth, based on and developed from his own life. The first-person
narrator in "Yuqing Sao" (Yuqing's Wife), for instance, is an observant
little boy who is catapulted into the adult world of illicit passion when
Yuqing Sao, an attractive young widow who is a servant of his family,
kills her lover and herself after she discovers his affair with another
woman.

In 1963, Bai went to the United States to study creative writing
through the International Writers' Workshop at the University of Iowa.
Two years later with a master's degree in hand, he accepted a teaching
post at the University of California at Santa Barbara, where he remained
until his retirement in 1994. While in Iowa, he wrote a series of stories
about Chinese expatriates, later collected in a book entitled *Niuyueke*
(New Yorkers). The reality of life as an expatriate, with it the sense of
dislocation, loss, and memory, is the predominant theme of *Niuyueke*. In
1973, Bai published *Taipei ren* (Taipei Characters), the most important
work of his career, winning him a large following in the communities
of the Chinese diaspora. The book has since been reprinted many times
by several publishers, both in Taiwan and on the mainland. The main
characters of *Taipei ren* are people who followed the Nationalist government to Taiwan. Many of them had enjoyed privileged lives on the
mainland as society dames, generals, government officials, bankers, or
industrialists. Bai examines how the past affects their lives by probing

into their longings, regrets, aching passions, melancholy, and nostalgia. There is a constant undercurrent of irony in these stories. As he relentlessly scrutinizes the complex emotions of his characters, Bai maintains a cool narrative distance, which enhances the tragic consequences of their situations. With *Taipei ren*, Bai has perfected the art of short story telling and the book displays his unique artistic sensibilities, impeccable artistry, and a keen moral vision. Bai has written one novel, *Niezi* (*Crystal Boys*), which depicts the underground world of homosexuals in Taipei.

Since his retirement, Bai has been devoting his time to reviving and promoting Kunqu Opera. He travels frequently across the Pacific Ocean to deliver lectures and speeches in Taiwan, Hong Kong, and China on literature, dramatic performances, and AIDS awareness. *See also* MODERNISTS.

BEI CUN, PEN NAME OF KANG HONG (1965–). Fiction and screenplay writer. Bei Cun grew up in Fujian and studied Chinese literature at Xiamen University. In the early 1990s he was an avant-garde writer, publishing a series of sketches, including "Taowangzhe shuo" (Says the Escapee), "Jiechizhe shuo" (Says the Kidnapper), "Pijiazhe shuo" (Says the Armored), and "Guixiangzhe shuo" (Says the Returnee), all of which focus on experimenting with innovative narrative techniques. This stylistic focus was later replaced by an intense interest in exploring the human soul, the meaning of life. Works such as *Shixi de he* (The River of Baptism), which depicts a poet's wandering experience, "Huanxiang" (Homecoming), an allegorical tale about the tragic fates of five poets, and "Zuihou de yishujia" (The Last Artist) all examaine human spirituality in its complicated manifestations. *Laomu de qin* (Laomu's Violin), and "Zhou Yu de hanjiao" (Zhou Yu's Shouts), which has been adapted into a movie, further explore the difficulties encountered in a spiritual journey. Salvation, as shown in the lives of the protagonists in these stories, lies in the individual's ability to find meaning in art/poetry, which proves to be elusive at best in an era of materialism and commodification.

Since 2003, Bei Cun has published several novels, including *Fennu* (Furor) about a young man's journey from the countryside to the city, from being an innocent and ambitious man to a criminal who finally comes to repent his actions while running away from the authorities, and *Gonglu shang de linghun* (Souls on Highways), a family saga unfolding in three generations, three countries, and three wars, connected by three highways. Compared with his earlier works, which tend to be dark and gloomy, these recent novels present life from a more upbeat and idealistic perspective, despite apparently tragic circumstances. Other than short stories and novels, Bei Cun has written screenplays as well as poetry. He currently works as an editor for *Fujian wenxue* (Fujian Literature).

BEI DAO, PEN NAME OF ZHAO ZHENKAI (1949–). Poet and essayist. Bei Dao is the most notable representative of the **Misty poets** associated with the underground journal *Jintian* (Today), which Bei Dao cofounded in 1978 with fellow poet **Mang Ke**. *Jintian* published works written by budding young poets who challenged the ideologically driven **socialist realist** tradition that had dominated Chinese literature since the 1950s. A Misty poem ordinarily contains oblique imagery and cryptic syntax. In their experiment with new techniques, the young poets opted for elusiveness and ambiguity of meaning, intentionally scrambling the relationship between the signifier and the signified to foreground the poetic language. In so doing, they hoped to cleanse the Chinese language that had been saturated with politics and communist ideology. In their effort to to remove the dogmatic, cliché-ridden expressions, they strove to replace the public, official language with a highly individualized one. *Jintian* nurtured a whole generation of poets, such as **Yang Lian**, **Gu Cheng**, **Duo Duo**, and **Shu Ting**, and helped establish Bei Dao's position as the leader of post-Mao poetry. Bei Dao was a favorite among college students, and one of his poems, "Huida" (Answer), a rebellious rejection of blind loyalty, became a battle cry for the prodemocracy movement in 1989. The activities of Bei Dao and the other Misty poets came to a halt in the aftermath of the crackdown on the Tian'anmen protests. *Jintian* was banned due to accusations of having instigated the protests, and its leading voices were silenced. Bei Dao, who was attending a conference in Berlin at the time, was forbidden to return to China. *Jintian* was resurrected in Stockholm in 1990 as a forum for expatriate Chinese writers. During his time abroad, Bei Dao has lectured at a number of universities in the West and his poems have been translated into several languages.

Bei Dao's poetry has gone through several phases, from defiant political outcry to personal ruminations about passion, love, and friendship, to the mourning of the bleak interior world, to ironic examinations of the human condition. The core of his poetry, however, has remained the same: to explore the intricate web of language and the nature of the self in relation to the emotional wounds inflicted by history and society. Unlike his hermetic poetry, Bei Dao's essays are easily accessible. In them, he offers his thoughts on a variety of topics, such as the stresses of exile, reminiscences about his friends, and recollections of his life in China. Bei Dao's poems and essays written since his exile have earned even more critical acclaim. For his uncompromised stance in defense of freedom of expression and his literary achievement, Bei Dao was inducted into the American Academy of Arts and Letters as an honorary member. He has been repeatedly nominated for the Nobel Prize for literature.

BI FEIYU (1964–). A Jiangsu native, Bi Feiyu graduated from Yangzhou Teachers' College in 1987. For his depiction of Chinese country life and his examination of the psyche of the Chinese peasants, Bi is considered an important newcomer in the **root-seeking** movement, although he started his career as an experimental writer. His novella "Gu dao" (The Solitary Island), in which a family legend intersects with national history, shows a writer more interested in narrative technique than plot and story. His later works, including award-winning stories "Buru qi de nüren" (Women in Lactation) and "Qingyi" (The Opera Singer), depart from experimentalism and embrace a realist style. Bi's novels include *Yumi* (Yumi), a trilogy about three sisters forced to quickly learn to fend for themselves when their village party secretary father falls from power as a result of sex scandals; *Pingyuan* (The Plain), which explores the mind-set of the peasants and their hard life in the 1970s, focusing on the vulnerability and despair of young people; *Tuina* (Massage), an account of the ordinary life led by a group of blind masseuses.

BI SHUMIN (1952–). Fiction writer. Born in Yili, Xinjiang, Bi Shumin joined the military at 16 upon graduation from the Beijing Foreign Languages School, where she majored in Russian. Bi spent the next 11 years in **Tibet**, working in the army first as a nurse, then a medic, and finally a doctor, until the 1980s, when she finished her military service and returned to Beijing. To nurture her budding literary interest, she studied creative writing at Beijing Normal University and received her master's in 1991. Later, she returned to the university and received her Ph.D. in psychology in 2002.

Bi began writing in the 1980s, inspired by her experience in Tibet. Her first publication "Kunlun shang" (Death in the Kunlun Mountain), a story about the sacrifices of the soldiers and officers stationed in Tibet, appeared in 1987 and she continued to write about the hardships endured by the Chinese military in the Tibetan plateau, especially by **women** in a predominantly male world. In recent years, Bi has been fascinated by the subject of human psychology. Her breakthrough story "Yuyue siwang" (*An Appointment with Death*) examines the experience of patients and their families when faced with incurable illnesses. Her novel *Zhengjiu rufang* (Saving the Breasts) explores the effects of breast cancer on women. Many of these works are based on her direct encounters with patients in her medical practice. Her recent novel *Nü xinli shi* (The Female Psychologist) tells how a psychologist maintains her professional authority when dealing with her patients who seek her advice while trying to sort out her own messy relationships with her husband and her lover.

BIAN ZHILIN (1910–2000). Poet, translator, and scholar. Born in Haimen, Jiangsu Province, Bian Zhilin studied English at Beijing University and went on to become a Shakespeare scholar and one of the most important poets in modern Chinese literature. While translating Western poetry into vernacular Chinese, Bian began writing poetry. His work caught the attention of **Xu Zhimo**, China's most prominent poet at the time, who admired Bian's innovative poems. In 1936, Bian collaborated with fellow Beijing University students **He Qifang** and **Li Guangtian** on a collection of poetry entitled *Hanyuan ji* (Hanyuan Collection), earning them the nickname "Three Musketeers of Hanyuan." In addition to writing free verse in the vernacular language, Bian explored new ways of writing modern regulated verse. Of all the poems Bian wrote during his career, the most memorable is the quatrain entitled "Duan Zhang" (The Broken Chapter) composed in 1934. It records the feelings of one single moment with images of a person standing on a bridge looking at a scene and another person (or persons) standing by a window looking at the one on the bridge while taking in the scenery around him or her.

The political atmosphere after 1949 permitted poets to write only propagandist poems and Bian soon abandoned poetry writing to focus instead on translation and scholarly work. His work on William Shakespeare's tragedies is considered an important contribution to Shakespearian studies in China. He is also credited with introducing a wide variety of Western literary works to Chinese readers.

BING XIN, A.K.A. PING HSIN, PEN NAME OF XIE BINGXIN (1900–1999). Born in Fuzhou, Bing Xin graduated from Yanjing University in Beijing with a bachelor's degree in literature and from Wellesley College in the United States with a master's in English literature. She began writing during the **May Fourth Movement** and had a long, distinguished career as a writer, translator, teacher, and public figure. Her creative writing includes poetry, prose, and short stories. In her early works, Bing Xin encouraged **women** to get an education not only as a way to obtain self-fulfillment but also to bring happiness and stability to the family. Her first story "Liangge jiating" (Two Families) portrays two housewives with different backgrounds: the educated woman is able to teach her children and provide understanding and comfort for her husband; the illiterate woman is only interested in spending money on jewelry and clothes and does not know how to bring up children or manage household finances. The family with the well-educated wife is happy while the one with the ignorant wife is unhappy. At a time when education for women was still rare, Bing Xin attempted to use her stories as a wake-up call to society. Her writings, as expressions of a wholesome, healthy, uplifting outlook, generally promote a positive attitude toward life and advocate love and kindness. Her series of poems *Fan xing* (Myriad Stars) are most emblematic of this worldview; she extols the love of family, the love of friends, and above all maternal love. In her view, love is capable of saving the world. The hero in "Chaoren" (The Superman), her best-known story, is a man saved by a loving relationship with a little boy. Bing Xin wrote many stories and poems for children; from the series *Ji xiao duzhu* (To Young Readers) to tales she wrote in the 1950s, she shows her young readers how important it is to love nature, learning, and family and friends.

– C –

CAN XUE, PEN NAME OF DENG XIAOHUA (1953–). Fiction writer. Born and raised in Changsha by intellectual parents working for the *Hunan Daily*, Can Xue moved with her family to a farm in the late 1950s when her father was labeled a rightist. During the famine that soon followed, the family suffered incredible hardships. The onset of the **Cultural Revolution** permanently ended Can Xue's formal schooling, leaving her with only a primary school education. Can Xue went to work in a factory and later quit her job to become a seamstress. She began writing in the early 1980s. A primary advocate for the Chinese **avant-garde** long before it became a trendy literary movement in China, Can Xue was a unique figure among contemporary Chinese writers. She takes pride in writing "pure literature" and single-mindedly pursues her own artistic vision, completely unaffected by either her critics or the market. With an imaginative mind, she has spun some of the most fantastic stories in contemporary Chinese literature. In her works, one can find traces of influence by Jorge Luis Borges and Franz Kafka. Her short stories, including "Shan shang de xiao wu" (A Little Hut on the Hill) and "Feizao" (Soap), and novellas such as "Canglao de fu yun" (*Old Floating Clouds*) and "Huang ni jie" (*Yellow Mud Street*), all written in the 1980s and variably called "gothic," "surrealistic," and "absurd," remain her best-known works. In these texts, dreams and fantasies appear to be tangible and believable. Focusing on the subconscious of the human mind, Can Xue has created a world that is invariably irrational, fragmented, and nightmarish, with no clear definition of time, space, and identity. Among the group of avant-garde writers who began writing experimental fiction in the 1980s, Can is arguably the only one who has maintained a cutting-edge approach to literature, continuing to produce the kind of work that compels the reader to participate in an intellectual exercise. *Bianjiang* (The Frontier), a recent novel that portrays the uncanny life of a small border town whose residents possess extraordinary abilities, is a testament to her sustained creative energy and her persistent effort at exploring the realm of the human psyche.

CAO JUREN (1900–1972). Essayist and fiction writer. Born in Zhejiang, Cao graduated from the Hangzhou Number One Teachers' College, a magnet for progressive thinkers at the time, and taught literature at several universities. He was an editor and journalist during the **Sino-Japanese War**. Cao moved to **Hong Kong** in 1950 and in his position as founder and editor of *Re feng* (Hot Breeze), a bimonthly literary journal, he published works of liberal writers who stayed on the mainland after 1949. Cao wrote a large quantity of works, most of which are essays and some fiction. He was also a literary critic.

CAO NAIQIAN (1949–). A Shanxi native, Cao began his literary career in the late 1980s when his short stories about rural Shanxi garnered praises from the veteran writer **Wang Zengqi**, who wrote an essay introducing his work to the public. The Wenjiayao stories, totaling more than 20, are based on life in the village at the border between Shanxi and Inner

Mongolia, where Cao lived for a year during the **Cultural Revolution** supervising the educated city youths sent there to perform physicial labor. These stories, published in some of China's major literary journals, won immediate critical acclaim in both China and **Taiwan** and attracted the attention of the Swedish Sinologist Goran Malmqvist, who helped promote Cao's work. Cao's realistic portrayal of destitution reveals some of the most horrific conditions of rural life in northern China. As a true realist, Cao presents Wenjiayao as it is—a village debilitated by poverty, with food and sex dominating the thoughts and conversations of the men. The stories contain unfiltered local ballads that express in a vivid and crude language sexual desire that burns inside the men in the village. "Nüren" (Women) and "Da pinhuo" (Bachelors' Potluck) are two of the stories in the Wenjiayao series. *Dao heiye xiang ni mei banfa* (*When I Think of You Late at Night, There's Nothing I Can Do*), a novel composed of five short stories, is arguably the best of Cao's work. It tells how the hunger for food and sex that ravages Wenjiayao turns one man into a criminal who rapes his own mother and forces a woman to offer her own body to alleviate her son's pent-up desire. It also exposes the abuse of power in the hands of village leaders. Cao's unfinished semiautobiographical novel, *Shangshi jiuzhang* (Nine Chapters of the Bygone Times), consists of eight short stories and one novella. In 2005, Cao was invited to participate in the International Writers Workshop at Hong Kong Baptist University.

CAO WENXUAN (1974–). Fiction writer. Born in rural Jiangsu, Cao Wenxuan graduated from the Chinese Department of Beijing University in the late 1970s. Since then, he has been teaching modern Chinese literature at his alma mater. A strong advocate for children's literature and a winner of several literary awards, including the Song Qingling Literature Prize and Bing Xin Literature Prize, Cao has published numerous stories and novels about Chinese adolescents. He writes in a lyrical style that appeals aesthetically to traditional sensibilities and his works portray everyday characters who experience life in its many facets and learn lessons about love, sacrifice, hard work, dignity, and judgment.

Shanyang bu chi tiantang cao (Goats Do Not Eat the Grass in Heaven) portrays the hard life of a boy as he follows adult migrant workers into the city; *Cao fangzi* (A Thatched House) examines the six years of elementary school life from the perspective of a little boy as he struggles to understand the world of the adults; *Hong wa* (Red Tiles), which won the National Book Award and Beijing Literature and Arts Award, portrays the simple and pure life of the countryside described in the words of a middle school student; *Xi mi* (Fine Rice), also set in rural China during the **Cultural Revolution**, tells how a country boy falls in love with a schoolteacher. Most representative of Cao's aesthetics is *Tian piao* (A Downpour), a novel about a love triangle between two men and one woman. In this book, Cao describes more than a dozen forms of rain in a style that accentuates his traditional sensibility. While situating a story of desire and human nature in the midst of the Cultural Revolution, Cao minimizes the historical background, skirting around the social destruction and political turmoil, and chooses to focus on a love story in which personal ambition pales next to romantic sentiments and even death is turned into an artistic experience.

CAO YU, A.K.A. TSAO YU, PEN NAME OF WAN JIABAO (1910–1996). Playwright. Born in Tianjin into an official family, Cao Yu was the most important playwright in 20th century China and the driving force behind the success of *hua ju* (**spoken drama**), a transplanted theatrical form introduced from the West to China during the first decade of the 20th century. Some of his plays, particularly those written in the 1930s, including *Leiyu* (*Thunderstorm*), a four-act tragedy about a family ripped apart by secret lives and opposing ideologies, and *Richu* (*Sunrise*) about the contrasting worlds of a society woman and a prostitute both driven to death by dark social forces, are Chinese classics and are still performed in China's theaters. *Beijing ren* (*Peking Man*), which portrays an old declining family, is considered the best play he wrote during the 1940s. Cao Yu's dramatic skills were influenced by Greek tragedies and works by Henrik Ibsen and Eugene O'Neill. However, the lyrical sensibility and the dramatic language as well as the social consciousness expressed are quintessentially Chinese.

After 1949, Cao Yu served as president of the Central Institute of Theater and Beijing People's Art Theater and continued to write, but none of the plays he produced during this period reached the same level of success and popularity as his earlier works.

CAO ZHILIAN, A.K.A. JERLIAN TSAO (1969–). Fiction writer. A graduate from National **Taiwan** University and the University of California at Berkeley, Cao Zhilian represents the new generation of "Internet writers" whose works are published online before they are picked up by traditional print publishers. Cao has written two novels and some short stories; they all can be found in paper form. *Mou dai fengliu* (The Romance of a Certain Era), published online in 1996, was conceived when she was researching for her Ph.D. dissertation on the social transformation in the city of Suzhou during the Ming dynasty (1368–1644). Set in the 16th century, it depicts the nebulous relationships among several characters. The experimental book resembles a collection of stories or essays rather than a traditional novel. The structure is loose and free, typical of Web writings, allowing the reader to read in a random order. The book is filled with details of landscape, food, clothing, entertainment, and other aspects of life in the Ming, and the tales of romance, political intrigue, and family feuds are woven in a language of classical grace and refinement. There is also a great deal of latitude and fluidity when the narrative travels through time and space. *Yinxiang shu* (A Book of Impressions), a more extreme experimentation than her previous work, is a novel without a story. The central theme of the book is the changing cultures of the living environment and the individual's relationship to them, focusing on Taipei, Berkeley, Hong Kong, and mainland China but without mentioning their specific names. The narrative strategy is designed to foreground the intimate, experiential connection between the self and the physical locale. What propels the narrative movement, however, is the language, the written word. In this work, Cao sets out to prove that a novel can be made with only words and imageries. Without the development and climax of a storyline, and without a protagonist, the novel relies on the beauty of the language to create humor, irony, and a sense of sorrow. *Tang chu de huaban* (Pedals of the Early Tang) is a collection of her early stories. *See also* WOMEN.

CHEN BAICHEN (1908–1994). Playwright and fiction writer. Chen Baichen was born into a merchant family in Huanyin, Jiangsu Province. Influenced by the **May Fourth Movement**, Chen began writing new poetry and fiction in middle school. His first work, a short story, was published in 1925 in *Xiaoshuo shijie* (Fiction World). Chen attended the Shanghai Institute of Arts and the South China Institute of Arts, working closely with **Tian Han** and others to promote a new theater and to build the Chinese film industry. A member of the **Left-wing Association of Chinese Writers**, which he joined in 1930, Chen worked with progressive theater troupes including Minzhong jushe (The Mass Theater), Nanguo (South China), and Modeng jushe (Modern Theater). He joined the Communist Youth League and was arrested in 1932 for his political involvement. While serving his prison sentence, Chen wrote short stories and some one-act plays.

When the **Sino-Japanese War** broke out in 1937, Chen moved to Sichuan and continued his work in the theater, leading and performing with troupes such as the Shanghai Film Troupe and the China Dramatic Arts Society. Many of the plays he wrote during this period denounced Japanese atrocities and aimed at boosting national morale. After the war, Chen returned to Shanghai and helped found the Kunlun Film Studio. He joined the Chinese Communist Party in 1950 and was appointed art director of the Shanghai Film Studio. He moved to Beijing in 1952 to take up the position of director of playwriting under the Ministry of Culture and later he was transferred to the Chinese Writers' Association. In 1966, Chen moved to Nanjing and worked in the Jiangsu Provincial Association of Culture. He left his government job in 1978 to become a professor of dramatic arts and chairman of the Chinese Language and Literature Department of Nanjing University, a position he held until his retirement.

Chen had a long and productive career. From the 1930s to the 1980s, he wrote more than 50 plays and screenplays. He is best known for his comedies and historical plays. Many of his comedies fall into the category of political satire, poking fun at the absurdities found in society under the Nationalist government. *Luan shi nannü* (Men and Women in Wild Times) mocks the degeneration of social mores; *Jiehun jingxingqu* (March to Marriage) disparages the repressive Nationalist regime; *Sheng guan tu* (Becoming Officials), a three-act play, satirizes the bureaucracy and corruption at the local level; *Sui han tu* (A Tale of Winter) centers on the futile effort of an idealistic medical doctor determined to eradicate tuberculosis. Chen's films include *Xingfu kuangxiangqu* (Rhapsody of Happiness), about the miserable urban life after the Sino-Japanese War, and *Wuya yu maque* (The Crow and the Sparrow), which presents the total collapse of the economy and social order under Chiang Kai-shek's government on the eve of the Communist victory. Chen's historical plays are critiques of some well-known figures in China's past, focusing on the power struggle at the highest level. *Shi Dakai de molu* (Shi Dakai at the End of His Life) and *Jintian cun* (Jintian Village) deal with conflicts within the leadership of the Taiping uprising in the 19th century; *Da feng ge* (Ode to the Gale), written in 1979, portrays the political struggle within the imperial court in the beginning years of the Western Han (206 B.C.–23 A.D.).

In addition to his plays, Chen also wrote novels and short stories, most of which expose social ills and express sympathy for the working poor. His first novel, *Xuanwo* (Whirlpool), was published in 1928, followed by three more: *Yige kuanglang de nüzi* (An Unruly Woman), *Zui'e zhi hua* (Flowers of Evil), and *Guilai* (Homecoming), all written under the influence of the **Mandarin Ducks and Butterflies school**. All would be later dismissed by him as nothing but "making a fuss about an imaginary illness" with no relevance to reality. *See also* SPOKEN DRAMA.

CHEN CUN, PEN NAME OF YANG YIHUA (1954–). Fiction writer. A Shanghai native, Chen Cun was sent in 1971 to a village in Anhui, where he stayed until 1975, when an illness allowed him to return to Shanghai. He studied political science at Shanghai Teachers' College and worked for several years in the city government. He is currently a member of the Shanghai Writers' Association. Because of a spinal disease that has permanently bent his back, he jokingly calls himself "Curve Man," a nickname he sometimes uses as a pen name.

Chen Cun deals with issues in everyday urban existence, and his stories are populated by ordinary folks who lead mundane lives without apparent drama. He is best known for his portrayals of teenagers in *Shaonan shaonü yigong qige* (Young Men and Women: Seven in Total), which tackles dilemmas faced by high school graduates who fail the notoriously grueling college entrance exams. In his characteristically humorous and mocking tone, he conveys the despair and rebelliousness of youths who try to maintain their equilibrium under tremendous social and parental pressure. His stories are not plot driven; the fragmented parts are connected by an ironic language that serves to direct and energize the narrative. *Xianhua he* (Fresh Flowers) is typical of Chen's style. Without major events or a sustained plot, the book is a journal kept by a writer, sick at home, who records what he does and sees everyday, such as eating, drinking, sleeping, shopping for groceries, brushing his teeth, taking a bath, writing letters, making love, watching TV, and other such trivial occurrences. By cataloging banal trifles, Chen Cun aims to strip life of its pretense and return it to its essence, laying bare man's vulnerabilities.

Chen Cun is also a prolific essayist. He has written biting but good-natured satires, creating a persona who does not take himself too seriously while making fun of other people's follies. His essays are collected in *Wanren zishu* (Confessions of the Curve Man) and *Sishi hushuo* (Making Nonsense at Forty).

CHEN DONGDONG (1961–). Poet. Born in Shanghai, Chen Dongdong graduated from Shanghai Normal University with a B.A. in Chinese literature. Considered a representative of the **Generation III poets** and often put in the camp of *xueyuan pai* (academic school), a loosely connected group based in college campuses that includes **Xi Chuan, Zang Di**, and **Wang Jiaxin**, Chen has worked as a teacher, an editor for opera and poetry journals, and a website designer among other careers. He began writing at the age of 20 and is known for having invented the terms *xiju gan* (comic effect) and *lishi changjing hua* (dramatized history). In poems such as "Xi ju" (Comedy) and "Chuntian: dubai he changing" (Spring: Monologues and Scenes), he creates a dreamy, dramatized world constructed with exquisite images, descriptions of scenes, and dialogues. The measured rhythm, refined musicality, and elegant sensuality that characterize Chen's work are reminiscent of classical Chinese poetry. In "Shuzhuang jing" (Mirror) and "Dian deng" (Lighting the Lamp), the poet sets up vignettes of domestic intimacy, similar to those found in Song dynasty *Ci* poetry. Chen's experiment with dramatization and ancient Chinese materials is most evident in "Liu shui" (Flowing Water), a long poem inspired by an ancient melody based on a legendary tale about music. Among the Generation III poets, Chen is believed to have the most classical sensitivity; however, the interplay between reality and imagination in his works is undoubtedly modern, and the syntax of his poems, along with his unconventional use of punctuation, reveals an experimental poet at work.

CHEN JIANGONG (1949–). Fiction writer, essayist, and screenplay writer. Born in Guangxi Province, Chen Jiangong moved to Beijing in 1957, when his economist father took a teaching position at the People's University. In 1977, Chen was admitted to Beijing University, ending his 10-year career as a coal miner. In the early 1980s, several of his short stories won prestigious awards, establishing him as a promising young writer. Chen writes in the realistic mode and his works reflect his experience as a laborer and college student. He is particularly noted for his Beijing-flavored stories. Influenced by **Lao She**, also a Beijing resident, Chen uses an urban, street language consisting of traditional expressions and trendy slang, vividly capturing the unique features of the witty Beijing vernacular. His works include *Miluan de xingkong* (A Star-studded Dazzling Sky), *Danfeng yan* (Beautiful Eyes), *Quanmao* (*Curly Hair*), and *Beijing ziwei* (Beijing Flavor).

CHEN RAN (1962–). Fiction writer. Born and raised in Beijing, Chen Ran is considered one of China's foremost feminist writers. She has written a number of stories that examine aspects of a **woman**'s role and her shifting relationship to the world and the individuals around her. Chen's female protagonists, all educated urbanites, are spiritual wanderers alienated from the outside world—depressed, lonely, hypersensitive, and rebellious. Her best-known work is *Siren shenghuo* (*A Private Life*), a psychological portrayal of a precocious, idiosyncratic adolescent girl growing up in an era of political upheaval. In this novel, the historical realities recede into the background, and the focus is on the coming of age of the protagonist, most notably her sexual awakening and youthful individuality. A Freudian psychoanalytic overtone and homoerotic sensuality give the novel a unique perspective into the inner world of the individual. Likewise, *Shengsheng duanduan* (Broken Sounds), a fictional account told in the diary form, presents the author's observations on accidental occurrences in everyday life. In a distinctly intellectual voice, the narrator comments on seemingly randomly selected topics, often trivial events that trigger her thoughts and imagination, and frequently digresses from the mundane details to enter into a philosophical discourse.

Other works by Chen include short stories "Wunü yu tade mengzhong zhi men" (The Witch and the Door in Her Dream), "Maishui nü he shougua ren" (The Wheat-ear Woman and the Widow), "Fan qiang dou shi men" (All Walls Are Ears), "Ling yi zhi erduo de qiaoji sheng" (The Knocking Sounds of the Other Ear), and "Pokai" (Broken). These tales feature single women who live by themselves, foregrounding a woman's lonely battle against the outside world and the dysfunctional human relationships characterized by betrayal, suspicion, and miscommunication. As Chen moves further into the inner world of her characters in her exploration of the female body and the human mind, her writings become more probing and pensive, noted also for their unique imageries and the contrast between the lived and dreamed realities. These are characteristics that help put Chen in the ranks of China's **avant-garde** writers.

CHEN RUOXI, A.K.A. CH'EN JO-HSI (1938–). Born and raised in rural **Taiwan**, Chen Ruoxi spent her childhood years under the influence of a patriotic father who refused to learn Japanese when the island was under Japanese occupation and who instilled in his young daughter a strong sense of pride in the Chinese culture. At the National Taiwan University where she was a student in the Foreign Languages Department, Chen began to write fiction and was a cofounder of the journal *Xiandai wenxue* (Modern Literature). Her exposure to Western modernism led her to adopt some of its artistic visions and narrative techniques in her own writing. In general, however, her works are much more indebted to realism, grounded in true-to-life characters, a simple language, and indigenous cultural traits. Her literary style can be traced to her rural upbringing. She has a deep feeling for the countryside and for the traditions that sustain its continued survival. One of the stories she wrote in her college days, "Zuihou yexi" (The Last Evening Show), laments the decline of the local culture through the accounts of the fall of a Taiwanese opera star's popularity.

In 1961, Chen went to study in the United States, where the views of the People's Republic of China were not nearly as negative as in her native Taiwan. Echoing the dissident sentiments felt by Taiwanese intellectuals against the high-handed policies of the Nationalist government, Chen became an ardent supporter of Maoist China. At Johns Hopkins University, she met her future husband, Duan Shiyao, a Ph.D. student in fluid mechanics. The young idealistic couple decided to expatriate to China. They arrived in Beijing in October 1966, at the outbreak of the **Cultural Revolution**. Instead of being welcomed by the Communists, they were suspected of being imperialist spies sent by America to sabotage socialist China. While Duan was sent to a farm to be reeducated, Chen remained in their home at the Hydraulic Engineering College in Nanjing, taking care of children whose parents, like Duan, were undergoing labor reform in the countryside. Disillusioned with communism, the couple left China in 1973 with their children and subsequently settled in Hong Kong. Chen's first story, "Yin Xianzhang" (*The Execution of Mayor Yin*), was published in 1974 and was followed by more "Cultural Revolution stories." These stories were enthusiastically received in Hong Kong and Taiwan, where they were taken as anti-Communist, a message the author insisted was unintended.

After moving to the United States in 1979, Chen published several books about Chinese immigrants trying to survive and succeed in their new country. Notable among them are *Zhi hun* (Marriage on Paper), which relates how a phony marriage between a woman from Shanghai and an American man turns into a true and caring partnership, *Tuwei* (Breakout) about the problems faced by well-eduated Chinese immigrants in San Francisco, *Yuanjian* (Foresight), which describes the pursuit of the American dream and its heavy toll on the individuals and their families, and *Er Hu* (Two Men Named Hu), which portrays two Chinese American couples. In 1995, Chen returned to her native Taiwan. Inspired by the charitable work done by Buddhist women there, Chen wrote *Hui xin lian* (The Lotus of Kindness), depicting the journey of three nuns from one family.

CHEN YINGZHEN, A.K.A. CH'EN YING-CHEN, PEN NAME OF CHEN YONGSHAN (1937–). Fiction writer. Chen Yingzhen attended Tamkang University and graduated from the National **Taiwan** University. He began his literary career in 1959 and has published mostly short stories portraying life in small villages and towns of Taiwan. In 1968, Chen, accused of "pro-communist activities," was found guilty and sentenced to seven years in prison.

As a literary figure, Chen is a leading voice in the **nativist** literary movement in Taiwan. Going against the modernist trend promoted by his professors and fellow students at the Foreign Languages Department of the National Taiwan University, Chen chose to adhere to the realist tradition by writing about the harsh realities of rural poverty. Treating literature as an outlet of social and moral conviction, Chen depicts the sufferings and alienation of Taiwanese farmers who are forced into insolvency by encroaching modernization and an unscrupulous business class. Chen also takes jabs at Taiwan's attempt to Americanize and the devastating effect it has on local culture. "Jiangjun zu" (Generals), one of his best-known stories, about a local drum and gong band that plays at funerals, laments the loss of a close-knit, traditional community in industrializing Taiwan. In Chen's writings, there is often the opposition between idealism and materialism. A politically engaged writer, Chen is often believed to have represented the social conscience of Taiwan during the repressive reign of Chiang Kai-shek.

CHEN ZHONGSHI (1942–). Fiction and prose writer. Fame came to Chen Zhongshi late in life. Prior to the publication of *Bai lu yuan* (The White Deer Plain), which won the Mao Dun Literature Prize, he was an obscure writer leading a quiet life in Xi'an in northwestern China. The novel changed his career almost overnight. Noted for its stylistic clarity and memorable characters, the novel addresses the issue of morality in Chinese society, particularly the role Confucianism plays in rural communities. In the view of the **May Fourth** generation, Confucianism was seen as the culprit responsible for China's decline; it was blamed for having emasculated the Chinese nation, turning it into "the sick man of the Orient." This verdict held sway decades after the May Fourth Movement. It is no surprise that when the **root-seekers** began their search for cultural heritage in the 1980s, they opted to overlook this most important tradition. Chen set out to rectify the situation. In *Bai lu yuan,* a novel about the sweeping changes taking place in northwestern China's countryside during the 20th century, Chen attributes the disintegration of social order to the abandonment of Confucian values. In his effort to reevaluate the role Confucianism plays in Chinese society, Chen presents the ancient teaching as a positive force in building and maintaining social stability and in serving as an indispensable moral compass. In addition to *Bai lu yuan*, Chen has written many short stories and essays.

CHENG FANGWU (1897–1984). Poet, fiction writer, and playwright. One of the founders of the **Creation Society**, Cheng Fangwu spent his formative years (1910–1921) in Japan, where he teamed with **Guo Moruo**, **Yu Dafu**, and other Chinese students to promote radical changes in China's political, social, and literary institutions. After he returned to China, Cheng moved to Guangzhou, the center of political activities at the time, and taught at Guangdong University and the Huangpu Military Academy. In 1927, after the alliance between the Nationalists and the Communists fell apart, Cheng fled to Paris, where he joined the Chinese Communist Party (CCP) and became the editor for *Chi guang* (Red Light), an internal magazine published by the party's Berlin and Paris branches. Upon his return to China in 1931, Cheng was assigned to key posts within the CCP, including party secretary of Hong'an County, director of the Central Party School, and president of United University of Northern China. After 1949, Cheng worked exclusively in higher education, serving as a university president.

Cheng's literary career was rather short, with a small output of writings mostly published in the 1920s when he was actively involved in the Creation Society. He wrote short stories and poems, promoting a "revolutionary literature" with the explicit purpose of effecting political and social change. Later when he was working in the Communist headquarters in northern Shaanxi, he wrote plays and songs to boost morale in service to the Communist cause. In his last years, he published memoirs about his revolutionary career such as *Changzheng huiyi lu* (A Memoir of the Long March), adding to the long list of personal accounts written by veteran Communists about this important chapter in the CCP history. More influential than his creative works are his commentaries and critical essays, which represent the mainstream Marxist tradition of the Chinese literary establishment. *See also* LEFT-WING ASSOCIATION OF CHINESE WRITERS; SPOKEN DRAMA.

CHENG NAISHAN (1946–). Novelist. Born in Shanghai, Cheng Naishan moved to **Hong Kong** with her family in 1949, but returned to her birthplace in 1956. She graduated from the Shanghai College of Education and taught English at a high school for 10 years before moving back to Hong Kong in the 1990s. Cheng's literary career is closely tied to Shanghai, which provides material and inspiration for her works. Many of her writings about the city deal with wealthy families, similar to her own, who remained in the city after the Communist victory. A member of this once privileged class, Cheng knows intimately how they have fared throughout the decades of political vicissitudes. *Lan wu* (*The Blue House*) focuses on the family of the former owner of Shanghai's largest steel mill and how their lives change in the aftermath of the revolution. Along the same line, Cheng planned to write a trilogy about an influential business tycoon and his descendents. The first book, *Jinrongjia* (*The Banker*), published in 1993 and based on her own grandfather's life, is set against the background of the **Sino-Japanese War** (1937–1945) during which the protagonist tries to avert a financial disaster by maneuvering among his business rivals, the puppet Chinese government, and the Japanese occupiers. The novel also introduces the banker's five children, setting the stage for the events that will unfold in the sequels.

A recurring theme in Cheng's works is the clash of social classes. In *Tiaoqin shi* (*The Piano Tuner*), Cheng tells about the relationship between the son of a piano tuner and the daughter of a former capitalist who find themselves separated by an invisible wall despite their physical proximity. Her most recent work, *Shanghai tange* (Shanghai Tango), recounts the glorious days of old Shanghai with its vibrant commercial culture revolving around clubs, bars, cafés, sumptuous banquets, horse races, and other grand entertainment.

CHI LI (1957–). Novelist. A popular writer whose works deal with daily lives of Chinese urbanites, Chi Li lives in Wuhan in central China and writes about the city and its residents. Her works are realistic portrayals of life in China today, addressing issues such as love and marriage, jobs, housing, children's education, food, sickness, and so on. Her style is simple and straightforward. Among her publications are *Butan aiqing* (Apart from Love) and *Kouhong* (Lipstick).

CHI ZIJIAN (1964–). Fiction writer. Chi Zijian is native to China's northeast, which she considers "the soul" of her creative imagination. Since she published her first story in the mid-1980s, Chi has produced several collections of stories and essays and a number of novels. Growing up in the remote mountainous region of Heilongjiang, Chi prefers quiet, simple country living to the thrill of urban life, a sentiment reflected in her writings. She writes in a plain but sensual language, telling stories based on her observations of life around her, particularly the folklores and customs of her hometown. She appreciates the small pleasures of what nature has to offer. Like a poet, she picks out the imperceptible bits and pieces of life and turns them into aesthetic moments. Because of the pronounced features of sentimentality, intimacy, melancholy, and nostalgia, Chi's stories often read like romantic poems. Even her novels bear characteristics of lyrical poetry; *Mangmang qiancheng* (Uncertain Prospects) and *Chen zhong xiangche huanghun* (Morning Bells Ring through Dusk) are some examples.

Wei Manzhouguo (The Puppet State of Manchuria), on the other hand, marks a radical departure from her previous endeavors. Instead of the usual concern over the individual life in contemporary rural northeast, Chi turns her attention to an important period in the region's and the nation's history. The book does not directly treat the armed resistance against the Japanese during World War II, but deals with the daily lives of the characters, from historical figures such as Emperor Puyi and guerrilla general Yang Jingyu to fictional characters who represent the ordinary folks who had to carry on with their lives under the Japanese occupation. The novel also contains references to regional customs such as the drum dance and the river lantern festival. Another ambitious novel, *E'erguna He you an* (On the Right Bank of the Argun River), an epic story narrated in the voice of a 90-year-old woman, the head of an Oroqen tribe living at the Sino-Russian border, is about the century-old history of how a traditional community tried to survive and maintain its lifestyle and human spirit under the pressure of outside forces. *Chuanyue yunceng de qinglang* (Sunshine Through Clouds), told from the perspective of a dog, is one of her rare acts of experimentation with a different form of narration. *See also* WOMEN.

CIVIL WAR (1945–1949). The ideological split between the Kuomintang (KMT), also known as the Nationalist Party, and the Chinese Communist Party (CCP) went back to 1927, when their cooperation during the Northern Expedition, whose purpose was to defeat the northern warlords and unify China, proved to be short-lived. Sensing the danger of the Communist influence within the ranks of his army, General Chiang Kai-shek broke away from the alliance and began a campaign to purge the CCP members and the leftists within the KMT. Afterward, the two parties fought intermittently, with the weaker CCP driven underground in urban areas and to the countryside to fight guerrilla wars. When the **Sino-Japanese War** broke out, the two sides formed an alliance for the second time. After the Japanese surrender, the confrontation between the KMT and the CCP resumed in a full-scale war. Fueled by a growing discontent in the nation about rampant government corruption and hyperinflation, the CCP, now better armed and with bases in rural China more consolidated, won the Civil War and gained control of the mainland (plus Hainan Island), while the KMT managed to retain the territories of the island of Taiwan, the Pescadores (Penghu), and several small islands off the coast of Fujian. To this day, the two sides remain divided.

The impact of the Civil War on modern Chinese literature was profound, not in the sense that the war was a subject matter for Chinese literature but that the ideological and political split between the Nationalists and Communists allowed Chinese literature written from the 1950s to the 1970s to have a freer and less controlled development in **Taiwan**, particularly with the modernist experiments, while the mainland preoccupied itself with ideological writings guided by the principles of **socialist realism**.

CREATION SOCIETY (CHUANGZAO SHE). Founded in 1921, the Creation Society was an influential literary organization. Its members included **Guo Moruo**, **Yu Dafu**, and other prominent names. In its early stage, it endorsed authentic expression with an emphasis on subjective, personal, and romantic sentiments. After 1925, as the Communist ideology gained popularity among Chinese intellectuals, the Creation Society promoted a form of "revolutionary literature," which influenced an entire generation of writers and readers. When it was finally closed down by the Nationalist government, many of its members joined the **Left-wing Association of Chinese Writers**. *See also* CHENG FANGWU; FENG NAICHAO; TIAN HAN; YANG HANSHENG; YE LINGFENG.

CRESCENT SOCIETY (XIN YUE PAI/SHE). Named after the journal, *Xin yue* (Crescent), which published writings by liberal-minded intellectuals, the Crescent Society represented an influential trend in 20th-century intellectual development. In social thought, it embraced humanistic and moderate reforms; in literature, it promoted modernist innovations, epitomized by **Xu Zhimo**, whose Romantic poems transformed Chinese poetry. All of its prominent members had been educated in Great Britain and the United States and were professors at Beijing's major universities, including **Hu Shi**, **Wen Yiduo**, and **Lin Huiyin**. Largely confined to academia, its influence began to diminish when *Xin yue* ceased publication in 1933.

CULTURAL REVOLUTION (WENHUA DA GEMING), FULL NAME: THE GREAT PROLETARIAN CULTURAL REVOLUTION (1966–1976). In the aftermath of his failed economic policies of the Great Leap Forward in the late 1950s, Mao Zedong was forced to stay on the political sidelines. Unsatisfied with the lost power and uneasy about the "antisocialist" tendencies within the Chinese Communist Party (CCP), Mao launched in the mid-1960s an offensive in an attempt to "purify" the CCP and regain control of the state. Mao believed that in a socialist society there always existed class struggle and the possibility of the return of capitalism and imperialism; hence the need for continuous revolutions. Mao's theory sparked two different interpretations within the party. The moderates perceived class struggle to be in the lower stratums of society where the enemies were those already overthrown: the rich peasants, the counterrevolutionaries, and the bourgeois intellectuals. The radical faction, on the other hand, wanted to extend class struggle to the highest levels of the government and to expose enemies among those still in power—the "capitalist roaders." In order to eliminate his political opponents, Mao sided with the radical faction during the beginning years of the Cultural Revolution. The Red Guards, all young students, were encouraged by the left-wing radicals to bring down government authorities in Beijing and in the provinces, which resulted in serious civil disorder, total collapse of the economy, and massive destruction of cultural institutions.

The aborted coup mounted by Mao's appointed successor, Lin Biao, in September 1971, eroded the influences of the left-wing radicals and led to the rehabilitation of disgraced former party leaders, including Deng Xiaoping, who was reinstated as a vice premier in April 1973. In 1976, three of the most senior party leaders passed away: Premier Zhou Enlai in January, Zhu De (then chairman of the Standing Committee of the National People's Congress) in July, followed by Mao Zedong in September. The country was also visited by an unprecedented natural disaster in that year: an earthquake devastated the city of Tangshan in Hebei Province, confirming the popular Chinese belief that the "mandate of heaven" was withdrawn from the rulers. In less than a month after Mao's death, the radical Gang of Four, led by Mao's wife Jiang Qing, were arrested, bringing the Cultural Revolution to an end. In 1981, the Central Committee of the Chinese Communist Party officially condemned the Cultural Revolution as a "serious national disaster launched and led by Mao Zedong and exploited by Lin Biao and Jiang Qing and their counterrevolutionary cliques."

During the Cultural Revolution, literary activities nearly came to a halt, with veteran writers thrown in the labor camps as in the case of **Ding Ling**, tortured to death as happened to **Zhao Shuli**, driven to suicide such as **Lao She**, or in most cases, forced to put down the pen due to the harsh political atmosphere. Very few came out of it unscathed. Those who managed to remain afloat were required to write politically mandated works. The so-called proletarian art in the form of revolutionary model operas, produced under the direct guidance of Mao's wife Jiang Qing, influenced the literary field in a number of ways: works were often created by a group of people and therefore bore no individual authorship; radical ideological themes, particularly class struggle, and larger-than-life heroes such as those portrayed in such novels as *Ouyang Hai zhi ge* (The Song of Ouyang Hai) and *Huanghai hong shao* (The Red Sentry of the Yellow Sea) were the only mode of expression. One of the handful of writers who emerged during the Cultural Revolution as standard-bearers of the era was **Hao Ran**, the most celebrated writer at the time. His novels about class struggle and enlightened peasants in the countryside were widely promoted by the authorities. *Jinguang da dao* (The Golden Road), *Yanyang tian* (*The Bright Clouds*), and *Xishao ernü* (Sons and Daughters of Xisha) were among the very few novels allowed on the shelves of bookstores.

When the Cultural Revolution ended, the serious damage it had done to the country's political and cultural institutions and the devastating effects it had on the the Chinese national psyche have been extensively explored in literature, first in the so-called **scar literature** represented by **Liu Xinwu**, Lu Xinhua, and others, and later by writers exiled to the Chinese frontier or labor camps, such as **Wang Meng** and **Zhang Xianliang**, and most prominently by the large number of educated youths sent to the countryside, such as **Ah Cheng, Zhang Chengzhi, Liang Xiaosheng, Han Shaogong**, and **Wang Xiaobo**. *See also* BEI DAO; CAN XUE; CHEN RUOXI; DENG YOUMEI; FENG JICAI; GAO XIAOSHENG; GAO XINGJIAN; GU CHENG; GU HUA; HE LIWEI; JING FU; KE YUNLU; LAO SHE; LI GUANGTIAN; LIANG XIAOSHENG; LU WENFU; LU XING'ER; MANG KE; SHEN RONG; SHIZHI; SU TONG; TIAN HAN; WANG ANYI; XIAO JUN; YAN GELING; YAN LIANKE; YANG JIANG; YANG LIAN; YE ZHAOYAN; YU HUA; ZHANG JIE; ZHANG KANGKANG; ZHENG YI.

– D –

DAI WANGSHU (1905–1950). Poet. Born in Hangzhou, Dai Wangshu studied literature and French in college and became one of the foremost modern Chinese poets. His first poem "Ninglei chu men" (Leaving Home in Tears) appeared in the inaugurating issue of *Yinluo* (A Jade Necklace), a literary journal he founded with his friends. Dai spent three years in France and was influenced by French symbolist poets, especially Paul Verlaine, whose style appealed to Dai's classical sensibilities. In 1929, his first collection of poetry, *Wode jiyi* (My Memories), was published and one of the poems, "Yu xiang" (A Rainy Alley), became an instant favorite among both critics and readers and remains one of the beloved modern poems. Other works, such as "A Dream Seeker" and "Bird of Paradise," helped elevate Dai to the ranks of China's leading poets. Disillusionment and melancholy are signature themes of his early poetry, expressed in a sentimental voice and a colloquial language interspersed with rhythms commonly found in classical Chinese poetry.

A significant contributor to the development of modern vernacular poetry, Dai showed an unwavering attention to form, which he considered to be the essence of poetry. He succeeded in creating a new poetic form that draws from both classical Chinese tradition and modern Western styles such as those used by the English Romantics and the French symbolists. He edited *Xiandai shi feng* (Modern Poetic Styles) and was a founder of *Xin shi* (New Poetry), platforms for Chinese experimental poetry and translations of Western works. Credited with introducing many French writers to the Chinese public, he was also an avid reader and translator of Spanish and Russian literature. Dai died of illness the year after the People's Republic of China was established. *See also* MODERNISTS.

DENG YOUMEI (1931–). Novelist. Though a veteran writer, Deng Youmei did not come to prominence until the early 1980s when he published a series of stories based on folklore and old traditions of Beijing. "Huashuo Taoran Ting" (Talking about Taoranting Park), *Nawu* (Nawu), *Yan hu* (*Snuff Bottles*), and "Xunzhao Hua'r Han" (Looking for Han the Forger) are among his best-known works. Thematically and aesthetically, these stories opened a new direction for post-Mao literature. Instead of writing directly about the destructive **Cultural Revolution**, a popular literary trend that was later given the name **scar literature**, Deng found inspiration in the old customs of Beijing formed by centuries of history as the political and cultural capital of the country, and particularly through the Manchu influences of the Qing dynasty. The main character in *Nawu* is a descendant of Manchu nobility who is an expert in many things, from cockfights and dog races to Peking opera and ancient art, everything except for the basic skills that could help him make a living at the time. "Xunzhao Hua'r Han" portrays the vicissitudes in the life of an antiques connoisseur. "Huashuo Taoran Ting" is set against the political backdrop of the 1970s, but the focus is on four old men practicing tai chi in the park. Deng makes good use of traditional institutions and objects, such as theaters, old academies, antiques, paintings, and calligraphies through which his characters interact with one another to form social connections. For his effort in searching for the old ways of life characteristic of a specific locale, Deng is considered one of the forerunners of the **root-seeking** movement in the post-Mao era. He took as models classical Chinese literature and art, such as *Hong lou meng* (*A Dream of Red Mansions*), *Shuihu zhuan* (*The Water Margin*), and the painting "Qingming shanghe tu" (The Scene of the Upper River at Qingming), which focus on presenting multiple facets of life in a particular place with attention to details that carry significant relevance to history.

Deng is a self-educated man who learned to write in the Communist army, which he joined in the early 1940s. After he left the army in 1949, he worked as a playwright in the Beijing People's Art Theater. Like many of his contemporary writers, Deng followed the dictates of the party and wrote stories and plays to serve the socialist cause. In 1957, when intellectuals were purged for having criticized the party bureaucracy, Deng was labeled a rightist and was dismissed from his job. The difficult years he had spent before being fully cleared in 1976 gave him many opportunities to get to know people from all walks of life who became material for his most memorable works.

DING LING, A.K.A. TING LING, PEN NAME OF JIANG BING-ZHI (1904–1986). Fiction writer. One of the most influential and most studied writers in modern Chinese literature, Ding Ling led a rich and colorful life that in many ways mirrored the journey progressive Chinese intellectuals took during the 20th century. Born in a small town in Hunan Province, Ding Ling was fortunate enough to have a liberal and fiercely independent mother who became the headmistress of a primary school when most **women** at the time stayed home. The **May Fourth Movement** of 1919 had a great impact on young Ding Ling. In 1921, she openly challenged tradition by publishing an article in a newspaper denouncing her uncle's refusal to dissolve her engagement to his son. She won her freedom and the victory made her aware of the power of the pen. In the spring of 1922, she traveled to Shanghai and Nanjing to pursue further education. She later moved to Beijing and attended literature classes taught by **Lu Xun** and other eminent writers. Ding Ling applied for admission to an art school but failed the entrance exam. She also toyed with the idea of becoming a movie actress. Dejected and confused, Ding Ling began to write novels partly out of loneliness and partly out of dissatisfaction with the society that provided very few opportunities for women.

In 1927, Ding Ling's first story, "Meng Ke" (A Woman Named Meng Ke), appeared in *Fiction Monthly*, a major literary journal. The following year, she published *Shafei nüshi de riji* (*Miss Sophie's Diary*), one of her best-known works, followed by more short stories about women. Ding Ling's works reflect the pulse of the times. The problems faced by women, especially young intellectual women, are at the center of her stories. "Meng Ke," *Shafei nushi de riji*, and another story, "Shu-jia zhongxin" (Summer Vacation), are all about the new generation of educated women who emerged after the May Fourth Movement. Shafei, for example, rebels against her family and its feudal ethics in pursuit of love and the meaning of life on her own terms. **Mao Dun**, a powerful critical voice of the time, remarked that Shafei is "representative of the rebellious young women who are abused and injured by the times." With an impressive body of works, Ding Ling quickly became a rising star. In 1932, she joined the **Left-wing Association of Chinese Writers** and the Communist Party the following year, thus beginning her lifelong association with the Communist cause.

"Tianjiachong" (Tianjiachong Village), a short story published in July 1931, marked a transition in Ding Ling's literary career. She replaces the self-absorbed, sentimental bourgeois heroine portrayed in her early works with the socially engaged, politically active intellectual woman. The protagonist of this story is an educated young woman from a landed family who goes to a rural village to educate and mobilize the peasants. For the first time in her writing career, Ding Ling places an educated woman in the midst of the working class, depicting her role in the communist revolution. As Ding Ling became increasingly devoted to communism, her writing became more dominated by ideology. Between 1931 and 1933, Ding Ling wrote 11 short stories on the miserable conditions of the workers and peasants and their rebellious struggles guided by the Communist Party. Ding Ling abandoned the gloomy sentiments displayed in her earlier works and instead embraced an optimistic outlook. These stories were considered important achievements for the left-wing literary movement and subsequently made Ding Ling a target of the Nationalist government. In May 1933, she was abducted and spent three years in captivity in a secret location before finally managing to flee in September 1936 to the Communist base in northern Shaanxi.

Ding Ling's arrival in the Communist-held region began a new chapter of her life. She was warmly greeted by the leaders of the Communist Party and soon developed friendships with Mao Zedóng and other high-ranking officials and generals. After the Japanese invasion, Ding Ling's work revolved around the war effort. She wrote for and edited newspapers and literary journals in an attempt to mobilize the masses and boost morale. The most representative of her writings in this period are seven short stories, including "Wozai xiacun de shihou" (*When I*

Was in the Xia Village). While the country was still embroiled in the **Civil War**, Ding Ling joined a land reform work team in the Communist-controlled north. She immersed herself in the life of the peasants, making investigations, visiting the poor, and participating in their work. She accumulated firsthand material that would later be used to write *Taiyang zhao zai Sanggan he shang* (*The Sun Shines over the Sanggan River*), a novel about the complexity of land reform, which won the Soviet Union's Stalin Prize (second place) in 1951.

After the founding of the People's Republic of China, Ding Ling held many official positions, including party secretary of the National Writers' Association and director of the Literary and Art Division of the Propaganda Ministry. The articles, essays, commentaries, and some short stories she wrote during this period received little critical notice and in the late 1950s Ding Ling was exiled to remote farms until 1977, when she was restored to her former positions and returned to Beijing. *See also* SINO-JAPANESE WAR; WOMEN.

DING XILIN (1893–1974). Playwright. Trained as a scientist, Ding Xilin was a rare case in Chinese literary circles. He was a student of physics and mathematics at the University of Birmingham from 1914 to 1920 and taught physics at universities in China throughout his life. After 1949, he held several official titles: representative to the People's Congress, vice minister of culture, director of Beijing Library, and member of the standing committee of the Association of Chinese Playwrights.

Ding was interested in literature at a young age, but it was his sojourn in Great Britain that gave him the opportunity to read a wide variety of Western works that inspired him to write plays. In the 1920s, Ding was arguably the greatest playwright on the stage of *aimei ju* (the amateur play), a precursor to the modern **spoken drama**. His first play, *Yizhi mafeng* (*A Wasp*), a romantic comedy written in 1923, pokes fun at social taboos that prohibit young people from finding their own marriage partners. Its success motivated him to produce more works: *Qin'ai de zhangfu* (*Dear Husband*), *Jiu hou* (*Flushed with Wine*), *Yapo* (*Oppression*), and *Xia le yizhi yan* (One Eye Blinded), all written in the 1920s. He continued to write in the 1930s and 1940s, and his last work came out in 1961. In addition to *Yizhi mafeng*, his best-known plays are *Yapo*, about two young people pretending to be married in order to satisfy the landlord who refuses to take in unmarried young tenants, and *San kuai qian guobi* (Three Dollars), which features a university student showing his indignation at a rich lady who demands from her servant a payment of three dollars for having broken her vase. Ding wrote mostly one-act comedies, satirizing the small injustices and social conventions in everyday life. Although they contain evidences of leftist ideology, his plays are subtle in their message and focus on class, gender, and generational conflicts. Ding prefers a simple plot, unexpected resolution, and a humorous but elegant vernacular language to create comic moments.

Ding was a man of many talents. Other than his profession as a physicist and his success in the theater, he also dabbled in language reform, having invented a system that uses character strokes for looking up words in a dictionary, a system that has been put to new use for entering Chinese characters with a computer.

DONG QIZHANG, A.K.A. DUNG KAI CHEUNG (1967–). Fiction writer. Born and raised in **Hong Kong**, Dong Qizhang received his master's degree in comparative literature from Hong Kong University. One of the most talented writers coming out of Hong Kong, Dong has produced an impressive output of works, most of which are novellas and novels. He is the recipient of numerous awards, including Taiwan's prestigious Unitas Literature Award.

His first award-winning novella "Anzhuo zhenni" (Androgyny) describes a female scientist who runs away from an unhappy marriage and lives in a remote mountain to research a rare type of lizard. As a modern, independent **woman** with strong feminist beliefs, she rejects the traditional role expected of her and refuses to be a "baby-making machine," a role into which her loveless marriage has essentially reduced her. Dong devotes a good amount of pages to the nature and habits of the androgynous lizard, which represents the woman's radical feminist position: without relying on men to reproduce, women could forever forsake male oppression and become truly independent. After the success of "Androgyny," Dong continued to explore gender identity in *Shuang shen* (A Hermaphrodite), a novel reminiscent of Virginia Woolf's *Orlando*. The protagonist wakes up one morning to find himself metamorphed into a female body and in so doing he/she gains a unique perspective into the multiplicity of human nature. In deconstructing the conventional ideas of gender differences, the novel makes references to Chinese myths about animals that embody both the *yin* and the *yang*.

Dong's novels are ambitious in terms of both scope of subjects and degree of innovation. Although they are rooted in Hong Kong realities, Dong is more interested in examining universal issues within history—not just human history but the history of the universe. The sheer vastness of intellectual territory his novels encompass is breathtaking and unprecedented in modern Chinese literature. *Tian gong kai wu: Xuxu ru zhen* (The Beginning of Things: The True Life of Xuxu) and *Shijian fan shi: Yaci zhi guang* (A Complex History of Time: Yaci's Light), parts one and two of his *Ziran shi sanbuqu* (Trilogy of a Natural History) represent such a multicourse feast (part three is yet to be published). These novels are set in Hong Kong but the issues covered in them are undoubtedly universal. What concerns Dong is human behavior in the material work and individual conduct in the development of civilizations. He studies material culture by looking at how the radio, telephone, sewing machine, automobile, typewriter, camera, book, and other daily goods have been invented and made and their relationship with the individual, the family, and the city. Through the portrayal of the life and work of the writer/protagonist, he also examines the dynamics between the creator/writer and the created/character.

Often characterized as postmodern, Dong's works are influenced by Jorge Luis Borges and Italo Calvino. Like these masters, Dong loves to push the limits of novel writing to the extreme. He sets out to break barriers between different genres, mixing, in his cauldron of fiction, scientific, philosophical, literary, sociological, and political discourses. Part of the reason that he stretches across so many fields is that each new discovery stimulates his imagination, renews his creativity, and provides a refreshing angle from which to examine the world around him.

DUANMU HONGLIANG, PEN NAME FOR CAO JINGPING (1912–1996). Fiction writer, playwright, and essayist. Born in Liaoning Province in northeast China, Duanmu Hongliang began writing fiction while studying history at Qinghua University in Beijing. Along with **Xiao Hong**, to whom he was briefly married, **Xiao Jun**, and other young writers from the Japanese-occupied Manchuria, Duanmu fled his homeland and wandered throughout China during the war years. He joined the **Left-wing Association of Chinese Writers** and became one of its most prominent voices.

Before 1949, Duanmu wrote mostly fiction. He aimed at capturing the spirit of his homeland by emphasizing its natural beauty and its hardy, earthy people. Duanmu is known for his passion for the land and the poetic language he uses to describe it. The work that best characterizes his art is his first novel, *Kerqinqi caoyuan* (The Khorchin Grassland), published in 1933. The book relates the rise and fall of a landed family on the eve of the Japanese invasion. Praised for its use of local dialect and its depiction of life in the northeast, the novel garnered admiration from important figures in the community of progressive intellectuals. Other notable works include his first short story, "Cilu hu de youyu" (The Sorrows of the Egret Lake), which depicts life in the northeast under Japanese occupation, "Liming de yanjing" (Eyes of Daybreak), and "Zao chun" (An Early Spring), about simple country folks. After 1949, Duanmu wrote mostly plays and political and literary essays. His most noteworthy accomplishment during the period is a fictionalized biography of Cao Xueqin, author of the most prominent novel in classical Chinese literature, *Hong lou meng* (*A Dream of Red Mansions*). Duanmu died as he was working on the third volume. *See also* SINO-JAPANESE WAR; SPOKEN DRAMA.

DUO DUO, PEN NAME OF SU SHIZHENG (1951–). Poet. Born and raised in Beijing, Duo Duo spent two years in rural Hebei during the **Cultural Revolution**. As one of the main **Misty poets**, Duo Duo has gone through many changes in his life and in his art. A founding member of the Today group, along with **Bei Dao** and **Mang Ke**, Duo Duo rose to fame in the 1980s but was forced to leave China in June 1989 when the Chinese government cracked down on the **Tian'anmen Prodemocracy Movement** with which Duo Duo was associated. Fifteen years later, however, he was not only allowed to return to China to live and teach, but the official Xinhua News Agency honored him with its 2004 Poet of the Year Award.

Duo Duo's poetic style has also undergone several changes, from the terse and cryptic political verse of his early career to the prosaic philosophical lines in recent years. His early experimental poems, such as "Mi zhou" (Honey Week) and "Zhi taiyang" (To the Sun), written in the 1970s and 1980s, are considered important pieces in the underground poetry movement, both in terms of style and vision. His later poems, particularly those written in the 1990s, such as "Guo hai" (Crossing the Sea), "Tamen" (They), and "Guilai" (Homecoming), while consistent with the poet's love for symbols and imageries, pay more attention to the exploration of the mysteries of life. Many years of living in the West have left deep imprints on his poetry. He has dealt with the theme of exile and alienation and, more important, his sojourn exposed him to poetic traditions that have produced prominent poets such as Charles Baudelaire, Sylvia Plath, and others who have influenced his work. Written exclusively in Chinese, Duo Duo's poems have been translated into many languages.

– E –

ERYUE HE, PEN NAME OF LING JIEFANG (1945–). Novelist. Born in Xiyang, Shanxi Province, Eryue. After high school, he joined the army, where he stayed for the next 10 years. Currently he lives in Henan and is the deputy chairman of the Writers' Association of Henan. Arguably the most popular and one of the most commercially successful writers in China today, Eryue He is a household name, in part because of the TV movies made from his historical novels. His reputation goes beyond China to reach all of the major Chinese communities in the rest of the world. His novels have been reprinted more than a dozen times, not including a variety of pirated editions. He has won many prestigious awards, including the Best Historical Novel Prize. His work is based on China's dynastic history, specifically the reigns of three Qing emperors: Kangxi, Yongzheng, and Qianlong, covering 140 years of a powerful empire. The three novels, *Kangxi Dadi* (Kangxi: the Great Emperor), *Yongzheng Huangdi* (Emperor Yongzheng), and *Qianlong Huangdi* (Emperor Qianlong), totaling 10 volumes and taking him 20 years to write, center on power struggles behind the walls of the imperial court. At the same time, they unfold a broad canvas of characters from all walks of life: concubines, officials, scholars, peasants, businessmen, and many others. Because of their large scope, the novels are considered encyclopedias of the Qing dynasty. Thoroughly researched, these novels, while re-creating history, convey the author's conflicted feelings about traditional culture; his portrayals of an empire from its youth to the beginning of its decline reveal a sense of nostalgia and a lamentation at the irretrievable vitality of a great era. Heavily influenced by classical Chinese novels, particularly Cao Xueqin's *Hong lou meng* (*A Dream of Red Mansions*), Eryue He believes that historical novels should be built on real historical events and enhanced through imaginative treatment of circumstances.

– F –

FAN WEN (1962–). Fiction and prose writer. Born in Zigong, Sichuan Province, Fan Wen received a B.A. in Chinese from Southwestern Education University in 1985. A member of the Chinese Writers' Association, Fan currently lives in Kunming and is the associate editor of *Wenxue jie* (The Literary Field). His early works, mostly fiction, began to appear in 1986, with a majority of the stories depicting contemporary Chinese life and novels portraying historical figures and events. His 1999 novel, *Qing guan Hairui* (Hairui: An Honest Official), is based on a well-known Ming dynasty scholar-official. Fan's fame, however, rests largely on two novels about Tibetans and other ethnic minorities in the southwest, *Shui ru dadi* (Land of Harmony) and *Beimin dadi* (Land of Compassion), both inspired by his numerous trips to **Tibet**, including the Tibet Expedition sponsored by Yunnan Press in 1999 to promote the history and culture of the region. Fan was especially familiar with an area in Yunnan Province that borders the Tibetan Autonomous Region, where ancient traders made their living by journeying between Lhasa and the hinterland through the famous Tea and Horse Route along the narrow valley of the Lanchang River. *Shui ru dadi* is set in eastern Tibet in a town called Yanjin, named after its ancient salt industry, where the Tibetans have lived side by side with the Naxis, the Chinese, and and others for hundreds of years. Several religious practices, including Tibetan Buddhism, Dongba, and Christianity, fought oftentimes violently for the hearts and minds of the locals in the first half of the 20th century. The novel unfolds a multiethnic, multicultural history hitherto unknown to many Chinese. *Beimin dadi* tells of the spiritual odyssey of an ordinary man who becomes a holy monk through extraordinary trials, including the deaths of all his loved ones. Influenced by Gabriel García Márquez and magic realism in Latin American literature, Fan's novels are imbued with mysterious events and supernatural exploits that reflect Tibetan beliefs in the supernatural. An amateur anthropologist, Fan frequently inserts his field research notes, including interviews and sketches, into the fictional narrative. In addition to his fictional works, Fan has written two travelogues that also deal with Tibetan history and culture: *Cangmang gu dao: hui bu qu de lishi bei ying* (Endless Ancient Path: Inerasable Shadow of History) and *Zangdong tanxian shouji* (Notes of an Expedition in Eastern Tibet).

FAN XIAOQING (1955–). Fiction writer. Born and raised in the southern city of Suzhou, Fan Xiaoqing spent several years in the countryside after high school. In 1977 she entered Jiangsu Teachers' College as a Chinese major and four years later joined its faculty. She became a professional writer in 1985 and serves at present as the deputy director of Jiangsu Writers' Association. Fan is a prolific writer and has received numerous awards for her short stories and novels. In the 1980s, she was celebrated for her portrayals of social relationships and lifestyles in the alleys of Suzhou in such works as *Kudang xiang fengliu ji* (The Romantic Life in the Crotch Alley) and *Lao an* (Old Shores), about the life of rickshaw workers during the beginning years of the post-Mao era. In the 1990s, she turned her attention to examining the muddy waters of Chinese bureaucracy in what has been called her "political novels," the best known of which are *Nü tongzhi* (A Female Comrade), *Bai ri yangguang* (One Hundred Days of Sunlight), and *Chengshi biaoqing* (The Facial Expressions of a City), all dealing with intricate relationships within the governmental system that puts the individual's ideals and moral standards in direct conflict with the expectations of the political power structure. The difficult negotiations and compromises her characters are forced to make in order to survive reveal some of the fundamental flaws of the system. Fan's style is generally naturalistic, accessible to the general readership, and her stories and novels describe characters and subjects close to everyday contemporary life. She is considered a "restrained" writer whose views on society and human nature tend to be moderate, even though her subject matter is often political. Fan also writes scripts for film and television. *See also* WOMEN.

FANG FANG, PEN NAME OF WANG FANG (1955–). Fiction writer. Fang Fang graduated from Wuhan University where she majored in Chinese. Often mentioned with **Chi Li**, another Wuhan writer, Fang is noted for her "new realist" stories, which present contemporary urban life with an accessible style. Her novellas *Taohua can* (Brilliant Are the Peach Blossoms), *Fengjing* (Scenery), and *Luori* (Sunset), among others, are all about life in the city of Wuhan. She portrays the difficulties of survival for the urban poor and the rivalries and distrust that exist among friends and family. Caught in the midst of abject poverty, her characters struggle in a spiritual quagmire, out of which they are unable or unwilling to extract themselves. Economic and social injustice breeds hatred and distorts human nature so that those few who have managed to climb out of their miserable conditions have succeeded only through dishonorable and ruthless means. In this seemingly hopeless urban slum, traditional morals struggle to prevail. In her novella *Wanjian chuan xin* (Ten Thousand Arrows Piercing the Heart), Fang Fang portrays a flawed character who redeems herself by doing hard manual labor to provide for her family. Throughout her career since the 1980s, while depicting urban life, Fang Fang has consistently focused her attention on **women,** investigating the disconnect between their dreams and reality. In the urban slums and the white-collar world, Fang Fang finds multidimensioned women who struggle to come to terms with their emotional needs under enormous social and economic pressure. The unambiguous empathy for women and their conditions shown in the stories manifests the author's feminist stance.

FEI MA (1936–), PEN NAME OF MA WEIYI. Poet. Born in Taizhong, **Taiwan,** Fei Ma moved with his family, soon after birth, back to his ancestral village in Guangdong. In 1948, he followed his father back to Taiwan, leaving behind on the mainland his mother, whom he would not see again for 30 years. He graduated with a Ph.D. in nuclear engineering from the University of Wisconsin, and has made a living as a nuclear energy researcher, but has made his fame as a poet. He was a member of the Bamboo Hat Society, the only mainlander among its exclusively Taiwanese membership. Considered a "black horse" in Taiwanese poetry, Fei Ma wrote poems in the 1950s and 1960s that showed compassion and concern for society and people, in direct opposition to the modernist and surrealist trends prevalent in Taiwan's poetry circles. In accordance with the Bamboo Hats' emphasis on social criticism, Fei Ma's poems take into account the social responsibility of the poet to his society in order to move his readers. Philosophical in its tone and realistic in its description, Fei Ma's poetry embraces the modern. In his opinion, modern poetry should strive to achieve four goals: social relevance, symbolism, originality, and economy of words. *Zai fengcheng* (*In the Wind City*), *Lu* (Road), and *Dudu yousheng de mati* (Sounds of the Horse Hoofs) are some of his publications.

FEI MING, PEN NAME OF FENG WENBING (1901–1967). Fiction writer and poet. A student of **Zhou Zuoren,** Fei Ming was a unique writer, well known in 1930s and the 1940s. His influence could be felt in the works of younger writers such as **Shen Congwen** and **Wang Zengqi,** two prominent writers in modern Chinese literature. However, as modern Chinese literature became increasingly realistic and utilitarian, Fei Ming's subjective, personal narratives became somewhat irrelevant and his name remained unmentioned for several decades until the 1990s, when his works reemerged from layers of dust.

Buddhism, classical Chinese poetry, and modern Western literature informed much of Fei Ming's work. Fei Ming was born in Huangmei, Hubei Province, an important place in the development of Chinese Buddhism because it was there that the Fourth, Fifth, and Sixth Patriarchs had practiced. Furthermore, the Fifth Patriarch was a Huangmei native. As a child, Fei Ming often accompanied his grandmother to the local temples. When he entered Beijing University in 1922, he was a frequent interlocutor with **Hu Shi**, who was writing a book on Zen Buddhism, and his teacher Zhou Zuoren was also a Buddhist. With a profound knowledge of Buddhist sutras, Fei Ming earned the respect of learned monks with whom he debated and shared ideas. He especially gravitated toward the ancient Chinese literary tradition that embraced the belief in simplicity and spontaneity advocated by Zen Buddhism as found in works by such preeminent poets as Wang Wei and Su Shi. While a student in the Foreign Languages Department of Beijing University, Fei Ming was exposed to symbolism and stream of consciousness, which coincided with some of the concepts embodied in Zen Buddhism and Tang poetry. What Fei Ming strove to achieve in his work was an artistic vision, a spiritual revelation, or a sensual image. His narrative is terse and compact, a feature that relates more to lyrical prose than to fiction, putting the emphasis on subjective feelings aroused through acute senses rather than mimetic descriptions of characters and intricate arrangements of plots. Noted for his economy of words, Fei Ming is celebrated for his ability to convey, through a simple, unadorned language, a profound outlook on life and society.

Fei Ming's earlier works, such as the short stories in *Zhulin de gushi* (Bamboo Grove Stories) and the novel *Qiao* (*Bridge*), paint scenes of a pastoral life, often viewed from the perspective of an innocent child, or simple country person, whose heart is portrayed as pure, uncluttered by worldly concerns and thus closest to the highest form of truth. Seeking peace and simplicity is at the core of these stories. Fei Ming's later works *Moxuyou xiansheng zhuan* (Biography of Mr. Nothing) and *Moxuyou xiansheng zuo feiji yihou* (After Mr. Nothing Takes a Ride in a Plane) are in many ways portraits of his own life. Here Fei Ming's protagonist no longer lives in a utopian world as those in his earlier works do; Mr. Nothing leads an ordinary life, going to the market, teaching Chinese, writing an essay, among other daily routines. What this character displays is a sense of total surrender, a sort of free flow, without any deliberate effort to achieve something, even freedom itself. Mr. Nothing is, after all, a manifestation of the Zen state of being.

FEIFEISM (FEIFEI ZHUYI). Established in Sichuan in 1986, Feifei (meaning "no no," a phrase coined by the group), represents a counter-cultural movement in poetry. Named after its journal, *Feifei* (Rejection), it includes a large number of poets scattered around the country. To be considered a Feifeist, a poet has to subscribe to the ideals promoted by *Feifei*, whose mission is to challenge the social and literary norms of the country. The Feifeist movement, which has flourished under ideological as well as market pressures, can be divided into two stages. The first, which lasted from 1986 to 1989, was characterized by its radical, subversive stance made evident by its proclamation of anticulture, antisublime, and antirhetoric. In 1988, **Zhou Lunyou**, who cofounded the movement, published his most contentious essay, "Fan jiazhi" (Anti-value), in the third issue of *Feifei*, announcing the intention to wage a war against all forms of establishment. He advocated targeting culture and its privileged concepts such as beauty, harmony, symmetry, completion, truth, and style in order to carry out a systematic subversion of conventional semantics. To accomplish this mission, Zhou and his colleagues engaged in the invention of new words and the deliberate use of unseemly expressions. Representing Feifei's vision and aesthetics are Zhou's own poems, in particular "Ziyou fangkuai" (Freedom Squares) and "Tou xiang" (Head Portrait), Yang Li's "Gao chu" (The Summit), Lan Ma's "Shi de jie" (The Demarcation of the World), and "Zu shi" (A Set of Poems) by He Xiaozhu.

Since 1989, the Feifeists have adopted a new tactic, advocating "personal writing" that calls for "pure Chinese language," uncorrupted by Western influences. This nationalistic assertion emphasizes the need to shift away from the preoccupation with the West, which has dominated Chinese intellectual thought and expression since the beginning of the 20th century. The Feifeist poets see no need to esteem the great masters of the West; instead, they position themselves as perpetual innovators and each writing act is projected as a fresh beginning, a "zero point." Chen Yaping, Chen Xiaofan, and Yuan Yong emerged as prominent members of the movement. Chen Yaping's poems "Yingxiang sanbuqu"

(Trilogy of Influence) are particularly important in defining Feifeism's position at this stage.

FENG JICAI (1942–). Novelist and painter. Multitalented, Feng Jicai has tried his hand at professional basketball, painting, the study of folk art, and a successful writing career launched in the 1970s with historical novels. Driven by a desire to preserve the memory of the **Cultural Revolution**, the most important historical event in his lifetime, Feng wrote fictional accounts of the tumultuous era, including *Pu hua de qi lu* (A Strayed Path Covered with Flowers), *Ah!* (Ah!), and *Ganxie shenghuo* (Thanks to Life), exposing the devastating effect of blind political idealism on human relationships. He also collected real stories of people who suffered in the Cultural Revolution and published their experiences in *Yibaige ren de shi nian* (*Ten Years of Madness: Oral Histories of China's Cultural Revolution*).

Driven by the same historical impulse but writing in a completely new narrative style, Feng created *Shen bian* (*The Miraculous Pigtail*), a story about a legendary hero at the turn of the 20th century, and *Sancun jinlian* (*The Three-Inch Golden Lotus*), a tragic tale of a **woman** whose life reflects the contradictions and conflicts involved in the practice of foot-binding. *Shen bian* is a mixture of the picaresque and the realist modes and it has the characteristics of the classical Chinese historical novels with a Robin Hood–type hero. It is also a symbolic novel, with the hero's pigtail representing both the backwardness and the tenacity of the Chinese. *Sancun jinlian,* by focusing on foot-binding, explores the complexity of tradition in society. The bound feet represent both suffering and pride in the lives of women who have internalized male-centered aesthetics and values. Feng writes in a seemingly effortless style that appeals to popular taste but also wins critical acclaim. *See also* ROOT-SEEKING.

FENG NAICHAO (1901–1983). Poet and fiction writer. Born in Yokohama, Japan, to parents who were prominent members of the local Chinese community, Feng Naichao studied philosophy and art history at Tokyo University. While in college, he participated in the activities of a Marxist society organized by Japanese students, where he was exposed to leftist literary theories of the Soviet Union. In 1926, his poems began to appear in *Chuangzao yuekan* (The Creation Monthly). In the following year, invited by **Cheng Fangwu**, Feng went to China to edit *Chuangzao yuekan* and other progressive journals. He joined the Chinese Communist Party in 1928. A founding member of the **Left-wing Association of Chinese Writers**, Feng edited the Chinese Communist Party's journal *Hong qi zhoukan* (The Red Flag Weekly) for several years. After 1949, he held several relatively minor positions in the central government. In 1950, he was appointed vice president of Sun Yat-sen University and lived in Guangzhou till 1975, when he moved to Beijing to work as a consultant to Beijing Library.

Among his creative works the most significant is his poetry collection *Hong sha deng* (The Lamp with a Red Shade), published in 1928, which established his reputation as a symbolist poet. He was adept at using obscure imageries and the attention he gave to sound and color as well as the dark and gloomy sentiments expressed in his poems invoke comparisons with French symbolist poets, whose decadent aesthetics had a strong influence on Feng. In addition to these **modernist** poems, Feng also wrote some "revolutionary" verses that focus on exposing social injustice. His short stories, collected in two volumes that were published in 1929, exhibit strong modernist tendencies.

FENG XUEFENG, A.K.A. FENG HSUE-FENG (1903–1976). Poet, literary theoretician, fiction writer, and member of the Lakeside Poetry Society. Born in Yiwu, Zhejiang Province, Feng Xuefeng was a student at the Hangzhou Number One Teachers' College when he joined the Morning Light Society, a literary organization founded by **Zhu Ziqing** and others, and began writing modern poetry. In 1925, Feng went to Beijing to study Japanese at Beijing University. Two years later, he joined the Communist Party and subsequently became a founding member of the **Left-wing Association of Chinese Writers** and served as its party secretary. In 1934, Feng participated in the Communist Red Army's Long March, and two years later he was sent to Shanghai to help run the underground party branch office. During the famous debate of the late 1920s between national literature and defense literature, Feng stood firmly on **Lu Xun**'s side. He was critical of those within the Left-wing Association who declared that Lu Xun's national literature was outdated and thus had become an obstacle for the advancement of revolutionary literature. Throughout the 1930s and 1940s, Feng was a leading critical voice in left-wing literary circles. After 1949, he held many important positions including president and editor-in-chief of the People's Literature Press and vice president of the Chinese Writers' Association. From 1954 to

1976, when he died of lung cancer, Feng suffered from a series of political persecutions and spent many years in prison.

Feng was a prolific writer with many talents. Among his works are poems, lyrical essays, parables, fiction, a screenplay, and a large number of critical and theoretical works on modern Chinese literature, including critiques of Lu Xun. His poems written in the early 1920s during the Lakeside years convey an uplifting, bright outlook on life and love, filled with youthful enthusiasm and a palpable drive. His later poems written in 1941 while in prison express the strong convictions of a Communist revolutionary. He was the first person to write modern parables. Most noteworthy is his theoretical and critical work in which he lay foundations for socialist literary criticism. *See also* CIVIL WAR.

FENG YUANJUN (1900–1974). Fiction writer. Born in rural Henan, Feng Yuanjun learned classical Chinese literature at a young age from her brother Feng Youlan, who would become one of the most influential philosophers in 20th century China. After graduating from Beijing Normal University in 1923, Feng went on to receive her postgraduate degree from Beijing University two years later and her Ph.D. in literary studies from the University of Paris in 1935. She taught Chinese literature at several prestigious Chinese universities, including Jinling University for Women, Fudan University, Sun Yat-sen University, and Wuhan University, and from 1949 to her death she worked at Shandong University.

Feng began writing fiction in 1923, resulting in the publication of three collections of short stories, *Juan shi* (Xanthiums), *Chun hen* (Traces of Spring), and *Jie hui* (Destruction). These romantic tales decry traditional values and advocate rights for **women** to seek their freedom in love and marriage. The central conflict of these stories is usually between the young educated female protagonist who desires romantic love and personal liberty and her conventional parents. "Gejue" (*Separation*) is representative of such tales. On one side of the clash stands the heroine determined to rebel against an arranged marriage and pursue personal happiness at all costs and on the other is the collective will of her family equally determined to uphold traditional values. The heroine is forced to choose between her lover and her family, a conflict beyond any hope of compromise. The description of the sufferings inflicted upon her by this irresolvable clash forms the core of the narrative. Like most of Feng's stories, "Gejue" is written in the form of letters, a convenient tool to directly express the feelings of the narrator/protagonist. The first-person narrative is Feng's preferred form and as such the focus of her stories is not on plot development but on the feelings and thoughts of the characters, often triggered by scenes that surround them, a common feature found in classical Chinese poetry and plays.

An accomplished scholar in classical Chinese literature, Feng turned completely away from creative writing to focus on her academic work after the publication of *Chun hen* in 1929 and made a significant contribution to the study of traditional Chinese theater. Her scholarly publications include *Zhongguo wenxue shi* (History of Chinese Literature) and *Gu ju shuo hui* (On Classical Chinese Plays).

FENG ZHI, A.K.A. FENG CHI, PEN NAME OF FENG CHENZHI (1905–1993). Poet. Known for his sonnets, Feng Zhi was a meticulous stylist, a scholar-poet. His poems, mostly expressions of his inner thoughts, are philosophical in nature, no doubt affected by his postgraduate studies at the University of Heidelburg. A scholar of German literature, philosophy, and art, Feng favored works by Johann Wolfgang von Goethe, Rainer Maria Rilke, Søren Kierkegaard, and Friedrich Nietzsche, and existentialism particularly influenced his thinking.

Feng began writing poetry when he was a student at Beijing University in the early 1920s. His poems bear the marks of a strong influence by the **May Fourth Movement**. His first poetry collection, *Zuori zhi ge* (Songs of Yesterday), was published in 1927. From 1930 to 1935, while in Germany on a government scholarship, Feng put aside his creative work to concentrate on his Ph.D. studies. He resumed his literary career after he came back to China. Some of his best poems were written during this period. "Qi lu" (Strayed Path) is typical of his style: a meditative voice contained in a terse and compact form. Feng is well known for his sonnets modeled after the English genre. Besides poetry, Feng also wrote a large number of essays and two fictional works based on historical figures: *Wu Zixu* (Wu Zixu) and *Du Fu zhuan* (A Biography of Du Fu). He was also a noted translator of German literature.

FENG ZIKAI, PEN NAME OF FENG RUI (1898–1975). Essayist and painter. Better known as an artist, Feng Zikai graduated from Hangzhou Number One Teachers' College. He studied music and art in Japan before returning to China in 1922 to work as an art teacher and editor. Feng rose to fame following publications of his paintings, cartoons, and essays. He continued to write and paint after 1949 while holding several official posts. His early essays aim to expose social evils such as hypocrisy, selfishness, and vulgarity and to praise the innocence, purity, and intelligence of children. His later essays are characterized by humor and vigorous sentiments.

– G –

GAO JIANQUN (1954–). Novelist and essayist. A Shanxi native, Gao Jianqun is a prolific writer, having published about two dozen novellas, such as "Yaoyuan de bai fangzi" (The White House in the Distance) and "Diaoxiang" (The Statues), and several collections of essays, including *Xiongnu he Xiongnu yiwai* (The Huns and Others) and *Wo zai beifang shouge sixiang* (I Am Harvesting Ideas in the North), and most significantly his novels about the ancient nomadic peoples of Central Asia. Gao lives in Xi'an and is the deputy director of the Shaanxi Writers Association.

As one of a growing number of writers devoted to depicting the cultural landscape of China's Loess Steppe in the northwest, Gao has produced an impressive amount of writings on the people and cultures of the region, most notable of which is *Zuihou yige Xiongnu* (The Last Huns), part 1 of his Trilogy of the Great Northwest, which also includes *Zuihou de minjian* (The Last Folk World) and *Zuihou de yuan xing* (The Last Long-Distance Trip). *Zuihou yige Xiongnu* centers on three generations of one family purportedly descended from the Huns, a Eurasian nomadic people who once conquered the Chinese and the Romans but left behind no written record of their own history. How could such a powerful people disappear into the tunnel of time without a trace on the land they used to dominate? This novel attempts to answer that question by piecing together historical references, folklore, and an imagined family saga. With a sweeping introduction of the history and legends of the Huns, including their rise and fall in Europe, and a fictionalized account of the fate of two lovers, a Hun soldier and a Han woman who are believed to be ancestors of the main characters, the novel proceeds to provide a geohistory of the region in the 20th century, from the Republican period to the post-Mao era, focusing on the early decades when the Communist Party was building its Soviet-style base in northern Shaanxi. Loosely based on local archives and folklore, the novel depicts the harsh natural environment and difficult living conditions that mold the resilient and restless character of the people. *Zuihou de minjian* was first published as *Liuliu Zhen* (Liuliu Township), about a mediation office that settles conflicts and arguments among the townspeople, ranging from small thefts to criminal cases. From these civil cases, a rich tapestry of cultural traditions is revealed. *Zuihou de yuan xing* combines the narrative techniques of a martial arts novel and a detective story to tell an entertaining tale of intrigue and adventure, with events triggered by the discovery of a female corpse dug out from the grave, which travels for seven days on the road before finally being returned to the woman's husband.

A more historically based work is *Hu ma bei feng—damo zhuan* (Nomads' Horses and the Northern Wind—History of the Great Desert), an epic novel that deals with the rise and fall of ancient nomadic peoples in central Asia, including the Shanshan kingdom with its capital in Loulan, an oasis town founded in the second century B.C. that flourished for 800 years before vanishing into the sand, the Western Xia kingdom (1038–1227), and Genghis Khan's mighty empire. The novel recreates the interactions between the Han Chinese agricultural society and the nomadic culture, portraying the latter as the force that helped sustain the Chinese civilization by periodically pumping fresh blood and energy into the Han culture whenever it began to show signs of decline.

GAO XIAOSHENG (1928–1999). Fiction writer. Born in rural Jiangsu, Gao Xiaosheng began writing poetry, fiction, and plays in the 1950s, which, instead of attracting critical attention, earned him a rightist label in 1958. He was sent back to the countryside for reform through physical labor until 1979 when the party's new policy returned him to his old post. In the 1980s, two of his stories earned him national recognition, "Li Shunda zaowu" (*Li Shunda Builds a House*) and "Chen Huansheng shangcheng" (Chen Huansheng's Adventure in Town), both dealing with the changes brought about by Deng Xiaoping's economic reforms in the Chinese countryside. Li Shunda is an honest peasant whose modest ambition to build a house for himself and his family is repeatedly thwarted by unpredictable political campaigns including the Great Leap Forward and the **Cultural Revolution**, which result in the devastation of the country's economy and morality. Experience has taught Li valuable lessons and when the new era of economic reform arrives, Li, now a smarter man, knows how to work the system. Chen Huansheng's transformation, from a simple workhorse who never questioned authority to a man learning to become his own master, is emblematic of the difficulties that accompany the Chinese peasantry on their journey toward selfhood in the new era of economic reforms. A son of peasants, Gao is keenly aware of both the strengths and weaknesses of Chinese peasants. He understands that the reforms offer the peasants unprecedented opportunities but they also pose serious challenges to the peasants' traditional way of thinking. Gao captures their sense of disorientation and fear. His stories, noted for their detached humor and ironic overtones, offer a scathing condemnation of capricious government policies and poke fun at the peasants' lack of consciousness.

GAO XINGJIAN (1940–). Playwright, fiction writer, critic, and painter. The winner of the 2000 Nobel Prize for literature, Gao Xingjian is widely credited with introducing "absurd theater" into China's dramatic performance. In addition, a small brochure he wrote on narrative techniques in modern Western literature stimulated discussions in the 1980s on modernism and led to a pervasive experimentation in fictional narratives in China.

Gao was born in Ganzhou, Jiangxi Province, when his family was fleeing from the Japanese invasion. He studied French at the Beijing Institute of Foreign Languages and worked as a translator for the China International Bookstore. During the **Cultural Revolution**, Gao was sent to a reeducation camp and could not publish his writings until 1979, when Deng Xiaoping's reforms brought more freedom for the country. Gao rose to fame as an innovative dramatist while working for the Beijing People's Art Theater; from 1982 to 1986 he wrote and produced a series of trend-setting plays, which were largely influenced by Bertolt Brecht, Antonin Artaud, and Samuel Beckett, including *Juedui xinhao* (Signal of Alarm), *Chezhan* (*Bus Stop*) in collaboration with Liu Huiyuan, *Ye ren* (Wild Man), and *Bi an* (The Other Shore). The antispiritual pollution campaign in 1986 halted his creative endeavors and Gao was forced to take a 10-month hiatus during which he embarked on a walking tour in the mountains of southwestern China. Gao left China in 1987 and settled in Paris, supporting himself with his paintings. After the government's crackdown on the **Tian'anmen Prodemocracy Movement** in 1989, Gao wrote a play, *Taowang* (Fugitives), denouncing the brutality of the Communist regime. The play landed him on the blacklist of the Chinese government, which declared him persona non grata.

Since the 1990s, Gao has written and directed a number of plays, including *Shengsi jie* (Between Life and Death), *Duihua yu fanjie* (*Dialogue and Rebuttal*), *Zhoumo sichongzou* (Weekend Quartet), *Yeyoushen* (Nocturnal Wanderer), and *Bayue xue* (August Snow), some of which were originally written in French. Nearly all of Gao's plays, particularly those written since the 1990s, and to some extent his novels, contain an introspective character who often steps outside himself or herself to examine the meaning of subjectivity, thus constructing a type of nihilist view on language and consciousness. Although Gao's plays have been staged all over the world, only three have ever been performed in China.

Gao has written two novels. *Ling shan* (*Soul Mountain*) is a meditative narrative recording a journey through space and time in search of a spiritual anchor. The book, which reflects his 1986 trip to Sichuan, was begun in 1982 in China and finished in 1990 in France. His autobiographical novel, *Yige ren de shengjing* (*One Man's Bible*), deals with the inner turmoil of a political exile through his relationships with two women. *See also* SPOKEN DRAMA.

GE FEI, PEN NAME OF LIU YONG (1964–). Fiction writer. Native of Jiangsu Province with a Ph.D. from East China Normal University, Ge Fei built his reputation as an **avant-garde** writer with intellectual prowess. He came into fame in the 1980s with his experimental stories, particularly *Mi zhou* (The Enigmatic Boat) and *Hese Niaoqun* (Flock of Brown Birds), which are regarded as representative texts of the Chinese avant-garde movement. He developed a style characterized by its circular movement and its tendency for abstraction, inspired in part by the works of Argentine writer Jorge Luis Borges. He also deliberately leaves out key elements in the plot, complicating the meaning of the text. In terms of language, Ge Fei retains much of the Chinese classical heritage with its stress on lyricism and refinement.

Ge Fei's novels written after 1990 are more accessible but still bear the traces of his early experimental fiction. In *Diren* (The Enemy), a mystery novel in which the main character tries to find out who set the fire that destroyed his family's business many years ago, the perpetrator is never identified but the characters mysteriously die one after the other. *Yuwang de qizhi* (The Flag of Desire), a philosophical rumination, deals with man's vulnerability, alienation, fear, and loneliness. Ge Fei's latest novel, *Renmian taohua* (A Beautiful Face Like a Peach Blossom), drops the philosophical propensity of his previous works to tell the story of a young woman and her romantic relationship with a revolutionary at the beginning of the 20th century, the last years of the turbulent reign of Emperor Guangxu (1871–1908). In this love story intertwined with history, Ge Fei crafts a utopian tale laced with exquisite sensuality and poetic sentiments.

Ge Fei's scholarly works include *Xiaoshuo yishu mianmian guan* (Various Facets of the Art of Fiction) and *Xiaoshuo xushi yanjiu* (Studies of Narrative Techniques in Fiction). He has been teaching literature at Qinghua University in Beijing since 2000.

GENERATION III POETS (DI SAN DAI SHIREN), A.K.A. NEW GENERATION/POST-MISTY/POST–NEW WAVE/CONTEMPORARY EXPERIMENTAL POETS. The generic term covers diverse poetry societies, including the influential **Feifeists** (Rejectionists) led by Sichuan poets **Zhou Lunyou**, Lan Ma, and others; the Xin chuantong (Neotraditionalists), also based in Sichuan, with **Ouyang Jianghe** and Liao Yiwu as its leading advocates; the Mang han (Reckless Man), also concentrated in Sichuan, headed by Wan Xia, Hu Dong, and others; the Tamen (They) in Nanjing, represented by **Han Dong, Yu Jian**, Wang Yin, and others; and the Haipai (Shanghai school) embodied in the works of **Chen Dongdong**, Momo, Meng Lang, and others. The term also includes many individual poets who do not officially belong to any of the above organizations, such as **Zhang Zao, Zhai Yongming, Wang Jiaxin**, and **Xi Chuan**.

For the Generation III poets, the year 1986 was a turning point. "Zhongguo xiandan shi qunti da zhan" (The Grand Showcase of Chinese Modern Poetry Movements) organized by Xu Jingya, editor for *Shenzhen qingnian bao* (Shenzhen Youth Daily), and Jiang Weiyang, editor for *Anhui Shige bao yuekan* (Anhui Poetry Monthly) provided a platform to display their work. In both theory and practice, Generation III poets differ from those of Generation I who were direct products of the **May Fourth Movement** and whose poetry is dominated by romanticism and ideology. They also depart from Generation II, better known as the **Misty poets**, the first group of modernist poets to have emerged on the mainland since 1949, who rose in rebellion against the political indoctrinations of the Mao era and whose work is essentially poetic expression of social protest. Although the Generation III poets have inherited the creative energies of the Misty poets, in contrast, their vision and tastes are postmodern, largely based on plebeian, nonheroic, antisublime sentiments. They have among themselves critics and theorists, such as Tang Xiaodu, **Zhou Lunyou**, Wang Jiaxin, and Yang Chunguang, who promote their work. The best of Generation III have persisted in their efforts to create cutting-edge, experimental poetry, refusing to be co-opted into the mainstream culture. In both form and content, they reject the preoccupation with culture, history, ideology, and aestheticism that dominated the work of the previous generations. They favor trivial, pedestrian themes, and in extreme cases, unseemly colloquialisms in an effort to deconstruct the formal properties of the Chinese language and invent some new dimensions of rhythm and meaning. The controversial work generated by these subversive poets challenges the definition of Chinese poetics. Since the late 1990s, the movement has further diversified and individualized. *See also* XIAO KAIYU.

GU CHENG (1956–1993). Poet. Born in Beijing, Gu Cheng began writing poetry when he was a child living on a remote farm in Shandong where his family, exiled from the capital, took residence at the time. He was brought to prominence in the 1980s when his first collection of poetry, *Hei yanjin* (Eyes of Darkness), was published. A member of the **Misty** poetry group, Gu was known, for his brilliant lyricism and complex metaphors. Called a "poet of fairy tales," he created in his early poems a poetic persona who looked at the world through the innocent but sorrowful eyes of a child. From the mid-1980s, his poems became increasingly experimental and their meanings harder to fathom.

Gu was invited to the West for a cultural exchange in 1987, and the following year he took a visiting position at Auckland University in New Zealand. After the Chinese government's crackdown on the **Tian'anmen Prodemocracy Movement** in 1989, Gu and his wife decided to stay in New Zealand; Gu quit his teaching job and retreated to a remote island. In 1992, he visited Europe and taught at a German university. In 1993, he committed suicide after killing his wife. He left behind a large number of poems, essays, drawings, calligraphies, and a posthumously published novel *Ying'er* (*Ying'er: The Kingdom of Daughters*), coauthored with his wife, which is a disjointed account of his infatuation with a young woman and his life after he left China.

GU HUA (1942–). Fiction writer. Born in a small village in Hunan Province, Gu Hua is noted for stories interwoven with traditional folklores and ballads that nurtured him as a child. Many of his works, including

Furong zhen (*A Small Town Called Hibiscus*), have been adapted into movies and operas.

During his early career, Gu came under the influence of the rigid ideological restrictions on literature and art under Mao Zedong and these political doctrines put limits on Gu's artistic talent. Most of his works published between 1962 and 1977 were written with an eye to the political message. As a child of poor peasants, he took the task of propagating the policies of the Communist Party seriously. He wrote about class struggle and sang the praises of the progressive forces represented by the Chinese Communist Party and the working class it led. He strove to portray life as bright and full of hope and to create a new kind of hero who could be a shining example for his readers. After 1978, as China was undergoing fundamental changes, Gu abandoned the old way of writing and turned to the memories of his childhood for inspiration. The result was a series of stories set against the background of rural Hunan, a land with which he was intimately familiar.

Gu's main works were published between 1979 and 1982, including *Pa man qingteng de xiaowu* (Log Cabin Overgrown with Creepers), a story of forest workers and their divergent attitudes toward life, *Futu shan* (Mount Futu), about a demobilized soldier who returns to his native village in the midst of a famine caused by misguided economic policies, and *Furong zhen* (*A Small Town Called Hibiscus*), a love story unfolding in four political campaigns waged one after another after 1949. These works have refreshingly real characters whose world is defined by local dialects, local customs, and local histories as well as human emotions. A writer with a strong sense of social mission, Gu seeks to reflect reality and to portray characters whose lives intersect with China's major social and political changes. *See also* SOCIALIST REALISM; CULTURAL REVOLUTION.

GUO MORUO, A.K.A. KUO MO-JO (1892–1978). Poet, playwright, and historian. Born in a small town in Sichuan Province, Guo Moruo left home to study medicine in Japan in 1914. Like **Lu Xun**, he gave up his medical career for literature and politics. He participated in the Northern Expedition (1926–1927) to end the rule of warlords and was involved in the Nanchang Uprising organized by the Communists. When the revolution failed, Guo fled to Japan, where he stayed until the **Sino-Japanese War** broke out. He returned to China and joined the anti-Japanese resistance. In 1949, he was appointed president of the Academy of Sciences and remained in that post until his death in 1978.

An influential figure in modern Chinese literature, particularly in its early period, Guo was a cofounder of the **Creation Society**. His poem "Nüshen" (Goddess) reveals signs of divergent influences from Walt Whitman to Rabindranath Tagore. Excessive exuberance marks his lyrical style. Among his dramatic works, *Qu Yuan* (Qu Yuan), based on the tragic life of the ancient poet, and *Cai Wenji* (Cai Wenji), based on another historical figure, are his most successful. He was more at home in poetry than in drama. He continued to write in the midst of a busy schedule tending to state affairs after the Communist victory. His reputation, however, was permanently marred by the less than admirable role he played in carrying out Mao Zedong's cultural policies.

His scholarly achievements, on the other hand, are well recognized. While his Marxist approach is not without its limitations, his research on inscriptions on oracle bones and bronze vessels did yield important discoveries in the understanding of ancient Chinese language, history, and material culture. *See also* MAY FOURTH MOVEMENT; SPOKEN DRAMA.

– H –

HAI XIN, PEN NAME OF ZHENG XINXIONG (1930–). A Guangdong native, Hai Xin came to **Hong Kong** in his youth and overcame many obstacles before succeeding in teaching himself to write. He primarily writes fiction about life in the lower social and economic echelons. His novels and short stories are realistic depictions of Hong Kong residents and their daily survival, providing important material for the study of Hong Kong society, in the same milieu and style of **Lü Lun** and **Shu Xiangcheng**. A prolific writer, Hai Xin has more than 20 titles to his name, including collections of short stories, novellas, and many full-length novels. His best-known work is *Tangxi sandai ming hua* (Three Generations of Famous Courtesans in Tangxi), which traces the changes taking place in the once well-known red-light district of Tangxi. Through the individual stories of three generations of courtesans and prostitutes, the author re-creates the history of Hong Kong. The influential *Hao men han men kong men* (The Gates of Wealth, Poverty, and Emptiness) is a novel about moral conventions. The heroine is a wealthy jeweler's daughter who spends 17 years in a nunnery. She chooses the monastic life as a means to escape from a messy romantic relationship with a hairdresser, the son of a servant for her family. As she passes through the three "gates," metaphors for three different social circles, she encounters not only different lifestyles but also different philosophies of life. Using her voice to represent the authorial perspective, Hai Xin passes moral judgment on the values that permeate the Hong Kong society.

HAI ZI, PEN NAME OF CHA HAISHENG (1964–1989). Poet. Born in rural Anhui, Hai Zi entered Beijing University at the age of 15, much younger than the national norm. For a son of a peasant family, this was especially rare. Four years later, with a degree in law, he began an academic career teaching law at a university in Beijing. He started writing poetry in his junior year at Beijing University and quickly gained fame as a powerful and creative voice. Increasingly withdrawn from society, he moved to a village outside Beijing and wrote feverishly; isolated from the outside word, his poetry became his only companion. While he derived a lot of satisfaction from his writing, he was frequently plagued by anxiety, loneliness, poverty, and misunderstanding. The mounting pressure he imposed on himself eventually drove him to suicide on his 25th birthday, cutting short a brilliant career as one of the most gifted poetic voices coming after the **Misty poets**. His death was especially poignant in an age seen as obsessed with materialism.

During his short life, Hai Zi wrote many poems, a play, and some essays. He took special pride in his long poems, seven in total. These long poems convey a tragic, heroic vision. *Taiyang* (The Sun), representative of this group of poems, expresses a sense of religiosity, fatalism, and universality. In his lyrical as well as dramatic poetry, Hai Zi is obsessed with death and its dark images. As the son of peasants, he is also intimately connected to the land. One of his long poems, *Tudi* (The Earth), and his lyrical wheat series are manifestations of a person intertwined with rural, agrarian life.

HAN DONG (1961–). Poet and fiction writer. Born in Nanjing, Han Dong moved to rural Jiangsu with his family when he was eight years old. He began writing poetry during his college years. After graduating from the Philosophy Department of Shandong University in 1982, Han taught Marxism at a college in Nanjing until 1993, when he quit his job to become a full-time writer. In 1985, he and some friends, including

Yu Jian, founded the poetry journal *Tamen* (They). A representative of the **Generation III** poets and a rising star in the experimental literary movement, Han advocated a plebian style of poetry that expresses everyday sentiments. "Youguan da yan ta" (About the Great Wild Goose Pagoda) and "Yi jianguo da hai" (You Have Seen the Sea) are characteristic of his prosaic poems, with more emphasis placed on conceptualization than semantic innovation. In recent years, Han has turned to writing fiction and has published two novels: *Zha gen* (Taking Roots), featuring a family forced to move to the countryside from the city during the **Cultural Revolution**, and *Wo he ni* (You and I) about a man tracing a memory of a love affair. Han's novels are characteristically meticulous in their description of minute, and at times, dry details.

HAN HAN (1982–). Novelist. A popular writer, Han Han has many fans among young readers in China. In 1999, when he was about to publish his first novel, *San chong men* (Three Doors), which portrays a small-town school that focuses exclusively on science subjects at the expense of humanities courses, leaving in despair science-challenged students, the author, like his protagonist, was a high school student who was failing his classes. Han subsequently dropped out of school to become a professional writer. Nearly all his stories and novels deal with contemporary youth culture in urban centers, particularly the dreams and troubles of high school and college students. In many ways, Han represents the generation born in the 1980s, a demographic that grew up in the economic boom era in a global consumer society fundamentally different from that of their parents' generation. Another novel, *Xiang shaonian la feichi* (Flying like Wind), depicts the growing pains of a high school dropout who becomes a member of an underground company that does business in book pirating; *Yi zuo chengchi* (A City), a novel considered by the author to be his best work so far, focuses on a group of rebellious students who lead a seemingly carefree life, running after girls, cars, and performance art. In the view of many critics, Han represents a modern, "fast-food" culture without substance and his antitradition posture belies a willing submission and subscription to consumerism and mass culture. That his books are phenomenal market successes only enhances that image. However, Han's novels, characterized by loose plots and sharp and satirical language, could be read as a serious indictment of the Chinese education system for stifling students' creativity and individuality. In a society that values book learning and encourages conformity, Han is also considered a negative example to teenagers who want to quit school to become their own free agents.

HAN SHAOGONG (1953–). Novelist. Han Shaogong gained his literary fame by writing about his native land, Hunan, in southern China. In the 1980s, with the publication of his novellas *Bababa* (Pa Pa Pa) and *Nününü* (Woman Woman Woman) and a critical essay entitled "Roots of Literature," Han placed himself at the center of a literary movement later named **root-seeking**. Together with **Ah Cheng, Jia Pingwa**, and many other post-Mao young writers, Han sought to rediscover the lost traditions of ancient Chinese culture and literature. Having spent several years as an educated youth in the Hunan countryside where the legend of Qu Yuan, one of China's most beloved poets, was a treasured folklore, he began to pay attention to traces of the ancient Chu culture, a southern tradition known for its vibrant shamanistic imagination as opposed to the more pragmatic Confucian northern tradition. In the folklores and dialects of the Miao people and the villages hidden in the mountains, isolated from modern civilization, Han believed that he had found the remains of the ancient Chu culture.

Although most critics do not group Han with China's **avant-garde** writers, he is truly postmodern in his approach to narrative innovation. While most of the root-seekers settled for the realistic mode, Han chose a separate path. The lack of specific historical reference and the supernatural elements in his novellas *Bababa* and *Nününü*, though inspired by ancient shamanistic traditions, are undoubtedly influenced by the magic realism of Latin American literature. In relating an allegorical tale about the decline of a tribe, *Bababa* calls for the spirit of the patrilinial masculine. *Nününü*, on the other hand, expresses the desire for the return of the primordial feminine, a mixture of the beautiful and the grotesque womanhood. Han's later works, especially *Maqiao cidian* (*A Dictionary of Maqiao*) and more recently *Anshi* (Hints), go even furth er in redefining the nature of fiction. Indeed, these are highly unusual fictional works. *Maqiao cidian* is written in the form of a dictionary, with more than 100 lexicon entries. It describes and analyzes the provenance of local expressions, popular myths, local history, and colorful personalities; the result is an assortment of stories loosely strung together to offer glimpses of a rural community struggling to survive the onslaught of radical changes brought by the **Cultural Revolution.**

Han juxtaposes the local speech with the highly politicized official language. The clashes of these two modes of expression produce many hilarious moments, making ironic comments on the absurdities of that era. In *Anshi*, Han continues the search for the subconscious continent associated with but beyond language. He explores the possibilities of escaping the control of signs and meanings by identifying the absurd in the midst of the normal and the microhistories buried within everyday speech. Han was awarded France's Chevalier de l'Ordre des Arts et des Lettres in 2003.

HAO RAN, PEN NAME OF LIANG JINGUANG (1932–2007). Novelist. Born in the industrial mining town of Tangshan, Hao Ran, orphaned at 12, grew up in a rural village and had only three years of formal schooling. He joined the Communist Youth League in 1949 and later worked as a journalist and editor for newspapers and magazines including *Hebei ribao* (Hebei Daily) and *Hong qi zazhi* (The Red Flag). He became a professional writer and a member of the Beijing Cultural Association in 1964.

Hao Ran began his career in the 1950s by writing about the progress made in the countryside under the leadership of Mao Zedong and the Chinese Communist Party. Two works, *Yanyang tian* (*Bright Clouds*) and *Jinguang dadao* (*The Golden Road: A Story of One Village in the Uncertain Days after Land Reforms*), made Hao the most famous writer during the **Cultural Revolution**. Both works deal with the success of land reform and collectivization in China's rural communities, focusing on class struggle and the conflict within the party between progressives and conservatives.

Written in the style of **socialist realism**, these novels portray village leaders as "perfect heroes" who represent the new, awakened peasants who are grateful to Mao Zedong and the party for having liberated them and who follow the party's policies unwaveringly. Hao Ran's other works written during this era include *Xisha ernü* (Sons and Daughters of Xisha) and *Baihua chuan* (The River of Flowers), both written under the auspices of Mao's wife Jiang Qing and her associates. Since the fall of the Gang of Four, Hao has published a number of short story collections and two novels, *Shanshui qing* (Love of the Land) and *Cangsheng* (The Common People), with the latter winning a special award for Chinese popular literature in 1991. All of Hao Ran's major works concern peasant life, with which he is intimately connected.

Hao Ran's standing in the history of modern Chinese literature is a hotly debated topic. His admirers consider him a bona fide realist writer whose works accurately reflect the enthusiasm and adulation the Chinese peasants had for the Communist Party and its socialist revolution. His detractors, on the other hand, dismiss his works written before and during the Cultural Revolution as distortions of rural reality, which advocate, with simplistic and crude techniques, for the leftist policies that have proved to be disastrous for China's rural economy. The debate notwithstanding, that Hao continued to succeed in the post-Mao era shows that he was a writer with real talent. Apparently tired of politics and the shadows cast over him by his past, Hao Ran moved out of the capital to a small town in Hebei in 1986 and lived there until his death.

HE LIWEI (1954–). Fiction writer, poet, and cartoonist. Born in Changsha, He Liwei graduated from Hunan Teachers' College. He was a poet before he began writing fiction. His stories, with poetic titles such as "Xiaocheng wu gushi" (No Story in a Small Town) and "Hua fei hua" (The Flower Is No Flower), tend to deemphasize plots and instead focus on language. His first story "Baise niao" (White Birds), which won the 1985 Best Short Story Award, tells about the innocent life of two little boys who are completely unaware of the chaos of the **Cultural Revolution** unfolding around them. Their world is solitary but sunny and peaceful, filled with the fragrance of wildflowers, pebbles on riverbanks, and white birds flying in the blue sky. To contrast the adult's cruel world with the children's serene environment represented a new approach to writing about the Cultural Revolution, making the memory of the era even more frightening. Like a classical imagistic poem, the meaning of the story is hidden in the imageries symbolizing the beauty of childhood. This lyrical approach to fiction writing appears in most of He's stories.

If He intended his short stories to be sonatas, he envisioned his novellas as symphonies. He liked to string together several independent stories in one text to express the main theme. *Guang he yingzi* (Light and Shadow), *Gen aiqing kaikai wanxiao* (Joking with Love), and *Beifang luoxue nanfang luoxue* (It Snows in the North and It Snows in the South), all about love and marriage, are structured in the same manner. He currently lives in Changsha and is the chairman of the Hunan Writers' Association. *See also* ROOT-SEEKING LITERATURE.

HE QIFANG (1912–1977). Poet and essayist. Born in Wanxian, Sichuan Province, He Qifang left home for Shanghai in 1927. While studying in a middle school, he wrote symbolic poetry to express his feelings about youth and romantic love. In 1931, he went to Beijing University to study philosophy. In the 1930s, He was known as a poet of refined and sophisticated sensibilities; he was influenced by the **Crescent Society** poets, especially **Xu Zhimo** and **Wen Yiduo,** and the modernist poets **Dai Wangshu** and **Liu Na'ou.** He was also a fan of French symbolist poetry and later he found inspiration in T. S. Eliot's "The Wasteland." He admired the imagistic precision of classical Chinese poetry and set off to find a poetic language that was capable of achieving the perfect combination of color, scene, allusion, and meaning. His early poetry, some of which was published in *Hanyuan ji* (Hanyuan Collection), a collaboration with **Bian Zhilin** and **Li Guangtian**, was characterized by its exquisite craftsmanship and graceful sensibility. His prose works, particularly those collected in *Hua meng lu* (Visualizing Dreams), make liberal use of symbols and images to create a coherent literary vision. At the outbreak of the **Sino-Japanese War,** He returned to Sichuan to teach but he continued to write poetry and essays. In 1938, He went with Bian Zhilin and **Sha Ting** to the Communist base in Yan'an and soon after was appointed chairman of the Literature Department at the Lu Xun Institute of Arts. During this time, he published a poetry collection entitled *Ye ge he baitian de ge* (Songs of Day and Night) and a collection of essays *Xinghuo ji* (Sparks), launching a successful career as a Communist poet. After 1949, He headed, at different times, the Literary Research Institute of the Chinese Academy of Social Sciences and the Chinese Writers' Association.

Joining the Communist revolution changed his writing style in a fundamental way. His poems and essays became more direct in meaning and his language more accessible. Most important, he acquired a voice that was vigorous and passionate in its praise of the Communist revolution. Some of the poems and prose he wrote after his arrival in Yan'an, including "Wo gechang Yan'an" (I Sing of Yan'an) and "Shenghuo shi duome guangkuo" (Great Life), expressing his optimism about communism, remain classics of socialist romanticism in China. After he attended the 1942 Yan'an Forum on Literature and Art at which Mao Zedong delivered his famous speech setting the guidelines for Communist literature and arts, He's creative work took another turn, this time toward the sole purpose of conveying political messages instead of expressing spontaneous feelings and sentiments. The lessons he learned from the conference and the subsequent political purges within the Communist ranks left indelible marks on He's literary work. Most of his writing after 1942 and especially since 1949 is political in nature. *See also* MODERNISTS.

HONG FENG (1957–). Fiction writer. Born and raised in a small town of Jilin Province in China's northeast, Hong Feng is often mentioned in the company of **Ma Yuan**, the most prominent Chinese experimental fiction writer, also from the northeast. The stories he wrote in the 1980s are regarded as representative works of China's **avant-garde** literature. "Bensang" (Going to a Funeral), a story of a son attending his father's funeral, uses an ironic voice to dismantle the authority of the father by a rebellious son, symbolizing the call for an end to the blind political idealism of the Mao era. "Hanhai" (The Great Sea) shares some of the concerns of the **root-seekers** in its depictions of folk customs in China's northeastern borders. In his more recent works, *Shengsi yuehui* (Critical Rendezvous), which recounts a man's history of sexual relationships with several women, and *Zhongnian dixian* (The Last Defense of Middle Age) about the dangerous world of sex, power, and money, Hong takes a completely different approach. Instead of writing for the elitist few, he aims to entertain the populace both in terms of subject matter and narrative method.

HONG KONG. What was known as the British Crown Colony of Hong Kong includes the island of Hong Kong, which the Qing government ceded to Great Britain in 1842 after it lost the Opium War (1839–1841), Kowloon, ceded in 1862, and the New Territories, leased to the British in 1898. Under British rule, Hong Kong prospered and became one of the most important shipping, trading, and financial centers in the world. For most of its colonial history, Hong Kong enjoyed peace and prosperity, with the exception of World War II when Japan invaded and occupied the city from 1941 to 1945. Since 1997, when China reclaimed its sovereignty over the territory, Hong Kong has remained an important international port and financial center under communist rule.

During the late 19th century and the greater part of the 20th century, Hong Kong was a place to recoup and regroup for revolutionaries and political activists opposing first the Qing, then the Nationalists and the Communists, and a safe haven for ordinary refugees running from China's seemingly never-ending troubles. The first wave of large-scale immigration from the mainland took place after the outbreak of the **Sino-Japanese War**. Refugees fleeing the devastations of the war included writers and artists, **Xia Yan, Ye Lingfeng, Xiao Hong**, and **Mu Shiying** among them. The second wave came after World War II, when mainland China plunged into a **Civil War** after Japan surrendered. Some left-leaning writers and artists on the run from the pursuit of the Nationalist government took refuge in Hong Kong and helped build the city's film and publishing industries. **Wu Zuguang**, for example, escaped from Chongqing to Hong Kong and continued his career there as a playwright and a filmmaker. Toward the end of the war as the Nationalists faced imminent defeat and soon after the establishment of the People's Republic of China, another wave of immigration hit Hong Kong, bringing with it wealthy businessmen, intellectuals, and others fearful of Mao Zedong and his Communist regime. **Jin Yong** and **Xu Xu**, who arrived respectively in 1948 and 1950, were among those who made it to Hong Kong during this crucial political transition in modern Chinese history. Among the earlier refugees, some returned to the mainland after 1949; others eventually moved to Taiwan; many, however, chose to remain in Hong Kong. During the 1950s and 1960s, Hong Kong's literary scene was dominated by these settlers from the mainland who formed the core of the first generation of writers.

In contrast to its impressive success in building the economy, the British did very little to encourage Hong Kong's literary enterprise. Unlike other British colonies, Hong Kong's English literary tradition is virtually nonexistent. Ironically, this lack of interest on the part of the colonial rulers gave an unintended opportunity for literature in Chinese to survive. Although a particular kind of popular literature, famous for its knight-errant novels and historical romances represented by Jin Yong and **Liang Yusheng**, formed the mainstay of Hong Kong's publishing industry, serious literature did manage to stay alive in the 1950s and 1960s largely through newspaper supplements and magazines, resulting in some truly innovative literature. **Liu Yichang**'s "Jiu tu" (An Alcoholic) and **Zhang Ailing**'s *Yuan nü* (*The Rouge of the North*) were serialized in *Xing dao ribao* (The Xing Dao Daily); *Huaqiao wenyi* (Overseas Chinese Literature and Art), one of the many literary magazines in Hong Kong, published works from **Taiwan** including modernist poems by **Ji Xian, Luo Fu**, and **Zheng Chouyu**.

While most of the literary writings in the 1950s and 1960s tended to speak to the centers (China and Taiwan) from the marginal space of Hong Kong, there were writers, such as **Shu Xiangcheng** and Liu Yichang, who attempted to grapple with Hong Kong's cultural uniqueness and its identity. Since the 1970s, with the first generation of writers fully assimilated and new generations of writers emerging, Hong Kong as a subject matter has become the central locus in the literary imagination of writers such as **Liang Bingjun, Li Bihua, Xi Xi, Shi Shuqing, Huang Biyun, Dong Qizhang,** and **Zhong Xiaoyang,** whose works explore the city's past and present as well as its ills and promises to form a type of "urban literature" that gives voice to a city whose "marginality" is at the core of its being. The degree of sophistication and seriousness, and the spirit of experimentalism, manifested in their works shows that Hong Kong, despite being called "a cultural desert," has made a significant contribution to modern Chinese literature. *See also* CAO JUREN; CHEN RUOXI; CHENG NAISHAN; HAI XIN; HUO DA; JIN YI; KUN NAN; LÜ LUN; NI KUANG; PING LU; SIMA CHANGFENG; TANG REN; WANG PU; XIA YI; XIAO TONG; XU SU; YI SHU; ZHANG JUNMO.

HONG LINGFEI (1901–1933). Novelist. Considered one of the pioneers who promoted a "proletarian literature" in the 1920s, Hong Lingfei was a key figure in the **Left-wing Association of Chinese Writers**. He participated in subversive activities, making him a target of the Nationalist government, which executed him in 1933. Most of his publications are fiction, dealing with Communist activism and the life of young intellectuals within the ranks of the revolution. *Liuwang* (Exile), a story about a young man fleeing from the government's arrest warrant, is largely based on his own life. *Da hai* (The Sea), published in 1930 about a peasant uprising, tells the story of three young peasants who are transformed from simple farmhands to conscious revolutionaries with strong political convictions and ideals. Like many left-wing writings, this novel is ideologically driven and intended to sing praises for the peasants who, the author believed, were pillars of the Chinese revolution. With detailed descriptions of their journey, the novel reflects the radical changes that took place in the Chinese countryside during the first few decades of the 20th century.

HONG SHEN (1894–1955). Play and screenplay writer. One of the pioneers of modern Chinese theater and cinema, Hong Shen graduated from Qinghua University, where he joined a theater club to promote the modern *huaju* (**spoken drama**), a progeny of the Western play introduced to

Chinese audiences in the early 20th century. In 1916, Hong went to the United States to study ceramic arts and three years later he entered Harvard as the first Chinese student in history to major in performing arts in the United States. After finishing his program at Harvard, he performed with various groups in New York and in 1922 Hong returned to China. The following year, he staged his first play *Zhao yanwang* (Mr. Zhao the Terrible), starring himself as the peasant-turned-murderer, and thus began a lifelong career transforming the Chinese theater. Hong was the first to use the term *huaju*, a word he coined in 1924 for the new play he and his colleagues were promoting. He founded Fudan ju she (Fudan Theater Society) and was a member of Nan guo she (South China Society) led by **Tian Han**, **Ouyang Yuqian**, and painter Xu Beihong, and the **Left-wing Association of Chinese Writers.** In the Chinese theater of the 1920s and 1930s, Hong was one of the most prominent names. As a director, he used not only his own scripts but also those of his colleagues, including **Yang Hansheng**'s plays *Li Xiucheng zhi si* (The Death of Li Xiucheng) and *Caomang yingxiong* (The Rebel Hero). During the dozen years he worked for Bright Stars, one of the first film companies in China, he made more than 30 movies, including the first Chinese sound movie *Ge nü Hong Mudan* (Red Peony the Singsong Girl). Last but not least, he was an accomplished actor, starring in plays and films, many written by him, including *Ji ming zao kan tian* (The Cock Crows in the Morning), a film set in the final years of the **Sino-Japanese War** about a group of travelers gathered in a country inn.

Hong's early writings can be regarded as psychological plays; they include *Shao nainai de shanzi* (Young Mistress's Fan), which is based on Oscar Wilde's *Lady Windermere's Fan*, and *Aiqing he huangjin* (Love and Gold), a tragedy about a bank clerk who dumps his true love to marry the daughter of the bank manager but commits suicide when his former girlfriend shows up at his wedding and kills herself in front of the newlyweds. Later, Hong turned to writing plays that were primarily concerned with sociopolitical issues, championing, among other progressive causes, the liberation of **women** and the poor. *Yapo* (Oppression) and *Nü quan* (Women's Rights) fall under this category. Other works with similar focus include his best film *Jie hou taohua* (Peach Blossoms after the Calamity), which reflects the colonial history of Qingdao through the tragic experience of a former Qing dynasty official who tries to protect his retirement home from foreigners and *Xin* *jiu Shanghai* (Shanghai Old and New), a comedy that centers on the lives of several tenants in a Shanghai apartment, all struggling to make a living. Hong died in Beijing from lung cancer. *See also* MAY FOURTH MOVEMENT; NEW CULTURE MOVEMENT; SPOKEN DRAMA.

HONG YING (1962–). Novelist and poet. Born in Chongqing, Sichuan Province, Hong Ying grew up in the squalid urban slums depicted in her memoir, *Ji'e de nü'er* (*Daughter of the River*). She began writing poetry in the early 1980s and a few years later received formal training at both the Lu Xun Creative Writing Academy and Fudan University. In 1991, she left China to study in London and has been living there since then.

The publication in 1997 of her memoir, *Ji'e de nü'er*, brought Hong instant fame. In the book, she describes her coming-of-age in a historical period ravaged by poverty and political repression. Set in the era of the great famine caused by the misguided policies of the Great Leap Forward in the late 1950s, the **Cultural Revolution** in the 1960s, and the 1989 **Tian'anmen Prodemocracy Movement**, the book is nonetheless more about the heroine's struggle for liberty, both intellectual and sexual, than an exposé of the totalitarianism of the Mao era. Following the success of her memoir, Hong published several novels in quick succession. *K* (*K: The Art of Love*), an erotic novel, is based on the love affair between **Ling Shuhua**, a well-known Chinese writer, and Julian Bell, son of Vanessa Bell and nephew of Virginia Woolf. *Ah Nan* (Ananda) mixes a detective story, an adventure novel, and a tragic love story with a philosophical and religious quest for enlightenment. The nod to Buddhism found in *Ah Nan* continues into her next novel, *Kongque de jiaohan* (Peacock Cries), in which the concept of reincarnation makes its way into the political, environmental, and sexual tensions surrounding the Three Gorges Dam Project. Hong's latest works include *Shanghai wang* (Ruler of Shanghai) and *Shanghai zhi si* (Death in Shanghai). She is a prolific and popular writer who enjoys a large following both in **Taiwan** and on the mainland. *See also* WOMEN.

HU FAYUN (1949–). Fiction and prose writer. Born in Wuhan, Hu Fayun graduated from Wuhan University with a B.A. in Chinese. He has worked as a welder, an accountant, and an office worker, and has spent several years in the countryside. Among his stories are "Si yu hechang" (Death from a Chorus), "Yinni zhe" (The Recluse), "Laohai shizong" (The Disappearance of Laohai). His best-known work is *Ruyan@sars.com*, a novel hailed by some critics as the most profound work of literature in China today and its author as the conscience of the Chinese intellectual. The protagonist is a middle-aged widow whose writings published on the Internet jeopardize her relationship with the man she loves since they pose a threat to his political career. While SARS plagues Chinese cities, a struggle unfolds between the powers of the government on the one hand and the liberal, antiestablishment forces on the other. The most severe criticism, however, is reserved for China's educated elites and their cynicism and cowardice. For its condemnation of Chinese politics and culture, Hu initially had difficulty finding a publisher willing to take the risk, and the novel only came out in book form three years after it was first posted online.

HU JIAN (1983–). Fiction writer. Born in Wuhan, Hubei Province, Hu Jian became known first in cyberspace where he began posting his work in 2001, attracting a sizable following among young readers. When his novella "Chong'er" (The Favorite Son) appeared in 2002 under the pen name Ci Xiaodao in *Mengya* (Sprouts), a journal geared to young readers, Hu's reputation grew. In the same year, a collection of novellas, *Fen qing shidai* (The Era of Angry Youths), about rebels and heroes in Chinese history, also came out. Promoted as a ticket that would win the author admission to Beijing University, the book caused a media storm around the criteria of Chinese college admissions. In the end, Hu was accepted by Wuhan University, from which he graduated with a bachelor's degree in Chinese.

Hu has been influenced by **Wang Xiaobo**, whose highly imaginative prose and sardonic wit find their way into Hu's *Fen qing shidai*. Hu's essay "Du mu qiao shang de baogao" (A Report on the Single-Plank Bridge), which exposes the problems in the Chinese education system, also shares Wang's characteristically rigorous and unrelenting style. *Qiang huo: jianmie feitu shouce* (Gunfire: A Handbook for Annihilating Mobsters), a collection of essays about crimes, terrorism, and weaponry that he had published online and in his column in *Nanfang dushi bao* (The Southern City Daily), came out in book form in 2006.

Characterized as a young man with an old soul, Hu is admired for his sophisticated intellect hidden behind a humorous and playful language. His observations of history and reality reveal an understanding about life and its sufferings.

HU LANCHENG (1906–1981). Prose writer. Known as the man who was once married to the renowned writer **Zhang Ailing**, Hu Lancheng was a very talented man in his own right. He came to prominence in the 1940s as a political commentator and art and literary connoisseur as well as a "traitor" who worked for the Japanese-controlled puppet government in wartime China. When the war ended, Hu escaped to Japan. In 1974, he went to **Taiwan** to teach at the University of Chinese Culture and developed a friendship with **Zhu Xining** and helped nurture the literary aspirations of Zhu's two daughters, **Zhu Tianwen** and **Zhu Tianxin**. Two years later, Hu returned to Japan, where he lived until his death.

Hu's literary achievement was overshadowed by his reputation as a traditional littérateur who dabbled in everything and was marred by his notoriety as a collaborator with the Japanese and an incorrigible womanizer, an aspect of his life candidly recorded in his confessional memoir, *Jinsheng jinshi* (*This Life, These Times*). His memoir details his experiences in politics and romance and contains a chapter on Zhang Ailing, providing valuable material for scholars who study Zhang and her work. In recent years, there has been a reevaluation of Hu's work. He is now generally considered a writer of refined prose and an erudite man with an unusal intellectual depth and literary sensibility. He has published several collections of prose on a wide range of topics, including *Chan shi yizhi hua* (Zen Is a Flower), a well-received scholarly work on Zen Buddhism.

HU SHI (1891–1962). Poet. Hu Shi was one of the most prominent leaders of the **May Fourth New Culture Movement**. Born and raised in rural Anhui Province, Hu won a government scholarship in 1910 to study in the United States. Initially enrolled at Cornell University to study agriculture, he soon changed his major to philosophy. In 1915, he was admitted to Columbia University and studied under John Dewey. After receiving his Ph.D. in 1917, Hu returned to China to take up a teaching post at Beijing University and to edit *Xin qingnian* (The New Youth), an influential progressive journal. He soon became a prominent leader in the campaign to reform Chinese literature and language. As an ardent and tireless promoter of a new literature, Hu published numerous articles championing the vernacular language. His ideas for reforming Chinese poetry were based on his knowledge of Chinese and Western literary history. He argued that all great poets had broken away from established traditions and that this was true for Li Po or William Wordsworth. Furthermore, he believed, any transformation in poetry had to start with form and language. The fixed rhyming schemes, which had once been revolutionary, had gone stale and fossilized. Likewise, he told his readers, classical Chinese, which had been used for thousands of years, was equally confining and restrictive. Just as Dante Alighieri had broken away from Latin in favor of a living speech, he proposed that Chinese poets should adopt the vernacular as the language of poetry. While proselytizing through essays and articles, Hu wrote poems that experimented with new forms and styles. *Changshi ji* (Experiments), a collection of poems published in 1920, established his reputation as the first vernacular poet in modern Chinese literature. He also wrote *Zhongshen dashi* (A Marriage Proposal), a play based on Henrik Ibsen's *A Doll's House*.

Hu had a distinguished career as a scholar of Chinese philosophy, literature, and intellectual history. His scholarly publications, including *Zhongguo zhexue shi dagang* (An Outline of the History of Chinese Philosophy), *Baihua wenxue shi* (History of Vernacular Literature), and *The Development of the Logical Method in Ancient China*, which was written in English, are wide-ranging. He also had a long-lasting relationship with Chiang Kai-shek's Nationalist government, serving, among other official capacities, as its ambassador to the United States from 1938 to 1942 and the president of the Academia Sinica from 1957 until his death in 1962. *See also* SPOKEN DRAMA; TAIWAN.

HU YEPIN (1903–1931). Fiction writer, poet, and playwright. A Fujian native and self-educated man, Hu Yepin had a brief but venturesome life. He was enrolled in the naval academy in Yantai, Shandong Province, and when the academy was disbanded, he was barely 15 years old. He drifted to Beijing and for a while scraped out a living as an apprentice in a jewelry store. Despite his ordeals, Hu read and wrote feverishly and eventually found his calling in literature. He was friends with **Shen Congwen** and was married to **Ding Ling**, also a struggling writer at the time. Among the **May Fourth** generation writers, Hu was one of the few who possessed an ease with the new vernacular language. His prose flows naturally, without the awkward mixture of the classical and the vernacular, a common feature in the works of many of his contemporaries.

Hu's early writings reflect his own sense of despair over poverty and hopelessness that permeate the Chinese society at the time. These semiautobiographical stories, featuring young intellectuals beaten down by the challenges in life, are loaded with romantic sentimentalism and self-pity. "Wang he chu qu" (Where to Go), a self-portrayal published in the mid-1920s, depicts the hard life of a young writer, an idealistic vagabond who struggles through poverty, loneliness, and callous treatment from his countrymen. The despondency felt by this character comes from dire economic conditions rather than unrequited romantic love as portrayed by many May Fourth writers. Another prominent cast of characters in Hu's writings are the working poor in both the city and the countryside. "Yu zhong" (In the Rain) depicts a rickshaw puller's miseries inflicted by bandits and unruly soldiers; "Hai'an bian" (The Seashore) paints a vignette of a fisherman struggling in a thunderstorm as he returns home from the market; "Huo zhuzi" (A Pearl in the Brain), arguably his best work, tells an allegorical tale about how superstition leads to the murder of a poor man whose unusually shaped head is said to contain a pearl, a desired object in the eyes of his fellow villagers.

In all of Hu's stories, everything works against the poor: natural disasters, social unrest, human greed, and their own traditional beliefs, an observation reminiscent of **Lu Xun**'s criticism of the fatuity of the Chinese national character. Hu's instinctual reaction against social injustice predisposed him toward the Communist ideology. He joined the Chinese Communist Party in 1930, and in the same year published a novella *Dao Mosike qu* (To Moscow) and a novel *Guangming zai women qianmian* (A Bright Future), seeking political solutions to China's social problems. His activities in the **Left-wing Association of Chinese Writers** put him on the government's blacklist. He was arrested in 1931 and subsequently executed.

HUANG BIYUN, A.K.A. WONG BIK WAN (1961–). Fiction and prose writer. Born and raised in **Hong Kong**, Huang Biyun graduated from the Chinese University of Hong Kong and later studied French in Paris and criminology at Hong Kong University. She has worked as a journalist, an editor, and a freelance writer. A writer of talent and depth, Huang has won numerous literary awards in Hong Kong and **Taiwan**. Her narrative art is characteristically intricate, often written with multiple voices and several references of time and space to reflect multiple views and possibilities.

Huang depicts the world and life in general from a fundamentally pessimistic angle. She is widely regarded as a writer fond of telling tragic tales of the unseemly and the morbid aspects of modern urban society and human desire. For her portrayals of the depravity of the human condition and the brutal forces in the world and within the human psyche, critics find in her works a unique "aesthetics of violence." Her protagonists, mostly **women**, are all alone, disconnected from others and isolated from the outside world. Lost souls struggling with the world and within themselves, they are burdened and depressed by the wickedness of the world and haunted by the dark secrets they carry inside themselves. Many of her stories published in the mid-1990s and collected in *Qihou* (Afterwards), including "Qi jiemie" (Seven Sisters) and *Wenrou yu baolie* (Tenderness and Violence), are set in foreign lands and focus on the characters' sense of homelessness and spiritual vagrancy. The feeling of uncertainty associated with being on the road away from home reflects the condition of human existence according to the author. Another story, "Shi cheng" (*Losing the City*), portrays the fear felt by Hong Kong residents as 1997 looms near. As anxiety escalates to desperation, the city falls into the abyss of rampant criminality, with human behavior at its worst, but life has to go on. As in her other works, a sense of helplessness and resignation runs throughout "Shi cheng." For a more philosophical treatment of human behavior, one could turn to *Qi zong zui* (Seven Counts of Crime), which examines the Christian concept of the original sin.

Huang's more recent works show an obvious move toward a more pronounced feminist position. *Lienü tu* (Portraits of Impetuous Women) portrays three generations of Hong Kong women as they each experience the major changes in modern Hong Kong history, including the Japanese occupation from 1941 to 1945, the violent and rebellious 1960s, and the handover of 1997. Other novels that treat issues specifically concerning women include *Shi er nüse* (Twelve Forms of Female Seduction), *Wu ai ji* (Without Love), and *Xue Kamen* (Bloody Carmen).

HUANG CHUNMING, A.K.A. HWANG CHUN-MING (1939–). Fiction writer. A native of **Taiwan**, Huang Chunming is one of the most prominent Taiwanese writers. His short stories are among some of the best works written in modern Chinese. The clash between urban and rural values is an ever-present theme in his works; as a leading voice in the **nativist** movement in Taiwan, Huang shows a nuanced understanding of the rural communities of the island and its poor and disadvantaged residents. His characters are rendered poignantly real in their merits and shortcomings. His description of the Taiwanese countryside is far from the bucolic paradise sung by Romantic poets; it is a poverty-stricken, unbearably harsh place to live. Huang's riveting tales portray the little people in the villages and small towns callously pushed aside by urban spread and made poorer as a result of Taiwan's economic boom and rapid modernization. "Nisi yizhi lao mao" (*The Drowning of an Old Cat*), a tragic tale about an old villager's futile attempt to prevent city people from building a swimming pool next to the village's auspicious well, is directly concerned with the erosion of a traditional lifestyle by the encroachment of urbanization. "Erzi de da wan'ou" (*His Son's Big Doll*) exposes the dehumanizing effects of commercialism in its description of the anguish felt in the heart of a man commodified as a "sandwich man" dressed as such an advertisement.

Keenly aware of the erosion of traditional practices and attitudes brought on by disruptive changes, Huang is nostalgic about the vanishing rural virtues in traditional Taiwanese communities. However, he is unsentimental about his feelings. He writes humorously and shows a close affinity with his characters, who show a remarkable likeness to his friends and relatives in the small town of Luodong, where he grew up. Huang is noted for his moral vision as well as his originality as a storyteller. He uses metaphors to delineate the problems faced by his characters. "Xuan" (Ringworm), a tale about a rural family struggling in dire poverty, paints a scene of misery by focusing on ringworms, a symbol of poverty and passive attitude on the part of the poor.

HUANG FAN (1950–). Born in Taipei, Huang Fan became publicly recognized in 1979 when he published the political short story "Lai Suo" (*The Story of Lai Suo*). He was one of the most influential and innovative writers in **Taiwan** during the 1980s. As an experiment with the narrative art, Huang often introduces real people or events into his otherwise fictitious tales.

Throughout his career, Huang's eye is trained on the helpless "little" people who are caught in the power struggles of politicians. He also portrays social outcasts in modern urban life. Influenced by American writers such as Saul Bellow, Huang uses his writing to dissect postindustrial society and its alienating effects on humanity.

HUANG JINSHU, A.K.A. HUANG KIN-CHEW (1967–). Fiction and prose writer. One of the prominent Chinese-Malaysian writers, Huang Jinshu was born and raised in Malaysia. Like **Li Yongping** and **Zhang**

Guixing, he went to study in Taiwan and launched his literary career there. He has made a name for himself as an innovative writer who challenges existing narrative techniques and as an unapologetically aggressive and sometimes impetuous critic. His fictional works are recognized for their sophisticated symbolism, allegory, and irony as well as elaborate narrative schemes. Some of his stories are set in the rainforest of Southeast Asia and others in metropolitan Taipei, both intersecting with the author's sense of self-identity. Most notable are his portrayals of the Chinese immigrants in Malaysia and their struggle to maintain cultural and linguistic identities while trying to succeed in a foreign land. Huang's fictional publications include *Meng yu zhu yu liming* (Dreams and Pigs and Dawn), *Wu an ming* (Black Dim Dark), *You dao zhi dao* (From Island to Island), *Ke bei* (Inscribed Back), and *Tu yu huo* (Earth and Fire). *Fenshao* (Setting on Fire), a collection of essays written over a span of 17 years (1989–2006) and published in 2007, expresses the author's views on a wide variety of subjects, including history, culture, and self and nation. Huang's scholarly publications include *Huangyan huo zhenli de jiyi: dangdai Zhongwen xiaoshuo lun ji* (The Art of Lies or Truth: Essays on Contemporary Chinese Language Literature) and *Ma Hua wenxue yu zhongguoxing* (Malaysian Chinese Literature and Chineseness).

HUO DA (1945–). Novelist and journalist. Born in Beijing to a Muslim family, Huo Da studied English in college and worked for the Bureau of Cultural Relics. She has held many official titles, among them member of the People's Congress and member of the National Political Consultative Conference. Her novel *Musilin de zangli* (A Muslim Funeral) won the prestigious Mao Dun Literature Prize. Many of her reportages have also won national awards.

Huo is interested in painting grand pictures of historical development. All of her novels deal with critical junctures in the past and are fictional representations of history. *Musilin de zangli* focuses on three generations of one Muslim family in the 20th century. What makes this novel unique is its treatment of religion and identity negotiated by Chinese Muslims in mainstream Chinese society. *Hong chen* (Red Dust) is a sympathetic portrayal of a former prostitute in a Beijing neighborhood during the **Cultural Revolution**. The epic *Bu tian lie* (Patching Up the Sky) presents the heroic revolt against the British at the beginning of colonial **Hong Kong**. Her other fictional works include *Nianlun* (Growth

Rings), *Chenfu* (Vicissitudes), and *Hun gui hechu* (Where Is the Home for the Soul) and numerous short stories and novellas. Huo is a writer with a strong sense of social responsibility. Her large number of report-ages deal with problems faced by ordinary people, such as the lack of protection for consumer rights recounted in *Wanjia youle* (Worries and Delights of the People), and other issues that impact ordinary citizens.

– J –

JI XIAN (1913–), A.K.A. CHI HSIEN, PEN NAME OF LU YU. Poet. Born in Qingyuan, Hebei Province, Ji Xian graduated from Suzhou Art School in 1933. Early in his career, Ji Xian, under the pen name Lu Yishi (Louis), published *Yishi shi ji* (Poems by Yishi), *Chufa* (Setting Out), and *Xiatian* (Summer), among other poetry collections. In the 1930s and early 1940s, he was an active member of a circle of poets who advocated "a completely new poetry" both in form and in content, a free verse invested with modern consciousness. He founded *Huo shan* (Mountain of Fire) and *Shi lingtu* (Territory of Poetry), and cofounded *Xin shi* (New Poetry) with **Dai Wangshu**, using these journals as a platform to advance the development of modern Chinese poetry. In Japanese-occupied Shanghai, Ji Xian published many poems and criti-cal essays and became a rising star.

In 1948, he went to **Taiwan** and began a 25-year teaching career in a Taipei middle school, where he worked until his retirement in 1973, while continuing to pursue an active writing career under the new pen name, Ji Xian. He assumed stewardship in Taiwan's modernist poetry movement and with *Xiandai shi* (Modern Poetry), a literary quarterly he cofounded in 1953, he promoted "cross-transplantation" in an attempt to bring Western modernist concepts and techniques to Chinese poetry. He favored the poetics of Baudelaire and preferred poetry of ideas to poetry of emotions.

Ji Xian has had a long and distinguished career. From the early 20th century to the 21st century, from the mainland to Taiwan and finally to the United States in 1976, he has faithfully adhered to the principle that poetry is an elitist art form of personal expression and that it should be separated from political propaganda or the representation of popular sentiments. His own poems can be decadent, crisp, playful, or humorous. *See also* MODERN POETRY MOVEMENT IN TAIWAN; MODERNISTS.

JIA PINGWA (1952–). Fiction writer and essayist. One of the most prolific writers in China today and the winner of several international prizes, including the Pegasus Prize for Literature, Jia has been active in the contemporary Chinese literary scene for almost three decades. A native of Shaanxi Province, Jia grew up in the countryside with a schoolteacher father and a peasant mother. The area around Xi'an boasts a rich history of having served as the capital for several dynasties in Chinese history, and vestiges of this glorious past can still be found in not only the many imperial tombs and ancient city walls in the region but also in the customs, arts, and dialects of the people. Jia has successfully capitalized on the abundance of cultural heritage his native land has to offer and has written extensively about the rural communities he knows initimately.

Jia's Shangzhou stories established him as a serious writer of literature. Inspired by trips into the mountainous countryside where he encountered remnants of the ancient past, these pieces explore the region's cultural as well as natural landscape. Jia places his characters in the context of the economic reforms since the 1970s in order to examine the conflict between agrarian society and the modern world due to rapid industrialization. While the themes in these stories are not unique, the style is entirely his own. Known for his "elegant prose," a mode of expression that finds its roots in classical Chinese literature, particularly the essays of the Ming and Qing dynasties, Jia uses a language that is both rustic and archaic, reflecting the actual speech in the area and thus giving these stories a deep sense of history and tradition. *Layue Zhengyue* (The Last and First Months of a Year) centers on a retired village schoolteacher who stubbornly refuses to accept the changes brought to the village by one of his former students. The clash between the old and the new values each character represents is revealed through a series of events that take place around the Chinese New Year. Other novels of Jia's such as *Shangzhou* (Shangzhou) and *Fuzao* (Turbulence) and stories such as "Jiwowa renjia" (People of Jiwowa), "Xiaoyue Qianben" (The Story of Xiao Yue), and "Guafu" (The Widow) all received critical acclaim. Among these, *Shangzhou* is the most innovative. The book consists of eight chapters and each chapter contains three episodes. The first episode of each chapter deals exclusively with local history, describing in great detail Shangzhou's mountains and rivers, local conditions and customs, historical anecdotes, and social changes. Only in the last two episodes does the love story become the primary plot. This arrangement foregrounds the local history, giving it the legitimacy to stand alone without the story, and treating Shangzhou as a character.

In 1993, the publication of *Fei du* (The Capital City in Ruins), an exposé of high society's decadence, thrust the author into a stormy controversy. Jia was publicly ridiculed and the novel was soon banned. *Fei du* is about four libertines in an ancient city whose hedonistic lifestyles remind the reader of the celebrity scholars of ancient China who spent their days writing poetry, visiting sing-song girls, and enjoying great patronage. Accused of celebrating this way of life and exhibiting undisguised sexual acts, the novel was compared to *Jin ping mei (Plum in the Gold Vase)*, a Ming dynasty novel known for its explicit sexual scenes. After *Fei du,* Jia has published several books, all with limited success, including the most recent, *Qin qiang* (Qin Qiang: the Shaanxi Opera), which has received mixed reviews. Some hailed it as a fitting "elegy" for the disappearing agrarian life; others were critical of its structural flaws.

Qin Qiang, a local opera popular among peasants, provides the backdrop for a story about the Shaanxi peasants in the era of reforms and urbanization. The story is narrated by a madman who is obsessed with a beautiful Qin Qiang opera actress from his village. He moves among the inhabitants of the village like a ghost, seeing and hearing everything. Through the madman's grievances against his rival, the husband of the actress, the author accentuates the contrast between the values of the city and those of the countryside and the dilemmas faced by the peasants when their traditional way of life is threatened by the encroachment of modernization. Other than the madman's intervention, the book is a naturalistic portrayal of village life made vivid by the bawdy, earthy local dialect.

Jia is a superb essayist with strong classical literary sensibilities. He is also an avid antique collector and a reputable calligrapher. *See also* ROOT-SEEKING LITERATURE.

JIAN XIAN'AI (1906–1994). Fiction writer, poet, and essayist. Born into a scholar-official family in the southwestern province of Guizhou, Jian Xian'ai left his hometown at the age of 13 to study in Beijing. Although he only lived at home for less than four years, rural Guizhou is featured prominently in his work. Through the **Literary Research Society**, which he joined in 1926, he became acquainted with prominent literary figures like **Zhu Ziqing, Shen Chongwen,** and **Xu Zhimo.** Although Jian studied economics at Beijing University, he became interested in literature as a way to dispel loneliness. His first attempt was as a short story writer. *Zhao wu* (Morning Fog), his first short story collection, was published in 1927. It consists of re-creations of his childhood world as he remembered it. Marked by melancholy and sentimentalism, these stories capture the colors and scents of a mountain village in Guizhou and express the pathos and nostalgia of a wanderer away from home. "Dao jia de wanshang" (The Homecoming Night) tells the tale of a young man returning home only to find his family's circumstances greatly reduced. The sorrows for the loss of a much more cheerful life palpate throughout the text. "Shui zang" (Water Burial) tells of a custom in his hometown through the death of a young man sentenced to drown as a punishment for theft. While depicting the callousness of the villagers who enjoy watching this barbaric practice, Jian focuses on the young man's mother, who waits for her son's return, unaware of what is happening to him, contrasting her maternal love with a cruel custom. Jian's criticism of the traditional practice was clearly influenced by the iconoclastic positions held by **May Fourth New Culture** proponents such as **Lu Xun,** who showed an interest in Jian's work and observed the authentic feelings of nostalgia in his writings.

In 1928, Jian returned to Guizhou and spent three months in his hometown, an experience that changed him and the style of his writing. No longer lingering over the private feelings of homesickness, his new stories sought to come to grips with the difficult life led by the working poor. "Yanba ke" (The Salt Carrier), "Zai Guizhou dao shang" (The Roads of Guizhou), "Du" (River Crossing), and other stories describe the hardships of sedan carriers, salt sellers, men and women, victims of poverty, barbaric traditions, and social ills. "Xiangjian de beiju" (A Tragedy in the Countryside), "Chouchu" (Hesitation), and "Yan zai" (Salt Shortage), all published in the mid-1930s, deal with social structure and class hierarchy, portraying a province plagued by fights among the warlords, its countryside under constant threats from bandits, rampant use of opium, an economy in shambles, and the people struggling to survive. For these hometown stories, Jian is considered one of the forerunners of **nativist** literature.

The two decades of the 1920s and 1930s were Jian's most productive years. When the Japanese troops invaded Beijing, Jian gave up his job at Beijing Songpo Library and returned with his family to his hometown and lived there until his death. Finding the atmosphere in the relatively peaceful mountain province too apathetic for his liking, Jian wrote essays and poems in an attempt to galvanize the population to join the anti-Japanese war effort. As the most important writer in Guizhou, Jian also worked as a teacher, a professor, a school principal, an editor, and a government official. He was also a critic of the theater, an interest he cultivated under the influence of his friend and classmate **Li Jianwu** when both were middle school students in Beijing.

JIANG GUANGCI, A.K.A. JIANG GUANGCHI (1901–1931). Novelist and poet. One of the most prominent Communist writers, Jiang Guangci, a son of a salt merchant in Anhui Province, went to Moscow in 1921 to study political economics and there he joined the Communist Party in the following year. In 1924, he returned to China to play a key role in promoting a proletarian revolutionary literature that would express the needs and sentiments of the great masses during the critical juncture of the nation's political transformation. Jiang became a member of the **Creation Society** and the **Left-wing Association of Chinese Writers**. *Shaonian piaopo zhe* (A Young Drifter), a novella published in 1925, features a country boy who goes to the city in search of a good life but dies in an uprising. The story exposes dark social realities and points out a path of hope for change in the form of radical revolution. In 1927, Jiang finished *Duanku dang* (Des Sans-culottes: The Party without Knee Breeches), about a workers' uprising in Shanghai. The title of the story, which emphasizes the inherent link between economic poverty and revolution, comes from a name referring to a group of impoverished rebels during the French Revolution.

Jiang's most complex work is *Lisa de aiyuan* (Lisa's Sorrows), published in 1929. The story is told from the perspective of a Russian aristocratic woman whose romantic dream is shattered by the Bolshevik victory, which took away her privileged lifestyle and sent her and her once dashing husband into exile in Shanghai. In the Chinese city, economic destitution forces her into prostitution and finally death from syphilis. The story's professed objective is to demonstrate that communism, not monarchy, is the future, a theme driven home through the positive example of the protagonist's sister, a revolutionary who has chosen a very different path. At the time of its publication, however, the story and its author received sharp criticism from the leftist camp, which accused Jiang of showing sympathy for Russian aristocracy. *Lisa de aiyuan* became one of the reasons for the CCP to revoke Jiang's membership, which, however, did not stop Jiang from continuing to promote Communist ideals.

Jiang's last work, *Paoxiao le de tudi* (A Roaring Land), later renamed *Tianye de feng* (The Storm from the Fields), portrays a peasant uprising in Jiangxi led by the Communist Party. Jiang's other publications include *Xin meng* (A New Dream), known as the "first collection of revolutionary poetry" in Chinese literature. Jiang's fictional works tend to follow the formula of the so-called revolution plus love, which places a romantic love story in the midst of revolutionary activities, whereas his poems express strong emotions of a rebellious youth who detests traditional values and embraces radical communist ideology. Jiang's detractors dismiss his work as simplistic and hollow, charging that his "literature for the masses" was cooked up in the cafés of Shanghai and his proletarian characters do not speak the language of the common people.

In many ways, Jiang was a man of his times, extremely popular in his lifetime; his novel *Chongchu yun wei de yueliang* (The Moon That Breaks out of the Clouds), written when he was recovering from tuberculosis in Japan, was reprinted six times in 1930 alone. Since then Jiang's reputation has taken a downward turn. The dismissal from the party made Jiang a suspect in the Mao era, and in the post-Mao period his political literature no longer holds the same appeal as it did in the 1930s; his is an all but forgotten name talked only about in literary history books. Jiang died of illness in Shanghai. *See also* MAY FOURTH MOVEMENT; NEW CULTURE MOVEMENT.

JIANG HE, PEN NAME OF YU YOUZE (1949–). Poet. One of the main **Misty poets**, Jiang He grew up in Beijing and was sent to the countryside in 1968 after graduating from high school. His first published poem, "Xingxing bianzouqu" (The Star Variations), is considered one of the representative poems of the 1980s, when he and his fellow poets energized the Chinese literary scene with their innovative style. These poems embodied the national consciousness and commanded public attention. Jiang's poetry represents his generation's understanding of the enlightened self and gives expression to its sense of mission.

He shows in his verses a strong awareness of historical imperatives, creating some of the best-remembered political lyrics from that period, including "Jinianbei" (Monument) and the epic "Taiyang he ta de fanguang" (The Sun and Its Reflection), projecting the self onto the image of the nation through history, myths, and legends. Jiang He has been living in the United States since 1988.

JIANG RONG (1946–). Fiction writer. As one of the first group of educated teenagers sent from Chinese cities to the grassland of Inner Mongolia during the **Cultural Revolution**, Jiang Rong learned to herd sheep, ride horses, and most important of all, love and respect the most feared and revered Mongolian wolf. He developed a fascination with the wild animal and came to understand why the Mongolian nomads worshiped wolves. Many years later, this extraordinary experience resulted in a novel. *Lang Tuteng* (*Wolf Totem*), published in 2004, tells the tale of Chen Zhen, a Beijing youth who comes to Inner Mongolia to escape the chaos of the Cultural Revolution, which is turning the capital into an inferno, uninhabitable for kids from educated families such as Chen. While learning to become a nomad from his Mongolian surrogate father, Chen attempts to unravel the secrets behind military conquests led by Genghis Khan and his troops. The novel evokes comparisons between agrarian and nomadic lifestyles and beliefs, questioning the myths of the Han Chinese culture whose staunch defenders have proselytized its "civilizing" conversions of the "barbarian" peoples. The narrator argues that the Han "sheep culture," which depends upon farming, is meek and anemic when brought face-to-face with the vigorous "wolf culture" of the nomads. He proposes that the nomadic cultures have continuously injected fresh blood into the Chinese civilization, helping it maintain its vitality. In the novel, the protagonist learns to appreciate the wild wolves and uncovers the similarities between human nature and animal instincts, as the fearless wolves reflect the qualities that help the Mongols win wars and overcome the harsh environment. Reminiscent of Jack London's *The Call of the Wild*, the novel is a eulogy for the primordial spirit, a tribute to the myth of the hero who survives hardships and challenges by strength and courage as well as instinctual intelligence, which still appeals to the modern man. While London's story centers on the "decivilization" of the animal, Jiang's novel focuses on man's return to the primitive. As the Mongolian grassland has been reduced to deserts, packs of wolves roaming the open space are scenes of the past.

For that reason, the novel is also an elegy for the endangered ecosystems of our world.

JIANG ZILONG (1941–). Fiction writer. A Tianjin native, Jiang Zilong has worked in a factory, served in the navy, edited a literary journal, and held various leading positions in the Chinese Writers' Association. These rich life experiences, particularly his years in China's machinery industries, have inspired his writing. He came into prominence in 1979 with the publication of "Qiao Changzhang shangren ji" (Manager Qiao Assumes Office at the Factory), a short story about the difficulties within a factory as it embarks on a painful reform in order to stay solvent. In the next few years, he wrote "Kaituo zhe" (The Trailblazer), "Chi chen huang lü qing lan zi" (*All the Colors of the Rainbow*), "Yan Zhao beige" (Lament of the North), and "Guo wan piao pen jiaoxiangqu" (A Symphony of Everyday Life), establishing his reputation as a writer who best portrays the initial stages of the reform era. Since the early 1970s, he has published more than 80 books, most of which treat how the economic reforms have impacted the nation's industries and urban citizenry. Manager Qiao has come to represent the courageous lower-level cadres who rose to the challenge to revive the stagnant economy by carrying out painful but necessary reforms to the outmoded manufacturing base in the wake of the **Cultural Revolution**. *Renqi* (Being Human) centers on the housing reform in a big city to expose the fierce and despicable maneuvers for power and self-interest fought within various government agencies and among individuals from the mayor to the average resident. *Kongdong* (Emptiness), a novel based on a family of two generations of doctors in Shanxi, portrays the tradition of Chinese medicine, which is utilized to stop the spread of tuberculosis at the turn of the new millennium. *Nongmin diguo* (The Peasant Empire), a major departure from the author's urban writings, describes how a smart peasant leads his fellow villagers out of poverty, building the "richest village in the country," but fails to escape the fate of many peasant leaders throughout Chinese history who are doomed by the corruption of power and money. The moral of the rise and fall of the village leader is that no matter how clever and how hardworking, the individual is fated to fail because he is still a "peasant" shackled by his or her own limitations and shortcomings as well as social prejudices. In that sense, the tragedy of the peasant is a lesson for China, a country still mostly populated by the peasantry.

JIN YI, A.K.A. YUNYUN, PEN NAMES OF ZHANG CHU (1927–). Fiction and prose writer, playwright, and poet. A **Hong Kong** native, Jin Yi is a prolific author of mainly novels and novellas. He began writing plays in 1949 and later concentrated on fictional work, dealing with the concerns of youth, such as jobs, friendship, love, and other worries that tend to occupy a young person's mind, as well as the life of the working class. His later works treat larger issues of Hong Kong's history and society. Jin Yi's publications include *Tong xin jie* (True-Love Knot), *Nu hai tong zhou* (On the Same Boat in the Turbulent Sea), *Cuoshi* (Blunder), and *Xianggang shui shang yi jia ren* (A Family on the Hong Kong River). One of his novels, *Yingfeng qü* (Singing against the Wind), has been translated into Thai and serialized in a newspaper in Thailand, helping to spread his reputation to Southeast Asia. Jin Yi worked as a journalist and an editor for several Hong Kong newspapers including *Wenhui Daily.*

JIN YONG, PEN NAME OF ZHA LIANGYONG (1924–). Novelist, screenplay writer, and newspaperman. Arguably the best-known and most widely read Chinese writer, Jin Yong was born in Zhejiang and finished his college education in Chongqing, the war capital during the **Sino-Japanese** conflict. He worked as a journalist, editor, and translator for various news organizations and moved to **Hong Kong** in 1948 to serve as a translator of international news for *Dagong Daily.*

Inspired by **Liang Yusheng**'s martial arts novels, Jin Yong wrote *Shujian enchou lu* (*The Book and the Sword*) and its success led to many more novels. His works combine traditional features, such as the theme of revenge and magical elements found in late Qing martial arts novels, with the chivalry and romantic love of 18th-century British and French novels. After Deng Xiaoping implemented his open-door policy, Jin Yong gained millions of readers in the mainland. It seems that everyone, from college professors to transient workers, reads his books. He is a household name in not only Hong Kong, **Taiwan,** and the mainland, but also throughout the Chinese diapora. He is also well known in many other Asian countries and overseas through the many kung fu movies based on his books. The popularity of Jin Yong's works does not seem to diminish as Chinese society undergoes radical transformations through its modernization campaigns.

In addition to martial arts novels, Jin Yong has written several screenplays, including *Juedai jiaren* (The Peerless Beauty), *Wuye qinsheng*

(Sound of Music at Midnight), and *San lian* (Three Loves). He is also a newspaperman and founder of *Mingbao Daily* and the Mingbao publishing house.

JING FU, PEN NAME OF GUO JINGFU (1942–). Novelist and essayist. Like his more famous colleague **Jia Pingwa**, Jing Fu was born in Shangzhou, Shaanxi Province, and like Jia, he has also written extensively about the rural societies of the northwestern province, having published many short stories, essays, and novels. His best-known work is *Bali qing chou* (Feud in Bali), a novel that portrays the entangled relationships of two families in a small town in southern Shaanxi from the 1950s to the 1980s. While centering on two women's unfortunate experiences and unhappy marriages, the novel reflects the starvation of the 1950s, the destruction of the **Cultural Revolution**, and the reform era, offering a glimpse into the vulnerability and lack of recourse in the lives of ordinary people and the destruction of family as a result of terrible abuses of power and human cruelty. Jing Fu's recent work is an environmental novel, *Lu ming* (The Cries of Deer), which portrays a young man's arduous journey to fulfill his father's dying wish to release a herd of badly abused deer back to the forest. Characteristic of Jing Fu's style, the novel mixes the sensational with the serious, resulting in a popular, entertaining novel with a nod to social criticism. Jing Fu sees environmental problems as the biggest challenge of the 21st century for humankind and plans to write more on the issue.

JULY SCHOOL (QIYUE PAI). A literary school formed in the first half of the 20th century around the journal *Qi yue* (July), which was founded and edited by Hu Feng, a Marxist theoretician who advocated "guofang wenxue" (literature for national defense) and later urged writers to focus on spontaneous, natural responses found in human behavior and historical events. This subjective stance was severely criticized by members of the left-wing literary circles, who believed that literature should faithfully serve the Communist Party's political agendas. In the campaign against intellectuals in the early 1950s, Hu and his followers were condemned as counterrevolutionaries.

– K –

KE YUNLU, PEN NAME FOR BAO GUOLU (1946–). Novelist. One of the most prolific and popular novelists in China today, Ke Yunlu has written more than a dozen novels since 1980. *Xin xing* (A Rising Star), published in 1984, and the television show based on it earned Ke his national fame. The novel portrays a county party secretary and the difficulties he encounters in the Chinese bureaucracy notorious for its corruption, inefficiency, and nepotism. With this and other novels about the inner workings of Chinese political and social system, Ke soon came to be known as an astute interpreter of Chinese officialdom; his novels, particularly *Ye yu zhou* (Night and Day) and *Shuai yu rong* (Fall and Rise), both depicting the complexities of life in Beijing in the 1980s, have been deemed "must reads" for those who wish to understand Chinese politics and social relationships.

In addition to his works on contemporary politics, Ke has published several novels about the tumultuous years of the **Cultural Revolution**. *Heishanbao gang jian* (History of Heishanbao) paints a village in the throes of absolute tyranny where the leader catalogs his conquests in politics and sex in secret codes. *Furong guo* (The Hibiscus Country) offers a panoramic view of Chinese society, from the capital city to a small village, from high-ranking officials to the common people, in particular the young Red Guards later sent to China's remote countryside. Also set in the Cultural Revolution but focusing on the experience of young people growing up in an era of political radicalism and social destruction, Ke has written *Xisheng* (Sacrifice), whose young protagonists struggle to fulfill political idealism and romantic love at a time of moral confusion, *Mengmei* (Obscuration), a tragic tale set in a small southern town that depicts the sexual awakening of a boy through his relationship with an older woman and how they are destroyed by an unforgiving society, and *Nage xiatian ni gan le shenme* (What Did You Do That Summer), an investigation of the tragic fate of a schoolteacher who was beaten to death in the name of justice by his rebellious students who live to regret their atrocious act. Picking up the coming-of-age theme, *Fuqin xianyi ren* (Suspect Fathers), published in 2005, examines the maturing process of a boy as he interacts with the opposite sex and with the older generation, and *Chenggong zhe* (A Success Story) is about the experience of a young man of humble beginnings who achieves material success at the expense of moral and spiritual integrity.

Ke is a man of many interests. He has forayed into such areas as psychology and mysticism. His curiosity about the workings of the human mind has resulted in a psychological novel, *Jidu zhi yanjiu* (A Study of Jealousy), featuring a gathering of writers, a social group the author considers to be the most susceptible to jealousy. His foray into the study of *qigong*, a system of deep-breathing exercises thought to possess miraculous powers, led to the publication of a novel, *Da qigong shi* (The Qigong Master), which, along with his other metaphysical writings, caused a great deal of controversy.

KONG JIESHENG (1952–). Fiction and prose writer. Born and raised in Guangzhou, Kong Jiesheng was sent to work for four years in rural Guangdong, an experience that became the source of his writing. In the late 1970s, Kong won several awards for his stories before he published his best-known work, "Nanfang de an" (The Shores of the South), in 1982. The story portrays several educated youths learning life's important lessons from their experiences during and after the turbulent years of the **Cultural Revolution**. Two years later, another novella, "Da linmang" (The Great Forest), about the tragic fate of five educated youths on the state farms of Hainan Island, also garnered national notice.

KUN NAN, A.K.A. YEDONG, PEN NAMES OF CEN KUNNAN (1935–). Poet and fiction and prose writer. A **Hong Kong** native, Kun Nan wrote for newspapers in his youth and cofounded several literary journals including *Shi duo* (Blossoms of Poetry) and *Xin sichao* (New Trends). In 1955 he published his first story, "Wen: chuang shiji de guanmian" (Kiss: The Royal Crown of Genesis). He has written two novels, *Di de men* (The Earth's Gate) and *Tiantang wu zai zu xia* (Heaven Dances under the Feet), and a short story collection *Xi jing de fengliu* (The Romantic Life of Playing with Whales). Throughout his career, Kun Nan has been interested in examining the effects of modernity on the psychological state of Hong Kong residents. In his attempts to find the moral and spiritual anchor that would protect people from the forces that alienate them from society and from themselves, Kun Nan represents the voice of the intellectual struggling to come to grips with his cultural identity under the dual pressure of colonialism and commercialism. His heroes begin as idealistic hopefuls, go through trials and tests, and finally as their dreams are dashed become utterly disillusioned. This pervasive hopelessness reflects what the author considers the prevailing views held by Hong Kong intellectuals in the 1950s and 1960s.

– L –

LAI HE, A.K.A. LAI HO (1894–1943). Fiction writer and poet. Born and raised in Japanese- colonized **Taiwan**, Lai graduated from medical school and practiced medicine throughout his life. From 1917 to 1919, he worked in a hospital in Xiamen, Fujian Province, where his Chinese was much improved as he became increasingly drawn to nationalist causes. After his return to Taiwan, Lai became involved in anti-Japanese activities, attracting the attention of the Japanese authorities, who arrested him in 1924. In 1941, he was again arrested and with his health destroyed during the two-year prison term, Lai died shortly after he was released from prison.

Under the influence of the **May Fourth Movement**, Lai was made aware of the important role literature could play in awakening the nationalist consciousness of the people; throughout his career he insisted on addressing contemporary political and social issues. As one of the first generation of Taiwanese writers, Lai began by writing stories in Japanese, as well as classical-style poetry in Chinese, a skill he had honed at a young age from a private tutor. After joining forces with other new literary movement proponents, including Zhang Wojun, Huang Chaoqun, and **Yang Kui**, Lai adopted the vernacular as a medium for his poetry and fiction to describe the collapse of the old social order and the sufferings of the poor, and above all, to expose the injustice the people of Taiwan suffered under the Japanese, reflecting his nationalist sentiments.

Lai's first story, "Dou nao re" (Festivity), shares the same concern of his mainland contemporaries who were passionate about eradicating the problems within traditional Chinese culture. The story satirizes the grandiose competitions held at religious festivals in rural Taiwan, depicting them as superstitious and pointless, a view similar to **Lu Xun's** criticism of the deficiency of the Chinese cultural trait. Other stories, however, focus on the economic exploitation and cultural assimilation policies imposed by the Japanese. Told in the realist mode, these stories are characterized by their biting satire and poignant symbolism. "Yi gan chen zai" (The Man with a Steelyard), considered his representative work, tells the story of a vegetable seller who struggles to make a living but ends up in jail on charges brought against him by a Japanese policeman who accuses him of cheating with a dishonest steelyard. His wife has to borrow money to bail him out, which further reduces the family's financial circumstances. Unable to climb out of his dire situation, the vegetable seller kills the policeman and then himself. The irony that a steelyard, a symbol of fairness, leads to injustice is an indication of Lai's narrative art. "Re shi" (Making Trouble), centers on the Japanese police chief's chickens, which are in the habit of running into the neighbor's yard to eat the vegetables. For fear of causing any trouble, the neighbor stomps the ground in an attempt to scare the chickens away. Nevertheless, the Taiwanese family is still charged with chicken theft. Lai points out that in the Japanese-occupied Taiwan, there is no justice for the Taiwanese people and the only way out for them is to break free of their oppressors.

Unlike the subtle and satirical tone found in his fictional work, the voice in Lai's poetry is direct and indignant, lamenting the ill fate of the Taiwanese people and denouncing the Japanese. "Juewu de xisheng" (The Awakened Sacrifice) is a political poem written to show support for the sugarcane farmers suppressed by the Japanese. "Nanguo aige" (The Song of Sorrow from the South) is also a battle cry against the colonizers. While writing stories and essays, Lai also took up editing for newspapers and literary journals through which he helped nurture young Taiwanese writers, earning him the honor of being called the "wet-nurse and father of modern Taiwanese literature."

LAI SHENGCHUAN, A.K.A. STAN LAI (1954–). Born in Washington, D.C., Lai Shengchuan moved to **Taiwan** in 1966 with his family when his diplomat father received a new assignment in the foreign ministry of the Republic of China. He moved back to the United States in 1978 to study dramatic art at the University of California at Berkeley. After he received his Ph.D. in 1983, Lai accepted a teaching post at the newly established National Art Institute in Taipei. It did not take long for Lai to make a name for himself. The pivotal moment came in 1985 when his Performance Workshop Theater staged his *Na yi ye women shuo xiangsheng* (That Night We Performed Crosstalk), which was an overnight hit. A few years later, he created more "crosstalk" plays: *Zhe yi ye shui you lai shuo xiangsheng* (Tonight Who Will Perform Crosstalk, 1989); *You yi ye tamen shuo xiangsheng* (One More Night They Performed Crosstalk, 1997); and *Qian xi ye women shuo xiangsheng* (On the Eve of the Millennium We Perform Crosstalk, 2000). By using a traditional art form, crosstalk, Lai created modern plays that look at the collective memory of the Chinese people and their views of history, tradition, and life in general. In *Na yi ye women shuo xiangsheng,* two crosstalk performers masquerade as the great crosstalk masters who have been invited to give a performance but fail to show up, alluding to the disappearance of tradition in modern Taiwan society. *Qian xi ye women shuo xiangsheng* covers two historical periods. The first episode takes place at the end of the 19th century with two crosstalk artists engaging in a conversation with a Manchu noble; in the second episode, the same theater is moved to Taipei and on the eve of the millennium the performance of a pair of crosstalkers is interrupted by a politician campaigning for a seat in the Taiwan parliament. The crosstalk series breathed life into an old form that had virtually disappeared in Taiwan.

In total, Lai has created almost 30 plays, including his most famous *An lian taohua yuan* (Pining . . . In Peach Blossom Land; 1986), a comedy that involves two theater groups mistakenly booked into the same theater for dress rehearsal, one performing *An lian* (Secret Love), a serious drama set in present-day Taiwan about a dying elderly man longing to see his first love from whom he was separated in 1949, and the other *Taohua yuan* (Peach Blossom Land), a farce that parodies a lyrical prose work written by a fourth-century Chinese poet about a man stumbling into a utopian world of peace and tranquility. The scheduling conflict reflects the more serious philosophical differences between the two groups forced by circumstances to share the same stage. As a result, chaos and madness ensue, creating some hilarious theatrical moments that underscore the contending views in the Chinese world with regard to visions of longing, memory, diaspora, identity, and life. In his eight-hour epic drama *Ru meng zhi meng* (A Dream Like a Dream; 2000), Lai sets up a narrative structure in which past and present, dream and reality intersect to create a fantastic world in which the characters engage in thoughtful reflections on national and cultural identity, which is shaped by history and shifting changes in politics, the experience of home, exile, and immigration. This poetic play about self-transcendence is clearly influenced by Tibetan Buddhism, which Lai has been studying for years. Lai's other plays include *Yuanhuan wuyu* (Circle Story; 1987), *Xi you ji* (Journey to the West; 1987), *Huitou shi bi an* (The Island and the Other Shore; 1989), *Taiwan guai tan* (Strange Tales from Taiwan; 1991), *Hongse de tian kong* (Red Sky; 1994), *Xiansheng kai ge men* (Please Open the Door, Sir; 1998), and *Wo he ta he ta he ta* (Me and Him and Him and Him; 1998).

Arguably, the most influential playwright/director alive today in the Chinese-speaking world, Lai has not only revived Taiwan's theater but also brought enthusiasm and excitement to theaters in China and in the Chinese diaspora. Lai's dramatic aesthetics—the multilayered structure, highly theatrical language, symbolic stage design, humor, romantic mood, free-flowing mise-en-scène, cultural implications, deep sense of tragedy, and persistent attempt at wrestling with some profound and abstract ideas—have far-reaching impacts in the Chinese theater. His plays, which are often compared to works by Tony Kushner, Robert Lepage, and Peter Brook, have toured internationally and have been well received. For his achievement as an artist and his leadership in the Taiwanese theater, Lai has twice (1988, 2001) received Taiwan's highest award for the arts, the National Arts Award. *See also* SPOKEN DRAMA.

LAO SHE, PEN NAME OF SHU QINGCHUN (1899–1966). Novelist. A Beijing native of Manchu nationality, Lao She lost his father, who fought the Boxers as a garrison soldier in the imperial army. As a child, Lao mingled with rickshaw pullers, peddlers, street singers, and other such lower-class people and learned the language and culture of the street, which would become the center of his writing. Upon graduation from the Beijing Normal School in 1918, Lao She was made principal of a primary school. In the following year, the **May Fourth Movement** broke out. Not an active participant, Lao She was nevertheless inspired by the ideas promoted by its proponents: democracy, science, and personal emancipation.

In the summer of 1924, Lao She took up a position as a lecturer in the School of Oriental and African Studies at the University of London. This trip would prove to be pivotal in his writing career. Inspired by the English novels he had read, particularly those written by Charles Dickens, Lao She tried his hand at writing novels. Adept at telling the stories of the middle and lower classes in Beijing, Lao She depicted in his early works the little people and their struggle for life in the midst of poverty and oppression. The protagonist of *Lao Zhang de zhexue* (Mr. Zhang's Philosophy) is a scoundrel whose actions are motivated by greed. While deriding Mr. Zhang's lack of morality, Lao She treats him as a comic character, giving him a touch of humanity, and thus accentuating the ordinariness of human depravity. The ignorant and incompetent youth in *Zhaozi yue* (*Thus Spake Master Zhao*) is another one of Lao She's flawed characters who idles away his life at mahjong tables and opera houses, seemingly unaffected by the changes brought to China by the May Fourth Movement. *Er Ma (Mr. Ma and Son: A Sojourn in London)*, a novel that reflects the author's own encounters with the Chinese expatriates in London, chronicles the misfortunes of a man and his son who go to London to run a gift shop. The son is patriotic, proud of being Chinese, but the father worships the West and emulates everything Western. A skilled storyteller and a master of Beijing folklore and dialect, Lao She proves in these novels that he is also a master satirist.

After he returned to China, Lao She published several books including *Mao cheng ji* (*Cat Country: A Satirical Novel of China in the 1930s*), a satirical novel focusing on the cat people's destruction of their educational and political systems out of sheer indifference and their complete abandonment of culture in favor of perpetual revolution. The novel conveys his deep concern for the Chinese society plagued by xenophobia, on the one hand, and the rush to embrace Western culture, on the other. *Lihun* (Divorce) exposes the injustice of the bureaucratic system through the portrayal of two office clerks, the old-fashioned Big Brother Zhang and the crafty Little Zhao. Lao She is a master storyteller with a great sense of humor and keen moral insights, and nowhere is this talent of his applied more aptly than in the novel *Luotuo Xiangzi* (*Camel Xiangzi*), a tragic story of a rickshaw puller. Xiangzi migrates from the countryside to Beijing hoping to make a better life for himself through hard work. His fortune fluctuates, until he is reduced to total disillusionment. Xiangzi's descent from an ambitious and honest young entrepreneur to a virtual beggar deprived of pride and self-respect represents the physical and moral destruction of the individual at the hands of society's evils. The vivid characters and the lively language they speak make the novel a uniquely realistic portrayal of city life.

Among Lao She's works written during the **Sino-Japanese War**, *Si shi tongtang* (Four Generations under One Roof) stands out. Inspired by the experience of his family while living in Japanese-occupied Beijing, this monumental novel depicts the hardships, humiliation, and unconquerable spirit of Chinese citizens in their resistance against Japanese aggression. The author's juxtaposition of the disintegration of a traditional family of four generations under one roof with a beaten nation under foreign occupation highlights the plight of the Chinese people.

After the war, Lao She and the playwright **Cao Yu** went to America on a lecture tour as guests of the U.S. State Department. When his year-long contract expired, Lao She remained in the United States, where he finished *Si shi tongtang*, wrote *Gushu yiren* (*The Drum Singers*), and assisted Ida Pruitt and Helena Kuo in translating them into English. In December 1949, Lao She returned to Beijing. A much-celebrated writer in Communist China, Lao She assumed a string of largely honorary appointments, including vice president of the Association of Chinese Writers and Artists and vice president of the Chinese Writers' Association. Despite his busy official schedules, Lao She continued to write, mainly plays, among which *Longxu gou* (*Beard Ditch*) and particularly *Cha guan* (*Teahouse: A Play in Three Acts*) have received critical acclaim. Lao She's final work was an unfinished novel entitled *Zhenghong qi xia* (*Beneath the Red Banner*), which was published in 1980, 14 years after the author's death. It chronicles the decline of the bannermen, the original military troops of the Manchu rulers. At the onset of the tumultuous **Cultural Revolution**, Lao She became one of the first targets of the Red Guards. He committed suicide by drowning himself in a lake on the outskirts of Beijing, tragically ending a life of literary eminence. *See also* SPOKEN DRAMA.

LEFT-WING ASSOCIATION OF CHINESE WRITERS (ZHONG-GUO ZUOYI ZUOJIA LIANMENG). Established in 1930 in Shanghai, the progressive association absorbed members from other organizations, such as the **Creation Society**. Founding members included **Lu Xun**, **Mao Dun**, **Xia Yan**, **Yu Dafu**, **Feng Naichao**, **Feng Xuefeng**, **Tian Han**, **Jiang Guangci**, **Yang Hansheng**, **Hong Lingfei**, and others. Its mission was to promote a "revolutionary literature" that opposed traditional society and reactionary forces and to support progressive young writers.

It attracted writers who were fully committed to the idea of literature serving the revolutionary cause. In the initial stage of the movement, the writers were primarily focused on ideology and less concerned about artistry, a practice most evident in the works by Jiang Guangci, **Rou Shi**, and **Hu Yepin**. Emerging after these writers were more sophisticated practitioners such as **Mao Dun**, **Ding Ling**, **Zhang Tianyi**, **Sha Ting**, and **Wu Zuxiang**, who leaned more toward critical realism and were more nuanced in their approach to the art of storytelling.

The organization effectively used its many publications, *Tuohuangzhe* (The Pioneer), *Mengya yuekan* (Sprouts Monthly), *Qianshao* (The Front Line), *Beidou* (The Dipper), and *Xiaoshuo yuebao* (Fiction

Monthly), to attack literary groups that it considered "bourgeois" and "reactionary," such as the **Crescent Society**. It was undisputedly the most influential literary organization during the 1930s. Although it was disbanded in 1936 in order to form the united front against the Japanese, its impact continued to be felt in the People's Republic of China all the way through the 1970s. *See also* CHEN BAICHEN; DUANMU HONGLING; HONG SHEN; OUYANG SHAN; OUYANG YUQIAN; SPOKEN DRAMA; WANG LUYAN; XIAO JUN; YE LINGFENG; YU LING; ZHOU ERFU; ZHOU LIBO.

LI ANG, PEN NAME OF SHI SHUDUAN (1952–). Fiction writer. A native of **Taiwan**, Li Ang studied philosophy at the University of Chinese Culture in Taiwan and attended the University of Oregon in the United States, majoring in dramatic arts. She published her first story in 1968 while still a high school student. Influenced by Western modernism introduced to Taiwan in the 1960s and 1970s, Li Ang was interested in exploring the inner workings of the individual, such as described in the subtly erotic story "*Hua ji*" (*Flower Season*), about a teenage girl's sexual fantasies. Li Ang is noted for her social writings about the fate of the individual when he or she comes into conflict with the established norms of society, particularly in the form of the clash of values between Western and traditional Chinese beliefs. As Taiwan underwent rapid modernization, Li Ang was increasingly aware of the horrific conditions of **women** who were victims of superstition, violence, and sexual brutality. Her best-known work is the controversial novella, *Sha fu* (*The Butcher's Wife*), a gripping story about a peasant woman who learns to empower herself against her abusive husband. When the story first came out in 1982, it caused a great storm. While it won the prestigious Unitas Fiction Award, the work was criticized for being "immoral" and sensational because of its bold exposition of sexuality and its militant feminist stance. The publication of the book in English in 1986 made Li Ang an internationally recognized writer.

LI BIHUA, A.K.A. LEE BIK-WA, LILIAN LEE (1959–). Fiction and film script writer and essayist. Born to a big, well-established family, Li Bihua showed literary talents at an early age. She is a prolific writer, having published many collections of essays, including *Hong chen* (Red Dust), *Jing hua* (Flower in the Mirror), and dozens of fictional works, several of which have been adapted into films, including the internationally renowned *Bawang bie ji* (*Farewell My Concubine*), which won an award at the Cannes Film Festival in 1993. A major theme in her work is romantic love, and in her more recent stories she turns her attention to portraying men's betrayal of love, a move influenced by feminism. No other story more clearly expresses this feminist stance than *Yanzhi kou* (Rouge), in which a ghost, a former sing-song girl, haunts the streets of **Hong Kong** in search of her lover, heir to a grocery fortune, who is supposed to have died with her in a double suicide. Other stories that treat the same theme include *Pan Jinlian zhi qianshi jinsheng* (The Past and Present Lives of a Seductress), *Chuandao Fangzi (The Last Manchu Princess)*, *Qing she* (Green Snake), and finally *Bawang bie ji*, her most famous work. Li currently lives in Canada. *See also* WOMEN.

LI ER (1966–). Fiction writer. Known primarily for his novels *Huaqiang* (Trickery) and *Shiliushu shang jie yingtao* (Cherries Grown on a Pomegranate Tree), Li Er worked for several years in the academic field upon graduation from the Chinese Department of East China Normal University in 1987. He is currently an editor at the literary journal *Mangyuan* (Wilderness). While in college, he was exposed to a wide variety of works by foreign writers, including Franz Kafka, Italo Calvino, Jorge Luis Borges, Gabriel García Márquez, Milan Kundera, Saul Bellow, and Václav Havel. He was also influenced by his friend and mentor **Ge Fei**, then a young lecturer at East China Normal University.

The main character (in absentia) of *Huaqiang*, published in 2001, is a man named Ge Ren, a translator, linguist, poet, and Communist revolutionary who died in the mid-1940s. In the vein of a detective novel, the work revolves around the mystery of Ge Ren's death through the accounts of three narrators whose own lives intertwined at some point with the protagonist's. The three versions of Ge Ren's story are collected and compiled by another narrator, the only descendant of the protagonist. The first narrator, a doctor who once serviced the Communist troops in northern Shaanxi, tells his part of the story in the 1940s as he escapes to Hong Kong as a result of a brutal internal purge within the Communist Party. The second narrator, a former underground Communist Party member being interrogated in a labor camp in 1970, recalls Ge Ren's family history and his early life as a romantic youth and progressive intellectual. The third narrator, a Communist army general turned Nationalist, delivers his version upon his triumphant return to China in 2000 as an honored guest of the party he once betrayed. The twists and turns of events in the lives of the narrators make mockery of the rivalries and wars between parties and countries. The novel suggests that if yesterday's enemy is today's friend, history has simply played a cruel joke (shua huaqiang) on all those involved in the zealous struggles in the past. It is no coincidence that the name Ge Ren sounds exactly like *geren* (individual) in the Henan dialect, which is the author's native tongue, invoking the allusion that the story of Ge Ren is the story of every individual who has gone through the social and political upheavals of modern China. The novel goes on to indicate that the notion of an individual in control of his or her own destiny is simply an illusion and coincidences and accidental choices leading to dramatically different consequences are the ultimate determinants of a person's life. History, as the title of the last chapter points out, is "written by the victor." *Huaqiang* is thus a metaphor for the follies of politics, the fortuity of life, and the unreliability of memory, history, and reality.

While *Huaqiang* deals primarily with the irony of history, *Shiliushu shang jie yingtao* (Cherries Grown on a Pomegranate Tree) addresses how traditional culture intersects with modern values in the present. The novel centers on the manipulation of influence in a village election in northern China. Everyone, from the current village head to the former village head, from the director of security to the accountant, from the village doctor to the school principal, from the Communist Youth League secretary to the average villager, has a stake in the game and tries to steer the outcome in his or her favor. The campaign shows that rural politics is every bit as complicated as any presidential election and a peasant is as sophisticated as any big-game politician. What the novel focuses on, however, is not the political implications of a village election, which as a new phenomenon in China is interesting in itself, but on how traditional values, which have sustained rural communities, are at odds with modern concepts of fairness and ethics. The unexpected election result reveals some hidden forces at work that bring to naught the individual's painstaking efforts to control the flow of events.

Li Er uses satire, irony, dark humor, and paradox to highlight the follies of human behavior. In many ways he is a philosopher of life who sees incongruity between intention and outcome, between words and action; his work questions the criteria for distinguishing right from wrong, truth from lie, and reality from fiction. Cherries grow on a pomegranate tree or a man bites a dog—ludicrous? Maybe or maybe not. In addition to his novels, Li Er has published many short stories and novellas collected under such titles as *Raoshe de yaba* (A Talkative Mute) and

Yiwang (Oblivion) as well as prose work. Some of Li Er's works have been translated into German.

LI GUANGTIAN (1906–1968). Essayist and poet. Born in Zouping, Shandong Province, Li Guangtian came under the influence of the **May Fourth New Culture Movement** while a student at the Jinan Number One Teachers' School. He began writing poetry and prose after becoming a student at Beijing University. *Hanyuan ji* (Hanyuan Collection), a poetry collection that contains works by Li and fellow Beijing University students **Bian Zhilin** and **He Qifang**, established his fame, though he later wrote more prose than poetry. In 1935, when he graduated from Beijing University, he returned to Jinan and continued to write while holding a teaching job. After the **Sino-Japanese War** broke out, Li wandered in Sichuan for several years before joining the faculty of the Southwest United University in Kunming. During this time, he wrote the novel *Yinli* (Gravitation), in addition to several collections of essays including *Huisheng* (Echoes), *Huanxi tu* (Picture of Happiness), and *Guanmu ji* (Shrubs). Li's essays are characterized by simplicity and naturalness, and they impart a sense of freedom of movement and an earthy touch with reality. After the war, he taught at Nankai University and Qinghua University. He joined the Communist Party in 1948, and in 1952 he was appointed president of Yunnan University and moved back to Kunming. At the height of the **Cultural Revolution**, Li became a victim of political persecution and was found dead in a lake in a northern suburb of Kunming. *See also* MODERNISTS.

LI GUOWEN (1930–). Fiction and prose writer. Like many writers of his generation, Li Guowen's career was interrupted by political campaigns. Li published his first work in 1957 but soon he was branded a rightist and sent to labor in a railway construction company. He did not resume his writing until 1976 at the end of the **Cultural Revolution**. After graduating in 1949 from the Nanjing School of Dramatic Arts with a degree in playwriting, Li worked for many years in the performing arts circle. He is, however, better known for his fiction and prose writings than his theater scripts. *Dongtian li de chuntian* (Spring in Winter), winner of the Mao Dun Literature Prize in 1982, covers a span of four decades of social change through the memory of a veteran revolutionary cadre who returns to the place where he fought as a guerrilla soldier to investigate the death of his wife, who was assassinated 40 years ago. *Huayuan jie wu hao* (Number 5 Garden Street), another novel, centers on a grand Russian-style mansion that has witnessed modern Chinese history through the lives of its influential occupants. His stories "Yue shi" (The Eclipse) and "Wei lou ji shi" (The Story of Unsafe Buildings) have also won prestigious awards in China. In recent years, Li has devoted a significant amount of his energy to his prose work, publishing several collections of essays, including *Da ya cun yan* (Elegant Rustic Talk), which won the Lu Xun Literature Prize, and *Li Guowen shuo Tang* (The Tang Dynasty), a collection of essays on the historical figures and events of that ancient era, one of his many publications that showcase his passion in revisiting Chinese history and civilization and drawing lessons from the past.

LI HANGYU (1957–). Fiction writer. A Hangzhou native, Li Hangyu is known as one of the pioneers of **root-seeking literature**. His article "Liyili women de gen" (Sorting Out our Roots), along with those by **Ah Cheng**, **Han Shaogong**, **Zheng Yi**, and **Zheng Wanlong**, all published in 1985, advocated a literature that sought inspiration in the nation's ancient past. In the 1980s, he was famous for his root-seeking stories about the customs and cultures along the Qiantang River, fictionalized as the Gechuan River, which runs in the vicinity of his native Hangzhou. The stories in his Gechuan River series including "Gechuanjiang shang renjia" (A Family on the Gechuan River), "Zuihou yige yulao'r, (*The Last Angler*), and "Shazao yifeng" (The Relics of Shazao) are set against the background of the economic reform era but reach back to the ancient history and customs unique to this region. Of particular importance is "Zuihou yige yulao'r," which portrays a man alienated and marginalized by society but determined to stick to the old ways. Coming from a tradition that has existed for generations in the area, Fukui, the last fisherman, rejects modernization and the lifestyles it represents. As factories dump pollutants into the river, fish die, and the fishermen who rely on the river begin to lose their livelihood. The others find ways to adapt to changing times by farm-raising fish or working for the factories, but Fukui refuses, despite being ridiculed by his fellow villagers. At the end of the story, he floats to the middle of the river in his small boat, content in the thought that he will die in the embrace of the river he calls his "mistress." He is the last witness to a once beautiful and plentiful river, a world in which man and nature coexisted in harmony. Underneath Li's descriptions of the local customs and traditions is a dirge for a bygone era forever lost to the irresistible and crushing forces of modernity. In his Gechuan River stories, Li finds the soul of the river culture in its spirit of wandering and unrestrained flow. He uses symbolism and myths as well as the vernacular language of the area to capture that spirit. Li has devoted his entire career to creating a tableau of the way of life along the Qiantang River of Zhengjiang, including his most recent prose work on the history and customs of the city of Hangzhou.

LI JIANWU, A.K.A. LIU XIWEI (1906–1982). Playwright and fiction writer. A graduate of Qinghua University and a member of the **Literary Research Society**, Li studied Western literature in college and spent two years in Paris in the early 1930s. A cofounder of the Shanghai Experimental Theater, Li was one of the key figures who promoted the modern speech play. After the founding of the People's Republic of China, Li worked for 10 years (1954–1964) at the Literature Research Institute of Beijing University and spent the rest of his career at the Foreign Literature Research Institute of the Chinese Academy of Social Sciences.

A prolific writer, having published numerous books, both creative and scholarly, Li had a diverse career as a fiction writer, a translator and scholar of French and Russian literature, a playwright, a director, an actor, and theater critic. Many of his fictional works, including novels *Tanzi* (The Crock and Other Stories) and *Xin bing* (Worries), are about the urban working class and the 1911 Republican revolution for which his own father gave his life. His translations include works by Gustave Flaubert, Molière, and Maxim Gorky. To this day, his translation of Flaubert's *Madame Bovary* remains the standard Chinese edition. Li was a noted essayist; one of his essays, "Yu zhong deng Taishan" (Climbing Mount Tai in the Rain), is a staple in middle school textbooks. Nowhere, however, is his accomplishment more prominent than in the theater. In his student days, Li had already shown a strong interest in performing arts. While studying at Qinghua University, he served as director of its theater club and performed in many plays. He later wrote and adapted more than 40 plays and is considered one of the founding fathers of modern Chinese theater.

Li was profoundly influenced by French playwrights, especially Molière, many of whose works he translated into Chinese. In the 1920s, Li wrote mostly one-act plays about the urban poor, such as *Muqin de meng* (A Mother's Dreams). After his trip to France in the 1930s, Li began to write multiple-act plays that dealt with a wide range of subjects, including important political and historical events past and present. He also paid more attention to the structure of his plays. *Zhe bu guo shi chuntian (It's Only Spring)*, considered his best work, interweaves a romantic tale with a revolutionary story. The plot revolves around a police chief's wife who manages to get her former lover a job as a secretary in her husband's department, hoping to rekindle the old flame. The lover, however, turns out to be an underground revolutionary being pursued by the police. When his cover is blown, she bribes the police to get him out of the city. The power of the play derives from the high drama achieved through a clever manipulation of contradictions and complex relationships among the characters as well as a seamless structure and witty language.

Created in the realist mode, Li's heroes are multidimensional human beings with flaws as well as virtues. The police chief's wife, for example, is selfish and delusional but empathetic. The characters' imperfections not only make them plausible but also give rise to tensions that inevitably lead to dramatic climaxes. Li emphasizes plot development and favors suspense and unexpected outcomes, relying on them to create dramatic moments. Because of the sophisticated artistry, Li's plays continue to draw attention while the political plays by many of his contemporaries have been more or less forgotten. *See also* MAY FOURTH MOVEMENT; NEW CULTURE MOVEMENT; SPOKEN DRAMA.

LI JIEREN (1891–1962). Novelist and translator of French literature. For his love of French literature and its influence on his writings, Li Jieren was called the "Chinese Zola" and the "Oriental Flaubert." Like his fellow Sichuanese writer, **Sha Ting**, he made extensive use of his native dialect, also earning him the reputation as a chronicler of the city of Chengdu.

From 1915 to 1919, when the **May Fourth New Culture Movement** was gaining momentum, Li worked as an editor and chief commentator for newspapers and did his part in assaulting the old Chinese traditions and spreading progressive ideas in provincial Chengdu. He wrote a great number of editorials and essays and published about one hundred stories written in both classical and vernacular Chinese, brief sketches that expose corruption in the government. In these early works, Li's gift as a storyteller is already evident. His presentation of realistic characters and events by making skillful use of the vernacular, his ability to create a biting political satire, and his drawing on the elements both of classical Chinese and foreign literature made Li a unique talent in the early days of modern Chinese literature.

In 1919, Li went to France to study French literature and began translating works by French writers, including Gustave Flaubert and Guy de Maupassant, into Chinese. During his stay in France he wrote one novella, *Tongqing* (Sympathy), based on his stay in a hospital for the poor in Paris. After he returned to China in 1924, Li wrote more short stories, most of them satirical pieces that poke fun at local warlords. His main accomplishment, however, is his historical trilogy based on major historical events before and after the 1911 Revolution: *Si shui wei lan* (*Ripples across a Stagnant Water*), part 1 of the trilogy, encompasses the years between 1894 and 1901. The story takes place in Tianhui, the northern suburb of Chengdu, a sleepy town stirred up by the Boxer Rebellion. For its grand scale, its sophisticated artistry, its successful portrayal of characters, and its creative use of colorful local language, *Si shui wei lan* is arguably the best early modern Chinese novel. Another work, *Baofengyu qian* (Before the Storm), continues to trace the history from 1901 to the eve of the 1911 Revolution. Moving the stage from a small town to the provincial capital, the author describes the intensification of social problems that threaten the tottering Manchu dynasty and the changes of intellectualism in the impending storm of the revolution. A third historical work, *Da bo* (The Great Wave) centers on the 1911 Revolution. With the Railroad Protection movement as the key event, the novel focuses on the political and military affairs and important historical figures of that period. In all three novels, Li takes pains to situate historical events in a richly described social life, because he recognizes that there is a strong correlation between historical changes and human activities, between what happens on the national stage and what happens in a person's private life.

Despite his deep entrenchment in Western literature, Li does not show the usual Europeanized tendency found in many of the works of his contemporaries, including those of **Lu Xun**. For all the various comparisons and analogies between his work and European fiction, all made on reasonable grounds, his characters are quintessentially Chinese. In his novels, there is a perfect fusion of Western and Chinese traditions, resulting in an art entirely of Li's unique style. After the founding of the People's Republic, Li held many posts in the government, including deputy mayor of Chengdu and vice president of the Association of

Sichuan Writers and Artists. During this time he revised his trilogy to make it more in tune with the new society, a move driven by ideological reasons instead of artistic vision.

LI JINFA (1900–1976). Poet, fiction writer, and sculptor. Li Jinfa grew up in Meixian, Guangdong Province, in a large family headed by his peasant/merchant father who had spent several years in Mauritius running a small shop. Educated in Guangdong, Hong Kong, and Shanghai, Li Jinfa later studied art in Paris, where he came under the influence of French symbolists, particularly Charles Baudelaire, whose "Les Fleurs du Mal" left a strong impression on the budding poet. The first symbolist poet in modern China, Li created some of the most obscure lines in early modern Chinese poetry, utterly confounding his readers. His poetry is known for its "bizarre" images and "irrational" associations. The poems collected in *Wei yu* (Drizzle), published in 1925, show evidence of symbolist influence in their abundant images of the grotesque, such as corpses, skeletons, bloodstains, cold nights, muddy roads, dead leaves, and so on. Like Charles Baudelaire, Li aestheticizes the unseemly and turns it into the sublime. "Ye zhi ge" (Song of the Night), "Qi fu" (The Abandoned Woman), and "Shenghuo" (Life) are among his best-known poems. He taught art in Hangzhou and Guangzhou, and in the late 1940s, he served as a diplomat stationed in Iran and Iraq for the Nationalist government. When the Communists won the Civil War, Li immigrated to the United States and made a living in New Jersey raising chickens. He died in New York. *See also* MODERNISTS.

LI PEIFU (1953–). Novelist. Born in Henan, Li Peifu began his literary career in the late 1970s. He has written extensively about China's northern countryside with its strong adherence to traditions and its persistent struggle to leave behind the poverty that has plagued the lives of its peasants for generations. Having lived in rural communities, Li understands the nature and the soul of the Chinese peasantry and his portrayals of country life are both realistic and profound. *Yang de men* (The Gate of Sheep), a novel banned by the government shortly after its release, paints a dark picture of what it is like when an agrarian community achieves economic prosperity. The book's negative portrayal of Chinese traditional society echoes the iconoclastic stance voiced in the works by **Lu Xun** and **Ba Jin**. The return to the critical tradition of the **May Fourth Movement** registers a revolt against the **socialist realism**

of the Mao era, which glorified the peasants as enlightened revolution-aries. In *Yang de men*, Li's Hujia Bao is a village controlled by one man, who rules his charges like "God watching over His flock," as the title suggests. On the surface, Hujia Bao is a Communist utopia, with no exploitation, no corruption, and no poverty. Underneath the blissful surface, however, is the reality of the authoritarianism of the village head, who does not hesitate to crush the slightest sign of defection and whose political network built through decades of painstaking cultivation reaches all the way from his village to the capital. The novel portrays the villagers as well-fed, subservient sheep and the various levels of govern-ment officials as greedy wolves who use their positions only to serve their personal interest. Also concerning the countryside, *Lishi jiazu* (The Li Clan) is a saga that chronicles the rise and fall of a large clan.

With the same focus on how power operates in society, Li has shed light on life in urban China. His novel *Chengshi baipishu* (White Paper on a City) is told from the perspective of a mad girl whose unusually acute senses allow her to uncover the absurdities and the lack of spiritual anchor of modern city life. Additionally, *Cheng de deng* (City Lights) depicts the arduous journey of country youths on the way to becoming urbanites. A more recent novel, *Dengdeng linghun* (Wait for the Soul), deals with the ruthless competitions within the business world and how power corrupts humanity. It portrays a businessman whose success and downfall are brought about by his personal ambition and hunger for power. A prolific writer primarily interested in portraying the nature of power in society, Li has written several volumes of novellas and short stories in addition to these influential novels.

LI RUI (1950–). Fiction writer and essayist. Born in Beijing, Li Rui lives in Shanxi, which features prominently in many of his writings. Widely considered one of the best writers in contemporary China, Li did not come to fame until the 1990s, even though he was already a published author in the mid-1970s. *Houtu* (The Solid Earth) is a series of short stories about poor peasants whose character traits contain both shrewd-ness and ignorance, which Li came to know intimately while working in the countryside as an educted youth during the **Cultural Revolution**. Also set in the countryside, *Wufeng zhishu* (Windless Trees) depicts a northern village inhabited by dwarfs whose calm life is disrupted by the arrival of two outsiders: an ardent revolutionary city youth and a beg-gar girl from the neighboring province. Li's historical novel, *Yincheng* *gushi* (*Silver City*), set at the beginning of the 20th century when the Qing dynasty was at its last breath, ponders the tumultuous modern Chinese history and the country's propensity for violence. By examining brutal revolutions, the book calls into question the rationality of using radical political movements as a necessary and natural vehicle to bring about social justice and economic prosperity.

A skilled storyteller attentive to narrative structure and the use of language, Li shows affinities with classical Chinese literature in its brevity and precision and in its expression of both the lyrical and rational sentiments. *See also* ROOT-SEEKING LITERATURE.

LI SHASHA, PEN NAME OF BI LIZI (1982–). Fiction and prose writer. Born in a village in Hunan Province, Li Shasha graduated from Northwestern University in Xi'an in 2004. Li belongs to the generation of the Internet, which launched his career. While still a freshman in college, Li began posting poems and stories online. Nicknamed "the Teenage **Shen Congwen**," he became known initially for his childhood stories about rural Hunan, a subject Shen had explored in the 1930s and 1940s. Another influence comes from **Wang Xiaobo**, whose unbridled imagination and liberal spirit can be detected most notably in Li's *Hong X* (Red X)—"red x" referring to the error mark written by teachers on student papers—a coming-of-age novel that portrays a rebellious teenager who, after being dismissed from school, experiences an existential and spiritual crisis while struggling to overcome hunger, deception, and his own self-destructive behavior. Another work of Li's, *Bei dangzuo gui de ren* (Ghosts in the City), a collection of essays, consists of two parts: reminiscences of the western Hunan countryside and his observations of life in the city of Xi'an. In general, his essays are held in better regard by critics. The most memorable ones include "Wo zui nan wang de yishuang nüren de shou" (An Unforgettable Pair of Women's Hands) about a child's vague awareness of romantic love, "Bei dangzuo gui de ren" on the hard life of migrant workers in the city, "Liang ge shaonian" (Two Teens) about country kids, "Yige xi'ai chuzou de pengyou" (A Friend Who Loves to Leave Home) about a wanderlust attracted by the outside world, and "Dakou gudu" (Foreign Music CDs and the Ancient Capital) about his impressions of modern youth culture in Xi'an.

Li received the 2005 Chinese Language Literature and Media Award. He also attracted international attention when he was featured in an article in *Time* magazine in June 2006, which calls him a "ghost writer" who represents the millions of country folks who have streamed into China's big urban centers. Chinese critics have praised his natural, effortless prose that captures the beauty and innocence of a rustic world and his vivid depiction of the dreams of rural youths lured away from their villages by the promise of modern life. A talented voice among the post-1980s generation, whose majority grew up in the cities and tend to focus narrowly on teenage rebels and personal angst, Li, who was raised in the countryside but now works in Guangzhou as a journalist, is uniquely poised to tackle the issues faced by Chinese youths outside the confines of school and romantic love. His work touches the core of Chinese modernization and the prices its youth and its country poor have to pay. For the depth of his work and his highly imaginative prose, Li is widely considered one of the most promising writers among his contemporaries.

LI YONGPING (1947–). A Chinese Malaysian growing up in Sarawak, Li Yongping moved to **Taiwan**, where he earned a degree in English literature from National Taiwan University. He later received a doctoral degree in comparative literature from Washington University in St. Louis. Li's major work is a group of stories first published serially in the 1970s and later collected under the title of *Jiling chunqiu* (Retribution: The Jiling Chronicles). It is considered a masterpiece of Chinese modernist literature with its emphasis on exquisite linguistic precision and emotional complexity as well as its intricate structure, metaphorical richness, and intense imagery. Set in a small town of uncertain locality, the novel tells a story of crime and revenge, dominated by primitive impulses, religious rituals, and karmic retribution. The victim is Changsheng, wife of a coffin maker, whose family lives in the midst of the town's brothel district. On the day of the town's biggest festival—the greeting of Guanyin, the Goddess of Mercy—Changsheng is raped while making offerings to Guanyin in hopes of increasing her chances of bearing a son. Out of shame, Changsheng commits suicide. Her death sets her enraged husband off on a violent rampage.

Li's other works include *Haidong Qing: Taipei de yige yuyan* (Haidong Qing: An Allegory of Taipei), which tells the experience of a Chinese Malaysian in Taipei, in his own words: "looking for China . . . for the roots of the Chinese." The novel provides an interesting case for the study of Chinese diasporic literature. Issues such as cultural identity and literary heritage are at the core of this work. In the process of searching for self-identity, the narrator projects an illusion of Chinese culture, made possible by self-indulgence in the pursuit of linguistic aesthetics. Through the protagonist's wanderings, the novel also explores how multinational corporations expand to the Third World and the serious implications for the local culture. Li is an absolute stylist in pursuit of "a pure, poetic language" inspired by the terse and compact classical Chinese, in sharp contrast to the verbose Westernized style prominent in modern Chinese expression.

LIANG BINGJUN, A.K.A. LIANG BINGGUAN, LEUNG PING-KWAN, P. K. LEUNG, AND YESI (1947–). Poet and fiction and prose writer. A **Hong Kong** native, Liang Bingjun received his Ph.D. in comparative literature from the University of California at San Diego in 1984. He began writing while still a middle school student and was a co-founder of several literary journals, including *Da muzhi* (The Thumb). Since receiving his Ph.D., Liang has held teaching and research positions at universities in Canada, Germany, Japan, Switzerland, the United States, and China. Currently, he teaches literature at Lingnan University in his native city. A well-known figure in the cultural circles of Hong Kong, **Taiwan,** and the mainland, Liang is a prolific writer engaged in both creative and critical writings. He has published numerous books of poetry, prose, and fiction, including *Lei sheng yu chan ming* (Thunder and Songs of Cicadas), *Youli de shi* (Poetry of Dissociation), *Dong xi* (East West), *Dao he dalu* (The Island and the Mainland), *Jiyi de chengshi xugou de chengshi* (A City Remembered and a City Imagined), and *Bulage de mingxinpian* (Postcards from Prague).

Liang is a powerful intellectual voice representing the spirit of Hong Kong. Familiar with the city's history and life, Liang understands the marginalized position assigned to Hong Kong by both the British colonizers and the Chinese mainlanders. He attempts to grapple with the definition of "home" and "country" in his poems, essays, and fiction. Written with characteristically modernist techniques and published under the pen name of Yesi, his fictional works capture the essence of colonial Hong Kong in a highly imaginative way. Liang is among the first generation of home-grown writers to explore the issue of identity in the cultural and linguistic hodgepodge. He continues to examine the sense of loss and complexity of identity politics in posthandover, postcolonial Hong Kong. For his sustained effort at exploring the meaning and the perplexity of life in the multicultural and multilingual city,

Liang is regarded as one of the best interpreters of the so-called Hong Kong consciousness, which is molded by the paradigms of colonialism and the myth of nationalism imposed upon its residents during its colonial history.

LIANG SHIQIU (1902–1987). Prose writer. A prominent scholar, translator, and lexicographer, Liang had studied in the 1920s at Colorado College, Columbia University, and Harvard University before returning to China to teach at Beijing University and Shandong University, among other institutions of higher learning. While at Harvard, he came under the influence of Irving Babbitt, whose theories of literature had a lasting influence on Liang. Diametrically opposed to the utilitarian brand of literature promoted by **left-wing** writers, Liang allied himself with intellectuals and writers such as **Hu Shi** and **Xu Zhimo**, who shared his belief in the aesthetic purpose of literature, pitting himself against **Lu Xun** and others in a heated debate about the function and direction of modern Chinese literature. He was a cofounder of the **Crescent Society** and began writing essays in the 1940s with his first collection published in 1949 entitled *Yashe xiaopin* (Sketches from a Refined Cottage). He continued to publish several more collections of essays after moving to **Taiwan** in 1949, where he taught English and served as dean of the College of Humanities at the National Taiwan Normal University until his retirement in 1966. Liang's crowning achievements, however, are his translation of the complete works of Shakespeare, which took him nearly 40 years to finish, and an English-Chinese dictionary widely circulated in the Chinese-speaking world. An erudite scholar and literary critic, Liang was at home in both Chinese and English literary traditions, evident in his prolificacy in translation and scholarly and creative writings. Liang died in Taipei. *See also* MAY FOURTH MOVEMENT; NEW CULTURE MOVEMENT.

LIANG XIAOSHENG (1949–). Novelist. Born into a working-class family in Harbin, Heilongjiang Province, Liang Xiaosheng is known primarily for his portraits of the Red Guards and the educated youth, the same generation to which Liang belongs. He spent several years working on the state farms of Beidahuang (the Great Northern Wilderness), a region in the northeastern frontier bordering the former Soviet Union, an experience that informs most of his writing. After graduating from Fudan University with a degree in creative writing, Liang worked as an editor in the Beijing Film Studio and a screenplay writer in the Chinese

Children's Film Studio. Currently, he teaches at the Chinese Culture University in Beijing.

The themes of innocence and victimization run throughout Liang's work. He portrays his generation as innocent youths taught to think of themselves as heroes and their sacrifices as necessary for the improvement of humanity. While lamenting the romantic idealism of the era, Liang describes the collapse of the utopian edifice built through years of political indoctrination, making his generation's sense of loss and disillusionment excruciatingly tragic. *Jinye you baofeng xue* (Snowstorm Tonight), *Napian shenqi de tudi* (Wondrous Land), and *Xue cheng* (City of Snow) portray the difficult but romantic lives of the educated youth battling the harsh conditions of the northeastern wilderness and the eventual disillusionment when the farms were disbanded and the educated youth returned en masse to the cities. Continuing to focus on the fate of the educated youth in his later works, Liang depicts their sense of dislocation and alienation in a society centered on consumerism and market globalization. The sense of nostalgia and loss expressed in works such as *Yige hongweibing de zibai* (Confession of a Red Guard) reflects the feelings of the disfranchised former Red Guards, now middle aged, struggling to survive in an increasingly materialistic society. Other works, such as *Fu cheng* (A Restless City) and *Jiusan duanxiang* (Random Thoughts of 1993), satirize the greediness and bureaucratic backbiting of the new economic era and express a pessimistic view of the corrupt and unjust Chinese society. Liang is a writer with a strong sense of social responsibility and his impassioned cries for the underprivileged class show his commitment to using literature as a vehicle to champion social justice. *See also* CULTURAL REVOLUTION.

LIANG YUSHENG, PEN NAME OF CHEN WENTONG (1926–2009). Liang Yusheng graduated in 1949 from Lingnan University in Guangzhou with a degree in economics. Soon after, he became a translator and editor for a **Hong Kong** newspaper. Liang came to fame in 1952 when his martial arts novel *Long hu dou jinghua* (Dragon and Tiger Fight in the Capital) was published. The new techniques he employs in the novel had great appeal to the public and Liang is credited for having pioneered a new way of writing martial arts novels. For the next 30 years, Liang produced, on average, one book a year. His novels are invariably based on historical sources. *Pingzong xiaying lu* (Tracks of the Chivalric Wanderer) is based on General Yu Qian (1398–1457) of the Ming dynasty. *Nüdi qiying zhuan* (Biography of the Heroic Empress) is set in the turbulent years of the reign of Empress Wu (624–705) of the Tang dynasty. At the center of Liang's novels is a contention for supremacy among different forces within the world of martial arts, which Liang then puts within larger historical events, such as dynastic changes and peasants' uprisings. Liang also pays attention to his characters' psychological states and their inner worlds of feelings and emotions, which are absent in traditional martial arts novels, thus enhancing the literary value of his novels. Liang died in Sydney, Australia, where he had lived since the 1980s.

LIAO HUIYING (1952–). Although not a self-professed feminist, from the very beginning of her career Liao has put **women**'s lives at the center of her writing. Focusing on women caught in **Taiwan**'s transition to modernity in the 1970s and 1980s, a period that saw a nascent feminist movement on the island, Liao describes incongruities between traditional expectations and modern realities faced by women in their struggle for economic independence as well as equality and respect in relationships. She treats controversial issues such as chastity, sexual libertinism, sexual abuse, and the birth of children out of wedlock. Written in the realist mode, her stories challenge social mores and promote the women's independence movement. The short story "Youma caizi" (*Seed of Rape Plant*), much of which is based on her own relationship with her mother, portrays the life of a traditional woman who has endured a loveless marriage and has resigned herself to her hard lot. Although she has raised her daughter on the belief that women are like colza seeds and take root wherever the wind blows them, the college-educated young woman has taken a very different path, becoming a successful career woman and enjoying a loving relationship. This change tackles the age-old Chinese practice of privileging sons over daughters and points out that education is the only means by which women can rise above their traditional roles. It also represents the author's attempt at resolving her own love-hate relationship with her mother. Liao's novel *Bu gui lu* (The Road of No Return) features a lonely 24-year-old woman who falls in love with a married middle-aged man. Through the pain and guilt that accompany their illicit affair, the story emphasizes the importance of women having a strong sense of self in order to cultivate enduring and meaningful relationships.

LIN BAI, PEN NAME OF LIN BAIWEI (1958–). Novelist. Born in Guangxi and graduated from Wuhan University, Lin Bai is noted for her bold descriptions of sexuality and the female body. *Yigeren de zhanzheng* (One Individual's War), an autobiographical novel decried as pornography when it was released, is a feminist declaration of independence. In the words of the heroine: "An individual's war means a hand that slaps itself, a wall that blocks itself, a flower that ruins itself . . . a **woman** that marries herself." The novel, now considered a major feminist work, details the life of a girl from the age of five, when she begins to explore her own body, to her middle-age years. The expression of the protagonist's hidden desires and emotions reveals the author's deliberate attempt to challenge a cultural taboo against the public display of personal feelings about sex and sexuality. Other similar works by Lin include "Pingzhong zhi shui" (Water in the Bottle), a languorous tale about lesbian love, and *Zhiming de feixiang* (A Fatal Flight), an intense love story that ends violently. Her most recent work, *Funü xianliao lu* (Records of Women's Gossips), is an oral history of rural women told in their own colloquial voices.

LIN HAIYIN (1918–2001). Fiction writer and essayist. Born in Osaka, Japan, Lin Haiyin moved with her parents to Beijing in 1923 where they lived until 1948. After her father, an educated Taiwanese, died in Beijing, Lin worked as a journalist to support her family. In 1948, Lin and her husband, Huang Fan (Xia Chengying), took their three children to **Taiwan**. Lin worked as an editor for a newspaper and later for an independent press. She played a crucial role in fostering a new generation of Taiwanese writers including **Zhong Lihe** and **Huang Chunming**. Lin died in Taiwan.

Though she began to write in Beijing, Lin's literary career did not take off until the 1950s, when she settled in Taipei. Most of Lin's works written between the 1950s and 1960s are based on her memories of her life in Beijing. *Cheng nan jiu shi* (*Memories of Peking: Southside Stories*), a memoir of her childhood, is Lin's most important work. It consists of reminiscences about her years in Beijing and vignettes of people she met in her neighborhood. Lin presents a vivid picture of local customs and living conditions of Beijing during the early 20th century. There is a strong sense of nostalgia running through these stories. Scenes such as Mama Song riding a donkey back to her hometown, kids playing by the neighborhood well, and the thief hiding in the haystack are what made up the lives of lower-class society in Beijing. These and other scenes are watched from the perspective of an innocent child. Besides her Beijing stories, Lin wrote children's literature, including some fairy tales and a large number of essays. *See also* WOMEN.

LIN HUIYIN (1903–1955). Poet, fiction writer, architect, and architectural historian. Born in Fujian Province to an official family, Lin Huiyin grew up in Beijing. In 1919 at the age of 16, her diplomat father took her to Europe. There she attended St. Mary's College in London and was introduced to her father's circle of literary friends including the poet **Xu Zhimo**, who courted her persistently but failed to win her hand. In 1925, she went to the United States with her then fiancé Liang Sicheng, son of the eminent political reform leader Liang Qichao, where she studied architecture at the University of Pennsylvania and stage design at Yale. After coming back to Beijing, the couple became the most important figures in the preservation and study of traditional Chinese architecture. After 1949, Lin taught architecture at Qinghua University and helped design the national emblem and the Monument of the People's Heroes, which stands in the center of Tian'anmen Square. She died of illness in Beijing.

Lin was active in the **Crescent Society**, of which Xu Zhimo was a prominent member, and her living room was the most famous literary and cultural salon in Beijing. She wrote numerous poems, six short stories, and one play, and translated English literature into Chinese. Her poems, while showing traces of Xu's influence in their romantic spirit, retain her own exquisite touch. "Ni shi renjian siyue tian" (You Are the Days of April) is her best-known poem. Her short story "Jiushijiu du zhong" (Ninety-nine Degrees) describes a hot summer day in the city of Beijing. The story captures the minute details of a birthday party, a wedding, a police station, and the death of a poor porter, all effortlessly strung together to present a vivid picture of the reality of the city. In another story, "Jiong" (Embarrassment), Lin uses the modern technique of stream of consciousness to reveal the emotional turmoil of a middle-aged professor who has to hide his improper feelings for the young daughter of his friend. Despite the small quantity of her literary output, these and other works provide enough evidence for Lin to be considered a talented writer. *See also* WOMEN.

LIN JINLAN (1923–). Fiction writer and playwright. Born in Wenzhou, Zhejiang Province, Lin began his literary career as a playwright. His first collection of plays, *Bugu* (The Cuckoo Bird), was published in 1956, and in the following decades he mostly wrote short stories about the contemporary lives of intellectuals or simple country folks. Lin places a strong emphasis on plot and language and his stories are noted for their flawless structure and graceful style. In the 1980s, he wrote a series of stories collected in *Aidengqiao fengqing* (The Customs of the Short-Bench-Bridge), which portrayed the rural communities of his native Zhejiang Province. Other works of his include *Chun lei* (Thunder in the Spring) and *Man cheng fei hua* (Flowers Flying All Over the City), both short story collections. *See also* ROOT-SEEKING LITERATURE; SPOKEN DRAMA.

LIN YAODE (1962–1996). Poet, fiction and prose writer, and critic. Graduate of Furen University in **Taiwan**, Lin Yaode was considered a literary prodigy. In his short life of 34 years, he published more than 30 books and won numerous awards. His writing career, which began when he was a teenager, spanned several genres and areas. At the time of his death, Lin had achieved fame as one of the most versatile and influential writers and critics in Taiwan. He is especially remembered as a tireless promoter of postmodern urban literature, which he saw as a continuation of the 1930s' **New Sensibility school** represented by such writers as **Shi Zhecun, Liu Na'ou**, and **Mu Shiying**, and the **modernist poetry movement** spearheaded by **Ji Xian** and others in Taiwan in the 1950s. He positioned himself as the movement's theorist, practitioner, and critic. In his fiction, including *E dixing* (*The Ugly Land*) and *Da dong qu* (The Great Eastern District), considered representative works of urban literature, he treats the city not just as a theme but also a text written and read by the author. His essays collected under the title of *Migong lingjian* (Parts of the Labyrinth) present the city as a composite of spaces as well as human beings, a modern "labyrinth" in which a person loses direction.

Another important issue that Lin was passionately involved in was the work of deconstructing history in general and literary history in particular. He was by all accounts an ambitious literary historian who challenged and subverted well-established interpretations by eminent scholars such as C. T. Hsia. The epic *Yijiusiqi gaosha baihe* (1947—The Taiwanese Lily) is particularly significant in that it represents Lin's broad attempt at examining how history, literary or political, is constructed. The work looks at the February 28th (1945) Incident from the perspective of an indigenous Taiwanese representing the marginalized people whose voice has been routinely silenced in official or popular history. The narration of the past as it appears in the book is predicated on the juxtaposition of several systems of reference, such as aboriginal myths, European imperialism, Japanese colonialism, and the Han Chinese cultural paradigm. His skepticism toward so-called definitive history or authoritative interpretation is most evident in this work.

Lin was also a highly regarded science fiction writer, having spun some incredibly imaginative tales including *Shijian long* (The Time Dragon), a futuristic treatment of human capacity for destruction. His propensity for the description of violence, of unrestrained savagery, often compared with French writers Marquis de Sade, Comte de Lautréamont, and Georges Bataille, has drawn a good deal of attention and created some controversy. Lin's poetry, characterized as symbolic, has received much critical acclaim.

LIN YUTANG (1895–1976). Novelist, essayist, translator, and editor. Lin was born in Fujian and raised by Christian parents. He was educated at St. Johns University in Shanghai and at Harvard and received his Ph.D. in 1923 from the University of Leipzig. Lin spent many years in the United States, wrote most of his major works in English, and was regarded as a significant interpreter of Chinese culture. His nonfictional books, initially published in English, include *My Country and My People, The Importance of Living,* and *Pleasures of a Nonconformist.* Among his novels are *Chinatown Family, Moment in Peking,* and *The Flight of the Innocents.* In the 1920s and 1930s, Lin edited and wrote essays (in Chinese) for *Yu si* (Words and Language) and other journals in which he advocated a philosophy of "loafing," and a sensual literary style, in complete opposition to the socially engaged literature promoted by mainstream writers such as **Lu Xun** and **Mao Dun.** Along with **Zhou Zuoren,** Lin promoted a personal approach to literature, which had many followers in the 1920s and 1930s.

LING SHUHUA (1900–1990). Fiction writer and painter. Born in Beijing, educated at Beijing University and in Japan and England, Ling wrote mostly short stories. Though not a prolific writer, Ling created some of the most unforgettable stories that capture the frustration of Chinese **women** caught in a traditional way of life. "Xiu zhen" (*The Embroidered Pillows*) and "Zhongqiu zhi ye" (*The Night of Mid-Autumn Festival*) are among her best stories. Her friendship with Julian Bell, son of Vanessa Bell and nephew of Virginia Woolf, enabled her to form enduring relationships with members of the Bloomsbury group. Encouraged by Virginia Woolf, with whom she corresponded, Ling wrote a memoir in English, *Ancient Melodies*, about her childhood growing up in an influential Beijing family headed by her scholar-official father, with his six wives and 10 children. Partially because of this privileged background and particially because of the narrow focus on women's domestic life in her writing, Ling is generally considered a "guixiu zuojia" (writer of the boudoir). She was also an accomplished artist, thanks to the training she received in her early childhood. She moved to London in the late 1940s with her husband, Chen Xiying, a scholar and a diplomat for the Nationalist government. She died in Beijing.

LITERARY RESEARCH SOCIETY (WENXUE YANJIU HUI). One of the earliest literary organizations in 20th-century China, the Literary Research Society was founded in 1921. Even at its inception, it was unambiguous about its undertaking: to inject a dose of seriousness into contemporary literature. This stance was in part a response to the so-called **Mandarin Ducks and Butterflies school** (yuanyang hudie pai) of literature, the main purpose of which was entertainment. Many of its founding members, including **Zheng Zhenduo, Mao Dun, Ye Shengtao**, and **Zhou Zuoren**, were prominent figures in the **May Fourth New Culture Movement**. Through their efforts, the Literary Research Society soon became the country's most influential literary association, attracting a large number of well-known writers and intellectuals such as **Wang Luyan, Xie Bingxin, Lao She, Liu Bannong, Xu Zhimo**, and others.

Mao Dun, a leading literary critic and a fiction writer, transformed *Xiaoshuo yuebao* (Fiction Monthly) after he became its editor in 1921, making it the main platform to promote the missions of the Literary Research Society by publishing works of authors who believed in "literature for life" (wenxue wei rensheng), a literature that offered realistic portrayals of contemporary life and sober examinations of social problems in an attempt to advance changes in society. To steer the development of modern Chinese literature in that direction, the Literary Research Society used its publications and various book clubs to introduce foreign literatures to its members and the general public, particularly realist works from Russia, Europe, Japan, and India. Writers whose works the Literary Research Society translated included Hans Christian

Andersen, Lord Byron, Leo Tolstoy, Anton Chekhov, Maxim Gorky, Ivan Turgenev, Roman Roland, Guy de Maupassant, Henrik Ibsen, Henryk Sienkiewicz, Rabindranath Tagore, George Bernard Shaw, Oscar Wilde, and many others. When *Fiction Monthly* stopped publication in 1932, the Literary Research Society was also dissolved.

LIU BAIYU (1916–2005). Prose and fiction writer. A prominent writer in the Mao era, Liu Baiyu held many important posts within the Chinese Communist Party, including Party secretary of the Chinese Writers Association and deputy minister of culture. He joined the Chinese Communist revolution soon after Japan invaded China and began his lifelong work in the Communist army, with which he fought in the **Sino-Japanese War**, the **Civil War**, and the Korean War.

A passionate believer in a utilitarian literature that serves the socialist cause and ideological principles of the Communist Party, Liu devoted his whole life to creating works that aimed to inspire and uplift the national spirit. The lyrical essay "Richu" (*Sunrise*), a staple of school textbooks in China, is representative of his work. It describes his experience on board an airplane from Moscow to Tashkent, a trip that allowed him to witness sunrise from the sky. From the descriptions of sunrise in nature, Liu moves on to talk about the "sunrise" in the hearts of the Chinese people. The rising sun thus becomes a symbol of a new China, a new society, a new life, and the youthful energy and idealism of the Chinese people, echoing the speech made by Mao Zedong to Chinese students studying in Moscow in which Mao compares the Chinese youths to the morning sun, full of promise and hope. A romanticist at heart, Liu sees the world in black and white contrasts in which good always triumphs over evil.

Other than lyrical prose, Liu also wrote fiction and reportages. His war novel *Di'er ge taiyang* (The Second Sun) is about the Communist troops crossing the Yangtze and marching down south to take control of Wuhan and Hunan from the hands of the Nationalist army and the personal sacrifices made by several generals to secure the Communist victory. The novel won the 1991 Mao Dun Literature Prize. An admirer of Dante, Johann Wolfgang von Goethe, Ivan Turgenev, and Victor Hugo, Liu favored hyperbole as well as expansive scenes and imageries and is best remembered for his lyrical essays that extol the beauty of the natural world, the value of life, the goodness of human nature, and a harmonious society. *See also* SOCIALIST REALISM.

LIU BANNONG (1891–1934). Poet and linguist. The son of a teacher, Liu Bannong was born in Jiangyin, Jiangsu Province. In 1912, he went to Shanghai to work as an editor and began publishing poetry and essays in newspapers and magazines. In 1916, his work debuted in *New Youth*, the most influential journal of the **May Fourth New Culture Movement**. His essay "My Views on the Change of Written Chinese," published in the May 1917 issue, was a significant piece in promoting modern Chinese language and literature. The same year, Liu took a teaching post at Beijing University, where he began his experimentations with using colloquial expressions and folk songs in his poetry. Under his urging, the *Beijing University Monthly* published folk ballads collected from all over the country, including the 20 "Boat Songs" Liu gathered from his native Jiangyin. In 1920, Liu went to London to study and in the following year moved to Paris where he majored in linguistics at the University of Paris. Upon receiving his Ph.D. in 1925, Liu went back to China to continue his research on Chinese language and popular literature. In 1934, while on a research trip to the northwest, Liu fell ill and died a few months later in Beijing.

Liu is credited with elevating folk literature to the mainstream. Through his research, his translations, and his own creative endeavors, Liu introduced lowbrow forms to institutions of higher learning. His campaign to bring down the ivory tower became part of the agenda of the **New Culture Movement** and helped establish his prominent role in modern Chinese intellectual development.

LIU HENG (1954–). Novelist. Raised in a village on the outskirts of Beijing, Liu Heng worked as a farmer and a factory worker and served in the military. He is a realist writer, best known for his novellas. Most of his early stories deal with rural communities and their basic needs for daily survival. According to Liu, Chinese country life consists of four essential ingredients: food, sex, physical strength, and dreams. "Gouri de liangshi" (*Dogshit Food*) concerns starvation in the countryside. *Fuxi fuxi* (Forbidden Love), which has been adapted into the erotic movie *Ju Dou* by Zhang Yimo, examines the conflict between instinctual sexual desire and social taboos in a traditional society. *Canghe bairimeng* (*Green River Daydreams*) deals with the aspirations that provide spiritual sustenance for the daily life of the peasants. As a novel that goes beyond the description of village life, *Canghe bairimeng* is the author's ambitious attempt at reconstructing the cultural heritage of the Chinese peasantry. *Qiuju da guansi* (Qiuju Goes to Court), which is the source for another of Zhang Yimo's movies, portrays a peasant woman fighting stubbornly against the injustice done to her family by the village head.

Later Liu turned his attention to urban problems. His social novel *Bai wo* (White Whirls) explores the emotional and psychological conflicts of an ambitious research scientist who is trying to negotiate between a marriage to a dutiful wife and an affair with another woman. By putting the issue of sexuality under the microscope, Liu attempts to examine the soul of the Chinese intellectual in modern-day society. Another novel, *Heide xue* (*Black Snow*), probes the problems faced by a young juvenile delinquent. *Pinzui Zhang Damin de xingfu shenghuo* (The Happy Life of Loquacious Zhang Damin), a popular novel about a Beijing resident of the lower social echelon, has received some critical attention. *See also* ROOT-SEEKING LITERATURE.

LIU NA'OU (1900–1939). Fiction and screenplay writer. Born in Japan, Liu Na'ou spent his first 16 years in **Taiwan**. He later studied Japanese literature in Tokyo, where he was exposed to the writings of the Japanese New Sensibility school. He went to Shanghai in 1926 and studied French at Zhendan University. Liu was closely associated with **Mu Shiying** and **Shi Zhecun**, modernist writers in the **New Sensibility school** who were active in Shanghai in the 1930s. He was the first to introduce into China the French writer Paul Morand, who influenced his work. Liu wrote about the city and its lures, and his only collection of short stories, entitled *Dushi fengjingxian* (Skylines of the City), foregrounds the material aspects of modern life in the metropolis. Scenes that are of particular importance to urban existence include ballrooms and cafés, where Liu's characters interact with one another and where their personalities are shaped and defined. Like his friend Mu Shiying, Liu was particularly interested in the character of the femme fatale, a symbol of eros. Many of his stories revolve around a triangular relationship, with two men in pursuit of one woman, competing for her attention with luxury goods. His characters are trendy men and women, partaking of the vices of modern consumer culture represented by sex, automobiles, and ballrooms. The Shanghai of Liu's stories is a Westernized cosmopolis, not much different from the cities in Europe and America in terms of modern amenities and materialist obsession. One story, "Reqing zhigu" (The Essence of Love), features a Frenchman as its protagonist in search of an oriental beauty.

As a publisher of journals and books, Liu was an ardent promoter of modernist literature. He was also interested in film. He founded the journal *Xiandai dianying* (The Modern Film) and wrote and directed a few romantic movies. Liu was assassinated in 1940, allegedly by Shanghai gangsters.

LIU SUOLA (1955–). Composer, singer, and fiction writer. Growing up during the **Cultural Revolution**, Liu Suola wrote her first story in 1984, a few years after graduating from the Central Conservatory of Music, where she studied composition and piano. Trained in classical music, she finds rock and roll and the blues more fitting to her rebellious spirit. Pursuing her dual career of musician and writer, Liu has been successful in both endeavors, though recently she has spent more energy on her experimental music. Her literary output consists of fictional works, most of which are novellas. "Ni biewu xuanze" (You Have No Choice) is about life in a music school where students feel frustrated with the authoritarian environment. It highlights the tensions in Chinese society between high-handed repression and uncontrollable creative spirit and gives voice to the sense of futility and discontent felt by the "lost generation" born in the 1960s and 1970s. A short novel, *Hundun jia ligeleng* (*Chaos and All That*), based on her sojourn in London, reflects the eclectic influences in the author's life, from street profanities to political mumbo jumbo, from Chinese operas to Western rock lyrics. Narrated by an émigré artist who lives in London, the story records events that took place in Beijing in the memories of the protagonist. Another novel, *Nüzhen tang* (Soup of the Female Chastity), is a collage of an assortment of genres, including myths, travel notes, drama, poetry, folk songs, newspaper articles, and screenplays. The novel tells a futuristic story that takes place four thousand years from now.

Liu's other publications include "Lantian lühai" (*Blue Sky and Green Sea*) and "Xunzhao ge wang" (*In Search of the King of Singers*). In all her works, the influences of Jack Kerouac, J. D. Salinger, Albert Camus, and Joseph Heller, whose works she read in the early 1980s, are easily detected. Her heroes are artist rebels who share many similarities with the author herself.

Liu currently lives in New York. She continues to write and perform music and has released three albums. *See also* WOMEN.

LIU XINWU (1942–). Fiction writer and essayist. In the immediate post-Mao era, Liu Xinwu was one of the most prominent literary names, identified as the representative writer of **scar literature** for his numerous stories exposing the damage left by the **Cultural Revolution**. His first story, "Ban zhuren" (*Class Counsellor*) was published in 1977, a year before Lu Xinhua's "Shangheng" (The Scar), which gives the movement its name. "Ban zhuren" explores the harmful influence of the Cultural Revolution on the minds of the Chinese youth. Through the portrayal of two teenagers and their reactions to a love scene in the novel *Gadfly* by Ethel Lilian Voynich, the story denounces the crime of ultraleftist policies and beseeches the society to save its children. This call echoes the cry **Lu Xun** voiced 60 years earlier in "Kuangren riji" (*The Diary of a Madman*) to save the children from Confucian ethical codes. This connection lends "Ban zhuren" an unmistakable sense of history and serves as a warning to the public that the old demons have come back in disguise to threaten the spiritual health of the children. "Aiqing de weizhi" (The Status of Love), "Xinglai ba, didi" (*Awake, My Brother*), and "Ai mei yipian shuye" (*I Love Every Green Leaf*) are among Liu's "scar" stories.

Liu later turned to write a series of stories about Beijing life. The idealized characters in his scar works are replaced with characters that are more realistic. Absent also is the motivation to expose social problems. The best known among this group of writings is *Zhonggu lou* (*The Bell and Drum Towers*), which recounts the past and present of several families in a neighborhood located in an old section of Beijing. Liu adopts a unique angle of observation that allows him to devote minute attention to each one of the 30 or so characters. The lack of a central character gives the text a polyphonic feel, allowing the reader a panoramic view of a society in action.

As a writer, Liu is particularly good at taking the pulse of society. He is aware of what the pressing issues of the day are and knows how to address them effectively. For this talent, he is considered a writer of social literature and tends to appeal to a large number of readers. As editor-in-chief of *People's Literature*, he has also exerted a strong influence in the development of Chinese literature.

LIU YICHANG, PEN NAME OF LIU TONGYI (1918–). Fiction writer, essayist, and newspaperman. Born in Shanghai, Liu Yichang was born in Shanghai and graduated from St. Johns University in 1981. All his life he worked as a journalist and editor. He moved to **Hong Kong** in 1948 and wrote for the *Xingdao Evening* and a few years later he went to

Singapore to edit a newspaper there. Returning to Hong Kong in 1957, Liu continued his writing career. Other than the large quantity of articles he wrote for newspapers, Liu devoted much of his time to his creative work. His novel *Jiutu* (An Alcoholic) is considered the first Chinese novel to use the technique of stream of consciousness. The protagonist is a writer, not unlike the author himself, forced by circumstances to give up his literary dreams to write popular, tasteless novels. As his notoriety rises, he sinks low spiritually. The random, disjointed remarks made in his drunken state are the most revealing of his psyche. When he sobers up, he has to face reality. Between drunkenness and sobriety, between illusion and reality, lies the inconvenient truth that ideals are hard to realize in real life.

Liu's other notable works include another novel, *Taoci* (Chinaware), four collections of novellas and short stories: *Tiantang yu diyu* (Heaven and Hell), *Si nei* (Inside the Temple), *Yi jiu jiu qi* (Nineteen Ninety-seven), and *Chun yu* (Spring Rain). Liu's fictional works are noted for their penchant for avant-gardism and experimentalism, representing the modernist movement in Hong Kong. Liu has had a long, prolific career in literature and journalism. He is also noted for his success at building bridges between Chinese-speaking communities by publishing literature written in Chinese from all over the world during his tenure as the editor-in-chief and director of *Hong Kong Literature* from 1985 to 2002.

LIU ZHENYUN (1958–). Fiction writer. Born in Yanjin, Henan Province, Liu Zhenyun was a schoolteacher and an army soldier before attending Beijing University. Upon graduation, he was assigned to work for the *Peasant Daily*. From 1989 to 1991, Liu was a graduate student at the Lu Xun Institute of Literature. He currently lives in Beijing.

Liu began publishing in 1982, the year he graduated from college, but fame did not find him until the late 1980s, when his short story "Yidi jimao" (Ground Covered with Chicken Feathers) was published. The story, told in a naturalistic manner, presents the tedious and hopeless life of an office worker in the city. A later novel, *Shouji* (Cell Phone), a satirical treatment of corruption that penetrates every aspect of social life, brought him to the height of his fame when it was adapted into a movie.

Similar thematic concerns dominate many of his works written in the 1990s, most notably the series of stories centered on his hometown. These poignant stories examine the makeup of the nation's culture by analyzing the pervasive abuse of power in society. In *Guxiang tianxia huanghua* (Hometown Filled with Yellow Flowers), the pursuit of the coveted job of village head has caused hatred and cost lives for generations between two families. Since the position brings power and power brings unlimited access, both families are willing to sacrifice their lives for it. *Guxiang xiangchu liuchuan zhong* (Hometown Interacting with Legends) connects the present with the past by bringing historical figures, such as Cao Cao (155–220) of the Three Kingdoms and Empress Dowager Cixi (1838–1908) of the Qing, side by side with the village's party secretary. However, the author reserves his sharpest criticism for the masses for their complacency. *Guxiang mian he huaduo* (Hometown Noodles and Flowers) examines, in the author's typical mocking voice, history and its webs of connections in which whoever has the power of speech has control of everything else. *Yiqiang feihua* (All Bullshit) expands Liu's interest in cultural inquiries into a philosophical reflection on language. The novel is an allegorical tale about a group of imaginative people in the lower echelons of society who love to picture themselves in a different kind of life but are frightened by their own thoughts. In order to cure the fear, they try to return to normalcy by talking about their real life only to find the words to be nothing but pure nonsense. Suspecting that they have gone crazy, they leave home to look for the cause of their insanity.

Liu is one of the most creative voices in modern Chinese literature. He is noted for his superb ability to retain satirical intervention without shortchanging a realistic representation of life. The comic element often found in his works serves to enhance the sense of absurdity in everyday life. *Wo jia Liu Yuejin* (My Name Is Liu Yuejin) turns upside down the logic of "the survival of the fittest" by giving the "sheep" a chance to defeat the "wolves." Liu Yuejin is a cook on a construction site. While looking for his lost bag, he chances upon another bag that contains a computer disk whose content, once revealed, would potentially destroy the lives of several important people. A hide-and-seek game ensues, ending in the triumph of the kind and harmless protagonist.

LU LING (1923–1994). Novelist and playwright. For the appearances of his writings in *Qi yue* (July), a literary journal edited by Hu Feng in the 1930s and 1940s, Lu Ling was forever associated with the so-called **July school** and suffered because of it. His best work is the novel *Caizhu de ernümen* (Sons and Daughters of a Landlord), about a prominent family being ruined when the children vie with one another for the family inheritance. Through the vicissitudes in the fortunes of the sons and daughters of a powerful landlord, the novel reveals the intricate historical path modern Chinese intellectuals have followed. The descriptions of violent internal conflicts and the tortured psychological states of the characters are strikingly original for early modern Chinese literature. Other important fictional works by Lu include *Ji'e de Guo Su'e* (The Hungry Guo Su'e), a novella praised by critics for its expression of basic humanity, and *Woniu zai jingji shang* (A Snail in Thorns), a psychological study of a pathetic character who hovers between spiritual paralysis and utter savagery, as well as "Luo Dadou de yisheng" (The Life of Luo Dadou), about the degenerated son of an old family, and "Yuyan" (Prediction), which deals with the tragic fate of a woman who works far away from her family. Lu's best-known play is a four-act tragedy written in 1947 entitled *Yunque* (Skylark), which established him as a leading dramatist.

In 1954, Lu Ling was jailed as one of the core members of the "Hu Feng Anti-Party Clique," tragically ending a brilliant career. He spent the next 20 years in prison, until Hu Feng's rehabilitation in the late 1970s allowed Lu Ling to be released. From the early 1980s, Lu Ling tried his hand at poetry and prose, but old age and poor health owing to many years of nightmarish life in prison made it impossible for him to recapture the vitality of his past. His earlier works, banned for decades, have now been made available. *See also* SPOKEN DRAMA.

LÜ LUN, PEN NAME OF LI LINFENG (1911–). Born into a sailor's family in **Hong Kong**, Lü Lun participated in the Northern Expedition. After he returned to Hong Kong, he began to publish essays and short stories in local newspapers. When the film industry moved to Hong Kong as Japan invaded Shanghai, Lü Lun began to write screenplays, producing films with such household names as *Chun can hua wei luo* (Flowers Still in Bloom when Spring Ends), *Xian duan qü zhong* (Broken Strings End the Song), *Pengmen shunü* (Lady from a Humble Abode), and *Dadi de ernü* (Sons and Daughters of the Land). When Japan occupied Hong Kong, Lü Lun fled to Guangdong and spent three years teaching at an elementary school. When Japan surrendered, he returned to Hong Kong and continued to work in the newspaper industry.

As a native Hong Kong writer, Lü lun devoted his talents to depicting his city and its residents. An eyewitness to Hong Kong's changes in the 20th century, Lü provides valuable insights into the soul of the city.

LU QIAO, PEN NAME OF WU NASUN (1919–2002). Fiction and prose writer. Born in Beijing and educated at the Southwest United University in Kunming, Lu Qiao left China in 1945 for the United States and graduated with a Ph.D. in art history from Yale University in 1954. Lu Qiao spent most of his professional life teaching art history at American universities. His scholarly publications are written in English, while his fiction and prose work is exclusively in Chinese, mostly written in the mid-20th century. Lu's best-known work is a novel, *Wei yang ge* (The Unfinished Song), completed in the mid-1940s during the **Sino-Japanese War** (1937–1945) and published in 1957 in Hong Kong. The book is based on his own student days in Kunming, when the Japanese invasion forced the professors and students of China's three elitist universities—Beijing University and Qinghua University in Beijing and Nankai University in Tianjin—to take refuge in the remote southwestern city. It centers on the students and the professors and local residents with whom they interact on a daily basis. Although the idealized student life is not altogether divorced from the war raging outside the bucolic campus, the author takes pains to deemphasize the national crisis, focusing instead on friendships and the pursuit of spiritual fulfillment. The novel evolves around four characters, all with attractive personalities and each in his or her own way working toward the goal of self-improvement and moral and ethical perfection. Lyrical and romantic in style, the novel is a eulogy for youth: a song of innocence. Lu Qiao's other stories and essays are collected in *Ren zi* (Son), *Chan qing shu* (Letters of Regrets), and *Shi chen ju* (Living in the Mundane World).

LU WENFU (1927–2005). Fiction writer. Born in Suzhou, a city he loved and devoted his whole career to depicting, Lu Wenfu worked for many years as a journalist and magazine editor and served as president of the Jiangsu Writers' Association and vice president of the Chinese Writers' Association. His literary career began in the 1950s with short stories about life in the small alleys of Suzhou, the most famous of which is "Xiao xiang shen chu" (*Deep within a Lane*). He is best known as the author of "Meishi jia" (*The Gourmet*), a novella about Suzhou cuisine and food culture. By all accounts, Lu was an old-fashioned gentleman who remained unaffected by the rampant ideological and dogmatic literature. What interested him throughout his career was the laid-back, simple but elegant lifestyle of the Suzhou residents. His prose is graceful, and his observations of the details of ordinary life are precise and full of wisdom. For his success in portraying the customs and traditions of Suzhou, he was called an "urban root-seeker," an honor he shared with other writers such as **Deng Youmei**, who wrote about the disappearing traditional life of old Beijing. *See also* ROOT-SEEKING LITERATURE.

LU XING'ER (1949–2004). Fiction writer, essayist, and playwright. Born and educated in Shanghai, Lu Xing'er was one of the urban youths sent to work in Beidahuang in the northeast. For 10 years she worked on a state farm, until she tested into the Central Institute of Theater in 1978. After graduation, she worked as a playwright for the Chinese Children's Art Theater. Later she served as an editor for Shanghai Literary Forum. She has published four novels and a number of collections of stories and prose.

In post-Mao literature, Lu Xing'er is known for her vivid portraits of **women**, particularly educated women, in modern Chinese society. Many of her female characters are successful but unhappy professionals, dissatisfied with the world around them. Like Lu Xing'er, these women belong to a generation brought up to believe in self-sacrifice and in the pursuit of ideals. They find the values of today's consumerism contrary to their convictions. Lu presents women in their struggle for self-respect and paints an ideal image of women, one that embodies awakened consciousness and a strong sense of purpose in life. Some of her stories are autobiographical, expressing her views about male chauvinism and the difficulties women face in their professional and personal lives. Other stories depict the aspirations of ordinary women, including *Liu gei shiji de wen* (A Kiss to the Century), *Huilou li de tonghua* (Fairy Tales in a Grey Building), *Nüren bu tiansheng* (No One Is Born to Be a Woman), and "Ah, Qingniao" (*Oh, Blue Bird*). *See also* CULTURAL REVOLUTION; SPOKEN DRAMA.

LU XUN, A.K.A. LU HSUN, PEN NAME OF ZHOU SHUREN (1881–1936). Fiction writer, essayist, and poet. A leader in the **May Fourth New Culture Movement** and father of modern Chinese fiction, Lu Xun remains a cultural icon in China. Three of his formal residences have been turned into museums and his books incorporated into textbooks, read and memorized by millions of children in Chinese schools. In life and after death, he has had a sizable following, both in the official and academic circles. Born into a scholar-official family in Shaoxing, Zhejiang Province, Lu Xun received a traditional education in the Confucian classics. As a child, he witnessed the decline of his family, which might have contributed to his decision to enroll in the Jiangnan Naval Academy in Nanjing, a school that offered generous scholarships. As he was fully immersed in a curriculum that emphasized science and technology, Lu Xun became fascinated by Theodore Huxley's *Evolution and Ethics*, translated into Chinese by Yan Fu. Upon graduation, Lu Xun received a government scholarship to study medicine in Japan. He frequented the anti-Qing gatherings organized by Chinese revolutionaries in Tokyo and became increasingly aware of the inadequacies of Chinese political and cultural systems. Soon convinced that medical science was not what the people of a weak and backward nation needed, he gave up his medical training and began using his pen, instead of the scalpel, to try to cure the nation of its spiritual diseases. Through publishing translations of European and Russian works by such well-known figures as Friedrich Nietzsche, Lord Byron, Percy B. Shelley, and Alexander Pushkin, Lu Xun and his comrades attempted to raise the spirit of the Chinese people and to encourage them to throw off the social and cultural shackles that inhibited their minds and souls. Literature became an expedient tool with which Lu Xun dissected his nation's problems.

When **Hu Shi**, Chen Duxiu, and others used the magazine *Xin qingnian* (New Youth) as their platform to wage a literary revolution, Lu Xun submitted "Kuangren riji" (*Diary of a Madman*) to be published in its May 1918 issue and later became one of the editors of *Xin qingnian.* "Kuangren riji" was written in the vernacular, the language advocated by the New Culture and New Literature proponents. As the first short story written in the modern style in Chinese fiction, its publication was a milestone. Lu Xun's genius in this work lies in his ability to convey an iconoclastic vision in a style that combines realism and symbolism, mixed with a pastiche of psychological theory and medical knowledge, maintaining throughout the narrative a cool distance of irony. The story contains a highly provocative message that denounces the long history of Chinese civilization as one that has been engaged in "eating people," pronounced by a man who ostensibly suffers from a persecution complex. Further complicating the narrative is the preface, written in classical Chinese, claiming that the diseased man has fully recovered and is awaiting a new assignment by the government. With its narrative complexity and rich symbolism, "Kuangren riji" took a solid first step in the development of modern Chinese fiction. This and other short stories, including "Kong Yiji" (The Scholar), "Guxiang" (Hometown), and "Yao" (Medicine), later collected in *Nahan* (*Call to Arms*), put Lu Xun in the forefront of an iconoclastic movement whose main target of criticism was Confucianism and its impact on the national character of the Chinese. These stories established Lu Xun as an innovative writer and a great thinker who understood what afflicted the Chinese culture and people, earning him the accolade "the soul of the nation."

Between 1924 and 1925, Lu Xun finished 11 short stories, collected and published in 1926 under the title *Panghuang* (Wandering). Most of the stories in this collection are about Chinese intellectuals and their sufferings, struggles, and failures. Juansheng and Zijun, the two young lovers in "Shangshi" (Regrets for the Past), best embody the hopes and disappointments of this class of people. They defy their families in pursuit of emancipation and individual freedom, but their marriage comes apart eventually, unable to survive the poverty that dogs them and the hopelessness pervasive in society. In the end, Zijun returns to her father's house and soon dies in sadness and depression. Juansheng falls into deep remorse and grief. Their tragedy comes to represent the failure of individuality and reform embraced by the May Fourth generation of intellectuals.

In these two collections, *Nahan* and *Panghuang*, Lu Xun reveals to his readers a civilization in crisis. Its intellectual elites are impotent and its masses ignorant. Superstition, blind loyalty to tradition, inertia, cruelty to one another, easy resignation to fate, total lack of individuality, and a host of other problems force China to its knees, reducing it to a weakened and anemic nation, sick to its core. The memorable characters Lu Xun created, including the fervent revolutionaries such as the madman and the young man of the Xia family, the troubled intellectuals such as the narrators in "Guxiang" and "Zhufu," the humiliated, old-fashioned scholar Kong Yiji, the miserable Xianglin Sao, and most important, the quintessential representative of the Chinese peasants, Ah Q, drive home the idea that the Chinese culture needs to be overhauled and replaced with something completely different. For his consistent effort at disseminating this message, Lu Xun has been called the "flag bearer of the New Culture Movement." In addition to short stories, Lu Xun wrote a large number of essays in which he debated with conservatives and lashed out at foes, earning him the reputation of a sharp-tongued polemicist. The style of his essays is impeccable and the tone biting and satirical. Compared to his fictional works, his essays are greater in number and cover a much wider range of subjects.

Lu Xun's legacy rests not only on his writings—three collections of fiction and 14 collections of essays, as well as poems, translations, and scholarly work—but also on his mentoring of young writers. He left a literary heritage that still exerts a powerful influence on Chinese writers today. He has come to embody the intellectual conscience of 20th-century China. However, being a fiercely independent man, proud and unforgiving, Lu Xun also had many detractors. His involvement with the **left-wing** literary circle endeared him to the Communists but antagonized the Nationalists. For many years, his books were banned in **Taiwan**. His critics find him confrontational and his body of literary output thin. Yet, even those who intensely dislike him cannot deny his significant influence on modern Chinese literature. *See also* ZHOU ZUOREN.

LU YAO, PEN NAME OF WANG WEIGUO (1949–1992). Novelist. Born into a poor peasant family in Shaanxi, Lu Yao left the countryside to attend Yan'an University in 1973 as a Chinese major. After graduation, he worked as a journalist and later as an editor for the journal *Shaanxi wenyi* (Shaanxi Literature and Art). In 1980 he published a novella, "Jing tian dong di de yi mu" (An Earth-Shattering Episode), which won a national prize. Two years later the short novel *Ren sheng* (Life) was published and shortly after a movie based on the novel was made, making Lu Yao a household name. In 1992, a year after he finished his most ambitious work, *Pingfan de shijie* (An Ordinary World), a novel that won the Mao Dun Literature Prize, Lu Yao died at the age of 42.

Having grown up in the poor and conservative countryside and worked his way into the city, Lu Yao understood on a personal level the extraordinary challenges and moral quandaries faced by educated youths of rural backgrounds. He wrote about the economic reform that lured young peasants into the cities, forcing them to change their traditional ways of thinking in order to find their place in the new economy and new social order. *Ren sheng* tells about the emotional journey of Gao Jialin, a high school graduate, as fate throws him back and forth between his native village and the city and between a simple, submissive country girl and a sophisticated, independent city woman. With his dreams repeatedly dashed, Gao finally realizes that he belongs to the soil that nurtured him, and his future rests with the poor and backward countryside that waits for him, and the educated country youths like him, to transform. Similarly, *Pingfan de shijie* deals with the great transformations taking place in rural communities and the surrounding small towns since Deng Xiaoping's reform. The novel covers the first decade of the reform era when China underwent fundamental changes in its economic, social, and cultural spheres. Lu Yao wrote in the realist tradition, and as an idealist he firmly believed in the future of the country.

LU YIN (1899–1934). Fiction writer and essayist. Lu Yin attended a missionary school and participated in the **May Fourth Movement** while a student at the Beijing Normal University for Women. In her short literary career, Lu Yin wrote fiction and essays in which she expressed her views on traditional ethics, particularly those designed to confine **women**. The main theme of her work concerns the oppression of women and their arduous struggle for love and independence. More often than not their efforts end in failure, in part because of their own feeling of paralysis in a society that does not value the needs of the individual. Critics have attributed the melancholy mood of her stories to a lack of love in her childhood and her bumpy journey to matrimony. Indeed, few of her heroes are able to obtain happiness, reflecting Lu Yin's pessimistic philosophy on life. Lu Yin casts her characters' romantic relationships against the background of a larger social transformation that took place in the early part of the 20th century, when traditional modes of life clashed violently with changes brought about by modernity. The road to romantic love, as described by Lu Yin, is full of suffering, but for women, the alternative path of career fulfillment is equally unattainable.

Lu Yin wrote in an unadorned style, often relying on the form of letters or diary to carry the narrative structure. "Lishi de riji" (The Diary of Lishi), "Haibing guren" (*An Old Acquaintance by the Sea*), "Jimo" (Loneliness), and many other stories all share this narrative feature. Her best work, "Xiangya jiezhi" (An Ivory Ring), also contains a fairly large portion of diary entries. It was written in memory of her friend Shi Pingmei, with the intention of leaving a record of a life that the author likens to that of "a tragic and beautiful poem." The essentially true-to-life narrative revolves around Zhang Qinzhu, the fictional character modeled after Shi Pingmei. Beautiful and talented, Zhang attracts the attention of a devious man who is trapped in an unhappy marriage arranged by his parents. His relentless pursuit wins her heart before she discovers that he already has a wife and two children. Still emotionally entangled with him, Zhang meets another man, who also falls in love with her and who takes steps to end a loveless marriage only to be told upon his return that Zhang does not want to marry him. Sick and heartbroken, he kills himself. Regrets and remorse soon drive Zhang also to her grave. Lu Yin's sympathy for the heroine is obvious. She had a similar relationship—her first husband also had a wife when they married. Lu Yin understood the sufferings borne by both the traditional wife and the modern, liberated woman. To some extent, she is also sympathetic to the man who is caught between his duty to his family and his desire to seek happiness. Lu Yin died at the young age of 35 from a botched surgery during childbirth, ending a promising career.

LUO FU, A.K.A. LO FU, PEN NAME OF MO LUOFU (1928–). Poet and essayist. Born in Hengyang, Hunan Province, Luo Fu joined the army during the **Sino-Japanese War** (1937–1945) and moved to **Taiwan** with the Nationalist government. He graduated from the English Department of Tamkang University, and in the 1950s Luo Fu and his friends Zhang Mo and **Ya Xian** founded *Xin shiji* (New Epoch), a poetry journal that had a lasting influence on Taiwan's literary development. A central figure in the modernist movement in Taiwan, and winner of many awards including the National Award for Literature and Art of Taiwan, Luo Fu is a prolific writer, having published more than a dozen collections of poetry and several collections of prose and critical essays, as well as many translations. In his early career, Luo Fu was a surrealist influenced by the French modernists, especially Charles Baudelaire, Arthur Rimbaud, Paul Valéry, and Guillaume Apollinaire. He was also fond of the work by Wallace Stevens, in whose verses Luo Fu found a kindred spirit. He was fascinated by Rainer Maria Rilke, whose profound religious sensibility influenced his own work; Luo Fu has acknowledged his debt to the German poet, pointing out that one of his early poems, "Shi shi zhi siwang" (*Death in a Stone Cell*), and his recent epic poem "Piao mu" (Driftwood) have traces of Rilke in them. In Luo Fi's more recent work, there emerges a new sense of clarity and serenity, much of which has to do with his rediscovery of the Chinese poetic tradition, which allows the poet to tap into those great resources as he continues to innovate and perfect his art.

In 1996, Luo Fu moved to Vancouver, Canada. This new environment has inspired him to explore fresh territories with regard to the meaning and essence of life. "Piao mu," composed during this period, is an intimate look at his personal life as an expatriate and a drifter, first from the mainland to Taiwan and then from Taiwan to Canada. It is also an expression of his artistic aspirations as well as his outlook on life. Luo Fu is a master of the Chinese language, a skilled linguistic magician. Having written many mesmerizing verses, Luo Fu has been called "a poetry wizard."

LUO YIJUN (1967–). Fiction writer. Born and raised in **Taiwan**, Luo Yijun received his bachelor's degree in creative writing from the Chinese Culture University and his master's from the National Taiwan Institute of Arts. As an undergraduate student, Luo studied under several established writers, including **Zhang Dachun**, whose postmodern style of writing had a strong impact on the budding writer. In 1993, Luo published his first book, *Hong zi tuan* (The League of the Red Letter), which contains six stories, most of which are metafiction focusing on narrative techniques, obviously influenced by such writers as Jorge Luis Borges, Italo Calvino, and Zhang Dachun. A book published in 1998 whimsically entitled *Qi meng gou* (Wife Dreaming of the Dog) established a key feature of his style, an offshoot of the Japanese *Shishosetsu*—the I-novel, which has been appropriated by other Chinese writers, most notably **Yu Dafu**.

Charactristic of the I-novel, the first-person narrator of Luo's stories resorts to unrelenting self-exposure and self-analysis of the most private, and often dark, world, and in so doing moves freely between the depth of his psychological state and external reality, merging the private with the public. Representative of this style of his work are *Yueqiu xing-shi* (The Moon Tribe) and *Qian beihuai* (Expressions of Sorrow). The former is a collection of stories that explore the emotional attachment and the memories the author's father's generation has with the mainland they left behind when they came to Taiwan with the Nationalist government. The focus is on the son's perception of his Taiwanese mother and mainlander father by "freezing" the flow of time in order to experience the intensity of emotions and feelings. *Qian beiluai*, a controversial work in the form of letters between the living (the narrator) and the dead (**Qiu Miaojin**, a lesbian writer who committed suicide), is a book on death and dying, a metaphysical reflection on the concept of time and the act of writing as an attempt to escape the doomed end. In theme and subject matter, this work is reminiscent of **Zhu Tianwen**'s *Huang ren shouji* (*Notes of a Desolate Man*).

Luo's best work is generally agreed to be the two-volume *Xixia lüguan* (The Hotel of the Ancient Xixia Empire), a novel that pulls together and magnifies the narrative styles and themes of his previous works. At the root of the novel is his reflection of the dilemma faced by his generation of Chinese born in Taiwan to parents who fled the mainland in the 1950s, an existential condition that has been experienced by others in the history of humankind, including the ancient people who created Western Xia (1038–1227)—once a powerful empire with its own written language, culture, and political system—and dominated western China. This nomadic people, known as Dangxiang or Tangut, left almost no trace of their existence, and in many ways Luo's father's generation, cut off for decades from their homes, families, communities, and their native land, mirrors the Danxiangs, facing the threat of leaving no mark in the memories of their offspring. Indeed, Luo has remarked that his own generation may be the last one still retaining some attachment to the mainland and to the traditions of their fathers' generation. As such, the population faces imminent extinction, as once happened to the Dangxiang. Luo's novel weaves two plots, one having to do with a cavalry fleeing south as Western Xia was being destroyed by the Mongols and another following the second generation of the mainlanders in Taiwan. The author works with inventive narrative freedom, cutting sharply between the two time periods, subjecting reality to the time-bending torsions of memory and legends while pointing out that human history, or the memory of human history, is like a hotel that has put up travelers, each of whom may or may not have left behind a story, a fragmented story at best.

Luo is clearly one of the most imaginative writers coming out of Taiwan. His creativity, abundant imagination, unrestrained style, and provocative subjects of sexuality, violence, and dark family history have won him numerous awards, such as the Best Book Award given by *Lianhe Daily*, making him a significant figure in modern Chinese literature. Luo's other fictional works include *Disange wuzhe* (The Third Dancer), *Yuanfang* (Faraway), and *Women zi ye'an de jiuguan likai* (At Night We Left a Dark Pub) as well as fairy tales, plays, and poetry.

– M –

MA FENG (1922–2004). Fiction writer. Ma Feng was one of the so-called potato school writers, all from Shanxi Province, known for writing about and for the rural masses. Throughout his career, Ma closely followed Mao Zedong's call to use literature as a tool to serve the people. With this mission in mind, he set out to write stories that would be appreciated by ordinary peasants. For Ma, folk literature was an inexhaustible source of artistic creation, and it played an important role in the formation of his literary style: plain, humorous, and easy to understand. *Lüliang shan yingxiong zhuan* (Heroes of Mount Lüliang), coauthored with Xi Rong, another potato school writer, is Ma's best-known work, written in a style reminiscent of traditional chapter novels, particularly *Shuihu zhuan* (*The Water Margin*). His later works are better representations of the realist mode in terms of artistic vision and narrative technique. In the 1950s and early 1960s, Ma's reputation was at its peak. Many of his stories were household names, such as "Women cun li de nianqing ren" (The Young People in Our Village) and "Wode diyige shangji" (My First Boss). All his life, Ma loved the peasants and never forgot his responsibility to represent their interests and speak to them in their language. Whether in characterization, choice of expression, or the organization of the interwoven details, Ma displays the best of his skill in the combination of realistic content with a form inspired by folk traditions. His humorous style also finds its fullest expression in the short story. Ma was also a screenplay writer, having turned several of his own stories into popular movies.

Of his publications, Ma once said, "If judged separately, no story of mine is good enough in terms of thematic development or characterization, but taking all my stories as a whole, the reader can have a general view of what happened in the lives of the Chinese peasants in the course of more than thirty years." *See also* SOCIALIST REALISM.

MA JIAN (1953–). Fiction writer and essayist. Born in Qingdao, Shandong Province, Ma Jian is one of the most independent writers in modern Chinese literature. Throughout his career, Ma has been noted for his defiant acts against authority. In the early 1980s, he attracted the government's attention for his nonconformist paintings and "freewheeling" lifestyle. He took his vows in 1983 with the Beijing Buddhist Association. The following year he quit his job as a photojournalist for the state-owned magazine, *Chinese Workers*, to travel to **Tibet** through the Chinese hinterland. He came to prominence in 1987 with the publication of his controversial "Liangchu ni de shetai huo kongkong dangdang" (*Stick Out Your Tongue*) in *People's Literature*, which partially caused the author's eventual exile. The story records Ma's close encounters with Tibetan culture, which both fascinated and horrified him. Unable to publish his work in China, he left for **Hong Kong**, and when the British colony was handed over to China in 1997, he went to Germany and later to England, where he still resides.

Widely reputed as a dissident writer, Ma believes that the soul of modern Chinese literature is a profound political consciousness and that the core of his own writing is a strong conviction in individualism and in the emancipation of the self. His works are critical of the lack of freedom in China and the debilitating effects of totalitarianism on the lives of ordinary people. *Hong chen* (*Red Dust*), winner of the 2002 Thomas Cook Travel Book Award, is an insightful and moving account of his three-year trek from Beijing to Tibet in the wake of a personal crisis that involved a divorce and a political purge. More than a travelogue, the book reveals the author's skepticism about everything from communism to Buddhism. His novel *Lamian zhe* (*The Noodle Maker*) consists of a series of stories about people living in the shadows of an authoritarian government after the 1989 crackdown on the **Tian'anmen Prodemocracy Movement**. The tone of the book is satirical, targeting the bizarre and cruel realities in contemporary Chinese society. Based on the same political event is his most recent book, *Beijing zhiwuren* (*Beijing Coma*), a novel that centers on a student demonstrator who remains in a coma for 10 years after being shot in the head during the Tian'anmen crackdown. When he wakes up, he is faced with a country that has changed beyond recognition: a nation suffering from a collective amnesia about what happened 10 years ago and consumed with the pursuit of material wealth. The novel is full of black humor, a prominent feature in Ma's work, mocking the absurdities and capriciousness in an oppressive society. Ma's other fictional works include *Yuan bei* (The Stele of Lamentation), *Jiutiao chalu* (Nine Crossroads), and *Ni la goushi* (Dog Shit).

MA LIHUA (1953–). Poet, prose and fiction writer. Her writing career is built entirely upon her 25-year experience living and working in **Tibet**, where she went in 1976 immediately after graduating from Lingyi

Teachers' College in Shandong Province. Along with other Chinese college graduates recruited by the government to serve as teachers, technical experts, doctors, and government officials, Ma was assigned to work first as an administrator and then as an editor for *Xizang wenxue* (Tibetan Literature), a journal publishing literary works written in Chinese. She traveled extensively on assignments, eventually covering every county (over 70) in the Tibetan Autonomous Region. Since 2003, she has been working as general editor for Tibetan Studies Press in Beijing.

In the initial phase of her encounter with Tibet, Ma belonged, in her own words, to "the last generation of Chinese romantic poets." Tibet provided a fantasy world into which she projected her own dreams. Later when she became interested in anthropology, Ma turned to prose writing. As she traversed the Tibetan plateau and met a wide spectrum of Tibetan people, she became one of the region's best-known spokespersons and advocates. Her cultural reportages and travel notes, which resulted from solid field research, portray Tibetan customs in vivid details. Because of the unique literary sensibility displayed in these works, Ma is credited for having built a bridge between anthropology and literature and has been called a "literary anthropologist." Her most important prose works include *Zangbei youli* (*Glimpses of Northern Tibet*), *Xixing Ahli* (Journey Westward to Ali), *Linghun xiang feng* (The Soul Is like the Wind), and *Zangdong hong shanmai* (The Red Mountains in Eastern Tibet). Her poems are collected in *Wo de taiyang* (My Sun) and her essays in *Zhui ni dao gaoyuan* (Following You to the Tibetan Plateau). She is also a noted scholar on Tibetan literature, having published *Xueyu wenhua yu Xizang wenxue* (The Culture of the Snow Land and Tibetan Literature). Ma's recent publication, *Ruyi gaodi* (The Highland of Dreams), is a fictional work inspired by the personal account of Chen Quzhen, a Qing military officer sent into Tibet in the early 20th century. Chen wrote the memoir in 1936 to record his extraordinary ordeal in Tibet. In her book, Ma mixes real historical events with fiction, and past with present, creating a postmodern work in which fictitious contemporary characters are cast as reincarnations of historical figures to recover a deeply buried past laden with mystery, violence, courage, ambition, geopolitics, and romantic love. *See also* WOMEN.

MA YUAN (1953–). Fiction writer. After graduating from Liaoning University in northeast China, where he studied Chinese literature, Ma Yuan went to **Tibet** to work as a journalist. The experience proved to be pivotal for his literary career. Lhasa in the 1980s was a lively place of artistic fermentation, and in Tibetan culture Ma found the perfect launchpad for his fictional experiment.

Regarded as one of the most important pioneers of China's **avant-garde literature**, Ma is credited for helping to turn the writer's focus from what stories to tell to how to tell a story. His writings, inspired by Tibetan religion and mysticism, are among the most influential works from the 1980s. Reacting against the dictates of **socialist realism**, which had dominated China's literary discourse for decades, Ma experimented with literary forms and narrative strategies, thanks in part to the availability of modern Western literature in Chinese translation, among them works by Jorge Luis Borges, which exerted a strong influence on Ma. He is noted for his labyrinthine narrative style, with the narrator, often identified as "Ma Yuan, the Chinese, who writes fiction," working to expose the fictitious nature of storytelling. His texts have complex, multileveled structures, mixing the fantastic with realistic elements. Ma's stories are concerned less with Tibet than with his personal vision of fiction and his Borgesian metafiction style accentuates a new awareness of narrative technique. "Lasa he de nüshen" (The Goddess of the Lhasa River), "Die zhiyao de sanzhong fangfa" (*More Ways Than One to Make a Kite*), and "Gangdisi de youhuo" (The Lure of the Gantise) are among his best-known stories. Since he left Tibet in 1989, Ma has made television shows and taught creative writing. Although he has not produced more fictional work, he has published two collections of essays, *Xugou zhi dao* (The Knife of Fiction) and *Yuedu dashi* (Reading the Masters), on his views on literature and his approach to creative writing.

MANDARIN DUCKS AND BUTTERFLIES SCHOOL (YUAN-YANG HUDIE PAI). This term, coined in the **May Fourth** era, refers to middlebrow romantic fiction writers at the end of the 19th century and the beginning of the 20th century, a time that witnessed great debates about the role literature played in society. While the Mandarin Ducks and Butterflies school saw literature as purely a venue of entertainment, the May Fourth leaders regarded it as a serious expression of the self and a realistic portrayal of life, ideals advocated by the **Creation Society**, the **Literary Research Society,** and the **Left-wing Association of Chinese Writers**. Although rejected by the elite, the Mandarin Ducks and Butterflies school writers enjoyed popular success. With their journal,

Saturday (Libailiu), for which they were also called the Saturday school (Libanliu pai), they were able to flood the streets with their laid-back, entertaining tales of love and betrayal. **Zhang Henshui**, Zhou Shou'ou, and Bao Xiaotian were some of the most popular writers of the group.

MANG KE, PEN NAME OF JIANG SHIWEI (1950–). Poet and painter. Born in Shenyang and raised in Beijing, Mang Ke was sent to rural Hebei at the age of 16, riding in the same horse carriage with **Duo Duo**. It was in the countryside that he began to write poetry. In 1976, Mang Ke returned to Beijing and two years later joined forces with other young poets including Bei Dao and Duo Duo to found *Jintian* (Today), an important venue for experimental poetry, which would become known as **Misty poetry**. Later on, as most of his friends and colleagues settled down one after another, Mang Ke continued his vagabond life in Beijing, making short and frequent trips abroad to participate in poetry festivals. Some 30 years after he published his first poem, Mang Ke turned to painting and achieved remarkable success in his new medium.

Mang Ke is a natural poet who relies almost exclusively on instinct rather than on learning. Abundant with natural imagery and pulsating with the rhythm of the earth and waters, many of his poems reflect his years in the countryside, which inspired him and nurtured his romantic view of life. Even his political poems, such as "Yangguang zhong de xiangrikui" (The Sunflower in the Sunlight) and "Tiankong" (The Sky), which boldly challenge absolutism and ideological tyranny, exude the smell and the sound of nature. Other than poetry, Mang Ke has written a novel based on his experience in rural Hebei as well as many essays, including his most recent work, *Qiao! Zhe xie ren* (Memories), which reminisces about his generation and some of its vivid characters. *See also* CULTURAL REVOLUTION.

MAO DUN, A.K.A. MAO TUN, PEN NAME OF SHEN DERONG (1896–1981). Fiction writer and literary critic. A forerunner in the **New Culture Movement** in early 20th-century China and a proponent of literary realism, Mao Dun made significant contributions to the development of modern Chinese literature. Through his own writings and his work as a translator, editor, and publisher, as a literary critic and theoretician, and finally as the minister of culture from 1949 to 1964, he left indelible marks in nearly every aspect of the literary and artistic endeavors of modern China.

Like the rest of his generation, Mao Dun received an education in a mixture of classics and modern thought. After graduating from Beijing University in 1916, Mao took a job as a translator and editor at the Commercial Press, where he stayed until 1925. His main achievement there was the transformation of the journal *Xiaoshuo yuebao* (Fiction Monthly), making it a major force in promoting a "literature for life," in direct opposition to what was advocated by the members of the **Mandarin Duck and Butterflies school** and the Saturday school, who held the view that the main purpose of literature was to entertain. Mao Dun's essay "On Proletarian Art," published serially in *Wenxue zhoukan* (Literature Weekly) in 1925, established his reputation as a Marxist theoretician. It asserts that art must faithfully reflect reality and meet the needs of its time. In a class-based society, a proletarian writer must identify with the lot of the common people, to educate and inspire them in their struggle for social justice and national independence. He or she must understand the unity of form and content, which requires that new ideas be expressed in new forms, an example of which is Maxim Gorky, whose works, Mao Dun believes, perfectly combine aesthetics and the aspirations of the proletariat. In this essay, Mao Dun delineates a form of realism for modern Chinese literature and art that influenced a whole generation of Chinese writers.

The trilogy Mao Dun wrote in the late 1920s, *Huanmei* (Disillusionment), *Dongyao* (Wavering), and *Zhuiqiu* (Aspirations), describes the experience of Chinese youth during the different stages of the revolution that aimed to unify a China ravaged by civil wars among its warlords. The 1930s saw the best of Mao Dun's writings, including *Ziye* (*Midnight*), a milestone in his literary career. The story takes place in 1930 when Chinese industrialists found themselves in direct conflict not only with foreign imperialist interests but also with workers' strikes and peasants' riots. The broad scope of the work, with its numerous characters from a wide spectrum of social classes and several plot lines, makes the novel Mao Dun's most ambitious undertaking. Mao Dun is noted for his skill at depicting the psychological depth of his characters with a few strokes. This *baimiao* style is reminiscent of the classical novels the author was extremely fond of as a child. In the same year, Mao Dun published *Linjia puzi* (*The Lin Family Shop*), "Chun can" (*Spring Silkworms*), "Qiushou" (Autumn Harvest), and "Can dong" (The Last of Winter), all conceived to show sympathy for the oppressed and to cry for social justice. *Linjia puzi*, a tightly structured story, is about the bankruptcy of a small shop in a small town. Mr. Lin, an honest, hardworking man, is forced out of business by corrupt government officials and greedy creditors. "Chuncan," "Qiushou," and "Candong" are three independent but consecutive short stories about village life. They portray a family of silkworm raisers headed by Old Tongbao and trace their fall from financial stability to bankruptcy, from self-sufficient peasants to poor farmhands. The stories present a vivid picture of economic distress and unrest in rural Chinese communities. "Chuncan," which focuses on the tragic lot of Old Tongbao, is a flawlessly crafted story. The moving descriptions of the family tending silkworms from hatching eggs to harvesting cocoons are some of the finest moments of the story.

Mao Dun's most influential work during the **Sino-Japanese War** is *Fushi* (Corruption). The political novel is severely critical of the Nationalist government, exposing the maliciousness and cunning of the special agents working for the government who suppress the democratic movement while indulging in a depraved lifestyle. Despite its overtly political tone, *Fushi* contains some interesting formalistic innovations. It is written in diary form, narrated by a minor female secret agent of the government. This unique perspective allows the author to concentrate on psychological exploration rather than the minute descriptions and plot expositions commonly found in his writings. Mao Dun also employs the narrative style of stream of consciousness with its characteristics of free association, inverted time order, and dreams or hallucinations. These techniques enrich the psychological realism of the novel.

After his death, a memorial fund in Mao Dun's honor was established to recognize notable achievements in Chinese literature. It is the most prestigious literary prize in China.

MAY FOURTH MOVEMENT (WUSI YUNDONG). The treaties of the Versailles Conference, signed on 28 April 1919, awarding Japan the former German leasehold of Jiaozhou, Shandong Province, triggered protests by university students in Beijing on 4 May. More demonstrations and strikes soon spread to other parts of China, followed by a nationwide boycott of Japanese goods. What began as a patriotic and anti-imperialist mass protest evolved into a national movement to reevaluate the entirety of Chinese civilization. Intellectuals attacked traditional values, identifying them as reasons for China's backwardness, and looked to the West for ideas with which to transform their nation.

The movement later split into two factions: the leftists and the liberals. The former, represented by Chen Duxiu and Li Dazhao, favored political action and established the Chinese Communist Party while the latter advocated a gradual change, emphasizing "enlightenment" as promoted by Columbia University graduate **Hu Shi**.

The May Fourth Movement left a profound impact not only on Chinese social and political life but also on Chinese intellectual, cultural, and literary thought. It is fair to say that modern Chinese literature was born in the May Fourth Movement and generations of Chinese writers came under its direct influence. The two writers who most represent the May Fourth spirit are **Lu Xun** and **Ba Jin**, Lu Xun for his strong indictment of the "man-eating" Confucian culture and Ba Jin for his portrayal of rebellious youths trying to break away from the confines of the traditional family and embrace social changes. *See also* AI QING; AI WU; BING XIN; CHEN BAICHEN; DING LING; FENG XUEFENG; FENG ZHI; HONG SHEN; HU YEPIN; JIAN XIAN'AI; JIANG GUANGCI; LAI HE; LAO SHE; LI JIEREN; MAO DUN; NEW CULTURE MOVEMENT; WANG JINGZHI; WANG LUYAN; WANG TONGZHAO; WEN YIDUO; XIA YAN; XU DISHAN; XU ZHIMO; YANG HANSHENG; YE SHENGTAO; YU DAFU; YU PINGBO; ZHAO SHULI; ZHENG ZHENDUO; ZHOU LIBO; ZHU ZIQING.

MEI NIANG, PEN NAME FOR SUN JIARUI (1920–). Fiction and prose writer. In the 1940s, Mei Niang was as famous as **Zhang Ailing**, one based in the north (Changchun and Beijing) and the other the south (Shanghai) and both living in the Japanese-occupied territories during the **Sino-Japanese War**. Mei Niang was born in Vladivostok, where her father, a successful businessman fluent in three foreign languages—Russian, Japanese and English—was working for a railway company. Her parents had met in Vladivostok and after Mei Niang was born they moved to Changchun, where his father's first wife lived. Though Mei Niang's parents doted on her, they soon passed away, leaving her in the care of the unkind first wife. Growing up as a daughter of a concubine, Mei Niang understood the nature of traditional society, particularly the position of young **women** within a large extended family. Her pen name "Mei Niang" (literally, Plum Blossom Girl) is a homophone for "having no mother," bearing testimony to the pain she suffered in her childhood. Later, she would repeatedly revisit this theme in her stories. While Mei Niang was an elementary school student, the Japanese army occupied northeastern China, making the young Mei Niang vaguely aware of a national tragedy. Most of the characters she created in her writings are women caught in the chaos of war, victims of misfortunes at both the personal and national levels. Mei Niang achieved her literary success at a very young age. Her first collection of short stories, *Xiajie ji* (Young Ladies), was published when she was merely 16 years old. At 24, she won the Japanese-sponsored Greater Asian Literature Prize for "Xie" (Crab), a semiautobiographical novella about the disintegration of a traditional family, a common theme in the May Fourth literature written by **Ba Jin**, **Lao She**, **Lu Ling**, and others. Mei Niang's writings reflect the realities of China in the 1930s and 1940s, often seen through the eyes of a sensitive, educated young woman. Her stories on the fate of women such as "Yu" (Fish), "Bang" (Clam), and "Chun dao renjian" (Spring Has Arrived) render vivid portrayals of the changing world in which "the consciousness of women" was beginning to emerge as a social and cultural phenomenon, despite the oppressive restraints imposed on them by society. By the time "Zhuru" (The Midget) appeared, Mei Niang was a well-known writer who had perfected the art of short story writing in the realist mode and whose vision had gone well beyond the confines of marriage and romance. In addition to short stories and novellas, Mei Niang also attempted full-length novels, *Ye hehua kai* (Night Lily) and *Xiao furen* (Little Women), both unfinished, deal with women's search for security and love in their relationships with men.

In many ways, Mei Niang's life was emblematic of the upheavals of 20th-century China. As a new woman growing up in the aftermath of the **May Fourth Movement**, she received a good education in Changchun and later in Japan, opportunities unavailable to her mother's generation. She became a young widow in 1948 when her husband's ship capsized on the way to **Taiwan**, leaving behind Mei Niang and their three young children. Instead of staying in Taiwan or going to Japan, Mei Niang took her children back to Beijing, which was now under the control of the Communists. She was assigned to work for the Agricultural Film Studio as a scriptwriter and editor. In the 1950s, she produced some children's picture books. During the subsequent political campaigns, Mei Niang managed to survive all kinds of appalling treatment, but two of her children died. Even as she was warmly welcomed into the circle of writers in the early 1950s, Mei Niang had already come under suspicion as "a traitor writer," an unsubstantiated allegation thrown at those who kept working in the Japanese-occupied territories during the war. Mei

Niang's writings, like those of the other authors accused of collaborating with the Japanese, were largely ignored, for they did not fit in the national narrative of patriotism and resistance. For decades, the name Mei Niang was erased from the history of modern Chinese literature. When she resurfaced in the early 1980s, most readers had never heard of her. Since then, not only have her old works been reissued, but her new writings, mostly essays, reminiscing about the past and sharing her travels and knowledge about the world, have also been published.

METSO (1966–). Poet, prose and fiction writer. One of the rising stars of **Tibetan** writers writing in Chinese, Metso grew up in Qinghai Province. Although her writings began to appear in the late 1980s, it is her 1997 novel *Taiyang buluo* (The Sun Tribe) that made her a national name. The novel depicts two Tibetan tribes in Amdo when the northwest was under the warlord Ma Bufang's control during the early decades of the 20th century. In the past, historical or literary discourses that dealt with this region and this period tended to focus on the Hui Muslim and the Han population, pushing the Tibetans out to the margin. With this novel, the author reclaims her people's history by placing the Tibetans at the center of this turbulent era to examine the Tibetan national character as well as issues such as education and modernity and their effect on cultural traditions. Another novel, *Yueliang yingdi* (The Moon Camp), describes life in a small Tibetan town, highlighting the romantic relationships of several residents. Like *Taiyang buluo*, Metso sets the story in the 20th century when the outside world began to crack open the isolated Tibetan society. History, however, is always kept in the background in Metso's romantic novels. Nevertheless, through the stories of love and desire, Metso unravels the tragic history of the Tibetan nation, as she has done in *Taiyang buluo* and *Yueliang yingdi*.

Metso's short stories and novellas, on the other hand, feature contemporary middle-class Tibetan **women**. Into these love stories she injects a dose of religiosity, turning them into quests for the meaning of life. Borrowing from the Buddhist concept of reincarnation, Metso creates characters that live in multiple manifestations, each adding a layer to the existence of another and further complicating their psychological depth. The author's dexterous play of different voices against one another departs from the realist mode adopted in her novels and gives the stories, such as "Shexiang" (Muskiness) and "Chujia ren" (Those Who Have Taken the Buddhist Vow), a measure of experimentalism.

MISTY POETRY (MENGLONG SHI), MISTY POETS (MENGLONG SHIREN). *Menglong*, which could also be translated as "obscure" or "enigmatic," implies that the meaning of a poem is not transparent, and that the poet's intention is not spelled out clearly for the benefit of the reader. The emergence of Misty poetry in the late 1970s marked a major literary breakthrough in post-Mao China with profound ramifications. Nearly all of the Misty poets were urban youths who had been sent to the countryside during the **Cultural Revolution**. The harsh realities of rural life led them to question their faith in authority and the isolated countryside stimulated their literary sensibilities. To express their aspirations for freedom and spirituality in their writing, they were the first to protest against authoritarianism and ideological tyranny in the thaw of the post-Mao era. **Bei Dao**'s 1972 poem "The Answer" represented the voice of skepticism and the defiance of his generation. The political relaxation in the late 1970s made it possible for the underground poets to have an open forum where they could publish their own work. Bei Dao and **Mang Ke** established *Jintian* (Today), a literary journal for experimental work.

To break away from the literary practices defined by Maoist doctrine, the Misty poets emphasized the individual and the private over the political and the collective. Influenced by Western literature, they wrote imagistic, elliptical, and often ambiguous poetry, without the didactic messages and political slogans that had dominated the literature of the Mao era. In the Antispiritual Pollution Campaign of 1983, Misty poetry was singled out for criticism by the authorities. Subsequently in the aftermath of the crackdown on the **Tian'anmen Prodemocracy Movement**, *Jintian* was banned and many of the Misty poets went into exile. Years later, *Jintian* resumed publication abroad. Prominent among the Misty poets are **Bei Dao, Duo Duo, Gu Cheng, Jiang He, Mang Ke, Shu Ting, Yan Li, Yang Lian**, and **Yu Jian**.

MO YAN, PEN NAME OF GUAN MOYAN (1956–). Novelist. Born in Gaomi, Shandong Province, Mo Yan received a B.A. from the Literature Department of the People's Liberation Army's Academy of Arts and Literature in 1981 and an M.A. from Beijing Normal University. He is undoubtedly one of the most creative and most prolific Chinese writers today. Noted for his magical realist style that takes astonishing, imaginative flights, Mo Yan has acknowledged his debt to Gabriel García Márquez and William Faulkner, whose art invoking the power of a

specific locale with its own mystical norms and logic offers Mo inspir-
ing models. In many ways, Mo Yan's success lies in his extraordinary
talent for transforming the crude and earthy into something sublime,
through prose just as precise, to achieve a kind of lyric joy that perme-
ates his works. The otherwise disconcerting dichotomy between the
sublime and the grotesque is thus obliterated, producing an aesthetic
experience that is both uplifting and challenging. Mo Yan's sensibility
is often characterized as grandiose and masculine, for his literary world
is filled with larger-than-life heroes who flaunt their primeval personalities. Bawdy language, violent sexual conquests, relentless revenge,
and savage behavior all mingle to form epic-scale sagas. Matching
his strong themes, his language, with its characteristic intensity and
exuberance, cascades downward like a torrential stream mingled with
fantastical flights of imagination. Beginning with his first short story,
"Touming de hong luobu" (The Translucent Red Carrot), Mo Yan has
consistently exhibited an uncanny ability to move at ease in and out of
two modes of narrative: the realist and the surrealist. This trademark
can be found even in his most realist stories. He continues to push the
limits of narrative innovation in his more recent novel *Tanxiang xing*
(Sandalwood Torture) in which he uses a large amount of colloquial
expression and rhymed prose, lending the text well to oral recitation. He
has a unique style completely his own, easily recognizable.

The most successful of Mo Yan's works are his historical romances,
including *Hong gaoliang* (*Red Sorghum*), set during the **Sino-Japanese
War**, *Tanxiang xing* (Sandalwood Torture), a love story rendered with
descriptions of horrific tortures during the Boxer Rebellion of 1900,
and *Feng ru fei tun* (*Big Breasts and Wide Hips*), a celebration of the
female through the chronicle of the life of a sexually potent, fertile,
and wise woman who lives from the end of the Qing to the post-Mao
era. Mo Yan is also known for his surrealist novels, such as *Jiu guo*
(*Republic of Wine*), which pokes fun at the Chinese obsession with
food and the "cannibalistic" culture vehemently denounced by **Lu Xun**
40 years before, *Tiantang suantai zhi ge* (*The Garlic Ballads*), set in
rural China of the 1980s, when a bumper harvest of garlic precipitates a
series of disastrous events, and *Sishi yi pao* (Forty-one Bombs), a story
told by a butcher's son about growing up in a village and the moral and
social problems brought about by modernization and commercialism
in contemporary China. Mo Yan extols the primordial forces that, in
his opinion, have been suppressed by two thousand years of Confucian

civilization. He celebrates the unbridled natural forces within man; he considers the libido the essential drive for survival. His search for a primitive self in the memories of his native Gaomi is thought to be a metaphorical search for the Chinese national spirit. Termed an "explosion of life's energies," Mo Yan's works resonate with the prevalent view held in China that the ancient Chinese race has degenerated, suffocated by layers of restrictions, its blood flow clogged and its life force exhausted. What the Chinese badly need, Mo Yan suggests, is the strong pulses of life, the awakened primordial forces, the "red sorghum," the "big breasts and wide hips," in order to rejuvenate itself.

Mo Yan's most recent book, *Shengsi pilao* (Fatigue of Life and Death), an examination of the relationship between the peasant and the land, departs from his previous works in that it contains much less violence and is more contemplative. Considered by many as his best work, the story is narrated by a former landlord executed during land reform in 1950. Unwilling to admit that he committed any crime other than being rich, he is reincarnated into various domestic animals who observe up close the changes in his home village during the subsequent 50 years. *See also* ROOT-SEEKING LITERATURE.

MODERN POETRY MOVEMENT IN TAIWAN. In the decade from the mid-1950s to the mid-1960s, **Taiwan** saw the emergence of four major poetry societies that played significant roles at different junctures of the modern poetry movement: the Modernists, the Blue Stars led by Tan Zihao, **Yu Guangzhong**, and others; the Creationists, represented by Zhang Mo, **Luo Fu**, and **Ya Xian**; and the Regionalists, also called *Li* (Bamboo Hats). The modernist movement was spearheaded by **Ji Xian**, who founded *Xiandai shi* (Modern Poetry) in 1953. Three years later, the Modernist Society (Xiandai pai) was formally established, drawing a membership of more than a hundred poets. In their mission statement, the Modernists proclaimed their avant-garde position, emphasizing "horizontal transplantation" (learning directly from Western literature) rather than vertical transmission (inheriting from Chinese traditions), and the discovery of new content, form, tools and methods. They advocated wholesale Westernization and looked for inspiration in Western poetry since Charles Baudelaire. The modernist movement could be regarded as a continuation of the cause pursued by **Dai Wangshu** and his colleagues, including Ji Xian, two decades earlier in Shanghai. The radical departure from Chinese tradition, along with the exclusive emphasis on intellect rather than emotions, made the Modern- ists easy targets for criticism. In 1959, Ji Xian left the Modernist Society and the journal he founded, *Xiandai shi*, was closed down in 1964, end- ing a decade of its influence in Taiwan's poetry movement.

Another group, the Blue Stars Society, was founded in 1954 and dis- banded in 1964. In the course of 10 years, it attracted many promising poets and published several dozen poetry collections. Less radical than the Modernists, the Blue Stars were apposed to indiscriminate adop- tion of Western traditions, choosing instead to emphasize the creation of "pure poetry" based on personal perceptions of life. While the Blue Stars also adopted Western modernist techniques, they perceived poetry as the expression of the individual self in concert with national spirit and cultural heritage.

The third influential poetry society was the Creationists, most of its members coming from the military in southern Taiwan. The society was established in 1954 and its journal, *Chuang shiji* (Creationists), was founded in October of the same year. Intended as a correction to the Modernists, the Creationists rejected absolute "intellectualism" or absolute "emotionalism" in favor of imageries and symbols. In the late 1950s, when the influence of the other two societies began to wane, the Creationists abandoned their earlier positions and opted for "surrealism" in an attempt to move poetry from relying on reason and rationality to a focus on aesthetics. In 1969, financial difficulties forced them to close down *Chuang shiji*, which would be revived in 1972 with a renewed emphasis on tradition and reality.

While the above three societies were more or less drawn to the idea of pure poetry, the few regionalist groups, most prominently Li, the Bamboo Hats, tried to call attention to the social realities of Taiwan. The emergence of the Bamboo Hats marked the rising of a unique Tai- wanese consciousness and identity. Its bimonthly, *Li*, from which the name for the group was derived, was one of the most influential poetry publications in Taiwan during the time. With its emphasis on Taiwan's history, geography, and reality, the journal published poems that con- tained social messages, regional flavor, and colloquial language. Other prominent members include Lin Hengtai, **Fei Ma**, Du Guoqing, Huang Hesheng, and **Zheng Chouyu**.

MODERNISTS (XIANDAI PAI). In 1931, the publisher Xiandai shuju (Modern Books) put out *Xiandai yuekan* (Modern Monthly) and shortly after **Dai Wangshu** founded *Xin shi* (New Poetry). These two journals became the main venues for modernist writings. Authors whose works were published in these two journals became known as belonging to the modernists (xiandai pai). Poetry was by far the dominant genre in modernist literature and characterized by symbolism, graceful language, and romantic sentiments. Among its representative poets were **Dai Wangshu, Li Jinfa, Ai Qing, He Qifang**, and **Li Guangtian**. The term also refers to the literary movement in **Taiwan** some 30 years later, when a group of faculty and students at the Foreign Languages Department of the National Taiwan University launched *Xiandai wenxue* (Modern Literature), a magazine that systematically introduced Western modernist writings and published works by Taiwan's own modernist writers. **Bai Xianyong** and **Wang Wenxing** are among the founders of the movement. *See also* CHEN RUOXI; OUYANG ZI.

MU DAN, PEN NAME OF ZHA LIANGZHENG (1919–1977). Poet. Born in Tianjin, Mu Dan studied Western literature at Qinghua University. When Japan invaded China, he followed his university to the southwestern city of Kunming to continue his studies. After receiving his bachelor's from the National Southwestern Associated University in 1940, he joined the Chinese Expedition Force to Burma to aid the British troops fighting against the Japanese Imperial Army, a traumatic experience that nearly cost him his life. In 1949, he enrolled in the University of Chicago and three years later he was awarded a master's degree in English literature. A year after that, he returned to Tianjin to teach at the Foreign Languages Department of Nankai University. During the Anti-Rightist Campaign in the late 1950s, Mu Dan was stripped of his teaching responsibilities and assigned to work as a librarian, a post he held until a heart attack took his life in 1977.

Mu Dan's literary reputation rests solely on three poetry collections published in the 1940s: *Tanxianzhe* (The Explorer), *Mu Dan shi ji 1939–1945* (Collected Poems by Mu Dan 1939–1945), and *Qi* (Flags). Influenced by T. S. Eliot, W. H. Auden, and William Butler Yeats, Mu Dan's poetic voice is meditative, philosophical, ironic, and at times abstract, questioning the meaning of life and dealing with issues concerning the self, the soul, and the spiritual. Although he did write some patriotic poems such as "Zan mei" (A Song of Praise), he was much more adept at treating existential subjects such as alienation and tragic human existence. Mu's poetic persona is often portrayed as lost, alienated, and fractured, as shown in "Cong xuwu dao chongshi" (From Nihilism to Substantiation). "Fangkong dong de shuqing shi" (Lyrics of an Air-raid Shelter), a poem written during the **Sino-Japanese War**, while expressing compassion, patriotism, and hope, does not echo the heroic, indignant sentimentalism of much of the Chinese poetry produced at the time.

Mu Dan understood the anxiety Chinese intellectuals felt as their country transitioned from the established order in which they were firmly anchored to the new, unpredictable world. While the sense of alienation expressed in his poems is firmly grounded in Chinese reality, he saw the Chinese experience as part of a human dilemma. In "She de youhuo" (The Seduction of the Snake), a parody of the Biblical story, Mu Dan readily embraces the Christian notion of original sin to convey both the Chinese intellectual's spiritual crisis and the universal human condition. As a poet experimenting with a new form and a new language, Mu Dan did not attempt to bridge the old and the new. Indeed, his poems, whether in form or content, show little influence from the Chinese poetic tradition.

Like **Shen Congwen**, **Feng Zhi**, and many others who gave up creative writing after 1949 and turned instead to the politically safer academic writing or translation work, Mu Dan wrote only a few poems after he returned to China from the United States. He devoted his energy to translating Russian and English literature. Among the authors he translated are Alexander Pushkin, Lord Byron, Percy Bysshe Shelley, and John Keats. His translation of Byron's *Don Juan*, which he finished in the 1970s, is widely considered a masterpiece in its own right. Mu Dan's literary accomplishment was largely ignored in the People's Republic of China until the 1980s, when the rediscovered poet was hailed as the most innovative **modernist** poet in 20th-century China.

MU SHIYING (1912–1940). Fiction writer. Born in Zhejiang, Mu Shiying spent his childhood in Shanghai with his banker father. While a student at Guanghua University majoring in Chinese language and literature, Mu was deeply engrossed in modern Western literature as well as works by Japanese New Sensibility school writers, especially those by Yokomitsu Riichi, which informed much of his work. He published his first story "Zanmen de shijie" (Our World) in 1930. Another story, "Gong mu" (Public Cemetery), made the pages of the first issue of *Xiandai* (Modernity), a literary journal that advocated for

Chinese modernism, establishing Mu as one of the prominent writers in the Chinese modernist movement, now often mentioned in the company of **Shi Zhecun** and **Liu Na'ou** as a prominent **New Sensibility** (Xin Ganjue pai) writer. The stories in his first collection of fiction, entitled *Nan bei ji* (The North and South Poles), explore the rough world of pirates, salt merchants, gang members, cabbies, beggars, and other such figures who talk dirty and act tough. In his second collection, *Gong mu* (The Public Cemetery), he turns to the subtle feelings and emotions of urban bourgeois life, a central subject for all New Sensibility writers. He put great emphasis on the exploration of the individual psyche and the perception of reality through the senses and thus won critical acclaim. His stories feature Freudian psychoanalysis, focusing on love, marriage, and sexuality as a medium through which to explore the theme of alienation in modern city life. His stories collected in *Baijin de nüti suxiang* (The Platinum Female Statue), *Yezonghui li de wuge ren* (The Five People in the Night Club), and *Shanghai de hubuwu* (Shanghai's Fox Trot) represent some of the best New Sensibility writings. Many of Mu's stories feature the femme fatale who represents the lethal eros of the modern city that abandons middle-class men after it has seduced them, leaving them in a state of confusion and despondence.

In the aftermath of the Japanese invasion, Mu went to **Hong Kong** but soon returned to Shanghai in 1939 to work for a newspaper run by the puppet government of Wang Jingwei, who collaborated with the Japanese. The following year, Mu was assassinated, allegedly by Chiang Kai-shek's secret service. His name was not cleared until the 1970s, when new evidence surfaced that he had been sent by the Nationalist government to infiltrate the puppet administration.

– N –

NATIVISTS (XIANGTU PAI). Wang Luyan (1901–1944) is widely considered the first of the Chinese nativist writers to explore the unique culture of his native land and to write about the effects of industrial forces that threatened the survival of rural communities in prerevolutionary China. After the 1920s, Chinese nativist literature evolved into several different forms. In sharp contrast to **Lu Xun**, who portrayed the countryside as the bastion of traditional values that inflicted serious damage to the Chinese national spirit, **Shen Congwen** depicted rural western Hunan as a pastoral refuge against modernization and Westernization. Meanwhile, the Communists promoted peasant literature, resulting in a number of writers whose works are characterized by their unique regional flavors. **Zhao Shuli** and his Shanxi Potato school and **Sun Li** and his Hebei Lotus Lake school were two of the most influential regional literary groups. In **Taiwan** after 1949, there was a group of writers emerging from the countryside who stood up against the influential trend of Westernization in Taiwanese literature by writing about traditional rural communities pushed to the fringes by Taiwan's modernization process. Their work met with strong resistance, and in some cases ridicule, from the elitist camp, which was dominated by pro-Western and **modernist** writers. The 1977 debates on nativist literature carried out between Peng Ge, **Zhu Xining**, and **Yu Guangzhong** on one side and Ye Shitao, **Chen Yingzhen**, and Wang Tuo on the other highlighted the differences in the two groups' aesthetic and political views. In the years that followed the debates, the nativists gradually gained a strong foothold in Taiwan, producing among the group such prominent names as **Huang Chunming**, **Wang Zhenhe**, and Chen Yingzhen. The nativist movement in its various forms and manifestations has influenced the **root-seeking literature** on the mainland since the 1980s.

NEW CULTURE MOVEMENT (XIN WENHUA YUNDONG). Associated with the **May Fourth Movement** and motivated by an urgent sense of cultural endangerment, the New Culture Movement was born in 1915 when Chen Duxiu founded *Qingnian zazhi* (Youth Magazine), renamed *Xin qingnian* (New Youth) a year later. In its first issue, Chen urged the nation's youths to throw away the "feudalist" shackles that had restricted the Chinese mind for more than a thousand years and to adopt Western concepts of democracy and science. He challenged them to be "independent instead of slavish," "progressive instead of conservative," "outgoing instead of withdrawn," "down-to-earth instead of pretentious," "scientific instead of imaginary," and "open instead of unreceptive to the rest of the world." When Chen accepted the offer of Cai Yuanpei, president of Beijing University, the center of the New Culture Movement shifted from Shanghai to Beijing. Cai, a liberal-minded administrator, recruited some of the nation's best minds for his university, including **Hu Shi**, Li Dazhao, Qian Xuantong, **Liu Bannong**,

Zhou Zuoren, and **Lu Xun**. These and other prominent intellectuals helped make Beijing University a breeding ground for the New Culture Movement.

In addition to the campaign for social reforms based on "Mr. Democracy" and "Mr. Science," which included educational reforms and the emancipation of **women**, the New Culture advocates waged a literary campaign to promote a new literature written in the vernacular instead of classical Chinese, which had a stranglehold on Chinese political, intellectual, and literary discourses. This linguistic reform, advocated by Hu and others, went far beyond the restructuring of the language; it had profound ramifications for the Chinese society as a whole. With classical Chinese taken down from its lofty pedestal, the authority of the classics and their intellectual and moral hold on the Chinese consciousness were loosened. The modernization of the country, the New Culture proponents argued, demanded a new written language and a new literature that was accessible to the broad masses not just the intellectual elite. In the 1917 February issue, Chen published "Wenxue geming lun" (On Literary Revolution), in which he defined the new literature as being "unassuming and expressive," "fresh and honest," and "plain and popular," a people's literature that was realistic and socially engaged. *Xin qingnian* was the chief venue for publishing new literary works. Pioneering writings such as Hu's vernacular poems and Lu Xun's short stories made their first appearances in *Xin qingnian*. These and other progressive writings offered critical examinations of age-old Chinese traditions, especially Confucianism, and advocated learning from the West, some going so far as to call for total Westernization.

Extremely popular among the educated youths, *Xin qingnian* inspired many reform-minded political activists such as Mao Zedong, who was introduced to Marxism by the magazine, as well as literary youths such as **Ba Jin**, who came into contact with it in the remote southwestern city of Chengdu. Largely confined to the intellectual elite, the New Culture Movement nevertheless brought widespread changes to Chinese society. In the beginning, the movement focused on attacking traditional thoughts and practices and bringing in new ideas and concepts from abroad. As some of the leaders became increasingly radicalized and opted for political action, as exemplified by Chen and Li, who went on to become founders of the Chinese Communist Party, the movement branched off in two separate directions: with Hu, Zhou, and others interested in gradual and intellectual enlightenment and Chen, Li, Lu Xun, and others pushing for political radicalism.

NEW GENERATION WRITERS (XIN SHENG DAI ZUOJIA). A term used for young writers who were born in the 1970s or 1980s, the latter also called "the post-1980s generation" (bashi niandai hou zuojia). Many among the group became famous at a young age, often while still in high school. In many ways, this is the generation of the Internet, which launched many careers by publishing works online and attracting a sizable following among Web surfers. It is also the generation of market economy, with youth magazines such as *Mengya* (Sprouts) promoting and marketing literary stars. The works by this new generation of writers are known for explicit, sometimes sensationalist, sexual content, distinctly unabashed exhibition of materialism, and self-absorption. Initially rejected by the mainstream literary establishment, the best among them have gradually gained recognition from critics for their increasingly sophisticated treatment of youth culture in contemporary society. The best known and most commercially successful among this generation of writers are **Wei Hui** and **Han Han**. *See also* HU JIAN; LI SHASHA; SU DE; XIAO FAN; YAN GE; ZHANG YUERAN.

NEW SENSIBILITY SCHOOL (XIN GANGJUE PAI). Active in the 1930s and 1940s, the New Sensibility writers, most prominently **Shi Zhecun**, **Mu Shiying**, and **Liu Na'ou**, wrote about the lives of the young and flamboyant generation in the bustling metropolis of Shanghai, exploring the workings of the individual psyche and the perception of reality through the senses. Their focus on sensual experiences and the musicality of language set them apart from other modernist writers who shared their obsession with modern urban life with its dance halls, cafés, and movie theaters.

NI KUANG, A.K.A. NI YIMING, NI CONG, WEI SILI, AND SHA WENG (1935–). A prolific writer of science fiction, fantastic tales, martial arts novels, and popular romances, Ni Kuang was born in Shanghai and moved to **Hong Kong** in 1957. Since 1992, he has been living in San Francisco. In the early 1960s, encouraged by **Jin Yong**, he began writing science fiction, becoming arguably the best-known science fiction writer in the Chinese-speaking world. His *Weisili Xilie* (The Wellesley Series) and *Shentan Gaosi xilie* (Goss the Great Detective) have won him a large following among Chinese readers. As movies turned into a major entertainment venue in Hong Kong, Ni embarked on a successful career writing for the film industry. He has written more than 300 film scripts. Known also for his anti-Communist stance, Ni is believed to have said, "To be patriotic, one must be opposed to Communism and to be opposed to Communism is patriotic."

NIE GANNU (1903–1986). Essayist, poet, and short story writer. Known for his wit and extraordinary talent, Nie Gannu spent his youth in the 1920s working as a secretary in the Nationalist army, teaching school in Malaysia, editing newspapers in Burma, training as a cadet in the Huangpu Military Academy in Guangzhou, and studying at Sun Yat-sen University in Moscow. In the 1930s, he joined the **Left-wing Association of Chinese Writers** and the Communist Party and spent several months in prison in Japan for his anti-Japanese activities. In the 1930s and 1940s, while editing progressive newspapers and journals, he wrote political essays, satirizing the Nationalist government and its attacks on the Communists. He also wrote about social injustice and the plight of **women**. For his sharp and biting language, Nie is widely considered the number two essayist, after **Lu Xun**, in modern Chinese literature, writing in the genre of satirical essay. After 1949, Nie worked as editor for the *Wenhui Daily* in **Hong Kong** and the People's Literature Press in Beijing. A proud and independent man, he was considered by the authorities as "unruly" and "liberal" and suffered a great deal during the various political campaigns of the People's Republic of China, despite being a veteran party member and having a long-standing friendship with many of the top leaders. In his later years, Nie wrote many poems in the classical style. Because of his personal integrity and the acute political insights he expressed in his writings, his work has attracted renewed interest in recent years. Other than his essays, Nie also wrote short stories and critical essays on classical Chinese novels.

NIE HUALING (1925–). Fiction and prose writer. Born in Hubei Province, Nie Hualing graduated from Central University with a degree in English. She moved to **Taiwan** in 1949 to work as a literary editor for *Ziyou Zhongguo* (Free China), a bimonthly journal that promoted liberal ideals, and soon after began to publish stories. In 1964, Nie went to the United States to participate in the Writers' Workshop at the University of Iowa. In 1967, Nie and her future husband, Paul Engle, established the International Writing Program, which attracted many writers from all over the world. During the 21 years the couple ran the program, hundreds of writers were invited to Iowa City, including more than 80 from **Hong Kong**, Taiwan, and the mainland. For their tireless effort to promote exchange among writers of different cultures and countries, Nie and Engle received numerous awards, including the Award for Distinguished Service to the Arts from the Governors Association. Nie retired from the University of Iowa in 1988.

Nie's best-known work is a fictional piece entitled *Sangqing yu Taohong* (*Mulberry and Peach: Two Women of China*) about a **woman**'s transformation from innocent youth to hardened middle age. Mulberry and Peach, two different aspects of the same person, represent self-alienation of the individual, calling into question the meaning of self-identity. Told in the form of journal entries and letters, the story centers on the theme of exile, underscoring the attempt to flee from various kinds of predicament, both external and internal. Another work, *San sheng san shi* (Three Lives in Three Worlds), is an autobiographical account of the author's life in China, Taiwan, and the United States. For her portrayals of strong female characters, Nie is regarded as one of the forerunners of Taiwan's feminist movement.

– O –

OUYANG JIANGHE (1956–). Poet and poetry critic. Like many of the **Generation III** poets, Ouyang Jianghe grew up in Sichuan. He is from a military family and served for nine years in the army. Ouyang is deeply indebted to classical Chinese poetry, having committed to memory hundreds of poems. Prior to "Xuan guan" (Cliff Burials), published in 1985 and which he regards as the watershed in his career, his early poetry pays homage to his cultural heritage, with an emphasis on the dichotomy between Sichuan's ancient shamanist heritage and centralized imperial power, as well as the interplay between modern and classical Chinese. The change after "Xuan guan" to contemporary themes without the weight of history opened for the poet an outlet to explore the relationship between word and object. "Shouqiang" (The Handgun), which brings into focus the temporal and conceptual quality of the physical entity, is representative of these later poems.

Ouyang's view of poetics is articulated in *Zhan zai xugou zhe bian* (On the Side of Fabrication), a collection of essays on contemporary Chinese poetry, including critiques of **Bei Dao** and fellow Sichuanese poets **Zhai Yongming** and Bai Hua. Echoing American poet Wallace Stevens, Ouyang asserts that the highest form of reality can be achieved only through the intervention of creative agency and that poetry, because of its total dependence on the perception of the individual mind, contains more truth than any other genre.

OUYANG SHAN, PEN NAME OF YANG FENGQI (1908–2000). Novelist. Ouyang Shan is often compared with **Lao She,** for they began their literary careers at about the same time, with Ouyang writing about urban life in the southern city of Guangzhou and Lao She, the northern city of Beijing. This is, however, where the similarities end. Ouyang Shan, because of his membership in the **Left-wing Association of Chinese Writers,** had strong Marxist leanings and his writings clearly reflect his political orientation. Most of the fictional works he published in the 1920s and early 1930s were romantic tales with a revolutionary theme.

Ouyang's first novel, *Meigui can le* (The Roses Have Faded), a sentimental tale influenced by Johann Wolfgang von Goethe's *The Sorrows of Young Werther,* tells of the tragic love between a university student and a young woman, interspersed with indignant outcries against imperialism. *Ai zhi benliu* (The Current of Love) shows greater artistic merit in depicting a young man's entanglement with two women, one poor and the other rich. This tragic story exposes the cruelty of high society and shows sympathy for the lower class, an ideological preoccupation that continues into his later works, such as *Gao Ganda* (Gao Ganda) and *Yidai fengliu* (A Whole Generation of Heroes). *Gao Ganda,* which records the agricultural cooperative movement in the Communist-controlled northwest, was his first novel written in response to the directives issued by Mao Zedong at the Yan'an Forum on Literature and Art in 1942. The voluminous *Yidai fengliu,* consisting of five parts, is his most ambitious project. It portrays the complicated relations among three families during the period from 1919 to 1949. *San jia xiang (The Three-Family Lane),* the first volume of the series, is generally considered the best of Ouyang's work for its panoramic view of Chinese society at the beginning of the 20th century and its successful portrayal of distinctive characters.

Ouyang considered his writings after the mid-1930s, when he joined the Left-wing Association of Chinese Writers, "new realism," and those published after 1942, when he attended the Forum on Literature and Art, "revolutionary realism." Both advocate a seemingly self-contradictory principle: "Characters must not be separated from reality and they must be made to stand higher than they really are." This approach, taken by many other Communist writers, dominates much of Ouyang's work. *See also* SOCIALIST REALISM.

OUYANG YUQIAN (1889–1962). Play and screenplay writer. One of the founders of modern Chinese theater and cinema, Ouyang Yuqian often acted in the plays he wrote and directed and his impact on Chinese performing arts is profound. Ouyang spent his teenage years studying in Japan, where he joined a theater club. In 1906, he began training to be a Peking opera actor at the age of 17 and launched his professional acting career nine years later. His success at playing the female role earned him eminence comparable to that of Mei Lanfang, the legendary Peking opera actor who also impersonated women onstage. Ouyang expanded the Peking opera repertoire with several of his own pieces, including *Pan Jinlian* (Pan Jinlian: A Seductress), *Daiyu zang hua* (Flower Burial), and *Yuanyang jian* (A Pair of Swords), as well as offering performance techniques and stage installations shaped according to his own aesthetics.

From the opera stage, Ouyang moved on to transform the Chinese theater, introducing *huaju* (**spoken drama**), a new form influenced by the Western genre of play. He wrote and directed historical plays such as *Mulan cong jun* (A Woman Warrior) and *Tao hua shan* (The Peach-Blossom Fan). Having established his reputation in the theater, Ouyang entered the film industry, again writing, directing, and sometimes acting in his own films. *Tianya genü* (A Female Street Singer), *Qingming shijie* (At the Qingming Festival), *Xin taohua shan* (A New Version of the Peach-Blossom Fan), and *Yehuo chunfeng* (Blustery Wind and Wildfire in Spring) are among his most memorable films. In keeping with the spirit of the times, these films promote progressive agendas such as the emancipation of **women** and national salvation. After 1949, Ouyang held several positions in the Chinese theater and academia, including president of the Chinese Academy of Theater and chairman of the Chinese Dance Association. See also LEFT-WING ASSOCIATION OF CHINESE WRITERS; SINO-JAPANESE WAR; SPOKEN DRAMA.

OUYANG ZI, A. K. A OUYANG TZE, PEN NAME OF HONG ZHI-HUI (1939–). Fiction writer and literary critic. Born in Japan, Ouyang

Zi went to National **Taiwan** University. Along with fellow students **Bai Xianyong**, **Wang Wenxing**, and **Chen Ruoxi**, she edited a literary magazine called *Xiandai wenxue* (Modern Literature), which was the main venue for Taiwan's modernist writings. Most of Ouyang's creative endeavors are short stories of an experimental nature that make liberal use of modernist techniques such as stream of consciousness, multiple perspectives, and symbolism. Her best critical writing is a study of Bai Xianyong's *Taipei ren* (Taipei Characters). *See also* MODERNISTS; WOMEN.

– P –

PAN JUN (1957–). Fiction writer. Born in a small town in Anhui Province, Pan Jun had a difficult and lonely childhood. His artist father, labeled a rightist one year after Pan was born, was sent to live in the countryside separated from his family for the next 18 years. Pan became known as an **avant-garde** writer in the late 1980s when his experimental fiction was first published, including "Nanfang de qingxu" (The Mood in the South), "Xianjin" (Trap), and "Sanyue yiri" (March the First), all about humanity's fear and anxiety about surviving in the world. Other notable works written during this period include *Baise shalong* (A White Salon)*,* "Liudong de shatan" (Moving Beach), and most important, *Feng* (Wind), which culminates his innovative effort with narrative techniques. *Feng* is written in three different narratives, representing respectively the historical perspective, the imagined world, and reality. Interlocked, they deconstruct one another, destroying the illusion that each has painstakingly created.

At the height of his success, Pan put his writing career on hold to join the business rush in the south, and in 1996, when he was financially secure, Pan resumed writing. In the second phase of his creative endeavor, Pan has produced an impressive range of works, from experimental plays to historical novels. The most significant is an autobiographical novel entitled *Dubai yu shoushi* (Soliloquy and Hand Gestures), in which the author and the narrator collapse to create a confessional narrative. In this tale about a writer who returns to his hometown after a long absence and reminisces about the past 30 years of his life, Pan explores self-imposed exile and historical imperative, themes that have preoccupied much of his work. The novel also manifests the author's fascination with formalistic features through the integration of verbal narration with visual images of his own art, a talent developed during the years Pan spent in the countryside after high school. Other such innovative stories include novellas *Lan bao* (Blue Castle), *Chong tong* (Two Pupils in the Eye), *Qiusheng fu* (Ode to Autumn), and *Taohua liushui* (Peach Blossoms and Flowing Water).

Pan's most recent book, *Sixing baogao* (A Report on the Death Penalty), as its title indicates, examines tradition, law, and practice with regard to the death penalty. Pan cites many international cases, including the O. J. Simpson trial in the United States, to provide a comparative framework for the Chinese cases he focuses on. Inspired by an incident in which an innocent man was beaten to death while in police custody, the book represents the author's concern over the lack of justice and compassion in China's legal system.

PING LU (1953–). Fiction writer. Born in Gaoxiong, Taiwan, Ping Lu studied psychology at National Taiwan University and statistics at the University of Iowa. While working as a statistician for the United States Postal Service, Ping published stories in Taiwanese newspapers. One short story, "Yumi tian zhi si" (*Death in a Cornfield*), won first prize in a fiction competition sponsored by the *United Daily News*. Ping has worked as editor and professor of journalism and creative writing in **Taiwan,** and since 2002 she has been living in **Hong Kong.** Of her prose fiction, the 1995 novel *Xing dao tianya* (Marriage Made in Revolution), about Sun Yat-sen and Song Qingling, and her 2002 novel about the pop singer Deng Lijun, are the best known.

– Q –

QIAN ZHONGSHU (1910–1998). Born in Wuxi, Jiangsu Province, Qian studied literature at Qinghua University. In 1935, he went to England with his bride, **Yang Jiang,** and two years later earned a baccalaureus litterarum (bachelor of literature) degree from the University of Oxford with a thesis on the image of China in English literature of the 17th and 18th centuries. Soon after, the couple moved to France for further study and research. They returned to China in 1938 and began a long career in academia. Called "the most learned man in 20th-century China," and famous for his extensive knowledge of both Western and Chinese literature and thought, Qian acquired the reputation of an erudite scholar bent over books in his study, showing no interest in the outside world.

Qian saw himself foremost as a scholar and devoted his entire career to studying literary works, both Chinese and Western. His scholarly publications include an exegetical book on Song dynasty poetry, *Song shi xuan zhu* (Annotated Poetry of the Song), a study of poetry *Tan Yi Lu* (On the Art of Poetry), and the voluminous *Guan zhui bian* (Studies of the Classics), which evaluates the Chinese classics from a comparative perspective, drawing contrasts with Western classics. Written in classical Chinese in the style of reading notes, *Guan zhui bian* represents the author's accumulated wisdom resulting from a lifetime study of literature, history, and philosophy. Qian's creative endeavors, on the other hand, resulted in a relatively small body of works: a novel, several short stories all written before 1949, a collection of essays, and poems composed in the classical style. Hardly prolific, Qian is nevertheless a household name, thanks to the television movie based on his novel, *Wei cheng (Fortress Besieged)*. The novel makes fun of Chinese intellectuals, particularly those who have returned to China from abroad, for their lack of self-awareness and their failures at everything from marriage to career in a tumultuous country struggling for survival under Japanese occupation. In the protagonist, a college professor, Qian casts an image of the Chinese intellectual with good intentions whose downfall is assured because of his selfish, lowly, and petty nature. *See also* NEW CULTURE MOVEMENT; SINO-JAPANESE WAR.

QIDENG SHENG, PEN NAME OF LIU WUXIONG (1939–). A **Taiwan** native, Qideng Sheng graduated from Taipei Normal College with a degree in art. He is noted for his controversial **modernist** writings, most published in the 1960s and 1970s and known for their loose structure and idiosyncratic, abstruse language. With little attention to plots, his stories, told often in the first-person subjective voice, read like lyrical essays. His protagonists, loners standing at the edge of society, tell the reader the minute details of their lives and innermost feelings, appealing directly to the reader's sympathy. Letters and interior monologues as used in *Tanlang de shuxin* (Letters from Tanlang) and *Simu weiwei* (Whispers of Love) are typical of Qideng's narrative style. Other works include *Wo ai hei yanzhu* (I Love Black Eyes), his best-known work about the alienated youth in modern Taiwanese society, and *Shahe* *bei ge* (Sad Songs of the Sha River), recollections by a disillusioned musician suffering from acute lung disease. Other than fiction, Qideng has also written poetry.

QIONG YAO, PEN NAME OF CHEN ZHE (1938–). Romance novelist. Born in Chengdu, Sichuan Province, Qiong Yao arrived in **Taiwan** with her family in 1949. Her first collection of short stories, *Chuang wai* (Outside the Window), was published in 1963 and since then she has written numerous novels, many of which have been adapted into popular movies or television series. Arguably the most popular romance novelists in the Chinese-speaking world, Qiong Yao places the development of a romantic relationship between the protagonists at the heart of all her novels, focusing on falling in love and the courtship, as well as the encounter and resolution of conflicts that are presented in the form of a triangular relationship, parental rejection, or misunderstanding between the lovers. Nearly all her novels emphasize the feelings of the female protagonist, often an innocent and beautiful girl, who makes unconditional commitment to the romantic relationship; her faith and good behavior are always rewarded in the end. In celebrating romantic love, Qiong Yao's novels tend to neglect sociopolitical considerations. In her novels, both the conflict and the climax are directly related to the core theme of love. In 1970s Taiwan under martial law of the authoritarian government, and in 1980s mainland just coming out of the political and ideological tight control of the Mao era, her novels, with their unequivocal emphasis on the true emotions shared by a young couple, were a breath of fresh air for teenagers learning about love and romantic relationships. *See also* WOMEN.

QIU MIAOJIN (1969–1995). Fiction and prose writer. Despite a short life, Qiu Miaojin has left behind a notable legacy in contemporary Chinese literature. Her writings, along with her tragic death, have shed new light on the predicament gays and lesbians faced in Taiwanese society despite the significant gains in the perception and acceptance of homosexuality made in urban **Taiwan** in recent decades. Qiu graduated from National Taiwan University with a bachelor's degree in psychology. While studying in Paris, she committed suicide. She left behind four books: *Gui de kuanghuan* (Revelries of Ghosts), *Eyu shouji* (Notes of an Alligator), *Jimo de qunzhong* (A Solitary Crowd), *Mengmate yishu* (Letters Written in Montmartre before Death), and a diary, *Qiu Miaojin riji* (Diary of Qiu Miaojin), the last two items posthumously published.

Of these works, *Eyu shouji* is the best, generally considered a Chinese classic on lesbian culture, whose reputation is so widespread that the name of its main character, Lazi—coined from Les(bian)—has been adopted as a self-reference by Chinese lesbians. The allegorical, semi-autobiographical novel traces the four undergraduate years of Lazi's life, as she ponders the dubious integrity of the self in relation to sexual identity and the role of writing—ideas that function for her as a means to explain away her emptiness and self-doubt as well as a way by which she can derive meaning out of a confused life. Lazi's propensity for dark ruminations over her homosexual and homoerotic feelings is juxtaposed with the humorous, self-effacing disposition of the other main character, Alligator. Throughout the novel, Lazi's first-person mythopoeic voice is frequently intersected by the lighthearted tone of Alligator, who represents an entity at odds with society, unsure of its sexual orientation and uncomfortable with its appearance, a strange species on the verge of extinction now being chased and gazed at by the public, a mirror image of Lazi. Both characters fade away after having been repeatedly persecuted, indicating that death and destruction are inevitable outcomes of a precarious existence.

Mengmate yishu contains 20 letters and journal entries Qiu wrote in France shortly before she took her own life. They are distressed professions of her strong feelings for the woman who betrayed her. The outpouring of her innermost emotions and the description of her tortured experience trying to come to terms with her lover's betrayal reveal her views on the meaning of love, life, and art, and paint a self-portrait of the author as she struggled desperately between salvation and destruction. Similarly, *Qiu Miaojin riji* is also self-writing at its most candid. On the other hand, both *Gui de kuanghuan* and *Jimo de qunzhong* are collections of short stories about an alienated and rebellious population rejected by mainstream society. At the heart of Qiu's work lies the author's recognition that the nature of passion and love intensifies human existence in both its most beautiful and most monstrous moments.

– R –

ROOT-SEEKING LITERATURE (XUNGEN WENXUE). A literary movement that began in the early 1980s, root-seeking has been the most pervasive and influential literary trend in post-Mao Chinese literature.

The poet **Yang Lian** was perhaps the first to express the need for Chinese literature to come to terms with China's cultural heritage. In his poems written around 1982, such as "Banpo" (Banpo: the Neolithic Age) and "Dunhuang" (The Dunhuang Caves), Yang sets out to discover the nation's past buried deep in the ancient lands and to examine its implications for the Chinese literary imagination. At around the same time, **Wang Meng** published his Xingjiang stories *Zai Yili* (In Yili), which, while recounting his experience in exile in the remote northwest, introduces the unique cultures of the Uygurs and the Kazaks. **Wang Zengqi** creates in "Da nao jishi" (Notes about the Great Mire) a pastoral world steeped in Chinese traditional virtues. Soon after, many writers, particularly those who had spent years during the **Cultural Revolution** in rural China as educated youths, eagerly joined the movement. **Jia Pingwa**'s "Shangzhou chu lu" (Stories of Shangzhou), **Zhang Chengzhi**'s *Beifang de he* (*The River in the North*), **Ah Cheng**'s *Qi qang* (*The King of Chess*), **Wang Anyi**'s *Xiao Bao zhuang* (*Bao Town*), **Li Hangyu**'s "Zuihou yige yulao'r" (*The Last Fisherman*), and many other works all came out at once, creating a phenomenon that caught the immediate attention of literary critics. A conference was held in Hangzhou in 1984 to discuss the significance of this cultural and literary phenomenon and explore new methods in fiction writing. In the following year, several writers, including Ah Cheng, **Zheng Yi**, **Han Shaogong**, **Zheng Wanlong**, and Li Hangyu, published their "root-seeking proclamations." Among them, Han's article, "Wenxue de gen" (Roots of Literature), which gave the movement its name, was the most influential and widely regarded as the unofficial "manifesto" of root-seeking literature. Using the example of the rich ancient Chu culture known for its highly imaginative and mystical shamanistic traditions, Han urged his fellow writers to "transcend reality" and to explore "the mysteries that define the development of a nation and of human existence." In the view of Han and his colleagues, there was a gap between the ancient past and the present, and in the 20th century, China had experienced a period of amnesia, in which the nation's rich past was erased from the collective memory of the Chinese. The responsibility of a writer, they believed, was to help the nation reconnect to its past, to "sort out," in the words of Li Hangyu, the cultural roots. Only by doing so, they argued, would Chinese literature be able to "dialogue" with the rest of the world. The goal of the root-seekers, therefore, was to search for authentic Chinese national roots in order to claim a spot in the global literary scene.

The primary locus of root-seeking literature is the Chinese country-side, where the political winds that swept China during the past century had only limited success. Agrarian society is thought to be the heart of Chinese culture, uncorrupted by Western influences and therefore retaining the primordial energies of humanity. Unlike the earlier **nativists** (xiangtu pai), the root-seekers were not satisfied with realistic representations of rural life and regional customs. Influenced by a wealth of literary traditions from the West and particularly by Latin American magic realism, they identified ancient Chinese traditions as a source of a new literature that addressed profound, universal issues while expressing a subjective vision of art and life. **Mo Yan**'s Gaomi stories celebrate the exuberant primordial energies and affirm the masculine vigor as opposed to the physical inferiority of the meek and "civilized" Confucian tradition; **Tashi Dawa**'s Tibetan tales unfold a world of mysteries and religious practices, and Han Shaogong's *Bababa* (Pa pa pa) depicts an isolated community in the remote mountains of Hunan where the villagers' behavior is controlled by irrational, superstitious beliefs, unaffected by the events in the outside world. Although the ancient roots that inspired the root-seekers were most often found in remote rural China, they also existed in the cities and were uncovered by "the urban root-seekers." **Deng Youmei** of Beijing and **Lu Wenfu** of Suzhou were the most representative of the group. Deng's portraits of the Manchu descendents and Lu Wenfu's stories about the history and customs of Suzhou not only record in vivid detail the vanishing or vanished cultures but also examine their impact on the people and the society they left behind.

Although the root-seeking movement reached the height of popularity in the 1980s, its impact is still felt at present. From its ranks have emerged some of the best writers in China today and the ancient cultures that inspired the root-seekers to continue to provide inspiration for Chinese writers. *See also* CHEN ZHONGSHI; LI RUI; LIN JINLAN; FENG JICAI; JIA PINGWA; LIU HENG; SU TONG; NATIVISTS; YU HUA; YE ZHAOYAN; ZHENG CHENGZHI; ZHANG WEI.

ROU SHI, PEN NAME OF ZHAO PINGFU (1902–1931). Poet and fiction writer. Born in Zhejiang, Rou Shi attended Hangzhou Number One Teachers' College, where he became a member of Chen Guang She (The Morning Sun Association), a progressive literary organization. After graduating, he taught at various schools and continued to write in his spare time. The short stories he wrote expressed his frustration with the state of the country. In Shanghai, he became acquainted with **Lu Xun**, who invited him to edit *Yu si* (Words and Language). He was a founding member of the **Left-wing Association of Chinese Writers** and the Chinese Communist Party. He was arrested by the Nationalist government and executed in prison along with four other left-wing writers. Of his fictional works, "Wei nuli de muqin" (Slave Mother) is best known. It describes a peasant woman's sad life and calls for the liberation of the working poor. Other works include "San jiemei" (Three Sisters) and *Jiu shidai zhi si* (Death of the Old Era) as well as a poetry collection, *Zhan* (Fight). He also translated literature from Denmark, the Soviet Union, and Eastern Europe. *See also* CIVIL WAR.

RU ZHIJUAN (1925–1998). Fiction writer. Ru Zhijuan belonged to the generation of writers who were nurtured by the Communist revolution. Born into a poor family in Shanghai, Ru lost her parents at a young age. She received some schooling in Christian missionary schools until her elder brother took her with him to join the Communist army in 1944. She was a performer and a playwright in the army's art troupe and worked as a nurse during battles. After she left the army in 1955, she was an editor for a literary journal in Shanghai until 1960, when she became a professional writer. She was the party secretary of the Shanghai Writers' Association before her death at the age of 73.

Ru is best remembered for her short story "Baihe hua" (Lilies on the Quilt) published in 1958. The story is based on the author's experience in the late 1940s when the Communists were fighting the **Civil War** with the Nationalists. Instead of the battlefield, the story focuses on what happens in the background. The simple plot involves a young soldier going to a village to borrow quilts for the wounded solders and meeting a family's young bride. It is an innocent romantic story, with its subtle juxtaposition of a beautiful young woman enjoying the sweet love of her new marriage and a naive 19-year-old man ignorant of sexual matters. Treating a war story in such a fashion is uncharacteristic of Communist literature and it is no surprise that the story was singled out in the 1960s as an indication of the author's bourgeois sentimentality. Ru wrote other stories but none captured the same kind of attention as "Baihe hua."

Among Ru's works published after the **Cultural Revolution**, the best known is "Jianji cuole de gushi" (The Incorrectly Edited Story), an exposé of the mismanagement of rural economy during the Mao era, focusing on two characters in an agricultural commune who represent the opposing forces within the party between the self-serving ideologues and the truth-seeking realists. Ru's writings tend to pay more attention to characterization than plot development. She is a writer of subtle emotions and her language is straightforward but vivid and fresh. *See also* WOMEN.

– S –

SAN MAO, PEN NAME OF CHEN PING (1943–1991). Born in Chongqing, the wartime capital of the Republic of China, San Mao moved to **Taiwan** with her parents. A precocious child, she had trouble fitting into the public school of Taipei and was subsequently home-schooled. She began publishing stories in her teens, but did not gain fame until the release of her first book, *Sahala de gushi* (The Sahara Tales), which records her personal experience in the African desert. Most of her later works are also based on her own experiences abroad. *Wan shui qian shan zhoubian* (Trip to South and Central America) is a travel journal commissioned by the *Lianhe Daily* after San Mao returned to Taiwan in the wake of her Spanish husband's sudden death in a drowning accident. San Mao taught creative writing at the Chinese Culture University and delivered guest lectures all over Taiwan. Her popularity reached new heights after she committed suicide in a Taipei hospital. *See also* WOMEN.

SCAR LITERATURE (SHANGHEN WENXUE). Derived from the title of a short story written by Lu Xinhua and published in 1978, the term refers to literature written in the late 1970s and early 1980s that treats the devastating effects of the **Cultural Revolution**—the "scars" it left on the minds and souls of the Chinese youth. **Liu Xinwu**'s "Ban zhuren" (The Homeroom Teacher) is another work that helped define the humanistic literary movement. While the mainstream of scar literature exposes the negative impact of political movements in the past decades, others focus on the moral and spiritual rectitude of the individual and the compassion of ordinary people. Cong Weixi's "Da qiang xia de hong yulan" (The Red Magnolia under the High Wall) and **Zhang Xianliang**'s "Tu lao qinghua" (Love in a Prison) reflect the fortitude of the political prisoners as they endure trauma and torture; **Zhang Jie**'s "Senlin li lai de haizi" (A Boy from the Forest) and Ye Weilin's "Zai meiyou hangbiao de heliu shang" (On the River without a Navigation Mark) shed light on the triumph of the human spirit and love despite difficult circumstances. *See also* WANG MENG; FENG JICAI.

SEBO (1956–). Fiction writer. Born in Chengdu, Sichuan Province, Sebo spent his childhood in Fenghuang, Hunan Province. In 1973, he went to the northeastern province of Liaoning to study medicine, and after graduation in 1975 he worked for several years as a medic in various parts of **Tibet**. Sebo started writing in the early 1980s. His short stories, such as "Yuanxing rizi" (*Circular Days*) and "Zai zhe shang chuan" (*Getting on the Boat Here*) portray capricious characters at odds with both Tibetan culture and outside influences. The illusive world created by Sebo reflects the predicament of modern-day Tibet as well as his philosophical views about life. Some critics consider Sebo an existentialist for his pessimistic characters engaged in a perpetual search on a lonely, circular journey. Sebo's works, firmly anchored in Tibetan culture, explore the clash of civilizations and cultures and what that clash means to the survival of indigenous traditions. His Tibet is full of contradictions and complexities, different from the utopian world portrayed by some of his fellow Tibetan writers. Like many young writers in the post-Mao era, Sebo is influenced by Western literature, such as works by Italo Calvino, Jorge Luis Borges, Milan Kundera, and William Faulkner. Sebo currently lives in Chengdu, Sichuan Province.

SHA TING (1904–1992). Novelist. Born in northwestern Sichuan, Sha Ting is best known as a chronicler of the agrarian society of his hometown. His works can be roughly divided into two categories: the ideological stories, written in response to Communist Party policies, and the hometown stories, based on people and events he personally encountered. From the very beginning of his career, Sha tried to fit his writing to the templates of the proletarian literature advocated by **Mao Dun** and others in the **Left-wing Association of Chinese Writers**, which he joined in 1932. His eagerness to embrace its ideology may have contributed to the dogmatic and moralizing style found in some of his writings. Yet, throughout his life, Sha struggled to stay close to his birthplace, repeatedly abandoning a promising political career, often to the chagrin of party leaders and his friends, in order to return to his roots for creative inspiration. Deep in his heart, he did not see himself as a politician and he got greater satisfaction from writing novels than from being a bureaucrat. His best works are those inspired by the real people of his hometown, who serve as prototypes for his characters. He was less of an imaginative writer than a keen observer and superb portraitist.

The characters that populate his hometown stories are peasants, local gangsters, landlords, government officials, and small-town intellectuals: the wide spectrum of people he met while growing up and through his uncle, the leader of the Society of Brotherhood, a well-known gang in Sichuan. The tone he often adopts in these tales is humorous and at times satirical. His satire is subtle; he never lashes out directly but lets his characters speak for themselves. "Zai qixiangju chaguan li" (In the Teahouse), a short story written in 1940, exposes the collaborations between the local gangsters and military officers. The political purpose of the story is to expose and satirize behaviors that hinder social reforms and the war effort. The message is conveyed not through moralizing and explicit propaganda, but through the words and acts of the characters. Sha does not rely on lengthy descriptions or psychological analysis to portray his characters; rather, his stories consist mostly of vivid dialogues in colloquial speech.

Tao jin ji (Gold Rush), written in 1942 and considered his best work, is the first of his many novels. The story revolves around a piece of land that is the center of a fight among local gentry, gangsters, and officials. *Tao jin ji* is a consummate study of local customs, language, and social networks, as well as the author's understanding of his own roots. Sha laments the ignorance and selfishness of small-town Chinese, whose energy and cleverness are misplaced. Instead of uniting to fight against the Japanese, they go to extreme lengths to destroy each other in order to protect their own interests. The inspiration for *Kun shou ji* (Caged Animals), a novel about elementary school teachers in rural Sichuan, came from his brother-in-law, whose elopement with the concubine of a wealthy landlord, leaving behind a wife and three children, caused a stir in town. Sha was intimately familiar with rural schoolteachers, his wife and his mother-in-law having taught in the country for many years, and was sympathetic to what they had to endure in such an isolated environment. *Huanxiang ji* (Homecoming), finished during the **Civil War**, focuses on the negative consequences of the Nationalist government's conscription campaign in the countryside.

After 1949, Sha tried to keep up with the times by writing about the accomplishments and transformations taking place in the country, but his work failed to achieve the same force and appeal as his hometown stories. In the 1980s, he refocused his attention on Sichuan, resulting in *Hong shi tan* (The Red Rock Beach), a novel regarded as the sequel to *Tao jin ji*. While the older book describes an old order essentially untouched by external events, the new book rings its death toll. In *Hong shi tan,* those who used to rule the insulated agrarian world make their last desperate attempt in the 1950s to hold on to power. Sha was much more at home and much more enthusiastic about portraying the old era than the new one he helped to usher in.

SHEN CONGWEN (1902–1988). Fiction writer. A self-described "country bumpkin," Shen Congwen hailed from the backwaters of a mountain town in western Hunan. Following the local tradition, he enlisted in the army at the age of 14, hoping to succeed in the military like his paternal grandfather who had risen through the ranks to become a general. Disillusioned by military life and uninterested in spending the rest of his time in small towns, he left the army and went to Beijing to seek a new life. With only an elementary school education, he could not pass the college entrance exams, so he audited classes. While attending lectures at Beijing University and devouring books in the city library, he began to write pastoral stories. By the end of the 1930s, he was one of the most respected Chinese writers. Fiercely independent, he was wary of political interference, which, he maintained, would rob literature of its soul. In the 1930s, at the height of his career, he infuriated his colleagues by criticizing the lack of individuality and frivolous pursuits of modern writers, which catapulted him to the center of a heated debate. He was denounced by both the left and the right; the left accused him of misleading the youth by encouraging them to withdraw from society; the right found his call for a literature of "flesh and blood" too ideological.

For his writings, Shen drew mostly from the wealth of his early experiences, the host of people he had met as he roamed western Hunan as a soldier and the old customs and street scenes that fascinated him as a child, to illustrate a world in direct contrast to modern urban life. This pastoral landscape is simple, but not simplistic. The world of the mountain villages in western Hunan that appears in some of his stories seems timeless, untouched by Confucian morality or modern concepts, and runs according to a different set of rules and values. The child bride in "Xiaoxiao" (Xiao Xiao) escapes a severe punishment when her out-of-wedlock pregnancy is discovered by her in-laws. Shen does not depict Xiaoxiao as either a victim of or a rebel against traditional morality, however, as a progressive writer would do: her life is spared partly because the head of her family "has not read Confucius." In "Bian cheng" (Border Town), another masterpiece of Shen's, he depicts an idyllic world inhabited by characters, the rich and the poor alike, who are kindhearted, generous, and trustworthy.

Other than the stories reminiscent of his hometown, Shen also wrote about city life, including "Shengshi de taitai" (The Gentleman's Wife) and "Ba jun tu" (A Portrait of Eight Steeds). Unlike the sincere, nostalgic tone in his hometown stories, a satirical voice describes the urban scene, making fun of the lack of morality in the polite society of high officials, university professors, and college students who maintain an exterior of propriety and intelligence underneath which hides their mean and vulgar nature. While exposing the sordid side of high society, the author also depicts the lives of the lower classes, particularly the struggle of folks from the countryside, like himself, for dignity and respect. In general, his city stories never reached the same degree of achievement as his rural tales.

After a painful period of soul-searching, Shen concluded in 1949 that his pen was out of date and he could not transform himself fast enough to keep up with the new society. He stopped writing fiction and sociopolitical essays altogether and reinvented himself as an expert in the field of antiquities. His work resulted in several groundbreaking scholarly books on ancient Chinese silk, costumes, lacquer, mirrors, and other cultural relics. Shen made a successful career as a scholar of antiquities but is best remembered as one of the greatest writers of 20th-century China. *See also* NEW CULTURE MOVEMENT; NATIVISTS.

SHEN RONG (1936–). Fiction writer. Shen was born in Hankou, Hubei, and had an eventful childhood due to the wars and political upheavals that surrounded her. She moved with her parents from one place to another and eventually settled in Chongqing. After 1949, she worked as an assistant in a publishing house and studied Russian at the Beijing Institute of Russian Studies. Shen began writing in the 1970s under the influence of **socialist realism**. Her best work in the 1970s is "Yongyuan shi chuntian" (The Eternal Spring). Set against the background of the decades between the **Sino-Japanese War** and the **Cultural Revolution**, the story portrays a female revolutionary cadre. Shen's breakthrough, however, did not come until the publication of *Ren dao zhongnian* (At Middle Age), a story about the difficulties faced by middle-aged professionals as a result of the collusion of political ideology with pervasive bureaucracy. When the story was turned into a movie, Shen became an instant celebrity.

After *Ren dao zhongnian,* Shen continued to write about the damages the Cultural Revolution did to the nation. *Rendao laonian* (At Old Age) was published in 1991 when Chinese society had undergone fundamental changes since the late 1970s. The three main characters, all professional **women** who were college classmates in the 1950s, experience a sense of loss and disillusionment in the midst of a rapidly commercializing society. Unable to fit into the new world, they have only one consolation: their memories of the idealistic 1950s when they, like the newly founded country, were optimistic and full of energy.

SHI SHUQING, A.K.A. SHI SHU-CH'ING (1945–). Novelist. Born and educated in **Taiwan**, Shi Shuqing, whose influence crosses the geographical and political boundaries separating Taiwan, **Hong Kong**, and the mainland, began her literary career with stories about her native Lugang, a small town in Taiwan. Tales such as "Bihu" (Gecko), "Ci Guanyin" (The Porcelain Guanyin), and "Nixiangmen de jidian" (The Fiesta of the Clay Statues) are teeming with characters who are physically and psychologically disfigured and whose world is rampant with madness, psychosis, morbidity, and death. With these gothic stories, Shi was recognized as an experimental, avant-garde writer interested in exploring the alienating effects of modern society on the lives of the individual, a theme that would make recurring appearances in her later works. After Shi moved to New York to study theater at the City University of New York, she wrote a series of stories on immigrants' lives in the global capitalist economy.

In 1979, Shi settled in Hong Kong, which became the setting for some of her major works, including stories collected in *Xianggang de gushi* (Hong Kong Stories) such as the novella "Weiduoliya julebu" (The Victoria Club). Her most celebrated books on Hong Kong are her *Xianggang sanbuqu* (The Hong Kong Trilogy). This ambitious project traces four generations of one family from the late 19th century, when the British took possession of Hong Kong, to 1997 when the city was handed over to the Chinese. The protagonist is a **woman** named Huang

Deyun, whose metamorphosis from a village girl, kidnapped and sold into prostitution, to a powerful businesswoman serves as a representation of Hong Kong during its turbulent century of colonial possession, as it changed from its humble beginnings as a plague-ridden port to a gleaming metropolis, the "pearl" on the crown of the British Empire. Grand in its epic scale, the novel is also a rich study of race and gender, providing interesting material for postcolonial and feminist studies.

In *Weixun caizhuang* (Blush of Intoxication), her first novel since her return to Taiwan, Shi turns her attention to the process of Westernization. The novel treats the business of importing Western wine and its consumption in Taiwanese society during the late 1990s, delivering a powerful exposé of the culture of a wine market created and manipulated by a group of imaginative but shady business dealers.

SHI TIESHENG (1951–). Fiction writer and essayist. After middle school, Shi Tiesheng left Beijing and went to work in a village in Shaanxi, where he stayed until an illness brought him back to the capital. For 10 years after that, he worked in a small factory. Shi gained fame in the early 1980s with a series of lyrical stories, including "Wo de yuaoyuan de qingpingwan" (*My Far Away Qingpingwan*), which is based on his life in the village. Shi casts an affectionate eye on his characters: the honest farmers who know nothing but hard work and suffering and the equally innocent city youths who have come to accept the harsh realities of the northwestern loess. In a controlled but loving tone of voice, Shi calmly relates the small aspirations of rural people.

Laowu xiaoji (Record of an Old House), an autobiographical novel, relates the first few years of his life in the factory after he was paralyzed from the waist down. The straightforward narrative style Shi uses for this work has been adopted in many of his other stories. The novel *Wuxu biji* (Notes of Discussions of Impractical Matters), published in 1996, is widely considered his best work. Other writings include prose pieces about his personal struggle with illness, such as *Bing xi suibi* (Fragments Written between Illnesses) and "Wo yu ditan" (*In the Temple of the Earth*), a touching confessional essay that records how little scenes in the park changed his perspective on life and prevented him from committing suicide. Years of living in a wrecked body made him prone to melancholic ruminations but his illness also made him more philosophical with regard to the meaning of life and death, a frequent theme in his writings.

SHI TUO, A.K.A. LU FEN, PEN NAMES OF WANG CHANGJIAN (1910–1988). Fiction and screenplay writer and essayist. Shi Tuo spent his childhood in the backwaters of the eastern Henan countryside. In 1931, he went to Beijing and his involvement in the protests against Japanese aggression led to the publications of his first short stories. Encouraged by **Ding Ling**, Shi continued writing stories that exposed the evils of the government and the bitter sufferings of the poor. In 1937, his story "Gu" (Rice) won the Dagong Daily Prize, marking the beginning of the most productive period of his career, which saw the publications of three more collections of short stories: *Limen shiji* (Notes of Limen), *Yeniao ji* (Wild Birds), and *Luori guang* (Light of the Setting Sun). Shi's stories contain vivid descriptions of scenery, a distinct local flavor, and a biting satirical tone, but, lacking in plot development, they are essentially lyrical prose. In the 1940s, Shi, living in the Japanese-occupied Shanghai, began to work on longer pieces, producing one novella and two novels, *Jiehun* (Getting Married) and *Ma Lan* (Ma Lan), which are considered his representative works. He also wrote screenplays during this period.

After 1949, Shi worked as a screenplay writer and editor for the Shanghai Film Studio and became a member of the Shanghai Writers' Association. He published one novel, *Lishi wuqing* (History Is Unsympathetic) and some historical plays, including *Ximen Bao* (Ximen Bao), before the outbreak of the **Cultural Revolution**. *See also* SINO-JAPANESE WAR.

SHI ZHECUN (1905–2003). Fiction writer, poet, essayist, translator, and scholar. As an artist, no one among his contemporaries was more inventive than She Zhecun. From composing classical poetry to creating modern verses, from his **Mandarin Ducks and Butterflies** (Yuanyang hudie) tales, to his **New Sensibility** (xin ganjue) stories, he put his energy to narrative innovations and is credited for having spearheaded the modernist movement in 20th-century Chinese literature. Best remembered for his psychoanalytical fiction, Shi was one of the first Chinese writers to use Western modernist techniques such as stream of consciousness and montage in his writings. Among his fictional work, "Jiangjun de tou" (The General's Head), a historical tale, and "Meiyu zhi xi" (*One Rainy Evening*), a languorous story about a chance meeting between a man and a woman, are some of the best illustrations of modernist literature. With their exquisite descriptions of the psychological interiors of the characters, Shi's works depart in a significant manner from the mainstream of modern Chinese literature.

After 1937, Shi gave up creative writing altogether for an academic career, becoming a prominent scholar on classical Chinese literature. In the Mao era, his name was erased from books on modern Chinese literature. He resurfaced in the 1980s, however, and his books were put back on the shelves of libraries and bookstores. Shi was equally at home inside the "four windows" (in his own words) he had opened: the study of classical literature, creative writing and editing, foreign literature translation and introduction, and ancient tombstone inscriptions. *See also* CULTURAL REVOLUTION; MODERNISTS.

SHIZHI, PEN NAME OF GUO LUSHENG (1948–). Poet. Born into a military family, Shizhi began writing verses when he was in the third grade. Considered the most influential poet in the underground poetry movement during the **Cultural Revolution**, Shizhi expressed the spirit of defiance as early as the late 1960s. A forerunner of post-Mao poetry, he has influenced **Bei Dao**, **Yan Li**, and many others of the **Misty** genera-tion,. His exuberant poems, such as "Xiangxin weilai" (*Trust the Future*), "Yu'er sanbuqu" (Fish Trilogy), and "Si dian ling ba fen de Beijing" (Bei-jing at 4:08) were hand-copied and circulated widely among the educated youth, showing them the dark realities of the era and giving them hope for a better future. In 1973, Shizhi was diagnosed with schizophrenia and has spent much of his time institutionalized since the 1980s. He began using the pen name Shizhi (forefinger) in 1978, signifying his indifference to the public's finger pointing because of his mental illness. He continued to write after being institutionalized, and his poems appeared in the under-ground poetry journal *Today*, founded by Bei Dao, **Mang Ke**, and others. He became a member of the Chinese Association of Writers in 1997 while still in the Beijing No. 3 Social Welfare House, a mental ward outside the city. Shizhi attributed his intellectual and political independence to his ill-ness: "Since I wear the hat of being insane, I can do whatever I want to: to be absolutely independent in thought and spirit, like a horse in the sky traveling at its own speed and direction without any restraint, all because I am insane." He is indeed known as the "mad poet."

SHU TING (1952–). Born in Fujian, Shu Ting rose to fame in the early 1980s as the most prominent female poet among the **Misty poets**. Shu began to write in the years of the **Cultural Revolution** when she was working among peasants. Compared with the poems written by other

Misty poets, her work is much more accessible and less abstruse. *Shuangwei chuan* (The Double-masted Boat), *Hui changge de yiweihua* (The Singing Iris), and *Shizuniao* (Archaeopteryx) are some of her poetry collections. She has also published several collections of essays.

For her association with the underground literary journal *Jintian* (Today), Shu came under attack during the Antispiritual Pollution Campaign in the late 1980s. While many other Misty poets have left China and obtained foreign citizenships, Shu has remained in China. *See also* WOMEN.

SHU XIANGCHENG, PEN NAME OF WANG SHENQUAN (1921–1999). Poet, novelist, essayist, and painter. A native of **Hong Kong**, Shu began publishing vernacular poetry and short stories in the 1930s while still a college student. When Hong Kong fell into the hands of the Japanese in 1942, Shu went to the mainland and stayed on till after Japan surrendered. The difficult experiences he suffered during these years while traveling through the Chinese hinterland provided rich material for a novel, *Jianku de xingcheng* (An Arduous Journey), and other works. In 1948, Shu returned to Hong Kong and soon reached the most productive period of his career. While working at his daytime job in the office of various businesses, he wrote at night, resulting in a large number of stories, poems, and essays, published under more than a dozen pen names to avoid jeopardizing his job and to protect his identity when researching for new stories. Shu's work also benefited from his many trips abroad, including his participation in the 1977 International Writers' Workshop at the University of Iowa.

A realist writer, Shu was a true believer in the representational mode. He practiced an art that sought to reflect life truthfully. Born and raised in Hong Kong, he was familiar with the history and environment of the city, and the thoughts and customs of its residents, and tried to re-create them in his works. For many years, Shu remained Hong Kong's favorite writer, whose works were appreciated by a wide spectrum of readers. Most of his fictional works deal with life in the lower echelons of society with its squalid conditions as well as its energy and humanism. "Liyu men de wu" (Mist over the Carp Gate) is a nostalgic tale about a man returning to his hometown with fond memories of the past. *Bali liang'an* (On the Banks of the Seine), inspired by his trip to Paris, features a French artist whose aspirations are repeatedly dashed by a materialistic society. Although set in a foreign land, this story resonates with the feelings Shu had about the fate of artists in Hong Kong, where true art found no sympathetic audience and all artistic forms were in danger of being commercialized. *Taiyang xiashan le* (The Sun Has Set), serialized in a literary journal in 1961, was published in 1984 on the mainland under the new title *Gangdao dajie de beihou* (Behind the Main Streets of Hong Kong). It tells the story of a poor but ambitious man who succeeds in life through perseverance and hard work.

Shu applied the techniques of realism to his painting as well as his poetry. His poems illustrate slices of Hong Kong life, expressing the poet's love and affection for the island. A fan of Cantonese opera and folk music, Shu transfers its rhythm and cadence to his poetry, which depicts the grotesque vulgarity of modern existence, denounces its morbid dehumanization, and calls for a return to the embrace of Mother Nature.

SIMA CHANGFENG, PEN NAME OF HU XINPING (1922–1980). Born in the northeast, Sima Changfeng left the mainland for **Hong Kong** on the eve of the Communist victory. He worked as an editor and taught literature in colleges and published mostly essays and some short stories from the mid-1950s to the late 1970s. He died in Canada. His early works are reminiscences of his childhood and youth, and in the latter part of his career, he focused on creating belles lettres that appealed to sophisticated sensibilities. Sima also wrote scholarly works, including a three-volume history of modern Chinese literature.

SINO-JAPANESE WAR (1937–1945). In the 19th century while the Qing dynasty was deeply mired in its domestic and international problems, Japan was strengthening its modernization project and expanding its imperial army. By the end of the century, it had become the most powerful nation in Asia. Following the examples of Western colonial powers, Japan set out to conquer China and the rest of Asia in an effort to fulfill its own imperial ambitions. When the Europeans marched into China after the Boxer Rebellion and proceeded to carve up the country and divide the bounty among them, Japan was an active participant. Having been defeated in the first Sino-Japanese War (1894–1895), the Qing was forced to cede **Taiwan** to Japan. After the Russo-Japanese War (1904–1905), Japan replaced Russia as the dominant force in southern Manchuria. When World War I (1914–1918) ended, Japan took control of Qingdao, in the Shandong peninsula, from Germany. In addition to these territories, Japan acquired concessions in Tianjin and Shanghai.

In 1931, the Manchurian Incident or Mukden Incident, which involved the bombing of the Japanese-controlled railroad near Shenyang (then known as Mukden), gave Japan the pretext to set up a puppet government, called Manchukuo, headed by Puyi, the deposed last emperor of the Qing. Japan then pressured Chiang Kai-shek's government to recognize Manchuria as an autonomous entity. Preoccupied with consolidating his power, Chiang Kai-shek was initially reluctant to engage the Japanese in military confrontations, and Japan, using the security of Manchukuo as justification, soon moved in to occupy Rehe (Jehol), Chahar, and the areas surrounding Beijing. Growing anti-Japanese sentiments in the country led to Chiang's kidnapping in Xi'an by General Zhang Xueliang in December 1936, forcing Chiang to form a coalition with the Communists. In 1937, the Japanese army pushed toward Beijing and was met with resistance from the Nationalist army at what is known as the Marco Polo Bridge in the southern suburb of Beijing. The Marco Polo Bridge Incident marked the beginning of a full-scale war between China and Japan. In no time, large Chinese territories fell into Japanese hands, and the Nationalist government was forced to retreat to Chongqiing, where they set up the war capital. From 1937 to 1941, China fought the Japanese alone. After Japan attacked Pearl Harbor in December 1941, the Sino-Japanese conflict folded into the larger theater of World War II and the Chinese military began to receive aid from the Allied forces.

The full-scale Sino-Japanese War lasted for eight years, costing immeasurable human and economic loss. It also changed the political landscape of China, leaving a lasting impact on the future of the country. Faced with an outside enemy, the ruling Nationalist Party and the Communists put aside their differences and built a united front against the Japanese. By the end of the war, the Communists had gained enough strength to pose a real threat to the Nationalists. The ink of the peace treaty was barely dry before the two sides plunged into a **civil war** that would continue for four years.

During the Sino-Japanese War, literary production reached an all-time high, both at the battlefront and in the Japanese-occupied territories. The antiwar sentiments merged into the leftist movement and became the mainstream of Chinese literature. Writers such as **Xiao Hong, Xiao Jun**, and **Duanmu Hongliang**, refugees from war-torn Manchuria, and Communist writers such as **Zhao Shuli**, emerged as new stars. The "national defense literature" (guofang wenxue), so termed by Zhou Yang and **Zhou Libo** to highlight the patriotic spirit, spread to film and theater, which were nearly taken over by the **left-wing** camp spearheaded by **Tian Han, Xia Yan, Ouyang Yuqian, Yang Hansheng**, and others. At the other end of the spectrum, writers in the Japanese-occupied territories such as **Zhang Ailing, Su Qing, Mei Niang**, and others pursued a path separate from the mainstream by focusing on the self, the family, romantic love, and social mores.

SOCIALIST REALISM. Endorsed by Mao Zedong in 1942 at the Yan'an Forum on Literature and Art, this aesthetic doctrine guided Chinese writers for nearly four decades, from the 1940s through the 1970s. A combination of realism and romanticism, socialist realism requires writers to treat subject matter that is in the mainstream of the national agenda. It holds the view that literature should reflect reality in a true-to-life fashion (which explains the popular practice of living with peasants in order to write about the countryside). Furthermore, it must articulate predetermined ideological objectives, leading to the creation of stereotyped and romanticized heroes. *See also* DING LING; SUN LI; ZHAO SHULI; SHA TING; HAO RAN; LIU BAIYU; OUYANG SHAN; SHEN RONG; ZHOU ERFU; ZHOU LIBO.

SPOKEN DRAMA. As precursors to spoken drama, *xin ju* (new play) and *wenming xi* (civilized drama), which were popular at the beginning of the 20th century, acted as bridges between traditional Chinese opera and the modern spoken genre, containing somes features of the older form such as improvisation and all-male casting but without the singing and music. The collegiate *aimei ju* (amateur play), which reached its height of popularity in the 1920s, was performed by students in school assembly halls. Fully scripted and often with an all-female cast, it was one step closer to spoken drama. **Hong Shen** is credited for naming the modern theatrical form *hua ju* (spoken drama) in 1928, when it began to be performed professionally in public theaters. It is the dramatic form of William Shakespeare, Henrik Ibsen, Molière, George Bernard Shaw, and other Western playwrights, which was transplanted to the Chinese stage.

The Chinese spoken drama is generally believed to have started in Japan, where in 1907 a group of Chinese students led by Li Shutong performed *Chahua nü (The Lady of the Camellias)*, an adaptation of the French play by Alexandre Dumas, fils. Later in the same year, another drama society staged *Uncle Tom's Cabin* in Shanghai. The early practitioners of the spoken drama were progressive youths inspired by

Ibsen, whose plays, conceived to reflect social reality, became models for the Chinese playwrights. *A Doll's House* was especially influential in its call for the emancipation of **women**, a significant component in the **New Culture Movement**. The popularity of the spoken drama was closely connected to the agenda of national revival and modernization the **May Fourth** intellectuals put forward to address what they believed to be a critical national crisis. For the survival of the nation, ordinary Chinese had to be enlightened and educated. Theater as a popular form of entertainment was seen by the reform-minded intellectuals as one of the most effective means to get their message to the masses directly and expeditiously. Chen Duxiu, founder of the Chinese Communist Party and the progressive journal *New Youth*, advocated transforming the traditional theater into a revolutionary venue, "a big classroom" with actors working as "important teachers."

Changing the traditional Chinese theater, however, proved to be a nearly impossible task. Entrenched in its own conventions and styles, the operative form relied heavily on old tales and historical romances for material. Therefore, what the audience focused on was the art of the performance, not the message of the play, as they were already familiar with the stories and moral lessons. To be able to go on the stage, the actors had to have received rigorous training, often from a young age, in a highly stylized form that involved singing, dancing, acrobatics, and acting. The props and costumes were also specialized. These features intrinsic to the traditional theater posed serious challenges to the reform-minded dramatists, who were faced with an ancient art form loaded with specific stylistics and preconditioned expectations. What the New Culture Movement looked for was a nimble form that required no particular professional training and easily adapted to different stage settings and social issues. The Western play met the needs of the progressive intellectuals perfectly. It was no accident that most of the early works of the new genre were staged in schools by amateur student actors, before a professional theater emerged in the late 1920s.

From translations or adaptations of Western plays, the Chinese playwrights moved to creating some memorable works of their own. Among the trailblazers were **Tian Han**, **Hong Shen**, **Guo Moruo**, and **Cao Yu**, and together with the professional troupes led by **Ouyang Yuqian**, **Xia Yan**, and others, they successfully transplanted a Western theatrical form and ensured for it a permanent place in the Chinese theater. A century later, the spoken drama still shares the stage with traditional operas. *See*

also CHEN BAICHEN; CHENG FANGWU; DING XILIN; DUANMU
HONGLIANG; GAO XINGJIAN; LAI SHENGCHUAN; LAO SHE;
LEFT-WING ASSOCIATION OF CHINESE WRITERS; LI JIANWU;
LIN JINLAN; LU LING; LU XING'ER; WEI MINGLUN; WOMEN;
WU ZUGUANG; XU XU; YANG HANSHENG; YANG JIANG; YE
LINGFENG; YU JIAN; YU LING; ZHANG XIAOFENG.

SU DE, PEN NAME OF WANG YI (1981–). Fiction writer. Born and
raised in Shanghai, Su De began writing short stories and essays at the
age of 14. She attended the Young Writers' Workshop at the Lu Xun Institute of Literature and graduated from East China Normal University.
Like **Xiao Fan** and many other post-1980s generation writers, Su De's
career was launched by *Mengya* (Sprouts), a literary journal for young
readers. Her first story, "Wo shi Lanse" (I Am Blue), a sentimental tale
about a girl named Blue, appeared in 2001 in *Mengya*, which put out
more of her stories in the following years. Her work also appeared on
the Internet, mostly on www.rongshuxia.com, a popular literary website
that has published several of her stories. After she had attracted a sizable following among online readers, Su De was then embraced by the
mainstream literary establishment. In 2002, Zhishi Press issued *Yan zhe
wo huangliang de e* (Along My Desolate Forehead), a collection of short
stories. The following year saw the publication of another short story
collection, *Ci malu shang wo yao shuo gushi* (I Want to Tell Stories
in the Streets). *Ganggui shang de aiqing* (Love on the Rails), hailed as
her best work so far, came out in 2004. In 2005, *Shu* (Atonement) was
published.

Nearly all of Su De's stories are about urban youths and their emotional ups and downs. Most of her characters come from broken families
and lead lonely lives; they are vulnerable and cynical, sensitive and
cruel, with deep psychological scars. "Yan shi" (Gone like Smoke), for
example, addresses passionate love and the confusion, inner turmoil,
and depression associated with sexual desire. *Ganggui shang de aiqing*
is a tragic story of two star-crossed lovers who grew up as brother and
sister but share no blood relations. Their "incestuous" affair drives their
parents to death. Feelings of guilt force the lovers apart, like two rails
traveling in the same direction but never connecting. In the end, depression drives the young man to suicide and the young woman into self-
imposed exile. Su De is noted for the skillfully woven labyrinthine plots
and the sophisticated language that represent her narrative style, as well

as the nuanced portrayals of distrustful and insecure teenage characters who are featured prominently in her writings. *See also* WOMEN.

SU QING, PEN NAME OF FENG YUNZHUANG (1914–1982). Essayist, fiction writer, and playwright. In Japanese-occupied Shanghai, Su Qing was as well known as her friend, **Zhang Ailing**. *Jiehun shi nian* (Ten Years of Marriage), a novel based on her own unhappy marriage, made her famous in Shanghai. In both her fiction and her newspaper columns, she wrote about the difficulties of everyday life for **women**, particularly career women like herself. She also talked about women's sexual desire in undisguised language. Stories such as "Liang tiao yu" (Two Fish), "Xiong qian de mimi" (Secrets), and "Fei e" (Moth), all told in the first-person narrative and drawn from her personal life, represent some of the most audacious expressions of sexuality found in Chinese literature of the 1940s. A divorced single mother raising children on her own, she distrusts marriage as an institution and proposes that it should not be the only viable option for women or men and that cohabitation should be socially acceptable. Her style of writing is plain and straightforward, painting her characters with bold, simple strokes. In addition to her autobiographical novel *Jiehun shi nian*, her other well-received books include the novella *Qi lu jia ren* (A Beauty on the Wrong Path), and the short story collection *Tao* (Waves). She depicts the pragmatism of career women, their self-consciousness, and their anxieties. After 1949, Su stayed on in Shanghai and wrote plays for the Shanghai Yueju Opera Troupe. The changed political environment, however, made it difficult for her to continue her creative work and she underwent a series of political persecutions until she finally died in poverty and sickness, unable to witness the revived interest in her writings.

SU TONG, PEN NAME OF TONG ZHONGGUI (1963–). Novelist. Su Tong began writing in the early 1980s while a student in the Chinese Department of Beijing Normal University. Although he had published several experimental works before, it was *Yijiusansinian de taowang* (The Escapes in 1934) that established his reputation as an **avant-garde** writer. He is better known for his "neohistorical" fiction. *Yingsu zhi jia* (The Poppy Growers) is a dark tale about a family whose downfall is brought about by lust and murder, symbolized by the crop they grow. *Qiqie chengqun* (*Raise the Red Lantern*) details the fate of **women** in a traditional household. *Mi* (*Rice*) is an engrossing story of a farm boy who amasses a fortune and loses it all through sexual conquest and murder. *Hongfen* (*Rouge*), about two former prostitutes and their entangled relationship with a man, portrays the social transformations that take place in the early years of the People's Republic. *Wo de diwang shengya* (*My Life as Emperor*), tells the account of an emperor's meteoric life in a fictitious dynasty, from supreme ruler to a poor acrobat, making a living on the streets. In these neohistorical dramas, Su Tong gravitates toward the past, taking advantage of the unfamiliarity provided by temporal distance to exercise his fertile imagination. In these texts, Su Tong proposes a new interpretation of history, one that is driven by forces of sexual synergy and mysterious transgressions.

Su Tong's other preoccupation is his childhood memories, which has resulted in a series of stories centered on a fabricated neighborhood, called Xiangchunshu Street, in a southern city. The brutal realities of this place include illicit sex, dark secrets, insanity, and inexplicable deaths, as presented in such stories as "Shujia xiongdi" (*The Shu Brothers*), "Nanfang de duoluo" (The Degeneration of the South), "Ciqing shidai" (The Era of Tattoos), "Chengbei didai" (The Northern Part of the Town), and the loosely structured novel, *Fengyangshu shange* (The Song of Maple and Poplar Trees). In these works, Su keeps the official history of the **Cultural Revolution** in the background and focuses on creating a personal history of the 1960s, a time of his own coming of age. What is real is the palpable memory of inexplicable violence, the colors and smells of the neighborhood river, the desolation, the loneliness, the poverty, the chaos, and the vague awakening of sexual desire that make up a sad but innocent childhood. In his recent novel *She weishenme hui fei* (Why Can Snakes Fly), Su examines contemporary life. This allegorical story centers on a local bully hired to collect debts for a company. The tale begins with the mysterious appearances of a young woman and trainloads of snakes that invade the city. Human corpses mingled with snake skeletons are juxtaposed with the fate of the woman, whose dreams of becoming a star end in a life of prostitution.

One of the most creative voices in modern Chinese literature, Su Tong is noted for his profound analysis of human nature and for his memorable portraits of women. The lyricism, sensuality, and allegorical nature of his work are also frequently cited as evidence of his gift as a writer. *See also* ROOT-SEEKING LITERATURE.

SU WEIZHEN (1954–). Fiction writer. Born in **Taiwan**, Su Weizhen graduated from a school of film and theater run by the military in Taipei and received her Ph.D. from the Chinese University of Hong Kong. She currently teaches literature at the Chinese University of Culture in Taipei. Su spent more than 10 years in the army, which provided material for her early work. Her best stories, however, are not about soldiers but about young lovers, focusing especially on female desire and sexuality. Her stories, such as "Pei ta yiduan" (Accompany Him Awhile), "Hongyan yi lao" (Lost Youth), and "Shijian nüzi" (Women in the World), often portray **women** entangled in passionate romances that end tragically. Psychosis, insanity, disappearance, and death permeate her stories, enveloping them in darkness. Her female protagonists willingly and unregretfully throw themselves into the passions and perils of relationships with abandonment, and their single-mindedness accentuates the power and darkness of sexual love. Su's aesthetic of passion is most powerfully expressed in *Chenmo zhi dao* (An Island of Silence), which depicts the female mind and body as a proud and aloof island, silent on the surface but turbulent underneath. Although Su's subject is passion of the heart, her tone is invariably controlled and ironic. Her other main works include *Fengbi de daoyu* (An Island in Isolation), *Moshu shike* (Magic Moment), and *Likai Tongfang* (Leaving the Residential Compound for Military Families).

SU XUELIN (1897–1999). Fiction and prose writer. Educated in Beijing and France, Su Xuelin spent the last 47 years of her life in **Taiwan**. Su had a long list of publications, mostly scholarly work on classical and modern Chinese literature. Her creative writings include *Lütian* (The Green Sky), a collection of essays, *Ji xin* (The Thorn Heart), an autobiographical novel, and *Chantui ji* (Cicada's Exuviae), a collection of historical tales. Her critical essays on her contemporaries such as **Lu Xun**, **Yu Dafu**, **Lu Yin**, **Xu Zhimo**, **Bing Xin**, and many others offer unique perspectives into their lives and their works. *See also* MAY FOURTH MOVEMENT; WOMEN.

SUN GANLU (1959–). Fiction writer and essayist. Based in Shanghai, Sun Ganlu is arguably the most radical practitioner of China's **avant-garde** literature. His stories, especially those published in the late 1980s, including "Wo shi shaonian jiutanzi" (*I Am a Young Drunkard*), "Xinshi zhi han" (A Mail Carrier's Letter), and a novella *Qing nüren caimi* (Inviting Women to Solve a Puzzle), show strong indications of influence by Jorge Luis Borges. With no beginnings or endings other than seemingly free streams of impressions strung together, these texts defy fundamental rules that govern traditional storytelling. *Qing nüren caimi*, for example, contains a secondary text, "Tiaowang shi-jian xiaoshi" (Looking from a Distance at the Disappearance of Time), which moves in and out of the main text, serving as its narrative content and at the same time mocking and deconstructing its premises. There is also the absence of character development in the story, usually considered an essential feature of fictional art. Like pieces in a jigsaw puzzle, the characters are movable and can replace one another and even the roles of reader and narrator are interchangeable. *Qing nüren caimi* is metafiction, intended primarily to provide a self-exposition of the narrative construct. Such a narrative posture is a defiant reaction to the dominance of **socialist realism** in Maoist literature, which privileges content over form. However, having served its historical purpose, this kind of purely formalistic exercise is impossible to sustain. Indeed, many of the writers who began their careers as experimentalists quickly moved on to incorporate at least some elements of traditional storytelling into their later work; **Su Tong** and **Yu Hua** are two good examples. The transition has proved more arduous for Sun, however.

Sun's first novel, *Huxi* (Breathing), published in 1997, though still retaining some of the experimental features of his earlier work, has a traceable plot and a story to tell. His latest work, another novel, *Shaonü qunxiang* (Portraits of Maidens), part of which has been published, relies on a sharply tuned language to depict and ponder identifiable contemporary issues. Sun is a writer with an enormous talent for inventing a discourse that is deliberate, intricate, uniquely his own, characterized by its long-winded syntax and its epigrammatic phrases. A long-time resident of Shanghai, Sun was a farmer and a postal worker before becoming a member of the Shanghai Writers' Association. He currently lives in the city.

SUN LI (1913–2002). Novelist and essayist. The Baiyangdian Lake area where Sun Li spent much of his time before and after the **Sino-Japanese War** formed the backdrop for many of his stories. Sun joined the Communist army in 1942 and thus began his long association with the Communists. Many of his stories were written during the war, depicting the villagers of the Baiyangdian Lake area in their heroic struggle against the Japanese army. He later wrote about the land reform policy. When the People's Liberation Army took Tianjin in 1949, Sun went to the city with the troops, and in the years that followed he worked at the

Tianjin Daily. In the 1950s he published some of his major works, including *Fengyun jishi* (*Stormy Years*), a novel about Chinese peasants' resistance against the Japanese, and *Tie mu qianzhuan* (*Blacksmith and Carpenter*), a novella portraying the waxing and waning of the friendship between two men over a period of 20 years.

The general tendency of Sun's art is to lean heavily toward creating positive characters to inspire his readers and to offer them stories that glorify the spirit of the nation, which fit the templates of **socialist realism**. In the 1950s, Sun's aesthetic was influential among young writers and helped form the so-called Lotus Lake school, consisting of a group of writers based in northern China who emphasized the use of poetic language to extol the beauty of the land and the admirable qualities of the peasants.

– T –

TAI JINGNONG (1903–1990). Essayist, fiction writer, and calligrapher. While studying literature at Beijing University, Tai Jingnong published his first collection of short stories, *Di zhi zi* (Son of the Earth), about the tragic lives of the peasants, which placed him among the pioneers of the so-called rural writers (xiangtu zuojia), although he was by then a member of the intelligentsia. Friends with **Lu Xun**, with whom he shared a penchant for ironic detachment and for the use of imageries, Tai devoted a good portion of his professional career to assessing Lu's contribution to Chinese literature. In 1946, he accepted a position at National Taiwan University. When the Nationalist government retreated to the island in 1949, he found himself unable to return to the mainland and consequently spent the rest of his life in Taipei. His friendship with Lu Xun, whose works were banned in **Taiwan**, and his association with progressive forces in the 1930s and early 1940s compromised Tai's sense of security, resulting in his decision to shift his creative energy to calligraphy, which led to impressive successes and public recognition. In the final years of his life, Tai resumed his writing career, producing mostly essays that record his thoughts on history and friendships, among other matters.

TAIWAN. After the first **Sino-Japanese War** (1894–1895), Taiwan was ceded to Japan and remained a Japanese colony until 1945 when Japan was defeated at the end of World War II and ordered to surrender the island to the Republic of China controlled by Chiang Kai-shek's Kuomintang (KMT) party. The military occupation created tensions between the newcomers and the Taiwanese, culminating in the February 28 Incident of 1947, during which the KMT administration in Taipei brutally suppressed the Taiwanese demonstrators who were protesting against its enonomic policies, ushering in the era of White Terror. In 1949 after the KMT lost the **Civil War** against the Communists, Chiang Kai-shek and his government retreated to Taiwan and moved the capital from Nanjing to Taipei, while continuing to claim sovereignty over the whole of China and planning to take back the mainland from the Communists in three years. Martial law was declared, giving the KMT absolute power to rule the island. The international community continued to recognize Chiang's Republic of China (ROC) as the legitimate representative of China until 1971 when the ROC lost its seat in the United Nations to the People's Republic of China (PRC). When Chiang died in 1975, his son Chiang Ching-kuo assumed the presidency. Under his leadership, Taiwan experienced a great economic boom, rising to become one of the so-called little Asian tigers, and political liberalization that resulted in the lifting of martial law in 1987.

The younger Chiang's handpicked vice president and successor Lee Teng-hui, whose proindependence position later caused his expulsion from the KMT, was the first democratically elected president of Taiwan. Under Lee, Taiwan underwent greater democratization and localization. Laws and practices with a bias against the Taiwanese were changed and local culture, history, and language were promoted to cultivate a Taiwanese, rather than a Chinese, identity. In 2000, Chen Shui-bian, of the Democratic Progressive Party (DPP), was elected president, the first president outside the KMT. At present, Taiwan remains extremely polarized, with the pan-green coalition of parties pushing for official Taiwan independence and the pan-blue coalition of parties favoring status quo or eventual reunification of China.

The first generation of modern Taiwanese literature emerged during the Japanese occupation and conveyed a sense of national pride in addition to anti-Japanese sentiments. Many of the works were influenced by the **May Fourth Movement** from the mainland. When the KMT lost the Civil War, a large number of intellectuals and writers retreated to the island with the Nationalist government, pumping fresh blood into the literary vein of the island. Mirroring the political divide that gripped the island, Taiwanese literature witnessed a heated debate between the **nativists** and the **modernists**, which raged for nearly two decades from the mid-1960s to the end of the 1970s. While the modernists were largely pro-KMT urbanites and intellectual elites from the mainland with Westernized literary sensibilities, the nativists represented the discontented local population and rural consciousness. These two strands competed for supremacy in the literary development of Taiwan and each delivered some remarkable performances. *See also* BAI XIANYONG; CHEN RUOXI; CHEN YINGZHEN; FEI MA; HU LANCHENG; HUANG CHUNMING; HUANG FAN; HUANG JINSHU; JI XIAN; LAI HE; LAI SHENGCHUAN; LI ANG; LI YONGPING; LIAO HUIYING; LIN HAIYIN; LIN YAODE; LUO FU; LUO YIJUN; MODERN POETRY MOVEMENT IN TAIWAN; NIE HUALING; OUYANG ZI; PING LU; QIDENG SHENG; QIONG YAO; QIU MIAOJIN; SAN MAO; SHI SHUQING; SU WEIZHEN; SU XUELIN; WANG WENXING; WANG ZHENHE; XI MURONG; XIAO LIHONG; XIE BINGYING; YA XIAN; YANG KUI; YANG MU; YU GUANGZHONG; YU LIHUA; YUAN QIONGQIONG; ZHANG DACHUN; ZHANG GUIXING; ZHANG XIAOFENG; ZHANG XIGUO; ZHENG CHOUYU; ZHONG LIHE; ZHONG ZHAOZHEN; ZHU TIANWEN; ZHU TIANXIN; ZHU XINING.

TANG REN, PEN NAME OF YAN QINGSHU (1919–1980). Novelist. Born in Jiangsu, Tang Ren was a journalist during and after the **Sino-Japanese War**. He moved to **Hong Kong** in 1950 and continued to work for newspapers. Tang Ren was a prolific writer, and during the 30 years of his career he published more than 50 books and many essays and articles in newspapers and journals. His best-known work is a historical novel based on the life of Chiang Kai-shek. His *Jinling chunmeng* (Spring Dream at Nanjing) and its sequel *Caoshan canmeng* (The Unfinished Dream at the Grass Mountain) remain two of the most popular books in modern Chinese literature. Other books of his, similar in theme and style, include *Jiang houzhu milu* (Secret Records of the Ex-Emperor Chiang) and *Beiyang junfa yanyi* (The Historical Romance of the Northern Warlords). His novels about life in the mainland before 1949 include *Funiushan enchou ji* (Love and Hate at the Crouching Cow Mountain). He also wrote about **Taiwan** in two novels, *Zai hai de nabian* (On the Other Side of the Sea) and *Huoshao dao* (Fire Island). Tang Ren depicts the lives of former officials of the Nationalist government who choose to stay in Hong Kong in *Ren zha* (Human Dregs) and *Xianggang wuyan xia* (Under the Hong Kong Eaves). Among his novels about Hong Kong society are *Xianggang daheng* (A Hong Kong Tycoon) and *Wo shi yike yaoqianshu* (I Am a Money Tree). His stories are set against important historical and political backgrounds, full of drama and legends. Tang has also written several screenplays, some of which have been made into movies.

TASHI DAWA (1959–). Fiction writer. Born in Batang, a Tibetan region in Sichuan Province, to a Tibetan father and a Chinese mother, Tashi Dawa grew up in Chongqing and had a typical Chinese education. He published his first story in 1978 and has since made **Tibet** the central focus of his work. He currently lives in Lhasa and is the vice president of the Tibetan Writers' Association. He is one of the most recognized names among Tibetan writers in China, noted for his magic realist stories.

As the **root-seeking** movement spread over Chinese art and literary circles during the 1980s, Tibet became a mecca for artists and writers seeking inspiration, and Tashi joined the pilgrimage. Unlike **Ma Yuan**, a Chinese writer famous for his Tibetan stories who used Tibet as a background for his innovative fiction, Tashi searched for the religious and mystic traditions of Tibetan culture and recreated them in his tales. In many of the stories collected in *Xizang: Ji zai pishengkou shang de hun (Tibet: A Soul Knotted on a Leather)* and *Xizang, yinmi de suiyue* (Tibet: The Hidden Years) realistic narrative and fantasy are seamlessly intertwined, a style he likened to Tibetan storytelling traditions influenced by Buddhism in which time and action are nothing but an illusion. In two of his stories, he borrows from Tibetan cultural practice by building the plots on the number 108, alluding to the number of Tibetan prayer beads: *Xizang: Ji zai pisheng shang de hun* tells stories that happen in 108 days and *Xizang: yinmi de suiyue*, a novella, chronicles events that take place in Tibet from 1877 to 1985, 108 years in total. Tashi's later works are more concerned about contemporary Tibetan life. *Yemao zouguo manman suiyue* (A Wild Cats' Long Journey) presents a Tibet that is on the march to modernity. No longer mysterious, it is a world full of incongruities and absurdities brought about by modernization and economic reforms. The urban Tibetan youths, descendants of former serfs and serf owners, have joined the force of capitalist globalization, leaving behind their traditional way of life. *Saodong de Xiangbala* (Turbulent Shambala), a more complex narrative and arguably his best work, deals with confrontations, negotiations, and compromises between two cultural paradigms in Tibetan society, represented by two types of characters: the ones who operate within the bounds of a realistic world and the ones with supernatural powers who transcend time and space. The second group acts as a mediator in the lives of the first group, leading them to a spiritual but illusive realm. In the act of embracing or rejecting the other, they reveal a Tibetan society caught in a tug-of-war between the old and the new, the local and the global. *See also* AVANT-GARDE.

TIAN HAN (1898–1968). Playwright, poet, and filmmaker. A pioneer of the modern Chinese play, Tian Han made significant contributions to modern Chinese theater and the impact he left on Chinese cultural life is well documented. The numerous plays and films he wrote and directed should guarantee him a prominent position in the history of modern Chinese theater, not to mention the number of art organizations and societies he cofounded. Tian came from a poor family in Changsha, Hunan Province. While studying in Tokyo, he helped found the **Creation Society** with **Guo Moruo** and others. After he returned to China in 1924, Tian, with the help of his wife, founded the literary journal *Nan guo banyue kan* (South China Biweekly). Later with Xu Beihong, a painter, and **Ouyang Yuqian**, a playwright and actor, he founded Nan guo she (South China Society), which energized and guided the movement to modernize the Chinese theater. A founding member of the **Left-wing Society of Chinese Writers** and the Left-wing Association of Chinese Playwrights, Tian was also a political activist. During the **Sino-Japanese War**, he and his troupe toured cities in the interior to boost national morale, performing *Lugou qiao* (The Marco Polo Bridge), a play he wrote and directed, and other patriotic plays. After the Communist victory in 1949, Tian was appointed director of arts in the Ministry of Culture, a position he held until the **Cultural Revolution** abruptly and brutally ended his life.

Tian was a prolific writer, having created some 100 works, including *Kafei dian zhi yi ye* (One Night at the Café), written in 1920 while he was studying in Japan, *Ming you zhi si* (The Death of a Famous Actor), based on the real life of a Peking opera actor, and *Suzhou ye hua* (*One Evening in Suzhou*). Several of Tian's early plays feature artists who make the pursuit of artistic perfection the ultimate goal in life. Liu Zhensheng in *Ming you zhi si* refuses to compromise his art in a society full of people willing to sell their souls in exchange for wealth and influence; the poet in *Gu tan de shengyin* (The Sound of an Old Pond) jumps into an ancient pond in despair because its malevolent spirit has seduced the dancing girl he saved from materialist corruption; Bai Wei in *Hu shang de beiju* (*A West Lake Tragedy*) commits suicide after she finishes reading the tragic story written by her former lover. Through these plays, Tian tells his audience that true art is worth dying for, as, in the words of his character, "life is short but art is timeless." As his involvement in progressive literature deepened, Tian began to produce plays that dealt less with abstract concepts but more with real sociopolitical issues. *Suzhou ye hua*, *Jiang cun xiao jing* (A Vignette of a Village by the River), *Nian ye fan* (New Year's Eve Dinner), and other critical realist plays seek to locate the roots of poverty and broken families in the sociopolitical system. Further signs of his political commitment are seen in his "revolutionary" plays such as *Gu Zhenghong zhi si* (The Death of Gu Zhenghong), *Yijiusan'er nian de yueguang qu* (The Moonlight Sonata of 1932), *Mei yu* (The Rainy Season), *Wufan zhi qian* (Before Lunch), and *Baofeng yu zhong de qi ge nüxing* (Seven Women in a Thunderstorm), all focusing on the working class and its organized uprisings against exploitation and oppression. Tian also worked with historical materials, turning the lives of memorable characters into plays such as *Guan Hanqin* (Playwright Guan Hanqin) and *Wencheng gongzhu* (Princess Wencheng).

Modeled after Western plays such as those by William Shakespeare, Henrik Ibsen, and George Bernard Shaw, the modern plays by Tian and his colleagues aspire to reflect real life and address contemporary issues, with actors speaking a language understood by the average person on the streets, in order to inspire the audience into action. The result is a mode that combines realism with romantic zest, a style that dominated Chinese plays and, to a lesser extent, movies until the 1980s and is still evident in Chinese theater today. *See also* MAY FOURTH MOVEMENT; SOCIALIST REALISM; SPOKEN DRAMA.

TIAN'ANMEN PRODEMOCRACY MOVEMENT (1989). Triggered by the death of Hu Yaobang, a liberal-minded Communist Party leader who had been forced to resign in January of 1988 as the secretary of the Chinese Communist Party, the protest movement started with Beijing college students and intellectuals who were dissatisfied with the pace of the reforms initiated by Deng Xiaoping in the late 1970s. The movement quickly gained the support of urban industrial workers angry about inflation and government corruption. In large numbers, the students gathered in Tian'anmen Square in the center of Beijing, demanding that the party revise its judgment on Hu and political, not just economic, reforms be instituted to bring democracy to China. An editorial in the *Renmin ribao* (People's Daily), the official newspaper of the government, which accused the protesters of "plotting civil unrest" and causing "turmoil," sent the students into a hunger strike to demand that the newspaper retract its statement and that a dialogue between their representatives and the party leaders be held to address their concerns.

There were different opinions within the leadership as to how to deal with these demands. The liberal faction, represented by party secretary Zhao Ziyang, who made an appearance in the square to urge students to stop their hunger strike, preferred dialogue while the hardliners, represented by Premier Li Peng, pushed for military crackdown. Deng Xiaoping, the paramount leader, and other party elders who feared that a lenient approach would encourage "bourgeois liberalism," which would in turn challenge the Communist Party's stranglehold on power, sided with the hardliners. Tanks rolled onto the square and soldiers fired at the protesters. The bloody crackdown was followed by a political cleanup throughout the country. The violent suppression of the prodemocracy movement outraged the international community and the Chinese government found itself the target of widespread condemnation. The leaders of the protest movement were either put in jail or forced to flee to the West. Many writers who expressed sympathy for the protesters or were protesters themselves went into exile, including most of the **Misty poets**. Except for a few who eventually returned to China to live, most of these writers have chosen to stay in the West but continue to write in Chinese. The experience of exile has no doubt enriched their understanding of life and literature, and furthermore, their presence in the West has helped broaden the appeal of Chinese literature in the West. *See also* BEI DAO; GU CHENG; YANG LIAN; DUO DUO; GAO XINGJIAN; MA JIAN; YAN LI; YO YO; ZHENG YI.

TIBET. As part of the People's Republic of China, Tibet is situated in the western part of the country and is known as the "roof of the world," a nickname that comes from the majestic Himalayan mountains and the high altitude of the region. The Chinese word *Zang* (Tibet/Tibetan) generally refers to two entities: the first is the Tibetan Autonomous Region, which covers what is historically known as U-Zang or central Tibet; the second is U-Zang plus Amdo and Kham in Qinghai, Gansu, Sichuan, and Yunnan provinces, where ethnic Tibetans also live. The Tibetan cultural influence stretches also to Sikkim and Ladkh in present-day India as well as Bhutan and Nepal. What constitutes Tibet is a hotly debated issue between the Chinese government and the Tibetan government in exile, which was set up in Dharamsala, India, in 1959, when the 14th Dalai Lama and his followers fled Tibet after a failed revolt against the Chinese Communists. To Tibetan exiles, Tibet encompasses all Tibetan cultural spheres, excluding the communities in Bhutan, India, and Nepal; to the Chinese government, Tibet means the Tibetan Autonomous Region, while the Tibetan communities in Gansu, Qinghai, Sichuan, and Yunnan are given autonomous status under the jurisdiction of the named provinces.

Tibet has a long and rich history. Songtsan Gampo (617–650) was the first Tibetan leader to unite the different warring tribes into one of the most powerful kingdoms in Asia and established a centralized government in Lhasa. During his reign, Buddhism took root in Tibet and replaced the indigenous religion, the Bön. In the reign of Lang Dharma (815–843), the Bön made a brief and bloody comeback, resulting in widespread persecutions of Buddhists. In 846, when Lang Dharma was assassinated, the Tibetan kingdom disintegrated into an assortment of principalities headed by various nobilities of the old kingdom. For the next four centuries Tibet remained divided, until the 13th century when the Mongol empire extended its influence and control to Tibet.

During the centuries of political instability in Tibet, Buddhism, however, had the opportunity to recover and grow. Various sects emerged, Nyingma (the ancient sect), Kagyu (the oral sect), and most important, Sakya (the grey earth sect), whose fifth-generation master, Phagpa (1235–1280), became the spiritual teacher of Kublai Khan (1215–1294), the ruler of the Mongol Yuan dynasty (1279–1368). With the support and protection of Kublai Khan, Phagpa and Sakya rose to the top of political power in all of Tibet. Phagpa is also credited with having invented the Mongolian written language. The Ming (1368–1644), which succeeded the Yuan, generally administered Tibet in a similar fashion as the Mongols, adopting a policy that emphasized a respect for its religion and a reliance on conferring honorary titles and other appeasement measures to keep Tibet nominally within the empire.

In the Qing dynasty (1644–1911), the Manchu rulers tightened their grip on Tibet through several measures that included incorporating Amdo and eastern Kham into neighboring Chinese provinces, installing a resident commissioner to Lhasa, and supporting Guluk (the way of virtue or the yellow hat sect) in the feud among various Tibetan Buddhist sects, requiring that the reincarnations of its major lamas, including the Dalai Lama and the Panchen Lama, be approved by the central government in Beijing, a practice that began in the reign of Qianlong Emperor (1711–1799). Despite these interventionist measures, the Manchus by and large allowed Tibet to remain an autonomous entity. In the 19th and early 20th centuries, Tibet was unwittingly dragged into the "Great Game," a power struggle among Great Britain, Russia, and China. In 1904, a British army led by Colonel Francis Younghusband invaded Lhasa with the pretext that Russia was increasing its influence in Tibet. The British succeeded in annexing to British India 90,000 square kilometers of traditional Tibetan territory in southern Tibet, which is in the present-day Indian state of Arunachal Pradesh, while recognizing Chinese suzerainty over Tibet.

The Guluk school, with its emphasis on the Vinaya and scholarly pursuits, was funded by Tsongkhapa (1357–1419), whose legacy continues into the modern age. From the time when Qianlong decreed the supremacy of the Guluk sect to the Chinese Communist takeover in the 1950s, Tibet had a system of theocracy in which all political and economic power was concentrated in the hands of the clergy and the aristocracy it supported. In the late 1950s, the Chinese government instituted socialism and Tibet was fully brought under the centralized rule of Beijing, forcing the 14th Dalai Lama and his followers to flee in 1959 to India, where they set up the Tibetan exile government in Dharamsala. The political standoff between the Chinese government and the Tibetan exile government is yet to be resolved.

While there was a great deal of interest in Tibet in the West, shown in the many travelogues, memoirs, and fictional accounts written by missionaries, adventurists, scientists, military officers, and spies disguised as pilgrims or businessmen, Tibet, curiously, did not register in the literary imagination of the Chinese, except for a handful of cases. All that changed in the early 1980s, when Beijing started recruiting college graduates to work in Tibet as government officials and professionals. The move attracted people with wanderlust from Chinese cities, looking for exotic life and adventure. Tibet became the ultimate destination for aspiring writers and artists who would later depict their experience in literature and paintings. Following this wave, Tibetan writers who had received a Chinese education began to write about their own culture in the Chinese language, which eventually led to the creation of a new narrative literature written in Tibetan. Traditionally, Tibetan literature consists of Buddhist tales translated from Sanskrit texts as well as a rich body of oral legends and chronicles, the most famous of which is the *Tale of Gesar*, said to be the longest epic in the world. The new Tibetan literature, which is still in its infancy, attempts to reflect Tibetan life in a realistic manner while taking inspiration from its rich heritage of oral and religious literature.

Influenced by magic realism of Latin America, Chinese fiction from Tibet explores the mysteries of its culture in a multitude of styles. **Ma Yuan**, an **avant-garde** writer, treats Tibet as a background against which to unfold his experiments in storytelling; **Tashi Dawa** mixes history with legends; **Ah Lai** deals with some of the major events in modern history that affected Tibetans living in western Sichuan; **Fan Wen** traces the spiritual and religious paths of eastern Tibet; **Ma Lihua** chronicles Tibet's social and economic changes. Chinese literature from Tibet unfolds a brilliant canvas, rich with colors and textures, occupying a major spot in the literary imagination of contemporary China. *See also* BI SHUMIN; MA JIAN; METSO; SEBO; WOESER; YA GELING; YANG LIAN; YANG ZHIJUN; YANGDON.

TIE NING (1957–). Novelist. Tie Ning grew up in the turbulent years of the **Cultural Revolution** and worked for four years among peasants in a village. In her early writing career, Tie focused on the northern countryside with which she is intimately familiar. "Oh, Xiang Xue" (*Ah, Fragrant Snow*), a sentimental tale published in 1982, made her a national name. This short story describes the coming of modernity to the Chinese countryside during the post-Mao era, as represented by the arrival of a train at a remote village. While selling fruits and eggs to passengers when the train stops at her village, Xiang Xue, along with other young girls, gets a glimpse of what the outside world looks like. Encouraged by **Sun Li**, a veteran writer also based in Hebei who liked the lyricism and the optimistic tone of the story, Tie published in the following year "Meiyou niukou de hong chenshan" (A Red Shirt without Buttons), one of her best-known works. Once again, with a young girl as her protagonist, the author portrays an independent youth who, after some mental anguish, gives up being a model student to wear a red shirt among the uniformity of blues and greys. The story captures the spirit of the new era, when nonconformist behavior was beginning to emerge.

Three other works published in the 1980s marked the beginning of Tie's long engagement with the subject of feminine subjectivity. "Maijie Duo" (*Haystacks*) concentrates on the fate of **women** in a village and the tragedy of their failed marriages. "Mianhua duo" (Cotton Stacks), another of her stories about rural women, centers on three female characters in the 1930s whose tragic fate is tied to the traditional world defined by male agendas. *Meigui men* (Gate of Roses), her first full-length novel, pays attention to female sexuality while depicting the dark side of human relationships. Most characters in these works survive in a male-centered society in which a "good" woman fulfils her maternal role while a "bad" one lets her sexuality get out of control. Tie is adept at exploring the restricted world inhabited by tradition-bound rural women, the small pleasures they extract from monotonous everyday life, and the enormous sacrifices they make for their families and communities.

Tie's focus on women and their role in society continued into the next two decades. *Yongyuan you duoyuan* (How Long Is Forever), published in 1999, shifts the spotlight onto a woman born and bred in the city who finds her traditional virtues, such as honesty and kindness, unsuited to the changing times of commercialism. *Da yu nü* (A Woman of Experience), published in the following year, examines the personal life of a middle-aged woman who has been abandoned by her film star husband. In both novels, the protagonists are treated as victims not just of men but also of other women, an indication that the author believes that the age of innocence, of mutual trust that she wrote about at the beginning of her career, is gone forever.

Tie's best work, *Ben Hua* (Native Cotton), is set in the chaotic early Republican period. The story centers on a family in a village where the main crop is *ben hua*, a low-yielding but resilient local cotton. The patriarch is a peasant boy whose meteoric rise to the powerful position of a high-ranking military officer is a local legend. Because of its ties to the outside world, the village is at the crossroad of tradition and modernity. While Christian missionaries introduce new water pumps to the villagers, girls from poor families continue the age-old custom of sleeping with strangers in exchange for cotton during harvest season. The peaceful lifestyle is disrupted by the entry of the superior cotton introduced from Japan, which is closely followed by the Japanese Imperial Army's invasion of China. The novel ends with the family losing two of its members to Japanese brutality.

Tie was president of the Hebei Writers' Association and in 2006 was elected president of the Chinese Writers' Association, the first woman to hold that position. See also SINO-JAPANESE WAR.

– W –

WANG ANYI (1954–). Novelist. Daughter of **Ru Zhijuan**, also a writer, Wang Anyi grew up in Shanghai. In 1970, after graduating from middle school, she went to the countryside of Jiangsu to be reeducated by the peasants. Two years later, she joined a performance troupe in the industrial city of Xuzhou. By the time she returned to Shanghai to work as an editor of a children's magazine, she already had several stories to her name. One of the most diverse and influential writers in contemporary China, Wang has continued to reinvent herself, evolving from a sentimental storyteller to an experimental writer and astute commentator on social mores. It is hard to categorize her work in one or another representational mode. Her love stories, best represented by *Xiaocheng zhi lian* (*Love in a Small Town*), subscribe to the realist mode. *Xiao baozhuan* (*Baotown*), on the other hand, mixes legends with reality to create a sense of permanence that transcends time and space, giving the story an allegorical dimension. Likewise, *Fuxi yu muxi de shenhua* (Patrilinial and Matrilineal Myths) is told with a similar ironic detachment, despite its professed autobiographical content. The most imaginative of Wang's writings is *Jishi yu xugou* (The Real and the Fictitious), in which the author traces her family history by mixing historical record with her own imagination. In the process of locating her maternal ancestry, Wang examines her own sense of place in the metropolis of Shanghai. As metafiction, the work is not only a highly fictionalized account of clan history but also a self-conscious commentary on the act of writing, which is equated to mythmaking.

In between the popular and the experimental narrative modes lies Wang's most ambitious project: reinventing Shanghai, where she grew up and still resides. In *Changheng ge* (*The Song of Everlasting Sorrow: A Novel of Shanghai*), *Meitou* (Meitou), *Fuping* (Fuping), *Tao zhi yaoyao* (The Dazzling Peach Blossoms), and other works,

Shanghai becomes a character with a soul of its own, both shaping and shaped by the lives its residents lead. Despite its size, the Shanghai in Wang's works is surprisingly intimate, approachable, a city characterized by its bourgeois taste and material culture as seen in its architecture, mannerisms, and etiquettes. Her mundane Shanghai is comforting and alluring despite the social and political changes to its appearance, like the protagonist of *Changhen ge,* whose downward spiraling life spans several decades of modern Chinese history, from when she was a glamorous winner of a beauty pageant in the 1940s to her ordinary life in the 1980s. Critics see some similarities between Wang and **Zhang Ailing**, who wrote about Shanghai in the 1940s. Both are captivated by the city and its social manners. They represent the so-called Shanghai school of writing, whose characteristics include detailed descriptions of daily life, a focus on the middle class, a fascination with urban existence, and an obsession with the pragmatic side of living.

With her most recent novel, *Qimeng shidai* (The Era of Enlightenment), Wang revisits her early days as an educated youth in the countryside by re-creating the experience of several urban youths in the heyday of the **Cultural Revolution**. Hailed as a record of a "spiritual odyssey" of a generation of Chinese, the novel captures the idealism and the confusion associated with the 1960s. Laden with discursive commentaries and observations, it highlights the author's perspective on history and the individuals trapped in it. *See also* ROOT-SEEKING LITERATURE; WOMEN.

WANG DINGJUN (1927–). Prose writer. One of the most influential and prolific prose writers in contemporary Chinese literature, Wang Dingjun was born in Shandong and spent his early youth in the Nationalist army, which he joined during the **Sino-Japanese War**. At the end of the **Civil War**, he followed the government to **Taiwan** and worked as a writer and editor for radio and newspapers. He has been living in the New York City area since emigrating to the United States in the 1970s. Wang's creative oeuvre consists of mostly essays. For an essayist, the best source of inspiration is life experience of which Wang has had an abundant amount. He has gone through earthshaking events in modern Chinese history, fought two wars, and having been uprooted several times in his life, endured long separations from his family, friends, and cultural environment. In addition to these painful but valuable life-changing experiences, he possesses a curious mind that enjoys prob-ing into history, society, and human behavior.

Many of his essays express a strong sense of nostalgia. Ever since he left his home in Shandong more than half a century ago, Wang has never returned to it in person but has never stopped writing about it. To Wang, home is a "piece of art" that he has "imagined, carved, polished and em-bellished" during more than half of his lifetime. It is his spiritual anchor. The concept of home in his writing is not just the village in Shandong but has extended to encompass China with its rich history and culture, including its beauty and its sufferings. *Jiaoyin* (*Footprints*), *Shan li shan wai* (Inside and Outside the Mountains), *Zuo xin fang de xuanwo* (Swirls of the Left Atrium of the Heart), *Hai shui tian ya Zhongguoren* (The Ocean, the Edge of the Sky, and the Chinese) are all expressions of his love for his home and his home country. Another prominent theme of his writings is humanity. He enjoys "people watching." Every human being, according to Wang, is a slide of "scenery" that he never tires of observing and describing. From these observations, Wang de-rives lessons about society, human nature, and the psyche of a nation. Works such as *Zhongnian* (Middle Age), *Qingren yan* (The Eyes of a Lover), *Sui liuli* (Broken Colored Glaze), *Women xiandai ren* (We the Modern People), and *Rensheng* (Life) belong to this category. Taiwan also features prominently in his writings in which he bears witness to the island's march to modernization and its impact on the environment and the people.

Wang has worked with all genres of prose writing, including the lyri-cal essay, narrative essay, and satirical essay. In his essays, he employs the techniques commonly used in poetry, fiction, and drama. His lan-guage is colloquial and succinct. In addition to a long list of publications of prose work, Wang has also written short stories collected in *Danshen wendu* (Body Heat of Unmarried Men) and *Toushi* (X Ray).

WANG HAILING (1952–). Novelist. Born in Shandong, Wang Hailing joined the military at the age of 16 and spent 14 years stationed on a tiny island. To help pass the time, she took up writing. Her breakthrough came in the 1990s with the family drama *Qian shou* (Holding Your Hands), which was made into a television series, earning Wang national fame. She followed it with two more best sellers, *Zhongguo shi lihun* (Divorce: Chinese Style), a novel about marital problems encountered by three couples, which was also turned into a popular television series, and *Xin jiehun shidai* (The Era of New Marriage), which centers on the members of an intellectual family and their unconventional romantic relationships, such as the widowed father with a young, uneducated maid from the countryside and the son with an older woman. Wang writes in a realist style and deals with love and conflict in contemporary Chinese families. With a unique understanding of interpersonal and familial relationships in Chinese society, she has become a popular writer widely considered "the number one interpreter of Chinese marriage." *See also* WOMEN.

WANG JIAXIN (1957–). Poet. Born in Hubei, Wang Jiaxin graduated from the Chinese Department of Wuhan University. From 1985 to 1990, he edited *Shi kan* (Poetry), the main poetry journal in China. After spending two years in England in the early 1990s, Wang returned to China to teach literary theory and comparative literature at Beijing Educational College. A representative of the so-called academic poets mostly based in Beijing, Wang has been writing poetry since the 1980s, when the influence of Misty poetry was at its height. For this reason, he is considered, by some literary critics, one of the Misty poets. However, Wang's reputation as a poet was not widely recognized until his sojourn in and return from Europe. One of the recurring subjects in his poetry written during this period is the émigré experience. In a series of poems paying homage to, or in dialogue with, poets such as Ezra Pound, William Butler Yeats, Joseph Brodsky, Boris Pasternak, Czeslaw Miłosz, and others, Wang identifies with them in feelings of alienation and rootlessnesss. Chinese poets who have influenced his work include Feng Zhi, also a scholar-poet of an older generation. See also GENERATION III POETS.

WANG JINGZHI (1902–1996). Poet and a member of the Lakeside Poetry Society. Born in Jixi, Anhui Province, Wang attended a trade school before enrolling in the Number One Hangzhou Teachers' College. As the **May Fourth Movement** unfolded, Wang was attracted by its call for personal emancipation and freedom. His best-known poem, "Hui zhi feng" (Hui's Wind), which is also the title of his first collection of poetry, is a self-confessing poem about his first love. Never before had anyone been so honest and unashamed about expressing sexual desire. This defiant act against established Confucian decorum reverberated in Chinese society. As **Zhu Ziqing** later described it, he "threw an extremely powerful bomb into the middle of old social morality." At the age of 20, Wang became an influential poet, mentored by prominent figures such as **Lu Xun,** who helped him revise his work, **Hu Shi,** who wrote the preface for his first collection of poetry, and **Zhou Zuoren,** who graced the book with calligraphy. When Wang was attacked by conservative moralists, these flag bearers of the May Fourth **New Culture Movement** rose in his defense. Lu Xun called Wang's poems "sounds of nature." After the success of *Hui zhi feng*, Wang published *Jimo de guo* (The Lonely Country), another collection of love poems, and three fictional works: *Yesu de fenfu* (Advice of Jesus), *Fu yu nü* (Father and Daughter), and *Cuiying ji qifu de gushi* (The Story of Cuiying and Her Husband), all written in 1926. Swept up in the wave of revolution of the 1920s, Wang began work in the propaganda department of the Northern Expedition Army, but soon left. Unlike the other Lakeside poets, he lacked an enthusiasm for politics. He later taught literature at various schools and universities.

After the founding of the People's Republic of China, Wang worked as an editor for the Classics Department of the Beijing People's Press and became a member of the Chinese Writers' Association on the payroll of the state. However, the new society required poetry for the masses, while Wang's forte was expressions of personal passion and emotions. He managed to produce a meager pamphlet of 21 poems. On the eve of the **Cultural Revolution,** Wang returned to Hangzhou where he lived an anonymous life until the end of the 1970s. In 1982, when the Lakeside Poetry Society celebrated its 50th anniversary, Wang was elected chairman of the newly revived organization. *Liu mei yuan* (Encounters with Six Beauties), poems about his relationships with six women in his youthful days, was published four months before his death. To the very end of his life, Wang believed that the central subject of poetry should be love and passion.

WANG LUYAN, A.K.A. LU YAN (1902–1944). Fiction writer. One of the early **nativist** writers in modern Chinese literature, Wang Luyan was born in a village in eastern Zhejiang and left home for Shanghai at the age of 15 to work as a shop apprentice. Three years later, he joined a work-study group in Beijing where he audited classes at Beijing University and taught himself Esperanto while trying to make a living by selling small wares and washing clothes. Attracted to the leftist literary doctrines in the 1930s, Wang became a member of the **Left-wing Association of Chinese Writers.**

Wang began his career by writing romantic tales. Later, as he became increasingly captivated by Marxist ideas, he adopted some of the leftist tendencies in his works. The novel *Ye huo* (Wildfire), renamed *Fennu de xiangcun* (The Enraged Countryside), foregrounds class struggle in line with the Communist Party's interpretation of social hierarchy. While his works written during this phase have more or less gone out of fashion, his stories about his hometown, all written in the late 1920s and early 1930s, have secured him a place in the history of modern Chinese literature.

Inspired by the memories of his childhood, these stories paint a vivid picture of rural Zhejiang with realistic details describing customs and habits of village life and capturing the beauty and complexity of the countryside. The most prominent characters in these stories are small merchants who struggle to stay solvent as industrial forces and local powers nibble away at their traditional way of life. "Huangjin" (Gold) is about such a middle-class character whose respected status in his village is compromised when he does not receive money his son is supposed to have wired to him. Once the money does not materialize, he becomes the laughingstock of his fellow villagers. Clearly, in this society, a man is judged by the amount of wealth he possesses. "Qiao shang" (*On the Bridge*) tells the story of a small businessman, like Lao Tongbao in Mao Dun's "Silkworm," driven to bankruptcy by big companies with foreign machines and investments. Several of Wang's hometown stories describe the customs of the seaside communities of eastern Zhejiang. "Juying de chujia" (Juying's Wedding) portrays the local tradition of marrying a woman to a dead man; "Cha lu" (Fork in a Road) tells about a fight between two villages as they carry the deity Guandi in a procession to purge evil spirits. "Shu ya" (The Teeth of a Mouse) describes the local custom of "mice giving away daughters for marriage" to drive rodents to the neighbor's house. These stories invoke a sense of nostalgia for a bygone world with all its attractions and imperfections.

In addition to these hometown stories for which he is best remembered, Wang also wrote essays and translated literature written originally in Esperanto. During the **Sino-Japanese War**, Wang drifted from place to place and finally died in Guilin from tuberculosis.

WANG MENG (1934–). Fiction writer. In the early 1950s, Wang Meng, a young, idealistic Communist, wrote "Zuzhibu laide nianqing ren" (A Young Man from the Organization Department), the story that got him into trouble in 1957 during the Anti-Rightist Campaign. He was exiled to Xinjiang in 1963 and lived there for more than 15 years before being allowed to return to Beijing in 1978. Since then, he has turned out more than 20 volumes of works, with varying degrees of critical success. He has held many official positions in the government, including minister of culture.

Before his exile, Wang had only a handful of short stories to his name. A novel, *Qingchun wansui* (Long Live Youth), begun in 1953, did not come out until 1979; its publication delayed, apparently, by its author's political troubles. His best works were completed after 1978. In many ways, Wang has been a trendsetter. He is widely credited with leading the way in the late 1970s and early 1980s in appropriating Western modernist techniques such as stream of consciousness and the expression of the absurd, and his Xinjiang stories are believed to have helped open up the field of **root-seeking literature**.

One of his experimental stories is "Hudie" (*The Butterfly*), in which Wang examines social, political, and personal transformation by focusing on how his characters lose and regain their self-identity. The bulk of the narrative is sustained by the internal musings of the protagonist, who returns to Beijing after a long political exile in a remote mountain village. While the length of time covered by the novel is only two days, the character's mental activities, set off by external events, cover a span of 30 years of his life. *Huodong bian renxing* (Movement Shapes Human Figures) is arguably Wang's best work. Unlike his many experimental stories, the novel is written in the mode of psychological realism. Through the tragic saga of four generations of the Ni family, Wang ponders issues such as the meaning of revolution and history, personal destiny, the clash of civilizations, and tradition as opposed to modernity.

Wang's series of four novels, *Lian'ai de jijie* (The Season of Love), *Shi lian de jijie* (The Season of Lost Love), *Chouchu de jijie* (The Season of Hesitation), and *Kuanghuan de jijie* (The Season of Revelry), took him less than a decade to complete. They chronicle the journey of a Chinese intellectual from the founding of the People's Republic to the end of the **Cultural Revolution**, representing the author's view on the relationship of the intellectual to the Communist revolution. Essentially, these novels are semiautobiographical in nature, in that they mirror the author's own trajectory from an ardent supporter of the revolution in the early days of the People's Republic to a victim of its political campaigns. They were conceived, in the words of the author, as the "spiritual history of [his] generation." The author examines the price one has to pay for decisions made at various crucial junctures in history. Whether one chooses to cooperate with those in power or remain independent ultimately determines the state of one's soul. *Qing hu* (The Green Fox), a novel portraying the meteoric rise of a middle-aged woman writer and her failed quest for love in the midst of a male-centered literary circle, is a tragic story told in a playful, satirical language. In this novel, Wang intensifies the facetious narrative voice used in some of his short stories. The dominant syntax, built by repetition and parallelism, results in a hyperbolic style and heightens the cynical tone. In writing about the absurd behaviors of his fellow writers, Wang turns the Chinese literary circle into a ludicrous circus.

WANG PU (1950–). Fiction and prose writer. Born in **Hong Kong**, Wang Pu went with her parents to the mainland at the age of one. She received her Ph.D. in literature from China Eastern Normal University in Shanghai. In 1989, she moved back to Hong Kong and worked as a newspaper editor and a college professor. She currently lives in Shenzhen.

Wang's writing career began in the early 1980s when her stories appeared in literary journals in Changsha, where she lived. Her first collection of short stories, *Nüren de gushi* (Women's Stories), was published in 1993 after she had moved back to Hong Kong. Told in the first-person point of view, these stories deal with the elusive nature of love and how an emotionally deprived childhood intensifies the desire for intimacy and romance. Wang's prose work *Xianggang nüren* (Hong Kong Women) invokes the heady, glamorous fusion of East and West in the ordinary lives of **women** of Hong Kong. Her award-winning novels *Buchong jiyi* (Supplementary Memories) and *Yao Jiu chuanqi* (The Story of My Uncle) are set against the background of mainland China and inspired by the memories of her childhood and youth. Another novel, *Xiang Meili zai Shanghai* (Emily Hahn in Shanghai), looks at the colorful life of the American writer, particularly her romantic entanglement in the 1930s with Shao Xunmei, a Chinese poet and publisher. Wang uses a refined language in both her prose and fiction. While her fiction contains the characteristics of her graceful prose, her essays read like short stories with well-developed plots.

WANG SHUO (1958–). Novelist. Born and raised in Beijing, Wang Shuo, known for his so-called hooligan literature, has written stinging satires with real moral implications. *Wan'r de jiushi xintiao* (*Playing for Thrills*), one of his early novels, is a tour de force of psychological realism. The protagonist, an unsuccessful writer, becomes the prime suspect in a murder case that took place 10 years earlier. Unsure if he indeed committed the crime, he searches for old friends for verification. The sense of guilt he feels, coupled with the burden of not knowing the truth, places the protagonist in a moral dilemma. *Qianwan bie ba wo dang ren* (*Please Don't Call Me Human*), a dark satire about Chinese nationalism, delivers a timely remonstration against misplaced national pride. The story describes the search for and the absurd training of a man groomed to win back China's national pride by defeating an American in a wrestling match. These early successes made Wang a darling of the media. He began churning out, in quick succession, television scripts that led to great commercial success.

WANG TONGZHAO (1897–1957). Fiction writer. A Shandong native and graduate of the University of China in Beijing, Wang Tongzhao worked all his life teaching literature and editing magazines and journals. He participated in the **May Fourth Movement** and was one of the founders of the **Literary Research Society**. His early stories, mostly romantic and sentimental outpourings, revolve around the theme of love and beauty, describing youthful passion and despair. *Yi ye* (One Leaf), his first novella published in 1922, features a young man from an old gentry family. Poor health and a sensitive disposition make him acutely aware of social injustice and misery around him. At college he is antisocial, distrustful of his peers. Although a pessimist and fatalist at heart, he eventually discovers love: love for his mother and sisters and the love he and his friends have for one another, which brings him hope and gives him faith in the world. Another novella, *Huanghun* (At Dusk), is about a college graduate hired by his uncle to run a textile manufacturing company in their hometown where he meets the uncle's two young concubines. Sympathetic to their predicament, he helps them escape their bondage. One of the women commits suicide upon reading her husband's search announcement in the newspaper and the other strikes out on her own and eventually becomes an opera star. In many ways, the story reflects the sense of obligation the May Fourth intellectuals felt toward their countrymen, as illustrated through the young man's effort to liberate the women from an unhappy marriage as well as through the clash between generations in the same family and the pertinacity of traditional practices.

Wang's later works focus on the sufferings of the working class, reflecting the influence of critical realism on Chinese writers. His 1932 novel *Shan yu* (Rain in the Mountain), set in rural northern China in the 1920s and 1930s, focuses on the disintegration of the agrarian way of life, as a result of civil unrest, exploitation, and heavy taxation at the hands of the government, and on the awakening of the peasants as they discover the source of their plight. Toward the end of the novel, the protagonist, a destitute farmer, leaves the countryside to seek his fortune in the city where he is faced with more challenges. The protagonist comes to grips with reality by joining the revolution. Another novel, *Chun hua* (Spring Blossoms), portrays the impact of the May Fourth Movement on the educated youths. In addition to fiction, Wang also published several collections of essays, poems, and plays, including *Ye xing ji* (Night Travel) and *Qu lai xi* (Leaving and Returning).

In 1934, Wang went to Europe and spent several months studying literature in London. After he returned to China a year later and through the years of the **Sino-Japanese War**, Wang worked as an editor and continued to pursue his literary career. When Japan surrendered, Wang returned to his native Shandong and taught Chinese literature at Shandong University. After 1949, he held several official positions, including director of Shandong Provincial Cultural Bureau.

WANG WENXING, A.K.A. WANG WEN-HSIN (1939–). Fiction writer and critic. Wang Wenxing was born in Fujian and grew up in **Taiwan**. He received his B.A. from National Taiwan University, then a bastion of Taiwan's modernist movement, and an M.A. in creative writing from the University of Iowa. Besides several collections of short stories, Wang has also published two novels, *Jia bian (Family Catastrophe)* and *Bei hai de ren (Backed against the Sea)*, which are major works in Taiwan's modernist literature. Wang is noted for his bold stylistic and linguistic experimentations.

When *Jia bian* was published in 1972, it caused a great controversy. It was considered an assault on traditional Chinese family values, particularly its long-held Confucian tradition of filial piety. Its stylistic peculiarities also came under fire. The story dramatizes stresses on the modern Taiwan family by highlighting the problems between husbands and wives and between parents and children. It starts with the unexpected disappearance of the father and continues through the various attempts that his wife and son make to bring him home. The novel's focus is on the son's guilty feelings about his mistreatment of his father, unfolding the tormented psychology of a rebellious young man who strives to break free from the controlling grip of traditional ethics. *Bei hai de ren* is an even more audacious revolt against the realist tradition of storytelling. Characterized as a Joycean novel in its absolute disregard for readability, it is the most radical departure from the standard form of the novel in modern Chinese literature. *See also* MODERNISTS.

WANG XIAOBO (1952–1997). Fiction writer and essayist. Born in Beijing, Wang Xiaobo spent several years as an educated youth in the countryside of Shandong and Xishuanbanna, a tropical region in remote Yunnan, and later attended the University of Pittsburgh. He went back to Beijing in 1988 with a master's degree and for the next few years taught sociology and statistics in Beijing universities. His sudden death from a heart attack at the height of his career was widely mourned and considered a great loss to Chinese literature.

Wang's sardonic wit, his ironic narrative style, and his profound examination of the interplay between power and sex are brilliantly captured in his Xishuanbanna stories, set in the lush landscape of the border region of Yunnan during the **Cultural Revolution**. *Huangjin shidai* (The Gold Times), *Baiyin shidai* (The Silver Times), *Qingtong shidai* (The Bronze Times), and the unfinished novel *Heitie shidai* (The Iron Times) are his main fictional works. In his characteristically satirical tone, Wang mocks the absurdities of life in Maoist China, where ideology trumped basic human needs and stifled creativity. Of these works, *Huangjin shidai* and *Qingtong shidai* are the best in representing Wang's style. *Huangjin shidai* is based on his personal experience as an educated youth in Xishuanbanna and later as a worker in a small factory in a Beijing suburb. *Qingtong shidai*, on the other hand, is a fictitious novel in which the narrator makes frequent references to fantastic classical Chinese tales within a story about contemporary life. Other than these novels, Wang also wrote short stories and many essays. He made a foray into the movie industry with his screenplay *Donggong xigong* (East Palace West Palace), a movie about homosexuality and power, which won the Best Screenplay Award at the 1996 Mar del Plata (Argentina) International Film Festival. As an independent thinker who preferred to remain on the periphery of society, Wang waged a lonely and courageous battle through his essays in his declarations against the power of the state and the seduction of the market.

WANG XIAONI (1955–). Poet, fiction and essay writer. Born in Changchun in northeast China, Wang Xiaoni worked as a literary editor after receiving her B.A. from Jilin University. She moved to Shenzhen in 1985 and is currently on the faculty of Hainan University. Wang is widely recognized in China for her poetry; among the honors she has received is the 2002 Poetry Prize sponsored by the country's three most influential poetry journals. Her early poems are devoted to the expression of agrarian life. As she moves to include a wider spectrum of themes, she maintains a fascination with the rural spirit of innocence and simplicity. She is particularly interested in the details of everyday life and much of her imagery is drawn from the world around her. Wang's poetry, written in a plain but precise language, expresses a gentle and graceful sensibility, a personal voice that emphasizes intimate feelings and emotions. The most important of her fictional works is *Fangyuan sishi li* (Twenty Kilometers Radius), which tells, in a fragmented style, a realistic story of educated urban youth living in the countryside, where the dire conditions of extreme poverty and lack of hope force young people to resort to cruel measures in order to survive. *See also* WOMEN.

WANG XIAOYING (1947–). Fiction writer. Born in Zhejiang Province, Wang Xiaoying spent several years on a tea farm in Anhui as an educated youth. She entered East China Normal University in 1978 to study Chinese literature. Upon graduation, she was assigned to work as an editor for a Shanghai literary journal. Since 1985, she has been a member of the Shanghai Writers' Association. Her major works include the novellas *Xinghe* (The Milky Way), *Suiyue youyou* (Times in the Past), and *Yilu fengchen* (A Journey of Hardships), and the novels *Ni weishui bianhu* (Whom Are You Defending), *Wemen cengjing xiangai* (Once Upon a Time We Were in Love), and *Danqing yin* (Inspired by Art). Wang's style of writing is realistic and her works primarily deal with contemporary life, issues such as love, marriage, and work, as well as changes in human relationships during the age of globalization. *See also* WOMEN.

WANG XUFENG (1955–). Novelist. Winner of the Mao Dun Literature Award, Wang Xufeng is known for the "tea trilogy," a project that took her 10 years to complete. She grew up in Zhejiang, which has a long tea-growing history, and has worked in a tea museum in Hangzhou. An expert in tea culture, from its growing to its appreciation in high society, Wang has turned her knowledge into a saga of a Hangzhou family's relationship with tea for the past 150 years. Part 1 of the trilogy, *Nanfang you jiamu* (Quality Tea Grows in the South), focuses on the sociopolitical changes affecting the tea growers in the late Qing dynasty; part 2, *Bu ye hou* (The Marquis of the Night), is set against the background of the **Sino-Japanese War**, and part 3, *Zhu cao wei cheng* (A City Surrounded by Plants), deals with the tumultuous years of the **Cultural Revolution.** The main theme of the trilogy is how civilization conquers brutality and culture survives violence. Tea represents the human spirit. Well researched and rich with details about growing, picking, making, and drinking tea, the tea trilogy is considered more than a fictional work; it is regarded also as a scholarly work written by a specialist in the field. *See also* WOMEN.

WANG ZENGQI (1920–1997). Fiction writer and playwright. Born in Gaoyou, Jiangsu Province, Wang attended Southwest United University in Kunming during the **Sino-Japanese War** and studied with **Shen Congwen**, who greatly influenced his writing. Wang was one of the very few writers whose career spanned nearly half a century. He published his first story in the 1940s, and continued to write during the **Cultural Revolution** and into the 1980s. From 1962 until his death, his official job was writing librettos for the Beijing Opera Troupe. He was one of the main writers of *Shajia bang* (The Shajia Creek), a revolutionary opera promoted by Mao's wife Jiang Qing. Wang reached the height of his creative career in the post-Mao era, with the publication of numerous short stories and essays. He is noted for his graceful style and lyrical sensibility, a legacy seen as passed down from Shen Congwen. A kind of godfather figure in the **root-seeking** movement of the 1980s, Wang also shared Shen's interest in cultures far removed from modernity, which were further explored by younger writers such as **Han Shaogong** and **Zheng Wanlong**.

Wang grew up in a landed family that was deeply rooted in Chinese traditions. His father was an easygoing man of many talents, a lover of literature and an accomplished musician, painter, calligrapher, and athlete, who greatly influenced his son. Like the rest of his generation, young Wang received both the traditional and modern forms of education. Toward the end of his career, however, it was Chinese traditions that had the greatest impact on his writing. His stories and essays are permeated with traditional sentiments. Many of his characters, such as the friends in "Suihan sanyou" (Three Friends in the Cold of Winter) exhibit the Confucian ideals of social engagement, moral uprightness, and human benevolence. The characters with Taoist inclinations are portrayed as having no ambitions other than living peacefully in the world and tending their personal interests: growing flowers, fishing, and cultivating artistic tastes. The laborers in "Da nao jishi" (A Tale of the Big Lake), an award-winning story, demonstrate contentedness with life and tolerance of others. "Fuchou" (Revenge), based on an account from the Buddhist sutras, tells how a fatal revenge is averted. "Youming zhong" (When the Death Bell Tolls), another story of Buddhist themes, conveys the compassion of monks. "Shoujie" (*The Love Story of a Young Monk*), which also won an award, portrays a monastic life without rigid rules. In the temple, the monks sing love songs, play cards, and even get married and have children. Leading a natural life of simplicity and freedom, they represent the ideals of Zen Buddhism as advocated and practiced by men of letters in ancient China. It was precisely this attitude toward life that helped Wang survive the decades of political vicissitudes. His personal convictions, which include kindness to others, living in harmony with society and nature, and a strong belief in humanity, are themes explored in his fiction and essays.

WANG ZHENHE, A.K.A. WANG CHEN-HO (1940–1990). Fiction writer. Born and educated in **Taiwan**, Wang Zhenhe is considered a **nativist** writer whose concerns for the lives of ordinary, downtrodden people feature prominently in Taiwan's realist tradition. He is also a superb satirist; humor runs through nearly all his works. "Jiazhuang yi niuche" (*An Oxcart for Dowry*) relates how a man gets an oxcart from a small garment merchant with whom his wife has been having an affair. All three characters live on the fringes of society, left behind by rapidly modernizing Taiwan. Wang depicts in a satirical language, but with great compassion, the tensions that exist in their everyday lives and their wretched conditions, including physical deformity as well as an apparent lack of morality. The comic voice is put to its full use in his novel *Meigui meigui wo ai ni* (*Rose, Rose I Love You*). Wang employs an alternately riotous, sardonic, and serious tone to address the issue of moral degradation in Taiwanese society. The novel sheds light on the exploitation of **women** in the prostitution industry boosted by the arrival of American G.I.s.

WEI HUI, PEN NAME OF ZHOU WEIHUI (1973–). Novelist. Born in Yuyao, Zhejiang Province, and graduated from Fudan University, Wei Hui is a representative of the **New Generation Writers** (Xin sheng dai zuojia). A self-described exhibitionist writer whose works deal with urban, materialistic life in contemporary China, Wei Hui is best known for her sexually explicit novels, *Shanghai baobei* (*Shanghai Baby*) and *Wode chan* (*Marrying Buddha*). Her books provide a window into the hedonistic lifestyle of modern materialistic youths obsessed with money, sex, and brand names, a far cry from the revolutionary idealism embraced by the older generations of the Mao era. *See also* WOMEN.

WEI MINGLUN (1941–). Playwright and essayist. Born and raised in small towns in Sichuan, Wei Minglun began making a living as a Sichuan opera actor when he was only nine years old. With virtually no formal education, he taught himself how to read and write and moved his way up to become a leading playwright in modern Chinese theater. He has won numerous prestigious awards and is widely known as a "wizard of the theater." Wei rose to prominence in the 1980s when he wrote and directed several influential Sichuan operas, including *Yi Dadan* (The Fearless Yi), *Pan Jinlian* (Pan Jinjian: The History of a Fallen Woman), and *Bashan xiucai* (The Talented Scholar of Sichuan). He continued to bring out more box office successes in the 1990s with the productions of *Xi zhao Qishan* (Sunset at Mount Qi), *Zhongguo gongzhu Dulanduo* (Dulanduo: A Chinese Princess), and *Bianlian* (Masque Changing).

Wei divides his plays into "**women**'s plays" and "men's plays." The most important among the former is the controversial *Pan Jinlian*, generally characterized as the pinnacle of the absurd in Chinese theater. *Pan Jinlian* is Wei's attempt to reexamine a despised woman from classical Chinese popular literature and give her a new interpretation. The play crosses boundaries of time and space and gathers, on the same stage, famous characters, both historical and fictional, including Empress Wu (624–705) of the Tang dynasty, author Shi Nai'an (1296?–1370?) of the Ming dynasty, Leo Tolstoy's Anna Karenina, Cao Xueqin's Jiao Baoyu, a county magistrate of ancient China, a present-day judge, and others. The interaction of these diverse characters results in "absurd" circumstances, such as 20th-century hooligans colluding with Ximen Qing, who is Pan's nemesis in Shi's novel, and Anna Karenina taking Pan Jinlian with her to commit a double suicide. Of the "men's plays," *Xi zhao Qishan* is the most representative of Wei's art. It once again shines critical light on a well-known figure, Zhuge Liang, of the classical novel *Sanguo Yanyi* (*Romance of the Three Kingdoms*). Through this beloved character, the play reassesses the moral attributes of the traditional Chinese literati. *See also* SPOKEN DRAMA.

WEN YIDUO, PEN NAME OF WEN JIAHUA (1899–1946). Poet. Before entering Qinghua University, Wen received a traditional education in Hubei, his home province. In 1922, he went to the United States to study fine arts and literature at the Chicago Art Institute. It was during this time that his first collection of poetry, *Hong zhu* (*Red Candle*), was published in China. He returned to Beijing in 1925 and became a literature professor. In 1928, his second collection, *Si shui* (Dead Water), was published. In the same year, he joined the **Crescent Society**. When the Japanese invaded China, Wen moved with his university to Kunming, Yunnan, where he became politically active. His public denounciation of the Nationalist government eventually cost him his life, when he was assassinated in 1946.

Wen's poetry reflects two aspects of his life. As a scholar and professor of Chinese literature, he paid attention to intrinsic elements of literary form. As a politically engaged intellectual, he showed a deep concern for his country and people. For these two reasons, he was regarded as both a "formalist" and "patriotic" poet. In reaction to the trendy practice of showing total disregard for form, he wrote essays to advocate "formal properties" for the new poetry. These essays as well as his poems established his position as a leader of modern poetry. *See also* NEW CULTURE MOVEMENT; SINO-JAPANESE WAR.

WOESER (1966–). Poet and prose writer. Woeser was born in Lhasa. Her father, a military officer with mixed Chinese and Tibetan parentage, joined the People's Liberation Army at the age of 13 and rose to be an army officer stationed in various places in **Tibet**, a position that afforded his daughter the opportunity to be educated in Sichuan Province from a young age. Woeser graduated from Southwestern College for Minorities, where she majored in Chinese language and literature. In 1990, she returned to Lhasa to edit *Xizang Wenxue* (Tibetan Literature) and began writing poetry. She was reconnected to her Tibetan heritage and became interested in Buddhism. In Lhasa, she had access to books smuggled into Tibet, including *In Exile from the Land of Snows: The Dalai Lama and Tibet since the Chinese Conquest* by John F. Avedon, which opened her eyes to a historical narrative about Tibet contrary to what she had received in her formal education. Such books transformed her into an activist, a public speaker for the suppressed Tibetan collective memory. *Shajie* (Revolution), an oral history of Tibet during the **Cultural Revolution**, publishes more than 300 photos taken by her father and the eyewitness accounts from her interviews, providing testimony about the widespread destruction of Tibetan culture. Her outspoken criticism of the Chinese government and her open admiration for the Dalai Lama jeopardized her position at *Xizang Wenxue* and her ability to publish in China. She has, however, been able to find publishers in Taiwan and Hong Kong.

Woeser's literary works, both poetry and prose, center on one theme: the eternal as represented in Tibetan Buddhism. In *Xizang: Jianghong se de ditu* (A Crimson Map), the author talks about the monasteries, the lamas, and the pilgrims and expresses her nostalgia for the disappearing Tibetan civilization. In *Xizang biji* (Notes of Tibet), a collection of essays and her best-known work, she explores the Tibetan consciousness. Her works document suppressed history, memorialize forgotten sufferings, and retrieve erased footprints. While recording her travels in Tibet to visit various sites and interview various personalities, she indulges in a personal and internal wandering, immersed in a world of dreams and memories. Her poetry is romantic and surreal, enhanced by the pathos of the Tibetan nation and by her own sense of loss and sentimentality. Her other works include a poetry collection, *Xizang zai shang* (Tibet: The High Plateau), *Ming wei Xizang de shi* (Poems Written for Tibet), and *Xizang jiyi* (Memories of Tibet). *See also* WOMEN.

WOMEN. In 20th-century China, the women's emancipation movement began as part of the modernization agenda of the **May Fourth Movement**, which sought to transform China into a modern nation. The May Fourth intellectuals called for the education of a whole generation of "new women," physically fit and mentally strong, to join the nation-building project. In order for women to participate in social reforms, traditional institutions that had subjugated them to practices such as foot-binding, arranged marriage, deprivation of education, and other forms of institutionalized discrimination against women had to be dismantled. On the political and legal front, reform-minded activists argued that since women's equality was predicated on economic independence, laws should be passed to guarantee women legal rights to inherit property, a privilege only sons could enjoy in previous societies. In the campaign to give women economic independence and freedom, consensual marriage and women's right to divorce their husbands were also put on the table. Based on the principles of gender equality and property ownership, the new legal codes passed in 1928 and 1929 granted Chinese women inheritance rights and freedom in marriage and divorce. The goals to acquire equal rights for education were also achieved. By the end of the 1920s, modern educational institutions at all levels were open to girls.

In the initial stage of the women's emancipation movement, progressive male intellectuals were major advocates and they used literature as an important tool to embolden and mobilize women. Henrik Ibsen's play *A Doll's House*, for example, was translated into Chinese and introduced by **Hu Shi** in the progressive journal *Xin qingnian* (New Youth) in 1918. Its main character Nora became synonymous with awakened and liberated women. Many characters modeled after Nora appeared in plays written by Chinese authors. **Ouyang Yuqian**'s *Pofu* (The Shrew) and *Pan Jinlian* (Pan Jinlian the Seductress) and Yuan Changying's *Kongque dongnan fei* (Southeast Flies the Peacock) all feature female characters who fight for personal independence. Encouraged by these examples, many Chinese women ran away from home to become free agents in their own right.

In no small measures, women's writings in the early 20th century appropriated the male discourse on women's emancipation, but soon they developed a voice of their own. While the writings of **Xie Bingying**, **Bing Xin**, **Lu Yin**, **Xiao Hong**, **Mei Niang**, and others clearly subscribe to much of the emancipation ethos promoted by male authors, embracing the struggle against arranged marriage, the right to education, and gender equality, works by **Ling Shuhua** and **Ding Ling**, while deploring the gender-specific confinements imposed on women by traditional societies, insisted that women's claim to subjectivity and intellect be accompanied by an emphasis on the development of strong female emotional and sexual desires. Later in the 1940s, **Su Qing** and **Zhang Ailing** brought women's writings to a whole new level. Su's prose, imploring her readers to understand the challenges faced by career women in the workplace as they struggled to make a living while defending their dignity and freedom, is surprisingly still relevant in today's society. Zhang Ailing, while depicting urban trivia, delves deep into the psyche of women and men as they engage each other in the game of love and desire.

In modern Chinese literary discourse, the women's emancipation movement that started in the early 20th century has never truly concluded to this day, and women's struggle for autonomy has been a recurring theme in women's writings. From **Yuan Qiongqiong, Li Ang**, and **Shi Shuqing** to **Chen Ran, Xu Xiaobin, Hong Ying**, and **Lin Bai**, the spotlight is focused on the female body in the belief that the raw intensity of female sexuality embodies women's sense of self and is therefore a crucial component of the female identity. If the emphasis on the female body is narrowly and internally focused, the fascination with the matrilineal found in the works by such writers as **Wang Anyi, Tie Ning, Zhang Jie**, and **Zhao Mei** is by definition grand and epical. Wang's *Jishi yu xugou* (The Real and the Fictitious) engages in mythmaking that takes the female narrator to where her maternal ancestry began—the grassland of the northern prairie; Tie's *Meigui men* (Gate of Roses), Zhang's *Wu zi* (No Written Word), Xu's *Yu she* (Feathered Snake), and Zhao's *Women jiazu de nüren* (Women in my Family) all trace back to their female ancestors to uncover the spring of strength or roots of madness that contribute to the current mental state of the female protagonists. By reclaiming or recreating the matrilineal records, which have been suppressed or erased by the male-dominated history-making enterprise, these women writers have attempted to rewrite not only individual clan history but also the history of the nation.

It goes without saying that not all women writers prefer to deal with women's bodies or matrilineal history, or the domestic scene, and every good writer possesses a highly individualized autonomous aesthetic. So characterizing women's writings in one way or another is no doubt risky. Nevertheless, there seems to be a remarkable consensus among critics with regard to the so-called feminine aesthetic of Zhang Ailing's writing—known for its meticulous focus on social trivia and its exquisite descriptiveness of the sounds and sights of the urban scene, a style much imitated, even by male writers. The notion of the domestic as the privileged topos for women writers, for better or for worse, is widely accepted as a trademark of the so-called Zhang (Ailing) style. Wang Aiyi, Yuan Qiongqiong, **Zhu Tianwen, Zhu Tianxin, Zhong Xiaoyang**, and **Bai Xianyong** are all considered heirs to this feminine aesthetic. *See also* AN QI; BI SHUMIN; CAN XUE; CAO ZHILIAN; CHEN RUOXI; CHENG NAISHAN; CHI LI; CHI ZIJIAN; FAN XIAOQING; FANG FANG; FENG YUANJUN; HUANG BIYUN; HUO DA; LI BIHUA; LIAO HUIYING; LIN HAIYIN; LIN HUIYIN; LIU SUOLA; LU XING'ER; MA LIHUA; METSO; NIE HUALING; OUYANG ZI; PING LU; RU ZHIJUAN; SAN MAO; SHEN RONG; SHU TING; SU DE; SU WEIZHEN; SU XUELIN; WANG HAILING; WANG PU; WANG XIAONI; WANG XIAOYING; WANG XUFENG; WEI HUI; WOESER; XI MURONG; XI XI; XIA YI; XIAO HONG; XIAO LIHONG; XU KUN; YAN GE; YAN GELING; YANG JIANG; YANGDON; YE GUANGQIN; YI SHU; YO YO; YU LIHUA; ZHAI YONGMING; ZHANG ER; ZHANG JIE; ZHANG KANGKANG; ZHANG XIAOFENG; ZHANG XIN; ZHANG XINXIN; ZHANG YUERAN; ZONG PU.

WU ZUGUANG (1917–2003). Playwright, and fiction and prose writer. A legendary figure in Chinese art and literary circles, Wu Zuguang was one of the last generation of Chinese men of letters who distinguished themselves in more than one area of Chinese cultural life. His career stretched across several disciplines: theater, film, poetry, calligraphy, and scholarly pursuits. Born in Beijing to a well-established family that prided itself for learning and literary accomplishments, Wu earned a reputation as a dramatist in the 1930s and 1940s with several critically acclaimed plays, including *Fengxue ye gui ren* (*Returning at a Snowy Night*), generally regarded as a masterpiece. Influenced by the **May Fourth New Culture Movement**, the play accentuates the conflicts between the pursuit of personal happiness and traditional values that choke individualism. The main characters, a Peking opera star and a concubine of a judge, fall in love with each other despite social pressures. When they muster enough courage to elope, they are dealt a fatal blow and their dreams for a happy life together end tragically.

Wu also adapted stories from classical Chinese literature and history into stage plays. *Zhengqi ge* (Song of Righteousness), about the 13th-century patriot Wen Tianxiang who fought the Mongols, the mythical love story *Niulang Zhinü* (The Cowherd and the Weaving Maid), and *Lin Chong ye ben* (Lin Chong Leaving at Night), based on the classical novel *Shui hu* (Water Margin), are all taken from existing sources. He also wrote opera scripts such as *San da Tao Sanchun* (*Tao Sanchun Receives Three Beatings*), *San guan yan* (Banquet at Three Passes), and

Hua wei mei (Match-Making Flowers). After the **Cultural Revolution**, Wu wrote *Chuang jianghu* (Crossing Rivers and Lakes), a play based on the eventful life of his wife, a famous opera star.

Although disinterested in politics, Wu got embroiled in a variety of political events. As early as the 1940s while working as an editor for *Xin min wanbao* (New Citizen Evening Post) in the war capital Chongqing, he published Mao Zedong's poem "Qin yuanchun: Xue" (Snow: To the Tune of Garden in Full Spring), an act that irritated the Nationalist government. Wu was forced to flee to **Hong Kong** to evade capture by secret agents and found a job working as a screenplay writer and director of film production companies. He made Hong Kong's first color film, *Guo hun* (The Soul of the Nation), which is based on his play *Zhengqi ge*. He turned another play of his, *Fengxue ye gui ren*, into a film as well. In 1949, Wu returned to Beijing to work as a screenplay writer and director at the Central Film Bureau.

Throughout the Mao era, Wu, an outspoken critic of bureaucracy and tyranny, became a target at every political campaign, starting with the Anti-Rightist Campaign in 1957 to the aftermath of the **Tian'anmen Prodemocracy Movement** in 1989. He was publicly insulted, beaten, exiled, and imprisoned; his house was ransacked and his wife reduced to life in a wheelchair. Through these ordeals, Wu refused to succumb to political expediency, as many others did, insisting on a life of moral conviction, which earned him much admiration. *See also* SPOKEN DRAMA.

WU ZUXIANG (1908–1994). Fiction writer and essayist. Born in Jingxian, Anhui Province, Wu Zuxiang became known in 1932 when his short story "Guanguan de bupin" (*Young Master's Tonic*) was published. He was then a student at Qinghua University. In the following years, Wu wrote more short stories collected in *Xiliu ji* (Western Willow) and *Fanyu ji* (After Meals). Wu's stories are characterized by their sardonic wit and satirical attacks on social evils, such as exploitation, corruption, and hypocrisy. During the **Sino-Japanese War**, he wrote a novel, *Shanhong* (Landslide), portraying the Chinese people's struggle against Japanese aggression. In the three decades after 1949, Wu taught at Beijing University and turned his attention to scholarly work on classical Chinese literature, especially the fiction of the Ming and Qing dynasties. In the post-Mao era, Wu resumed his creative work, producing several collections of essays.

– X –

XI CHUAN, PEN NAME OF LIU JUN (1960–). Poet. Widely considered one of the most innovative poets living in China today, Xi Chuan was born in Jiangsu and graduated from Beijing University with a B.A. in English. In their college days, Xi Chuan, **Hai Zi**, and Luo Yihe were nicknamed the "Three Musketeers" on the Beijing University campus for their poetic gifts. After Hai Zi's suicide, Xi Chuan undertook the project of collecting, editing, and publishing his friend's work. Xi Chuan's early work tends toward expansive, extravagant images, inspired by Li Po, the eighth-century poetical genius, earning him a reputation as a neoclassicist. An admirer of Jorge Luis Borges, Ezra Pound, and many other Western poets, Xi Chuan later combines the influences of European literature and traditional versification in a style that emphasizes clarity, precision, and rhythm, exemplified in poems such as "Yangguang xia de hai" (The Sea in the Sunlight), a modern sonnet in which the formal properties of a traditional form are adapted to modern Chinese to create a composite picture of dynamic images. "Xugou de jiapu" (Fabricated Pedigree), an allegorical poem, represents Xi Chuan's attempt at reexamining the self in relation to historical events. He also experiments with long narrative poems that make liberal use of colloquial expressions. Among the numerous awards he has received are the 1994 Modern Chinese Poetry Prize and the 2001 Lu Xun Literature Prize. He currently teaches at the Central Academy of Fine Arts in Beijing.

XI MURONG, (1943–). Poet, essayist, and painter. A descendent of Mongolian nobility, Xi was born in Sichuan. She left China for **Hong Kong** in 1949 and moved to **Taiwan** in 1955. Popular among young readers in Taiwan, Hong Kong, and the mainland, Xi's love poems, including those collected in *Qi li xiang (Seven-li scent)* and *Wuyuan de qingchun* (Unregrettable Youth), are sentimental and nostalgic in their refined expressions of the fragile and tumultuous emotions of adolescence. Xi has additionally published several collections of essays, including *Xinling de tansuo* (Soul-Searching). *See also* WOMEN.

XI XI, PEN NAME OF ZHANG YAN (1938-). Fiction writer, essayist, and poet. Born in Shanghai, Xi Xi moved with her family to **Hong Kong** in 1950. She made a living by teaching English in an elementary school and worked on her own writing on the side, until 1979, when she retired from her teaching job to focus on writing. Several of her works have won prestigious awards in **Taiwan**. Widely considered the most important literary figure in Hong Kong, Xi Xi was influenced by Western modernist and postmodernist literature. Known as a master of versatility, she enjoys experimenting with a variety of styles and subjects. *Huzi you lian* (Mustache Has a Face) is one of her most innovative stories, in which Xi Xi creates a character who does everything against the norm, often asking strange questions such as "why do wings have butterflies?" "Xiang wo zheyang de yige nüzi" (*A Girl Like Me*) is one of her better-known stories. It tells how the prejudices encountered in society create despondency and loneliness in the mind of a makeup artist who works in a funeral home. There is powerful psychological realism in the details of the character's inner turmoil and her resignation to her fate. Xi Xi has the uncanny ability to convey her condemnation of the dark side of human behavior with a light touch. Other stories concern a host of problems faced in city life, such as the lack of space in crammed housing situations and the city's relationship to the mainland.

Xi Xi has written several books featuring Hong Kong as the main character. Unique among these works is "Fu cheng zhi yi" (*Marvels of a Floating City*), an allegorical tale that deals with national identity and feelings of uncertainty, issues precipitated by the 1997 handover of Hong Kong to China. The image of the city hanging in the air without roots, without anchor, is an apt description of the state of the city in the 1980s as China and Great Britain negotiated over its future. The story is told as a fairy tale, aided by surrealist paintings to accentuate the sense of disorientation, insecurity, and trepidation felt by the residents. A more ambitious work is *Fei zhan* (*Flying Carpet: A Tale of Fertilla*), an epic about the century that took Hong Kong from a fishing village to an international metropolis. The central characters are two merchant families whose business and personal connections allow the novel to treat the city's past and present, its multiracial and multicultural history, its politics, economy, wars, immigration, archeology, science, education, and so on. The novel is also a Hong Kong history from the female perspective, captured vividly in the words of maidservants, housewives, businesswomen, and professionals, about how **women** break gender barriers to achieve material success and social equality. Most noteworthy in this novel is the author's narrative innovatition. The nonlinear narrative of the saga of the two families is interspersed with expositions on archeology, astronomy, botany, chemistry, musical instruments, and so forth. The fictional and nonfictional elements are interwoven into an allegorical novel, a medley of fables, chorography, scientific sketches, philosophical discussions, and other forms of discourse. Other works that focus on Hong Kong include *Wo cheng* (*My City*), a kaleidoscope of life in 1970s Hong Kong, *Hou niao* (Migratory Birds), about the transient lifestyle of some of the city's residents and what it means to their psychological well-being, and most important, Xi Xi has also written poems, some of which are collected in *Shi qing* (Stone Chimes), as well as several screenplays.

XIA YAN, A.K.A. HSIA YEN, PEN NAME OF SHEN NAIXI (1900–1995). Playwright and screenplay writer. A key figure in literature and performing arts of China, Xia Yan had a long distinguished career. In 1919, he participated in the **May Fourth Movement**. In the following year, he went to Japan on a government scholarship to study electrical engineering. While there, he joined the Nationalist Party and was in charge of the personnel department of its branch in Japan. Xia Yan returned to China in 1927 to work in the workers' movement while pursuing a career in literary translation. Two years later, he became a cofounder of the **Left-wing Association of Chinese Writers** and joined the Communist Party, eventually rising to become, among his numerous official and professional titles, deputy minister of culture and a member of the Political Consultative Conference in the People's Republic of China. As the undisputed leader of the left-wing film industry in the 1930s and 1940s, Xia Yan worked with his colleagues to establish a realist tradition that emphasized active engagement with national issues, leaving a strong legacy that continued into the post-Mao era.

Nearly all the screenplays Xia wrote address contemporary problems facing the nation. The central theme of *Kuang liu* (Violent Currents) is the sufferings of the peasants in the wake of the 1931 flood that ravaged six provinces along the Yangtze River; *Chun can* (*Spring Silkworms*) and *Lin jia puzi* (*The Lin Family Shop*), which are adapted from **Mao Dun**'s stories, deal with the hardships of small businesses under the dual oppression of capitalism and bureaucracy; *Shanghai ershi si xiaoshi* (Twenty-four Hours in Shanghai) puts into sharp contrast the extreme poverty of workers in a textile mill and the extravagant lifestyle of its owners; *Ya sui qian* (New Year's Eve Gift) focuses on a coin as it passes from one social scene to another, revealing the lives of different social classes of Shanghai.

Xia Yan's role in the movement to popularize the modern play is equally significant. From the 1920s through the 1940s, he tirelessly promoted the new play and wrote many scripts with varying degrees of success. Xia Yan's plays generally fall into two categories: the patriotic plays such as *Faxisi xijun* (The Fascist Germs) about a young Chinese scientist who throws himself into the resistant war against the Japanese after returning to China from Japan with his Japanese wife, only to find his homeland devastated by war, and *Lili cao* (The Luxuriant Grass) about the Chinese people's heroic struggle against the Japanese and plays about the lives of ordinary urbanites, including *Duhui de yi jiao* (A Corner of a Metropolis), *Yi nian jian* (In a Year), *Cangfu* (The Prostitute), and his best-known play, *Shanghai wuyan xia* (*Under the Eaves of Shanghai*), which revolves around the struggle for survival of five families living in an apartment building in Shanghai. Like his films, Xia Yan's plays portray Chinese society, focusing on the theme of patriotism and the conflicts between social and economic classes, with attention to details of daily life and realistic renditions of his characters' psychological state. Xia Yan died in Beijing at the age of 95, a well-respected and influential cultural icon. *See also* CIVIL WAR; NEW CULTURE MOVEMENT; SINO-JAPANESE WAR; SOCIALIST REALISM; SPOKEN DRAMA.

XIA YI, PEN NAME OF CHEN XUANWEN (1922–). Born in **Hong Kong**, Xia Yi studied at Southwestern United University in Kunming during the **Sino-Japanese War**. When the war ended, she continued her studies at Qinghua University in Beijing and began to publish essays and short stories. She returned to Hong Kong in 1948. In 1978, she attended the International Writers' Workshop at the University of Iowa. Xia Yi took material from daily life in Hong Kong and turned it into vivid stories and essays. She was particularly popular with the youth and female readers. Many of her novels are written in diary form, including *Xianggang xiaojie riji* (Diary of Miss Hong Kong), *Shaonü riji* (Diary of a Teenage Girl), *Qingchun riji* (Diary of Youth), and *Zhao xia riji* (Diary of Morning Clouds). *See also* WOMEN.

XIAO FAN, PEN NAME OF FAN JIZU (1982–). Fiction writer. Born and raised in Shanghai, Xiao Fan majored in philosophy at East China Normal University. Like many of his generation, in his early career, Xiao Fan admired **Wang Xiaobo** and imitated his unrestrained style and rebellious spirit. Later, he fell in love with the **avant-garde** aesthetics of

Yu Hua, **Su Tong**, and **Can Xue**. These influences are most evident in *Bu ji de tiankong* (The Unbridled Sky), a collection of short stories. Like **Su De** and others, Xiao Fan's career was launched in *Mengya* (Sprouts), a teen literary journal based in Shanghai, which published his story "Wo xiao shihou" (When I Was Little) when the author was 17 years old.

His first novel, *Wo de tutou laoshi* (My Bald Teacher), which tells an intricately woven postmodern tale about homosexual love, was published in his junior year in college. *Wo nianqing shi de nü pengyou* (The Girlfriend of My Youth) tells a suspenseful story of romantic love among two men and a woman. His second collection of stories, *Du yao shen tong* (Poison and Child Prodigy) came out in 2004 soon after he graduated from college. The title story portrays a precocious child who experiments with poison making to take his own life so that he could be together with his dead father. Characteristic of Xiao Fan's style, this sad tale is told in a playful, humorous tone. His most recent novel, *Mayi* (Ants) is about illusive love, violence, and cruelty in the experience of four teenagers whose lives are intertwined because of the history of their parents' complicated sexual relationships.

Focused on exploring the meaning of life and human nature, Xiao Fan shows equal fascination with the magic of storytelling by dazzling his readers with lively characters and intriguing plots. He favors the use of humor and hyperbole to deflect the seriousness of his subject and to create a unique world of young characters whose actions are driven by both innocent and sinister forces. The most prolific among his generation, Xiao Fan has published in some of the most prestigious literary journals, including *Shouhuo* (Harvest) and *Shiyue* (October), and with three novels to his name he is well positioned to attract readers beyond the circle of teenagers who admire his talent. *See also* NEW GENERATION WRITERS.

XIAO HONG, A.K.A. HSIAO HUNG (1911–1942). Born in a small town in northeastern China, Xiao Hong had a lonely childhood, which she later recorded in her autobiographical novel *Hulan he (Tales of Hulan River)*. Encouraged by **Xiao Jun**, a young writer who rescued her after her boyfriend abandoned her in a hotel, she began to write. Xiao Hong fell in love with Xiao Jun and the couple jointly published a collection of short stories. Unhappy with life in Harbin, which was then under Japanese occupation, the couple left the city in 1934 and began a vagrant life. The seaside city of Qingdao provided them with a welcome respite and there Xiao finished another short novel, *Shengsi chang* (*The Field of Life and Death*), portraying the lives of peasants and their resistance against the Japanese occupation in northeastern China. The couple also began corresponding with **Lu Xun**, seeking his advice on writing. They later went to Shanghai and became active in the **Left-wing Association of Chinese Writers**. When Japan invaded Shanghai, Xiao Hong fled to several cities and eventually landed in **Hong Kong**. By then, she had broken up with Xiao Jun and was living with **Duanmu Hongliang**, another writer from the northeast. Despite her professional success, Xiao Hong was plagued all her life by loneliness, insecurity, and poor health, which eventually killed her.

In her brief life, Xiao Hong wrote fiction and essays as well as a small number of poems and plays. *Hulan he zhuan* and *Shengsi chang* are her best-known works. Other works include *Shangshi jie* (The Market Street), a memoir of her life in Harbin, and *Ma Bole* (Ma Bole), a caricature of a spineless, contemptible man in the Japanese-occupied northeast. Both her fiction and her essays have a lyrical quality to them; graceful and polished, they represent a sensibility of innocence and simplicity. *See also* SINO-JAPANESE WAR.

XIAO JUN, A.K.A. HSIAO CHUN (1907–1988). Known for his stories about war-torn northeast China under Japanese occupation, Xiao Jun's name is inextricably linked with another writer from the same area, **Xiao Hong**. Both considered themselves disciples of **Lu Xun**, who helped promote their literary careers in the 1930s when the young writers were war refugees in Shanghai. Xiao Jun grew up in Changchun, a city in the northeast. He had some schooling and spent six years in the military before being dismissed for insubordination. While still in the military, Xiao tried his hand at writing short stories. In Harbin, Xiao Jun met and married Xiao Hong. They published at their own expense a joint collection of short stories of which six were written by Xiao Jun, portraying the working class living under the rule of the puppet government controlled by the Japanese. These immature stories contain strong emotions and indignant outbursts, characteristic of Xiao Jun's sensibility and style.

In the summer of 1934, Xiao Jun and Xiao Hong fled Harbin for Qingdao, where he completed his first major work, *Bayue de xiangcun* (*Village in August*), while Xiao Hong finished *Shengsi chang* (Life and Death), establishing their reputations as a rising literary couple. Xiao's novel portrays guerrillas fighting the Japanese in the northeast under the leadership of the Communist Party. The novel won the endorsement of Lu Xun for its patriotic theme, intensity of emotions delivered by a blunt and forceful language, and description of the beautiful northeast landscape, which found sympathetic readers in a country bracing itself for war. Xiao was eagerly embraced by the **left-wing** writers. During the war, Xiao Jun also wrote *Di san dai* (Generation III), later changed to *Guoqu de niandai* (The Past Years), a novel describing life in the northeast before the 1911 revolution, with a mountain village in western Liaoning as its backdrop. Xiao Jun attributes the peasants' suffering to a combination of forces, specifically exploitation by the landlord class and foreign interests, which collude with one another to keep the poor at the bottom of society. To change the lot of the peasants in a fundamental way, Xiao Jun suggests that a radical revolution has to take place. Artistically, *Di san dai* is a more mature work than *Bayue de xiangcun*, both of which are Xiao Jun's defining works. After the **Sino-Japanese War** was formally declared, Xiao Jun traveled through many cities, including Xi'an, where he and Xiao Hong broke up. After the war, Xiao Jun returned to the northeast and assumed the posts of president of the Lu Xun Art and Literature Institute at Northeastern University, head of the Lu Xun Culture Press, and editor-in-chief of the *Literature Newspaper*. Like many writers of his generation, Xiao Jun suffered political persecution from the late 1950s through the 1970s. In the midst of adversities, Xiao Jun wrote the novel *Wuyue de kuangshan* (*Coal Mines in May*) and another historical novel, *Wu Yue chunqiu shihua* (The History of the Wu and Yue States), which were published in the 1980s. *See also* CULTURAL REVOLUTION; LEFT-WING ASSOCIATION OF CHINESE WRITERS.

XIAO KAIYU (1960–). Poet. Born in rural Sichuan, Xiao Kaiyu is one of the representative poets of **Generation III**. Recognizing the indebtedness of modern Chinese poetry to the West as well as to China's ancient traditions, Xiao tackles the problem of self-identity, the raison d'etre of modern Chinese poetry and as an extension modern Chinese culture. Xiao represents Generation III's anxiety and perplexity over the destiny and mission of the intellectual. Sharing his generation's opposition to refinement and aestheticism in poetry, Xiao favors unfiltered colloquialism in his treatment of two main themes: the issue of culture as expressed in early poems such as "Hai shang huayuan" (Garden on the Sea) and "Hanren" (The Chinese), and the confrontation between the individual and society, as in "Yuanze" (Principle). Throughout his career, Xiao has been preoccupied with the relationship between poetic expression and reality, addressed in his main work, "Xiang Du Fu zhi-jing" (Saluting Du Fu), 10 individual poems in which the Tang dynasty poet witnesses, in anguish, "another China," a kaleidoscope of 20th-century social phenomena, which represents the poet's view on the anxi-ety and perplexity of Chinese culture. While interested in the spiritual and intellectual aspect of poetic expression, Xiao is equally if not more keen on the physical world. His poetry records a kaleidoscope of mate-rial phenomena, signaling his disapproval of the dismissive attitude of the Chinese intellectual elite toward material culture. The irony created in the clash of ideas gives Xiao's poetry an added layer of sophistication and helps define his view on the role of poetry not as a representation of truth and beauty but as an objective witness of reality. His poetry collections include *Dongwu yuan de kuangxi* (The Ecstasy of the Zoo) and *Xuexi zhi tian* (The Sweetness of Learning). Xiao has been living in Berlin since 1997 and has worked as a visiting professor in the Shanghai Conservatory of Music.

XIAO LIHONG, A.K.A., HSIAO LI-HUNG (1950–). Novelist. Xiao Lihong, born in Jiayi, **Taiwan**, became one of the most popular writ-ers in the late 1970s when **women** emerged as a powerful force in the island's literary field. The main characters of her writing are women situated in traditional Taiwanese societies, trying to negotiate between personal aspirations and familial and social responsibilities. Her first novel, *Guihua xiang* (The Cassia Flower Alley), published in 1977, is a portrayal of a woman from poor childhood to affluent old age, living a full life as a daughter, sister, wife, mother, sister-in-law, daughter-in-law, mother-in-law, friend, lover, and the head of a wealthy family in a small town of Taiwan. Through her performance in these roles, each making a unique demand on her physically and psychologically, Xiao's heroine displays a strong sense of self and fluid subjectivity full of emotional as well as moral complexities. Like *Guihua xiang*, her second novel, *Qian jiang you shui qian jiang yue* (*A Thousand Moons on a Thousand Rivers*), describes life in a large traditional family in rural Taiwan from the 1950s to the 1960s through the experience of the female protagonist, a young woman intimately attached to her native land and what it represents—love for the family and the community, respect for learning, tolerance, generosity, modesty, frugality, sincerity, moderation, and hard work—strong Confucian values. The novel won Taiwan's *Lianhe wenxue* award in 1980 for its "pure and implicit" descriptions of romantic love and its innovative language that combines classical Chinese lyricism with Taiwanese local dialect. *Bai shuo hu chun meng* (Spring Dreams at the White Water Lake), published in 1995, paints a picture of small-town life for several families intertwined through marriage and friendship. The characters come from all walks of life, such as the wife of the town bailiff, the fortune teller, the local doctor, the schoolteacher, the richest man in town, the carpenter, the electrician, the butcher, and many others, together contributing to a full view of a Taiwanese society in the late 1940s before the onset of modernization. The readers can derive from it a deeper understanding of the interconnectedness of all lives in a traditional community. For their representations of a bygone era, Xiao's novels have become part of the collective memory of a whole generation of Taiwanese who find echoes of their childhood in the relatively simple and innocent world Xiao created.

Despite her enormous popularity, Xiao for many years was considered a *guixiu zuojia* (writer of the boudoir) because of her focus on domesticity and romance and her refined traditional sensibilities. Since then, feminist critics have discovered the underlying social and political implications of her writing and given her overdue critical recognition.

XIAO TONG, PEN NAME OF SHENG JIANZHONG (1928–). Essayist and fiction writer. Educated in Shanghai and Beijing, Xiao Tong went to **Taiwan** in 1949 and edited a newspaper for a living. He settled in **Hong Kong** in 1961, working in the beginning as a screenplay writer and director for a film studio and later quitting his job to concentrate on his writing. He is a prolific writer who has worked in many literary genres. His greatest achievements are his essays and fiction. The most memorable of his essays were written in the 1970s, recording the several trips he made back to Beijing. As a fiction writer, he sticks strictly to the mimetic mode of expression and deals with contemporary realities.

XIE BINGYING, A.K.A. HSIEH PINGYING (1906–2000). Essayist and fiction writer. Known as a "**woman** soldier writer," Xie Bingying was well ahead of her times; not only did she receive a formal education afforded mostly to boys, she joined the army and fought in battles as early as the 1920s when foot-binding was a common practice for

Chinese girls. This rare accomplishment was due to her own determination as well as the support provided by her father, a well-known scholar and an open-minded educator, and her progressive brothers. Xie's first success at creative writing is a diary entitled *Congjun riji* (*War Diary*) published in 1927 and based on her own experience in the Northern Expedition (1926–1927), a military campaign led by the Nationalist Party and the Communist Party to end the rule of warlords and unify the country under the Nationalist leadership. The work was translated into English by **Lin Yutang**, winning Xie international fame. When Japan invaded China, Xie resumed her military service, this time heading an auxiliary company of women to provide medical services for the troops and report on the battles.

Xie was influenced by Western literature introduced to China during the **May Fourth Movement** and her two trips to Japan, in 1931 and 1935, allowed her to come into contact with Japanese feminist writings. Nearly all of her publications in the 1930s and 1940s champion women's liberation from the yoke of traditional morality. Most of Xie's writings are autobiographical. *Nü bing zizhuan* (Autobiography of a Female Soldier), *Nübing shi nian* (Ten Years of a Female Soldier's Life), and *Yige nüxing de fendou* (A Woman's Struggle for Independence) are all drawn from her life.

After she moved to **Taiwan** in 1948 to assume a teaching post at National Taiwan Normal University, Xie continued to be productive, turning out a large number of works, both fiction and prose, consisting of reminiscences of her early life such as *Wo de shaonian shidai* (My Teenage Years), *Guxiang* (Hometown), and *Wo de huiyi* (Remembrances); travelogues such as *Malaiya youji* (Travels to Malaysia) and *Jiujinshan de wu* (The Fog of San Francisco); and novels about romantic love, inlcuding *Hong dou* (Red Beans) and *Biyao zhi lian* (Biyao's Love). Xie lived in San Francisco from 1971 to her death in 2000. *See also* NEW CULTURE MOVEMENT.

XU DISHAN (1893–1941). Fiction writer and essayist. Born in **Taiwan**, Xu Dishan settled in Fujian with his family after Japan occupied the island. While a student at Yanjing University in Beijing, he took part in the **May Fourth Movement**. From 1923 to 1926, Xu studied religion and philosophy at Columbia University and Cambridge University. On his way back to China, he stopped in India to study Buddhism and Sanskrit. Upon his return to Beijing in 1927, he became a professor at his alma mater. He left Beijing in 1935 for a job at the University of Hong Kong and died six years later in the midst of the Japanese invasion of China.

Xu was a unique personality among his contemporaries. His background as a Christian and scholar of religious studies and his experience in south and southeast Asia gave him a distinctive perspective on life and the world. His early stories are known for their exotic settings. "Shangren fu" (*The Merchant's Wife*) is a tale of a Chinese woman who leaves her home in Fujian to look for her husband in Singapore who later sells her to a Muslim merchant from India. While expressing sympathy for the woman, the story does not put emphasis on the exploitation of women, a popular theme among May Fourth writers. Rather it conveys a magnanimous attitude toward life and suffering, revealed through the words of the protagonist. In his works, Xu focused on love, forgiveness, and a sense of harmony, reflecting his religious background. Even in his later and more socially oriented works, Xu adhered to the principle of understanding and kindness. "Chuntao" (*Spring Peach*) details the life of a woman with two husbands, an unusual arrangement caused by war and poverty and sustained by compassion. Xu created characters with complicated experiences and plots with many twists and turns. In addition to a small corpus of fictional works, Xu published several collections of essays. His best-known essay is "Luohuasheng" (Goober Peas), which has been included in school textbooks.

XU KUN (1965–). Fiction writer. Born in the city of Shenyang in the northeastern province of Liaoning, Xu began writing fiction in 1993, while pursuing an academic career in literary studies. She belongs to the so-called post-1960s generation that ascended to the literary stage in the 1990s. Her writing is often characterized as postmodern whose trademark is satire. Xu's protagonists are often intellectuals who have lost the center of gravity in their dealings with an unfamiliar cultural environment charged with energy and materialistic desires, a confusing and absurd world that causes her characters a great deal of anxiety. It is in the clashes of values that the "comic" effects of Xu's stories are achieved. In her stories, idealism surrenders to materialism and high-minded culture gives in to life's banalities. The intellectual wrestles with the contradictions within society as well as within the self. Xu's works contain no tragedy or heroism; instead, there is an abundant amount of mockery and cynicism. A winner of the Lu Xun Literature Prize in 2001, Xu writes almost exclusively about contemporary urban existence. Most of her writings are short stories. Some of the best-known titles include "Xianfeng" (The Avant-garde), "Zaoyu aiqing" (Encountering Love), and "Yi yu" (Sleep Talk). She has written a novel, *Nüwa* (The Goddess Nüwa), which portrays the life of a **woman** from 1930, when she was brought at the age of 10 as a child bride into her husband's family, to 1990, when she reigns over a clan of four generations under the same roof. As a family saga, the novel is often seen as the author's attempt to establish a feminist cultural nationalism in opposition to the predominant patrilineal and patriarchal discourse.

XU SU, PEN NAME OF XU BING (1924–1981). Novelist, essayist, and poet. Born in Jiangsu, Xu Su spent his childhood in the countryside and served in the Nationalist army during the **Sino-Japanese War**. He arrived in **Hong Kong** in 1950 and became the editor and founder of several publications. Most of his novels are based on his experience in the army and the patriotic activities of the Chinese youth during the Sino-Japanese War, though a few are about life in Hong Kong. They feature young lovers whose lives are intertwined with the fate of the nation, focusing on themes such as humanism, nationalism, and ethics. *Xingxing, Yueliang, Taiyang* (The Stars, the Moon, and the Sun), about the romantic relationships of one man and three women, expresses the author's idealistic conception of human nature. In *Yituan* (Suspicion), a story about betrayal and revenge, human nature is more complicated and harder to define and friendship is put to the test when the pursuit of love reveals the truth about humanity's moral weakness. Xu further explores the conflict between sexual passion and social constraints, questioning society's role in suppressing basic human instincts, in stories such as "Shi jie" (Ten Commandments) and "Di yi pian qiu ye" (The First Autumn Leaf). In addition to fiction, Xu also wrote many essays and poems.

XU XIAOBIN (1953–). Fiction writer. Born in Beijing and educated at the Central Institute of Finance, Xu Xiaobin began publishing short stories and novels in 1981. Most of her works are semiautobiographical. She belongs to a circle of young **women** writers who came to fame in the 1990s and who are noted for their introspective, self-focused narratives that mix fiction with their personal lives. This group includes some well-known names, such as **Chen Ran**, **Lin Bai**, and **Hong Ying**. Xu's fictional works not only show a tendency toward autobiography but also a persistent urge to probe into some of the fundamental questions about human existence. Interested in the inner world of women living on the peripheries of society, Xu portrays their feeble revolt against a corrupt world, often in the form of escape. While running away from society, her characters also run away from their true selves. They live in the real world but their souls wander out of their bodies, making them eccentric creatures unable to behave according to social conventions. These spiritual wanderings, often attributed to conditions created since time immemorial, endow Xu's novels with a mythical dimension.

What characterizes Xu's fiction is her probing of the inner world of women, the mystery of their desires and experiences, and their perception of the self in society and in history. *Dunhuang yimeng* (Lingering Dream of Dunhuang) places a romantic tale in an atmosphere of ancient history and mystic religiosity. The heroine, who seeks the meaning of life, achieves her goal by following her unadulterated instincts. *Shuangyu xingzuo* (Pisces), which explores the despair of women alienated from both society and home, is dominated by a sense of doom and fatalism. Xu is interested in history, but one that is personal not official. *Yu she* (Feathered Snake) tells the lives of five generations of women, spanning 100 years. In this introspective novel, Xu probes the makeup of the female psyche in relation to society and family history. The heroine's eccentric and violent behavior, representing her desperate attempt to break free from the chains that reined in her predecessors, shocks her family and alienates her from society. Forced to go through brain surgery to treat her insanity, she becomes "normal" but loses her creativity and gradually bleeds to death. *Deling gongzhu* (Princess Deling), a historical novel, is based on the real life of a Manchu diplomat's daughter, also an author of some repute. The central theme of *Deling gongzhu* is not driven by great events but by the inner workings of the characters and their emotional journeys through love and interpersonal relationships. For her unrelenting focus on the female perspective, Xu is regarded as one of the foremost feminist writers in China.

XU XU, A.K.A. HSU HSU, XU BOXU, XU YU (1908–1980). Novelist, playwright, and poet. Xu Xu studied philosophy and psychology at Beijing University and earned his Ph.D. from the University of Paris. He moved to **Hong Kong** in 1950. A prolific and versatile writer who enjoyed popularity in the 1930s and 1940s, Xu has been somewhat neglected for the last 50 years in China. This lack of attention might have something to do with a widely circulated statement that he made about his change of heart about Marxism: "Those who are not moved by Marxism at a young age are cold-blooded, but if they still make a fetish of it at middle age, they are idiots." His scope of writing includes poetry, prose, drama, and literary criticism, but his main achievements are in fiction.

During his stay in France, Xu wrote *Gui lian* (Ghost Love), his first novella, which earned him his reputation as a writer. It is a tale of a young man's fortuitous meeting with a woman in black who calls herself Ghost. This woman, originally a revolutionary and an assassin, escaped from prison and after spending several years abroad in exile has returned to China. Faced with the failure of the revolution and her lover's murder, she becomes withdrawn. Disguising herself as a ghost, she lives a reclusive existence in a dreary old house in the suburbs of Shanghai, and through the practice of meditation and yoga, she has gained a serene and elegant appearance. The young man woos her enthusiastically only to be refused. This novella contains all the ingredients of a popular story: a fantastic tale, intrigue, modern romance, and even a trendy revolutionary theme. It fully demonstrates the author's imagination and talent as well as his political instinct.

Xu's best-known novel is *Feng xiaoxiao* (The Wind Soughs and Sighs), published in 1943. Applying his favorite features of detective and romantic fiction combined with a patriotic message, the author tells the story of an individualistic young philosopher living in Japanese-occupied Shanghai and his relationships with three beautiful women: a Chinese dancing girl and two American women he has met at a birthday party at the home of an American couple, a military medical doctor and his Secret Service agent "wife." These romantic relationships are complicated by international and political intrigues. The novel ends with the protagonist joining the American Secret Service to fight the Japanese. The popularity of Xu's fiction largely rests upon his ability to sustain complex plots and his clever mixture of exoticism and a lyrical and philosophical mode of expression, which helps to avoid the triteness of the common detective plot or romantic story. The major shortcoming of his works, however, lies in their excessively stereotypical characters, which reduces their realistic impact.

Among Xu's large corpus of fiction are *Jibusai de youhuo* (Gypsy Temptation), *Yi jia* (A Family), *Beican shiji* (The Century of Misery), and *Wulan de emeng* (Wulan's Nightmare). Xu's plays include *Yue guang qu* (The Moonlight Sonata), *Ye hua* (Wildflower), *Gui xi* (Ghost

Play), and *Xiongdi* (Brothers). His poems appear in several collections, including *Jie huo ji* (Borrowing Fire) and *Deng long ji* (The Lamp). *See also* SPOKEN DRAMA.

XU ZHIMO, A.K.A. HSU CHI-MO (1897–1931). Poet. Xu Zhimo was born in Haining, Zhejiang Province, to a well-to-do family. In 1918, after studying at Beijing University, he went to the United States to study economics and finance, but a brief stint at Clark University only confirmed his distaste for the course of study his banker father had chosen for him. He subsequently transferred to Columbia University to study political science. Still unsatisfied, he left the United States to study at Cambridge University, where he fell in love with English romantic poetry. Inspired by poets such as Lord Byron, John Keats, and Percy Bysshe Shelley, he began to write his own poems. His two years in England were crucial in making a poet out of a young man who seemed to be drifting without a clear sense of direction. Both spiritually and emotionally, Xu became attached to Cambridge, to which he dedicated several lyric pieces, the best known among them being "Farewell, Cambridge" and "To Mansfield." In 1922, he returned to China and joined the **New Culture Movement** as its best poet.

Comparable to his literary reputation is the notoriety of Xu's entanglements with three women, a topic of several books, and recently, a movie and a television series. He married twice, first to Zhang Youyi, sister of a friend of his, whom he divorced while in Europe, angering his father. At Cambridge, he courted **Lin Huiyin.** Back in Beijing, he fell in love with Lu Xiaoman, who broke her engagement to a high-ranking government official to marry Xu. Although his divorce and second marriage went against social norms and aroused the wrath of conservatives, such as his own father and his mentor, Liang Qichao, Xu was accepted and even admired in intellectual and literary circles. He was considered a true romantic who not only embraced the romantic ideal in his poetry but also practiced it in his life.

Xu's poetry, though modern in its thematic and formal features and its vernacular language, retains the musicality of classical Chinese poetry. At a time when it was in vogue to align poetry with everyday speech, discarding formalistic concern with rhyme and rhythm, Xu believed that modern poetry had its own internal aesthetic principles that were different from those of prose. A prolific poet, Xu also worked as an editor for literary journals and taught at several universities before dying in a plane crash in 1931 at the age of 34. He left behind four collections of verse and several volumes of translations from various languages. *See also* CRESCENT SOCIETY.

– Y –

YA XIAN, A.K.A. YA HSIEN, PEN NAME FOR WANG QINGLIN (1932–). Poet. Born in Nanyang, Henan Province, Ya Xian, which means "mute strings," joined the Nationalist army in 1949 right before it retreated to **Taiwan**. He participated in the International Writing Program at the University of Iowa and received his master's degree from the University of Wisconsin at Madison. He edited the literary supplement of the *United Daily* in Taipei. He rose to fame in the 1950s, at a time of political oppression by Chiang Kai-shek's government, and continued to lead a productive career through the next two decades. Part of a modernist movement, Ya Xian's poetry bears evidence of a strong influence by European surrealism, with its heavy emphasis on allusion, metaphor, irony, and symbolism. Some of his poems, such as "Ru ge de xingban" (An Andante Ballad), "Yindu" (India), "Zai Zhongguo jie shang" (In the Streets of China), which are modernist reconstructions of folk ballads, make references to dreams and the subconscious, allowing the poet to move at will between the real and imagined world in order to reach an aesthetic realm beyond rationality and language.

YAN GE, PEN NAME OF DAI YUEXING (1984–). Fiction writer. One of the post-1980s generation writers, Yan Ge began publishing stories online at www.rongshuxia.com as a high school student. She later entered Sichuan University to study comparative literature and Chinese. She has won several awards, including first prize for the New Concept Composition Competition, which made her a popular name among young readers.

From the Chinese **avant-garde** writers, especially **Yu Hua**, **Su Tong**, **Ge Fei**, and **Ma Yuan**, Yan Ge learned narrative techniques to create stories that border on fantasy and reality, a style that is most evident in *Liangchen* (Good Times), generally considered her best work. The novel consists of ten independent stories centering on one character named Gu Liangcheng, who has multiple identities: as a librarian who loves his colleague simply because they are both outsiders in a suffocating small town, a beekeeper who possesses not a single bee, a playwright whose ideal of love can only be realized on stage, and a funeral home worker who keeps his profession a secret for fear of being rejected. According to the author, the ten manifestations of unattainable love described in the novel all come down to the longing she has for her mother whose death inspired her to write the book. Among Yan Ge's other works are *Yi shou zhi* (The Tale of Strange Animals), a fantastic story about animals with various human personalities, and *Guan He* (The Guan River), a novel set in ancient China that deals with separation, longing, betrayal, deception, and death in a sensual and languorous language. *See also* WOMEN.

YAN GELING (1956–). Novelist. Born in Shanghai, Yan Geling joined a military performance troupe as a dancer at the age of 12. This experience provides the background for some of her early work including "Mai hong pingguo de mang nüzi" (*The Blind Woman Selling Red Apples*), a gripping tale set in **Tibet** about cultural conflicts between the Han soldiers and local Tibetans. She began writing in the 1970s as a journalist covering the Sino-Vietnamese border war. Her first fictional story was published in the 1980s after she left the armed service. When she went to the United States in 1989 on a student visa, Yan was already a familiar name in China. She received her master's of fine arts in creative writing from Columbia College, Chicago. She currently lives in the United States and makes frequent trips back to China. Her books are written in Chinese and occasionally in English. Her writing is brisk, spare, and fluid.

Yan has written several stories about urban youth sent to China's far-flung countryside during the **Cultural Revolution**. *Cixing caodi* (Female Grassland) relates the heartbreaking fates of a group of city girls left on a remote grassland to raise horses for the cavalry. "Tian yu" (Celestial Bath) centers on a vulnerable city girl living among coarse herdsmen who exchanges her body for the opportunity to get back to the city.

Yan's protagonists are often young, vibrant, innocent women thrown into the company of unscrupulous men in a corrupt world. The protagonist of "Shaonü Xiaoyu" (A Girl Named Xiaoyu) is a simple-minded, good-hearted immigrant forced into a fake marriage by her boyfriend for the purpose of obtaining legal status. "Shui jia you nü chu zhangcheng" (Good-by, Innocence) tells a wrenching story about a gullible rural girl kidnapped and sold into prostitution who later becomes a murderer. *Fusang (The Lost Daughter of Happiness)*, a novel set in the 19th century, features a young woman from a Chinese village who is sold into prostitution in San Francisco's Chinatown. While telling the riveting story of the heroine's entangled relationship with a white man, the narrator frequently interrupts the narrative to speak directly with the protagonist, sharing feelings about her own interracial marriage. Yan's most recent novel, *Xiaoyi Duohe* (Aunt Duohe) is a moving tale about a young Japanese woman named Duohe who is sold at the end of World War II to be the second wife of the second son of the Zhang family. The Zhangs suffered many losses in the war: the eldest son was killed by the Japanese and the second son's first wife miscarried when the Japanese invaded their village, rendering her unable to bear children. The burden to ensure that the family line would continue falls on Duohe. She does not disappoint the Zhangs and in the end gives them three children. Since polygamy is outlawed in the new China, the family has to present Duohe to the outside world as the sister of the second daughter-in-law. To avoid suspicion, this unconventional family moves several times. Duohe, with her high standard of hygiene and a strong principle of right and wrong, and the Zhangs, who adopt a philosophy of life that takes things as they come and accepts life's adversities with no resistance, manage to stay together as a family for 40 years. Several of Yan's works have been turned into movies, including "Shaonü Xiaoyu," "Tian yu," "Shui jia you nü chu zhangcheng," and *Fusang. See also* WOMEN.

YAN LI (1954–). Poet, fiction and prose writer, artist. Born in Beijing, and a member of the **Misty poetry** movement, Yan Li began writing poetry in the early 1970s while being "rusticated" in rural Hebei. Friends with some of the major Misty poets, including **Bei Dao**, **Mang Ke**, and **Duo Duo**, Yan was active in promoting a modernist poetry with his innovative verses, which emphasize wit and black humor, by juxtaposing seemingly unrelated images to reveal the absurdity of the human condition. "Yi renlei de mingyi shengcun" (Surviving in the Name of Humanity), "Niuyue" (New York), and "Hei'an zhi ge" (Song of Darkness) are some of his best-known poems. As an organizer and participant in the Star art exhibitions, Yan, along with other artists, represented significant breakthroughs in post-Mao modern art. Yan's straddling of both poetry and art gave him a unique spot in the unofficial **avant-garde** movement. Although he is primarily recognized for his poetry and painting, Yan has also written essays and fiction. He moved to New York in 1985 and continued to write and paint. Two years later, he founded *Yi hang* (One Line), a poetry journal based in New York. He currently lives in New York and Shanghai.

YAN LIANKE (1958–). Novelist. Born in a small town in Henan Province, Yan Lianke joined the army in 1985. He later studied political science at Henan University and literature at the Military Institute of Arts. Yan began his career by writing about rural and army life. *Zuihou yiming nü zhiqing* (The Last Female Educated Youth) deals with the prices individuals have to pay due to forces beyond their own control. It focuses on a woman whose decision to leave the village, along with the rest of the urban youth, is complicated by her marriage to a local peasant. Other novels about rural China include *Riguang liunian* (Sunlight and the Fleeting Time), about a small village's painful and courageous journey to modernity, and an allegorical novel, *Shouhuo* (The Village of Shouhuo), in which the author uses a farcical and hyperbolic language to tell a sad tale of how a remote village inhabited by disabled residents is discovered and used for developing the economy of the county. Both of these two novels examine suffering and the meaning of life.

In dealing with military themes, Yan focuses on interpersonal relationships and the common concerns of daily life. *Xia Riluo* (Xia Riluo), set against the background of the border clash between China and Vietnam, focuses on two low-ranking military officers whose friendship is threatened when they are faced with the prospect that one of them could be promoted and the other forced to return to farming. The best known of his military fiction is *Wei renmin fuwu* (Serve the People), which tells the story of a soldier from the countryside who gains military honors and promotions by providing sexual favors to his commander's bored wife. The exchange of sex for political status makes a mockery of Mao's teaching, "Serve the people." For sexual arousal, the protagonists come up with "counterrevolutionary" acts such as smashing Chairman Mao statues. By turning Mao Zedong and the lofty Communist ideals into a game of debauchery, the novel offended the sensibilities of the authorities and was subsequently banned.

On Yan's long list of publications are *Jinlian nihao* (Hello, Jinlian), a parody of the tale about China's most infamous seductress, Pan Jinlian, who is featured in classical novels and operas, and *Jianying ru shui* (As Hard as Water), a story of two young Red Guards during the **Cultural**

Revolution whose steamy sex is carried out in the midst of their revolutionary destructive acts that provide stimulants for their insatiable carnal desire.

YANG HANSHENG A.K.A. HUA HAN, PEN NAMES OF OUYANG BENYI (1902–1993). Playwright and screenplay and fiction writer. One of the leaders of the leftist Chinese literary establishment, Yang Hansheng had a long career that spanned seven decades. A Sichuan native, Yang graduated from Shanghai University. He joined the Chinese Communist Party in 1925 and thereafter began his work as a career revolutionary activist. He was a political staff member in the Nationalist army when the Nationalists and the Communists were working together against the warlords and participated in the Communist-led Nanchang Uprising. In 1929, he was the party secretary of the **Left-wing Association of Chinese Writers.**

The trajectory of Yang's literary career was similar to that of other early revolutionary writers, such as **Hong Lingfei** and **Jiang Guangci,** who emerged from the **May Fourth Movement** to champion radical changes in Chinese society through their writings. Yang began as a fiction writer. From the romantic and revolutionary young intellectual hero who wallows in despair over personal and national predicaments to peasant/worker rebels, his protagonists changed as he became better acquainted with the objectives of the Communist revolution. A member of the **Creation Society,** Yang was a passionate advocate of a utilitarian literature that served the high purpose of the revolutionary cause. A prolific writer in the proletarian literary movement of the 1920s and the early 1930s, he published, under the pen name Hua Han, numerous stories, several novellas, and a novel. In these early works, Yang injects a heavy dose of romantic sentimentalism into his characters, resulting in the style of "revolution plus love," which characterizes the so-called proletarian literature (puluo wenxue) of the 1920s. *Nü qiu* (The Female Prisoner), written in the form of letters, is narrated by a woman put in prison after being accused of subversive activities. Another novella, *Liangge nüxing* (Two Women), deals with the choices young intellectuals make in the turbulent years of the late 1920s when factions, including the Nationalists, the Communists, and the various warlords, were vying with one another for political power. In his trilogy *Di quan* (The Underground Spring), published in 1930 and generally believed to be his best fictional work, Yang expands his scope to include peasants and workers in armed uprisings. Two years later when the novel was reissued, five prefaces, including one written by Yang himself, were attached. In their critiques of the work, **Mao Dun**, Qu Qiubai, and two other leftist critics used the novel as an example to assess the achievements and shortcomings of the proletarian literature, paying tribute to its clear political purpose but criticizing its stereotyped characters and unrealistic plots.

One cannot be certain whether these criticisms had contributed to Yang's move away from fiction to plays and screenplays, but starting from 1933 when he entered the Shanghai Yihua Film Studio until the end of his career, Yang devoted his creative energy to film and theater, turning out a total of more than 90 plays and screenplays under the pen name Yang Hansheng, which he adopted in 1933 when he wrote *Tieban hong lei lu* (Tears on the Iron Plate), a movie about Sichuan peasants rising against a local tyrant. Working closely with **Tian Han**, another leftist filmmaker and playwright, Yang wrote some of the best-known films and plays in the left-wing movement, including such classics as *Wan jia denghuo* (City Lights), a realistic portrayal of a middle-class family driven apart by economic pressure and typical domestic quarrels between the mother-in-law and the daughter-in-law, and *San Mao liulang ji* (A Young Vagabond) about the sad but dignified life of a street urchin, as well as plays based on the 19th-century Taiping peasant uprising: *Li Xiucheng zhi si* (The Death of Li Xiucheng), *Tian guo chun qiu* (The History of the Taiping Rebellion), and *Caomang yingxiong* (The Rebel Hero). Conceived as part of a national salvation agenda, the historical plays used the cautionary tales of the Taiping rebels to warn about infighting, urging the Chinese people to unite against their common enemy during the **Sino-Japanese War**. Later in the **Civil War**, Yang wrote plays to expose social injustice and to encourage rebellion against oppression, part of a national campaign orchestrated by the Communist Party. For many years during the wars, Yang worked for various theater and film companies. He was a founder of the Chinese Dramatic Arts Society (Zhonghua juyi she), established in 1941 to perform progressive plays in the areas controlled by the Nationalists. After 1949, Yang served as deputy chairman of the National Association of Culture as well as many other administrative and honorary positions in the government. *See also* SPOKEN DRAMA.

YANG JIANG, PEN NAME OF JIANG JIKANG (1911–). Prose and fiction writer, playwright, translator. Born in Beijing, Yang Jiang graduated from Dongwu University in Suzhou, Jiangsu Province. She met her future husband, **Qian Zhongshu**, while doing graduate work at Qinghua University. Soon after their wedding, the couple set off for England, and later for France, to study literature. After they returned to China, Yang taught literature at Qinghua University. After 1949, she worked at the Chinese Academy of Social Sciences until her retirement in 1989.

Prior to 1949, Yang wrote some plays, including the comedies *Chenxin yuyi* (To the Heart's Content) and *Nong jia cheng zhen* (Make-Believe Becomes Reality), and short stories. However, she was not widely known until the 1980s, when she was recognized with the publication of her memoir, *Ganxiao liu ji* (Six Chapters from My Life Downunder), which recounts the life of a group of intellectuals, including herself and her husband, Qian Zhongshu, sent to the countryside from 1969 to 1972 to undergo ideological education through physical labor. Another memoir published in 2003, entitled *Women sa* (The Three of Us), recalls the days when her husband and their daughter were still alive and describes in loving memory the warmth of an intellectual family and the power of their love for one another. The best known of her fictional work, *Xizao* (Shower), published in the 1980s, portrays a group of intellectuals who returned to China from abroad in the 1950s and how they survive the political campaigns aimed at the educated. Faced with hard choices that are made more excruciating because of their belief in the importance of morality and basic human decency, these scholars reveal, each in his or her own painful emotional tribulations, the fundamental needs of humanity.

In addition to her creative work, Yang is also a noted translator of English, French, and Spanish literature. Her translation of *Don Quixote* is regarded as the best rendition into Chinese of the Spanish masterpiece. *See also* CULTURAL REVOLUTION; SPOKEN DRAMA; WOMEN.

YANG KUI, A.K.A. YANG K'UEI (1905–1985). Fiction writer. A significant writer in colonial Taiwanese literature, Yang Kui grew up in Japanese-occupied **Taiwan**. He went to Japan in 1924 to study and while there he was thrown in prison for participating in the demonstrations against the government's mistreatment of Koreans in the country. In 1927, Yang returned to Taiwan and participated in protests against Japanese occupation, which got him arrested several times by the Japanese authorities. Yang cofounded, together with **Lai He** and others, the journal *Taiwan xin wenxue* (New Literature of Taiwan), which published works written in Chinese or Japanese. He introduced mainland writers to Taiwan by translating their works into Japanese. After Japan surrendered, Yang became an editor for the literary supplement of *Heping ribao* (Peace Daily) and continued to bring more **May Fourth** writers to the attention of readers in Taiwan, even entering into a collaborative venture with mainland writers to produce a magazine called *Wenhua jiaoliu* (Cultural Exchanges), which failed to materialize due to the change of political environment when Chiang Kai-shek and his government retreated to Taiwan.

In the aftermath of the February 28 Incident (1947), which resulted in a brutal crackdown by the Nationalist government on a massive protest movement mounted by Taiwanese against the government's discriminatory economic and political policies, corruption, and mistreatment of the people, Yang, along with his wife and many other demonstrators, was arrested and spent three months in jail. Once out of prison, he continued to promote the new Taiwanese literature in his creative and critical works. In 1949, he was sent back to jail, this time with a 12-year sentence, for his article "Heping xuanyan" (The Declaration of Peace), in which he advocated a peaceful resolution to the conflict between the Communists and the Nationalists and demanded that the prisoners involved in the February 28 demonstrations be released. While being kept on the infamous Green Island for political prisoners, Yang continued to ponder over issues concerning Taiwanese literature but did not produce much creative work. After his release from prison, Yang devoted the rest of his life to farming and rarely made public appearances either through writing or speech.

Yang was a realist writer with a strong sense of social commitment. His writing was meant to arouse sympathy for the oppressed and to move his readers to action in the fight against colonial rule. "Song bao fu" (*The Newspaper Carrier*), originally written in Japanese and later translated by the author himself into Chinese, is generally considered his representative work. The story relates the experience of a Taiwanese young man who has lost everything in Japanese-occupied Taiwan and who leaves his hometown for Tokyo, where he is further exploited. Based on the author's own experience as a student in Japan in the mid-1920s, when he delivered newspapers during the day and went to school at night, the story conveys an unambiguous message about class struggle and encourages the exploited to unite and fight for their rights. "E Mama chujia" (*Mother Goose Gets Married*) unravels the web of lies built around Japan's "Great East Asia Economic Prosperity" project by pointing out that the project is nothing but Japan's imperialist scheme to rob its colonies of their natural resources. Yang's other notable works include "Ya bu bian de meigui" (*The Indomitable Rose*) and "Lüdao jiashu" (*Letters from the Green Island*), both concerning his imprisonment.

Yang used to call himself "a humanistic socialist," an ideological leaning formed in his youth as a student in Japan. On account of his nationalist views, his works were considered political protests and therefore banned in Taiwan until the 1970s, when the **modernist** versus **nativist** literary debates brought them to light. *See also* CHEN YING-ZHEN; CIVIL WAR; HUANG CHUNMING; SINO-JAPANESE WAR; WANG ZHENHE.

YANG LIAN (1955–). Poet. Yang Lian was born in Bern, Switzerland, where his diplomat parents, representing the newly established People's Republic of China, were posted. He grew up in Beijing but spent several years in the countryside as an educated youth. Yang came to fame in the early 1980s, when he became one of the most prominent members of the **Misty poets.** Yang was in New Zealand with his wife, **YoYo,** in 1989 when the Chinese government cracked down on the student demonstration at Tian'anmen Square. He stayed in New Zealand until 1993 and eventually became a citizen. He later lived in Germany, Australia, and the United States, and since 1994, Yang has made London his home. His books were banned in the aftermath of the Tian'anmen demonstration, but in recent years he has travelled back to China and his poems have been published there. Winner of the 1999 Flaiano International Prize for Poetry, Yang enjoys an international reputation as one of the major voices representing modern Chinese poetry, and his work has been translated into many languages.

A man of talent and charisma, Yang has evolved into one of the most creative poets of the original Misty group. Yang has attempted to reinvigorate an interest in cultural heritage and make it relevant to modern consciousness. His well-known long poem, "Nuorilang," named after a waterfall in a national park in western Sichuan, ponders history and reality in the interplay of a natural phenomenon and a Tibetan myth. Other poems that explore the past in the present include "Banpo" (The Prehistoric Village), "Dayan ta" (The Wild Goose Pagoda), "Xizang" (Tibet), and "Dunhuang" (Dunhuang), all landmarks impregnated with rich history. Yang's attraction to such locales comes from his preoccupation with the meaning of culture and civilization in the highly abstract sense. This particular interest in tracing the infinite and the universal through ancient traditions has become more pronounced in his poetry written after he left China. *Yi,* a book-length poem and his most ambitious project, is inspired by the Taoist classic, *Yi jing* (*Book of Change*). The poem weaves together assorted images, encompassing the past, present, and future, making metaphysical inquiries about time and space. Yang also writes about exile, conceived not just as a form of political excommunication, but more cogently, as the essence of existence, complementing the fundamental concern of his poetry: the expression of the meaning of life and death. Noted particularly for his innovative use of the Chinese language, Yang's poetry is often abstruse, subscribing to its own logic and inner hermetic rationale.

YANG MU, PEN NAME OF WANG JINGXIAN (1940–). Poet, essayist, and translator. Born in **Taiwan**, Yang Mu began writing poetry in middle school. He graduated from Donghai University with a degree in English and from the University of Iowa with a master's degree in creative writing, and received his Ph.D. in comparative literature from the University of California at Berkeley. Yang has taught Chinese and comparative literature at the University of Washington, National Taiwan University, and Hong Kong University of Science and Technology, among other institutions of higher learning. He has had a long and distinguished career. That he has studied both classical Chinese poetry and Western poetic traditions is reflected in his own creative work. Among Western poets, the work of John Keats and William Butler Yeats highly influenced Yang. Keats's desire to return to an idealized and romanticized social order in the Middle Ages is echoed in Yang's eulogizing of nature worship among indigenous cultures in **Taiwan**. Yang also expressed his admiration for Yeats's innovative linguistic techniques. On the other end of the spectrum, classical Chinese poetry, from *Shi jing* (*The Book of Odes*) to the great poets of the Tang dynasty, has been a constant source of intellectual nourishment for him. Yang has systematically studied classical Chinese philosophy and literature and considered the Chinese poetic tradition an essential element in his blood and spirit; his Ph.D. dissertation was a study of *Shi jing.*

Yang's own poetry shows his familiarity with Chinese images and allusions, as well as its rhythms, and with a wide variety of forms and meters of English poetry. His poems are characterized by fragmented imageries that demand active participation from the imagination of readers to fill in the blanks. Yang is particularly noted for his experiments with integrating forms of poetry and lyrical prose, innovations partially inspired by the rhymed prose of the Six Dynasties (221–589) and early Chinese philosophical texts, which Yang studied during his college years. Most of all, he is known for his lasting interest in expressing the romantic spirit, for living a life that embraces the energy of rebelliousness. His poems and essays often deal with questions about life and death, truth and beauty, and the significance of spirituality. Similarly, his autobiography attempts to define the meaning of beauty through recollections of his early life in Taiwan. *See also* MODERN POETRY MOVEMENT IN TAIWAN.

YANG ZHIJUN (1955–). Fiction and prose writer. Yang Zhijun's literary career is built upon his many years of experience living and working in the **Tibetan** region of Qinghai. Although he has written extensively on the western frontier and its rich cultures, it is *Zang ao* (The Tibetan Mastiff) that won him national fame. The novel personifies the canine species famous for its ferocity and loyalty. The central characters are two packs of mastiffs, each belonging to a Tibetan nomadic tribe, who are civilized by their masters but still maintain their primordial nature. The brutal world of animals vividly portrayed in the novel resonates with the time-honored customs, including religious practices, of the Tibetan nomads. The mastiffs' fights among themselves for supreme leadership mirror tribal conflicts in the grassland and human relationships. *Zang ao 2* (The Tibetan Mastiff: Part 2) and *Zang ao 3* (The Tibetan Mastiff: Part 3) focus on the deep bond between the narrator's father, a Chinese who is a principal and teacher in a Tibetan nomadic community, and the mastiffs he rescues and raises. Through the description of the mastiffs' battles with wild wolves, who are despised in the Tibetan grassland for being greedy and selfish, and their heroic deeds during blizzards to protect their masters and herds of sheep and cattle, the novels foreground the spirit of loyalty and courage. The triology ends with the narrator's father leaving the grassland to return to Xining during the **Cultural Revolution** when the struggle for power in the human world brings devastating destruction to the mastiff population. In these novels, the mastiffs are endowed with humanlike intellect; the line between humans and animals is indistinguishable. Yang also makes liberal use of magic realism when he portrays Tibetan religious practices and traditional beliefs.

Yang is also known as an environmental activist with a series of writings on the devastation afflicting the Tibetan Plateau and the heavy price humans pay for their ambition to conquer nature. These works include "Huan hu bengkui" (The Collapse of the Lakeside), "Hai zuotian tuiqu" (The Ocean Receded Yesterday), and *Wu ren buluo* (A Tribe without Human). Like Ernest Hemingway, Yang examines the everlasting struggle of humankind with nature, through which to explore the meaning of life. The Tibetan Plateau, with its unique natural environment and rich cultural traditions, has been his inspiration. Whether he will continue to write about China's western frontier or find a new muse, now that he has settled in the modern coastal city of Qingdao, remains to be seen.

YANGDON (1963–). Fiction writer. Born in Lhasa, Yangdon is one of the younger generation of **Tibetan** writers writing in Chinese. She attended Beijing University, where she majored in Chinese literature, and after graduation she returned to Lhasa to work as an assistant editor for *Xizang wenxue* (Tibetan Literature), in which her stories began to appear in 1986. *Wu xingbie de shen* (*God without Gender*), a novel about a Tibetan aristocratic family published in 1994, is set in the mid-20th century. From the perspective of a precocious young girl, the novel looks at the life of the aristocracy. To render a realistic cultural landscape, Yangdon imbues her work with rich details, vividly capturing the customs of daily life in the aristocratic families and monasteries. In 1997, Yangdon won the Literature Prize for Minorities, and two years later a movie based on her novel was released. In her view, Tibetan culture has been misrepresented in Chinese literature, and as a writer her mission is to rectify the erroneous images and reclaim the ownership of Tibetan cultural representation. She shows a propensity for historical subjects, re-creating a past in contrast to the present. She attempts to retrieve the glorious Tibetan civilization by celebrating Tibetan heroes such as Songtsen Gampo, the founder of the Tibetan Empire, and Tseyang Syatso, the Sixth Dalai Lama, and in so doing she emphasizes her ethnic pride. Since 1994, Yangtsen has been working in Beijing at the Chinese Center for Tibetan Studies, where she works as an editor for China's Tibetan Studies Press.

YAO XUEYIN (1910–1999). Fiction writer. Born into a peasant family in Henan Province, Yao Xueyin began publishing stories in newspapers and literary journals during the 1930s. Most of his writings deal with the struggle of peasants in times of war and national strife. Yao's best-known work is *Li Zicheng* (The Legend of Li Zicheng), a historical novel that took him more than 30 years to finish, with the first volume published in 1963 and the last two volumes published in 1999 after the author's death. The novel is about the rise and fall of the peasant uprising led by Li Zicheng (1606–1645) at the end of the Ming dynasty (1368–1644). Yao paints a sympathetic portrait of the rebel leader while examining the reasons behind Li's success and failure. The views of Chinese history the book espouses are clearly in line with the Chinese Communist Party's ideological interpretations. Mao Zedong spoke highly of Yao's work and ordered his protection at a time when political pressure was mounting against the author during the **Cultural Revolution**. An important figure in the development of the genre of the historical novel, Yao has left a significant legacy in modern Chinese literature. To celebrate his contribution, the Chinese Ministry of Culture established the Yao Xueyin Historical Novel Prize in 2003, four years after his death.

YE GUANGQIN (1948–). Fiction and prose writer. Born into a Manchu family that counts among its ancestors numerous empresses and royal concubines during the Qing dynasty, the most famous being the notorious Empress Cixi, who presided over the empire during one of its most disastrous and vulnerable periods, Ye Guangqin has written about the descendants of that illustrious family and the remnant traditions gleaned from the decay of a collapsed empire.

Her best-known work is a novel *Cai sangzi* (Picking Mulberry Seeds), which is composed of 10 independent novellas telling the individual stories of 14 members of a Manchu noble family who were thrust into the whirlwind of the political and cultural upheavals in the 20th century. Ye's other notable works include *Shui fan Yuefu qiliang qu* (Memories of a Bleak Past), also dealing with family history, and *Xiaoyao jin* (A Laid-back Life) about life in the old Beijing neighborhoods that used to be occupied by descendants of the Manchu nobilities. Many of her stories have won prizes, including "Huanglian houpu" (Two Chinese Herbal Medicines), "Zui ye wuliao" (Bored while Drunk), and "Meng ye he ceng dao Xie Qiao" (No Return to Xie Qiao Even in a Dream), all cultural vignettes of traditional Beijing. Ye is admired for her graceful and sophisticated language as well as her unique ability to capture the scenes and sights of a bygone era. Ye has been living in Xi'an since 1968 and is the deputy director of the Xi'an Writers Association. *See also* WOMEN.

YE LINGFENG (1905–1975). Novelist and essayist. Born in Nanjing, Jiangsu Province, Ye studied painting in Shanghai in the 1920s and was a member of the **Creation Society**, sharing similar interests with the other Creationists, particularly **Yu Dafu**, whom Ye greatly admired. He edited several literary journals, including *Hongshui* (Flood), *Xiandai xiaoshuo* (Modern Novel), *Xiandai wenyi* (Modern Art), and *Wenyi huabao* (Art Pictorial). In 1930, he joined the **Left-wing Association of Chinese Writers** but lost his membership the following year due to lack of participation in its activities. Ye moved to **Hong Kong** in 1938 and continued to edit newspapers and magazines until his death in 1975.

A prolific writer, Ye published numerous novels, collections of short stories, and essays. Early in his career, Ye wrote romantic tales, such as *Hong de tianshi* (Red Angel) and *Wei wancheng de chanhuilu* (Unfinished Confessions). Later, especially after settling in Hong Kong, he showed a keen interest in local history. *Neng bu yi jiangnan* (Memory of the South of the River), *Xianggang fangwu zhi* (A Local History of Hong Kong), and *Xianggang jiushi* (Legends of Hong Kong) are some of his representative works. *See also* SPOKEN DRAMA.

YE SHENGTAO, PEN NAME OF YE SHAOJUN (1894–1988). Fiction writer, editor, and educator. Ye Shengtao was one of the few from the first generation of modern Chinese writers whose careers began in the early 20th century and continued through the 1980s. His main creative accomplishments are short stories and a novel, *Ni Huanzhi* (Ni Huanzhi the Schoolteacher), as well as children's literature. Best remembered as a consummate stylist, he composed unpretentious but richly textured prose.

Born in Suzhou, Ye grew up in a family supported by his father's meager income as a bookkeeper. At the age of 11, he took the very last civil service exam the Qing dynasty ever administered. Ye wrote his first stories, more than 20 in total, in classical Chinese. Some of these stories are in imitation of Washington Irving, whose short stories Ye admired. The **May Fourth Movement** of 1919 changed his outlook as well as the language he wrote in. As a key member of the **Literary Research Society**, working closely with **Mao Dun** and others, Ye became one of the pioneers of the New Literature movement, which advocated realism and vernacular language. In 1919, he wrote his first vernacular poem, "Chunyu" (Spring Rain), and published his first vernacular story, "Zhe ye shi yige ren" (Is This a Human Being?), about the misfortunes of a country woman, which echoes the theme of **Lu Xun**'s "Diary of a Madman" published nine months earlier. *Gemo* (Barrier), published in 1922, is the second collection of short stories of the New Literature, after *Chenlun* (*Sinking*) by **Yu Dafu**. *Huo zai* (Fire), his second collection of short stories, was published in 1923, followed closely by four more collections of short stories and one novel.

Ye is best known for his portrayals of schools and teachers in his short stories with which he expresses his views on education, shaped during his many years of teaching under the influence of the May Fourth Movement with its emphasis on science and democracy. These stories expose the ills of the traditional system of education. The characters, mostly teachers, are ridiculed either because they muddle through life like Mr. Wu in "Fan" (Meals) or because they are cruel and abusive, as the English teacher in "Yi er" (Adopted Son) and the history teacher in "Fengchao" (Agitation). Some of his characters, such as those in "Yunyi" (Dark Clouds), are empty-headed and idle away their time by filling their minds with silly love letters. Others degenerate into gamblers and engage in promiscuous activities, like those in "Xiaozhang" (The Headmaster). By attacking the old system, Ye advocates a new educational philosophy that instead of cramming students' heads with useless knowledge provides an environment conducive to the free development of children's intellects. To that end, the subservient role the student plays in the traditional system must be replaced by an equal and fair relationship between the teacher and the student, as advocated and carried out by the protagonist in Ye's novel *Ni Huanzhi* (Ni Huanzhi the Schoolteacher).

Ni Huanzhi, completed in 1928, is the author's only novel and one of the few full-length novels in early modern Chinese literature. In the May Fourth era the short story was the predominant genre while the novel, because of the technical difficulties demanded by its length, was not a popular choice for most writers. By the time *Ni Huanzhi* came out, there had been a dozen or so novels written, mostly medium-length texts, the most notable of which was Lu Xun's *Ah Q zhengzhuan* (*The True Story of Ah Q*). With the exception of Lu Xun's work, the other novels, in the words of Mao Dun, only touched "a tiny corner of a person's life." In

Ni Huanzhi, the author places the protagonist in the midst of the major events of a turbulent era and depicts a significant historical period from 1911 to 1927. Ni Huanzhi is an idealistic, reform-minded educator. Convinced that education is the hope of all hopes, he, together with the headmaster, experiments with new methodologies despite strong resistance from the staff and the parents. They teach practical knowledge and allow the students to develop their personalities in an open environment. Ni is a modern man living in a world still governed by traditional values. Neither his educational reform nor his marriage can succeed in such an environment. He dies, still young but already broken, longing for the bright day when "there must be people different from us."

In the field of children's literature, the short stories, fairy tales, and songs Ye wrote for children are still widely used in schools across the nation. Modern Chinese fairy tales, before Ye, were either rewritings of traditional mythical tales or translations from foreign texts. *Daocao ren* (Scarecrow), published in 1923, opened a new direction for the writing of fairy tales. Ye's fairy tales create a fantasy world imagined and perceived from the innocent perspectives of children. Nature and animals dominate these tales, and the morals of "beauty" and "love" are conveyed subtly.

As editor for literary journals, most notably *Xiaoshuo yuebao* (Fiction Monthly), Ye discovered and nurtured many new poets and novelists, and many prominent writers were his frequent contributors. During his tenure as editor of several influential journals and publishing houses, he helped publish some of the most prominent writings of modern Chinese literature.

YE WEILIAN, A.K.A. WAI-LIM YIP (1937–). Poet, essayist, translator, and scholar. Born in Zhongshan, Guangdong Province, Ye Weilian received his B.A. from National Taiwan University, his M.A. from the University of Iowa, and his Ph.D. from Princeton University. He currently teaches comparative literature at the University of California, San Diego. A poet and scholar, Ye has authored numerous books in Chinese and in English. In 1978, the media in **Taiwan** named him one of the 10 greatest modern Chinese poets. Ye is a poet of modernist sensibilities who also exhibits Taoist and Buddhist aesthetics; his poems are expressions of spontaneous feelings as well as philosophical and intellectual inquiries. Written in a variety of styles and on a wide range of themes, they capitalize on the poet's deep cultural roots and solid learning, both Chinese and Western. His essays, like his poems, are examples of belles lettres.

Ye is an influential scholar in comparative poetics. He is also a noted translator and scholar of Chinese poetry. His translation of Wang Wei's poetry, *Hiding the Universe: Poems of Wang Wei*, and particularly his anthology, *Chinese Poetry: Major Modes and Genres*, both published in the early 1970s, have been widely adopted in the classrooms of American colleges. Two other books of translations, *Modern Chinese Poetry, 1955–1965* and *Lyrics from Shelters: Modern Chinese Poetry 1930–1950*, which appeared respectively in 1976 and 1992, are also important scholarly contributions. He introduced Western modernist poets, including T. S. Eliot, to Chinese readers in the 1970s, helping launch Taiwan's modernist poetry. *See also* HONG KONG; MODERN POETRY MOVEMENT IN TAIWAN.

YE ZHAOYAN (1957–). Fiction writer. A Nanjing native and grandson of **Ye Shengtao**, Ye Zhaoyan graduated from Nanjing University and became known in the 1980s through the publication of several stories, including "Xuangua de lü pinguo" (A Hanging Green Apple), "Wuyue de huanghun" (Dusk in May), "Lüse kafeiguan" (A Green Café), and *Zaoshu de gushi* (The Story of a Date Tree), which established his reputation as an innovative stylist. Since then, he has written several novels, more short stories, and numerous essays. Like most young writers in the 1980s, Ye came under the influence of Latin American magic realism. "Zaoshu de gushi" echoes Gabriel García Márquez's *One Hundred Years of Solitude* in foregrounding the role of the narrator. This story features a woman and her chance encounters with several men at a time of great political uncertainty. The narrator tells the tragic story with many moments of lighthearted humor, emphasizing the helplessness of individuals facing their capricious and unpredictable fates.

His tales about old Nanjing under the poetic title of *Ye bo Qinhuai* (Anchored at Night in the Qinhuai River) paint cameos of personalities and scenes of Nanjing in the 1930s and 1940s. All four stories in the series have the city's famous sites for titles. "Zhuangyuan jing" (The Number One Scholar's Mirror) is a love story between a humble musician and a warlord's concubine. "Shizi pu" (The Shop at the Crossroad) portrays the sinister world of government and the successes and failures of romantic relationships among the city's upper class. "Zhuiyue lou" (The Moon Chasing Pavilion) tells of the courageous life of an old scholar who refuses to collaborate with the Japanese. "Banbian yin" (Half of a Camp) details the disintegration of a large established family after the Japanese defeat. Along the same line, Ye wrote *Hua ying* (The Shadow of Flowers), relating a moving tale about an old spinster who inherits a large fortune and is ruined as a result of the fierce fight between her and her relatives for control of the inheritance. The movie version of the story is Chen Kaige's *Feng yue* (Temptress Moon). *Hua sha* (The Ghost of Flowers) is the least traditional of Ye's neohistorical stories. The author injects the historical narration with a dose of contemporary sensibility by creating an ironic distance between the narrator and the characters. The story begins in the late Qing dynasty and ends half a century later in the Republican period, focusing on a local hero, who is executed for burning Christian churches and killing missionaries, and his posthumous son and half brother who terrorize a southern Chinese town. Among Ye's neohistorical stories, the best known is *Yijiusanqi nian de aiqing* (*Nanjing 1937: A Love Story*), a saga set on the eve of the Japanese massacre of Nanjing, about a passionate courtship launched by a determined former philanderer who is oblivious to the coming of the Japanese onslaught. Narrated with humor and with little sentimentality, the novel is a poignant personal story played out on a grand historical stage.

Ye has written several novels and novellas about contemporary life, notably the allegorical *Meiyou boli de huafang* (The Greenhouse without Glass) set during the **Cultural Revolution**, and *Women de xin duo wangu* (Our Hearts Are So Stubborn), which traces the sexual encounters of a man during his 40 years of life. *See also* ROOT-SEEKING MOVEMENT; SINO-JAPANESE WAR.

YI SHU, PEN NAME OF NI YISHU (1946–). Romance writer. Born in Shanghai, Yi Shu, younger sister of science fiction writer Ni Kuang, moved with her family to **Hong Kong** at the age of two. At 15, she was already a published author whose stories appeared in the literary supplements of local newspapers. After graduating from high school, Yi Shu worked as a journalist and editor for a movie magazine. In 1973, she went to England to study hotel management. After she returned to Hong Kong, she worked for a hotel and later for the Hong Kong government. Seven years later, she quit her job and moved to Canada. Yi Shu specializes in popular love stories. Some of her romantic tales have been turned into films. Among her numerous books are *Meigui de gushi* (The Story of Rose) and *Zhao hua xi shi* (Morning Flowers Gathered at Dawn). *See also* WOMEN.

YO YO, PEN NAME OF LIU YOUHONG (1955–). Fiction writer and essayist. Born in northwestern China, Yo Yo worked as an editor for an art publication in Beijing prior to going abroad with her husband, poet **Yang Lian.** They were in New Zealand when the Chinese government cracked down on the **Tian'anmen Prodemocracy Movement** on 4 June 1989. Ever since then, the couple has been living in the West, moving from place to place before finally settling down in London. Yo Yo began to write in the 1990s, which has resulted in many essays and short stories, as well as several novellas collected in *Renjing guihua* (Human Scenery and Ghost Speech), *Ta kanjian le liangge yueliang* (She Saw Two Moons), *Tishen lan diao* (Substitute Blues), and *Hunxi* (Marriage Game), and a novel, *Ghost Tide.* In many ways, her exile was the defining moment in her life and career. Many of her works deal with life in exile in its minute daily detail. Not only does she discuss her alienation from China, but also alienation as a human condition. The majority of her stories portray female characters who have to negotiate between marriage and personal space as well as malaise associated with modern life; the stories paint the interior landscape of the modern **women.** Yo Yo's recent novel, *Ghost Tide*, exposes the absurdities of life in the 1950s and 1960s when China was embroiled in political fanaticism. By identifying the strong current of traditional beliefs that runs under the surface of Communist ideals, the novel brings into focus the struggle of conscience that leaves deep psychological scars on Chinese people. Through irony, humor, and fantastic mysticism, Yo Yo laments the heavy tolls the Chinese have paid and are continuing to pay while ghosts of the distant and recent past haunt the land.

YOU FENGWEI (1943–). Fiction writer. A Shandong native and currently living in the city of Qingdao, You Fengwei has served in the army and worked in a factory. His literary career began in 1976 and since then he has published numerous short stories and novellas as well as novels. You has written about some of the most important events in 20th-century China, such as the **Sino-Japanese War** and the Anti-Rightist Campaign. Instead of sweeping historical accounts, You focuses on human conscience tested during critical moments of moral and political choices. His writings provoke serious reflections on the past and its connection to the present. His best-known work, *Zhongguo yijiuqwuqi* (China, 1957), a novel about how the cruel machine of the state sets out to destroy the soul of Chinese intellectuals, is hailed as a book of "intellectual and moral conscience" that has reopened a "wound" in modern Chinese history. The Anti-Rightist Campaign that began in 1957 is generally agreed to be a political operation that "castrated" the whole class of Chinese intellectuals by turning them from idealistic, liberal-minded thinkers into, in the words of the protagonist of the novel, "shameless dogs" begging for mercy at the feet of their masters. More than any other political campaign, it is responsible for brainwashing, humiliating, and breaking the spirit of the educated, the cream of society. The bulk of the poignant story takes place in a prison and a labor camp, with 20 years of events reflected through the words of the protagonist. While exposing the brutality of political persecution, the novel also laments the inherent weaknesses of Chinese intellectuals. *Yibo* (Legacy) narrates two related episodes in the protagonist's life: in 1949 when he was saved by a peasant in a harrowing escape from the communist-controlled mainland to Taiwan and then in the reform era when the man, now a Chinese American, goes back to the mainland to pay his debt by trying to help the peasant's son build a fruit-processing factory. *Niqiu* (Loach), a novel about migrant workers in Beijing, sheds light on the life of the underprivileged population trying to stay alive at the margins of society. *Se* (Seduction), another novel set in urban China, deals with the inner struggles of a successful businessman faced with all kinds of seduction that a modern city life throws his way: money, sex, power, and fame. In addition to novels, You has written many short stories, including those collected in *Yizhuang anjian de jizhong shuofa* (Several Versions of the Same Case).

YU DAFU, A.K.A. YU TA-FU (1896–1945). Fiction writer and poet. One of the most talented writers of the **May Fourth** era, Yu Dafu was a sentimental and lyrical fiction writer. His life, with three marriages, two divorces, and a tragic death, is the stuff that makes fiction. Born to a father who was a minor county official, Yu went to Japan at the age of 18 with his eldest brother, a judge in Beijing. He stayed there, off and on, for 10 years, earning a bachelor's degree in economics in 1922. His sojourn in Japan figures prominently in his most famous story, "Chenlun" (*Sinking*). He was, arguably, the most talented poet among modern Chinese writers who wrote in the classical style, though he never took his own poetry seriously.

By all accounts, his short story collection *Chenlun* (*Sinking*) was a landmark in modern Chinese literature. In addition to the title story, two other stories are included in the collection: "Nanqian" (Moving South) and "Yinhui se de si" (The Silver-grey Death). The book caused a storm and was derided as indecent for its overt sexual descriptions. Years later, Yu still complained about the "abuses and insults" his critics heaped upon him. However, when **Zhou Zuoren** wrote an article in the literary supplement of the *Beijing Morning News* defending the author, the tide of public opinion turned. The book became a commercial as well as a critical success. "Chenlun" is a medium-length story about a Chinese student studying in Japan who suffers from schizophrenia. Tormented by his nation's weakness and his own sexual inhibition, he cannot shake off a sense of inferiority that trails him like a shadow. He tries to overcome his psychological and physiological paralysis by going to brothels, but to no avail. In the end, death is the only solution. Before he drowns himself in the ocean, he cries out in the direction of China, "Oh my motherland, you are the reason why I die. Become rich and strong as soon as possible. You still have a lot of children who are suffering there." Yu injects into the sufferings of the individual a dose of national tragedy, turning the hero's illness into "the disease of the age." The semiautobiographical nature of "Chenlun" and the other two stories in the collection, and their frank descriptions of private feelings, especially sexual urges, earned the author the reputation of an exhibitionist. Yu did not deny the intimate connection between himself and his work. To him, all works of art were expressions of the self, a belief that reflects the aesthetics of the Chinese lyrical tradition as well as the influence from the Japanese *Shishosetsu*, the I-novel.

Yu's writings published after his return to China in 1922, though still intensely lyrical and sentimental, are much more removed from his personal life. The financial difficulties he had helped turn his attention to searching for social and political answers. "Chunfeng chenzui de wanshang" (*Nights of Spring Fever*), a short piece written in 1923, tells the story of a poor and frustrated intellectual who, living in a slum in Shanghai, gets to know a female worker employed in a cigarette factory. Similarly, "Bo dian" (A Humble Sacrifice) is about the encounter between an impoverished intellectual and a rickshaw puller in Beijing. Told in his preferred first-person narrative, stories such as these put the intellectual, who evidently embodies the sentiments of the writer himself, in the company of the working class, reflecting the progressive trend of the times.

The dominant theme, however, remains the loss of youth and love. In stories such as "Guoqu" (The Past) and "Chu ben" (Run Away), a dark and pessimistic tone reverberates throughout the narrative, a characteristic of Yu's writing that earned him the reputation of a "decadent" writer. In the early 1930s, Yu left the **left-wing** literary circle in Shanghai, against the advice of **Lu Xun**, and led a quiet family life in Hangzhou, where he wrote several stories. One of them is his personal favorite, "Chi guihua" (Late-Flowering Cassia), a lyrical tale about a man who falls in love with a vivacious woman whose unadorned beauty blends seamlessly with the idyllic environment where the air is tinged with the fragrance of blooming cassia. This picture of innocence and beauty is far removed from reality and a sharp contrast to the turmoil engulfing the author as well as the nation. The refined sensibility conveyed through the protagonist embodies the author's artistic self: subjective, sentimental, romantic, and spontaneous.

At the end of 1938, Yu went to Singapore, and during the next three years he worked as editor-in-chief for the literary supplement to the *Xinzhou Daily* and the *Weekly of the Overseas Chinese*. He wrote many short, poignant political and literary essays, along with travelogues and old-style poems. The **Sino-Japanese War** took a serious toll on Yu. His mother was starved to death and his eldest brother was assassinated by the Japanese. Just before the Pacific War ended, the Japanese military police arrested and murdered Yu in Indonesia. *See also* CREATION SOCIETY.

YU GUANGZHONG, A.K.A. YU KUANG-CHUNG (1928–). Poet, essayist, and translator. Born in Nanjing, Yu attended middle school in Sichuan during the **Sino-Japanese War** and studied at Jinling University and Xiamen University before moving to **Hong Kong** with his parents in 1949. A year later, the family moved to **Taiwan**, following the Nationalist government's retreat to the island. Yu graduated from the Foreign Languages Department of National Taiwan University and received a master's degree from the University of Iowa. From 1974 to 1985, he taught literature at the Chinese University of Hong Kong. He has lived in the United States twice as a Fulbright scholar. A noted poet, Yu is well received in China, Taiwan, and Hong Kong: places that are intimate, like "mother, wife, and lover," to him. His best-known poems include "Xiangchou" (Nostalgia), an emotional and melancholy verse about his longing for his homeland.

Throughout his career, Yu has moved back and forth between modernism and traditionalism. In many ways, his poetry reflects the major trends in Taiwan's literary development in the 20th century. In the late 1950s, when he was studying at the University of Iowa, Yu experimented with modernism and produced some abstract poems that betrayed a nihilist outlook. In the 1960s, he showed a strong desire to be connected with his cultural roots in poems such as "Qiaoda yue" (Percussion) and "Dang wo si shi" (At the Time of My Death). In the 1970s, he absorbed elements from folk songs and wrote such memorable lyrics as "Baiyu kugua" and continued his journey in search of history and cultural heritage, which resulted in "Yu yongheng bahe" (A Tug-of-War with Eternity), "Jiuguang tielu" (Railroad between Jiulong and Guang-zhou), "Xun Li Bai" (In Search of Li Bai), and "Ye tu Dongpo" (Reading Dongpo at Night). At the same time, he got embroiled in a political/literary storm. His article "Lang lai le" (*The Wolves Are Coming*), published in 1977, condemned Taiwan's **nativists** (xiangtu pai), especially one of the leading voices, **Chen Yingzhen**, for espousing values of proletarian literature promoted in Communist China, a damaging charge in a poltical environment of "white terror" created by the despotic rule of Chiang Kai-shek and his government.

Since the 1980s, Yu has "returned home" in more than one sense. With the publication of his poems on the mainland, he has been invited back to give lectures there, where the sense of nostalgia expressed in his poems finds adulating audiences. Yu is a versatile as well as prolific writer. His poetic style changes with his themes. Patriotic sentiment is often conveyed in bold and robust words and vigorous rhythms, while nostalgia and love are articulated with tender diction and languid cadence. His lyrical essays on a variety of topics have also won critical acclaim. He is a noted translator of Oscar Wilde, Ernest Hemingway, and many other English and American writers. He has won numerous literary awards in Taiwan, including the National Literary Award in Po-

etry and the Wu San-lian Literary Award in Prose. *See also* MODERN
POETRY MOVEMENT IN TAIWAN.

YU HUA (1960–). Fiction writer. Yu Hua is one of the best writers in
modern Chinese literature. Known primarily as a prominent **avant-garde**
writer whose experimental fiction focuses on narrative innovation, Yu
is a diverse author who has also worked with both traditional Chinese
literary forms and the realist genre. Born in Hangzhou, Zhejiang Province, Yu followed his parents at the age of three to Haiyan in northen
Zhejiang. He later studied medicine and worked for several years as a
dentist in a county hospital. Envious of the free life of a writer, he began
to write in 1983 and published his first story at the age of 25.

In the beginning of his career, Yu experimented with new narrative
techniques and showed an obsession with a clinical perspective on brutal
acts. "Yijiu baliu" (1986), a story about a man going insane, possibly as
a result of the persecutions he has been put through during the **Cultural
Revolution**, is a case in point. The excessive savage imageries of murder,
schizophrenia, and violence are presented graphically and salaciously.
Whether the thoughtless, unmitigated brutality depicted in the story has
some symbolic implications is a subject for debate, but it is obvious that
such a relentless cataloging of butchery reveals the author's fascination
with acts of violence. *Zai xiyu zhong huhuan* (*Cries in the Drizzle*) and
Xianshi yizhong (*One Kind of Reality*) both belong to this group of experimental writings. Yu has also tried to breathe some new life into the old
forms of traditional Chinese literature. His novel *Xianxue meihua* (Blood
and Plum Blossoms) is a parody of Chinese "knight errant" fiction (wuxia
xiaoshuo), and "Gudian aiqing" (Classical Love) is based on the traditional genre of "scholar and beauty fiction" (caizi jiaren xiaoshuo).

Yu's realist narratives are spellbinding tales with profound social
implications. *Huozhe* (*To Live*) and *Xu Sanguan mai xue ji* (*The
Chronicle of a Blood Merchant*) are two such powerful stories. Both
are about the survival of the little man in the face of unpredictable
twists of fate. *Huozhe* is a historical epic about Fugui, the spoiled
son of a rich family, who, unable to take destiny into his own hands,
drifts as a tragic figure in the violent currents of 20th-century Chinese history. Tribulations visit him and his family one after another.
He endures them all. Despite his many weaknesses, the basic human
decency within him enables Fugui to arrive at a state of dignity. Xu

Sanguan in *Xu Sanguan mai xue ji* is also a sympathetic but unappealing figure. Like Fugui, misfortunes reveal the human quality in him. When he is determined to sell his blood "all the way to Shanghai" to pay for his son's medical treatment, he is redeemed as a loving father. In both novels, there is an unmistakable indictment of an uncaring system in which the little man pays a heavy price for the smallest pleasures in life. In the same vein, *Xiongdi* (Brothers), his latest novel, tells the moving story of how a family of four, formed by a second marriage, survives the Cultural Revolution. Yu calls this novel "Dickinsonian," for its rich description of social mores and human love and spirit. *See also* ROOT-SEEKING LITERATURE.

YU JIAN (1954–). Poet, essayist, and playwright. Born and raised in Kunming, a laid-back city in the southwestern part of the country, generally not considered a hotbed for **avant-garde** literature, Yu Jian is one of the few poets who still possess the innovative spirit of **Misty poetry**. He has written some of the most interesting Chinese experimental poems, which are characteristically terse and concrete, but ambiguous. He adopts a syntax that contains few adjectives, with nouns acting as verbs. Some of his poems are politically provocative, notably "Ling dang'an" (File 0: The Archive Room), published in 1994 in the first issue of the foremost avant-garde literary journal, *Dajia* (Great Masters), which is based in Kunming. The poem is a biting commentary on dehumanized life in China under the constant watch of the state. From birth to death, a Chinese person's life is condensed to a secret file, constantly updated and hidden, its content unknown to the individual in question. Yu's work lends well to experimental theater. "Guanyu *Bi'an* de yici Hanyu cixing taolun" (A Study of the Linguistic Features of *The Other Shore*), his response to **Gao Xingjian**'s famous play, was staged by his friend Mou Sen, a renowned experimental theater director. Yu's play takes out the dramatic metaphysical content of the original play and challenges the longing for the "other shore" it expresses. Yu also collaborated with Mou in turning "Ling dang'an" into a play, which toured several cities outside China. Yu won first prize for the 14th Unitas New Poetry Award in **Taiwan**. Yu lives in Kunming and is a member of the Yunnan Writers' Association. *See also* GENERATION III POETS; SPOKEN DRAMA.

YU LIHUA (1931–). Born in Shanghai, Yu Lihua moved to **Taiwan** with her family in 1949. From the 1950s through the 1970s, Taiwan experienced an economic boom accompanied by a rush to modernize and Westernize. Students went in droves to America to study. Out of this generation emerged several writers whose works reflected this experience. **Bai Xianyong, Nie Hualing, Ouyang Zi, Zhang Xiguo,** and **Chen Ruoxi** all contributed to this "overseas student literature." Yu was the most representative of the group, owing to both the quantity and the depth of her works on this subject.

Most of her "overseas student" works were written in the decade from the late 1960s to the late 1970s, including *Yan* (Flame), *Kaoyan* (Test), *Fu jia de ernümen* (Children of the Fu Family), *Bian* (Change), and *You jian zhonglü you jian zhonglü* (Seeing the Palm Trees Again), which won Taiwan's Jiaxin Literature Prize. In describing the so-called lost generation of youths who struggled to define their identity, Yu focuses on their personal choices in love, family, and career. Faced with loneliness in a foreign land and hard decisions about whether to stay in America or to return to Taiwan, many of her characters are like Yu herself, having been uprooted many times in their lives, first in the mainland in the course of two wars, then moving to Taiwan, and finally to America. *You jian zhonglü you jian zhonglü* is her defining work. It features a journalism student who, with a Ph.D. in hand, returns to Taiwan to find his former sweetheart married to another man. He decides to stay nonetheless, because it is Taiwan that holds his roots and soul. In *Fu jia de ernümen*, another important work of Yu's, the five children of a well-to-do Taiwanese family represent four different types of overseas students: the Westernized ones who give up their ideals and cut off their ties to their Chinese roots in order to pursue worldly success; the ruined ones who fail to adapt themselves to American society; the disillusioned ones who, despite their professional success in America, cannot find spiritual satisfaction; and the awakened ones who return to Taiwan for a meaningful life, leaving behind the material comfort of America. In these characters, Yu emphasizes the sense of cultural belonging and the difficulty of maintaining one's cultural identity in a foreign land. Her latest novel, *Zai liqu yu daobie zhijian* (Between Departure and Farewell), depicts a group of Chinese American professors, some of whom have lost the vitality and moral fiber of their youth.

Other than her work about the Chinese émigré community, Yu has also written about her early experiences in China. *Meng hui Qing He* (Return to the Green River in a Dream), a novel set in a small town in Zhejiang during the **Sino-Japanese War**, centers on the squabbles of a large family of three generations and the tragic tale of a love triangle. *See also* CIVIL WAR; WOMEN.

YU LING (1907–1997). Playwright. A member of the **Left-wing Association of Chinese Writers**, Yu Ling was a progressive playwright and filmmaker in war-torn China of the 1930s and 1940s. When Japan invaded Shanghai in 1937 and the Chinese government abandoned the city, Yu Ling, together with **Ouyang Yuqian** and other artists who stayed behind, established Lan niao ju she (the Blue Bird Theater Club) and performed, among others, **Cao Yu**'s *Leiyu* (Thunderstorm) and *Ri chu* (Sunrise) as well as his own plays in the relatively safe French Concession district. Between 1937 and 1941, Yu wrote more than two dozen plays, some of which were later turned into films in Hong Kong and Shanghai.

Yu's works, characteristic of the times, overwhelmingly center on the theme of national salvation. *Ye Shanghai* (Dark Nights in Shanghai), which was staged in 1939 to mark the second anniversary of the Japanese invasion of Shanghai, portrays the chaos and destruction in Shanghai following the Japanese invasion; *Chang ye xing* (Travel during Long Nights), a four-act play, presents the different moral choices people are forced to make under Japanese rule; *Qiyue liu huo* (Fire in July), a five-act play staged in 1961, focuses on the heroic resistance against the Japanese put up by the people of Shanghai led by the Communist Party. A prolific playwright with more than 60 plays to his name, Yu served, after 1949, as director of the Shanghai Film Studio and president of the Shanghai Theater Academy. *See also* CIVIL WAR; SINO-JAPANESE WAR; SOCIALIST REALISM; SPOKEN DRAMA.

YU PINGBO (1900–1990). Poet and essayist. Born into an eminent scholar-official family, Yu Pingbo graduated from Beijing University in 1919 and briefly studied in England and the United States. As a member of several literary associations, including the New Trend Society (xinchao she) and **Literary Research Society**. In 1922, Yu worked with **Zhu Zhiqing, Zheng Zhenduo, Ye Shengtao**, and others to found *Shi* (Poetry), the first poetry journal since the **May Fourth Movement**. He was one of the major poets who advocated a "plebeian poetry," one that drew from the Chinese folk tradition, used an everyday language, and ignored the metric regulations of traditional poetics. Nevertheless, Yu was a new poet with quintessentially traditional sensibilities, a stylist who paid meticulous attention to the use of words and images. The poems collected in *Dong ye* (Winter Nights), published in 1922, are characteristically concise, fastidious, and graceful. They expressed his love for his hometown and for his friends and family. Yu was also a noted essayist, having published several collections of essays written in different genres ranging from belles lettres to travelogues, from philosophical musings to reading notes. His essays show traces of influence from **Zhou Zuoren**, with whom he shared a fondness for the individual's aesthetic experience, rather than a strong social consciousness.

Yu is best known as a distinguished scholar of classical Chinese literature who made significant contributions to the study of *Ci*, a subgenre of classical poetry, and particularly to the scholarship of *Hong lou meng* (*A Dream of Red Mansions*), an 18th-century novel generally considered the best fictional work in classical Chinese literature. After 1949, he taught Chinese literature at Beijing University and worked at the Chinese Literature Research Institute of the Chinese Academy of Social Sciences. *See also* NEW CULTURE MOVEMENT.

YU QIUYU (1946–). Essayist. One of the most popular writers in China today, Yu Qiuyu was educated in Shanghai and has spent a great part of his career teaching theater and drama in colleges. He rose to fame in the 1990s with a collection of essays on historical figures and events entitled *Wenhua ku lü* (A Difficult Journey across Cultures). Subsequently, he published more essays, which continue to draw a large readership. His work addresses a variety of topics, from ancient Greek culture to contemporary Shanghai life. Running through his numerous essays is the theme of patriotism from the perspective of a Chinese intellectual whose sense of responsibility for his nation and its cultural heritage echoes the so-called anxiety complex of the traditional scholar-official in ancient China. A controversial figure and academic celebrity whose essays are written for popular consumption, Yu has drawn many detractors, who accuse him of peddling cheap sentimentalism and showmanship, evidenced by his frequent television appearances and promotional events. In the meantime, however, his books are being sold in large quantities, making him one of the richest writers in China. In addition to essays, Yu has written books on the aesthetics of the theater.

YUAN QIONGQIONG, A.K.A. YUAN CH'IUNG-CH'IUNG (1950–). A product of the feminist movement that swept **Taiwan** from the 1970s to the 1980s, Yuan Qiongqiong used her writings to call attention to **women** in modern Taiwanese society. Her work reflects the social and cultural changes as women seek to achieve gender equality and self-identity by challenging the patriarchal tradition and its impact on women's psychological well-being. Focusing on women's attitudes toward love and sexuality, Yuan paints women trapped in unhappy relationships, struggling to find their own voices. "Ziji de tiankong" (A Sky of One's Own), published in 1996, traces the trajectory of the protagonist from a submissive and needy wife to a self-confident and financially independent woman after her divorce. Despite her sympathy for the feminist movement, Yuan did not see herself as a social commentator. In this respect, she is different from other feminist writers of Taiwan, such as **Li Ang** and **Liao Huiying**, whose writings have greater social and political implications. Yuan puts the spotlight on the individual's sexual or psychological frustrations. The best of her stories have a subtle and ironic tone. Her other published fictional works include short story collections *Chun shui chuan* (Spring Water Boat) and *Huanxiang zhi chong* (Fantasy Bug), as well as a novel, *Jin sheng yuan* (Predestined to Meet).

In addition to fiction, Yuan also writes poetry, essays, and film and television scripts. She has won several literary awards, including Taiwan's Unitas Literature Award.

– Z –

ZANG DI (1964–). Poet. Born and raised in Beijing, Zang Di received his B.A. and Ph.D. in Chinese from Beijing University and is currently teaching literature at his alma mater. Zang began writing poetry in his freshman year. His first poem, "Weiming hu" (The Weiming Lake), appeared in 1983 in a Beijing University journal and since then he has published more than 20 poems in the same journal. His poems are characterized by their slow, deliberate pace made possible through images gleaned from daily life, which are then stretched and multiplied in a flowing, prosaic, linguistic play. This particular emphasis on style suggests that poetry as a form of art is capable of opening up a multitude of angles from which the world can be experienced; the task for a poet is not merely to express his or her emotions but to explore all possible ways in which poetry interacts with the world through imagination. In this respect, Zang is a truly modern poet in the footsteps of poets such as John Ashbery, whose poetry shows the potential of the human mind.

Zang's poetry is sophisticated and philosophical. Winner of the Poetry Prize awarded by *Zuojia* (Writers) in 2000, among other honors, Zang is a prolific poet, having published several collections of poetry and prose. He also edited a Chinese translation of poems by Rainer Maria Rilke and several collections of contemporary Chinese poetry.

ZANG KEJIA (1905–2004). Poet. Zang Kejia was one of the most celebrated poets in Communist China. He came from an educated family in Shandong and received a traditional early education in his home village. Later, when he studied in the provincial capital, Zang was exposed to modern literature and was inspired to write his own vernacular poetry. In his youth, Zang was a fervent believer in radical social change. In 1926, he made his way to Wuhan, the center of revolution at the time. *Ziyou de xiezhao* (Portraiture of Freedom), a collection of poems, reflects this critical moment in his life, as well as in the nation's history. When the revolution failed, Zang returned to his hometown. From 1930 to 1934, he studied at Qingdao University and met many well-known writers, including **Wen Yiduo**, **Shen Congwen**, and **Lao She**, who were on the faculty. Zang benefited most from Wen's guidance. In 1933, Zang published his first poetry collection, *Laoyin* (Branding). The following three years saw the publication of three more of his collections: *Zui'e de heishou* (The Evil Black Hand), *Ziji de xiezhao* (Self-Portrait), and *Yunhe* (The Great Canal). These poems reveal the conditions of the countryside and the sufferings of the peasants and expose corruption within the Nationalist government. Most of them are short poems written in a powerful, vivid, colloquial language, representing some of the poet's best work. During the **Sino-Japanese War**, Zang joined the military as a civilian staff member. He wrote many poems to encourage the Chinese people in their struggle against Japanese aggression.

In 1942, Zang arrived in Chongqing, the war capital, where he continued to produce many collections of poems, including *Nitu de ge* (Song of the Soil) and a long poem "Gushu de huaduo" (The Flowers of an Ancient Tree). In 1945, a few days after he met Mao Zedong, who came to Chongqing for a meeting with Chiang Kai-shek, Zang wrote a poem in praise of the Communist leader: "Mao Zedong, ni shi yike daxing" (Mao Zedong, You Are a Big Star), which was published in *New China Daily*, the official newspaper of the Communists. He wrote many more adulating political poems after 1949. Within the Communist government, Zang acted as one of the enforcers of its policy on literature in his position as party secretary of the Chinese Writers' Association and the chief editor of *Shi kan*, a poetry journal.

ZHAI YONGMING (1955–). Poet. Considered one of the best female poets in China today, Zhai Yongming grew up in Chengdu, Sichuan Province. She entered the Chengdu Institute for Telecommunications and Engineering to study physics, a subject in which she had little interest. After graduating, she worked for several years at a research institute but occupied herself in her free time with writing poetry, which resulted in several collections. In 1986, Zhai resigned from the institute. She lived in the United States for a year in the early 1990s with her artist husband, and the sojourn inspired her travelogue, *Niuyue, Niuye yi xi* (New York and West of New York). After her return to Chengdu, she opened a bar that has become a literary salon for local poets and artists. For her writings about the female body and the dark female consciousness, particularly the melancholy but rebellious sentimentality voiced in *Nüren* (Women), Zhai is regarded as a feminist whose language is sensual and exquisite, and whose images are alluring. While her early poems express feelings of alienation, rejection, distrust, sadness, and desperation, her later poems tend to embrace the delights of life and human relationships. *See also* GENERATION III POETS; WOMEN.

ZHANG AILING, A.K.A., EILEEN CHANG (1921–1995). Fiction writer. Better known in the West as Eileen Chang, Zhang Ailing is widely considered the most talented woman writer in 20th-century China and celebrated for her relentless dissection of the tragic ironies of human experience. By birth, she should have had a pampered life, with a grandfather who was a high-ranking official in the late Qing government and a grandmother who was a daughter of Li Hongzhang, an influential Qing official. However, wealth and family prestige did not guarantee happiness, but a lonely childhood might have contributed to the making of an author. Her first published work is about her experience of being beaten and locked up by her father. Zhang, a reclusive figure who died all alone in her Los Angeles apartment at the age of 74, was interested in exploring the interior landscape of the individual and the decaying traditional way of life, no doubt inspired by her aristocratic background. In many ways, she epitomizes, both in her own life and in her works, the glamorous city of Shanghai in the 1930s and 1940s, a metropolis where East and West, old and new, converged.

Zhang graduated from a Christian high school in Shanghai in 1937, the same year the Japanese invaded the city. Her plan to study in England had to change because of the war in Europe. Instead, she entered the University of **Hong Kong**. During her third year at the university, Japan invaded the city. She returned to Shanghai and married **Hu Lancheng**, a writer and journalist later accused of collaborating with the Japanese. The couple eventually separated and Hu went to Japan while Zhang remained in China. With the excuse of resuming her studies in Hong Kong, she got permission to leave China in 1952. Three years later, she immigrated to the United States. There she married for the second time, to an American playwright. After he died, she lived alone until her death in 1995.

Zhang arrived at the height of her writing career in the mid-1940s. In 1943 alone, she finished eight stories, including "Qing cheng zhi lian" (*Love in a Fallen City*), the first important work that brought her fame, and "Jin suo" (*The Golden Cangue*), generally considered the best of her work. "Qing cheng zhi lian" centers around the heroine's life first as the mistress of a wealthy businessman, then as his wife, and finally as a divorced woman who is rejected by her own kin, who regard her divorce as a disgrace to the family. Zhang is skilled at presenting the complexity of the inner minds of women, and nowhere is that skill more evident than in the portrayal of Cao Qiqiao, the protagonist of "Jin suo." Cao's transformation from a lovely and innocent girl to a cold-blooded, neurotic widow is delivered with powerful psychological insights.

Unlike most of her contemporaries, Zhang was not preoccupied with the "big" theme of China's national salvation. Her lenses were always focused on the trivialities of life, the subtle feelings between men and **women**, and intricate manipulations within families. From these personal and familial perspectives, the author reveals the dilemma of being a woman in a society gingerly inching toward modernity. Her fascination with life's small details sprang from an appreciation of popular art and classical novels, especially *Hong lou meng* (*A Dream of Red Mansions*). Her works display a remarkable degree of psychological realism and narrative sophistication, and her use of imagery and symbolism as well as irony gives credence to her writing, making her one of the best writers in modern Chinese literature. In an essay entitled "Writing about Myself," she expresses her admiration for Western modernism: "Modern literature seems to be different from what we had in the past because it no longer stresses a thesis, but just tells a story from which the reader gets as much as he can or as much as the story can offer." Her stories and novels are examples of this new aesthetic concept.

In the 1940s, Zhang wrote many short pieces of prose, later collected in *Liuyan* (Gossips). While not all her stories and novels are autobiographical, her essays are all about her unhappy childhood, her parents' divorce, her dreams, what she learned in her early years, and her reflections on what she saw and heard. This collection affords us glimpses of the real Zhang, who loved the modern metropolis of Shanghai and its bustling urban life and played the part of a witty observer commenting on fashion, movies, dance, music, painting, and literature. Her essays show that she was intimately linked to the outside world, the variegated social sphere of Shanghai and Hong Kong in the chaotic 1940s. Some of Zhang's later works, written after she left China in 1952, carry political subtexts. *The Rice-Sprout Song*, a visceral portrayal of the famine directly caused by the land reform movement in rural China during the early 1950s, and *Naked Earth*, which critiques the destructive power of the Communist Party over human relationships, were commissioned by the United States Information Agency and published in Hong Kong in the mid-1950s. She wrote both novels in English and Chinese. During her stay in the United States from 1955, Zhang also tried to rewrite some of her early stories in English, including *The Rouge of the North*, an expanded rewrite of her much celebrated early novella—*The Golden Cangue*. In the 1970s, she wrote *Xiao tuanyuan* (A Small Reunion) but requested that the manuscript be destroyed in the event of her death. Against her dying wish, the novel was published in 2009 and has quickly gained recognition as among the best of her work. It is widely believed to be a fictionalized account of the author's own life growing up in a declining aristocratic family, her passionate but disillusioned love affair with Hu Lancheng, and her pervasive feeling of depression and darkness. Like Zhang's other works, the novel is also a perceptive study of human nature with all its contradictions and self-deceptions, tenacity and frailty, and all the good and bad that life brings to the individual. In Zhang's long career, she also ventured into filmscript writing for the Hong Kong movie industry as well as scholarly work on *Hong lou meng*, a translation into English and modern Chinese of *Haishang hua lie zhuan* (Biographies of the Shanghai Courtesans), a 19th-century novel originally written in the Suzhou vernacular.

Zhang's influence on Chinese literature is enormous. Among her many progenies are **Shi Shuqing**, **Zhu Tianwen**, **Zhu Tianxin**, **Wang**

Anyi, and **Zhong Xiaoyang**, all believed to have inheritated her legacy. A recent movie by the renowned diretor Ang Lee, *Lust, Caution*, which is based on Zhang's semiautobiographical story about romance, politics, and betrayal during the **Sino-Japanese War**, thrusted Zhang into the limelight of Western popular culture, a notoriety from which the reclusive author would have probably recoiled.

ZHANG CHENGZHI (1948–). Fiction writer, essayist, and painter. Trained as an archeologist and a historian at Beijing University and the Chinese Institute of Social Sciences, Zhang has made a successful career in creative writing. This multilingual, multitalented scholar-writer rose to fame in the late 1970s with the short story "Qishou wei shenme gechang muqin" (*Why Herdsmen Sing "Mother"*), a romantic tale based on the author's experience as an educated youth in Inner Mongolia between 1967 to 1972, which informs many of his other stories, including his best-known novella, *Hei junma* (*The Black Steed*). Set against the background of the Mongolian grassland, *Hei junma* revolves around the life of the hero and his relationship with a young girl and an elderly woman who has adopted them. It is a simple love story that reaches into the deep layers of traditional practices as they come into conflict with modern beliefs. The hero's profound love for his land and his people transcends his frustration with and disappointment in some of its ancient practices, which he has come to understand as sources that have sustained their traditional way of life. Other noteworthy works originating from Zhang's life as a herdsman include a novel, *Jin muchang* (The Golden Pasture), and some short stories. Zhang studied the history of China's northern ethnic minorities as a graduate student and apparently identified with many of the traits that define their characters, such as honesty, fortitude, and friendship. *Beifang de he* (*The River in the North*) represents his understanding of the spirit of the nation, as embodied in the river in the north—the Yellow River—with its energy and vigor. It is less a story than a long poem, largely carried by the stream of consciousness and subjective ruminations of the narrator, a college graduate who has spent years as an educated youth in China's northwest and who is preparing to take an exam for a postgraduate program in geology.

After *Hei junma* and *Beifang de he*, Zhang wrote an unconventional novel entitled *Xinling shi* (A History of the Soul), his most important work, which mixes fiction with poetry, history, and memoir. The main events of the narrative took place in the reign of Qianlong, emperor of the Qing dynasty, who launched successive brutal attacks on the Jahreyes, a subsect of Islamic Sufism, resulting in the latter's fierce rebellious uprisings and suicide missions against the Manchu empire. As the violent past casts a long shadow across this emotional account of the narrator's encounter with the Jahreyes, the author/narrator increasingly finds himself drawn to his ethnic and religious roots. Born in Beijing to a Muslim family, but raised in an atheist environment, Zhang was not encouraged to practice his religion. Considered a work of pain and love by the author, the book culminates Zhang's long journey in search of spiritual sanctuary, not just for himself but also for the Chinese nation. In his rigorous defense of the heterodox, Zhang denounces mainstream Chinese culture for the collapse of its moral order and its lack of spirituality. He vehemently proclaims that only the heterodoxy has what it takes to pump new blood into the decayed body that is the Chinese culture. A consistent theme that runs through all of Zhang's creative works is the defense of "the people." He identifies with the underprivileged and feels affinity with poor peasants and herdsmen who are marginalized in society. He sees himself as their champion. In middle age, Zhang appears to have lost none of the youthful idealism of his Red Guard days. A lonely fighter most of the time, he has been waging a war against materialism and moral degradation since.

Other than his creative works written in Chinese, Zhang has penned several poems in Mongolian, and three scholarly books in Japanese, dealing with nomadic life in Mongolia, Islam in China, and the Red Guards during the **Cultural Revolution**. *See also* ROOT-SEEKING LITERATURE.

ZHANG DACHUN, A.K.A., CHANG TA-CH'UN (1957–). Fiction writer and essayist. Zhang Dachun studied at Fu Jen Catholic University in **Taiwan** and worked as a journalist for the *China Times*. A popular writer and celebrity in Taiwan, Zhang has published numerous books and won several awards. His oeuvre ranges from political thrillers to detective mysteries, including *Gongyu daoyou* (*Apartment Tour Guide*), and the science fiction work, *Shijian zhou* (Axis of Time). Zhang is also an astute cultural commentator whose portraits of rebellious teenagers in stories such as "My Kid Sister" and "Wild Child" strike a chord in present-day society where dysfunctional families abound. Zhang's wry wit aptly captures the insanities of the modern youth culture in the tradition of J. D. Salinger. With his seemingly indifferent playfulness and humorous tone, Zhang subverts mainstream views by pointing out the disintegration of fibers that are supposed to tie society together and by so doing registers his deep disapproval of the political and social realities of contemporary Taiwan. In addition to his writing career, Zhang is also a television anchor and radio talk show host.

ZHANG ER, PEN NAME OF LI MINGXIA (1961–). Poet. Born in Beijing, Zhang Er came to the United States in 1986 and received her Ph.D. in molecular pharmacology from Cornell University. She is currently teaching at Evergreen State College in Washington State. She has published several collections of poetry including a bilingual edition, *Guanyu niao de duan shi / Verses on Bird.* For many years, Zhang lived in New York City, where she was actively involved in the poetry communities, giving public readings of her poems and participating and editing overseas Chinese poetry journals, such as *Yi hang* (One Line) and *Shi xiang* (The Poetic Phenomenon). She has published a series of vignettes of New York poets, introducing contemporary poets in the New York area to Chinese readers. Although written in her native language, Zhang's poems reflect her multicultural background, addressing issues such as language and self-identity. She has also translated and edited collections of modern Chinese poetry.

ZHANG GUIXING (1956–). Fiction writer. Born in Borneo, Malaysia, Zhang Guixing graduated from National Taiwan Normal University with a bachelor's degree in English. He became a permanent resident of **Taiwan** in 1982 and has been living and working there ever since. Like **Li Yongping**, Zhang went to Taiwan to study and found his calling in literature. As a "lü Tai Ma Hua zuojia" (Malaysian Chinese writer living in Taiwan), a term that aptly reflects the richness and complexity of his literary heritage, Zhang taps the multiple sources of Chinese, Malaysian, Taiwanese, and Western literary traditions. His first collection of short stories, *Fu hu* (Capturing the Tiger), already reflects this diverse background. What established his so-called tropical rainforest style, however, is *Keshan de ernü* (Keshan's Sons and Daughters), a collection of short stories about his homeland, such as "Wan dao, lanhua, and Zuolun qiang" (The Curvy Knife, the Orchid, and the Revolver), a story of the absurd that centers on a series of coincidences happening to a college student who returns from Taiwan to Malaysia only to find himself a target of kidnapping. Other works that pit the hero against the lush background of the rainforest and rubber plantations of Southeast Asia include *Qun xiang* (*Herds of Elephants*), a novel about a young man in search of his uncle, who is a guerrilla leader, and *Sailian zhi ge* (*Siren Song*), which explores youthful sexuality amid the violence of the wild rainforest.

As a Chinese Malaysian, Zhang is fascinated by the history of Chinese migration to Southeast Asia. His novels explore the reasons and the forces that led his ancestors to the South Seas and the consequences of their arduous journey. In *Wanpi jiazu* (*The Clown Dynasty*), he parodies the Biblical story of Noah's Ark as a metaphor for the journey of Chinese Malaysians who "floated" from southern China to Southeast Asia. The same theme runs in *Wo sinian de chang mian zhong de nan guo gongzhu* (*My South Seas Sleeping Beauty: A Tale of Memory and Longing*) and *Hou bei* (*The Primate Cup*), which expose the sufferings of the Chinese at the hands of the colonialists as well as the vicious fights and killings between the Chinese and the aborigines as a result of the brutal forces of Western industrial expansion. While he puts the blame on colonialism and capitalism for plundering the natural resources of the third world and directly causing ethnic strife, he goes further to show that the Chinese settlers and the locals are perfectly capable of prejudice and violence and that brutality is inherently human.

As Zhang critiques the history of colonialism in Southeast Asia, he describes sexuality as a form of male hegemony. Time and again in his novels, Zhang depicts the brutal force and power that men wield while making sexual conquests. By treating sexual desire as both salvation and moral degradation, his work bears signs of Christian influence. The mother in *Wo sinian de chang mian zhong de nan guo gongzhu* is the Eve of Eden, representing sin as well as innocence: the mother a prodigal son fondly remembers and the country to which a young man far away from home longs to return to have both lost their pristine quality. Eden has become a land of carnalism and paradise is filled with suffering and injustice.

Each one of Zhang's major works is a complex web, woven into which are myths, legends, parables, fairy tales, history, and personal memories. In his characteristically free-flowing, unrestrained style, Zhang has created an exuberant aesthetic befitting the verdant, foreboding rainforest he frequently depicts. As an author who deals with cultural identity and the dilemma of straddling multiple national borders, he represents in many ways the epitome of cultural globalism of the postmodern world.

ZHANG HENSHUI (1895–1967). Novelist. After the publication in 1919 of his first novel, *Nan guo xiangsi pu* (Love in Southern China), Zhang Henshui maintained an unchallenged status as the most popular novelist in China throughout the Republican period (1911–1949). Although his name faded on the mainland during the Mao era, he continued to enjoy a large readership in the rest of Chinese-speaking communities. Recent years have seen a revived interest in him on the mainland, with the publications of new editions of his works and several television dramas adapted from his novels.

A prolific writer with more than a hundred titles to his name, Zhang was a transitional figure, bridging the worlds of traditional and modern literature. His novels, written in the traditional style of Chinese vernacular fiction, rely heavily on suspenseful plots and smooth and accessible language to tell a good story. Grouped with the **Mandarin Ducks and Butterflies school,** which believed entertainment to be the mission of literature, Zhang is not considered a mainstream writer and his novels are generally regarded as lowbrow. Romantic stories such as *Chun ming wai shi* (Anecdote of a Sunny Spring), *Jinfen shijia* (The Family of Wealth), and *Tixiao yinyuan* (Fate in Tears and Laughter), are his representative works. During and after the **Sino-Japanese War**, his novels turned toward social satire and realistic portrayals of Chinese society in turmoil. *Bashiyi meng* (Eighty-one Dreams) is a representative work of this period. His novels written before 1949 were serialized in newspapers in Shanghai and Hong Kong. Zhang wrote a few novels after the Communist victory in 1949, including *Kongque dongnan fei* (The Peacocks Fly Southeast), *Feng qiu huang* (The Male Phoenix Courting the Female Phoenix), and *Qiu Jiang* (The Autumn River), all based on traditional tales. He died of a stroke in Beijing.

ZHANG JIE (1937–). Fiction writer. Zhang Jie emerged in the post-Mao era as a writer who helped chart a new course for Chinese literature. In the late 1970s, as the country was reversing Mao Zedong's political and economic policies, **scar literature** (shanghen wenxue), devoted to the portrayal of suffering during the **Cultural Revolution**, became a popular trend. Zhang found herself in the middle of the cathartic movement. Although the internal and external scars left by the catastrophic Cultural Revolution are kept in the background of her stories, the main purpose of her writing remains the same: to cleanse Chinese society of the negative influences imposed by the radical ideologies of the Cultural Revolution. While most of scar literature focuses on the sufferings, Zhang chooses to center on the triumph of the good and the noble. She strives to embrace life with enthusiasm, to show the unbending human spirit in the midst of adversities. "Senling li de yinyue" (The Music of the Forests) is typical of Zhang's early works, representing the author's belief in love, trust, and perseverance. "Ai shi buneng wangji de" (*Love Cannot Be Forgotten*), a story that advocates the ideal of love, caused a small whirlwind when it came out in 1980 for its positive portrayal of love outside marriage. Ideals such as truth, kindness, honor, and beauty are important elements in Zhang's writings. Owing to her dogged pursuit of these ideals, her characters tend to be one-dimensional.

Zhang, a writer with a strong sense of social responsibility, wants her writings to reflect the transformations her country has gone through, and to that end, she tends to cast her characters against the background of grand historical and social events. *Chenzhong de chibang* (*Heavy Wings*), her first novel, deals with economic reforms in urban China. Centering on the reform in the Ministry of Heavy Industry and its subsidiary, the Shu Guang Automobile Factory, Zhang exposes the complicated and entangled contradictions that arise in China's economy, politics, and culture, as they affect family, love, friendship, and marriage. The novel recreates the atmosphere of Chinese society in a time of great change and describes the complex nature of social reforms in the country. *Wu zi* (No Written Word), a semiautobiographical novel, focuses on the life of a woman writer; through her accounts of the marriages of several generations of women in her family, the novel reflects the turmoil of 20th-century China.

ZHANG JUNMO, PEN NAME OF ZHANG JINGYUN (1939–). Fiction and prose writer. Born in Guangdong, Zhang came to **Hong Kong** in 1946. He has been an editor and a newspaper columnist. Early in his career, Zhang wrote romantic novels and his later works reflect realities in Hong Kong, while his essays comment on the small delights and hardships in daily life. His publications include collections of fiction and prose such as *Yaoyuan de xingsu* (Distant Stars), *Xianggang ziye* (Hong Kong at Midnight), and *Cu kafei* (Coarse Coffee), as well as novels *Jianghu ke* (A Worldly Traveler), *Qingchun de chaqu* (An Interlude of Youth), and *Riluo shifen* (At Sunset). He also writes science fiction and detective novels. In recent years, Zhang has been involved in the study of jade and has coauthored several books on the history and culture of this highly valued precious stone.

ZHANG KANGKANG (1950–). Novelist. Born in Hangzhou, Zhang Kangkang was sent to the wilderness of the northeast to work on a state farm after graduating from middle school. Her first story "Deng" (Lamp) was published in 1972, followed by novels *Fenjie xian* (The Great Divide), *Dandan de chenwu* (The Light Morning Mist), *Beiji guang* (*Northern Lights*), and *Yinxing banlü* (*The Invisible Companion*), plus several short stories, including "Ai de quanli" (*The Right to Love*). Nearly all of these works portray lives of educated city youth sent to China's remote countryside. As a member of that generation, Zhang has captured its spirit through her descriptions of the hardships they endured, the idealism they were devoted to, and the purity and romanticism they embodied, as well as the disillusionment and uncertainty they had to confront. Among her later works are the controversial *Qing'ai hualang* (The Gallery of Romatic Love), *Chi tong dan zhu* (All Shades of Red), about progressive intellectuals in the first half of the turbulent 20th century, and *Zuo nü* (The Troublemaking Woman), which depicts an independent **woman** who refuses to conform to the female stereotypes prescribed by a male-centered society. Zhang currently lives in Harbin and is deputy chairwoman of the Heilongjiang Writers' Association. *See also* CULTURAL REVOLUTION.

ZHANG TIANYI (1906–1985). Fiction writer. Best known for his satirical short stories and children's literature, Zhang Tianyi was a key figure among the left-wing writers of the 1930s and 1940s. At the beginning of his career, he wrote chiefly comic and detective stories, some of which were published in *Saturday*, the stronghold of the **Mandarin Ducks and Butterflies school**, devoted to entertaining literature. Influenced by Marxism and **Lu Xun**'s stories, Zhang Tianyi underwent a profound ideological transformation and began to devote himself to the cause of the **Left-wing Association of Chinese Writers.**

Zhang Tianyi drew inspiration for his satire from *The Scholars* by Wu Jingzhi, a Qing dynasty writer, satirical stories by Lu Xun, and works by Russian writers Nicholai Gogol and Anton Chekhov. His characters are often caricatures drawn in precise detail through vivid images. He is an expert at employing sharp, witty, and at times, whimsical language to create these sketches.

When Zhang began writing for children, the field was flooded with reproductions of old fairy tales or stories copied from ancient Chinese books. Following the footsteps of **Ye Shengtao**, whose "Scarecrow," published 10 years earlier, was the first story in modern Chinese children's literature, Zhang believed that stories for children should change to keep up with the changing society. True to his leftist identity, he taught lessons of class struggle in tales such as "Dalin he Xiaolin" (*Big Lin and Little Lin*), describing the conflicts between the oppressed and the oppressors, singing the praises of the strength and wisdom of the working people, and exposing the avarice and cruelty of the exploiting upper class. With his sharp and humorous language, Zhang sought to inspire his young readers to distinguish right from wrong and to know what to love and what to hate.

ZHANG WEI (1956–). Novelist. Born in Longkou, a coastal town in the eastern Shandong peninsula, Zhang Wei has made his hometown and its surrounding area the central location for his creative endeavors. He adopts a lyrical voice in his short stories about the disappearing natural rural life, while his social novels are narrated in a somber tone. A prolific writer, he has won numerous awards both on the mainland and in Taiwan.

Zhang rose to fame in the 1980s with the publication of several influential novels dealing with reforms taking place in the countryside. *Gu chuan* (The Ancient Boat) focuses on how the new policies have changed the lives of a former landlord's children. *Qiutian de fennu* (The Wrath of Autumn) is about a lonely battle fought by a young man, also a former landlord's son, against the tyranny of the village's Communist Party secretary. Zhang's humanistic inclinations made him a natural heir to the **May Fourth** iconoclastic legacy, which called for the enlightenment of the ignorant populace. His writings in this period tend to be critical of the peasants' ignorance and slavish subservience to authority, which make modernization a difficult process in rural communities. He also explores the conditions that allowed totalitarianism to continue its dominance into the 1980s. As Deng Xiaoping's reforms led China further and further away from its agrarian past, and as modernization left behind a devastated environment, Zhang began to turn his critical gaze toward the alienating effects of modernity and commercialism, expressing an aching nostalgia for the lost pastoral landscape.

Beginning with *Jiuyue de yuyan* (*September's Fable*), and later in *Huainian yu zhuiji* (Yearnings and Remembrances), *Mogu qizhong* (Seven Kinds of Mushrooms), *Baihui* (Baihui), *Waisheng shu* (Letters), and *Neng bu yi shukui* (Remembering Hollyhock), Zhang explores the dichotomy between the countryside and the city, representing not only different lifestyles but also different worldviews. The old intellectual in *Waisheng shu* leaves his life in Beijing to find his ancestral home in a fishing village, leaving the center—the capital—for the fringe—the province—in order to cleanse his soul. The artist in *Neng bu yi shukui* is ruined because of his insatiable desires stimulated by a commercial culture; and only the hollyhock grown in the field can restore his health and creativity. By returning to the pastoral, Zhang's characters discover their "home," their spiritual anchor, in the villages and towns on the eastern coast. Similar themes can be found in his most recent novel, *Ciwei ge* (Song of a Hedgehog), which continues to explore the sense of loss felt by the individual when faced with the encroachment of modern commercial culture and the feeble but valiant resistence he puts up in order to find a place where he can lead his dream life and nurture his soul. The novel places the protagonist's life against the century of history of a seaside region. The protagonist, a man of traditional sensibilities, finds a farm by the sea and lives there as a self-sufficient gentleman farmer. In his spare time, he works on a historical book on his ancestors and their relationship with the land. Reality, however, eventually dashes his dream with his farm gone and his family succumbed to the pressure of modernity.

Forever an idealist, Zhang laments the loss of values in contemporary Chinese life. In his writings, he consistently tries to retrieve these ideals from the past. With his expression of the discontent of the modern world, Zhang is considered an important voice in the **root-seeking** movement. He has also written stories based on ancient historical events and figures, another persistent effort of his to reconstruct the moral values of Chinese culture by re-creating the local history of his hometown, the Shangdong Peninsula. Among these historical tales, *Yingzhou sixu lu* (Record of Thoughts on Yingzhou) and *Dong xun* (Inspection Tour to the East) are best known.

ZHANG XIANLIANG (1936–). Novelist. Born in Nanjing, Zhang Xianliang moved with his parents to Chongqing, the war capital, when he was a primary school student. After the Japanese surrendered, the family moved back to Nanjing, where Zhang attended middle school. In 1951, the family moved again, this time to Beijing. Having failed the college entrance exam, Zhang volunteered to go to the northwest. He worked as a secretary in a village in Gansu Province before being transferred in 1956 to the Gansu Cadres Cultural School to teach literature. Soon afterward, Zhang's life took a sudden turn for the worse. He was labeled a rightist because of a poem he published in 1957. For the next 22 years, he lived under a great shadow of distrust and was imprisoned for several years. After years of physical hardship and mental anguish, Zhang was finally rehabilitated in the late 1970s and he wrote several stories based on his experience at the labor camps. A powerful voice in the beginning years of the post-Mao era, Zhang's work is considered part of the **scar literature**. While other scar writers focused their attention on denouncing the dehumanizing effects of the **Cultural Revolution**, Zhang emphasizes the individual's moral triumph achieved by surviving hardships, which in many ways reflects his own life.

"Ling yu rou" (*Body and Soul*) portrays a young intellectual, Xu Linjun, who is a victim of the ultraleftist policies under Mao Zedong. Because of his wealthy family background, he is labeled a rightist just to meet a quota. Exiled to a remote farm, he survives the harsh conditions with the help of the peasants and the love of a woman. Years later, when his long-lost father returns to take him abroad, Xu decides to stay. This act of patriotism is seen as an affirmation of the true value of life and the strong sense of mission important for a Chinese intellectual. *Lühuashu* (*Mimosa*) and *Nanren de yiban shi nüren* (*Half of Man Is Woman*) are about the life of a political prisoner. *Lühuashu* details the events in the early 1960s, when Mao's economic policies of the Great Leap Forward produced disastrous results and nationwide famines and threatened the well-being of the country. Against this background, Zhang Yonglin, a rightist, is released from a labor reform camp and assigned to a remote and backward northwestern farm to work as a self-supporting laborer. He experiences all kinds of hardship but receives care and help from the villagers. Through physical labor and diligent study of Marxist works, Zhang Yonglin becomes a true believer in Marxism. The author infuses the severe realities the protagonist encounters with a degree of romanticism, finding beauty and lyricism in the bitter and crude life of the countryside and showing that a damaged heart can heal so long as there is beauty and love in life. The story shows the capacity and strength of the individual to transform himself and arrive at an introspective realization under adverse circumstances.

Nanren de yiban shi nüren continues to explore the experience of alienation and restoration of humanity. In this novel, the protagonist, Zhang Yonglin, has once again lost his freedom and the people around him are mere carcasses without the slightest sign of spirituality. Despondent, he is eventually saved by Huang Xianju, a woman with charm and passion, who awakens his desire for life. While enjoying his sexual recovery, he is tormented by a deep sense of shame. He questions the motive of his relationship with Huang, concluding that what they have between them is not love but lust. A divorce ensues and Zhang Yonglin embarks on a lonely journey in search of the true meaning of life, which, he believes, has to be completed alone. *Nanren de yiban shi nüren* highlights the need for spiritual as well as physical fulfillment in human life.

Xiguan siwang (*Getting Used to Dying*) further explores the themes of patriotism and the separation of body and soul. It is also a close examination of the consequences of trauma. A near-death experience in the past has permanently damaged the hero's psychological well-being. The shadow of death always hangs over his head, even when he is making love. Through a brilliant narrative device that switches between "you," "I," and "he" to represent the same individual, the author highlights his alienation and psychological and emotional wounds. Unlike Zhang's previous novels, which assert that life damaged can be made whole again, the tragic story of *Xiguan siwang* shows that not all broken pieces can be put together. Currently, Zhang Xianliang is the head of a film production company and chairman of the Ningxia Writers' Association. *See also* CULTURAL REVOLUTION.

ZHANG XIAOFENG (1941–). Prose and fiction writer and playwright. Born in Jinhua, Zhejiang Province, Zhang Xiaofeng moved to **Taiwan** at the age of eight. She graduated from Dongwu University and has taught at universities in Taiwan. Zhang is primarily known as a prose writer. Her lyrical essays, noted for their classical elegance, are highly regarded and very popular in all Chinese-speaking communities. She has published numerous essay collections including *Ditan de na yi duan* (At the Other End of the Carpet), *Bu xia hong tan zhi hou* (After Stepping Off the Red Carpet), *Ni hai meiyou ai guo* (You Have Not Loved), *Cong ni meili de liuyu* (From Your Beautiful River Valley), *Chu xue*

(The First Snow), *Yige nüren de aiqing guan* (A Woman's Perspective on Love), and *Shengjing zhi tapian* (The Rubbings of the Bible). Her essays express her love of Mother Nature, her sentimental attachment to the homeland, her appreciation of the value of life, and her persistent inquiry into the meaning of existence. In her works, the Chinese humanistic tradition and the Christian ideal of compassion are seamlessly blended, giving her prose a high degree of cultural refinement and universal appeal and making Zhang one of the best prose writers in modern Chinese literature.

In addition to her famous prose work, Zhang has written plays, including *He shi bi* (Mr. He's Jade) and *Wuling ren* (The Man from Wuling), and acted in them. She has also published several collections of short stories, including *Hong shoupa* (Red Handkerchief) and *Mei lan zhu ju* (Plum, Orchid, Bamboo, and Chrysanthemum). *See also* SPOKEN DRAMA; WOMEN.

ZHANG XIGUO, A.K.A. CHANG HSI-KUO, CHANG SHI-KUO (1944–). Fiction writer. Born in Chongqing, Sichuan, Zhang Xiguo moved to **Taiwan** in 1949 with his parents. He studied electrical engineering at National Taiwan University, which eventually brought him to the United States in 1966. He has taught engineering and computer science at the University of Illinois, Cornell University, and the University of Pittsburgh, while also turning out a great many novels.

Considered the best science fiction writer writing in Chinese, Zhang has produced a large number of works that make liberal use of his background in science and technology. The crown of his writing career rests on the series called *Youzi hun* (Soul of the Émigré), which includes *Xiangjiao chuan* (*Banana Boat*) and *Buxiu zhe* (The Incorruptible). The series consists of 12 stories, each of which is an experiment in form. Other works include *Kongzi zhi si* (The Death of Confucius), *Qi wang* (*The Chess King*), and *Rang weilai deng yi deng ba* (Let the Future Wait). Often mentioned in the company of Hong Kong science fiction writer **Ni Kuang**, whose stories aim at entertainment by focusing on plot development and the use of high-tech props, Zhang is thought to be much more serious in his attempts to tackle issues of great importance to humanity, even though his characters reside in an imaginary and alien world. Many of his novels can be read as critiques of Chinese history and society.

ZHANG XIN (1954–). Fiction writer. A member of the Guangzhou Literary Writing and Research Institute and a graduate of the Writers Workshop at Beijing University, Zhang Xin began publishing short stories and novellas in the late 1970s. A popular writer whose work depicts life and work of **women**, mostly professional women in the southern coastal cities, Zhang has received several awards for her stories and her collection of novellas. *Buyao wen wo cong nali lai* (Don't Ask Me Where I Come From) has won the Lu Xun Literature Award. Among her other publications are *Ai you ruhe* (What about Love), "Fuhua beihou" (Behind the Glamour), "Touru juese" (Getting into the Role), "Yongyuan de paihuai" (The Everlasting Hesitation), and "Juefei ouran" (*Certainly Not Coincidence*), all romantic tales of young women in contemporary urban China. *See also* WOMEN.

ZHANG XINXIN (1953–). Fiction and prose writer. Born in Nanjing, Zhang Xinxin grew up in Beijing in a military family. She has worked at a number of jobs including farmworker, soldier, nurse, television anchor, and theater director. Her literary career began in the early 1980s while she was a student at the Central Institute of Theater. She has been living in the United States since 1988.

Zhang's best-known work is the oral histories she and Sang Ye collected from their interviews of people of different social backgrounds, ranging from a professional basketball player to a former prostitute. Her style of writing has shifted from a subjective voice venting frustrations about men and society in her early stories, to that of a storyteller who enjoys weaving complicated tales such as "Wan yihui zuoze de baxi" (Playing a Thief's Game), to a narrative mode devoid of the authorial voice as in the oral histories. In recent years, Zhang has written mostly nonfiction, including a book based on her experience working for the Voice of America entitled *Wo zhidao de meiguo zhiyin* (The Voice of America That I Know). *See also* WOMEN.

ZHANG YUERAN (1982–). Fiction writer. Born in Ji'nan, Shandong Province, Zhang Yueran majored in English and law at Shandong University and studied computer science at National Singapore University. One of the post-1980s generation, Zhang began writing at a young age. After *Mengya* (Sprouts), a literary journal for young readers, published her stories, she became a popular teen writer. Winner of several awards including the Singapore Undergraduate Literature Prize (second place), Zhang has attracted the attention of mainstream literary journals and newspapers as well as established writers such as **Mo Yan**, who wrote the preface for one of her books.

Zhang's best-known work is *Yintao zhi yuan* (The Distance of Cherry), a sentimental, coming-of-age novel about two girls who grow up together and who experience friendship, love, and death. *Hong xie* (A Red Shoe), a tale of retribution, depicts the relationship between an assassin and a little girl who witnessed him murder her mother. *Shi niao* (The Story of the Revenge Bird) was inspired by Chinese mythology and the author's personal experience of the 2004 tsunami that devastated the countries bordering the Indian Ocean. The novel, set in the 17th century at the height of sea expeditions, portrays a Chinese woman who loses her memory in a tsunami as she journeys to Southeast Asia. Populated by colorful characters such as pirates, sing-song girls, eunuchs, and European missionaries, the novel creates a historical past and a South Seas landscape saturated with magic and fantasy. *See also* NEW GENERATION WRITERS; WOMEN.

ZHANG ZAO (1962–). Poet. One of the main representatives of the **Generation III poets**, Zhang Zao majored in English at Hunan Teachers' University and later received a master's degree from Sichuan Foreign Languages Institute, where he found himself in the midst of a lively circle of young poets and he began to write. Soon after he published his poems in 1979, Zhang was touted as one of the most gifted young poets of the time. While many of his fellow Generation III poets went southward to join the entrepreneurial frenzy, Zhang, driven by the same sense of restlessness, chose to go abroad in 1986 instead. He received his Ph.D. in comparative literature from Tubingen University in Germany, where he is now teaching. His success as a poet has much to do with his unique skill in creating aestheticism in the context of routine modern life. "Jing zhong" (In the Mirror), a short poem about beauty, idealism, memory, and regrets, is characteristic of this poetic vision. Though experimental in nature, Zhang's poems possess a quality of elegance. His language is deceptively plain and straightforward, but his imageries jump and skip, leaving room for the reader's imagination. His themes and images often come from classical literature, both Chinese and foreign. The poet persona acts as if he is an observer of these ancient literary scenes. Zhang is unique among contemporary Chinese poets in that he is conversant in several foreign languages, including English, German, French, and Russian, allowing him to have direct access to these literary traditions. Among the many awards he has received are the 1999 Anne Kao Prize for Lyric Poetry and the 1998–1999 Poetry Prize sponsored by the literary magazine *Zuojia* (Writers).

ZHAO MEI (1954–). Fiction and prose writer. Born in Tianjin, Zhao Mei received her bachelor's degree from the Chinese Department of Nankai University. She currently works for the journal *Wenxue ziyou tan* (Candid Comments on Literature). Since 1986 when her first story appeared, Zhao has published more than four collections of short stories and more than a dozen novels as well as several collections of essays. In 1998, she won the Lun Xun Literature Award for her prose work *Linghun zhi guang* (The Light of the Soul). Zhao has created many memorable **women** characters including those in her historical novels such as *Wu Zetian* (Empress Wu) and *Gaoyang gongzhu* (Princess Gaoyang), both legendary figures in Chinese history, and in fictional accounts such as *Women jiazu de nüren* (Women in my Family), which tells harrowing stories about the sufferings of women as well as their heroic triumphs. Another group of Zhao's works can be characterized as romantic novels, *Tianguo de lianren* (Lovers of the Sky) and *Shiji mo de qingren* (Lovers at the Fin de Siècle) among them.

Zhao's recent novel *Qiutian si yu dong ji* (Autumn Dies in Winter) is unique among her publications both in style and subject matter. Unlike her previous work, which places much emphasis on plot, *Qiutian si yu dong ji* is a cerebral work that relies heavily on intellectual ruminations. The novel features several Chinese scholars who study and interpret the literary works of Milan Kundera, who is the central figure in this novel. Kundera was introduced to Chinese readers in the 1980s as a radical and innovative writer who successfully challenged the literary and intellectual establishments of the West. To Chinese intellectuals in the 1980s who were looking for ways to break away from all sorts of constraints of the past decades, Kundera was no doubt an inspiration. Merely a decade later, however, as the novel shows, such a literary and intellectual icon has become less relevant. The change in the image of Kundera mirrors the change in Chinese society. Kundera, who used to be the spiritual and intellectual anchor is no longer able to sustain Chinese intellectuals, as the idealism of the 1980s has given in to the pressures of mundane but inescapable daily life. The novel contains lengthy academic discourses on Kundera and his fictional characters.

Zhao's works are characterized by her unfailingly graceful language and her ability to navigate between the expansive historical landscape and the subtleties of personal emotions.

ZHAO SHULI (1906–1970). Novelist. Zhao Shuli is undoubtedly the most celebrated name in the so-called potato school, a term given to writers, mostly of rural origins and active in the 1940s and 1950s, who represent peasant life in northern China with simple and straightforward language. Zhao owed much, if not all, of his success to the Chinese Communist Revolution and its professed literary policy to serve the needs of the peasants who were the backbone of its success. Zhao's reputation was established against this political and historical background.

Growing up poor in a peasant family in a village of Qinshui, Shanxi Province, Zhao had deep roots in rural life and understood its customs and traditions. As a child, he learned the Chinese classics from his grandfather, a failed Confucian scholar turned peasant, and from his father he acquired a lifelong love for Bangzi, a local opera, and the knowledge of herbal medicine. Until he attended, in 1925 at the age of 19, the Number Four Normal School of Shanxi, which was located in Changzhi, a small city close to his hometown, Zhao had lived in this agrarian society cut off from the outside world. While in Changzhi, he eagerly read progressive magazines such as *Xin qingnian* (New Youth), *Xiaoshuo yuebao* (Fiction Monthly), and *Chuangzao zhoukan* (Creation Weekly), as well as Chinese translations of books and brochures such as *The A.B.C of Communism* by Nicolai Bukharin and *Evolution and Ethics* by Thomas Huxley. Zhao joined the Chinese Communist Party in 1927. His writing career began with some stories written in imitation of Western literature, which was a typical practice in his generation shaped by the new culture of the **May Fourth Movement**. Influenced by **Lu Xun** and in response to the call of the **left-wing** movement to create a literature that dealt with real social issues, Zhao turned to his rural roots. Unlike most of the left-wing writers, Zhao came from the countryside and was familiar with the art forms that the country folks loved to see and hear. He argued that for progressive ideas to reach the countryside, two stumbling blocks had to be removed: the first, the old storybooks representing Confucian ethics and superstitious traditions; and the second, the prejudice among the cultural elite, who considered popular forms of folk entertainment vulgar. His mission was to create a new literature to replace the traditional tales that, in his view, were poisoning the peasants' minds. This new literature had to be understood and embraced by the peasants. Unlike most of the literature at the time, which dealt with the sentiments of the educated youth in a refined language, his stories would contain the smell of the yellow earth, written in a language that the peasants, like his father, would understand. Mao Zedong's talks at the Yan'an Forum on Literature and Art in 1942 helped catapult Zhao to the forefront of literature and art at the Communist base.

"Xiao Erhei jiehun" (*Little Erhei's Marriage*), published in 1943, is considered one of his best works. Set in the Communist-controlled Taihang Mountain area during the **Sino-Japanese War**, the story tells about a young peasant couple, Erhei and Xiaoqin, whose parents are opposed to their marriage because according to local superstition their fortunes do not match. In the end, love triumphs and the young couple, protected by the new marriage law, are able to wed. Encouraged by the success of the story, Zhao went on to write "Li Youcai banhua" (*Rhymes of Li Youcai*), in which he treats the power struggle between the landlord class and the poor peasants. In the character of Li Youcai, an awakened peasant, there is the shadow of the author's father, also a village musician. Li's rhymed ballads represent the old form of entertainment, now fully transformed to serve the cause of the revolution. This character crystallizes the proletarian artistic enterprise envisioned by the author.

"Xiao Erhei jiehun" and "Li Youcai banhua" firmly established Zhao's position as the preeminent peasant novelist. Their successes led to the novel *Li Jiazhuang de bianqian* (*Changes in Li Village*), written in 1945, which focuses on the growth of a young peasant boy as he and his fellow villagers fight against the Japanese army and its puppets. During the 17 years between the founding of the People's Republic of China and the **Cultural Revolution**, Zhao produced more short- and medium-length stories and another novel, *San li wan* (The Three-Mile Bend), all reflecting rural life. Although none of them reached the same level of success as his earlier stories, he was proud that his writings were in complete harmony with the party's policies and with the progress of Chinese society. His self-confidence was shattered in 1966, however, when the storm of the Cultural Revolution swept across the country and he became a victim. Zhao Shuli was tortured and died in prison in 1970. *See also* SOCIALIST REALISM.

ZHENG CHOUYU, A.K.A. CHENG CH'OU-YU, PEN NAMES OF ZHENG WENTAO (1933–). Poet. Born to a military family in Ji'nan,

Shandong Province, Zheng Chouyu moved to **Taiwan** with his family in 1949. After college, he worked at the Port of Jilong while pursuing his writing career. His poetry caught the attention of **Ji Xian**, who invited him to join the Modern Poetry Society. Zheng left Taiwan in 1968 at the invitation of the International Writing Program at the University of Iowa, where he received his M.A. He taught Chinese literature at Yale University from 1973 until his retirement. Zheng is known as a lyrical poet with the sensibility of a romantic wanderer, which he attributed to the trajectory of his life. His mastery of the Chinese language has also garnered widespread praises. "Cuowu" (Mistake), a love poem written in 1954, best captures his sense of rhythm and his ability to express the delicate moods and feelings of a man on a journey away from home. While Zheng is celebrated for his graceful and restrained style in dealing with subtle personal feelings, he is equally at home with conveying bold and unconstrained emotions. Zheng is a prolific poet and among his many poetry collections are *Yibo* (Legacy), *Yanren xing* (Journey of a Northerner), and *Jimo de ren zuo zhe kan hua* (A Seated Man of Solitude Views Flowers). Zheng sees his poetry as an expression of Confucian humanism, Taoist belief in the natural world, and the Buddhist practice of compassion. *See also* MODERN POETRY MOVEMENT IN TAIWAN.

ZHENG WANLONG (1944–). Fiction writer. Born in Heilongjiang, Zheng Wanlong spent his early childhood among the Eroqen huntsmen and gold miners in the mountains of the northeast. He moved to Beijing at the age of eight after his mother died. After graduating from Beijing Chemical Engineering School in 1963, he worked for 11 years as a technician in a fertilizer factory while writing poetry and short stories in his spare time. He was transferred to the Beijing Press in 1974 to work as an editor, an important step in his writing career. In 1980, he became a member of the Chinese Writers' Association and began to devote himself to writing full-time.

In the mid-1980s, Zheng joined the popular **root-seeking** movement with an article "Wo de gen" (My Roots) and with a series of stories based on the memories of his childhood encounters with life in the harsh environment of the Da Xing'an Mountains in Heilongjiang. These "strange tales from strange lands" (yi xiang yi wen) depict a world of danger and brutality, where men try to survive in the uninhabited hostile environment. Much like the world of the American Westerns, Zheng's northern frontier is governed by guns, liquor, and physical might. In this primitive world, men are pitted against nature and against one another. Far away from civilization, masculine vigor is celebrated while anything that relates to the civilized society is frowned upon. Having once killed a wolf with three kicks, the hero in "Lao Bangzi jiuguan" (*Old Stick's Wineshop*), a man proud of the 43 scars on his body, is feared and revered. To safeguard his tough-guy image, he disappears into the mountains so that he will be thought to have died in the wilderness hunting down animals, not from an illness, which is the real cause of his death. In these "strange lands" inhabited by mythological tribes, superstition rules alongside of sheer muscle. Customs such as worshiping a sulfuric smell depicted in "Huang yan" (Yellow Smoke) offer the reader a glimpse into the exotic traditions of the northern frontier.

Zheng currently lives in Beijing and writes film and television scripts.

ZHENG YI (1947–). Fiction and prose writer. Before his involvement in the 1989 **Tian'anmen Prodemocracy Movement** forced him into exile to the United States, Zheng Yi had been known as the author of "Feng" (*Maple*), a story about the **Cultural Revolution**, and *Lao jing (Old Well)*, a novella about a village in northern China and its persistant effort to drill for water. *Lao jing* was later adapted into a movie that won awards at several international film festivals. Since coming to the United States in 1993, Zheng, now an outspoken critic of the Chinese government, has turned to nonfiction writing. *Hongse jinianbei (Scarlet Memorial: Tales of Cannibalism in Modern China)* uncovers the dark secrets of cannibalism in Guangxi Province as a result of politically motivated policies in Guangxi during the **Cultural Revolution**. *Zhongguo zhi huimie: Zhongguo shengtai bengkui jinji baogao (China in Ruins: The Ecological Breakdown)* describes the serious damages that industrialization and modernization, particularly mismanagement, have inflicted on China's environment. One novel, *Shen shu* (Magic Tree), recounts the tumultuous state of the Chinese countryside since World War II up to the present.

In the beginning of his career, Zheng was a reputed writer of **scar literature**, and at present he is thought to be a dissident writer known for his sharp criticisms of the Communist government. The four years he spent in a village in Shanxi as an educated youth and his later life in exile are two critical sources of influence on his thinking and writing.

ZHENG ZHENDUO (1898–1958). Essayist, fiction writer, translator, and editor. Born into a poor family in Yongjia, Zhejiang Province, Zheng Zhentuo graduated from the Beijing Railway Management School. When the **May Fourth Movement** broke out, Zheng eagerly embraced its ideals. A leading voice in the **New Culture Movement**, Zheng was instrumental in promoting the development of modern Chinese literature. He was a founding member of several organizations, including the **Literary Research Society**, which advocated realism and opposed art for art's sake, and the Minzhong Xiju She (Society of People's Theater), which promoted **spoken drama**. Known for his work as editor of a variety of literary journals, including the influential *Fiction Monthly*, which was responsible for establishing trends in modern Chinese literature, Zheng called on Chinese writers to express authentic feelings and to produce works of "blood and tears." Zheng's own creative work consists of numerous essays including those collected under the title *Ouxing riji* (Diary of My European Journey), written in the late 1920s during his two-year exile in France on suspicion of Communist connections, and fictional works, "Qu huo zhe de daibu" (The Arrest of the Fire-Stealer) and "Jiating de gushi" (The Tale of a Family). Among his translations are Russian fiction, Greek myths, and Indian fables. After 1949, Zheng was appointed director of the Bureau of Cultural Relics, director of the Literary Research Institute of the Chinese Academy of Social Sciences, and deputy minister of culture, among other official positions. He died in a plane crash while leading a government delegation to visit Afghanistan and the Middle East.

ZHONG LIHE, A.K.A. CHUNG LI-HO (1915–1960). Fiction and prose writer. One of the most prominent writers from rural **Taiwan**, Zhong received a Japanese education, and after finishing middle school, he worked briefly on his father's farm, where he fell in love with a young farmhand. The love affair met with disapproval from his parents and the community, as the young couple shared the same surname, a significant detail that rendered their union "incestuous" according to local customs. Heartbroken, they left home, and eventually arrived on the mainland where they lived as husband and wife. When they returned to Taiwan in 1946, Zhong was already a published writer but still struggling financially. Most of Zhong's works, based on his own ordeals, were published posthumously. These autobiographical stories, such as "Lishan nongchang" (Lishan Farms) and "Yuanxiangren" (The Native), deal with social prejudice and financial difficulties in rural Taiwan, making Zhong a pioneer in Taiwan's **nativist** literary (xiangtu wenxue) movement. Zhong died at the age of 45 in the midst of poverty and illness.

ZHONG XIAOYANG (1962–). Fiction writer and essayist. Born in Guangzhou, Zhong Xiaoyang grew up in **Hong Kong** and graduated from the Film Department of the University of Michigan. She immigrated to Australia in 1991 but moved back to Hong Kong four years later. Zhong achieved her fame at a young age, having published several books—novels, short stories, essays, and poems—by the age of 25. Like **Taiwan's Zhu Tianwen** and **Zhu Tianxin**, whom she befriended when she went to Taipei in 1981 to accept the Unitas Literature Award for her novel *Ting che zan jie wen* (Stop the Car to Ask for Directions), Zhong is influenced by **Zhang Ailing**, whose exquisitely styled fiction captures the subtleties of modern urban life. Zhong wrote *Ting che zan jie wen* at the tender age of 18, but her prose is stunningly sophisticated, a result of her deep immersion in classical Chinese poetry and fiction, particularly the 18th-century novel *Hong lou meng* (*A Dream of Red Mansions*), a book that also greatly influenced Zhang Ailing. *Ting che zan jie wen* presents a portrait of a woman whose dream of love is thrice dashed by reality. Another novel, *Yi hen chuanqi* (Love in Eternal Regret), relates the collapse of a wealthy Hong Kong family caught in the fatal entanglement of romantic rivalry and intrigue. Published in 1996, the novel can be read as an allegory of the city's colonial history and an expression of anxiety about the imminent British handover of Hong Kong to China.

Much of Zhong's work deals with the emotional intensities of romantic relationships that end tragically, invoking the world inhabited by Zhang Ailing's characters. In a language that is at once evocative, meditative, and elegant, Zhong presents a modern urban life pointedly from a **woman**'s perspective. While describing the agonizing consequences of a lost love, Zhong celebrates the imperfection of human destiny. Characterized as gothic, Zhong's fiction is overwhelmingly concerned with the topos of decay and death, as shown by book titles such as *Ran shao zhi hou* (In the Wake of the Fire), a collection of short stories, and *Gao mu si hui ji* (Dead Wood and Burnt Ashes), a poetry collection.

ZHONG ZHAOZHENG, A.K.A. CHUNG CHAO-CHENG (1925–). Novelist. Zhong Zhaozheng was a member of the first generation of **Taiwan**ese writers that emerged after the Japanese occupation. His works, written in the tradition of social realism established by older writers such as Zhang Wojun, Wu Zhuliu, and others, ushered in a new generation of Taiwanese writers. Educated in the Japanese system, Zhong began learning written Chinese in his adult years and published his first work in Chinese in 1953.

Zhong mostly wrote short stories in the 1950s, depicting local customs and tradtions. In the 1960s, he turned to writing novels, publishing in installments his first book, *Lubing hua* (Lubing Flower). His most important works are *Zhuoliu sanbuqu* (Trilogy of Muddy Torrent) and *Taiwanren sanbuqu* (Trilogy of the Taiwanese), which portray life in Taiwan under Japanese occupation, bearing witness to the national mentality of that period. *Zhuoliu sanbuqu* is an autobiographical novel, and through the experience of the protagonist, a young man of some education, it depicts Taiwan during and after the Japanese occupation. The novel denounces the Japanese colonizers' hypocrisy and cruelty and describes a nascent nationalism among the Taiwanese and their search for identity.

Taiwanren sanbuqu, which took the author more than 10 years to write, is a saga of five generations of the Lu clan, whose ancestors came to Taiwan from Guangdong in the 18th century. Zhong links the patriotic anti-Japanese struggle on the island with the important historical events that occurred on the mainland between 1895, when Taiwan was ceded to Japan, and 1945, when Taiwan was restored to China. He treats the history of Taiwan by describing the heroic struggles of the Taiwanese under the Japanese occupation. This novel is unique in the history of Taiwanese literature in terms of the broad span of time it covers and its grand scale. For his numerous books about Taiwan, Zhong is regarded as an important chronicler of its history and a bard of its spirit.

ZHOU ERFU (1914–2004). Novelist and poet. Born in Nanjing, Jiangsu Province, Zhou Erfu joined the **Left-wing Association of Chinese Writers** in the mid-1930s as a student in the English Department of Guanghua University in Shanghai. After graduating from college in 1938, Zhou worked as an editor and journalist, initially in the Communist-controlled Yan'an in the northwest and later in Chongqing and Hong Kong. After 1949, he rose to the position of deputy minister of culture. While visiting Japan in 1985 as head of an official delegation, he visited the Yasukuni Shrine, which violated the Chinese government's diplomatic rule and resulted in the suspension of his party membership.

Although he began his literary career as a poet, publishing in 1934
Ye xing ji (Traveling at Night), a collection of poems, Zhou is best remembered for his novels, especially *Shanghai de zaochen* (*Morning in
Shanghai*), which portrays Shanghai's industrialists around the time of
the Communist takeover in 1949. Written in the mode of **socialist realism**, the novel offers a panoramic view of the city at an important historical moment. Through the changes in the life of the main character,
an ambitious textile mill owner, the novel reflects the difficult trajectory
of Chinese manufacturers in their effort to build a national industry
and their gradual conversion to socialism. Often compared with **Mao
Dun's** *Ziye* (*Midnight*), another novel that treats the same subject matter, Zhou's work is more ambitious with four volumes covering a wide
spectrum of diverse social classes from wealthy factory owners to struggling workers. Similar in scope is Zhou's historical novel *Changcheng
wan li tu* (A Portrait of the Great Wall), which is about the Chinese
people's heroic resistance to Japanese invasion in World War II. He
worked, off and on, for 16 years to finish the six-volume historical saga.
Zhou's other publications include *Baiqiu'en daifu* (*Doctor Norman Bethune*), a biographical novel based on the life of the Canadian doctor who
died while treating Chinese soldiers during the **Sino-Japanese War**,
another novel *Yan su ya* (The Swallow Cliff), and several collections of
short stories and essays.

ZHOU LIBO, PEN NAME OF ZHOU FENGXIANG (1908–1979).
Novelist. Born in rural Hunan, Zhou Libo graduated from Changsha
Number One Middle School, a liberal institution made famous by its
alumni such as Mao Zedong. While in school, Zhou was exposed to
progressive ideologies and his determination to pursue freedom and
independence was indicated by his chosen pen name—"Libo" is a transliteration of the English word *liberty*. In 1929, Zhou left Changsha for
Shanghai and entered Labor University to study economics. When his
involvement in the underground Communist activities was discovered
the following year, Zhou was promptly dismissed by the university. He
returned to Hunan and began to pursue a writing career. In 1931, he
went back to Shanghai to work as a proofreader for a publisher. A year
later, he was arrested for participating in the labor movement and was
later released on bail. Zhou became a member of the **Left-wing Association of Chinese Writers** and the Chinese Communist Party (CCP) in
1934. When the **Sino-Japanese War** broke out, Zhou worked as a war

correspondent and editor for *Kang zhan ribao* (Resistant War Daily) and *Jiuwang ribao* (National Salvation Daily), newspapers published by the CCP. At the end of 1939, Zhou was transferred to the CCP base in Yan'an and assumed the post as head of the editing and translation department of Yan'an Lu Xun Institute of Arts. He was present at the Yan'an Forum on Literature and Art held in 1942, at which Mao Zedong delivered his historic speeches. In the following years, Zhou was put in charge of the CCP's propaganda work, editing newspapers such as *Jiefang ribao* (Liberation Daily) and *Zhongyuan ribao* (Central Plains Daily). After 1949, Zhou worked for, among other organizations, the Chinese Writers' Association and served on the editorial board of the People's Literature Press.

Bao feng zhou yu (The Storm), written in 1948, and *Shan xiang ju bian* (*Great Changes in a Mountain Village*), published in 1959–1960, are Zhou's best-known works. Both novels deal with the land reform in the Chinese countryside carried out during the first few years of the Communist victory. *Bao feng zhou yu*, based on Zhou's personal experience from 1946 to 1948 as a member of a land reform team sent to the newly liberated northeast, describes how poor peasants are empowered when the Communists give them land taken from rich landlords. The enlightened peasants begin to take control of not only properties but also their destinies, winning victory over their own ignorance while overthrowing the landed class that exploited them and defeating local bandits who mount fierce attacks against the Communist-controlled region. Like Ding Ling's *Taiyang zhao zai Sanggan He shang* (The Sun Shines upon the Sanggan River), another work that deals with the land reform, *Bao feng zhou yu* was trumpeted as a masterpiece of **socialist realism** and placed third in the 1951 Stalin Literature Prize. The work was clearly influenced by Mikhail A. Sholokhov, the Soviet Nobel laureate whose novel *Seeds of Tomorrow* (volume 1 of *Virgin Soil Upturned*) Zhou translated into Chinese in the 1930s.

Shan xiang ju bian can be seen as a sequel to *Bao feng zhou yu* in that it reflects the immediate transformation taking place in the countryside after the land reform and depicts the social upheavals in the shift from private landownership to collectivization. Set in a village of his native Hunan, to which Zhou returned to live in 1955, the novel explores the arduous journey of the peasants as they gradually move to embrace collectivization, initially in the form of cooperatives and eventually communes. In portraying the collectivization movement as the second storm after the land reform, which shakes the foundation of rural China, the novel paints a society on its way to fundamentally transforming the peasantry into a powerful and enlightened force in socialist construction. Both novels are noted for the vivid portrayal of characters and the author's effortless mastery of regional dialects. Another notable work is *He chang shang* (On the Rice Threshing-Ground), which consists of sketches and stories written after he returned to Hunan and refocused his creative energy on rural communities as his writings about factory life had failed to garner critical attention. The pieces in the book highlight the optimism Chinese peasants feel toward their future and the harmonious rural communities and new customs established after the collective production system was put into effect.

After the **Cultural Revolution,** Zhou published "Xiangjiang yi ye" (One Night on the Xiang River), which won the 1977–1978 national prize for a short story. It describes a brilliant military campaign conducted by the Communist troops during the Sino-Japanese War. A loyal adherent to the party line throughout his life, Zhou was nevertheless an outspoken critic of the quality of contemporary Chinese writing. *See also* MAY FOURTH MOVEMENT; NEW CULTURE MOVEMENT.

ZHOU LUNYOU (1952–). Poet. A native of Xichang, Sichuan Province, Zhou Lunyou is the founder of **Feifeism** and its visionary and controversial theorist and spiritual leader. As chief editor of *Feifei* and *Feifei Criticism* as well as several collections of essays and poems, Zhou has guided the movement as its authoritative voice from its inception to the present. His importance is based not only on his own creative and theoretical work but also on his charisma, his devotion to poetry, his perseverance, and his self-confidence. Zhou's own poems, in particular "Ziyou fangkuai" (Freedom Squares) and "Tou xiang" (Head Portrait), represent the early stage of the Feifei movement. "Ziyou fangkuai" is a long text consisting of various genres, including lyrics, prose poetry, essays, quotations, insertions, and illustrations, randomly arranged like a collage, to achieve a kind of ecstatic chorus of words, images, and concepts. "Tou xiang" is about an artist who is trying to paint a head portrait in five ways, each version acting as a chapter of the long poem. In 1992, Zhou published another milestone essay, "Hongse xiezuo" (Red Writing), which aims its criticism at obsequious or escapist writers, including some former Feifeists who have surrendered to the establishment. Zhou challenges Chinese poets to write about real life, on forbidden themes, and against all forms of brutality. "Daofeng ershi shou" (Twenty Poems Written on the Blade) and "Dun ci" (Escape) embody this period of his creative work. "Daofeng ershi shou" deals with the meaning of brutality, its powerful effects on society, and the challenges it imposes on the individual. "Dun ci" uses many traditional rhetorical tropes, such as similes, analogies, parallelism, and reduplication, to subvert the accepted norms in order to return the language to its original meaning. *See also* GENERATION III POETS.

ZHOU MEISEN (1956–). Novelist and screenplay writer. Known for his "anti-corruption" or political novels, Zhou Meisen has written a number of works exposing the crimes committed when political power and money join forces, calling attention to the increasing economic gulf between the rich and the poor. For his realistic portrayal of China's corrupt bureaucracies, Zhou has become a target of attacks by some party officials, but since he has been careful to limit his criticism to officials at or below the provincial level, he has managed to squeeze through the severe scrutiny of governmental censorship. An ironic twist of his popularity is that one of his novels has won an award from the Communist Party's highest information control apparatus: the Ministry of Propaganda, both as a token of free expression and more likely an indication that corruption has caused concerns among the central leadership.

   Renjian zhengdao (The Right Path in the World), his first political novel, exposes the abuse of power in a province, while exploring the consequences of the market economy set in motion by Deng Xiaoping's reform policy. The success of *Renjian zhengdao* prompted Zhou to write *Tianxia caifu* (The Wealth of the World), focusing on the workings of the stock market and the people who profit from manipulating it, and *Zhongguo zhizao* (Made in China), reflecting the conflict between true reformers and corrupt officials. *Juedui quanli* (Absolute Power) centers on a city's party secretary, who has worked tirelessly to turn the city into an economic success and at the same time has allowed rampant corruption to go unchecked under his watch. Zhou's novels give the reader an excellent entry into the intricate web of Chinese bureaucracy with its political intrigues and conspiracies. Several of Zhou's novels have been turned into runaway hits on television that in turn fuel the sale of his books. The popularity of Zhou's works results from both the subject matter and the easy accessibility of his style.

Other than the political novels that have brought him fame, Zhou has written many historical novels, including *Zhong e* (Heavy Yoke), about the Chinese Trotskyists and other early revolutionaries in the early 1900s, and *Lunxian de tudi* (Land Fallen to the Enemy), on the Chinese people's struggle against Japanese aggression. There are also stories inspired by his own experience working in the coal mines of Xuzhou, Jiangsu Province, where he was born, including *Hei fen* (The Black Tomb) and *Yuan yu* (The Original Prison), both about the coal mining industry in the early 20th century. Before becoming a writer of best sellers, Zhou was an editor, businessman, and government official.

ZHOU ZUOREN, A.K.A. CHOU TSO-JEN (1885–1967). Essayist. Born in Shaoxing, Zhejiang Province, Zhou Zuoren was a leading intellectual in the 1920s, sharing the same fame as his elder brother **Lu Xun** as an important writer in the **New Culture Movement**. Like Lu Xun, he had received a traditional education before entering the Jiangnan Naval Academy in Nanjing. In 1906, Zhou joined Lu Xun in Japan. After coming back to China, he taught literature at Beijing University and was a founding member of the **Literary Research Society**. His work as editor of *Xin qingnian* (New Youth) and later *Yu si* (Words and Language), two major literary journals, as wells as his essays and translations, made him an influential figure in modern Chinese literature. Estranged from his brother because of a family dispute, Zhou became ideologically at odds with the mainstream literary trends, which his brother championed. He espoused traditional aesthetics that valued individualism rather than the national paradigm advocated by most of the **May Fourth** intellectuals, including his brother. In calling for tolerance in literature, he promoted freedom for writers to develop their own individual styles and themes, rather than subscribing to the set of formulas that dominated the intellectual and literary discourse of the day. In the 1930s and 1940s, he turned to writing humorous essays about the life of leisure, a major departure from the influential essays he had written in the 1920s. Further exacerbating his relationship with his fellow May Fourth comrades, Zhou collaborated with the Japanese during the **Sino-Japanese War**, for which he was sentenced to prison and his books were subsequently banned. Pardoned by the Communists in 1949, Zhou lived in obscurity, making a living by translating Greek and Japanese literature and writing about his famous brother. He died in Beijing.

ZHU TIANWEN, A.K.A. CHU T'IEN-WEN (1956–). Fiction and screenplay writer. One of the most talented writers from **Taiwan**, Zhu Tianwen was tutored, along with her two younger sisters, by their father, **Zhu Xining**, a writer and editor, and by **Hu Lancheng**, a litterateur with exquisite sensibilities, who taught them classical Chinese literature and shared the family's love for the writings of **Zhang Ailing**, with whom he lived in Shanghai in the late 1930s. The Zhu sisters grew up surrounded by books and were encouraged to write. While still in high school, Zhu began publishing stories in the literary supplements of Taiwan's major newspapers. Early in her career, she wrote about the experience of growing up in Taiwan, vividly portrayed in stories such as "Xiao Bi de gushi" (The Story of Xiao Bi), "Tongnian wangshi" (Childhood Memories), and "Beiqing shijie" (The World of Sadness). *Yanxia zhi du* (*A City in a Hot Summer*), which includes 14 short stories written in the 1980s, marks a new direction in Zhu's writing. In a somber tone, these stories comment on the alienating effects of modernization on the city of Taipei and its residents.

Greater critical acclaim came to Zhu with the publication of "Shiji mo de huali" (*Fin de Siècle Splendor*), which describes the high fashion and modern lifestyle of the protagonist, a former model, and her hopeless love affair with a married man. Zhu's real achievement in the story lies in her ability to create a lingering sense of loss and sadness without succumbing to sentimentalism. The extravagant language she uses in the story also befits the complexity of a cosmopolitan character. Similar in theme and style is her more recent work, *Huang ren shouji* (*Notes of a Desolate Man*), an award-winning and richly textured novel about a gay man trying to come to terms with his alienation from society while dealing with the impending death of his best friend who is suffering from AIDS. It is a cerebral book, packed with ruminations about Levi Strauss, Michel Foucault, T. S. Eliot, and other famous Western thinkers and literary personages, because the hero is steeped in Western culture as well as Chinese traditions. Homosexuality, though a focal point of the novel, serves only to highlight the dilemma faced by a highly educated, keenly sensitive Taiwanese intellectual in his inability to reconcile all the contradictions inherent in modern life. Like "Shiji mo de huali" and *Huang ren shouji, Wu yan* (Words of the Witch), Zhu's most recent book, examines modern life by centering on the complications of human relationships. Rich in its range of characters, the book is similar to a colorful Yamato-e painting, with its long scroll of scenes continuously and delicately illustrated.

Zhu is also an award-winning screenplay writer. She has worked extensively with Taiwan's eminent director Hou Hsiao-hsien on a number of internationally acclaimed films. *Haishang Hua* (Flowers of Shanghai) and *Tongnian wangshi* (Childhood Memories) are only two of the many collaborations between them. She is also an editor for *Sansan jikan* (The Threes), a literary journal, and Sansan shufang (The Threes Press), both founded by her and her sisters after she graduated from the English Department of Tamkang University. *See also* ZHU TIANXIN.

ZHU TIANXIN, A.K.A. CHU T'IEN-HSIN (1959–). Fiction writer. Born into a literary family in **Taiwan**, Zhu Tianxin is one of the three daughters of **Zhu Xining**, a well-known writer. Like her sister **Zhu Tianwen**, Zhu also published her first book at the age of 16 while still a high school student. She has since written several books and won a number of literary awards. Zhu studied history at National Taiwan University. A leading fiction writer in Taiwan, Zhu is also a literary editor.

Her autobiographical work, *Ji rang ge: Bei yi nü sannian ji* (Times of Peace and Comfort: Three Years at the Taipei Number One Middle School for Girls), remains a popular book among schoolgirls in Taiwan. Short stories in *Fangzhou shang de rizi* (Days on Board the Ark) and *Zuori dang wo nianqing shi* (Yesterday When I Was Young) and a novel *Weiliao* (Unfinished) are also about teenagers' friendships, tears, and laughter. In *Gu du* (The Ancient Capital), a collection of short stories, Zhu turns her attention to the displaced urban population living on the fringes of society, treating issues such as cultural and national identity. Through nostalgia, her characters attempt to construct their sense of self in relation to history, memory, and place. Many of her stories portray second- or third-generation mainlanders, particularly those who grew up in the *juancun* (military dependents' villages). These characters are forced to confront an identity crisis, having to reconcile two notions of home and nation: one defined by their own memories of childhood growing up in Taiwan and the other drilled into their heads by the older generation's nostalgic reminiscences of the lost mainland. *See also* HU LANCHENG; ZHANG AILING.

ZHU XINING, A.K.A. CHU HSI-NING (1927–1998). Fiction and prose writer and editor. Zhu studied art in Hangzhou but abandoned his studies to join the Nationalist army. When the government lost the **Civil War** and retreated to **Taiwan**, Zhu went along with the troops and had reached the rank of colonel by the time he left the army. Recognition came to him in the 1950s when his short stories were published. Many of his writings, though set in the mainland at the beginning of the 20th century, deal with the impact of modernity on the traditional way of life, a theme that resonated with the concerns shared by some intellectuals in Taiwan at the time. "Tien jiang" (*Molten Iron*), a gripping tale about a small town in northern China during the Qing dynasty, juxtaposes the arrival of modernity, represented by the coming of the train, with the gruesome death of a man determined to win back a salt production contract and with it his family's honor. His "irrational" behavior (self-mutilation that culminates in pouring hot, lavalike iron into his own mouth) is portrayed as a last desperate and futile attempt to hold on to the traditional way of life. A posthumously published novel, *Hua Taiping jia chuan* (The Hua Family Heritage), relates the changes in a Shandong village when Christian missionaries crack open the isolated, self-sufficient agrarian society. This novel reflects his family background. Zhu's grandfather, a preacher in his hometown in Shandong, was one of the first generation of Chinese Christians. Zhu is noted for his innovative techniques, his riveting plots, and his portrayals of Chinese country life. His aesthetics influenced a younger generation of writers, including **Zhang Dachun** and his daughters **Zhu Tianwen** and **Zhu Tianxin**.

ZHU ZIQING, A.K.A. CHU TZE-CH'ING (1898–1948). Essayist and poet. Born in Donghai, Jiangsu Province, Zhu Ziqing grew up in Yangzhou. He received a traditional education in his early childhood. In 1916, he attended Beijing University, where he participated in the **May Fourth Movement** and joined the New Tide Association, which was a main platform for modern literary work. After he graduated from Beijing University in 1920, Zhu taught at middle schools in Jiangsu and Zhejiang until 1925, when he joined the faculty at Qinghua University to teach Chinese literature, a job he held until a stomach ulcer took his life in 1948.

While caught in the center of a radical nationalist movement, Zhu was by nature a moderate intellectual, which he had in common with fellow southerners such as **Ye Shengtao**, who shared his enthusiasm for a new literature and had the same traditional literary sensibilities built upon a solid training in Chinese classics. Neither a radical reformer nor a conservative scholar, Zhu represented Chinese intellectuals among the May Fourth generation whose temperament was more in tune with Confucian gentlemanly virtues than with fervent revolutionary ideals or the liberal sentiments of Westernized intellectuals such as **Hu Shi** and **Xu Zhimo**. Zhu's essays and poems embrace traditional values and show an earthy intimacy with Chinese life. "Beiying" (The Silhouette), "He tang yue se" (Moonlit Lotus Pond), and "Jiang sheng li de Qinhuaihe" (The Qinhuai River in the Sound of Oars) are considered among the most brilliant lyrical essays in modern Chinese literature and have been read by generations of Chinese schoolchildren.

Zhu was one of the pioneering poets who experimented with using the vernacular as a poetic medium. He was also a founding member of *Shi Kan* (Poetry), China's first journal of modern poetry. Among his many poems, "Huimie" (Destruction), published in 1923, is the best known. Zhu's other publications include a collection of essays written after his 1931 trip to Europe and many scholarly essays on modern Chinese poetics and classical Chinese literature.

As the **Sino-Japanese War** broke out, Zhu followed his university as it retreated to Kunming where the difficulties of life and the assassination of his colleague **Wen Yiduo** by the government secret agents made Zhu more sympathetic to the Communist cause. In *Xinshi zahua* (Commentaries on New Poetry), Zhu speaks highly of the poems written by progressive poets Wen Yiduo, **Zang Kejia, Ai Qing**, and others and calls for literature to rally the nation in its resistance against Japanese aggression.

ZONG BAIHUA (1897–1986). Poet and essayist. Although in college Zong Baihua majored in medicine and studied philosophy and literature in his spare time, it was the latter that sustained his career and earned him a national name. Unlike **Lu Xun**, who gave up medicine to become a writer in order to save the soul of his countrymen, Zong went into aesthetics and literature more because of an imaginative propensity than a Confucian sense of social responsibility. In 1920, he went to Germany and studied with Max Dessoir and other eminent philosophers. He returned to China in 1925 and began a pioneering program to teach aesthetics as an academic discipline at Chinese universities. From 1952 till his death, he worked in the Philosophy Department of Beijing University. Known primarily for his contribution to aesthetic studies in China, Zong was a distinguished scholar familiar with both Western and Chinese philosophies. His theory that the core of Chinese aesthetics rests on the unification of opposite entities—"solidity-emptiness" and "finite-infinite"—paradigms espoused in Taoism and Buddhism, has a far-reaching influence in the world of Chinese academia and arts. His scholarly works include *Yi jing* (The Realm of Arts) and *Kangde yanjiu* (A Study of Kant). Zong was also a noted essayist. His best-known works are *Meixue de sanbu* (The Aesthetic Promenade), a collection of lyrical essays on aesthetics, and the letters included in *San ye ji* (Three Leaves: Correspondences of Tian Han, Zong Baihua, and Guo Moruo).

Zong displayed an interest in vernacular poetry as early as the late 1910s, when he was a student at Tongji University in Shanghai, where he joined the Chinese Youth Association and edited its magazine *Shaonian Zhongguo* (Chinese Youth). While studying in Germany, Zong began to write poetry, encouraged by Dessoir's emphasis on the aesthetic experience in nature and art. Most of the poems collected in *Liu yun xiao shi* (Floating Clouds: Short Poems), a book that attracted much attention in the 1920s and 1930s, were written during his sojourn in Germany. Although he was not nearly as prolific in his creative work as in his philosophical writings, he continued to write poetry after his return to China. His poems express his love of nature and the instantaneous perception of the beauty of the eternal universe through small joys in everyday life. Zong embraces Zen Buddhism in its celebration of the moment and the discovery of the philosophical and literary in the mundane. *See also* GUO MORUO; NEW CULTURE MOVEMENT; TIAN HAN.

ZONG PU, PEN NAME OF FENG ZONGPU (1928–). Fiction writer and essayist. Born in Beijing, Zong Pu grew up in an academic environment, moving from one university campus to another with her family, which was headed by her famous father, the renowned philosopher Feng Youlan (*1895–1990*). Although she published stories in the 1940s and 1950s, it is her work from the post-Mao era that has established her reputation as a creative writer.

Among her works are "Hong dou" (Red Beans), published in 1957, about the conflict of love and revolutionary ideals in a missionary school, "Xian shang de meng" (Dream on the Strings), about the chaotic years of the **Cultural Revolution**, and *Sansheng shi (Everlasting Rock)*, a love story set in the 1960s. Worth special mention are *Nan du ji* (Going South), about scholars who took divergent roads in the 1930s in Japanese-occupied Beijing, and its sequel, *Dong cang ji* (Hiding in the East), a novel chronicling the lives of China's intellectual elites, who are forced to retreat to the southwest during the **Sino-Japanese War**. Zong's protagonists are university professors, the group of people she knows intimately. Through the portrayal of their lives, Zong illustrates the spirituality of Chinese intellectuals who maintain moral purity in their pursuit of knowledge, scholarship, and aesthetic perfection. These traditional beliefs and practices give them the strength to survive social upheaval and transcend the chaos and madness of the age. They represent the best of Chinese culture, unbending and resilient in their quiet, unassuming ways. Zong writes in a style of gentle elegance, refined by her training in both Chinese classics and Western literature. The same style also characterizes her essays, the most endearing pieces of which are her sketches of well-known academics, including her distinguished father.

Bibliography

CONTENTS

Introduction   295
Primary Works (Individual Authors)   297
Anthologies   403
Surveys and General Critical Works   406
Critical Works on Individual Authors   411

INTRODUCTION

In a field as large as modern Chinese literature, there is understandably an incredible amount of material, works by authors and the scholars who study them. It is not feasible to include all notable works in this dictionary. Painstaking efforts, therefore, have been made to sift through the ocean of books and select only the most essential. The bibliography is divided into four categories: Primary Works (Individual Authors); Anthologies; Surveys and General Critical Works; and finally Critical Works on Individual Authors. While the first category contains both the Chinese originals and the English translations, the last three categories only include English publications. As this dictionary is intended primarily for English readers, emphasis is placed on works published in English.

For a reader coming to modern Chinese literature for the first time, the best place to start is perhaps a general introductory or survey book. Merle Goldman's *Modern Chinese Literature in the May Fourth Era*, and C. T. Hsia's *A History of Modern Chinese Fiction* should prove to be very helpful. Goldman's work is a historical examation of the first phase of modern Chinese literature, situating the authors and their works against the specific background of the era. Hsia's book, on the other hand, is a survey of exclusively fictional works, which covers up to the 1950s with the epilogue extending to the 1970s. While acknowledging the historical and political importance of these works, Hsia gives priority to assessing their literary value. Thus extensive plot summaries are provided, giving the reader a good sense of what a novel or story is about. For a closer look at the literature in the decades after the Nationalist retreat to Taiwan, Sun-sheng Yvonne Chang's *Modernism and the Nativist Resistance: Contemporary Chinese Fiction from Taiwan* treats the opposing ideological and aesthetic views of the two camps and their respective achievements. The volume edited by Wendy Larson and Anne Wedell-Wedellsbog, *Inside Out: Modernism and Postmodernism in Chinese Literary Culture*, and Xiaobing Tang's *Chinese Modernism: The Heroic and the Quotidian* should be interesting reads on new literature from the mainland since the 1980s.

For a sample of readings, the anthology edited by Joseph S. M. Lau and Howard Goldblatt, *The Columbia Anthology of Modern Chinese Literature*, is ideal, as it contains poetry, fiction, and essays up till the 1990s. If one wishes to focus on women writers, two anthologies edited by Amy D. Dooling and her colleague, *Writing Women in Modern China: An Anthology of Women's Literature from the Early Twentieth Century* and *Writing Women in Modern China: The Revolutionary Years, 1936–1976*, are recommended. If one is interested in the avant-garde writers in the mainland since the 1980s, Henry Zhao's *The Lost Boat: Avant-garde Fiction from China* includes names such as Ma Yuan, Ge Fei, Yu Hua, Su Tong, Can Xue, an altogether very fascinating collection. To get further acquainted with modern Chinese poetry, one can browse Michelle Yeh's *Anthology of Modern Chinese Poetry* and *Another Kind of Nation: An Anthology of Contemporary Chinese Poetry*, edited by Zhang Er and Chen Dongdong.

For plays (spoken drama), *Theater and Society: An Anthology of Contemporary Chinese Drama* edited by Yan Haiping would be a good place to start.

These critical surveys and anthologies should be able to guide readers to a few favorite names to explore further. The list may include fiction writers Lu Xun, Shen Congwen, Ba Jin, Mao Dun, Zhang Ailing, Wu Zhuoliu, Xiao Hong, Bai Xianyong, Wang Wenxing, Huang Chunming, Han Shaogong, Mo Yan, Su Tong, Yu Hua, Li Rui, Zhu Tianwen, Zhu Tianxin, Zhang Guixing, Li Yongping, Xi Xi, Wang Anyi, and Can Xue; poets Xu Zhimo, Dai Wangshu, Yang Mu, Bei Dao, Gu Cheng, Shu Ting, Yang Lian, Yu Jian, and Xi Chuan; playwrights Cao Yu, Lao She, Gao Xingjian, and Lai Shengchuan. Although the list should include many other names, unfortunately the English translations of their works are slow in coming. Keep an eye out for anyone that attracted your attention as you browsed through this dictionary.

The list of critical works is given here specifically for a reader interested in taking a more in-depth look at some of the works and literary trends. Marston Anderson's *Limits of Realism: Chinese Fiction in the Revolutionary Period* is a book intended for the academically inclined on how the Western realist tradition was transformed in the Chinese context. Leo Ou-fan Lee's *Voices from the Iron House*, David Der-wei Wang's *Fictional Realism in 20th-Century China: Mao Dun, Laoshe, Shen Congwen*, and Yi-Tsi Mei Feuerwerker's *Ding Ling's Fiction: Ideology and Narrative in Modern Chinese Literature* are devoted to the study of one or several authors. Xudong Zhang's *Chinese Modernism in the Era of Reforms* examines literature in the post-Mao era. For a scholarly work on modern Chinese poetry, take a look at Jiayan Mi's *Self-Fashioning and Reflexive Modernity in Modern Chinese Poetry*. For general feminist interpretations, Rey Chow's *Women and Chinese Modernity: The Politics of Reading Between West and East* and Amy D. Dooling's *Women's Literary Feminism in Twentieth Century China* may be helpful.

PRIMARY WORKS (INDIVIDUAL AUTHORS)

Ah Cheng

Qi wang (*King of Chess*). Beijing: Zuojia, 1998. [includes *Qi wang, Shu wang, Haizi wang*]

* * *

Three Kings. Tr. Bonnie McDougall. New York: Vintage/Ebury, 1990.

Ah Lai (Alai)

Ah Ba Ah Lai (Ah Ba and Ah Lai). Beijing: Zhongguo gongren, 2004.
Chen'ai luoding (*Red Poppies*). Beijing: Renmin wenxue, 1998.
Dadi de jieti (The Earth's Staircase). Kunming: Yunnan renmin, 2000.
Jiunian de xueji (Bloodstains from the Past). Beijing: Zuojia, 1989.
Kong shan (The Empty Mountain). Beijing: Renmin wenxue, 2005.
Kong shan 2 (The Empty Mountain, Book II). Beijing: Renmin wenxue, 2007.

* * *

Red Poppies. Trs. Howard Goldblatt and Sylvia Li-chun Lin. New York: Houghton Mifflin, 2002.
"Agu Dunba." Trs. Karen Gernant and Chen Zeping. *Conjunctions* 44 (2005): 69–80.
"The Locust Blossoms." Trs. Karen Gernant and Chen Zeping. *Conjunctions* 44 (2005): 81–89.
"The Wind over the Grasslands." In Herbert Batt, ed./tr., *Tales of Tibet: Sky Burials, Prayer Wheels, and Wind Horses*. Lanham, MD: Rowman & Littlefield, 2001, 189–204.

Ai Qing

Dayanhe—Wode baomu (Dayan River—My Wet-nurse). Shanghai: Qunzhong zazhi gongsi, 1936.
Beifang (North). Shanghai: Wensheng, 1942.
Huanhu ji (Cheering). Beijing: Xinhua shudian, 1950.
Xian gei xiangcun de shi (Ode to the Countryside). Beijing: Beimen, 1945.
Yuan chuntian zao dian lai (Wishing for an Early Spring). Guilin: Shiyi, 1944.

* * *

The Black Eel. Trs. Yang Xianyi and Robert Friend. Beijing: Panda Books, 1982.
Selected Poems by Ai Qing. Tr. Eugene Chen Ouyang. Bloomington: Indiana University Press, 1982.
Poems in Cyril Birch and Donald Keene, eds., *Anthology of Chinese Literature: From the Fourteenth Century to the Present Day.* New York: Grove Press, 1987, 362–68.

Ai Wu

Chuntian (Spring). Shanghai: Liangyou tushu, 1937.
Fengrao de yuanye (Fertile Plains). Chongqing: Ziqiang, 1946.
Nan xing ji (Journey to the South). Shanghai: Wenhua shenghuo, 1935.
Nan xing ji xin pian (New Chapters of Journey to the South). Kunming: Yunnan renmin, 1983.
Qiushou (Autumn Harvest). Shanghai: Dushu, 1942.
Ye jing (Night Scenes). Shanghai: Wenhua shenghuo, 1936.

* * *

Banana Vale. Beijing: Panda Books, 1994.
Homeward Journey and Other Stories. Beijing: Foreign Languages Press, 1957.
A New Home and Other Stories. Tr. Yeh Yung. Beijing: Foreign Languages Press, 1959.
Selected Stories by Ai Wu [English-Chinese edition]. Beijing: Chinese Literature Press, 1999.
Steeled and Tempered. Beijing: Foreign Languages Press, 1961.
"Return by Night." Tr. Raymond Hsu. *Renditions* 7 (1977): 39–44.

An Qi

Benpao de zhalan (Running Railings). Beijing: Zuojia, 1997.
Ge: Shui shang hong yue (Songs: Red Moon on Water). Hong Kong: Xuntong, 1993.

Xiang Dulasi yiyang shenghuo (Living in the Manner of Duras). Beijing: Zuojia, 2004.

Ba Jin

Hanye (Cold Night). Shanghai: Chengguang, 1949.
Jia (Family). Shanghai: Kaiming, 1933.
Miewang (Destruction). Shanghai: Kaiming, 1929.
Qi yuan (Garden of Repose). Shanghai: Wenhua shenghuo, 1944.
Suixiang lu (Record of Random Thoughts). Hong Kong: Sanlian, 1979.

* * *

Autumn in Spring and Other Stories. Beijing: Panda, 1981.
Family. Tr. Sidney Shapiro. Boston: Cheng & Tsui Company, 1990.
Garden of Repose [bilingual edition]. Tr. Jock Hoe. Boston: Cheng & Tsui Company, 2001.
Random Thoughts. Tr. G. Barme. Hong Kong: Joint, 1984.
Selected Works of Ba Jin. Tr. Jock Hoe. 2 vols. Beijing: Foreign Languages Press, 1988. [Includes *Family, Autumn, Trilogy; Garden of Repose*; and *Cold Night*]
Ward Four. Trs. Haili Kong and Howard Goldblatt. Boston: Cheng & Tsui Company, 1999.

Bai Xianyong

Jimo de shiqisui (Lonely at Seventeen). Taipei: Yuanjing, 1976.
Niezi (Crystal Boys). Taipei: Yuanjing, 1984.
Taipei ren (Taipei Characters). Taipei: Chenzhong, 1971.
Youyuan jingmeng (Wandering in the Garden and Waking from a Dream). Taipei: Yuanjing, 1982.
Zhexian ji (The Story of the Immortals). Taipei: Wenxing, 1967.

* * *

Crystal Boys. San Francisco: Gay Sunshine Press, 1989.
Wandering in the Garden and Waking from a Dream: Taipei Characters. Bloomington: Indiana University Press, 1982.

Bei Cun

Fashao (Running a Fever). Beijing: Shiyue wenyi, 2004.
Fennu (Furor). Beijing: Tuanjie, 2004.
Gonglu shang de linghun (Soul on the Highway). Beijing: Xinhua, 2005.
Shixi de he (The River of Baptism). Shanghai: Shanghai wenyi, 1993.

* * *

"The Big Drugstore." Tr. Caroline Mason. In Jing Wang, ed., *China's Avant-garde Fiction*. Durham, NC: Duke University Press, 1998, 217–34.

Bei Dao

Bodong (Waves). Guangzhou: Huacheng, 1986.
Guilai de moshengren (The Stranger Who Has Returned). Guangzhou: Huacheng, 1986.
Kai suo (*Unlock*). Taipei: Jiuge, 1999.
Lan fangzi (*Blue House*). Taipei: Jiuge, 1999.
Lingdu yishang de fengjing xian: Bei Dao shixuan 1993–1996 (Landscape Over Zero: Poems by Bei Dao 1993–1996). Taipei: Jiuge, 1996.
Wuye geshou: Bei Dao shixuan 1972–1994 (Midnight Singer: Selected Poems by Bei Dao 1972–1994). Taipei: Jiuge, 1994.

* * *

At the Sky's Edge: Poems 1991–1996 [bilingual edition]. Tr. David Hinton. New York: New Directions, 2001.
The August Sleepwalker. New York: New Directions, 2001.
Blue House: A Collections of Essay. Trs. Ted Huters and Fengying Ming. New York: Zephyr Press, 2000.
The Chinese Poetry of Bei Dao, 1978–2000: Resistance and Exile. Tr. Dian Li. Lewiston, NY: Edwin Mellen Press, 2006.
Forms of Distance. Tr. David Hinton. New York: New Directions, 1994.
Landscape Over Zero. Trs. David Hinton and Chen Yanbing. New York: New Directions, 1996.
Midnight's Gate: Essays. Trs. Matthew Fryslie and Christopher Mattison. New York: New Directions, 2005.
Old Snow. Trs. Bonnie S. McDougall and Chen Maiping. New York: New Directions, 1991.
Unlock. Trs. Eliot Weinberger and Iona Man Cheong. New York: New Directions, 2000.

Bi Feiyu

Pingyuan (The Plain). Jiangsu wenyi, 2005.
Qingyi (The Opera Singer). Wuhan: Changjiang wenyi, 2001.
Tuina (Massage). Beijing: Renmin wenxue, 2008.
Yumi (Yumi). Nanjing: Jiangsu wenyi, 2003.

Bi Shumin

Hong chufang (A Red Prescription). Beijing: Shiyue wenyi, 1997.
Nü xinli shi (A Female Psychologist). Chongqing: Chongqing chubanshe, 2007.

Xizang de gushi (Stories from Tibet). Beijing: Zhongguo sanxia, 2006.
Yuyue siwang (*An Appointment with Death*). Kunming: Yunnan renmin, 1996.
Zhengjiu rufang (Saving the Breasts). Beijing: Remin wenxue, 2003.

* * *

"An Appointment with Death." Trs. Qin Yaqing and Jin Li. *Chinese Literature* (Spring 1997).
"One Centimetre." In Carolyn Choa and David Su Li-qun, eds., *The Vintage Book of Contemporary Chinese Fiction*. New York: Vintage Books, 2001, 278–94.
"The Hitchhiker." *Chinese Literature* (Spring 1997).

Bian Zhilin

Bian Zhilin daibiao zuo (Selected Works by Bian Zhilin). Beijing: Huaxia, 1998.
Cangsang ji: Zalei sanwen 1936–1946 (Vicissitudes: Essays 1936–1946). Nanjing: Jiangsu renmin, 1982.
Hanyuan ji (Hanyuan Collection), with He Qifang and Li Guangtian. Shanghai: Shangwu, 1934.
Yumu ji (Fish-Eye Collection). Shanghai: Wenhua shenghuo, 1935.

* * *

The Carving of Insects. Ed. Mary M. Y. Fung; Trs. Mary M. Y. Fung and David Lunde. Hong Kong: Renditions Books, 2006.

Bing Xin

Bing Xin he ertong wenxue (Bin Xin and Children's Literature). Ed. Zhuo Ru. Shanghai: Shaonian ertong, 1990.
Bing Xin quanji (Complete Works by Bin Xing). Ed. Zhuo Ru. 8 vols. Fuzhou: Haixia wenyi, 1994.
Ji xiao duzhe (To Young Readers). Beijing: Beixin, 1926.

* * *

The Photograph. Beijing: Chinese Literature Press, 1992.
Selected Stories and Prose by Bing Xin [English-Chinese edition]. Beijing: Chinese Literature Press, 1999.
Spring Waters. Beijing: Grace Boynton, 1929.
Essays in Martin Woesler, ed., *20th Century Chinese Essays in Translation*. Bochum: Bochum University Press, 2000, 91–100. [selections from "Letters to Children"]
Poems in Kai-yu Hsu, ed., *Twentieth Century Chinese Poetry*. Garden City, NY: Doubleday, 1963, 16–23; Kenneth Rexroth and Ling Chung, eds./trs., *The Orchid Boat: Women Poets of China*. New York, McGraw-Hill, 1972.

Stories in Vivian Ling Hsu, ed., *Born of the Same Roots: Stories of Modern Chinese Women*. Bloomington: Indiana University Press, 1992, 44–61.

Can Xue

An ye (Dark Nights). Beijing: Huawen, 2006.
Bianjiang (The Frontier). Shanghai: Shanghai wenyi, 2008.
Canglao de fuyun (*Old Floating Clouds*). Beijing: Shidai wenyi, 2001.
Huangni jie (*Yellow Mud Street*). Taipei: Yuanshen, 1987.
Tiantang li de duihua (*Dialogue in Paradise*). Beijing: Zuojia, 1988.
Tuwei biaoyan (Breakout Performance). Shagnhai: Shanghai wenyi, 1990.
Wuxiang jie (Five Spices Street). Fuzhou: Haixia wenyi, 2002.
Zuihou de qingren (The Last Lover). Guangzhou: Huacheng, 2005.

* * *

Dialogues in Paradise. Trs. Ronald R. Janssen and Jian Zhang. Evanston, IL: Northwestern University Press, 1989.
The Embroidered Shoes: Stories. New York: Henry Holt and Company, 1997.
Old Floating Clouds: Two Novellas. Trs. Ronald R. Janssen and Jian Zhang. Evanston, IL: Northwestern University Press, 1991.
"The Land of Peach Blossoms." Trs. Karen Gernant and Chen Zeping. In Frank Stewart and Herbert J. Batt, eds., *The Mystified Boat and Other New Stories from China*. Special issue of *Manoa: A Pacific Journal of International Writing* 15, 2 (Winter 2003). Honolulu: University of Hawaii Press, 2004, 125–33.

Cao Juren

Jiudian (The Wine Shop). Hong Kong: Chuangkeng, 1954.
Qinhuai jiuwen lu (Old Stories of the Jinhuai River). Hong Kong: Sanyu, 1971–1972.
Wo yu wo de shijie (Me and My World). Hong Kong: Sanyu, 1972.

Cao Naiqian

Dao heiye xiang ni mei banfa: Wenjiayao fengjing (*When I Think of You Late at Night, There's Nothing I Can Do: Scenery of Wenjiayao*). Taipei: Tianxia wenhua, 2005.
Fo de gudu (Buddha's Solitude). Taiyuan: Beiyue wenyi, 1996.
Zuihou de cunzhuang (The Last Village). Taiyuan: Shanxi renmin, 2004.

* * *

"When I Think of You Late at Night, There's Nothing I Can Do." Tr. Howard Goldblatt. In Goldblatt, ed., *Chairman Mao Would Not Be Amused: Fiction from Today's China*. New York: Grove Press, 1995, 197–205.

Cao Wenxuan

Cao fangzi (A Thatched House). Nanjing: Jiangxu shaonian ertong, 1997.
Hong wa (Red Tiles). Beijing: Shiyue wenyi, 1998.
Qingtong kuihua (Bronze Sunflower). Nanjing: Jiangsu shaonian ertong, 2005.
Shanyang bu chi tiantang cao (Goats Do Not Eat the Grass in Heaven). Nanjing: Jiangsu shaonian ertong, 1991.
Tian piao (Downpour). Beijing: Changjiang wenyi, 2005.
Xi mi (Fine Rice). Shanghai: Shanghai wenyi, 2003.
Youyu de tianyuan (Melancholy Rusticity). Beijing: Shiyue wenyi, 1989.

Cao Yu

Beijing ren (*Peking Man*). Shanghai: Wenhua shenghuo, 1941.
Leiyu (*Thunderstorm*). Shanghai: Wenhua shenghuo, 1933.
Richu (*Sunrise*). Shanghai: Wenhua shenghuo, 1936.

* * *

Bright Skies. Tr. Chang Pei-chi. Beijing: Foreign Languages Press, 1960.
The Consort of Peace. Tr. Monica Lai. Hong Kong: Kelly Walsh, 1980.
Peking Man. Trs. Leslie Nai-kwai Lo et al. New York: Columbia University Press, 1986.
Sunrise: A Play in Four Acts. Tr. A. C. Barnes. Beijing: Foreign Languages Press, 1978.
Thunderstorm. Trs. Wang Tso-liang and A. C. Barnes. Beijing: Foreign Languages Press, 1958.
The Wilderness. Tr. Christopher C. Rand. Hong Kong: Hong Kong University Press, 1980.

Cao Zhilian

Mou dai fengliu (The Romance of a Certain Era). Taipei: Kaiyuan shuyin, 2004.
Tang chu de huaban (Pedals of the Early Tang). Taipei: Shangwu, 2006.
Yinxiang shu (A Book of Impressions). Taipei: Kaiyuan shuyin, 2004.

Chen Baichen

Jiehu jingxing qu (The March to Marriage: A Play in Four Acts). Beijing: Zhongguo xiju, 1963.
Luan shi nan nü (*Men and Women in Wild Times*: A Play in Three Acts). Shanghai: Shanghai zazhi gongsi, 1939.
Mo ku (Den of Monsters: A Play in Four Acts). Shanghai: Shenghuo shudian, 1928.

* * *

"Men and Women in Wild Times." In Edward Gunn, ed., *Twentieth-Century Chinese Drama: An Anthology.* Bloomington: Indiana University Press, 1983, 126–73.

Chen Cun

Chen Cun wenji (Collection of Essays by Chen Cun). Nanjing: Jiangsu wenyi, 1996.
Xianhua he (Fresh Flowers). Shanghai: Shanghai wenyi, 1997.

* * *

"Footsteps on the Roof." Tr. Hu Ying. In Howard Goldblatt, ed., *Chairman Mao Would Not Be Amused: Fiction from Today's China.* New York: Grove Press, 1995, 244–261.

Chen Dongdong

Ci de bianzou (Variations of Words). Shanghai: Dongfang, 1997.
Hai shen de yi ye (One Night in the Life of the Ocean God). Beijing: Gaige, 1997.
Mingjing de bufen (The Clear Part). Changsha: Hunan wenyi, 1997.

* * *

"From Lexicon, Nouns." Tr. Yanbing Chen. In Henry Y. H. Zhao, Yanbing Chen, and John Rosenwald, eds., *Fissures: Chinese Writing Today.* Brookline, MA: Zephyr Press, 2000, 142–43.
"Snow-Covered Sun" and "Finally." In Wang Ping, ed., *New Generation: Poems from China Today.* New York: Hanging Loose Press, 1999, 43–45.

Chen Jiangong

Beijing ziwei (Beijing Flavor). Beijing: Zhongguo chengshi, 1995.
Danfeng yan (*Phoenix Eyes*). Taipei: Linbai, 1986.
Miluan de xingkong (A Star-studded Dazzling Sky). Tianjin: Baihua wenyi, 1982.
Quanmao (*Curlylocks*). Bejing: Yanshan, 1998.

* * *

"Curlylocks." *Chinese Literature* (Summer 1988): 47–128.
"The Fluttering Flowered Scarf." Tr. Li Meiyu. *Chinese Literature* (Summer 1988): 186–213.

"Looking for Fun." In Jeanne Tai, ed./tr., *Spring Bamboo: A Collection of Contemporary Chinese Short Stories*. New York: Random House, 1989, 57–118.
"Number Nine Winch Handle Alley." Tr. Michael Day. In Michael S. Duke, ed., *Worlds of Modern Chinese Fiction*. Armonk, NY: M.E. Sharpe, 1991, 268–94.
"Phoenix Eyes." Tr. Ellen Hertz. In *Prize-Winning Stories from China, 1980–1981*. Beijing: Foreign Languages Press, 1985, 163–85.

Chen Ran

Ling yizhi erduo de qiaoji sheng (The Knocking Sounds of the Other Ear). Beijing: Zuojia, 2001.
Shengsheng duanduan (Broken Sounds). Beijing: Zuojia, 2000.
Siren shenghuo (*A Private Life*). Beijing: Zuojia, 1996.
Yu wangshi ganbei (Drink to the Past). Wuhan: Hubei cishu, 1993.
Zuichun li de yangguang (*Sunlight between the Lips*). Wuhan: Changjiang wenyi, 2001.

* * *

A Private Life. Tr. John Howard-Gibbon. New York: Columbia University Press, 2004.
"Sunshine Between the Lips." Tr. Shelley Wing Chan. In Howard Goldblatt, ed., *Chairman Mao Would Not Be Amused: Fiction from Today's China*. New York: Grove Press, 1995, 112–29.

Chen Ruoxi

Er Hu (Two Men Named Hu). Gaoxiong: Dunli, 1986.
Hui xin lian (The Lotus of a Compassionate Heart). Taipei: Jiuge, 2001.
Qingshui shen huijia (Aunt Qingshui Comes Home). Taipei: Luotuo, 1999.
Tuwei (Breakout). Taipei: Lianhe baoshe, 1983.
Yin xianzhang (The Execution of Mayor Yin). Taipei: Yuanjing, 1976.
Zhi hun (Marriage on Paper). Taipei: Zili wanbao, 1986.

* * *

The Execution of Mayor Yin, and Other Stories from the Great Proletarian Cultural Revolution. Trs. Nancy Ing and Howard Goldblatt. Bloomington: Indiana University Press, 1978.
Old Man and Other Stories. Hong Kong: Chinese University of Hong Kong, 1986.
The Short Stories of Chen Ruoxi: A Writer at the Crossroads. Tr. Hsin-sheng C. Kao. Lewiston, NY: Edwin Mellen Press, 1992.

Spirit Calling: Five Stories of Taiwan. Tr. Lucy H. M. Chen. Taipei: Heritage Press, 1962.

Chen Yingzhen

Lingdang hua (Bell Flowers). Taipei: Renjian, 1988.
Wo de didi Kangxiong (My Younger Brother Kangxiong). Taipei: Renjian, 1988.
Yexing huoche (Freight Cars Traveling at Night). Taipei: Yuanjing, 1984.

* * *

Exile at Home: Short Stories by Ch'en Ying-chen. Tr. Lucien Miller. Ann Arbor: Center for Chinese Studies, University of Michigan, 1986.

Chen Zhongshi

Bai lu yuan (White Deer Plain). Beijing: Renmin wenxue, 1993.

* * *

"Trust." In Helen Siu and Zelda Stern, eds., *Mao's Harvest: Voices from China's New Generation.* New York: Oxford University Press, 1983, 146–56.

Cheng Fangwu

Shou sui (New Year's Eve). Shanghai: Chuangzao she, 1929.
Liulang (Wandering: Short Stories, Poems, and Essays). Shanghai: Chuangzao she, 1927.
Cheng Fangwu shi xuan (Selected Poems by Cheng Fangwu). Beijing: Zhonggong zhongyang dangxiao, 1994.

* * *

"From a Literary Revolution to a Revolutionary Literature." Tr. Michael Gotz. In *Bulletin of Concerned Asian Scholars* (Jan.–Mar. 1976): 35–38; also in Kirk A. Denton, ed., *Modern Chinese Literary Thought.* Stanford: Stanford University Press, 1996, 269–75.
"The Mission of the New Literature." Tr. Nicholas A. Kaldis. In Kirk A. Denton, ed., *Modern Chinese Literary Thought.* Stanford: Stanford University Press, 1996, 247–54.

Cheng Naishan

Jinrongjia (The Banker). Shanghai: Shanghai wenyi, 1993.
Lan wu (The Blue House). Tianjin: Baihua wenyi, 1984.
Shanghai tange (Shanghai Tango). Shanghai: Xuelin, 2002.

Shanshui you xiangfeng (When Mountain and River Meet). Shanghai: Shanghai wenyi, 1999.

* * *   .

The Banker. Tr. Brittin Dean. San Francisco: China Books, 1993.
The Blue House. Beijing: Panda Books, 1989.
The Piano Tuner. Tr. Brittin Dean. San Francisco: China Books, 1989.

Chi Li

Bu tan aiqing (*Apart from Love*). Tianjin: Baihua, 1996.
Fannao rensheng (Worrisome Life). Beijing: Zuojia, 1989.
Kouhong (Lipstick). Nanjing: Jiangsu wenyi, 2000.
Wuya zhi ge: Chi Li daibiao zuo (Song of the Crow: Representative Works by Chi Li). Shenyang: Chunfeng wenyi, 2004.

* * *

"Trials and Tribulations." Tr. Stephen Fleming. *Chinese Literature* (Winter 1988): 112–60.
Apart from Love. Beijing: Panda Books, 1994.

Chi Zijian

Baixue de muyuan (The Cemetery in Snow). Kunming: Yunnan renmin, 1995.
Beiji cun tonghua (Fairy Tales of a Northern Village). Beijing: Zuojia, 1989.
Chen zhong xiangche huanghun (Morning Bells Ring through Dusk). Nanjing: Jiangsu wenyi, 1997.
E'erguna He you an (On the Right Bank of the Argun River). Beiijing: Shiyue wenxie, 2005.
Qingshui xichen (Clean Water Washing Off Dust). Beijing: Zhongguo wenlian, 2001.
Wei Manzhouguo (The Puppet State of Manchuria). Beijing: Renmin wenxue, 2004.

* * *

Figments of the Supernatural. Tr. Simon Patton. Sydney: James Joyce Press, 2004.
A Flock in the Wilderness: Beijing: Foreign Languages Press, 2005.

Dai Wangshu

Wode jiyi (My Memories). Shanghai: Shuimo shudian, 1929.
Wangshu cao (Writings of Wangshu). Shanghai: Xiandai, 1933.
Dai Wangshu shiji (Poetry of Dai Wangshu). Chengdu: Sichuan renmin, 1981.

* * *

Dai Wangshu: The Life and Poetry of a Chinese Modernist. Gregory Lee. Hong Kong: The Chinese University Press, 1989. [a study with extensive translations]

"Dai Wangshu's Poetic Theory." Tr. Kirk A. Denton. In Denton, ed., *Modern Chinese Literary Thought.* Stanford: Stanford University Press, 1996, 316–17.

Poems in Kai-yu Hsu, ed., *Twentieth Century Chinese Poetry: An Anthology.* Garden City, NY: Doubleday, 1963, 169–75.

Deng Youmei

Jing cheng nei wai (Inside and Outside the Capital). Beijing: Renmin wenxue, 1985.

Nawu (Nawu). Hong Kong: Mingchuang e, 1988.

Shuang mao tu (Picture of Two Cats). Beijing: Zuojia, 1994.

Xunzhao Hua'r Han (Looking for Painter Han). Tianjin: Baihua wenyi, 1984.

Yanhu (*Snuff Bottles*). Chengdu: Sichuan wenyi, 1985.

* * *

Snuff-Bottles and Other Stories. Tr. Gladys Yang. Beijing: Chinese Literature, 1986.

"Han the Forger." In Carolyn Choa and David Su Li-qun, eds., *The Vintage Book of Contemporary Chinese Fiction.* New York: Vintage Books, 2001, 191–204.

Ding Ling

Ding Ling quan ji (Complete Works by Ding Ling). Shijiazhuang: Hebei renmin, 2000.

Muqin (Mother). Shanghai: Liangyou, 1933.

Taiyang zhao zai Sanggan He shang (*The Sun Shines Over the Sanggan River*). Beijing: Renmin wenxue, 1951.

Wo zai Xia cun de shihou (*When I Was in the Xia Village*). Beijing: Sanlian, 1951.

Yige nüren (The Story of a Woman). Shanghai: Zhonghua shuju, 1930.

Zai hei'an zhong (In the Darkness). Shanghai: Kaiming, 1928. [includes "Meng Ke" (Meng Ke), "Shafei nüshi de riji" (*Miss Sophie's Diary*), "Shujia zhong" (Summer Vacation), and "Ah Mao guniang" (A Girl Called Ah Mao)]

Zisha riji (A Diary of Suicide). Shanghai: Guanghua, 1929.

* * *

I Myself Am a Woman: Selected Writings of Ding Ling. Ed. Tani E. Barlow with Gary J. Bjorge. Boston: Beacon Press, 1989.

Miss Sophie's Diary and Other Stories. Tr. W. J. F. Jenner. Beijing: Chinese Literature Press, 1985.

The Sun Shines Over the Sanggan River. Beijing: Foreign Languages Press, 1984.
"In the Hospital." Tr. Susan Vacca. *Renditions* 8 (1977): 123–35.
"When I Was in Xia Village." Tr. Gary J. Bjorge. In Joseph S. M. Lau and Howart Goldblatt, eds., *The Columbia Anthology of Modern Chinese Literature.* New York: Columbia University Press, 1995, 143–58.

Ding Xilin

Ding Xilin juzuo quan ji (Plays by Ding Xilin). 2 vols. Beijing: Zhongguo xiju, 1985.

* * *

"Dear Husband." Trs. Bonnie S. McDougall and Flora Lam. *Renditions* 69 (2008): 62–75.
"Flush with Wine." Trs. John B. Weinstein and Carsey Yee. MCLC Resource Center Publication (March 2004).
"Oppression." Tr. Joseph S. M. Lau. In Edward Gunn, ed., *Twentieth-Century Chinese Drama: An Anthology.* Bloomington: Indiana University Press, 1983, 41–51.

Dong Qizhang

Anzhuo zhenni (Androgyny). Taipei: Lianhe wenxue, 1996.
Di yi qian ling er ye: Shuo gongshi de gushi. (The 1002nd Night: The Story of Story-telling). Hong Kong: Tupo, 2005.
Ditu ji (The Atlas). Taipei: Lianhe wenxue, 1996.
Mingzi de meigui (The Roses of Names). Hong Kong: Pupu gongzuo fang, 1997.
Shijian zhi fan shi: Yaci zhi guang (A Complex History of Time: Yaci's Light). Taipei: Maitian, 2007.
Shuang shen (A Hermaphrodite). Taipei: Lianjing, 1997.
Shuo shu ren (The Story-teller). Hong Kong: Xiang jiang, 1997.
Tian dong kai wu: Xuxu ru zhen (The Beginning of Things: The True Life of Xuxu). Taipei: Maitian, 2005.
Tong dai ren (The Same Generation). Hong Kong: Sanren, 1998.
Yi yu jianshi (A Brief History of Lepisma saccharina). Taipei: Lianhe wenxue, 2002.

* * *

"The Atlas: Archaeology of an Imaginary City." Tr. Dung Kai Cheung. In Martha P. Y. Cheung, ed., *Hong Kong Collage: Contemporary Stories and Writing.* Hong Kong: Oxford University Press, 1998, 40–54.

"The Centaur of the East." Tr. Dung Kai Cheung. In Martha P. Y. Cheung, ed., *Hong Kong*
Collage: Contemporary Stories and Writing. Hong Kong: Oxford University Press, 1998, 202–4.
"A Government House with a View." Tr. Dung Kai Cheung. In Martha P. Y. Cheung, ed., *Hong Kong Collage: Contemporary Stories and Writing.* Hong Kong: Oxford University Press, 1998, 83–84.

Duanmu Hongliang

Da shidai: Duanmu Hongliang sishi niandai zuopin xuan (The Great Era: Works Written in the 1940s by Duanmu Hongliang). Taipei: Lixu wenhua, 1996.
Kerqinqi caoyuan (The Khorchin Grassland). Beijing: Renmin wenxue, 1997. [rpt. of the 1939 edition]
Duanmu Hongliang xiaoshuo xuan (Stories by Duanmu Hongliang). Beijing: Zuojia, 1993

* * *

Red Night. Tr. Howard Goldblatt. Beijing: Chinese Literature Press, 1988.
Selected Stories by Duanmu Hongliang. Beijing: Chinese Literature Press, 1999.
The Sorrows of Egret Lake—Selected Stories of Duanmu Hongliang [Chinese-English edition]. Trs. Howard Goldblatt and Haili Kong. Hong Kong: Chinese University Press, 2007.

Duo Duo

Amusitedan de heliu (Rivers in Amsterdam). Taiyuan: Beiyue wenyi, 2000.
Dache (Hitchhike). Tianjin: Baihua wenyi, 2004.
Duoduo shi xuan (Selected Poems by Duoduo). Guangzhou: Huacheng, 2005.

* * *

The Boy Who Catches Wasps—Translations of the Recent Poetry of Duoduo. Tr. Gregory Lee. Brookline, MA: Zephyr Press, 2002.
Crossing the Sea (Guo hai). Ed./tr. Lee Robinson and Yu Li Ming. Concord, ON: Anansi, 1998.
Looking Out from Death: From the Cultural Revolution to Tiananmen Square. Trs. Gregory Lee and John Cayley. London: Bloomsbury Pub. Ltd., 1989.
Statements: The New Chinese Poetry of Duo Duo. Trs. Gregory Lee and John Cayley. London: Wellsweep, 1989.

Eryue He

Kangxi Da di (Great Emperor Kangxi). Hong Kong: Huangguan, 1995.
Yongzheng Huangdi (Emperor Yongzheng). Wuhan: Changjiang wenyi, 1991.
Qianlong Huangdi (Emperor Qianlong). Taipei: Babilun, 1994.

* * *

Emperor Yongzheng [excerpts]. Tr. Xiong Zhenru. *Chinese Literature* (Autumn 1998).

Fan Wen

Beimin dadi (Land of Compassion). Beijing: Renmin wenxue, 2006.
Cangmang gu dao: hui bu qu de lishi bei ying (Endless Ancient Path: Inerasable Shadow of History). Kunming: Yunnan renmin, 2000.
Qing guan Hairui (Hairui: An Honest Official). Fuzhou: Haixia wenyi, 1999.
Shui ru dadi (Land of Harmony). Beijing: Renmin wenxue, 2004.
Zangdong tanxian shouji (Notes of an Expedition in Eastern Tibet). Tianjin: Xinlei, 2001.

Fan Xiaoqing

Bai ri yangguang (One Hundred Days of Sunlight). Nanjing: Jiangsu wenyi, 1997.
Chengshi biaoqing (The Facial Expressions of a City). Beijing: Zuojia, 2004.
Fei jia you nü (The Daughter of the Feis). Beijing: Renmin wenxue, 1995.
Kudang xiang fengliu ji (The Romantic Life of the Crotch Alley). Beijing: Zuojia, 1987.
Lao an (Old Shores). Beijing: Shiyue wenyi, 1992.
Nü tongzhi (A Female Comrade). Shenyang: Chunfeng wenyi, 2005.

* * *

"Return to Secular Life." In *Six Contemporary Chinese Women Writers, IV*. Beijing: Panda Books, 1995, 146–83.

Fang Fang

Luori (Sunset). Beijing: Qunzhong, 2004.
Xingyun liushui (Moving Clouds and Flowing Water). Wuhan: Changjiang wenyi, 1996.

Wuni hu nianpu (History of the Black Muddy River). Beijing: Renmin wenxue, 2000.

* * *

Three Novellas by Fang Fang: Contemporary Chinese Women Writers V. Beijing: Panda Books, 1996.

"Hints." Tr. Ling Yuan. *Chinese Literature* (Summer 1997).

Fei Ma

Dudu yousheng de mati (Sounds of the Horse Hoofs). Taipei: Li shikan she, 1986.

Fei ba, jingling (Fly, My Eidolon). Taizhong: Chenxing, 1992.

Fei Ma de shi (Poetry by Fei Ma). Guangzhou: Huangcheng, 2000.

Fei Ma shi xuan (Selected Poems by Fei Ma). Taipei: Shangwu, 1983.

Lu (Road). Taipei: Erya chubanshe, 1986.

* * *

Autumn Window. Chicago: Arbor Hill Press, 1995.

In the Wind City [Chinese-English edition]. Taipei: Li shikanshe, 1975.

Selected Short Poems by Fei Ma [Chinese-English edition]. Hong Kong: Yinhe, 2003.

Poems in Dominic Cheung, ed./tr., *The Isle Full of Noises: Modern Chinese Poetry from Taiwan.* New York: Columbia University Press, 1987, 117–20.

Fei Ming

Moxuyou Xiansheng zhuan (Biography of Mr. Nothing). Shanghai: Kaiming, 1932.

Qiao (Bridge). Shanghai: Kaiming, 1932.

Tao yuan (Peach Orchard). Shanghai: Kaiming, 1928.

Zao (Dates). Shanghai: Kaiming, 1931.

Zhulin de gushi (Bamboo Grove Stories). Beijing: Beixin, 1927.

* * *

Bridge [excerpt]. Tr. Christopher Smith. *Chinese Literature* (Spring 1990): 119–22.

"Caltrop Pond." Tr. Christopher Smith. *Chinese Literature* (Spring 1990): 113–18.

"Little Sister." In Chi-chen Wang, ed., *Contemporary Chinese Stories.* New York: Columbia University Press, 1944.

"On Modern Poetry." In Harold Acton and Chen Shih-hsiang, eds./trs., *Modern Chinese Poetry*. London: Duckworth, 1936.
"The Story of the Bamboo Grove." Tr. Li Guoqing. *Chinese Literature* (Spring 1990): 108–12.
Poems in Michelle Yeh, ed./tr., *Anthology of Modern Chinese Poetry*. New Haven: Yale University Press, 1992, 22–24.

Feng Jicai

Gao nüren he tade ai zhangfu (The Tall Woman and Her Short Husband). Shanghai: Shanghai wenyi, 1984.
Pu hua de qilu (A Branch Road Covered with Flowers). Beijing: Renmin wenxue, 1979.
Sancun jin lian (The Three-Inch Golden Lotus). Hong Kong: Xiangjiang, 1987.
Shen bian (The Miraculous Pigtail). Beijing: Zhongguo minjian wenyi, 1988.
Yibaige ren de shinian (Ten Years of Madness: Oral Histories of China's Cultural Revolution). Hong Kong: Xiangjiang, 1987.

* * *

Chrysanthemums and Other Stories by Feng Jicai. San Diego: Harcourt, Brace, Javanovich, 1985.
The Miraculous Pigtail. Beijing: Chinese Literature Press, 1987.
Ten Years of Madness: Oral Histories of China's Cultural Revolution. San Francisco: China Books, 1996.
The Three-Inch Golden Lotus. Tr. David Wakefield. Honolulu: University of Hawaii Press, 1992.

Feng Naichao

Hong sha deng (The Lamp with a Red Silk Shade). Shanghai: Chuangzao she, 1928.
Kuilei meiren (The Puppet Beauty). Shanghai: Changfeng shudian, 1929.
Fuxu (Compensation). Shanghai: Hubing shuju, 1929.
Mao Zengdong song (In Praise of Mao Zedong). Hong Kong: Haiyang shuwu, 1948.

Feng Xuefeng (Feng Hsue-feng)

Feng Xuefeng de shi (Poems by Feng Xuefeng). Beijing: Renmin wenxue, 1979.
Xuefeng yuyan (Parables by Xuefeng). Beijing: Renmin wenxue, 1953.

* * *

Poems and stories in Hualing Nieh, ed., *Literature of the Hundred Flowers. Volume II: Poetry and Fiction*. New York: Columbia University Press, 1981, 306–9.

Fables. San Francisco: China Books and Periodicals, 1983.

Feng Yuanjun

Chun hen (Traces of Spring). Shanghai: Beixin shuju, 1926.
Jie hui (After the Disaster). Shanghai: Beixin shuju, 1929.
Juan shi (Xanthiums). Shanghai: Beixin shuju, 1928.

* * *

"The Journey." In J. Anderson and T. Mumford, eds./trs., *Chinese Women Writers: A Collection of Short Stories by Chinese Women Writers of the 1920s and 1930s*. Beijing: Foreign Languages Press, 1985, 168–78.

"Separation." Tr. Janet Ng. In A. Dooling and K. Torgeson, eds., *Writing Women in Modern China: An Anthology of Women's Literature from the Early Twentieth Century*. New York: Columbia University Press, 1998, 105–113.

Feng Zhi (Feng Chi)

Feng Zhi shi xuan (Selected Poems by Feng Zhi). Chengdu: Sichuan renmin, 1980.
Shan shui (Mountains and Rivers). Chongqing: Guomin tushu, 1943.
Shisi hang ji (The Sonnets). Guilin: Mingrishe, 1942.
Zuori zhi ge (Songs of Yesterday). Shanghai: Beixin, 1927.

* * *

Poems in Cyril Birch and Donald Keene, eds., *Anthology of Chinese Literature: From the Fourteenth Century to the Present Day*. New York: Grove Press, 1987, 369–73; Kai-yu Hsu, ed., *Twentieth Century Chinese Poetry: An Anthology*. Garden City, NY: Doubleday, 1963, 131–49.

Feng Zikai

Chexiang shehui (A Community of Train Riders). Shanghai: Liangyou, 1935.
Jiaoshi riji (Diary of a Teacher). Chongqing: Wanguang, 1946.
Yuanyuantang suibi (Yuanyuantang Notes). Shanghai: Kaiming, 1939.

* * *

Essays in David Pollard, ed., *The Chinese Essay*. New York: Columbia University Press, 2000, 189–205.

Gao Jianqun

Chou rong qishi (A Melancholy Rider). Beijing: Zhongguo wenlian, 1998.
Hu ma bei feng—damo zhuan (Nomads' Horses and the Northern Wind—History of the Great Desert). Beijing: Dongfang, 2003.
Liuliu Zhen (The Liuliu Township). Xi'an: Shaanxi renmin, 1994.
Wo zai beifang shouge sixiang (I Am Harvesting Ideas in the North). Chengdu: Sichuan wenyi, 2000.
Xiongnu he Xiongnu yiwai (The Huns and Others). Xi'an: Shaanxi renmin jiaoyu, 1994.
Zuihou de yuan xing (The Last Long-Distance Trip). Beijing: Hualing, 2007.
Zuihou yige Xiongnu (The Last Huns). Beijing: Zuojia, 1992.

Gao Xiaosheng

Chen Huansheng shang cheng chu guo ji (Chen Huansheng Going to Town and Abroad). Shanghai: Shanghai wenyi, 1991.
Gao Xiaosheng daibiao zuo (Representative Works by Gao Xiaosheng). Zhengzhou: Huanghe wenyi, 1987.
Li Shunda zaowu (*Li Shunda Builds a House*). Nanjing: Jiangsu renmin, 1979.

* * *

The Broken Betrothal. Beijing: Panda Books, 1981.
"A Gift of Land." Tr. Howard Goldblatt. In Helen F. Siu, ed., *Furrows: Peasants, Intellectuals, and the State: Stories and Histories from Modern China.* Stanford: Stanford University Press, 1990, 163–80.
"Li Shunda Builds a House." Tr. Madelyn Ross. In Mason Y. H. Wang, ed., *Perspectives in Contemporary Chinese Literature.* University Center, MI: Green River Press, 1983, 193–228.

Gao Xingjian

Che zhan (*Bus Stop*). Taipei: Lianhe wenxue, 2001.
Ling shan (*Soul Mountain*). Taipei: Lianjing, 1990.
Shengsi jie (Between Life and Death). Taipei: Lianhe wenxue, 2001.
Yige ren de shengjing (*One Man's Bible*). Taipei: Lianjing, 1999.
Zhoumo sichongzou (Weekend Quartet). Taipei: Lianhe wenxue, 2001.

* * *

Buying a Fishing Rod for My Grandfather: Stories. Tr. Mabel Lee. London: Flamingo, 2002.
One Man's Bible: A Novel. Tr. Mabel Lee. London: Flamingo, 2002.

The Other Shore: Plays by Gao Xingjian. Tr. Gilbert C. F. Fong. Hong Kong: The Chinese University Press, 1999.
Soul Mountain. Tr. Mabel Lee. New York: HarperCollins, 1999.

Ge Fei

Diren (The Enemy). Guangzhou: Huacheng, 1991.
Renmian taohua (Peach-Blossom Face). Shenyang: Chunfeng wenyi, 2004.
Yuwang de qizhi (The Flag of Desire). Nanjing: Jiangsu wenyi, 1994.

* * *

"Encounter." In Herbert Batt, ed./tr., *Tales of Tibet: Sky Burials, Prayer Wheels, and Wind Horses.* Lanham, MD: Rowman & Littlefield, 2001, 77–104.
"Green Yellow." Tr. Eva Shan Chou. In Jing Wang, ed., *China's Avant-garde Fiction.* Durham, NC: Duke University Press, 1998, 23–42.
"Remembering Mr. Wu You." Tr. Howard Goldblatt. In Goldblatt, ed., *Chairman Mao Would Not Be Amused: Fiction from Today's China.* New York: Grove Press, 1995, 236–43.
Stories in Frank Stewart and Herbert J. Batt, eds., *The Mystified Boat and Other New Stories from China.* Special issue of *Manoa: A Pacific Journal of International Writing* 15, 2 (Winter 2003). Honolulu: University of Hawaii Press, 142–61. [includes "A Date in Purple Bamboo Park" and "The Mystified Boat"]

Gu Cheng

Gu Cheng shi quanbian (Collected Poems by Gu Cheng). Shanghai: Sanlian, 1999.
Hei yanjin (Eyes of Darkness). Beijing: Renmin wenxue, 1986.
Ying'er (*Ying'er: The Kingdom of Daughters*). Coauthored with Lei Mi. Beijing: Zuojia, 1993.

* * *

Nameless Flowers: Selected Poems of Gu Cheng. Tr. Aaron Crippen, with photographs by Hai Bo. New York: George Brazilier, 2005.
Sea of Dreams: The Selected Writings of Gu Cheng. Tr. with introduction by Joseph R. Allen. New York: New Directions, 2005.
Selected Poems by Gu Cheng. Ed. Seán Golden and Chu Chiyu. Hong Kong: Renditions Paperbacks, 1990.
Ying'er: The Kingdom of Daughters. Coauthored with Lei Mi. Tr. Li Xia. Dortmund: Projekt Verlag, 1995.

Gu Hua

Guhua duanpian zhongpian xiaoshuo ji (Collection of Short Stories and Novellas by Gu Hua). Beijing: Renmin wenxue, 1982.
Furong zhen (A Small Town Called Hibiscus). Beijing: Renmin wenxue, 1981.

* * *

Pagoda Ridge and Other Stories. Tr. Gladys Yang. Beijing: Chinese Literature, 1985.
A Small Town Called Hibiscus. Beijing: Panda Books, 1983.
Virgin Widows. Tr. Howard Goldblatt. Honolulu: University of Hawaii Press, 1996.

Guo Moruo (Kuo Mo-jo)

Guo Moruo juzuo (Plays by Guo Moruo). Hefei: Anhui wenyi, 1997.
Guo Moruo shige jingcui (Selected Poems by Guo Moruo). Changchun: Dongbei chaoxian minzu jiaoyu, 1993.

* * *

The Resurrection of Fêng-Huang. Trs. Harold Acton and Ch'en Shih-Hsiang. London: Oxford University Press, 1972.
Selected Poems from "The Goddesses." Trs. John Lester and A. C. Barnes. Beijing: Foreign Languages Press, 1958, 1978.

Hai Xin

Chen hui (Morning Sunshine). Hong Kong: Shanghai shuju, 1977.
Chu mai ying zi de ren (The Man Who Sells His Shadow). Guangzhou: Huacheng, 1985.
Hao men han men kong men (The Gates of Wealth, Poverty, and Emptiness). Hong Kong: Huoyi, 1998.
Jinse de laba (The Golden Horn). Hong Kong: Zhongliu, 1977.
Panni de nü'er (A Rebellious Daughter). Hong Kong: Shanghai shuju, 1976.
Shizi lukou (Crossroad). Hong Kong: Shanghai shuju, 1976.
Tangxi sandai ming hua (Three Generations of Famous Courtesans in Tangxi). Hong Kong: Tiandi tushu, 1992.
Xigua chengshu de shihou (When Watermelons Are Ripe). Hong Kang: Haiyang wenyishe, 1978.
Zise qianniuhua (Purple Morning Glory). Hong Kong: Shanghai shuju, 1978.

* * *

"Night Revels." Tr. Gu Yaxing. In Michael S. Duke, ed., *Worlds of Modern Chinese Fiction*. Armonk, NY: M.E. Sharpe, 1991, 305–10.

Hai Zi

Haizi shi quanbian (Collected Poems by Haizi). Ed. Xi Chuan. Shanghai: Sanlian, 1997.

* * *

An English Translation of Poems of the Contemporary Chinese Poet Hai Zi. Tr. Hong Zeng, Lewiston, NY: Edwin Mellen Press, 2005.

Han Dong

Baba zai tianshang kan wo (My Father Is Watching Me in Heaven). Shijiazhuang: Hebei jiaoyu, 2002.
Wo de Bolatu (My Plato). Xi'an: Shaanxi shifan daxue, 2000.
Wo he ni (You and Me). Shanghai: Shanghai wenyi, 2005.
Xi tian shang (The Western Sky). Shanghai: Shanghai renmin, 2007.
Zha gen (Taking Roots). Beijing: Renmin wenxue, 2003.

* * *

"The Duck Prophet." Tr. Yanbing Chen. In Henry Y. H. Zhao, Yanbing Chen, and John Rosenwald. *Fissures: Chinese Writing Today*. Brookline, MA: Zephyr Press, 2000, 281.
"Five Poems." Trs. Tony Prince and Tao Naikan. *Renditions* 57 (2002): 112–121.
"Learning to Write with a Brush." Tr. Michael Day. *PRISM International* (Vancouver) 36, 3 (Spring 1998).
"Mourning the Cat." Tr. Yanbing Chen. In Henry Y. H. Zhao, Yanbing Chen, and John Rosenwald. *Fissures: Chinese Writing Today*. Brookline, MA: Zephyr Press, 2000, 280.
"Taking Advantage." Tr. Desmond Skeel. In Henry Y. H. Zhao, Yanbing Chen, and John Rosenwald. *Fissures: Chinese Writing Today*. Brookline, MA: Zephyr Press, 2000, 183–211.

Han Han

San chong men (Three Doors). Beijing: Zuojia, 2000.
Xiang shaonian la feichi (Flying like Wind). Beijing: Zhongguo qingnian, 2002.
Yi zuo chengchi (A City). Nanchang: Ershiyi shiji, 2006.

Han Shaogong

Anshi (Hints). Beijing: Renmin wenxue, 2002.
Bababa (Pa Pa Pa). Beijing: Zuojia, 1996.
Gui qu lai (*Homecoming*). Beijing: Zuojia, 1996.
Maqiao Cidian (*A Dictionary of Maqiao*). Beijing: Zuojia, 1996.

* * *

A Dictionary of Maqiao. Tr. Julia Lovell. New York: Columbia University Press, 2003.
Homecoming and Other Stories. Hong Kong: Renditions, 1992.

Hao Ran

Cangsheng (The Common People). Beijing: Shiyue wenyi, 1988.
Jinguang dadao (*The Golden Road: A Story of One Village in the Uncertain Days after Land Reforms*). 4 vols. Beijing: Jinhua, 1994.
Yanyang tian (*Bright Clouds*). Beijing: Zuojia, 1965.

* * *

Bright Clouds. Beijing: Foreign Languages Press, 1974.
The Call of the Fledglings and Other Children's Stories. Beijing: Foreign Languages Press, 1974.
The Golden Road: A Story of One Village in the Uncertain Days after Land Reforms. Tr. Carma Hinton and Chris Gilmartin. Beijing: Foreign Languages Press, 1981.
Little Pebble Is Missing. Hong Kong: Chao Yang Publishing Company, 1973.

He Liwei

Guang he yingzi (Light and Shadow). Shijiazhuang: Huashan wenyi, 2000.
Gen aiqing kai wanxiao (Joking with Love). Beijing: Xin shijie, 2002.

He Qifang

Hanyuan ji (Hanyuan Collection), with Bian Zhilin and Li Guangtian. Shanghai: Shangwu, 1934.
Hua meng lu (Visualizing Dreams). Shanghai: Wenhua shenghuo, 1936.
Wo gechang Yan'an (I Sing of Yan'an). Hefei: Anhui jiaoyu, 1997.
Xinghuo ji (Sparks). Shanghia: Qunyi, 1946.
Yuyan (Prophesy). Shanghai: Wenhua shenghuo, 1945.
Ye ge he baitian de ge (Songs of Day and Night). Beijing: Renmin wenxue, 1952.

* * *

Paths in Dreams: Selected Prose and Poetry of Ho Ch'i-fang. Ed./tr. Bonnie S. McDougall. St. Lucia, Queensland: University of Queensland Press, 1976.

"Clouds." Tr. Bonnie McDougall. *Stand* (Newcastle) 15, 3 (1974).

"Elegy." Tr. David Pollard. In David Pollard, ed., *The Chinese Essay.* New York: Columbia University Press, 2000, 271–75.

Poems in Michelle Yeh, ed./tr., *Anthology of Modern Chinese Poetry.* New Haven: Yale University Press, 1992, 60–66.

Hong Feng

Hanhai (The Great Sea). Beijing: Zuojia, 1988.

Geming la geming la (Joining the Revolution). Shenyang: Chunfeng wenyi, 2004.

Ku jie (The Boundary of Bitterness). Shenyang: Chufeng wenyi, 1993.

Zhongnian dixian (The Last Defense of Middle Age). Kunming: Yunnan renmin, 2001.

* * *

"The Stream of Life." Tr. Michael Day. In Michael S. Duke, ed., *Worlds of Modern Chinese Fiction*, 63–75.

Hong Lingfei

Gui jia (Homecoming). Shanghai: Xiantai, 1929.

Liuwang (Exile). Shanghai: Xiandai, 1928.

Ming chao (The Ming Dynasty). Shanghai: Yadong, 1928.

Qianxian (The Front Line). Shanghai: Taidong shuju, 1928.

Hong Shen

Hong Shen juzuo xuan (Selected Plays by Hong Shen). Beijing: Renmin wenxue, 1954.

* * *

"Yama Chao" (Zhao Yanwang). In E. Gunn, ed., *Twentieth-Century Chinese Drama: An Anthology.* Bloomington: Indiana University Press, 1983, 10–40.

Hong Ying

Ah nan (Ananda). Changsha: Hunan wenyi, 2002.

Ji'e de nü'er (*Daughter of the River*). Beijing: Zhishi, 2003.

Kongque de jiaohan (Peacock Cries). Beijing: Zhishi, 2003.
Shanghai zhi si (Death in Shanghai). Taipei: Jiuge, 2005.

* * *

Daughter of the River. Tr. Howard Goldblatt. New York: Grove Press, 1999.
K: The Art of Love. Trs. Henry Zhao and Nicky Harman. London: Marion Boyars, 2002.
Summer of Betrayal. Tr. Martha Avery. New York: Farrar Straus and Giroux, 1997; London: Bloomsbury, 1997.

Hu Fayun

Ruyuan@sars.com. Beijing: Zhongguo guoji guangbo, 2006.
Si yu hechang (Death from a Chorus). Wuhan: Wuhan, 2006.

Hu Jian

Fen qing shidai (The Era of Angry Youths). Wuhan: Changjiang wenyi, 2002.
Qiang huo: jianmie feitu shouce (Gunfire: A Handbook for Annihilating Mobsters). Beijing: Zhongguo sanxia, 2006.

Hu Lancheng

Chan shi yizhi hua (Zen Is a Flower). Taipei: Sansan, 1979.
Jinsheng jinshi (This Life, These Times). Taipei: Yuanjing, 1976.
Shanhe suiyue (Times of My Country). Taipei: Sansan shufang, 1990.

* * *

"This Life, These Times" [excerpts]. Tr. D. E. Pollard. *Renditions* 45 (1996): 129–35.

Hu Shi

Changshi ji (Experiments). Beijing: Beijing University Press, 1920.
Hu Shi wen ji (Essays by Hu Shi). Taipei: Yuandong, 1953.
Hu Shi quan ji 11 wenxue (Complete Works by Hu Shi, vol. 11, Literature). Hefei: Anhui jiaoyu, 2003.

* * *

A Collection of Hu Shi's English Writings. Ed. Chou Chih-p'ing. Taibei: Yuanliu, 1995.
"The Greatest Event in Life" [Zhongshen dashi]. In E. Gunn, ed., *Twentieth-Century Chinese Drama: An Anthology.* Bloomington: Indiana University

Press, 1983, 1–9; also in A. E. Zucker, ed., *The Chinese Theater*. Boston: Little Brown, 1925, 119–28.

"The Literary Revolution in China." *Chinese Social and Political Science Review* 6, 2 (1922): 91–100.

"Some Modest Proposals for the Reform of Literature." In Denton, Kirk A., ed., *Modern Chinese Literary Thought*. Stanford: Stanford University Press, 1996, 123–39.

Poems in Hsu Kai-yu, ed., *Twentieth Century Chinese Poetry: An Anthology*. Garden City, NY: Doubleday, 1963, 1–3; Michelle Yeh, ed./tr., *Anthology of Modern Chinese Poetry*. New Haven: Yale University Press, 1992, 1.

Hu Yepin

Bieren de xingfu (Other People's Happiness). Shanghai: Huatong, 1929.

Dao Mosike qu (To Moscow). Shanghai: Guanghua, 1930.

Guangming zai women qianmian (A Bright Future). Shanghai: Chunqiu, 1930.

Huo Zhuzi (A Pearl in the Brain). Shanghai: Guanghua shuju, 1928.

* * *

"Living Together." Tr. George Kennedy. In Harold Isaacs, ed., *Straw Sandals: Chinese Short Stories, 1918–1933*. Cambridge, MA: MIT Press, 1974, 207–14.

"A Poor Man." In *Chinese Stories from the Thirties*, vol. 1. Beijing: Foreign Languages Press, 1982.

Huang Biyun

Lie nü tu (Portraits of Impetuous Women). Hong Kong: Tiandi tushu, 1999.

Shi er nüse (Twelve Forms of Female Seduction). Taipei: Maitian, 2000.

Qihou (Afterwards). Hong Kong: Tiandi tushu, 1994.

Qi zong jingmoi (Seven Kinds of Silence). Hong Kong: Taindi tushu, 1997.

Wenrou yu baolie (Gentle and Violent). Hong Kong: Taindi tushu, 1994.

Wu ai ji (Without Love). Taipei: Datian, 2001.

* * *

"Losing the City." Tr. Martha Cheung. In Martha P. Y. Cheung, ed., *Hong Kong Collage: Contemporary Stories and Writing*. Hong Kong: Oxford University Press, 1998, 205–32.

"Plenty and Sorrow." Tr. Janice Wickeri. In *Renditions* 47/48 (Spring/Autumn 1997): 53–72; also in *Hong Kong Stories: Old Themes and New Voices*. Hong Kong: Renditions, 1999, 126–158.

"She's Woman, I'm Woman." In Kwok-kan Tam, Terry Siu-Han Yip, and Wimal Dissanayake, eds., *A Place of One's Own: Stories of Self in China, Hong Kong, and Singapore*. New York: Oxford University Press, 1999, 287–300. Also as

"She's a Young Woman and So Am I." Tr. Naifei Ding, in Patricia Sieber, ed., *Red Is Not the Only Color: Contemporary Chinese Fiction on Love and Sex between Women, Collected Stories*. Lanham, MD: Rowman & Littlefield, 2001, 37–48.

Huang Chunming

Erzi de da wan'ou (*His Son's Big Doll*). Taipei: Xianrenzhang, 1969.
Kan hai de rizi (Days of Going to Sea). Hong Kong: Nüshen, 1985.
Shayonala zaijian (Sayonara, Goodbye). Taipei: Huangguan wenxue, 1985.

* * *

The Drowning of an Old Cat and Other Stories. Tr. Howard Goldblatt. Bloomington: Indiana University Press, 1980.
The Taste of Apples. Tr. Howard Goldblatt. New York: Columbia University Press, 2001.

Huang Fan

Caifa (The Plutocrat). Taipei: Xidao, 1990.
Cibei de ziwei (The Flavor of Compassion). Taipei: Lianhe baoshe, 1984.
Da shidai (The Great Epoch). Taipei: Shibao wenhua, 1982.
Da xue zhi zei (College Thieves). Taipei: Lianhe wenyi, 2004.
Fandui zhe (The Opposition). Taipei: Zili wanbao she, 1987.
Lai Suo (*Lai Suo*). Taipei: Shibao wenhua, 1979.
Shangxin cheng (City of Broken Hearts). Taipei: Zili wanbaoshe, 1982.
Zaoyu de guojia (A Manic-Depressive Country). Taipei: Lianhe wenxue, 2003.

* * *

"Lai Suo." Tr. Eric B. Cohen. In Michael S. Duke, *Worlds of Modern Chinese Fiction*. Armonk, NY: M.E. Sharpe, 1991, 76–98.
"A Man of Scruples, Shu-ming Fan, The Just and the Fair." Tr. Chen I-djen. *The Chinese Pen* (Autumn 1988): 59–82.
"A Rainy Night." Trs. Chou Chang Jun-mei and Eva Shan Chou. *The Chinese Pen* (Spring 1983): 1–26.
Poems in Jeff Twitchell, tr., *Original: Chinese Language-Poetry Group, A Writing Anthology*. Brighton, England: Parataxis Press, 1995, 90–93.

Huang Jinshu

Fenshao (Setting on Fire). Taipei: Maitian, 2007.
Huangyan huo zhenli de jiyi: dangdai Zhongwen xiaoshuo lun ji (The Art of Lies or Truth: Essays on Contemporary-Chinese Language Literature). Taipei: Maitian, 2003.

Ke bei (Inscribed Back). Taipei: Maotouying, 2001.
Meng yu zhu yu liming (Dreams and Pigs and Dawn). Taipei: Jiuge, 1994.
Tu yu huo (Earth and Fire). Taipei: Maitian, 2005.
Wu an ming (Black Dim Dark). Taipei: Jiuge, 1997.

Huo Da

Bu tian lie (Patching Up the Sky). Beijing: Beijing chubanshe, 1997.
Musilin de zangli (A Muslim Funeral). Beijing: Shiyue wenyi, 1988.
Wei chuan de hong jia yi (Red Bridal Gown). Beijing: Shiyue wenyi, 1995.

Ji Xian

Ji Xian jing pin (The Best Poems by Ji Xian). Beijing: Renmin wenxue, 1995.
Ji Xian zi xuan ji (Self-Selected Works by Ji Xian). Taipei: Liming wenhua, 1978.
Zhongnan Shan xia (At the Foot of the Zhongnan Mountain). Taipei: Shangwu, 1973.

* * *

Poems in Germain Groogenbroodt and Peter Stinso, eds., *China, China: Contemporary Poetry from Taiwan, Republic of China*. Ninove, Belgium: Point Books, 1986.

Jia Pingwa

Fei du (The Capital City in Ruins). Beijing: Zuojia, 1993.
Fuzao (Turbulence). Hong Kong: Tiandi, 1989.
Qin qiang (Qin Qiang: The Shaanxi Opera). Beijing: Zuojia, 2005.
Renshen, guangshan (Pregnancy and Going to the Mountains). Beijing: Zuojia, 1993.
Shangzhou san lu (Three Chapters of Shangzhou). Xi'an: Shaanxi lüyou, 2001.

* * *

The Castle. Tr. Shao-Pin Luo. Toronto: York Press, 1997.
The Heavenly Hound. Beijing: Panda Books, 1991.

Jian Xian'ai

Chouchu ji (Hesitation). Shanghai: Liangyou, 1936.
Huanxiang ji (Homecoming). Shanghai: Zhonghua shuju, 1934.
Jiu jia (A Wine Shop). Chongqing: Wanguang shuju, 1945.

Shan cheng ji (A Mountain City). Beijing: Zuojia, 1956.

Xiangjian de beiju (Tragedies in the Countryside). Shanghai: Shangwu yinshu guan, 1937.

Yan de gushi (Salt Stories). Chongqing:Wenhua shenghuo, 1940.

Zhao wu (Morning Fog). Shanghai: Beixin shuju, 1927.

Jiang Guangci

Ai Zhongguo (Crying for China). Hankou: Changjiang shudian, 1926.

Chongchu yun wei de yueliang (The Moon That Breaks out of the Clouds). Shanghai: Beixin shuju, 1930.

Duanku tang (The Short-Pants Party). Shanghai: Taidong shuju, 1927.

Jiang Guangci xiaoshuo quan ji (Complete Works of Jiang Guangci). Shanghai: Xin wenyi shudian, 1932.

Lisa de anyuan (Lisa's Sorrows). Shanghai: Xiandai shuju, 1929.

Tianye de feng (The Wind in the Fields). Shanghai: Hufeng shuju, 1932.

Xiang qing ji (Homesickness). Shangahi: Xiandai shuju, 1930.

* * *

"Hassan." In Harold Isaacs, ed., *Straw Sandals: Chinese Short Stories, 1918–1933*. Boston: MIT Press, 1974, 170–73.

Jiang He

Taiyang he ta de fanguang (The Sun and Its Reflection). Beijing: Renmin wenxue, 1988.

Poems in Yan Yuejun et al., eds., *Menglong shi xuan* (Collection of Misty Poems). Changchun: Chunfeng wenyi, 1986.

Poems in *Wu ren shi xuan* (Poems by Five Poets). Beijing: Zuojia, 1986.

* * *

"Cong zheli kaishi" (Begin from Here); "Jinianbei" (Monument); "Xing" (Star); and "Xingxing Bianzouqu" (Star Variations). Trs. Alisa Joyce, Ginger Li, and John Mingford. *Renditions* 23, 131–39.

"Meiyou xie wan de shi" (Unfinished Poem). Trs. Alisa Joyce, Ginger Li, and Yip Wai-lim. *Renditions* 19 & 20, 221–34.

Jiang Rong

Lang Tudeng (*Wolf Totem*). Wuhan: Changjiang wenyi, 2004.

* * *

Wolf Totem. Tr. Howard Goldblatt. New York: Penguin Books, 2009.

Jiang Zilong

Chi chen huang lü qing lan zi (*All the Colors of the Rainbow*). Tianjin: Baihua wenyi, 1981.
Kaituo zhe (The Trailblazer). Beijing: Zhongguo qingnian, 1981.
Kongdong (Emptiness). Beijing: Shiyue wenyi, 2001.
Nongmin diguo (The Peasant Empire). Beijing: Renmin wenxue, 2008.
Renqi (Being Human). Beijing: Zuojia, 2000.
She shen (God of Snakes). Tianjin: Baihua wenyi, 1986.
Yan Zhao beige (Lament of the North). Beijing: Zhongguo qingnian, 1985.

* * *

All the Colours of the Rainbow. Beijing: Panda Books, 1983.
"The Foundation." In Helen F. Siu and Zelda Stern, eds./trs. *Mao's Harvest: Voices from China's New Generation*. New York: Oxford University Press, 1983, 128–46.

Jin Yi

Cuoshi (Blunder). Guangzhou: Huacheng, 1984.
Sumiao Xianggang: huaijiu (Hong Kong Sketchbook: Nostalgia). Hong Kong: Sanlian, 1999.
Tong xin jie (True-Love Knot), *Nu hai tong zhou* (On the Same Boat in the Turbulent Sea). Hong Kong: Wenjia, 1975.
Xianggang shui shang yi jia ren (A Family on the Hong Kong River). Guangzhou: Huacheng, 1987.

Jin Yong

Feihu waizhuan (The Unofficial Biography of the Flying Fox). Hong Kong: Mingheshe, 1976.
Lu ding ji (*The Deer and the Cauldron*). Hong Kong: Mingheshe, 1976.
Tianlong babu (Eight Chapters of the Heavenly Dragon). Hong Kong: Mingheshe, 1976.
Xiao ao jianghu (Conquests at All Corners of the Country). Hong Kong: Mingheshe, 1976.
Yitian tulong ji (Slaying the Dragon Aided by Heaven). Hong Kong: Mingheshe, 1976.

* * *

The Book and the Sword. Tr. Graham Earnshaw. Hong Kong: Oxford University Press, 2004.

The Deer and the Cauldron: A Martial Arts Novel. Tr. John Minford. New York: Oxford University Press, 1997.
Foxy Volant of the Snowy Mountain. Tr. Olivia Mok. Hong Kong: Hong Kong University Press, 1996.
Return of the Condor Heroes. Tr. Eileen Zhong. Singapore: Asiapac, 1997.

Jing Fu

Bali qing chou (The Feuds in Bali). Beijing: Wenlian, 1993.
Jing Fu xiaoshuo jing xuan (Selected Stories and Novellas by Jing Fu). Xi'an: Taibai wenyi, 1996.
Lu ming (The Cries of Deer). Shanghai: Shanghai renmin, 2007.

Ke Yunlu

Chenggong zhe (A Success Story). Beijing: Zhongguo wenxue, 1998.
Da qigong shi (The Qigong Master). Beijing: Renmin wenxue, 1989.
Fuqin xianyi ren (Suspect Fathers). Beijing: Renmin wenxue, 2005.
Furong guo (The Hibiscus Country). Beijing: Dianying, 2000.
Heishanbao gang jian (The History of Heishanbao). Guangzhou: Huangcheng, 2000.
Jidu zhi yanjiu (A Study of Jealousy). Tianjin: Baihua wenyi, 1990.
Long nian dang'an (The Dragon Year Dossier). Beijing: Renmin wenxue, 2002.
Mengmei (Obscuration). Guangzhou: Huangcheng, 2000.
Nage xiatian ni gan le shenme (What Did You Do That Summer). Beijing: Gongren, 2002.
Shuai yu rong (Fall and Rise). Beijing: Renmin wenxue, 1987.
Xisheng (Sacrifice). Kunming: Yunnan, 2001.
Ye yu zhou (Night and Day). Beijing: Renmin wenxue, 1986.

Kong Jiesheng

Da linmang (The Great Forest: A Collection of Novellas). Guangzhou: Huacheng, 1986.
Putong nügong (An Ordinary Female Worker: A Collection of Short Stories). Shanghai: Shanghai wenyi, 1984.
Xi chuang ke meng (The Western Window: Dreams of a Traveler. A Collection of Essays). Nanchang: Jiangxi renmin, 1987.

* * *

"On Marriage." *Chinese Literature* 5 (1979): 3–24; also in Geremie Barme and Bennett Lee, trs., *The Wounded: New Stories of the Cultural Revolution.* Hong Kong: Joint Publishing, 1979, 25–54.
"On the Other Side of the Stream." In P. Link, ed., *Roses and Thorns: The Second Blooming of the Hundred Flowers in Chinese Fiction,* 1979–1980. Berkeley: University of California Press, 1984, 168–93.
"The Sleeping Lion." Tr. Susan McFadden. In Howard Goldblatt, ed., *Chairman Mao Would Not Be Amused: Fiction from Today's China.* New York: Grove Press, 1995, 269–95.

Kun Nan

Di de men (The Earth's Gate). Hong Kong: Qingwen shuwu, 2001.
Tiantang wu zai zu xia (Heaven Dances under the Feet). Hong Kong: Kehua, 2001; also in *San cheng ji xiaoshuo xilie di san ji Xiang Gang juan wu aiji* (Fiction Series on Three Cities, Part 3 — Hong Kong: Without Love), ed., Xu Zidong. Shanghai: Shanghai wenyi, 2006.
Xi jing de fengliu (The Romantic Life of Playing with Whales). Hong Kong: Yuelin, 1998.

Lai He (Lai Ho)

Lai He quan ji (Complete Works by Lai He). 6 vols. Taipei: Qianwei, 2000–2001.
Lai He xiaoshuo ji (Fictional Works by Lao He). Taipei: Hongfan, 1994.
Yi gan chen zai (The Man with a Steelyard: Short Stories by Lai He). Taipei: Hongfan, 1996.

* * *

Poems in *Taiwan Literature, English Translation Series* 15 (2004): 15–58; 155–76.

Lai Shengchuan

An lian tao hua yuan (Secret Love in Peach Blossom Land); *Hongse de tiankong* (Red Sky). Beijing: Dongfang, 2007.
Hui tou shi bi an (The Island and the Other Shore). Taipei: Huangguan, 1989.
Lai Shengchuan: Juchang (Lai Shengchuan: Theater). 4 vols. Taipei: Yuanzun wenhua, 1999.
Lai Shengchuan de chuangyi xue (Lai Shengchuan on Creativity). Beijing: Zhongxin, 2006)

Ru meng zhi meng (Dream Like a Dream). Taipei: Yuanliu, 2991.
Xi you ji : Zhongguo xian dai ge ju (Journey to the West: A Modern Chinese Musical). Taipei: Huangguan, 1988.

* * *

"Pining . . . In Peach Blossom Land" [An lian taohua yuan]. Tr. Martha Cheung. In Cheung and Jane Lai, eds., *An Anthology of Contemporary Chinese Drama.* New York: Oxford University Press, 1997, 375–453.

Lao She

Cha guan (*Teahouse*). Beijing: Xiju, 1958.
Er Ma (Mr. Ma and Son: A Sojourn in London). Shanghai: Shangwu, 1931.
Lao Zhang de zhexue (Mr. Zhang's Philosophy). Shanghai: Shangwu, 1939.
Si shi tongtang (Four Generations under One Roof). Tianijn: Baihua wenyi, 1959.

* * *

Beard Ditch. Beijing: Foreign Languages Press, 1956.
Beneath the Red Banner. Tr. Don J. Cohn. Beijing: Panda Books, 1982.
Blades of Grass: The Stories of Lao She. Trs. William Lyell and Sarah Wei-ming Chang.
Camel Xiangzi. Tr. Shi Xiaojing. Beijing: Foreign Languages Press, 2001.
Cat Country: A Satirical Novel of China in the 1930s. Tr. William Lyell. Columbus: Ohio State University Press, 1970.
Dragon Ma and Son: A Novel by Lao She (Er Ma). Tr. Jean M. James. San Francisco: Chinese Materials Center, 1980.
The Drum Singers. New York: Harcourt Brace, 1952.
Selected Stories by Lao She [English-Chinese edition]. Honolulu: University of Hawaii Press, 1999.
Teahouse: A Play in Three Acts. Tr. John Howard-Gibbon. Beijing: Foreign Langauges Press, 1984.
The Yellow Storm (Si shi tongtang). Tr. Ida Pruitt. New York: Harcourt, Brace and Co., 1951.

Li Ang

An ye (Dark Night). Taipiei: Shibao wenhua, 1985.
Mi yuan (The Garden of Seduction). Taipei: Maitian, 1998.
Sha fu: Lucheng gushi (The Butcher's Wife). Taipei: Lianhe baoshe, 1983.

* * *

The Butcher's Wife. San Francisco: North Point Press, 1986.
"Curvaceous Dolls." Tr. Howard Goldblatt. In Joseph S. M. Lau and Howard Goldblatt, eds., *The Columbia Anthology of Modern Chinese Literature.* New York: Columbia University Press, 1995, 360–72.

"Flower Season." Tr. Howard Goldblatt. *The Chinese Pen* (Summer 1980): 55–67.

Li Bihua

Bawang bie ji (*Farewell My Concubine*). Hong Kong: Tiandi tushu youxian gongsi, 1985.

Chuandao Fangzi: Manzhouguo xiaoyan (*The Last Princess of Manchuria*). Hong Kong: Tiandi, 1990.

Pan Jinlian zhi qianshi jinsheng (Past and Present Lives of a Seductress). Beijing: Renmin wenxue, 1999.

Qing she (The Green Snake). Hong Kong: Tiandi tushu youxian gongsi, 1986.

Yanzhi kou (Rouge). Hong Kong: Tiandi tushu youxian gongsi, 1986.

You seng (Seduction of a Monk). Beijing: Renmin wenxue chubanshe, 1995.

* * *

Farewell to My Concubine: A Novel. Tr. Andrea Lingenfelter. New York: William Morrow, 1993.

The Last Princess of Manchuria. Tr. Andrea Kelley. New York: William Morrow, 1992.

Li Er

Huaqiang (Trickery). Beijing: Renmin wenxue, 2002.

Raoshe de yaba (A Talkative Mute). Wuhan: Hubei jiaoyu, 2000.

Shiliushu shang jie yingtao (Cherries Grown on a Pomegranate Tree). Nanjing: Jiangsu wenyi, 2004.

Yiwang (Oblivion). Guilin: Lijiang, 2002.

Li Guangtian

Hanyuan ji (Hanyuan Collection), with Bian Zhilin and He Qifang. Shanghai: Shangwu, 1934.

Li Guangtian daibiao zuo (Representative Works of Li Guangtian). Zhengzhou: Huanghe wenyi, 1987.

* * *

A Pitiful Plaything and Other Essays. Beijing: Panda Books, 1982.

Li Guowen

Di yi bei ku jiu (The First Gulp of Bitter Wine: A Collection of Short Stories). Beijing: Renmin wenxue, 1982.

Da ya cun yan (Elegant Rustic Talk: A Collection of Essays). Shanghai: Dongfang chuban zhongxin, 2000.
Huayuan jie wu hao (Number 5 Garden Street). Beijing: Shiyue wenyi, 1984.
Dongtian li de chuntian (Spring in Winter). Beijing: Renmin wenxue, 1981.
Li Guowen shuo Tang (The Tang Dynasty). Beijing: Zhonghua shuju, 2006.

Li Hangyu

Bai li shu shasha xiang (The Rustling Sounds of the White Oak). Nanjing: Jiangsu renmin, 1985.
Lao Hangzhou: Hu shan renjian (Old Hangzhou: the Lake, the Mountain, and the People). Nanjing: Jiangsu meishu, 2000.
Zuihou yige yulao'r (*The Last Angler*). Beijing: Renmin wenxue, 1985.

* * *

"In a Little Corner of the World." Tr. Sally Vernon. In Henry Zhao, ed., *The Lost Boat: Avant-garde Fiction from China*. London: Wellsweep, 1993, 59–74.
"The Last Angler." Tr. Yu Fanqin. *Chinese Literature* (Autumn 1984): 40–51.
"The Old Customs of Brick Stove Beach." Tr. Kuang Wendong, *Chinese Literature* 12 (1983): 19–40.
"Seeking Roots among the Gechuan River." In Laifong Leung, ed., *Morning Sun: Interviews with Chinese Writers of the Lost Generation*. Armonk, NY: M.E. Sharpe, 1994, 88–96.

Li Jianwu

Sahuang shijia (A Family of Liars). Shanghai: Wenhua shenghuo, 1940.
Li Jianwu daibiao zuo (Selected Works by Li Jianwu). Beijing: Huaxia, 1999.
Qingchun (Youth). Shanghai: Wenhua shenghuo, 1948.
Qiu (Autumn). Shanghai: Wenhua shenghuo, 1946.
Zhe buguo shi chuntian (*It's Only Spring*). Shanghai: Wenhua shenghuo, 1946.

* * *

It's Only Spring and Thirteen Years. Tr. Tony Hyder. London: Bamboo, 1989.
"Springtime." In Edward Gunn, ed., *Twentieth-Century Chinese Drama: An Anthology*. Bloomington: Indiana University Press, 1983, 174–227.

Li Jieren

Baofeng yuqian (Before the Storm). Shanghai: Zhonghua shuju, 1936.
Da bo (The Great Wave). Shanghai: Zhonghua shuju, 1937.
Hao renjia (Good Families). Shanghai: Zhonghua shuju, 1936.
Li Jieren xuanji (Selected Works of Li Jieren). 5 vols. Chengdu: Sichuan renmin, 1980–1986.

Si shui wei lan (*Ripples across a Stagnant Water*). Shanghai: Zhonghua, 1935.
Tongqing (Sympathy). Shanghai: Zhonghua, 1934.

* * *

Ripples across a Stagnant Water. Beijing: Panda Books, 1990.

Li Jinfa

Li Jinfa shi ji (Collection of Poetry by Li Jinfa). Chengdu: Sichuan wenyi, 1987.
Wei Shike yu xiongshou (Sponger and Killer). Beijing: Beixin, 1927.
Wei xingfu er ge (Song of Happiness). Shanghai: Shangwu, 1926.
Wei yu (Drizzle). Beijing: Beixin, 1925.

* * *

"A Record of My Own Inspiration." Tr. Kirk A. Denton. In Denton, ed., *Modern
  Chinese
Literary Thought.* Stanford: Stanford University Press, 1996, 390–91.

Li Peifu

Cheng de deng (City Lights). Wuhan: Changjiang wenyi, 2003.
Chengshi baipishu (White Paper on Cities). Beijing: Renmin wenxue, 2001.
Dengdeng linghun (Wait for the Soul). Guangzhou: Huacheng, 2007.
Lishi jiazu (The Li Clan). Tianjin: Baihua wenyi, 1999.
Yang de men (The Gate of Sheep). Shenyang: Chufeng wenyi, 2004.

* * *

"The Adulterers." Tr. Charles A. Laughlin, with Jeanne Tai. In David Der-wei
  Wang, ed., *Running Wild: New Chinese Writers.* New York: Columbia University Press, 1994, 168–73.

Li Rui

Houtu: Lüliang shan yinxiang (The Solid Earth: Impressions of Mount Lüliang).
  Hangzhou: Zhejiang wenyi, 1989.
Jiu zhi (The Old Address). Shanghai: Shanghai wenyi, 1993.
Tian shang you kuai yun (A Patch of Cloud in the Sky). Nanjing: Jiangsu wenyi,
  2003.
Wufeng zhishu (Windless Trees). Jinan: Shandong wenyi, 2002.
Yincheng gushi (*Silver City*). Wuhan: Changjiang wenyi, 2002.

* * *

Silver City. Tr. H. Goldblatt. New York: Henry Holt, 1997.

Li Shasha

Hong X (Red X). Guangzhou: Huacheng, 2004.
Bei dangzuo gui de ren (The Man Taken to Be a Ghost). Beijing: Dongfang, 2004.

Li Yongping

Jiling chunqiu (*The Jiling Chronicles*). Taipei: Hongfan, 1986.
Haidong Qing: Taipei de yige yuyan (Haidong Qing: An Allegory of Taipei). Taipei: Lianhe wenxue, 1992.
Li Yongping zixuan ji (Works by Li Yongping from 1968–2002). Taipei: Maitian, 2003.

* * *

Retribution: The Jiling Chronicles. Trs. Howard Goldblatt and Sylvia Li-chun Lin. New York: Columbia University Press, 2003.
"At Fortune's Way." Trs. Susan Wan Dooling and Micah David Rapaport. In Joseph S. M. Lau and Howard Goldblatt, eds., *The Columbia Anthology of Modern Chinese Literature.* New York: Columbia University Press, 1995, 326–48.
"A La-tzu Woman." Tr. James Fu. In Chi Pang-yuan et al., eds., *An Anthology of Contemporary Chinese Literature.* 2 vols. Taipei: National Institute for Compilation and Translation, 1975: II: 459–70.
"The Rain from the Sun." In Joseph S. M. Lau, ed., *The Unbroken Chain: An Anthology of Taiwan Fiction Since 1926.* Bloomington: Indiana University Press, 1983, 232–49.

Liang Bingjun (Ye Si)

Bulage de ming xin pian: Yesi xiao shuo (Postcards from Prague: Fiction by Yesi). Hong Kong: Chuangjian, 1990.
Ban tu: Liang Bingjun shi xuan (Halfway: Selected Poems by Liang Bingjun). Hong Kong: Zuojia, 1995.
Dao he da lu (The Island and the Mainland: Fiction by Yesi). Hong Kong: Huahan wenhua, 1987.
Dong xi (East West: Poems by Liang Bingjun). Hong Kong: Oxford University Press, 2000.
Hui ge zao chen de hua (Pidgins' Morning Utterances: Fiction by Yesi). Taipei: Youshi wenhua, 1976.
Jian zhi (The Art of Paper-cutting: Stories by Yesi). Hong Kong: Suye, 1982.
Lei sheng yu chan ming (Thunder and Songs of Cicadas: Poems by Liang Bingjun). Hong Kong: Damuzhi banyuekan, 1978.
Shenhua wucan (Fairy Tales for Lunch). Taipei: Hongfan, 1979.

You li de shi (Poetry of Dissociation). Hong Kong: Oxford University Press, 1995.

* * *

City at the End of Time. Trs. Gordon T. Osing and Leung Ping-kwan. Hong Kong: Twilight Books, 1992.
Travelling with a Bitter Melon: Selected Poems (1973–1998) by Leung Ping-kwan. Ed. Martha P. Y. Cheung. Hong Kong: Asia 2000.
"Jasmin." Tr. P. K. Leung. *Renditions* 29/30 (Spring/August 1988): 235–56.
"Lotus Leaves: Seven Poems." Trs. Kwok Kwan Mun and Lo Kwai Cheung, with John Minford. *Renditions* 29/30 (Spring/August 1988): 210–21.
"Postcolonial Affairs of Food and the Heart." Trs. Jesse Chan and John Minford. *Persimmon* 1, 3 (Winter 2001): 42–57.
"The Sorrows of Lan Kwai Fong." Trs. Martha Cheung and P. K. Cheung. In Martha P. Y. Cheung, ed., *Hong Kong Collage: Contemporary Stories and Writing.* Hong Kong: Oxford University Press, 1998, 85–98.
"The Story of Hong Kong." Tr. Martha Cheung. In Martha P. Y. Cheung, ed., *Hong Kong Collage: Contemporary Stories and Writing.* Hong Kong: Oxford University Press, 1998, 3–16.
"Tasting Asia: Twelve Poems" (Chinese original and English Translation). Tr. P. K. Leung. *Modern Chinese Literature and Culture* 17, 1 (Spring 2005): 8–31.
"Transcendence and the Fax Machine." Tr. Jeanne Tai. In David Der-wei Wang, ed., *Running Wild: New Chinese Writers.* New York: Columbia University Press, 1994, 13–20.
"The Walled City in Kowloon: A Space We All Shared." Tr. Janice Wickeri. In Martha P. Y. Cheung, ed., *Hong Kong Collage: Contemporary Stories and Writing.* Hong Kong: Oxford University Press, 1998, 34–39.

Liang Shiqiu

Guanyu Lu Xun (On Lu Xun). Taipei: Aimei, 1970.
Huai yuan meng yi (Dreams and Remembrances of the Scholartree Garden). Taipei: Yuandong, 1974.
Liang Shiqiu lun wenxue (Liang Shiqiu on Literature). Taipei: Shibao, 1978.
Qinghua ba nian (Eight Years at Qinghua University). Taipei: Chongguang, 1962.
Yashe xiaopin (Sketches from a Refined Cottage). Taipei: Zhengzhong, 1949.
Yashe xiaopin xu ji (Sequel to Sketches from a Refined Cottage). Taipei: Zhengzhong, 1973.
Yashe xiaopin (Sketches from a Refined Cottage), vols. 3 and 4. Taipei: Zhengzhong, 1982, 1986.

* * *

From a Cottager's Sketchbook, vol. 1. Tr. Ta-tsun Chen. Hong Kong: Chinese University Press, 2005.

"Fusing with Nature." Tr. Kirk A. Denton. In Denton, ed., *Modern Chinese Literary Thought: Writings on Literature, 1893–1945.* Stanford: Stanford University Press, 1996, 213–17.

"The Generation Gap." Tr. Cynthia Wu Wilcox. *The Chinese Pen* (Autumn 1985): 33–39.

"Haircut." Tr. David Pollard, ed., *The Chinese Essay.* New York: Columbia University Press, 2000, 230–33.

"Listening to Plays." Tr. David Pollard. In Pollard, ed., *The Chinese Essay.* New York: Columbia University Press, 2000, 233–37.

"Literature and Revolution." Tr. Alison Bailey. In Kirk A. Denton, ed., *Modern Chinese Literary Thought: Writings on Literature, 1893–1945.* Stanford: Stanford University Press, 1996, 307–15.

"Men." Tr. Chao-ying Shih. *The Chinese Pen* (Spring 1974): 40–44.

"Sickness." Tr. David Pollard. In Pollard, ed., *The Chinese Essay.* New York: Columbia University Press, 2000, 227–30.

"Snow." Tr. Nancy E. Chapman and King-fai Tam. In Joseph S. M. Lau and Howard Goldblatt, eds., *The Columbia Anthology of Modern Chinese Literature.* New York: Columbia University Press, 1995, 664–67.

"Women." Tr. Chao-ying Shih. *The Chinese Pen* (Winter 1972): 23–29.

Liang Xiaosheng

Jinye you baofengxue: Liang Xiaosheng zhiqing xiaoshuo xuan (Snowstorm Tonight: Stories of the Educated Youths by Liang Xiaosheng). Beijing: Jingji ribao, 1997.

Xue cheng (Snow City). Beijing: Shiyue wenyi, 1988.

Yi ge Hong Weibing de zibai (Confession of a Red Guard). Chengdu: Sichuan wenyi, 1988.

Zhe shi yipian shenqi de tudi (A Land of Wonder and Mystery). Tianjin: Baihua wenyi, 1985.

* * *

The Black Button. Beijing: Panda Books, 1992.

Panic and Deaf: Two Modern Satires. Hanming Chen and James O. Belcher, eds./trs. Honolulu: University of Hawaii Press, 2000.

"Ice Dam." Tr. Christopher Smith. *Chinese Literature* (Spring 1990): 3–60.

"The Jet Ruler." Tr. Yang Nan. *Chinese Literature* 5 (1983): 35–50.

"A Land of Wonder and Mystery." Tr. Shen Zhen. *Chinese Literature* 5 (1983): 5–34.

Liang Yusheng

Baifa monü zhuan (Biography of the White-Haired Succuba). Hong Kong: Weiqiang, 1984.
Pingzong xiaying lu (Tracks of a Chivalric Wanderer). Hong Kong: Tiandi, 1984.
Qi jian xia Tianshan (Seven Swordsmen Leaving Mount Tianshan). Guangzhou: Guangzhou lüyou, 1985.
Yun hai yu gong yuan (The Cloud and the Jade Bow). Fuzhou: Fujian renmin, 1984.

Liao Huiying

Bu gui lu (No Return). Taipei: Lianhe baoshe, 1983.
Lanse di wu ji (The Fifth Blue Season). Taipei: Jiuge, 1988.
Luo chen (The Fallen Dust). Beijing: Renmin wenxue, 1988.
Mang dian (The Blind Spot). Taipei: Jiuge, 1986.
You ma caizi (*Seed of Rape Plant*). Taipei: Huangguan, 1983.

* * *

"Seed of Rape Plant." Tr. Chen I-djen. *The Chinese Pen* (Spring 1986): 1–33.

Lin Bai

Funü xianliao lu (Records of Women's Gossips). Beijing: Xinxing, 2005.
Pingzhong zhi shui (Water in the Bottle). Nanjing: Jiangsu wenyi, 1997.
Yigeren de zhanzheng (One Individual's War). Nanjing: Jiangsu wenyi, 1997.
Zhiming de feixiang (A Fatal Flight). Beijing: Taihai, 2001.

* * *

"The Seat on the Verandah." Tr. Hu Ying. In Frank Stewart and Herbert J. Batt, eds., *The Mystified Boat and Other New Stories from China*. Special issue of *Manoa: A Pacific Journal of International Writing* 15, 2 (Winter 2003). Honolulu: University of Hawaii Press, 2004, 83–109.

Lin Haiyin

Cheng nan jiu shi (*Memories of Peking: Southside Stories*). Taipei: Chun wenxue, 1960.
Hunyin de gushi (A Story of Marriage). Taipei: Chun wenxue, 1986.
Lü zao yu xian dan (*Green Seaweed and Salted Eggs*). Taipei: Chun wenxue, 1982.

Meng Zhu de lücheng (Meng Zhu's Journey) Taipei: Chun wenxue, 1967.
Zhuxin (Candlewick). Taipei: Chun wenxue, 1963.

* * *

Green Seaweed and Salted Eggs. Tr. Nancy C. Ing. Taipei: The Heritage Press, 1963.
Memories of Peking: South Side Stories. Tr. Nancy Ing and Chi Pang-yuan. Hong Kong: Chinese University Press, 1992.
"Buried with the Dead." Tr. Jane Parish Yang. *The Chinese Pen* (Winter 1980): 33–61.
"Gold Carp's Pleated Skirt." Tr. Hsiao Lien-ren. In Chi Pang-yuan et al., eds., *An Anthology of Contemporary Chinese Literature.* Taipei: National Institute for Compilation and Translation, 1975, II, 9–23.

Lin Huiyin

Lin Huiyin shi ji (Collection of Poems by Lin Huiyin). Beijing: Renmin wenxue, 1985.
Lin Huiyin xiaoshuo: Jiushijiu du zhong (Fiction by Lin Huiyin: Ninety-nine Degrees). Shanghai: Shanghai guji, 1999.
Lin zhong yige xia ye (A Summer Night in the Forest). Hong Kong: Sanlian shudian, 2001.

* * *

"Hsiu Hsiu." Tr. Janet Ng. In Janet Ng and Janice Wickeri, eds., *May Fourth Women Writers: Memoirs.* Hong Kong: Renditions, 1997, 19–34.
Three Poems in A. Dooling and K. Torgeson, eds., *Writing Women in Modern China: An Anthology of Women's Literature from the Early Twentieth Century.* New York: Columbia University Press, 1998, 303–5.

Lin Jinlan

Aidengqiao fengqing (The Customs of the Short-Bench-Bridge). Hangzhou: Zhejiang wenyi, 1987.
Luori hongmen (Sunset at the Red Gate). Beijing: Dazhong wenyi, 2000.
Chun lei (Thunder in the Spring). Beijing: Zuojia, 1958.
Man cheng fei hua (Flowers Adrift All Over the City). Guangzhou: Huacheng, 1987.

* * *

"Grassland." *Chinese Literature* 5 (1961): 84–96.
"Taiwan Girl." Tr. Sidney Shapiro. *Chinese Literature* 4 (1957): 3–19.

"The Transcript." Tr. Howard Goldblatt. In *Roses and Thorns: The Second Blooming of the Hundred Flowers in Chinese Fiction.* Perry Link, ed. Berkeley: University of California Press, 1984, 102–10.

Lin Yaode

Du shi zhi hong (The Demise of the City). Taipei: Hongguang, 1989.
Du shi zhongduan ji (The Terminals at the End of the City). Taipei: Shulin, 1988.
E dixing (*The Ugly Land*). Taipei: Xidai, 1988.
Yi jiu si jiu nian yihou (After 1949). Taipei: Erya, 1986.
Yin wan cheng xue (A Silver Bowl Holding Snow). Taipei: Hongfan, 1987.
Shijian long (The Time Dragon). Taipei: Shibao wenhua, 1994.
Da dong qu (The Great Eastern District). Taipei: Lianhe wenxue, 1995.

* * *

"A Dream of Copper." Tr. Daniel J. Bauer. In Pang-yuan Chi, ed., *Taiwan Literature in Chinese and English.* Taipei: Commonwealth Publishing, 1999, 287–316.
"The Ugly Land." Tr. Stephen H. West. *Renditions* 35–36 (1991): 188–97.
Poems in Michelle Yeh and N. G. D. Malmqvist, eds., *Frontier Taiwan: An Anthology of Modern Chinese Poetry.* New York: Columbia University Press, 2001, 460–65.

Lin Yutang

Jian fu ji (Cutting and Dusting). Beijing: Beixin, 1928.
Lin Yutang sanwen jingdian quanbian (Collection of Lin Yutang's Essays). Beijing: Jiuzhou, 1998.
Lin Yutang youmo wen xuan (Selected Essays of Humor by Lin Yutang). 2 vols. Ed. Lin Taiyi. Changchun: Shidai wenyi, 1995.

* * *

Between Tears & Laughter. New York: Blue Ribbon Books, 1945.
Chinatown Family. New York: J. Day Co., 1948.
The Flight of the Innocents. New York: Putnam, 1964.
The Importance of Living. New York: Reynal & Hitchcock, 1937.
A Leaf in the Storm: A Novel of War-Swept China. New York: J. Day Co., 1941.
Memoirs of an Octogenarian. Taipei: Mei Ya Publications, 1975.
Moment in Peking: A Novel of Contemporary Chinese Life. New York: J. Day Co., 1939.
Pleasures of a Nonconformist. London: Heinemann, 1962.
With Love & Irony. New York: J. Day Co., 1940.

Ling Shuhua

Aishanlu mengying (Dream in a Mountain-Lover's Hut). Singapore: Shijie shuju, 1960.
Hua zhi si (A Temple of Flowers). Beijing: Xinyue, 1929.
Ling Shuhua xiaoshuo ji. (Collection of Fiction by Ling Shuhua). Taipei: Hongfan, 1984.
Nüren (Women) Shanghai: Shangwu, 1930.
Xiao Ge'rliang (Little Brothers). Beijing: Liangyou, 1935.

* * *

Ancient Melodies. New York: Universe Books, 1988. [rpt. of the 1953 edition]
"Embroidered Pillow." Tr. Marie Chan. *Renditions* 4 (1975): 124–27.
"A Happy Occasion." Tr. Janet Ng. *Renditions* 46 (1996): 106–13.
"The Night of Mid-Autumn Festival." In Joseph S. M. Lau and Howard Goldblatt, eds., *The Columbia Anthology of Modern Chinese Literature.* New York: Columbia University Press, 1995.
"Once Upon a Time" and "Intoxicated." In A. Dooling and K. Torgeson, eds., *Writing Women in Modern China: An Anthology of Women's Literature from the Early Twentieth Century.* New York: Columbia University Press, 1998, 179–95.

Liu Baiyu

Caoyuan shang (The Grassland: Short Stories). Shanghai: Wenhua shenghuo, 1937.
Dier ge taiyang (The Second Sun). Beijing: Renmin wenxue, 1987.
Liu Baiyu sanwen xuan ji (Selected Lyrical Essays by Liu Baiyu). Tianjin: Baihua wenyi, 1993.
Xinling de licheng (The Journey of the Soul: A Biography). Beijing: Jiefangjun wenyi, 1994.
Wutaishan xia (At the Foot of the Wutai Mountain). Chongqing: Shenghuo shudian, 1939.

* * *

Flames Ahead. Beijing: Foreign Languages Press, 1954.
Six A.M. and Other Stories. Beijing: Foreign Languages Press, 1953.
"Drums Like Spring Thunder." Tr. Sidney Shapiro. *Chinese Literature* 7 (1960): 71–75.
"The Glow of Youth," Tr. Gladys Yang and Yang Hsien-yi. *Chinese Literature* 11 (1959): 5–57.
"A Heart-warming Snowy Night." Tr. Sidney Shapiro. *Chinese Literature* 2 (1959): 3–13; also in *I Knew All Along and Other Stories by Contemporary Chinese Writers.* Beijing: Foreign Languages Press, 1960, 147–57.

"Landmark." *Chinese Literature* 9 (1960): 17–32.
"The Most Marvelous Day in Her Life." Tr. Gladys Yang. *Chinese Literature* 12 (1964): 54–61.
"Night on the Grassland." Tr. Gladys Yang. *Chinese Literature* 12 (1964): 54–61.
"On the Dusty Highway." Tr. Tang Sheng. *Chinese Literature* 3 (1955): 52–59; also trans. as "On the Dusty Road," by Lucy O. Yang Boler. In Kai-yu Hsu, ed., *Literature of the People's Republic of China.* Bloomington: Indiana University Press, 1980, 125–32.
"Sunrise." Tr. Gladys Yang. *Chinese Literature* 11 (1960): 33–37.
"Typhoon." Tr. Sidney Shapiro. *Chinese Literature* 5 (1960): 3–11.

Liu Bannong

Liu Bannong shixuan (Poems by Liu Bannong). Beijing: Renmin wenxue, 1958.
Liu Bannong daibiao zuo (Selected Works by Liu Bannong). Zhengzhou: Huanghe wenyi, 1987.
Liu Bannong de Wafu ji (Tiles and Cauldrons). Beijing: Beixin, 1926.

Liu Heng

Bai wo (White Whirls). Wuhan: Changjaing wenyi, 1992.
Canghe bairimeng (*Green River Daydreams*). Beijing: Zuojia, 1993.
Fuxi fuxi (Forbidden Love). Beijing: Zuojia, 1993.
Gouri de liangshi (*Dogshit Food*). Beijing: Zuojia, 1993.
Heide xue (*Black Snow*). Beijing: Zuojia, 1993.

* * *

"Dogshit Food." Tr. Sabina Knight. In Joseph S. M. Lau and Howard Goldblatt, eds., *The Columbia Anthology of Modern Chinese Literature.* New York: Columbia University Press, 1995, 416–428.
Black Snow. Tr. Howard Goldblatt. New York: Atlantic Monthly Press, 1993.
Green River Daydreams: A Novel. Tr. Howard Goldblatt. New York: Grove Press, 2001.
The Obsessed. Tr. David Kwan. Beijing: Panda Books, 1991.

Liu Na'ou

Dushi fengjingxian (The Skylines of the City). Shanghai: Shuimo shudian, 1930.
Liu Na'ou xiaoshuo quan bian (Collection of Fiction by Liu Na'ou). Shanghai: Xuelin, 1997.

Liu Suola

Hundun jia ligeleng (*Chaos and All That*). Beijing: Zhongguo huaqiao, 1994.
Ni bie wu xuanze (You Have No Choice). Beijing: Taihai, 2001.

Nüzhen tang (The Soup of Female Chastity). Fuzhou: Haixia wenyi, 2003.
Xunzhao ge wang (*In Search of the King of Singers*). Changchun: Shidai wenyi, 2001.

* * *

Blue Sky, Green Sea and Other Stories. Tr. Martha Cheung. Hong Kong: Research Center for Translation, Chinese University of Hong Kong, 1993.
Chaos and All That: An Irreverent Novel. Tr. Richard King. Honolulu: Hawaii University Press, 1994.
"In Search of the King of Singers." Tr. Martha Cheung. *Renditions* 27/28 (1987): 208–34.

Liu Xinwu

Banzhuren (*The Class Counsellor*). Beijing: Zhongguo qingnian, 1979.
Gonggong qiche yongtandiao (*Bus Aria*). Beijing: Beijing renmin, 1986.
Zhonggu lou (*The Bell and Drum Towers*). Beijing: Beijing renmin, 1985.
Sipai lou (Sipai Tower). Shanghai: Shanghai wenyi, 2004.

* * *

Black Walls and Other Stories. Hong Kong: Chinese University of Hong Kong, 1990.
"The Bell and the Drum Towers." In Jianing Chen, ed. *Themes in Contemporary Chinese Literature.* Beijing: New World Press, 1993, 93–204.
"Bus Aria." Tr. Stephen Fleming. *Chinese Literature* (Winter 1986): 81–114.
"Class Counsellor" and "Awake, My Brother!" Trs. Geremie Barme and Bennett Lee. In *The Wounded: New Stories of the Cultural Revolution.* Hong Kong: Joint Publishing, 1979, 147–204.
"I Love Every Green Leaf." Tr. Betty Ting. In *Prize Winning Stories from China 1978–1979.* Beijing: Foreign Languages Press, 1981, 455–73.
"Overpass." In Helen F. Siu and Zelda Stern, eds., *Mao's Harvest: Voices from China's New Generation.* New York: Oxford University Press, 1983, 29–90.
"Ruyi." Tr. Richard Rigby. *Renditions* 25 (1986): 53–85.

Liu Yichang

Jiutu (An Alcoholic). Hong Kong: Haibing, 1963.
Si nei (In the Temple). Taipei: Youshi wenhua, 1977.
Taoci (Chinaware). Hong Kong: Wenxue yanjiushe, 1979.
Tiantang yu diyu (Heaven and Hell). Guangzhou: Huacheng, 1981.

* * *

The Cockroach and Other Stories. Hong Kong: Renditions, 1995.
"Intersection." Tr. Nancy Li. *Renditions* 29/30 (1988): 84–101.

Liu Zhenyun

Guanchang (The Corridors of Power). Beijing: Huayi, 1992.

Guxiangmian he huaduo (Hometown Noodles and Flowers). Beijing: Huayi, 1993.

Guxiang tianxia huanghua (Hometown Filled with Yellow Flowers). Beijing: Zhongguo qingnian, 1991.

Guxiang xiangchu liuchuan (Hometown Interacting with Legends). Beijing: Huayi, 1993.

Shouji (Cell Phone). Wuhan: Changjiang wenyi, 2003.

Wo jiao Liu Yuejin (My Name Is Liu Yuejin). Wuhan: Zhangjiang wenyi, 2007.

Yidi jimao (Ground Covered with Chicken Feathers). Beijing: Zhongguo qingnian, 1992.

Yiqiang feihua (All Bullshit). Beijing: Zhongguo gongren, 2002.

* * *

Stories in Paul White et al., eds./trs., *The Corridors of Power*. Beijing: Panda Books, 1994.

Lu Ling

Caizhu de ernümen (Sons and Daughters of a Landlord). Chongqing: Xiwang, 1945.

Chu xue (The First Snow). Yinchuan: Ningxia renmin, 1981.

Ji'e de Guo Su'e (The Hungry Guo Su'e). Guilin: Nantian, 1943.

Lu Ling juzuo xuan (Selected Plays of Lu Ling). Beijing: Zhongguo xiju, 1986.

Ranshao de huangdi (The Burning Waste Land). Shanghai: Zuozhe zhijia, 1950.

Yunque (Skylark). Shanghai: Xiwang, 1948.

* * *

"The Coffins." Tr. Jane Parrish Yang. In Joseph S. M. Lau et al., *Modern Chinese Stories and Novellas, 1919–1949*. New York: Columbia University Press, 1981, 510–26.

"First Snow." *Chinese Literature* 3 (1954).

Lü Lun

Hei Lila (Dark Lila). Shanghai: Zhongguo tushu, 1941.

Lianqü erchongzou (Love Duet). Hong Kong: Yimei, 1955.

Qiong xiang (A Destitute Neighborhood). Hong Kong: Wenyuan, 1953.

Wujin de ai (Boundless Love). Hong Kong: Hongyun, 1947.

Lu Qiao

She chen ju (Living in the Mundane World). Taipei: Shibao wenhua, 1998.
Wei yang ge (The Unfinished Song). Taipei: Shangwu, 1980.

Lu Wenfu

Er yu Zhou Tai (Running into Zhou Tai Twice). Shanghai: Shanghai wenyi, 1964.
Lu Wenfu daibiao zuo (Representative Works of Lu Wenfu). Zhengzhou: Huanghe wenyi, 1987.
Ren zhi wo (Shelters). Shanghai: Shanghai wenyi, 1995.
Shen xiang de pipa sheng (Music from Deep in the Alleys). Shanghai: Shanghai wenyi, 2005.
Wei qiang (*The Boundary Wall*). Tianjin: Baihua wenyi, 1984.
Xiao xiang shenchu (*Deep within a Lane*). Shanghai: Shanghai wenyi, 1980.

* * *

The Gourmet and Other Stories of Modern China. London: Readers International, 1979.
A World of Dreams. Beijing: Chinese Literature, 1986. [includes "A Weak Light," "Deep within a Lane," "Tang Qiaodi," "The Man From the Peddler's Family," "The Boundary Wall," "The Gourmet," "The Doorbell," and "A World of Dreams"]

Lu Xing'er

Ah, Qingniao (*Oh, Blue Bird*). Beijing: Shiyue wenyi, 1984.
Huilou li de tonghua (Fairy Tales in a Grey Building). Taiyuan: Beiyue wenyi, 1989.
Liu gei shiji de wen (A Kiss to the Century). Beijing: Shiyue wenyi, 1988.
Nüren bu tiansheng (No One Is Born to Be a Woman). Shanghai: Shanghai wenyi, 1989.
Nüren de guize (Women's Rules). Shijiangzhuang: Hebei Jiaoyu, 1995.

* * *

Oh! Blue Bird. Beijing: Panda Books, 1993.
The Mountain Flowers Have Bloomed Quietly. Beijing: Panda Books, 2005.
"The One and the Other." Tr. Joyce Song. *Chinese Literature* (Winter 1990): 60–73.
"The Sun Is Not Out Today." In Zhu Hong, ed./tr., *The Serenity of Whiteness: Stories by and about Women in Contemporary China*. New York: Ballantine

Books, 1991, 188–207. "Under One Roof." Tr. Shi Xiaojin. *Chinese Literature* (Winter 1990): 45–59.

Lu Xun (Lu Hsun)

Gushi xinbian (Old Tales Retold). Shanghai: Wenhua yu shenghuo, 1936.
Nahan (Call to Arms). Beijing: Beijing daxue xinchao she, 1923.
Panghuang (Wandering). Beijing: Beixin, 1926.
Yecao ji (Wild Grass). Beijing: Beixin, 1927.
Zhaohua xishi (Dawn Blossoms Plucked at Dusk). Beijing: Weimin, 1928.

* * *

Complete Poems: A Translation with Introduction and Annotation. Tr. David Y. Ch'en. Tempe: Center for Asian Studies, Arizona State University, 1988.
Dawn Blossoms Plucked at Dusk. Trs. Hsien-yi Yang and Gladys Yang. Peking: FLP, 1976.
Diary of a Madman and Other Stories. Tr. William Lyell. Honolulu: University of Hawaii Press, 1990.
Selected Stories of Lu Xun [English-Chinese edition]. Trs. Yang Xianyi and Gladys Yang. Beijing: Foreign Languages Press, 2000.
The True Story of Ah Q. Trs. Yang Xianyi and Gladys Yang. Boston: Cheng and Tsui, 1999.

Lu Yao

Ren sheng (Life). Beijing: Zhongguo qingnian, 1982.
Pingfan de shijie (An Ordinary World), vol. 1. Beijing: Zhongguo wenlian, 1986.
Lu Yao xiaoshuo ming zuo xian (Selected Novellas by Lu Yao). Beijing: Huaxia, 1995.

Lu Yin

Haibing guren (An Old Acquaintance by the Sea). Shanghai: Shangwu, 1925.
Lu Yin zizhuan (Autobiography of Lu Yin). Shanghai: Diyi, 1934.
Manli (A Woman Named Manli). Beijing: Beiping wenhua xueshe, 1927.
Meigui de ci (The Thorn of the Roses). Shanghai: Zhonghua shuju, 1933.
Nüren de xin (The Heart of a Woman). Shanghai: Shishe chubanbu, 1933.
Xiangya jiezhi (An Ivory Ring). Beijing: Shangwu, 1930.

* * *

"After Victory." In A. Dooling and K. Torgeson, eds./trs., *Writing Women in Modern China: An Anthology of Women's Literature from the Early Twentieth Century*. New York: Columbia University Press, 1997, 143–56.

"Autobiography (Excerpts)." Tr. Kristina Torgeson. In Janet Ng and Janice Wickeri, eds., *May Fourth Women Writers: Memoirs*. Hong Kong: Renditions, 1997, 94–119.

"News from the Seashore—A Letter to Shi Pingmei." In A. Dooling and K. Torgeson, eds./trs., *Writing Women in Modern China: An Anthology of Women's Literature from the Early Twentieth Century*. New York: Columbia University Press, 1997, 139–41.

Luo Fu

Piao mu (Drifwood). Taipei: Lianhe wenxue, 2001.
Shijian zhi shang (Scars of Time). Taipei: Shulin, 1993.
Xuebeng: Luo Fu shi xuan (Avalanche: Poems by Luo Fu). Taipei: Shulin, 1994.
Yiduo wu he (One Lotus Flower at Noon). Taipei: Jiuge, 1979.
Yinwei feng de yuangu: Luo Fu shi xuan 1955–1987 (All Because of the Wind: Poems by Luo Fu 1955–1987). Taipei: Jiuge, 1988.
Yueguang fangzi (Moonlit House). Taipei: Jiuge, 1990.

* * *

Death of a Stone Cell. Tr. John Balcom. Monterey, CA: Taoren Press, 1993.
Selected Poems of Lo Fu. Trs. Wai-lim Yip et al. Taipei: Flowers of Poetry Press, 1992.
Poems in Dominic Cheung, ed./tr., *The Isle Full of Noises: Modern Chinese Poetry from Taiwan*. New York: Columbia University Press, 1987, 62–72.

Luo Yijun

Disange wuzhe (The Third Dancer). Taipei: Lianhe wenxue, 1999.
He xiao xing shuo tonghua (Telling Fairy Tales to Little Stars). Taipei: Huangguan, 1994.
Hong zi tuan (The League of the Red Letter). Taipei: Lianhe wenxue, 1992.
Qi meng gou (Wife Dreaming of the Dog). Taipei: Yuanzun wenhua, 1998.
Qian beihuai (Expressions of Sorrow). Taipei: Maitian, 2001.
Wo'ailuo (Gaara). Taipei: INK, 2004.
Women (Us). Taipei: INK, 2004.
Women zi ye'an de jiuguan likai (At Night We Left a Dark Pub). Taipei: Huangguan, 1993.

Xixia lüguan (The Hotel of the Ancient Xixia Empire). Taipei: INK, 2008.
Yuanfang (Faraway). Taipei: INK, 2003.
Yueqiu xingshi (The Moon Tribe). Taipei: Lianhe wenxue, 2000.

Ma Feng

Cun chou (*Vendetta*). Beijing: Sanlian, 1950.
Ma Feng Wenji (Collected Works by Ma Feng). 6 vols. Beijing: Dazhong wenyi, 2000.
Taiyang ganggang chushan (*The Sun Has Risen*). Taiyuan: Shanxi renmin, 1961.
Wo de diyige shangji (My First Boss). Beijing: Renmin wenxue, 1958.
Women cun de nianqingren (The Young People in Our Village). Taiyuan: Shanxi renmin, 1959.

* * *

The Sun Has Risen. Beijing: Foreign Languages Press, 1961.
Vendetta. Beijing: Chinese Literature Press, 1989.

Ma Jian

Fasheng Guanxi (Relationship). Hong Kong: Xin shiji, 1997.
Jiutiao Chalu (Nine Crossroads). Taipei: Yuanliu, 1995.
Lamian zhe (*The Noodle Maker*). Hong Kong: Tiandi, 1994.
Langji Zhongguo (Wandering in China). Beijing: Xin shijie, 2002.
Rensheng Banlü (Companions for Life). Hong Kong: Xin shiji, 1996.

* * *

Beijing Coma: A Novel. Tr. Flora Drew. New York: Farrar, Straus and Giroux, 2008.
The Noodle Maker. London: Chatto and Windus, 2004.
Red Dust: A Path through China. Tr. Flora Drew. London: Chatto and Windus, 2001.
Stick Out Your Tongue. Tr. Flora Drew. New York: Farrar, Straus and Giroux, 2006.

Ma Lihua

Linghun xiang feng (The Soul Is like the Wind). Beijing: Zuojia, 1994.
Wo de taiyang (My Sun). Beijing: Renmin wenxue, 1988.
Xixing Ahli (Travel West to Ahli). Beijing: Zuojia, 1992.
Zangbei youli (*Glimpses of Northern Tibet*). Beijing: Jiefangjun wenyi, 1990.

Zangdong hong shanmai (The Red Mountains of Eastern Tibet). Beijing: Zhonguo shehui kexue, 2002.

* * *

Glimpses of Northern Tibet. Beijing: Chinese Literature Press, 1991.

Ma Yuan

Liangge nanren (Two Men). Haikou: Nanhai, 2000.
You shen (The Wandering Spirit). Hangzhou: Zhejiang wenyi, 2001.
Ximalaya gu ge (The Ancient Ballads of the Himalayas). Kunming: Yunnan renmin, 2003.
Xugou (*A Fiction*). Beijing: Zuojia, 1997.

* * *

"More Ways Than One to Make a Kite." Tr. Zhu Hong; "A Wandering Spirit." Tr. Caroline Mason. In Jing Wang, ed., *China's Avant-garde Fiction.* Durham, NC: Duke University Press, 1998, 246–83.
Stories in Herbert Batt, ed./tr., *Tales of Tibet: Sky Burials, Prayer Wheels, and Wind Horses.* Lanham, MD: Rowman & Littlefield, 2001, 5–76. [includes "Vagrant Spirit," "A Fiction," and "A Ballad of the Himalayas"]
Stories in Frank Stewart and Herbert J. Batt, eds. *The Mystified Boat and Other New Stories from China.* Special issue of *Manoa: A Pacific Journal of International Writing* 15, 2 (Winter 2003). Honolulu: University of Hawaii Press, 2004. [includes "The Master," "The Black Road," and "Under the Spell of the Gangtise Mountains"]
Stories in Henry Zhao, ed., *The Lost Boat: Avant-garde Fiction from China.* London: Wellsweep, 1993, 29–42; 101–44. [includes "Fabrications" and "Mistakes"]

Mang Ke

Mang Ke shi xuan. Beijing: Zhonguo wenlian, 1989.
Jintian shi na yi tian (What Day Is It Today). Beijing: Zuojia, 2001.
Yangguang zhong de xiangrikui (The Sunflower in the Sunlight). Guilin: Lijiang, 1988.
Ye shi (Wild Affairs). Beijing: Zuojia, 2001.

* * *

"A Poem Presented to October." Trs. Gordon T. Osing and De-An Wu Swihart. *Salt Hill* 5 (1998).

Mao Dun

Dongyao (Wavering). Shanghai: Shangwu, 1928.
Huanmie (Disillusion). Shanghai: Shangwu, 1928.
Zhuiqiu (Aspirations). Shanghai: Shangwu, 1928.
Ziye. (*Midnight*). Shanghai: Kaiming shudian, 1932.

* * *

Midnight. Beijing: Foreign Languages Press, 1979.
Rainbow. Berkeley: University of California Press, 1992.
Spring Silkworms and Other Stories by Mao Dun. Tr. Sydney Shapiro. Beijing: Chinese Literature Press, 1979.
The Vixen. Beijing: Panda Books, 1987.

Mei Niang

Mei Niang jin zuo ji shujian (Recent Essays and Letters by Mei Niang). Beijing: Tongxin, 2005.
Mei Niang xiaoshuo sanwen ji (Selected Stories and Essays by Mei Niang). Beijing: Beijing chubanshe, 1997.
Yu (Fish). Beijing: Xinmin yinshuguan, 1943.
Di'er dai (The Second Generation). Changchun: Yizhi shudian, 1940.
Xiajie ji (Young Ladies). Changchun: Yizhi shudian, 1936.
Xie (Crab). Beijing: Huabei zuojia xiehui, 1944.

Metso

Ren zai gaochu (At the Summit). Xi'an: Shaanxi shifan daxue, 2001.
Shexiang zhi ai (The Love of Muskiness). Lhasa: Xizang renmin, 2007.
Taiyang buluo (The Sun Tribe). Beijing: Zhongguo wenlian, 1995.
Taiyang shi (The Sun Stone). Xi'an: Taibai wenyi, 2005.
Yueliang yingdi (The Moon Camp). Beijing: Zhongguo wenlian, 2001.
Zangdi renfang: sange Kangba hanzi he yige Anduo nüzi de youli (Fragrant Tibet: Travels of Three Kham Men and One Amdo Woman). Qingdao: Qingdao, 2006.

Mo Yan

Feng ru fei tun (*Big Breasts and Wide Hips*). Beijing: Zuojia, 1996.
Hong gaoliang (*Red Sorghum*). Beijing: Zuojia, 1994.
Jiu guo (*Republic of Wine*). Haikou: Hainan, 2000.

Pilao shengsi (Fatigue of Life and Death). Beijing: Zuojia, 2006.
Tanxiang xing (Sandalwood Torture). Beijing: Zuoja, 2001.
Tiantang suantai zhi ge (*The Garlic Ballads*). Beijing: Zuojia, 1988.

* * *

Big Breasts and Wide Hips. Tr. Howard Goldblatt. New York: Arcade Pub., 2004.
Explosions and Other Stories. Trs. Janice Wickeri and Duncan Hewitt. Hong Kong: Renditions Paperbacks, 1991.
The Garlic Ballads. Tr. Howard Goldblatt. New York: Viking; London: Penguin, 1995.
Red Sorghum. Tr. Howard Goldblatt. London: Heinemann; New York: Viking, 1993.
The Republic of Wine: A Novel. Tr. Howard Goldblatt. New York: Arcade Pub., 2000.

Mu Dan

Qi (Flag). Shanghai: Wenhua shenghuo, 1948.
Tanxian dui (The Expedition). Kunming: Chongwen yinshuguan, 1945.
She de youhuo (The Temptation of the Snake). Zhulai: Zhulai chubanshe, 1997 (reissue).
Mu Dan shi ji 1939–1945 (Poems by Mu Dan 1939–1945). Beijing: Renmin wnexue chubanshe, 2001.

* * *

"Mu Tan: Eleven Poems." Tr. Pang Bingjun. *Renditions* 21/22 1984: 252–72.

Mu Shiying

Baijing de nüti shuxiang (The Platinum Female Statue). Shanghai: Xiandai, 1934. Rpt. Shanghai: Shanghai shudian, 1988.
Gong mu (The Public Cemetery). Shanghai: Shagnhai shuju, 1933.
Hei Mudan (Black Rose). Shaghai: Liangyou, 1934.
Nanbei ji (The North and South Poles). Shanghai: Hufeng, 1932.

* * *

"Black Whirlwind." Tr. Wiu-kit Wong. *Renditions* 37 (Spring 1992).
"Five in a Nightclub." Tr. Randy Trumbull. *Renditions* 37 (Spring 1992).
"The Shanghai Foxtrot (a fragment)." Tr. Sean Macdonald. *Modernism/Modernity* 11, 4 (Nov. 2004): 797–807.

Ni Kuang

Chen chuan (The Sunken Boat). Hong Kong: Mingchuang, 1985.
Dier zhong ren (The Second Kind of People). Hong Kong: Mingchuang, 1981.
Lan xue ren (Blue-blooded Man). Hong Kong: Mingchuang, 1985.
Mingyun (Fate). Hong Kong: Mingchuang, 1997.
Xun meng (Chasing a Dream). Hong Kong: Mingchuang, 1987.

* * *

"Antiques Alley: Two Short Stories." Tr. Don J. Cohn. *Renditions*, 29/30 (1988): 146–54.

Nie Gannu

Liang tiao lu (Two Roads). Shanghai: Qunyi, 1949.
Gannu xiaoshuo ji (Short Stories by Nie Gannu). Changsha: Hunan renmen, 1981.
Gannu sanwen (Lyrical Essays by Nie Gannu). Beijing: Renmin wenxue, 1981.
Gannu zawen xuan (Essays by Nie Gannu). Beijing: Renmin wenxue, 1955.
Nie Gannu quan ji (Complete Works of Nie Gannu). 10 vols. Wuhan: Wuhan chubanshe, 2004.

Nie Hualing

Lu yuan qingshi (Love at the Deer Corral). Taipei: Shibao, 1996.
Meng gu ji (Valley of Dreams). Hong Kong: Zhengwen chubanshe, 1965.
Qian shan wan shui chang liu (Beyond the Mountains, Forever Flows the River). Chengdu: Sichuan wenyi chubanshe, 1984.
San sheng san shi (Three Lives in Three Worlds). Tianjin: Baihua wenyi, 2004.
Sanshi nian hou (Home-return Thirty Years Later). Wuhan: Hubei renmin, 1980.
Sangqing yu Taohong (*Mulberry and Peach: Two Women of China*). Hong Kong: Youlian, 1976.
Shiqu Jin Lingzi (Losing Jing Lingzi). Taipei: Xueshen shuju, 1960.

* * *

Mulberry and Peach: Two Women of China. Trs. Jane Parish Yang and Linda Lappin. New York: The Feminist Press at CUNY, 1998; originally published by Beacon Press, Boston, 1988.

Ouyang Jianghe

Shiji mo de zhuiwen: 1900–2000 (Trace the Last Century). Zhengzhou: Daxiang, 2000.
Shui qu shui liu (Who Will Leave and Who Will Stay). Changsha: Hunan wenyi, 1997.

Touguo ciyu de boli: Ouyang Jianghe shi xuan (Through the Glass of Words: Poem by Ouyang Jianghe). Beijing: Gaige, 1997.
Zhan zai xugou zhe bian (On the Side of Fabrication). Shanghai: Sanlian, 2001.

* * *

"Our Hunger, Our Sleep." Trs. Yanbing Chen and John Rosenwald. In Henry Y. H. Zhao, Yanbing Chen, and John Rosenwald, eds., *Fissures: Chinese Writing Today*. Brookline, MA: Zephyr Press, 2000, 259–62.

Ouyang Shan

Gao Ganda (Gao Ganda). Hebei: Huabei xinhua shudian, 1947.
Ku dou (The Bitter Struggle), vol. 2 of *Yidai fengliu*. Guangzhou: Guangdong renmin, 1962.
Liu an hua ming (Light at the End of the Tunnel), vol. 3 of *Yidai fengliu*. Beijing: Renmin wenxue, 1981.
Meigui can le (The Roses Have Faded). Shanghai: Guanghua shudian, 1927.
Sanjia xiang (*Three-Family Lane*), vol. 1 of *Yidai fengliu* (A Whole Generation of Heroes). Guangzhou: Guangdong renmin, 1959.
Sheng di (The Sacred Land), vol. 4 of *Yidai fengliu*. Beijing: Renmin wenxue, 1985.
Taojun de qingren (Taojun's Lover). Shanghai: Guanghua, 1928.
Wannian chun (Eternal Spring), vol. 5 of *Yidai fengliu*. Guangzhou: Huacheng, 1985.

* * *

The Bright Future. Tr. Tang Sheng. Beijing: Foreign Languages Press, 1958.
Uncle Gao. Beijing: Foreign Languages Press, 1957.
"Three-Family Lane." *Chinese Literature* 5 (1961): 2–71; 6 (1961): 3–68.

Ouyang Yuqian

Ouyang Yuqian juzuo xuan (Collection of Plays by Ouyang Yuqian). Beijing: Renmin wenxue, 1956.
Pan Jinlian (Pan Jinlian: A Seductress). Shanghai: Xin dongfang, 1928.
Tao hua san (The Peach-Blossom Fan). Beijing: Zhongguo xiju chubanshe, 1957.
Yu mo (The Demon of Desire). Shanghai: Guomin shudian, 1939.

* * *

"Pan Chinlian." In Edward Gunn, ed., *Twentieth-Century Chinese Drama: An Anthology*. Bloomington: Indiana University Press, 1983, 52–75.

Ouyang Zi

Ouyang Zi ji (Collection of Short Stories by Ouyang Zi). Taipei: Qianwei, 1993.
Na chang toufa de nühai (That Long-Haired Girl). Taipei: Dalin, 1983.
Qiu ye (Autumn Leaves). Taipei: Erya, 1980.

* * *

"Meijung." Tr. Alexander Moosa. *The Chinese Pen* (Winter 1979): 68–85.

"The Net." Tr. the Author. In Joseph S. M. Lau, ed., *The Unbroken Chain: An Anthology of Taiwan Fiction Since 1926*. Bloomington: Indiana University Press, 1983, 185–94.

"Perfect Mother." Tr. Chu Limin. In Chi Pang-yuan et al., eds., *An Anthology of Contemporary Chinese Literature*. Taipei: National Institute for Compilation and Translation, 1975, II, 357–74.

"Prodigal Father." Tr. the Author. *The Chinese Pen* (Autumn 1974): 50–64.

"Vase." Tr. Chu Limin. In Chi Pang-yuan et al., eds., *An Anthology of Contemporary Chinese Literature*. Taipei: National Institute for Compilation and Translation, 1975, II, 345–56.

"The Wooden Beauty." Tr. Sally Lindfors. *The Chinese Pen* (Summer 1984): 74–82.

Pan Jun

Dubai yu shoushi (Soliloquy and Hand Gestures). Beijing: Renmin wenxue, 2000.

Feng (Wind). Zhengzhou: Henan renmin, 1993.

Pan Jun shiyan zuopin ji (Collection of Pan Jun's Experimental Works). 2 vols. Guangzhou: Huacheng, 2000.

Riyun (Solar Halo). Beijing: Renmin wenxue, 1989.

Sixing baogao (A Report on the Death Penalty). Beijing: Renmin wenxue, 2004.

Ping Lu

Wu yin feng xian (The Fifth Seal: A Collection of Short Stories). Taipei: Yuanshen, 1988.

Yumi tian zhi si (*Death in a Cornfield*). Beijing: Renmin wenxue, 1992.

* * *

"Death in a Cornfield." Tr. Chou Chang Jun-mei. *The Chinese Pen* (Winter 1985): 1–30.

"The Fifth Seal" (Wu yin feng xian). Tr. Nancy Du. *The Chinese Pen* (Summer 1994).

"Five Paths Through the Dusty World" (Hongchen wuzhu). Tr. Daniel J. Bauer. *The Chinese Pen* (Summer 1993); also in Pang-yuan Chi, ed., *Taiwan Literature in Chinese and English*. Taipei: Commonwealth Publishing, 1999, 155–76.

"The Legend of Master Hau." Tr. Nancy Du. *The Chinese Pen* (Summer 1995).

"The Name of the Isle" (Daoyu de mingzi). Tr. Gregory Gonsoulin. *Taiwan Literature English Translation Series* 1 (Aug. 1996).

Qian Zhongshu

Ren shou gui (Humans, Animals, and Ghosts). Shanghia: Kaiming, 1946.
Wei cheng (*Fortress Besieged*). Shanghai: Chenguang, 1947.

* * *

Cat: A Translation and Critical Introduction. Hong Kong: Joint Publishing, 2001.
Fortress Besieged. Trs. Jeanne Kelly and Nathan Mao. Bloomington: University of Indiana Press, 1979.
"The Inspiration." In Joseph S. M. Lau et al., eds., *Modern Chinese Stories and Novellas, 1919–1949.* New York: Columbia University Press, 1981.
"The Souvenir." In Joseph S. M. Lau et al., eds., *Modern Chinese Stories and Novellas, 1919–1949.* New York: Columbia University Press, 1981.
"Windows." Tr. Martin Woesler. In Woesler, ed., *20th Century Chinese Essays in Translation.* Bochum: Bochum University Press, 2000, 106–10.

Qideng Sheng

Bai ma (White Horse). Taipei: Yuanjing, 1986.
Cheng zhi mi (The Mystery of a City). Taipei: Yuanjing, 1986.
Jiangju (Impasse). Taipei: Yuanjing, 1986.
Jingshen binghuan (Mental Sickness). Taipei: Yuanjing, 1986.
Shahe bei ge (Sad Songs of the Sha River). Taipei: Yuanjing, 1976.
Wo ai hei yanzhu (I Love Black Eyes). Taipei: Yuanjing, 1986.
Yesu de yishu (Jesus' Art). Taipei: Hongfan, 1979.
Yindun zhe (The Loner). Taipei: Yuanjing, 1976.

* * *

"How Love Scatters: On the Publication of the First Collection of My Works." In Helmut Martin, ed., *Modern Chinese Writers: Self-Portrayals.* Armonk, NY: M.E. Sharpe, 1992, 196–202.

Qiong Yao

Chuang wai (Outside the Window). Taipei: Huangguan, 1989.
Huan zhu gege (The Princess Returning Pearls). Hong Kong: Huangguan, 1997.
Ji du xiyang hong (Sunsets). Huangguan, 1989.
Ting yuan shen shen (House with a Deep Courtyard). Taipei: Huangguan, 1969.
Yan yu meng meng (Rain and Mist). Taipei: Huangguan, 1975.
Yi lian you meng (A Curtain of Dreams). Taipei: Huangguan, 1990.

* * *

"In the Old Family House." Trs. Ren Zhong and Yuzhi Yang. In *Hometown and Childhood*. San Francisco: Long River Press, 2005, 115–22.

Qiu Miaojin

Gui de kuanghuan (Revelries of Ghosts). Taipei: Lianhe wenxue, 1991.
Eyu shouji (Notes of an Alligator). Taipei: Shibao, 1994.
Jimo de qunzhong (A Solitary Crowd). Taipei: Lianhe wenxue, 1995.
Mengmate yishu (Letters Written before Death). Taipei: Lianhe wenxue, 1996.
Qiu Miaojin riji (Diary of Qiu Miaojin). Taipei: INK, 2007.

Rou Shi

Eryue (February). Shanghai: Chunchao shuju, 1929. Rpt. Shanghai: Shanghai shudian, 1985.
Fengren (The Mad Man). Ningbo: Huasheng, 1925.
Jiu shidai zhi si (Death of the Old Era). Beijing: Beixin, 1929.

* * *

"A Slave Mother." In Harold Isaacs, ed., *Straw Sandals: Chinese Short Stories, 1918–1933*. Cambridge: MIT Press, 1974, 215–41.
"Threshold of Spring." Tr. Sidney Shapiro. *Chinese Literature* 6 (1963): 3–42; 7 (1963): 30–64.

Ru Zhijuan

Baihe hua (Lilies on the Quilt). Beijing: Renmin wenxue, 2000.

* * *

Lilies and Other Stories. Beijing: Panda Books, 1985.

San Mao

Beiying (Silhouette). Changsha: Hunan wenyi, 1987.
Daocao ren shouji (Notes of a Scarecrow). Hong Kong: Wuxingji, 1981.
Gungun hong chen (In the World of Desires). Hong Kong: Huangguan, 1991.
Kuqi de luotuo (A Sobbing Camel). Beijing: Zhongguo youyi, 1985.
Nao xue ji (Playing Truant). Hong Kong: Huangguan, 1991.
Sahala de gushi (The Sahara Tales). Hong Kong: Wuxingji, 1981.
Yu ji bu zai lai (The Rainy Season Will Not Come Again). Taipei: Huangguan, 1976.

* * *

"Nostalgia." Trs. Ren Zhong and Yuzhi Yang. In *Hometown and Childhood*. San Francisco: Long River Press, 2005, 21–24.

Sebo

Stories in Sebo, ed., *Zhizhe de chenmo* (The Silence of the Wise). Chengdu: Sichuan wenyi, 2002. [includes "Zai zheli shang chuan" (*Get the Boat Here*), "Huan ming" (Imagined Cry), "Xingqisan de gushi" (The Wednesday Story), "Bayue shi ge hao jijie" (August Is a Good Season), and "Nuobu Tsiring" (Nuobu Tsiring), 25–74.]

* * *

"The Circular Day." In Herbert Batt, ed./tr., *Tales of Tibet: Sky Burials, Prayer Wheels, and Wind Horses*. Lanham, MD: Rowman & Littlefield, 2001, 205–15.

"Get the Boat Here" *Manoa* 12, 2 (2000): 42–48.

Sha Ting

Huanxiang ji (Homecoming). Shanghai: Wenhua shenghuo, 1948.
Kun shou ji (Caged Animals). Chongqing: Xindi, 1945.
Tao jin ji (Gold Rush). Chongqing: Wenhua shenghuo, 1943.
Xiao Ai (Xiao Ai). Shanghai: Tianma, 1935.
Xiao cheng fengbo (Tempest in a Small Town). Chongqing: Dongfang, 1944.

* * *

"An Autumn Night." Tr. Gladys Yang. *Chinese Literature* 2 (1957): 88–98.
"The Contest." Tr. Gladys Yang. *Chinese Literature* 3 (1961): 61–77.
"The Way of the Beast." Tr. Ellen Yeung. In Helen Siu, ed., *Furrows: Peasants, Intellectuals and the State*. Stanford: Stanford University Press, 1990, 65–74.

Shen Congwen

Ba jun tu (The Portrait of Eight Stallions). Shanghai: Wenhua shenghuo, 1935.
Biancheng (Border Town). Shanghai: Wenhua shenghuo, 1934.
Fu fu (The Husband and Wife). Shanghai: Xin shidai, 1933.
Shan gui (The Mountain Spirit). Shanghai: Guanghua, 1928.
Yige nüjuyuan de shenghuo (The Life of an Actress). Shanghai: Dadong, 1931.

* * *

Imperfect Paradise: Fiction from Modern China. Ed. Jeffrey Kinkley. Honolulu: University of Hawaii Press, 1995.

Selected Short Stories of Shen Congwen [English-Chinese edition]. Tr. Jeffrey Kinkley. Hong Kong: Chinese University Press, 2004.

Shen Rong

Ren dao zhongnian: cong xiaoshuo dao dianying (At Middle Age: From Fiction to Film). Beijing: Zhongguo dianying, 1986.
Taizi cun de mimi (Secrets of Prince Village). Beijing: Renmin wenxue, 1983.
Yongyuan shi chuntian (Spring Forever). Beijing: Renmin wenxue, 1980.

* * *

At Middle Age. Beijing: Chinese Literature, 1987.
"The Freakish Girl." Tr. Gladys Yang. *Chinese Literature* (Spring 1988): 37–40.
"A Gift of Night Fragrance." Tr. Gladys Yang. *Chinese Literature* 5 (1989): 3–56.
"Ten Years Deducted." Tr. Gladys Yang. In Yang Bian, ed., *The Time Is Not Ripe: Contemporary China's Best Writers and Their Stories.* Beijing: Foreign Languages Press, 1991, 193–216.

Shi Shuqing (Shi Shu-ch'ing)

Naxie bumao de rizi (The Barren Years). Taipei: Hongfan, 1988.
Ta mingjiao hudie: Xianggang sanbuqu zhi yi (Her Name Is Butterfly: Hong Kong Trilogy, part 1). Taipei: Hongfan, 1993.
Bianshan yang zijing: Xianggang sanbuqu zhi er (Mountains Covered with Bauhinias: Hong Kong Trilogy, part 2). Taipei: Hongfan, 1995.
Jimo yunyuan: Xianggang sanbuqu zhi san (The Lonely Cloud Garden: Hong Kong Trilogy, part 3. Taipei: Hongfan, 1997.
Weiduoliya julebu (The Victoria Club). Taipei: Lianhe, 1998.
Weixun caizhuang (Blush of Intoxication). Taipei: Maitian, 1999.

* * *

The Barren Years and Other Short Stories and Plays. San Francisco: Chinese Materials Center, 1975.
City of the Queen: A Novel of Colonial Hong Kong. Trs. Howard Goldblatt and Sylvia Li-chun Lin. New York: Columbia University Press, 2005.

Shi Tiesheng

Bing xi suibi: Shi Tiesheng rensheng biji (Fragments Written between Illnesses: Essays on Life by Shi Tiesheng). Hong Kong: Sanlian, 2002.

Wo de yuaoyuan de qingpingwan (*My Far Away Qingpingwan*). Beijing: Shiyue wenyi, 1985.

Wuxu biji (Notes of Discussions of Impractical Matters). Shanghai: Shanghai wenyi, 1996.

* * *

Strings of Life. Beijing: Panda Books, 1991.

"Fate." In Carolyn Choa and David Su Li-qun, eds., *The Vintage Book of Contemporary Chinese Fiction*. New York: Vintage Books, 2001, 11–21.

"In the Temple of the Earth." Tr. Shi Junbao. *Chinese Literature* (Spring 1993): 105–17.

"Like a Banjo String." In Jeanne Tai, ed., *Spring Bamboo: A Collection of Contemporary Chinese Short Stories*. New York: Random House, 1989, 171–205.

"My Faraway Qingping Wan." Tr. Shen Zhen, *Chinese Literature* (Spring 1984): 61–76.

Shi Tuo

Yeniao ji (Wild Birds). Shanghai: Wenhua shenghuo, 1948.

Jiehun (Getting Married). Shanghai: Chenguang, 1949.

Guoyuan cheng ji (Records of an Orchard City). Shanghai: Shanghai chuban gongsi, 1946.

Lishi wuqing (History Is Unsympathetic). Shanghai: Shanghai chuban gongsi, 1951.

* * *

"Garden Balsam." Tr. Wang Ying. *Chinese Literature* 1 (Spring 1993): 118–122.

"A Kiss." In Theodore Huters, ed. *The Modern Chinese Short Story*. Armonk, NY: M.E. Sharpe, 1990.

Shi Zhecun

Beishan lou shi (Poems from the Northern Mountain Studio). Shangahi: Huadong shifan daxue, 2000.

Deng xia ji (Under the Light). Shanghai: Kaiming, 1937.

Jiangjun de tou (The General's Head). Shanghai: Xin zhongguo, 1932.

Meiyu zhi xi (*One Rainy Evening*). Shanghai: Xin zhongguo, 1936.

Shan nüren xingpin (The Character of a Kind Woman). Shanghai: Liangyou, 1933.

Shang yuan deng (Lanterns). Shanghai: Shuimo, 1929.

* * *

One Rainy Evening. Beijing: Panda Books, 1994.
"The True Oracle of the Pagoda." *Chinese Literature* 4 (Winter 1991): 131–45.
"The Waning Moon." In Chia-hua Yuan and Robert Payne, eds., *Contemporary Chinese Short Stories*. London: Noel Carrington, 1946, 41–47.

Shizhi

Shizhi (Guo Lusheng) Hei Dachun xiandai shuqingshi he ji (A Joint Collection of Lyric Poetry by Shizhi and Hei Dachun). Chengdu: Chengdu keji daxue, 1993.
Xiangxin weilai (Trust the Future). Guilin: Lijiang, 1988.

* * *

"Trust the Future." In David S. G. Goodman, ed., *Beijing Street Voices: The Poetry and Politics of China's Democracy Movement*. London: Marion Boyars, 1981, 139.

Shu Ting

Hui changge de yiweihua (The Singer Iris). Chengdu: Sichuan wenyi, 1986.
Shu Ting de shi (Poems by Shu Ting). Beijing: Renmin wenxue, 1994.

* * *

Mist of My Heart: Selected Poems of Shu Ting. Trs. Gordon T. Osing and De-an Wu Swihart. Ed. William O'Donnell. Beijing: Panda Books, 1995.
Shu Ting: Selected Poems. Ed. Eva Hung. Hong Kong: Renditions Paperbacks, 1994.

Shu Xiangcheng

Bali liang'an (On the Banks of the Seine). Hong Kong: Zhongliu, 1971.
Dushi shichao (City Poems). Hong Kong: Qishi niandai yuekanshe, 1972.
Jianku de xingcheng (An Arduous Journey). Hong Kong: Qishi niandai zazhishe, 1971.
Taiyang xiashan le (The Sun Has Set). Hong Kong: Nanyang, 1962.
Wu Xianggang (Misty Hong Kong). Hong Kong: Zhongnan, 1956.

* * *

"Seven Selected Poems." Tr. Eva Hung. *Renditions* 29/30 (Spring/Autumn 1988): 194–98.

Sima Changfeng

Shenggming de changliu: Sima Changfeng yizuo xuan (Life Goes On: Selected Essays by Sima Changfeng, posthumously published). Ed. Lin Jieqing. Hong Kong: Dangdai wenyi, 2004.

Su De

Ci malu shang wo yao shuo gushi (I Want to Tell Stories in the Streets). Hangzhou: Zhejiang wenyi, 2003.
Ganggui shang de aiqing (Love on the Rail). Changchun: Chunfeng wenyi, 2004.
Shu (Atonement). Shanghai: Shanghai yiwen, 2005.
Yan zhe wo huangliang de e (Along My Desolate Forehead). Beijing: Zhishi chubanshe, 2002.

Su Qing

Jiehun shinian (Ten Years of Marriage). Hefei: Anhui wenyi, 1997.
Su Qing wenji (Collected Works by Su Qing). 2 vols. Shanghai: Shanghai shudian, 1994.

* * *

"Waves." Tr. Cathy Silber. In Amy D. Dooling, ed., *Writing Women in Modern China: The Revolutionary Years, 1936–1976*. New York: Columbia University Press, 2005, 178–205.

Su Tong

Fengyangshu shange (The Song of Maple and Poplar Trees). Beijing: Zhognguo shehui kexue, 2001.
Hongfen (Rouge). Wuhan: Changjiang wenyi, 1992.
Mi (*Rice*). Hong Kong: Tiandi, 1992.
Qiqie chengqun (*Raise the Red Lantern*). Wuhan: Changjiang wenyi, 1992.
She weishenme hui fei (Why Can Snakes Fly). Kunming: Yunnan renmin, 2002.
Wo de diwang shengya (*My Life as Emperor*). Guagnzhou: Huacheng, 1993.
Yijiusansinian de taowang (The Escapes in 1934). Shanghai: Shanghai shehui kexue yuan, 1988.
Yingsu zhijia (The Poppy Growers). Shanghai: Shanghai wenyi, 2004.

* * *

My Life as Emperor. Tr. Howard Goldblatt. New York: Hyperion, 2005.
Raise the Red Lantern. Tr. Michael Duke. New York: William Morrow, 1993.
Rice. Tr. Howard Goldblatt. New York: William Morrow, 1995.
"The Brothers Shu." Tr. Howard Goldblatt. In Goldblatt, ed., *Chairman Mao Would Not Be Amused: Fiction from Today's China.* New York: Grove Press, 1995, 25–68.
"Death without a Burial Place." Trs. Karen Gernant and Chen Zeping. In Frank Stewart and Herbert J. Batt, eds., *The Mystified Boat and Other New Stories from China.* Special issue of *Manoa: A Pacific Journal of International Writing* 15, 2 (Winter 2003). Honolulu: University of Hawaii Press, 2004, 57–66.
"Flying Over Maple Village." Tr. Michael Duke. In Jing Wang, ed., *China's Avant-garde Fiction.* Durham, NC: Duke University Press, 1998, 147–59.

Su Weizhen

Aiqing rensheng (Life of Love). Taipei: Qianwei chubanshe, 1983.
Pei ta yi duan (Accompany Him Awhile). Taipei: Hongfan shudian youxian gongsi, 1983.
Fengbi de daoyu (An Island in Isolation). Taipei: Maitian chuban gufen youxian gongsi, 1996.
Chenmo zhi dao (An Island in Silence). Taipei: Shibao chuban qiye youxian gongsi, 1994.
Moshu shike (Magic Moment). Taipei: INK yinke chuban youxian gongsi, 2002.

* * *

"Broken Thread." Tr. Loretta C. Wang. *The Chinese Pen* (Autumn 1989): 69–91.
"Missing." Trs. Agnes Tang and Eva Hung. In Eva Hung, ed., *Contemporary Women Writers: Hong Kong and Taiwan.* Hong Kong: Renditions, 1990, 89–112.

Su Xuelin

Chantui ji (Cicada's Exuviations). Chongqing: Shangwu, 1945.
Fusheng shi ji (Ten Chapters of a Floating Life). Hefei: Anhui wenyi, 2005.
Ji xin (The Thorn Heart). Beijing: Beixin, 1929.
Lütian (The Green Sky) Beijing: Beixin, 1928.

* * *

"Harvest." In A. Dooling and K. Torgeson, eds., *Writing Women in Modern China: An Anthology of Women's Literature from the Early Twentieth Century.* New York: Columbia University Press, 1998, 201–7.

Sun Ganlu

Fangwen mengjing (Paying a Visit to Dreamland). Wuhan: Changjiang wenyi, 1993.
Huxi (Breathing). Guangzhou: Huacheng, 1997.
Qing nüren caimi (Inviting Women to Solve a Puzzle). *Shouhuo* 6, 1988.

* * *

"I Am a Young Drunkard." Tr. Kristina Torgeson. In Jing Wang, ed., *China's Avant-garde Fiction*. Durham, NC: Duke University Press, 1998, 235–45.

Sun Li

Baiyangdian Jishi (On the Baiyangdian Lake). Beijing: Zhongguo qingnian, 1958.
Cun ge (Rustic Songs). Beijing: Tianxia tushu, 1949.
Fengyun jishi (*Stormy Years*). Beijing: Renmin wenxue, 1951.
Tiemu qianzhuan (*Blacksmith and Carpenter*), vol. 1. Tianjin: Tianjin renmin, 1957.

* * *

Blacksmith and Carpenter. Trs. Sidney Shapiro and Gladys Yang. Beijing: Foreign Languages Press, 1982.
Lotus Creek and Other Stories. Beijing: Foreign Languages Press, 1982.
Selected Stories by Sun Li [English-Chinese edition]. Beijing: Chinese Literature Press, 1999.
Stormy Years. Beijing: Foreign Languages Press, 1982.

Tai Jingnong

Di zhi zi (Son of the Earth). Beijing: Renmin wenxue, 2000.
Jian ta zhe (The Man Who Built the Pagoda). Taipei: Yuanjing, 1990.
Longpo zawen (Essays by Tai Jingnong). Beijing: Sanlian, 2002.
Tai Jingnong shi ji (Selected Poems by Tai Jingnong). Hong Kong: Hanmoxuan, 2001.
Wo yu Laoshe yu jiu (Laoshe and I with Wine). Taipei: Lianjing, 1992.

Tang Ren

Beiyang junfa yanyi (Romance of the Northen Warlords). Changsha: Hunan renmin, 1985.
Fusheng ba ji (Eight Chapters of a Floating Life). Tianjin: Baijua wenyi, 1987.

Jinling chunmeng (Spring Dream at Nanjing). Shanghai: Shanghai wenhua, 1958.

Tashi Dawa

Gu hai lan jingfan (Blue Prayer Flags in the Ancient Sea). Kunming: Yunnan renmin, 2000.
Saodong de Xiangbala (The Turbulent Shambala). Beijing: Zuojia, 1993.
Xizang: Yinmi de suiyue (Tibet: The Hidden Years). Taipei: Yuanliu, 1991.

* * *

A Soul in Bondage: Stories from Tibet. Beijing: Panda Books, 1992.
"The Old Manor." Tr. Shi Junbao. *Chinese Literature* (Autumn 1991): 41–52.
"Over the River." Tr. Li Guoqing. *Chinese Literature* (Summer 1991): 3–10.
"Serenade on the Plateau." Tr. Yu Fanqin. In *Love That Burns on a Summer's Night.* Beijing: Chinese Literature Press, 1990, 77–87.
"The Silent Sage." Tr. Lei Ming. *Chinese Literature* (Autumn 1991): 53–57.
Stories in Herbet Batt, ed., *Tales of Tibet: Sky Burials, Prayer Wheels, and Wind Horses.* Lanham, MD: Rowman & Littlefield, 2001, 105–162. [includes "Tibet: A Soul Knotted on a Leather Thong," "The Glory of a Wind Horse," and "For Whom the Bell Tolls"]

Tian Han

Guan Hanqing (Playwright Guan Hanqing). Beijing: Zhongguo xiju chubanshe, 1958.
Tian Han xiju ji (Collection of Plays by Tian Han). Shanghai: Xiandai shuju, 1930.
Fu shi (The Floating Corpse). Shanghai: Shanghai zazhi gongsi, 1937.
Hui chun zhi qu (The Song of the Return of the Spring). Shanghai: Putong shudian, 1935.
Kafei dian zhi yi ye (One Night at the Café). Shanghai: Zhonghua shudian, 1924.
Liming zhi qian (Before Dawn). Shanghai: Beixin shuju, 1937.
Liren xing (Song of a Beauty). Beijing: Zhongguo xiju chubanshe, 1959.
Ming you zhi si (Death of a Famous Actor). Beijing xiju chubanshe, 1957.
Tian Han xiju ji (Collection of Plays by Tian Han). 5 vols. Shanghai: Xiandai shuju, 1933.

* * *

Kuang Han-ching: A Play [Guan Hanqing]. Beijing: Foreign Languages Press, 1961; also in Edward Gunn, ed., *Twentieth-Century Chinese Drama: An Anthology.* Bloomington: Indiana University Press, 1983, 324–80.

The White Snake: A Peking Opera. Trs. Yang and Yang. Beijing: Foreign Languages Press, 1957.

"The Night the Tiger Was Captured." Tr. Randy Barbara Kaplan. *Asian Theatre Journal* 11, 1 (1994): 1–34.

"One Evening in Soochow." In Ku Tsong-nee, ed., *Modern Chinese Plays.* Shanghai: The Commercial Press, 1941, 1–22.

"A West Lake Tragedy." In Ku Tsong-nee, ed., *Modern Chinese Plays.* Shanghai: The Commercial Press, 1941, 91–118.

Tie Ning

Ben hua (Native Cotton). Beijing: Renmin wenxue, 2006.

Da yu nü (A Woman Who Has Seen It All). Shenyang: Chunfeng wenyi, 2000.

Meiyou niukou de hong chenshan (A Red Shirt without Buttons). Beijing: Zhongguo qingnian, 1984.

Meigui men (Gate of Roses). Beijing: Zuojia, 1990.

Yongyuan you duoyuan (How Long Is Forever). Beijing: Jiefangjun wenyi, 2000.

* * *

Haystacks. Beijing: Panda Books, 1990.

"Ah, Fragrant Snow." Tr. Jianying Zha. *Fiction* 8, 2/3 (1987): 168–80.

Wang Anyi

Changhen ge (The Song of Everlasting Sorrow: A Novel of Shanghai). Beijing: Zuojia, 1999.

Jishi yu xugou (The Real and the Fictitious). Beijing: Renmin wenxue, 1993.

Qimeng shidai (The Era of Enlightenment). Beijing: Renmin wenxue, 2007.

Tao zhi yaoyao (The Dazzling Peach Blossoms). Shanghai: Shanghai wenyi, 2003.

Xiao baozhuan (Baotown). Shanghai: Shanghai wenyi, 1986.

* * *

Baotown. Tr. Martha Avery. New York: Viking Penguin, 1985.

Lapse of Time. Tr. Jeffrey Kinkley. San Francisco: China Books, 1988.

Love in Brocade Valley. Trs. Bonnie McDougall and Chen Maiping. New York: New Directions, 1992.

Love in a Small Town. Tr. Eva Hung. Hong Kong: Renditions, 1988.

Love on a Barren Mountain. Tr. Eva Hung. Hong Kong: Renditions, 1991.

The Song of Everlasting Sorrow: A Novel of Shanghai. Trs. Michael Berry and Susan Chan Egan. New York: Columbia University Press, 2008.

"Brothers." Tr. Diana B. Kingsbury. In *I Wish I Were a Wolf: The New Voice in Chinese Women's Literature.* Beijing: New World Press, 1994, 158–212.

"Death of an Artist." Tr. Hu Ying. In Frank Stewart and Herbert J. Batt, eds., *The Mystified Boat and Other New Stories from China*. Special issue of *Manoa: A Pacific Journal of International Writing* 15, 2 (Winter 2003). Honolulu: University of Hawaii Press, 2004, 135–41.

Wang Dingjun

Chang duan diao (Lyrics of Irregular Lines). Taipei: Wenxing, 1965.
Dan shen wen du (Body Heat of Unmarried Men). Taipei: Erya, 1988.
Feng yu yin qing: Wang Dingjun san wen jing xuan (Rain or Shine). Taipei: Erya, 2000.
Hai shui tian ya Zhongguo ren (The Ocean, the Edge of the Sky, and the Chinese). Taipei: Erya, 1982.
Kai fang de ren sheng (A Receptive Life). Taipei: Erya, 1975.
Kan bu tou de cheng shi (An Enigmatic City). Taipei: Erya, 1984.
Qingren yan (Lover's Eyes). Taipei: Dalin, 1970.
Ren sheng guan cha (Observations of Life). Taipei: Wenxing, 1965.
Shan li shan wai (Inside and Outside the Mountains). Taipei: Hongfan, 1984.
Sui liuli (Broken Colored Glaze). Taipei: Jiuge, 1978.
Wang Dingjun hui yi lu (Memoirs of Wang Dingjun). Taipei: Wushi tushu, 1995
Yishi liu (Stream of Consciousness). Taipei: Wushi tushu, 1990.
Shi shi yu qi (World Affairs and Chess). Taipei: Jingsheng wenwu gongsi, 1969.

* * *

"Footprints." Tr. David Pollard. In Pollard, ed., *The Chinese Essay*. New York: Columbia University Press, 2000, 300–03.
"The Last Word in Beauty and Ugliness." Tr. David Pollard. In Pollard, ed., *The Chinese Essay*. New York: Columbia University Press, 2000, 295–300.
"Marvelling at Life." Tr. Lily Liu. *The Chinese Pen* (Winter 1991): 26–32.
"On the Eve of Departure." Tr. Candice Pong. *The Chinese Pen* (Summer 1980): 43–54.
"A Patch of Sunlight." Tr. Nicolas Koss. In Pang-yuan Chi, ed., *Taiwan Literature in Chinese and English*. Taipei: Commonwealth Publishing, 1999, 1–26.
"Red Ribbons." Tr. Eve Markowitz. *The Chinese Pen* (Autumn 1979): 44–55.
"The Soil." Tr. Una Y. T. Chen. *The Chinese Pen* (Summer 1978): 57–78. Reprinted in Nancy Ing, ed., *Winter Plum: Contemporary Chinese Fiction*. Taipei: Chinese Materials Center, 1982, 393–411.
"The Wailing Chamber." Tr. Simon Chau. *Renditions* 8 (1977): 137–46.

Wang Hailing

Qian shou (Holding Your Hands). Beijing: Renmin wenxue, 1999.
Xin jiehun shidai (The Era of New Marriage). Wuhan: Changjiang wenyi, 2006.
Zhongguo shi lihun (Divorce: Chinese Style). Beijing: Beijing chubanshe, 2004.

Wang Jiaxin

Jinian (Rememberance). Wuhan: Changjiang wenyi, 1985.
Wang Jiaxin de shi (Poems by Wang Jiaxin). Beijing: Renmin wenxue, 2001.
Youdong xuanya (Moving over the Cliff). Changsha: Hunan wenyi, 1997.

* * *

Stairway: Selected Poems by Wang Jiaxin. Tr. John Cayley. London: Wellsweep, 1993. [available only as an electronic Expanded Book]
Poems in Wang Ping, ed., *New Generation: Poems from China Today.* New York: Hanging Loose Press, 1999, 119–21.

Wang Jingzhi

Hui zhi feng (Hui's Wind). Shanghai: Yadong tushuguan, 1922.
Jimo de guo (The Lonely Country). Shanghai: Kaiming, 1927.
Shi ershiyi shou (Twenty-one Poems). Beijing: Zuojia, 1958.
Yiyi xun—Wang Jingzhi qingshu (Ripples of Communications: Wang Jingzhi's Love Letters). Ed. Wang Baifei. Hangzhou: Zhejiang wenyi, 2002.

Wang Luyan

He bian (The Riverbank). Shanghai: Liangyou fuxing tushu, 1941.
Huangjin (Gold). Shanghai: Xin shengming shuju, 1928.
Lüren de xin (The Heart of the Traveler). Shanghai: Wenhua shenghuo, 1937.
Que shu ji (Sparrows and Mice). Shanghai: Wenhua shenghuo, 1935.
Tongnian de bei'ai (*The Sorrows of Childhood*). Shanghai: Wenhua shenghuo, 1931.
Wuding xia (Under the Roof). Shanghai: Xiandai shuju, 1934.
Ye huo (Wildfire) [*Fennu de xiangcun* (Enraged Countryside)]. Shanghai: Liangyou tushu, 1937.
Youzi (Grapefruit: Short Stories and Essays). Beijing: Beixin, 1926.

* * *

"On the Bridge" and "The Sorrows of Childhood" in Gladys Yang, tr. *Stories from the Thirties*, vol. 1. Beijing: Foreign Languages Press, 1982.

Wang Meng

Chouchu de jijie (The Season of Hesitation). Beijing: Renmin wenxue, 1995.
Dan huise de yanzhu—zai Yili (Light Grey Eyes—in Yili). Beijing: Zuojia, 1984.
Hu die (Butterfly). Taipei: Yuanjing, 1988.
Huodong bian renxing (Movement Shapes Human Figures). Beijing: Renmin wenxue, 1986.

Kuanghuan de jijie (The Season of Ecstasy). Beijing: Renmin wenxue, 2000.
Lian'ai de jijie (The Season of Love). Beijing: Renmin wenxue, 1993.
Qing hu (The Green Fox). Beijing: Renmin wenxue, 2004.
Qingchun wangsui (Long Live Youth). Beijing: Renmin wenxue, 1979.
Shilian de jijie (The Season of Abnormity). Beijing: Renmin wenxue, 1994.

* * *

Bolshevik Salute: A Modernist Chinese Novel. Tr. Wendy Larson. Seattle: University of Washington Press, 1990.
The Butterfly and Other Stories. Tr. Rui An. Beijing: Foreign Languages Press, 1983.
Snowball: Selected Works of Wang Meng, vol. 2. Trs. Cathy Silber and Deidre Huang. Beijing: Foreign Languages Press, 1989.
The Strain of Meeting: Selected Works of Wang Meng, vol. 1. Tr. Denis C. Mair. Beijing: Foreign Languages Press, 1989.
The Stubborn Porridge and Other Stories. Tr. Hong Zhu. New York: George Braziller, Inc., 1994.

Wang Pu

Bieren de chuangkou (The Windows of Others). Shanghai: Shanghai renmin, 1995.
Buchong jiyi (Supplementary Memories). Hong Kong: Tiandi tushu, 1997.
Nüren de gushi (Women's Stories). Shanghai: Baijia, 1992.
Xiang Meili zai Shanghai (Xiang Meili in Shanghai). Beijing: Renmin wenxue, 2005.
Xianggang nüren (Hong Kong Women). Shanghai: Dongfang chuban zhongxin, 2003.
Yao Jiu chuanqi (The Story of My Uncle). Hong Kong: Tiandi tushu, 1999.
Zhengli chouti (Cleaning Up the Drawers). Hong Kong: Tiandi tushu, 1995.

Wang Shuo

Wan'r de jiushi xintiao (*Playing for Thrills*). Beijing: Zuojia, 1989.
Wo shi ni baba (I Am Your Dad). Taipei: Maitian, 1993.

* * *

Playing for Thrills. Tr. Howard Goldblatt. New York: William Morrow, 1998.
Please Don't Call Me Human. Tr. Howard Goldblatt. New York: Hyperion East, 2000.

Wang Tongzhao

Chun hua (Spring Blossoms). Shanghai: Liangyou tushu, 1936.
Chun yu zhi ye (Spring Night in the Rain). Shanghai: Shangwu, 1930.

Yi ye (One Leaf). Shanghai: Shangwu, 1922.
Huanghun (At Dusk). Shanghai: Shangwu, 1926.
Shan yu (Rain in the Mountain). Shanghai: Kaiming shudian, 1933.
Tong xin (The Innocence of a Child). Shanghai: Shangwu, 1925.

* * *

"Fifty Dollars." In Harold Isaacs, ed., *Straw Sandals: Chinese Short Stories, 1918–1933*. Cambridge, MA: MIT Press, 1974, 2348–70.

Wang Wenxing (Wang Wen-hsin)

Bei hai de ren (*Backed against the Sea*). Taipei: Hongfan, 1981.
Jia bian (*Family Catastrophe*). Taipei: Hongfan, 1979.

* * *

Backed against the Sea. Tr. Edward Gunn. Ithaca, NY: East Asia Program, Cornell University, 1993.
Family Catastrophe. Tr. Susan Wan Dolling. Honolulu: University of Hawaii Press, 1995.

Wang Xiaobo

Baiyin shidai (The Silver Times). Guangzhou: Huacheng, 1997.
Huangjin shidai (The Gold Times). Taipei: Lianjing, 1992.
Qingtong shidai (The Bronze Times). Guangzhou: Huacheng, 1997.
Wo de jingshen jiayuan (*My Spiritual Garden*). Beijing: Wenhua yishu, 1997.

* * *

"My Spiritual Garden." *Contemporary Chinese Thought* 30, 3 (Spring 1999).

Wang Xiaoni

Fangyuan sishi li (Twenty Kilometers Radius). Beijing: Zuojia, 2003.
Fangzu Shenzhen (Exiled to Shenzhen). Kunming: Yunnan renmin, 1996.
Qingting yu sushuo (Listening and Confessing). Xiamen: Lujiang, 2006.
Ren niao di fei: Xiao Hong liuli de yi sheng (Humans and Birds Fly Low: Xiao Hong's Floating Life). Changchun: Changchun chubanshe, 1995.
Shou zhi yi zhi huang hua (Holding a Yellow Flower in Hand). Shanghai: Dongfang, 1997.
Wo de zhi li bao zhe wo de huo (My Fire Is Wrapped Up in My Paper). Shenyang: Chunfeng wenyi, 1997.

* * *

"At the Edge of a Field, a Pair of Shoes," "The Millstone." Trs. Gordon T. Osing and De-an Wu Swihart. *Salt Hill* 5 (1998).

"A Birthday Night," "Love," "Many, Many Pears." Tr. Michael Day. *The Drunken Boat.* (Spring/Summer, 2006).

Wang Xiaoying

Xiangsi niao (Lovebirds). Tianjin: Baihua wenyi, 1983.
Xin jianiang de jingzi (The Bride's Mirror). Beijing: Zhongguo qingnian, 1986.
Yilu fengchen (Journey of Hardships). Chongqing: Chongqing chubanshe, 1987.
Danqing yin (Inspired by Art). Beijing: Renmin wenxue, 1997.

* * *

Stories in Hugh Anderson, ed., *A Wind Across the Grass: Modern Chinese Writing with Fourteen Stories.* Ascot Vale, Australia: Red Rooster Press, 1985, 142–54.

Wang Xufeng

Cha ren sanbuqu (Tea Trilogy) [*Nanfang you jiamu* (Quality Tea Grows in the South); *Bu ye hou* (The Marquis of the Night); *Zhu cao wei cheng* (A City Surrounded by Plants)]. Beijing: Renmin wenxue, 2004.

Wang Zengqi

Yangshe de yewan (Nights in the Sheep Pen). Beijing: Zhongguo shaonian ertong, 1962.
Wang Zengqi duanpian xiaoshuo xuan (Selected Short Stories by Wang Zengqi). Beijing: Beijing chubanshe, 1982.
Wang Zengqi wenji (Collected Works by Wang Zengqi). 4 vols. Nanjing: Jiangsu wenyi, 1993.

* * *

Story After Supper. Beijing: Chinese Literature, 1990.
"Big Chan." In Carolyn Choa and David Su Li-qun, eds., *The Vintage Book of Contemporary Chinese Fiction.* New York: Vintage Books, 2001, 181–90.
"Buddhist Initiation." In Zhihua Fang, ed./tr., *Chinese Stories of the Twentieth Century.* New York: Garland Publishing, 1995, 173–201.
"The Love Story of a Young Monk" and "Story After Supper." Tr. Hu Zhihui and Shen Zhen. *Chinese Literature* 1 (1982): 58–96.

Wang Zhenhe (Wang Chen-ho)

Jiazhuang yi niuche (*An Ox-Cart for Dowry*). Taipei: Yuanjing, 1976.
Meigui meigui wo ai ni (*Rose, Rose I Love You*). Taipei: Yuanjing, 1984.

* * *

Rose, Rose, I Love You. Tr. Howard Goldblatt. New York: Columbia University Press, 1998.
"Auntie Lai-chun's Autumn Sorrows." Tr. Hsiao Lien-ren. *The Chinese Pen* (Winter 1975): 59–92.
"An Oxcart for Dowry." Trs. the Author and Jon Jackson. In Joseph S. M. Lau, ed., *Chinese Stories From Taiwan: 1960–1970.* New York: Columbia University Press, 1976, 75–99.
"Ghost, Northwind, Man." Tr. Nancy Ing. *The Chinese Pen* (Summer 1975): 1–22.
"Shangri-la." Tr. Michael S. Duke. *The Chinese Pen* (Spring 1983): 48–88.

Wei Hui

Shanghai baobei (*Shanghai Baby*). Shengyang: Chunfeng wenyi, 1999.
Wode chan (*Marrying Buddha*). Shanghai: Shanghai wenyi, 2004.

* * *

Marrying Buddha. Tr. Larissa Heinrich. London: Constable and Robinson, 2005.
Shanghai Baby. Tr. Bruce Humes. New York: Simon and Schuster, 2001.

Wei Minglun

Bashan gui hua (The Ghost Talk from Sichuan). Shanghai: Shanghai renmin, 1997.
Bashan xiucai (The Talented Scholar from Sichuan). Chengdu: Sichuan renmin, 1983.
Gui hua yu ye tan (Ghost Talk and Evening Chat). Beijing: Renmin wenxue, 2001.
Pan Jinlian (*Pan Jinlian: The History of a Fallen Woman*). Shanghai: Sanlian, 1987.
Wei Minglun juzuo sanbuqu (Three Plays by Wei Minglun). Taipei: Erya, 1995.
Yi Dadan (The Fearless Yi). Beijing: Zhongguo xiju, 1980.

* * *

"Pan Jinlian: The History of a Fallen Woman." In Haiping Yan, ed., *Theater and Society: An Anthology of Contemporary Chinese Drama.* Armonk, NY: M.E. Sharpe, 1998, 123–88.

Wen Yiduo

Hong zhu (Red Candle). Shanghai: Taidong, 1923.
Si shui (Dead Water). Shanghai: Xinyue, 1928.
Wen Yiduo quanji (Complete Works by Wen Yiduo). 4 vols. Shanghai: Kaiming, 1948.

* * *

Red Candle: Selected Poems by Wen I-to. Tr. Tao Tao Saunders. London: Cape, 1972.
Wen Yiduo: Selected Poetry and Prose. Beijing: Panda Books, 1990.
Poems in Cyril Birch and Donald Keene, eds., *Anthology of Chinese Literature: From the Fourteenth Century to the Present Day*. New York: Grove Press, 1987, 356–61.

Woeser

Ming wei Xizang de shi (Poems Written for Tibet). Taipei: Taiwan dakuai wenhua, 2006.
Shajie (Revolution). Taipei: Taiwan dakuai wenhua, 2006.
Xizang biji (Notes of Tibet). Guangzhou: Huacheng, 2003.
Xizang: Jianghong se de ditu (Tibet: A Crimson Map). Taipei: Shiying, 2003.
Xizang jiyi (Memories of Tibet). Taipei: Taiwan dakuai wenhua, 2006.
Xizang zai shang (The Highland of Tibet). Xining: Qinghai renmin, 1999.

Wu Zuguang

Fenghuang cheng (The City of Phoenix). Chongqing: Shenghuo shudian, 1939.
Fengxue ji (Wind and Snow: A Collection of Plays). Beijing: Renmin wenxue chubanshe, 1955.
Fengxue ye gui ren (*Returning in a Snowy Night*). Shanghai: Kaiming, 1944.
Wu Zuguang daibiao zuo (Selected Works by Wu Zuguang). Beijing: Huaxia chubansha, 1998.
Wu Zuguang xin ju ji (New Plays by Wu Zuguang). Hong Kong: Anding chubanshe, 1991.
Yishu de huaduo (Blossoms of Art: A Collection of Essays). Shanghai: Xin wenyi chubanshe, 1955.

* * *

The Three Beatings of Tao Sanchun, or 'A Shrew Untamed,' a traditional Peking Opera by Wu Zuguang. Shanghai: Shanghai Foreign Language Education Press, 1988.

"Against Those Who Wield the Scissors: A Plea for an End to Censorship." Tr. Michael S. Duke. In Helmut Martin, ed., *Modern Chinese Writers: Self-portrayals*. Armonk, NY: M.E. Sharpe, 1992, 35–40.
"On China's National Characteristics." In Geremie Barme, *New Ghosts, Old Dreams: Chinese Rebel Voices*. New York: Times Books, 1992, 363–73.

Wu Zuxiang

Xiliu ji (Western Willow). Shanghai: Shenghuo shudian, 1934.
Fanyu ji (After Meals). Shanghai: Wensheng, 1935.
Shanhong (Landslide). Chongqing: Wenyi jiangzhujin guanli weiyuanhui, 1943.
Shihuang ji (Gleaning and Collecting Scraps). Beijing: Beijing daxue, 1988.

* * *

Green Bamboo Heritage. Beijing: Panda Books, 1989.
"A Certain Day." Tr. Marston Anderson. In Helen Siu, ed., *Furrows: Peasants, Intellectuals and the State*. Stanford: Stanford University Press, 1990, 40–54.
Stories in Joseph Lau et al., eds., *Modern Chinese Stories and Novellas 1919–1949*. New York: Columbia University Press, 1981, 372–415. [includes "Fan Village," "Let There Be Peace," and "Young Master Gets His Tonic"]

Xi Chuan

Dayi Ruci (The Gist of Meaning). Changsha: Hunan wenyi, 1994.
Shen qian (Deep and Shallow). Beijing: Zhongguo heping, 2006.
Shui zi (Water Stain). Tianjin: Baihua wenyi, 2001.
Xi Chuan shi xuan. Beijing: Renmin wenxue, 1997.
Xugou de jiapu (Fabricated Pedigree). Beijing: Heping, 1997.
Yinmi de huihe (A Clandestine Meeting). Beijing: Gaige, 1997.
Zhonguo de meigui (China's Rose). Beijing: Zhonguo wenlian, 1991.

* * *

"Close Shots and Distant Birds." Trs. Xi Chuan and Inara Cedrins. *The Drunken Boat* (Spring/Summer 2006).
"What the Eagle Says." Tr. Maghiel van Crevel. *Seneca Review* 33, 2 (2003): 28–41.
Poems in *Renditions* 37 (1992): 138–41; 51 (1999); Tony Barnstone, ed. *Out of the Howling Storm: The New Chinese Poetry*. Hanover, CT: Wesleyan University Press, 1993, 125–30; *Heat* 2 (1996): 130–32; 8 (1998): 112–14; Wang Ping, ed. *New Generation:Poems from China Today*. New York: Hanging Loose Press, 1999, 143–50; Henry Y. H. Zhao, Yanbing Chen, and John Rosenwald, eds., *Fissures: Chinese Writing Today*. Brookline, MA: Zephyr Press, 2000, 28.

Xi Murong

Qili xiang (Seven-li scent). Taipei: Dadi, 1981.
Wode jia zai gaoyuan shang (My Home Is on a Plateau). Taipei: Yuanshen, 1990.
Wuyuan de qingchun (Unregrettable Youth). Taipei: Dadi, 1983.
Zai hei'an de heliu shang (*Across the Darkness of the River*). Haikou: Nanhai, 2003.

* * *

Across the Darkness of the River. Tr. Chang Shu-li. Copenhagen/Los Angeles: Green Integer, 2001.

Xi Xi

Fei zhan (*Flying Carpet: A Tale of Fertilla*). Taipei: Hongfan, 1996.
Hou niao (Migratory Birds). Taipei: Hongfan, 1991.
Huzi you lian (Mustache Has a Face). Taipei: Hongfan, 1986.
Meili dasha (The Beautiful Skyscrapers). Taipei: Hongfan, 1990.
Shaolu (Deer). Hong Kong: Suye, 1982.
Shi qing (Stone Chimes). Hong Kong: Suye, 1983.
Wo cheng (*My City*). Hong Kong: Suye, 1979.
Xiang wo zheyang de yige nüzi (*A Woman Like Me*). Taipei: Hongfan, 1984.

* * *

Flying Carpet: A Tale of Fertilla. Tr. Diana Yue. Hong Kong: Hong Kong University Press, 2000.
A Girl Like Me and Other Stories. Ed. Eva Hung. Hong Kong: Chinese University of Hong Kong, 1986.
Marvels of a Floating City and Other Stories: An Authorized Collection. Trs. Eva Hung and John and Esther Dent-Young. Hong Kong: Renditions, 1997.
My City: A Hong Kong Story. Tr. Eva Hung. Hong Kong: Renditions, 1993.

Xia Yan

Yi nian jian (In the Course of a Year). Shanghai: Kaiming shudian, 1950.
Kaoyan (*The Test*). Beijing: Renmin wenxue, 1955.
Shanghai wuyan xia (*Under the Eaves of Shanghai*). Shanghai: Shanghai zazhi gongsi, 1937.
Shuixiang yin (Song of the Village by the River). Chongqing: Qunyi chubanshe, 1942.
Shui xiang yin (Song of a River Town: A Four-Act Play). Chongqing: Qunyi chubanshe, 1942.

Xia Yan dianying juzuo ji (Screenplays by Xia Yan). Beijing: Zhongguo dianying, 1985.

Xia Yan juzuo ji (Plays by Xia Yan). Beijing: Zhongguo xiju, 1984.

* * *

The Test: A Play in Five Acts. Tr. Ying Yu. Beijing: Foreign Languages Press, 1956.

"Contract Labor." *Chinese Literature* 8 (1960): 47–63.

"Under Shanghai Eaves." In Edward Gunn, ed., *Twentieth-Century Chinese Drama: An Anthology.* Bloomington: Indiana University Press, 1983, 76–125; also translated as "Under the Eaves of Shanghai" by Yao Hsin-nung. *Renditions* 3 (1974): 128–48.

Xia Yi

Wo (Me). Beijing: Zhongguo youyi, 1986.

Xiwang zhi ge (Songs of Hope). Hong Kong: Shanbianshe, 1982.

Xianggang liang jiemie (Two Sisters of Hong Kong). Beijing: Zhongguo wenlian, 1985.

Xiao Fan

Bu ji de tiankong (The Unbridled Sky). Hangzhou: Zhejiang wenyi, 2003.

Wo de tutou laoshi (My Bald Teacher). Beijing: Zhongguo minzu sheying yishu, 2003.

Du yao shen tong (Poison and Child Geniuses). Shanghai: Dongfang, 2004.

Wo nianqing shi de nü pengyou (The Girlfriend of My Youth). Beijing: Zhonguo qingnian, 2005.

Mayi (Ants). Beijing: Zuojia, 2006.

Xiao Hong

Hulan he (Tales of Hulan River). Shanghai: Shanghai zazhi, 1941.

Kuangye de huhan (Cry in the Wilderness). Chongqing: Shanghai zazhi, 1940.

Ma Bole (Ma Bole). Chongqing: Da shidai, 1941.

Niu che shang (On the Ox Cart). Shanghai: Wenhua shenghuo, 1937.

Shangshi jie (The Market Street). Shanghai: Wenhua shenghuo, 1936.

Sheng si chang (Field of Life and Death). Shanghai: Rongguang, 1935.

* * *

Field of Life and Death and Tales of Hulan River. Tr. Howard Goldblatt. Boston: Cheng & Tsui, 2002.

Selected Stories of Xiao Hong. Bilingual Series in Modern Chinese Literature. Tr. Howard Goldblatt. Hong Kong: The Chinese University Press, 2005.

Xiao Jun

Bashe (Arduous Journey). Harbin: Heilongjiang wenxue yishu, 1979.
Bayue de xiangcun (Village in August). Shanghai: Zuojia shuwu, 1946.
Disan dai (The Third Generation). Shanghai: Wenhua shenghuo, 1946.
Jiang shang (On the River). Shanghai: Wenhua shenghuo, 1936.
Wuyue de kuangshan (Coal Mines in May). Beijing: Zuojia, 1954.
Yang (Sheep). Shanghai: Wenhua shenghuo, 1936.

* * *

Coal Mines in May [excerpts]. Tr. Howard Goldblatt. In Kai-yu Hsu, ed., *Literature of the People's Republic of China.* Bloomington: Indiana University Press, 1980, 198–206.
A Picture. Beijing: Foreign Languages Press, 1960.
Village in August. Tr. Evan King. New York: Smith and Durrell, 1942.
"Aboard the S.S. *Dairen Maru.*" In Edgar Snow, ed., *Living China.* New York: John Day and Co., 1937; Westport, CT: Hyperion Press, 1973, 207–11.
"Goats." In Joseph S. M. Lau, C. T. Hsia, and Leo Lee, eds, *Modern Chinese Stories and Novellas, 1919–1949.* New York: Columbia University Press, 1981, 352–69.
"The Third Gun." In Edgar Snow, ed., *Living China: Modern Chinese Stories.* New York: Reynal and Hitchcock, 1936, 212–19.

Xiao Kaiyu

Dongwuyuan de kuangxi (The Ecstasy of the Zoo). Beijing: Gaige, 1997.
Xiao Kaiyu de shi (Poems by Xiao Kaiyu). Beijing: Renmin wenxue, 2004.
Xuexi zhi tian (The Sweetness of Learning). Beijing: Gongren, 2000.

Xiao Lihong

Guihua xiang (The Cassia Flower Alley). Taipei: Lianjing, 1977.
Qian jiang you shui qian jiang yue (A Thousand Moons on a Thousand Rivers). Taipei: Lianjing, 1981.
Bai shui hu chun meng (Spring Dreams at White Water Lake). Taipei: Lianjing, 1996.

* * *

A Thousand Moons on a Thousand Rivers. Tr. Michelle Wu. New York: Columbia University Press, 2000.

Xiao Tong

Shang jing ji (Going to the Capital). Hong Kong: Wenfeng, 1978.
Wufeng lou suibi (Random Notes from the Windless Pavilion). Hong Kong: Daguang, 1970.
Xue, zai huiyi zhong (Snow in Memory). Hong Kong: Wenfeng, 1976.

Xie Bingying

Biyao zhi lian (Biyao's Love: A Novel). Taipei: Lixing, 1959.
Congjun riji (*War Diary*). Shanghai: Chundhao shuju, 1928.
Guxiang (My Hometown: Essays). Taipei: Lixing, 1957.
Hong dou (Red Beans: A Novel). Taipei: Hongqiao, 1954.
Weida de nüxing (Great Women: Short Stories). Shanghai: Guanghua, 1933.
Wo de shaonian shidai (My Teenage Years: Essays). Taipei: Zhengzhong, 1955.
Wo de xuesheng shenghuo (My Student Life: Essays). Shanghai: Guanghua, 1933.
Wu (Fog: Short Stories). Taipei: Danfang, 1955.
Yige nübing de zizhuan (Autobiography of a Female Soldier). Shanghai: Liangyou, 1936.
Yige nüxing de fendou (A Woman's Struggle for Independence: Essays). Hong Kong: Shijie wenhua, 1941.

* * *

Autobiography of a Chinese Girl. Tr. Tsui Chi. London: Allen and Unwin, 1943; rpt. London: Pandora, 1986.
Girl Rebel: The Autobiography of Hsieh Pingying, with Extracts from Her New War Diaries. Trs. Adet Lin and Anor Lin. New York: John Day and Co., 1940; rpt, New York: De Capo Press, 1975.
Excerpts from *War Diary.* Tr. Lin Yutang. In A. Dooling and K. Torgeson, eds., *Writing Women in Modern China: An Anthology of Women's Literature from the Early Twentieth Century.* New York: Columbia University Press, 1998, 255–62.
"The Girl Umeko." Tr. Hu Mingliang. In Amy D. Dooling, ed., *Writing Women in Modern China: The Revolutionary Years, 1936–1976.* New York: Columbia University Press, 2005, 95–111.
"Letters of a Chinese Amazon." In Yutang Lin, ed./tr., *Letters of a Chinese Amazon and War-Time Essays.* Shanghai: The Commercial Press, 1930, 3–47.
"Midpoint of an Ordinary Life." Tr. Shirley Chang. In Jing M. Wang, ed., *Jumping Through Hoops: Autobiographical Stories by Modern Chinese Women Writers.* Hong Kong: Hong Kong University Press, 2003, 151–66.

Xu Dishan

Chuntao (*Spring Peach*). Beijing: Renmin wenxue, 1963.
Kong shan ling yu (Empty Mountain and Miraculous Rain). Shanghai: Shangwu, 1925.
Shenmi qite yi yu qingyun (The Mysterious and Exotic: Collection of Fiction by Xu Dishan). Beijing: Wenlian, 1996.
Zhui wang lao zhu (The Spider Hard at Work Making a Net). Shanghai: Shangwu, 1925.

* * *

"Big Sister Liu." In *Chinese Stories from the Thirties*, vol. 1. Beijing: Foreign Languages Press, 1982.
"The Merchant's Wife." In Joseph S. M. Lau and Howard Goldblatt, eds., *The Columbia Anthology of Modern Chinese Literature*. New York: Columbia University Press, 1995, 21–34.
"Spring Peach." In Zhihua Fang, ed./tr., *Chinese Stories of the Twentieth Century*. New York: Garland Publishing, 1995, 173–201.

Xu Kun

Gouri de zuqiu (The Son-of-Bitch Soccer: Selected Works by Xu Kun). Beijing: Zhongguo qingnian, 2001.
Nüwa (The Goddess Nüwa). Shijiazhuang: Hebei jiaoyu, 1995.
Xianfeng (The Avant-garde). Taiyuan: Beiyue wenyi, 1995.
Xiao Qing shi yitiao yu (Xiao Qing Is a Fish). Beijing: Zhongguo wenlian, 2001.
Xingqing nannü (Passionate Men and Women: Selected Stories by Xu Kun). Beijing: Zhongguo qingnian, 2001.
Zaoyu aiqing (Encountering Love). Wuhan: Changjiang wenyi, 1997.

Xu Su

Di yipian luoye (The First Fallen Leaf). Beijing: Zhonguo youyi, 1985.
Xingxing yueliang taiyang (The Stars, the Moon, and the Sun). Hong Kong: Dangdai wenyi, 1999.

Xu Xiaobin

Dunhuang yimeng (Lingering Dream of Dunhuang). Beijing: Beijing, 1994.
Feichang qiutian: Xu Xiaobin zhongpian xiaoshuo xinzuo (An Unusual Autumn). Beijing: Zhongguo guangbo dianshi, 2005.
Yu she (Feathered Snake). Beijing: Renmin wenxue, 2004.

Deling gongzhu (Princess Deling). Beijing: Renmin wenxue, 2004.
Taiyang shizu (The Solar Tribe). Wuhan: Changjiang wenyi, 2001.

Xu Xu

Beican shiji (Century of Misery). Hong Kong: Liming, 1977.
Gui lian (In Love with a Ghost). Shanghai: Yechuang, 1938.
Jibusai youhuo (Gypsy Temptation). Shanghai: Yechuang shuwu, 1940.
Feng xiaoxiao (The Wind Soughs and Sighs). Shanghai: Huaizheng, 1946.
Xiongdi (Brothers). Shanghai: Yechuang shuwu, 1947.
Yan quan (Smoke Rings). Shanghai: Yechuang, 1946.
Ye hua (Wildflowers). Shanghai: Yechuang, 1947.
Yi jia (A Family). Shanghai: Yechuang, 1940.

* * *

Woman in the Mist and Two Other Tales. Tr. Eudora Yu. Hong Kong: Rainbow Press, 1963.

Xu Zhimo

Aimei xiao zha (Love Letters), with Lu Xiaoman. Shanghai: Liangyou, 1936.
Feilengcui de yi ye (One Night in Florence). Beijing: Xinyue shudian, 1927.
Luo shi (When Falling). Beijing: Beixin, 1926.
Qiu (Autumn). Shanghai: Liangyou, 1931.
Xu Zhimo daibiao zuo (Representative Works by Xu Zhimo). Shanghai: Santong, 1942.
Zhimo de shi (Collection of Poems by Zhimo). Shanghai: Zhonghua, 1925.

* * *

Poems in Cyril Birch and Donald Keene, eds., *Anthology of Chinese Literature: From the Fourteenth Century to the Present Day*. New York: Grove Press, 1987, 341–55; Kai-yu Hsu, ed., *Twentieth Century Chinese Poetry*. New York: Doubleday, 1963, 65–92; Michelle Yeh, ed., *Anthology of Modern Chinese Poetry*. New Haven: Yale University Press, 1994, 5–12.

Ya Xian

Ya Xian shi ji (Selected Poems by Ya Xian). Taipei: Hongfan shudian, 1981.

* * *

Salt: Poems. Tr. the Author. Iowa City: Windhover Press, University of Iowa, 1968.

Poems in Dominic Cheung, ed./tr., *The Isle Full of Noises: Modern Chinese Poetry from Taiwan*. New York: Columbia University Press, 1987, 79–83.

Yan Ge

Guan He (The Guan River). Beijing: Nanhai chuban gongsi, 2004.
Liang chen (Good Times). Wuhan: Changjian wenyi, 2005.
Yi shou zhi (The Tale of Strange Animals). Beijing: Zhongxin, 2006.

Yan Geling

Cixing caodi (Female Grassland). Shenyang: Chunfeng wenyi, 1998.
Fusang (*The Lost Daughter of Happiness*). Hong Kong: Tiandi, 1996.
Shui jia you nü chu zhangcheng (Goodby, Innocence). Beijing: Zhongyang bianyi, 2002.
Xiaoyi Duohe (Aunt Duohe). Beijing: Zuojia, 2008.

* * *

The Lost Daughter of Happiness. London: Faber and Faber, 2001.
"The Blind Woman Selling Red Apples." Tr. Herbert Batt. In Herbert Batt, ed., *Tales of Tibet: Sky Burials, Prayer Wheels, and Wind Horses*. Lanham, MD: Rowman & Littlefield, 2001, 225–33.

Yan Li

Mu yu de zaoyu (Experiences of the Mother Tongue). Shanghai: Shanghai wenyi, 2002.
Niuyue bu shi tiantang (New York Is No Paradise). Beijing: Huayi, 1996.
Yan Li shi xuan 1985–1989 (Selected Poems by Yan Li 1985–1989). Taipei: Shulin, 1991.
Yan Li shi xuan 1991–1995 (Selected Poems by Yan Li 1991–1995). Shanghai: Shanghai wenyi, 1995.

* * *

"Back Home." Tr. Denis Mair. *Literary Review* (Winter 2003).
"Starboy and I." Tr. Denis Mair. In Frank Stewart and Herbert J. Batt, eds., *The Mystified Boat and Other New Stories from China*. Special issue of *Manoa: A Pacific Journal of International Writing* 15, 2 (Winter 2003). Honolulu: University of Hawaii Press, 111–22.
"The Song of Aids." Tr. Denis Mair. *Talisman* 12 (1994).
Poems in Wang Ping, ed., *New Generation: Poems from China Today*. New York: Hanging Loose Press, 1999, 159–63.

Yan Lianke

Jianying ru shui (As Hard as Water). Wuhan: Changjiang wenyi, 2001.
Jinlian, nihao (Hello, Jinlian). Beijing: Zhongguo wenxue, 1997.
Riguang liunian (Sunlight and the Fleeting Time). Guangzhou: Huacheng, 1998.
Xia Riluo (Xia Riluo). Shenyang: Chunfeng wenyi, 2002.
Zuihou yiming nü zhiqing (The Last Female Educated Youth). Baihua wenyi, 1993.

Yang Hansheng

Caomang yingxiong (The Rebel Hero). Shanghai: Qunyi, 1949.
Li Xiucheng zhi si (The Death of Li Xiucheng: A Play in Four Acts). Hankou: Huazhong tushu gongsi, 1938.
Tianguo chunqiu (The History of the Taiping Rebellion). Chongqing: Qunyi, 1944.
Yang Hansheng juzuo xuan (Selected Plays by Yang Hansheng). Beijing: Renmin wenxue, 1957.
Yang Hansheng xuan ji di yi juan: duanpian xiaoshuo, zhongpian xiaoshuo (Selected Works by Yang Hansheng, vol. 1: Short Stories and Novellas). Chengdu: Sichuan renmin, 1982.

Yang Jiang

Ganxiao liu ji (Six Chapters from My Life Downunder). Beijing: Sanlian, 1981.
Women san'r (The Three of Us). Beijing: Sanlian, 2003.
Xizao (Baptism). Hong Kong: Sanlian, 1988.
Yang Jiang xiaoshuo ji (Short Stories by Yang Jiang). Haiko: Nanhai, 2001.

* * *

Baptism [Xizao]. Trs. Judith Armory and Shihua Yao. Hong Kong: Hong Kong University Press, 2007.
Lost in the Crowd: A Cultural Revolution Memoir. Tr. Geremie Barme. Melbourne: McPhee Gribble, 1989.
Six Chapters from My Life Downunder. Tr. H. Goldblatt. Seattle: University of Washington Press, 1984; also tr. Djang Chu as *Six Chapters of Life in a Cadre School: Memoirs from China's Cultural Revolution*. Boulder: Westview Press, 1986; tr. Geremie Barme with Bennett Lee as *A Cadre School Life: Six Chapters*. Hong Kong: Joint Publishing Co., 1982.
"Forging the Truth." Tr. Amy D. Dooling. In Dooling, ed., *Writing Women in Modern China The Revolutionary Years, 1936–1976*. New York: Columbia University Press, 2005, 112–77.

"Windswept Blossoms." In Edward Gunn, ed. *Twentieth-Century Chinese Drama: An Anthology.* Bloomington: Indiana University Press, 1983, 228–75.
Essays in David Pollard, ed., *The Chinese Essay.* New York: Columbia University Press, 2000. "The Art of Listening" [Tinghua de yishu], 260–64; "The Cloak of Invisibility" [Yin shen yi], 264–69.

Yang Kui

Yang Kui zuopin xuan ji (Selected Works by Yang Kui). Beijing: Renmin wenxue, 1985.
Yang Kui ji (Selected Stories by Yang Kui). Taipei: Qianwei, 1991.
Yang Kui quan ji (Complete Works by Yang Kui), ed., Peng Xiaoyan. Taipei: Guoli wenhua zichan baocun yanjiu zhongxin choubei chu, 1998.

* * *

"The Indomitable Rose." Tr. Daniel Tom. *The Chinese Pen* (Autumn 1978): 86–94.
"Mother Goose Gets Married." Tr. Jane Parish Yang. In Joseph S. M. Lau, ed., *The Unbroken Chain: An Anthology of Fiction from Taiwan.* Bloomington: Indiana University Press, 1983, 33–54.
"Mother Goose Gets Married" (from Japanese). Tr. Esther T. Hu. *Taiwan Literature, English Translation Series* no. 20 (2007): 73–100.
"Mud Dolls." In Rosemary Haddon, ed./tr., *Oxcart: Nativist Stories from Taiwan, 1934–1977.* Dortmund: Projekt Verlag, 1996, 73–84.
"The Newspaper Carrier." Tr. Robert Backus. *Taiwan Literature, English Translation Series* no. 21 (July 2007): 59–92.
"Paperboy." Tr. Rosemary Haddon. *Renditions* 43 (1995): 25–58.
"Remembering Dr. Lai Ho." Tr. Mary Treadway. *Taiwan Literature, English Translation Series* no. 2 (Dec. 1997): 59–66.

Yang Lian

Da hai tingzhi zhi chu (*Where the Sea Stands Still*). Shanghai: Shanghai wenyi, 1998.
Gui hua: Zhili de kongjian (Ghost Talk: Space of Intelligence). Shanghai: Shanghai wenyi, 1998.
Huang (Yellow). Beijing: Renmin wenxue, 1989.
Huang hun (Desolate Spirit). Shanghai: Shanghai wenyi, 1988.

* * *

The Dead in Exile. Tr. Mabel Lee. Kingston: Tiananmen Publications, 1990.
Masks and Crocodile. Tr. Mabel Lee. Sydney: University of Sydney East Asia Series. Wild Peony Press, 1990.

Non-Person Singular: Selected Poems of Yang Lian. Tr. Brian Holton. London: Wellsweep, 1994.
Notes of a Blissful Ghost. Tr. Brian Holton. Hong Kong: Renditions, 2002.
Where the Sea Stands Still: New Poems. Tr. Brian Holton. Newcastle upon Tyne: Bloodaxe Books/Dufour Editions, 1999.
YI [Yi]. Bilingual edition. Los Angeles: Sun & Moon Press, 2002.

Yang Mu

Beidou xing (Dipper). Taipei: Hongfan, 1986.
Jinji de youxi (Forbidden Games). Taipei: Hongfan, 1983.
Shiguang mingti (The Proposition of Time). Taipei: Hongfan, 1997.
Wanzheng de yuyan (Complete Allegories). Taipei: Hongfan, 1991.
Yang Mu shi ji (Poems by Yang Mu). Taipei: Hongfan, 1978.

* * *

Forbidden Games and Video Poems: The Poetry of Yang Mu and Lo Ch'ing. Tr. Joseph Roe Allen III. Seattle: University of Washington Press, 1993.
No Trace of the Gardener: Poems by Yang Mu. Trs. Laurence Smith and Michelle Yeh. New Haven: Yale University Press, 1998.
"Wu Feng." In Edward Gunn, ed. *Twentieth-Century Chinese Drama: An Anthology*. Bloomington: Indiana University Press, 1983, 475–513.
Poems in Domini Cheung, ed./tr., *The Isle Full of Noises: Modern Chinese Poetry from Taiwan*. New York: Columbia University Press, 1987, 35–47.

Yang Zhijun

Gaoyuan da jie shi (The Destruction of the Plateau). Beijing: Gongren, 2004. [includes "Hai zuotian tuiqu" (The Ocean Receded Yesterday) and "Huan hu bengkui" (The Collapse of the Lakeside)].
Qiaoxiang rentou gu (Beating the Human-Skull Drum). Beijing: Renmin wenxue, 2006.
Tianhuang (The Great Void). Dunhuang wenyi, 1994.
Wu ren buluo (The Tribe without Human). Beijing: Gongren, 2001.
Zang ao (The Tibetan Mastiff). Beijing: Renmin wenxue, 2005.
Zang ao 2 (The Tibetan Mastiff: Part 2). Beijing: Renmin wenxue, 2006.
Zang ao 3 (The Tibetan Mastiff: Part 3). Beijing: Renmin wenxue, 2007.

Yangdon

Wu xingbie de shen (*God without Gender*). Beijing: Zhongguo qingnian, 1994.

* * *

"God without Gender." In Herbert Batt, ed./tr., *Tales of Tibet: Sky Burials, Prayer Wheels, and Wind Horses*. Lanham, MD: Rowman & Littlefield, 2001, 177–88.

Yao Xueyin

Chongfeng (Reunion). Chongqing: Dongfang, 1943.
Chunnuan huakai de shihou (Spring Blossoms). Chongqing: Xiandan, 1944.
Li Zicheng (The Legend of Li Zicheng). Beijing: Zhongguo qingnian, 1999.

* * *

"Half a Cartload of Straw Short." Tr. Yeh Chun-chan. In *Three Seasons and Other Stories*. London: Staple Press, 1946, 73–84.

Ye Guangqin

Cai sangzi (Picking Mulberry Seeds). Beijing: Shiyue wenhua, 1999.
Mo yu qian sui Ye Guangqin zhongpian xiaoshuo xinzuo (Squid and other Stories by Ye Guangqin). Beijing: Zhongguo guangbo dianshi, 2005.
Meng ye he ceng dao Xie Qiao (No Return to Xie Qiao Even in a Dream). Beijing: Huawen, 2002.
Quanjia fu (A Happy Family). Beijing: Beijing chubanshe, 2001.
Shui fan Yuefu qiliang qu (Memories of a Bleak Past). Beijing: Xin shijie, 2002.
Xiaoyao jin (A Laid-back Life). Beijing: Wenhua yishu, 2007.

Ye Lingfeng

Juzi furen (Madame Juzi). Shanghai: Guanghua, 1927.
Hong de tianshi (Red Angel). Shanghai: Xiandai, 1930.
Shidai guniang (Modern Girl). Shanghai: Sishe, 1933.
Wei wancheng de chanhuilu (Unfinished Confessions). Shanghai: Jindai shudian, 1936.
Xianggang jiushi (Legends of Hong Kong). Hong Kong: Shanghai shuju, 1969.

Ye Shengtao

Cheng zhong (In the City). Shanghai: Kaiming, 1926.
Daocao ren (Scarecrow). Shanghai: Shangwu, 1923.
Gemo (Barrier). Shanghai: Shangwu, 1922.
Huo zai (Fire). Shanghai: Shangwu, 1923.
Ni Huanzhi (Ni Huanzhi the Schoolteacher). Shanghai: Kaiming, 1929.
Xian xia (Below the Line). Shanghai: Shangwu, 1925.

* * *

Selected Stories and Prose by Ye Shengtao. Beijing: Chinese Literature Press, 1999.

Ye Weilian

Hong ye de zhui xun (In Search of Red Leaves). Taipei: Dongda, 1997.
Hua kai de shengyin (The Sound of Flowers Blooming). Taipei: Siji, 1977.
Sanshi nian shi (Poems Written in Thirty Years). Taipei: Dongda, 1987.
Shanshui de yueding (Appoints with Mountains and Rivers). Taipei: Dongda, 1994.
Wang yiba xing (A Scoop of Stars). Taipei: Sanmin, 1998.
Ye hua de gushi (Tales of Wildflowers). Taipei: Zhongwai wenxue yuekanshe, 1975.
Yige Zhongguo de hai (One China's Sea). Taipei: Dongda, 1987.
Yu de weidao (The Taste of Rain). Taipei: Erya, 2006.

* * *

Between Landscapes: Poems by Wai-Lim Yip. Santa Fe: Pennywhistle Press, 1994.
Poems in Dominic Cheung, ed./tr., *The Isle Full of Noises: Modern Chinese Poetry from Taiwan.* New York: Columbia University Press, 1987, 84–92.

Ye Zhaoyan

Aiqing guize (Rules of Love). Nanjing: Jiangsu wenyi, 1994.
Hua sha (The Flower Spirit). Taipei: Maitian, 1998.
Hua ying (The Flower Shadows). Hong Kong: Tiandi, 1996.
Ye bo qinghuai (Anchored at Night in the Qinhuai River). Hangzhou: Zhejiang wenyi, 1991.
Yijiusanqi nian de aiqing (*Nanjing 1937: A Love Story*). Nanjing: Jiangsu wenyi, 1996.
Zao shu de gushi (The Story of a Date Tree). Nanjing: Jiangsu wenyi, 1994.

* * *

Nanjing 1937: A Love Story. Tr. Michael Berry. New York: Columbia University Press, 2003.

Yi Shu

Jiaming yu Meigui (Jiaming and Rose). Taipei: Linbai, 1989.
Jin fen shijie (The World of Wealth). Taipei: Linbai, 1991.

Shenghuo zhi lv (The Journey of Life). Taipei: Linbai, 1994.
Zhao hua xi shi (Morning Flowers Gathered at Dusk). Taipei: Linbai, 1987.

* * *

"Home-coming." Tr. Eva Hung. *Renditions* 29/30 (1988): 108–113.

Yo Yo

Renjing guihua (Human Scenery and Ghost Speech). Beijing: Zhongyang bianyi, 1994.
Ta kanjian le liangge yueliang (She Saw Two Moons). Changchun: Shidai wenyi, 1995.
Tishen lan diao (Substitute Blues). Beijing: Gongren, 2000.
He chao (River Tide). Taipei: Lianhe wenxue, 2001.
Hunxi (Marriage Game). Shanghai: Baijia, 2005.

* * *

Ghost Tide. Auckland, New Zealand: HarperCollins, 2005.

You Fengwei

Niqiu (Loach). Changchun: Chunfeng wenyi, 2002.
Se (Seduction). Shanghai: Shanghai wenyi, 2003.
Yibo (Legacy). Guangzhou: Huacheng, 2008.
Zhongguo yijiuwuqi (China, 1957). Shanghai: Shanghai wenyi, 2001.

Yu Dafu

Chenlun (*Sinking*). Shanghai: Taidong, 1921.
Dafu quanji (The Complete Works of Yu Dafu), vol. 1: *Hanhui ji* (Cold Ashes), vol. 2: *Jilei ji* (Chicken Ribs), vol. 3: *Guoqu ji* (The Past). Shanghai: Chuang-zaoshe, 1927.
Mi yang (The Stray Sheep). Beijing: Beixin, 1928.
Ta shi yige ruo nüzi (She Is a Weak Woman). Shanghai: Hufeng, 1932.
Weijue ji (Wild Plants). Beijing: Beixin, 1930.

* * *

"Sinking" [Chenlun]. Trs. Joseph S. M. Lau and C. T. Hsia. In Joseph S. M. Lau and Howard Goldblatt, eds., *The Columbia Anthology of Modern Chinese Literature*. New York: Columbia University Press, 1995, 44–69.
"The Winter Scene in Jiangnan." Tr. David Pollard. In Pollard, ed., *The Chinese Essay*. New York: Columbia University Press, 2000, 212–15.
Nights of Spring Fever and Other Writings. Beijing: Panda Books, 1984.

Yu Guangzhong

Bai yu ku gua (The White Jade Bitter Gourd). Taipei: Dadi, 1975.
Lanse de yumao (Blue Feathers). Taipei: Lanxing shishe, 1954.
Lian de lianxiang (The Association of the Lotus). Taipei: Wenxing, 1964.
Meng yu dili (Dream and Geography). Taipei: Hongfan, 1990.
Qiu zhi song (Ode to Autumn). Taipei: Jiuge, 1988.
Wu xing wu zu (No Stop to the Five Primordial Elements). Taipei: Jiuge, 1998.
Zai lengzhan de niandai (The Era of the Cold War). Taipei: Chun wenxue, 1970.
Zhang shang yu (Rain in the Palm). Taipei: Wenxing, 1964.

* * *

Acres of Barbed Wire—To China, in Day Dreams and Nightmares. Tr. the Author.
Taipei: Mei Ya Publications, 1971.
Night Watchman [bilingual edition]. Taipei: Jiuge, 1992.
"Remembering and Missing Taipei." Trs. Ren Zhong and Yuzhi Yang. In *Hometown and Childhood*. San Francisco: Long River Press, 2005, 143–52.
Essays in David Pollard, ed., *The Chinese Essay*. New York: Columbia Univer-
sity Press, 2000. "My Four Hypothetical Enemies" [Wo de sige jiaxiang di],
308–15; "Thus Friends Absent Speak" [Chisu cunxin], 305–08.
Essays in Martin Woesler, ed., *20th Century Chinese Essays in Translation*. Bochum: Bochum University Press, 2000. "Listening to the Cold Rain" [Tingting
na leng yu], 156–64; "Shatian Mountain Residence" [Shatian shan ju], 150–55;
"The Wolves Are Coming" [Lang laile], 165–68.
Poems in Dominic Cheung, ed./tr., *The Isle Full of Noises: Modern Chinese Poetry from Taiwan*. New York: Columbia University Press, 1987, 48–61.

Yu Hua

Huozhe (*To Live*). Taipei: Maitian, 1994.
Xianshi yizhong (*One Kind of Reality*). Beijing: Xin shijie, 1999.
Xiongdi (Brothers). Shanghai: Shanghai wenyi, 2005.
Xu Sanguan mai xue ji (*The Chronicle of a Blood Merchant*). Shanghai: Shanghai
wenyi, 2004.
Zai xiyu zhong huhuan (*Crying Out in the Drizzle*). Guangzhou: Huacheng,
1993.
Xianxue meihua (Fresh Blood and Plum Blossoms). Beijing: Xin shijie, 1999.

* * *

Chronicle of a Blood Merchant. Tr. Andrew F. Jones. New York: Pantheon Books,
2004.
Cries in the Drizzle. Knopf Publishing Group, 2007.
Pain and Punishments. Tr. Andrew F. Jones. Honolulu: University of Hawaii
Press, 1996.

To Live. Tr. Michael Berry. New York: Anchor Books, 2003.

"Death Narrative." Tr. Lucas Klein. In Frank Stewart and Herbert J. Batt, eds., *The Mystified Boat and Other New Stories from China.* Special issue of *Manoa: A Pacific Journal of International Writing* 15, 2 (Winter 2003). Honolulu: University of Hawaii Press, 2004, 162–67.

"The Noon of Howling Wind." Tr. Denis Mair. In Jing Wang, ed., *China's Avant-garde Fiction.* Durham, NC: Duke University Press, 1998, 69–73.

"One Kind of Reality." Tr. Helen Wang. In Henry Zhao, ed., *The Lost Boat: Avant-garde Fiction from China.* London: Wellsweep, 1993, 145–84.

Yu Jian

Jujue yinyu (Rejecting Metaphor). Kunming: Yunnan renmin, 2004.

Ling dang'an: changshi qi bu yu biantiao ji (File 0: Seven Long Poems and Notes). Kunming: Yunnan renmin, 2004.

Shi liushi shou (Sixty Poems). Kumning: Yunnan Renmin, 1989.

Yimei chuanguo tiankong de dingzi (A Nail through the Sky). Kunming: Yunnan renmin, 2004.

Zhengzai yanqian de shiwu (Familiar Scenes). Kunming: Yunnan renmin, 2004.

* * *

"File 0." Tr. Maghiel van Crevel. *Renditions* 56 (2001): 24–57

"Four Poems." Tr. Simon Patton. *Renditions* 46 (1996): 69–79.

Poems in Wang Ping, ed., *New Generation: Poems from China Today.* New York: Hanging Loose Press, 1999, 177–88.

Yu Lihua

Bian (Change). Hong Kong: Tiandi, 1980.

Fu jia de ernümen (Children of the Fu Family). Hong Kong: Taindi, 1981.

Gui (Return). Hong Kong: Tiandi, 1981.

Kaoyan (Test). Beijing: Renmin wenxue, 1982.

Meng hui Qing He (Return to the Green River in a Dream). Changsha: Hunan wenyi, 1987.

Yan (Flame). Hong Kong: Taindi, 1980.

You jian zhonglü you jian zonglü (Seeing the Palm Trees Again). Hong Kong: Tiandi, 1989.

* * *

"Glass Marbles Scattered All Over the Ground." Tr. Hsiao Lien-ren. In Chi Pang-yuan et al., eds., *An Anthology of Contemporary Chinese Literature.* Taipei: National Institute for Compilation and Translation, 1975, II, 161–73.

"In Liu Village." Trs. the Author and C. T. Hsia. In Joseph S. M. Lau, ed., *Chinese Stories From Taiwan: 1960–1970*. New York: Columbia University Press, 1976, 101–42.
"Nightfall." Trs. Vivian Hsu and Julia Fitzgerald. In Vivian Ling Hsu, ed., *Born of the Same Roots: Stories of Modern Chinese Women*. Bloomington: Indiana University Press, 1981, 194–209.
"Two Sisters." Trs. Hsin-sheng Kao and Michelle Yeh. In Kao, ed., *Nativism Overseas: Contemporary Chinese Women Writers*. Albany: SUNY, 1993, 57–80.

Yu Ling

Ye Shanghai (Dark Nights in Shanghai). Shanghai: Shanghai juchang yishu she, 1939.
Yu Ling juzuo ji (Plays by Yu Ling). 4 vols. Beijing: Zhongguo xiju chubanshe, 1984–1987.

Yu Pingbo

Dong ye (Winter Nights). Shanghai: Yadong tushuguan, 1922.
Yan zhi cao (Swallows and Grass). Beijing: Zhongguo wenlian, 1993, rpt.
Yu Pingbo shi quan bian (Collected Poems by Yu Pingbo). Hangzhou: Zhejiang wenyi, 1992.

* * *

Poems in Kai-yu Hsu, ed., *Twentieth Century Chinese Poetry: An Anthology*. Garden City, NY: Doubleday, 1963, 14–15.

Yu Qiuyu

Wenhua ku lü (A Difficult Journey across Culture). Shanghai: Zhishi, 1992.
Qiannian yi tan (A Sigh of One Thousand Years). Beijing: Zuojia, 2000.
Shan ju biji (Jottings in a Mountain Abode). Shanghai: Wenhui, 1998.
Wenming de suipian (Broken Pieces of Civilizations). Shenyang: Chunfen wenyi, 1994.

* * *

"The Message Man." Tr. David Pollard. *Renditions* 52 (1999): 13–20.
"The Night Boat." Trs. Ren Zhong and Yuzhi Yang. In *Hometown and Childhood*. San Francisco: Long River Press, 2005, 123–34.
"Shanghai People" [Shanghai ren]. Tr. David Pollard. In Pollard, ed., *The Chinese Essay*. New York: Columbia University Press, 2000, 351–61.

"A Taoist Parinirvana Stupa." *Chinese Literature* (Autumn 1998).
"West Lake: A Dream." *Chinese Literature* (Autumn 1998).
"The Vicissitude of Tianyi Pavilion." *Chinese Literature* (Autumn 1998).

Yuan Qiongqiong

Chun shui chuan (Spring Water Boat). Taipei: Hongfan, 1985.
Hongchen xinshi (Secrets in the Red Dust). Taipei: Erya, 1981.
Ziji de tiankong (A Sky of One's Own). Taipei: Hongfan, 1981.

* * *

"Adversity." Tr. Cynthia Wu Wilcox. *The Chinese Pen* (Winter 1985): 69–87.
"Beyond Words." Trs. Howard Goldblatt and Joseph Lau. *The Chinese Pen* (Summer 1983): 17–30.
"Even-Glow." Tr. Chen I-djen. *The Chinese Pen* (Summer 1985): 1–28.
"Fever." Tr. Felice Marcus. *Renditions* 52 (1999): 71–85.
"A Place of One's Own." Tr. Jane Parish Yang. In Michael S. Duke, ed., *Worlds of Modern Chinese Fiction*. Armonk, NY: M.E. Sharpe, 1991, 193–205.
"The Sky's Escape." Tr. Michael S. Duke. *The Chinese Pen* (Winter 1979): 1–24.

Zang Di

Yan yuan ji shi (Notes about the Beijing University Campus). Beijing: Wenhua yishu, 1998.
Feng chui cao dong (Grass Rustles in the Wind). Beijing: Zhongguo gongren, 2000.
Xinxian de jingji (Fresh Thorns). Beijing: Xin shijie, 2002.

* * *

Poems in Zhang Er and Che Dongdong, eds., *New Poems from China: Talisman Anthology of Contemporary Chinese Poetry*. Jersey City, NJ: Talisman House, 2006.

Zang Kejia

Laoyin (Branding). Beijing: Renmin wenxue, 1999.
Yunhe (The Great Canal). Shanghai, Wenhua shenghuo, 1937.
Zang Kejia shi xuan (Poems by Zang Kejia). Beijing: Renmin wenxue, 1986.

* * *

Poems in Robert Payne, ed., *Contemporary Chinese Poetry*. London: Routledge, 1947; Kai-yu Hsu, ed., *Twentieth Century Chinese Poetry: An Anthology*. Garden City, NY: Doubleday, 1963.

Zhai Yongming

Heiye li de su ge (The Unadorned Songs of Night). Beijing: Gaige, 1997.
Niuyue, Niuyue yi xi (New York and West of New York). Chengdu: Sichuan wenyi, 2003.
Nüren (Women). Guilin: Lijiang chubanshe, 1986.
Zai yiqie meigui zhi shang (On All Roses). Shenyang: Shenyang, 1992.
Zhai Yongming shi ji (Poems by Zhai Yongming). Chengdu: Chengdu, 1994.
Zhengru ni suo kan dao de (Just as You Have Witnessed). Guilin: Guangxi shifan daxue, 2004.
Zhongyu shi wo zhouzhuan bu ling (Unable to Cope). Shijiazhuang: Hebei jiaoyu, 2002.

* * *

"Jing'an Village." Trs. Tony Price and Tao Naikan. *Renditions* 52 (1999): 92–119.
Poems in Wang Ping, ed., *New Generation: Poems from China Today*. New York: Hanging Loose Press, 1999, 191–97.

Zhang Ailing

Ban sheng yuan (Eighteen Springs). Hong Kong: Huangguan, 1991.
Chi di zhi lian (*Naked Earth*). Hong Kong: Xiandai, 1976.
Chuanqi: Zhang Ailing duanpian xiaoshuo ji (Tales of Love: Short Stories by Zhang Ailing). Taipei: Huangguan, 1977.
Di yi lu xiang: Zhang Ailing duanpian xiaoshuo ji er (The First Incense Burning: Short Stories by Zhang Ailing, vol. 2). Taipei: Huangguan, 1991.
Jin suo ji (*The Golden Cangue*). Hong Kong: Nüshen, 1983.
Liu yan (*Written on Water*). Hong Kong: Huangguan, 1991.
Qing cheng zhi lian (*Love in a Fallen City*). Hong Kong: Huangguan, 1993.
Xiao tuanyuan (A Small Reunion). Hong Kong: Huangguan, 2009.
Yang ge (*The Rice-Sprout Song*). Taipei: Huangguan, 1976.

* * *

Lust, Caution: The Story. Tr. Julia Lowell. New York: Anchor Books, 2007.
Naked Earth. Hong Kong: Union Press, 1956.
The Rice-Sprout Song: A Novel of Modern China. Berkeley: University of California Press, 1998.
The Rouge of the North. Berkeley: University of California Press, 1998.
Traces of Love and Others Stories. Ed. Eva Hung. Hong Kong: Renditions Book, 2000.
Written on Water. Tr. Andrew F. Jones. New York: Columbia University Press, 2005.

"The Betrothal of Yindi." In Cyril Birch and Donald Keene, eds., *Anthology of Chinese Literature: From the Fourteenth Century to the Present Day*. New York: Grove Press, 1987, 443–47.
"The Golden Cangue." In Hsia et al., eds., *Modern Chinese Stories and Novellas 1919–1949*. New York: Columbia University Press, 1981, 530–59.
"Love in a Fallen City." Tr. Karen Kingsbury. *Renditions* 45 (Spring 1996).

Zhang Chengzhi

Beifang de he (*The River of the North*). Tianjin: Baihua wenyi, 1985.
Hei junma (*The Black Steed*). Wuhan: Changjiang wenyi, 1993.
Jin muchang (The Golden Pasture). Beijing: Zuojia, 1987.
Xinlin shi (A History of the Soul). Changsha: Hunan wenyi, 1999.

* * *

The Black Steed. Beijing: Chinese Literature Press, 1989.
"Dazzling Poma." Tr. Steven L. Riep. In Michael S. Duke, ed., *Worlds of Modern Chinese Fiction*. Armonk, NY: M.E. Sharpe, 1991, 329–38.
"The Love of Shata." *Chinese Literature* (Winter 1995): 169–183.
"The Nine Palaces." In Jeanne Tai, ed., *Spring Bamboo: A Collection of Contemporary Chinese Short Stories*. New York: Random House, 1989, 41–55.
"River of the North." Tr. Stephen Fleming. *Chinese Literature* (Summer 1987): 42–137.
"Why Herdsmen Sing about 'Mother.'" Tr. Xu Ying. In *Prize-Winning Stories from China 1978–1979*. Beijing: Foreign Languages Press, 1985, 123–35.

Zhang Dachun

Bing bian (A Pathological Change). Taipei: Shibao, 1990.
Gongyu daoyou (*A Guided Tour of an Apartment Complex*). Beijing: Wenhua yishu, 1986.
Sahuang de xingtu (A Lier). Taipei: Lianhe wenxue, 1996.

* * *

Wild Kids: Two Novels about Growing Up. Tr. Michael Berry. New York: Columbia University Press, 2000.
"The General's Monument." Trs. Ying-tsih Hwang and John Balcom. *The Chinese Pen* (Spring 1987): 58–84.
"A Guided Tour of an Apartment Complex." Tr. Chen I-djen. *The Chinese Pen* (Winter 1989): 1–24.

Zhang Er

Mei ren kanjian ni kanjian de jingzhi (The Sceneries Only You Saw). Xining: Qinghai renmin, 1999.
Shan yuan (Connected to Mountains). Taipei: Tangshan, 2005.
Shui zi (Words on Water). New York: Xin dalu, 2002.

* * *

Carved Water. Tr. Bob Holman. Kaneohe, HI: Tinfish Press, 2003.
Slight Progress. Tr. Rachel D. Levitsky. New York: Pleasure Boat Studio, 2006.
Verses on Bird. Tr. Rachel D. Levitsky. Brookline, MA: Zephyr Press, 2004.

Zhang Guixing

Fu hu (Capturing the Tiger). Taipei: Shibao, 1980.
Hou bei (The Primate Cup). Taipei: Lianhe wenxue, 2000.
Keshan de ernü (Keshan's Sons and Daughters). Taipei: Yuanliu, 1988.
Qun xiang (Herds of Elephants). Taipei: Shibao, 1998.
Sailian zhi ge (Siren Song). Taipei: Yuanliu, 1992.
Wanpi jiazu (The Clown Dynasty). Taipei: Lianhe wenxue, 1996.
Wo sinian de chang mian zhong de nan guo gongzhu (My South Seas Sleeping Beauty: A Tale of Memory and Longing). Taipei: Maitian, 2001.
Xue Liyang daifu (Dr. Xue Liyang). Taipei: Maitian, 1994.

* * *

My South Seas Sleeping Beauty: A Tale of Memory and Longing. Tr. Valerie Jaffe. New York: Columbia University Press, 2007.

Zhang Henshui

Bashiyi meng (Eighty-one Dreams). Taiyuan: Beiyue wenyi, 1993.
Chun ming wai shi (An Unofficial History of a Sunny Spring). Taiyuan: Beiyue wenyi, 1993.
Jinfen shijia (The Family of Wealth). Beijing: Tuanjie, 2003.
Ti xiao yinyuan (Fate in Tears and Laughter). Hong Kong: Xuelin, 1990.

* * *

Eighty-one Dreams [excerpts]. Tr. T. M. McClellan. *Renditions* 57 (2002): 35–67.
Fate in Tears and Laughter [excerpts]. Tr. Borthwick. In Liu Ts'un-yan, ed., *Chinese Middlebrow Fiction: Fiction from the Ch'ing and Early Republican Eras*. Hong Kong: The Chinese University Press, 1984, 255–87.

Shanghai Express: A Thirties Novel by Zhang Henshui. Tr. William Lyell. Honolulu: University of Hawaii Press, 1997.

Zhang Jie

Ai shi bu neng wangji de (*Love Must Not Be Forgotten*). Guangzhou: Guangdong renmin, 1980.
Chenzhong de chibang (*Heavy Wings*). Beijing: Renmin wenxue, 1982.
Fang zhou (*The Ark*). Beijing: Beijing chubanshe, 1983.
Wu zi (No Written Word). Beijing: Shiyue wenyi, 2002.

* * *

As Long as Nothing Happens Nothing Will. London: Virago, 1988.
Heavy Wings. Tr. Howard Goldblatt. New York: Grove Weidenfeld, 1989.
Love Must Not Be Forgotten. San Francisco: China Books, 1986.
"The Time Is Not Yet Ripe." Tr. Gladys Yang. In Yang Bian, ed., *The Time Is Not Ripe: Contemporary China's Best Writers and Their Stories*. Beijing: Foreign Languages Press, 1991, 260–80.

Zhang Junmo

Cu kafei (Coarse Coffee). Taipei: Yuanjing, 1979.
Rihuo shifen (At Sunset). Kong Kong: Chunfeng, 1967.
Xiangchou (Nostalgia). Hong Kong: Shanbian she, 1982.
Xianggang ziye (Hong Kong at Midnight). Guangzhou: Huacheng, 1986.
Yaoyuan de xingsu (Distant Stars). Kong Kong: Lufeng, 1978.

Zhang Kangkang

Chi tong dan zhu (All Shades of Red). Beijing: Renmin wenxue, 1995.
Qing'ai hualang (Gallery of Romantic Love). Shenyang: chunfeng wenyi, 1996.
Yinxing banlü (*Invisible Companion*). Beijing: Zuojia, 1986.

* * *

The Invisible Companion. Tr. Daniel Bryant. Hong Kong: New World Press, 1996.
Living With Their Past: Post-Urban Youth Fiction. Ed. Richard King. Hong Kong: Renditions, 2002.
"The Right to Love" [Ai de quanli]. In R. A. Roberts and Angela Knox, eds./trs., *One Half of the Sky: Selections from Contemporary Women Writers of China*. London: William Heinemann, 1987, 51–81.
"Northern Lights." Tr. Daniel Bryant. *Chinese Literature* (Winter 1988): 92–102.

Zhang Tianyi

Baoshi fuzi (The Father and the Son of the Baos). Shanghai: Santong, 1941.
Dalin he xiaolin (*Big Lin and Little Lin*). Beijing: Zhongguo shaonian ertong, 1956
Huawei xiansheng (Mr. Huawei). Beijing: Renmin wenxue, 1955.
San xiongdi (Three Brothers). Shanghai: Wenguang, 1937.
Yangjingbang qixia (Knights Errant Speaking Pidgin). Shanghai: Xinzhong, 1936.
Zai chengshi li (In the City). Shanghai: Liangyu, 1937.

* * *

Big Lin and Little Lin. Tr. Gladys Yang. Peking: Foreign Languages Press, 1958.
Snake-Bite & Other Children's Stories from China: 1949–1979. San Francisco: China Books and Periodicals, 1984.
Magic Gourd. Tr. Gladys Yang. Beijing: Foreign Languages Press, 1959.
"Mid-Autumn Festival." Tr. Ronald Miao. In Joseph S. M. Lau and Howard Goldblatt, eds., *The Columbia Anthology of Modern Chinese Literature.* New York: Columbia University Press, 1995, 136–42.
"Mr. Hua Wei." Trs. J. Vochala and I. Lervitova. *New Orient* 5, 4 (1966).
"A New Life." Tr. Carl Durley. *Renditions* 2 (1974): 31–49.

Zhang Wei

Baihui (Baihui). Beijing: Shiyue wenyi, 1994.
Ciwei ge (Song of a Hedgehog). Beijing: Renmin wenxue, 2007.
Gu chuan (The Ancient Boat). Beijing: Renmin wenxue, 1987.
Jiazu (The Clan). Shanghai: Shanghai wenyi, 1995.
Jiuyue de yuyan (*September's Fable*): Shanghai: Shanghai wenyi, 1993.
Neng bu yi shukui (Remembering Hollyhock). Wuhan: Changjiang wenyi, 2005.
Qiutian de fennu (The Wrath of Autumn). Beijing: Renmin wenxue, 1986.
Waisheng shu (Letters). Beijing: Zuojia, 2000.

* * *

September's Fable [excerpt]. Trs. Terrence Russell and Shawn Xian Ye. *Words Without Borders: The Online Magazine for International Literature.*

Zhang Xianliang

Ling yu rou (*Body and Soul*). Tianjin: Baihua wenyi, 1981.
Lühua shu (*Mimosa*). Beijing: Shiyue wenyi, 1984.
Nanren de yiban shi nüren (*Half of Man Is Woman*). Beijing: Zhongguo wenlian, 1985.
Xiguan siwang (*Getting Used to Dying*). Tianjin: Baihua wenyi, 1989.

* * *

Getting Used to Dying. Tr. M. Avery. London: Collins, 1991.
Grass Soup. Tr. M. Avery. London: Secker and Warburg, 1994.
Half of Man Is Woman. Tr. Martha Avery. New York: W. W. Norton, 1986.
Mimosa. Tr. G. Yang. Beijing: Panda Books, 1985.
My Bodhi Tree. Tr. Martha Avery. London: Secker and Warburg, 1996.
"Body and Soul." Tr. Phillip F. C. Williams. In W. C. Chau, ed., *Prize Winning Stories from China: 1980–81.* Beijing: Foreign Languages Press, 1985, 58–92.

Zhang Xiaofeng

Bu xia hong tan zhi hou (After Stepping Off the Red Carpet). Hong Kong: Daosheng, 1979.
Cong ni meili de liuyu (From Your Beautiful River Valley). Nanjing: Jiangsu wenyi, 2006.
Ditan de na yi duan (At the Other End of the Carpet). Taipei: Daosheng, 1983.
Ni hai meiyou ai guo (You Have Never Loved). Taipei: Dadi, 1987.
Qiuqian shang de nüzi (The Woman on the Swing). Guangzhou: Huancheng, 2005.
Xiaofeng xiaoshuo ji (Selected Stories by Zhang Xiaofeng). Taipei: Daosheng, 1976.

* * *

"Lumps of Coal." Tr. Jane Parish Yang. *The Chinese Pen* (Spring 1985): 33–60.
"A Variety of Lovely Things." Tr. Christopher Lupke. *The Chinese Pen* (Summer 1985): 63–73.

Zhang Xiguo

Boli shijie (The Glass World). Taipei: Hongfan, 1999.
Kongzi zhi si (Death of Confucius). Taipei: Hongfan, 1978.
Pi Mushi (Reverend Pi). Taipei: Hongfan, 1978.
Qi wang (The Chess King). Taipei: Hongfan, 1983.
Rang weilai deng yi deng ba (Let the Future Wait). Taipei: Hongfan, 1984.
Wu yu die (*Five Jade Disks*). Hong Kong: Zhishi, 1983.
Xiangjiao chuan (*Banana Boat*). Taipei: Hongfan, 1976.
Xingyun zu qu (The Star and Cloud Series). Taipei: Hongfan, 1980.

* * *

The Chess King. Tr. Ivan Zimmerman. Singapore: ASIAPAC Books Ltd., 1986.
The City Trilogy: Five Jade Disks, Defenders of the Dragon City, and Tale of a Feather. Tr. John Balcom. New York: Columbia University Press, 2003.

"Banana Boat." In Neal Robbins, ed., *Contemporary Chinese Fiction: Four Short Stories*. New Haven: Far Eastern Publications, Yale University, 1986.
"Flute." *The Chinese Pen* (Summer 1975): 55–77.

Zhang Xin

Ai you ruhe (What about Love). Tianjin: Baihua wenyi, 1998.
Ban ni dao liming (Staying with You till Dawn). Beijing: Jingji ribao, 1997.
Chengshi qingren (Lovers in the City). Beijing: Huayi, 1995.

* * *

"Certainly Not Coincidence." In *Six Contemporary Chinese Women Writers, IV*. Beijing: Panda Books, 1995, 264–74.
"Invincible Time." *Chinese Literature* (Spring 1997).
"What Hope For." *Chinese Literature* (Winter 1998).

Zhang Xinxin

Beijingren—yibaige putong ren de zishu (Beijingers: Lives of One Hundred Ordinary People), with Sang Ye. Shanghai: Shanghai wenyi, 1986.
Du bu dong xi (Solitary Journeys between the East and the West). Beijing: zhishi, 2000.
Women zhege nianji de meng (Dreams of Our Generation). Chengdu: Sichuan wenyi, 1985.

* * *

"A 'Bengal Tigress' Interviews Herself: A Panorama of Our Times from Within." Tr. Ellen Lai-shan Yeung. In Helmut Martin, ed., *Modern Chinese Writers: Self-portrayals*. Armonk, NY: M.E. Sharpe, 1992, 137–46.
"The Dreams of Our Generation" and "Selections from Beijing's People." Eds./trs. Edward Gunn, Donna Jung, and Patricia Farr. Ithaca, NY: Cornell East Asia Papers, 1986.
"Dust." Tr. W. J. F. Jenner. *Renditions* 27/28 (1987): 163–73.
"How Did I Miss You?" Tr. Angela Knox. In R. A. Roberts and Angela Knox, eds., *One Half of the Sky*. Heinemann: London, 1987, 92–124.
"Theatrical Effects." Tr. Jeffrey C. Kinkley. *Fiction* 8, 2/3 (1987): 146–65.

Zhang Yueran

Hong xie (Red Shoes). Shanghai: Yiwen, 2006.
Kuihua zou shi zai 1890 (Sunflowers Lost in 1890). Beijing: Zuojia, 2003.
Shi ai (Ten Love Stories). Beijing: Zuojia, 2004.
Shi niao (The Story of the Revenge Bird). Shanghai: Guangming riban chubanshe, 2006.

Zhang Zao

Chun qiu lai xin (Letters from Spring and Autumn). Beijing: Wenhua yishu chubanshe, 2000.

* * *

"Night View of New York." Tr. Yanbing Chen. In Henry Y. H. Zhao, Yanbing Chen, and John Rosenwald, eds., *Fissures: Chinese Writing Today*. Brookline, MA: Zephyr Press, 2000, 144–46.
Poems in Zhang Er and Chen Dongdong, eds., *Another Kind of Nation: An Anthology of Contemporary Chinese Poetry*. Jersey City, NJ: Talisman House, 2007.

Zhao Mei

Lang yuan (The Garden). Shenyang: Chunfeng wenyi, 1994.
Linghun zhi guang (The Light of the Soul). Zhengzhou: Henan wenyi, 2002.
Qiutian si yu dong ji (Autumn Dies in Winter). Chengdu: Sichuan wenyi, 2005.
Shiji mo de qingren (Lovers at the Fin de Siècle) Nanjing: Jiangsu wenyi, 1998.
Tianguo de lianren (Lover of the Sky). Beijing: Zuojia, 1993.
Tiankong meiyou yanse (The Sky Has No Color). Tianjin: Bai hua wen yi chu ban she, 1998.
Women jiazu de nüren (Women in My Family). Shengyang: Chunfeng wenyi, 1998.
Wu Zetian (Empress Wu Zetian). Wuhan: Changjiang wenyi, 2007.

Zhao Shuli

Li jia zhuang de bianqian (*Changes in Li Village*). Shanxi: Huabei xinhua shudian, 1946.
Li Youcai banhua (*Rhymes of Li Youcai*). Shanxi: Huabei xinhua shudian, 1943.
San li wan (The Three-Mile Bend). Beijing: Renmin wenxue, 1958.
Xiaoerhe jiehun (*Little Erhei's Marriage*). Shanxi: Huabei xinhua shudian, 1943.

* * *

Changes in Li Village. Tr. Gladys Yang. Beijing: Foreign Languages Press, 1954.
Rhymes of Li Youcai and Other Stories. Tr. Gladys Yang. Beijing: Foreign Languages Press, 1980.
Sanliwan Village. Tr. Gladys Yang. Beijing: Foreign Languages Press, 1964.
"Little Erhei's Marriage." *Chinese Literature* 5 (1979): 28–54.

Zheng Chouyu

Yibo (Legacy). Taipei: Shangwu, 1966. *Yanren xing* (Journey of a Northerner). Taipei: Hongfan, 1980.

Jimo de ren zuo zhe kan hua (A Man of Solitude Views Flowers While Seated). Taipei: Hongfan, 1993.

Zheng Chouyu shi xuan (Poems by Zheng Chouyu). Beijing: Zhongguo youyi, 1984.

* * *

Poems in Domini Cheung, ed./tr., *The Isle Full of Noises: Modern Chinese Poetry from Taiwan*. New York: Columbia University Press, 1987, 73–83.

Zheng Wanlong

Hong ye, zai shan na bian (Red Leaves over the Other Side of the Mountain). Chengdu: Sichuan renmin, 1983.

Shengming de tuteng (Totem of Life). Beijing: Zhongguo wenlian, 1989.

Youren qiaomen (Someone Is Knocking on the Door). Shenyang: Chunfeng wenyi, 1986.

Zheng Wanlong xiaoshuo xuan (Stories by Zheng Wanlong). Beijing: Beijing chubanshe, 1982.

* * *

Strange Tales from Strange Lands. Tr. Kam Louie. Ithaca, NY: Cornell East Asia Series, 1993.

"The Clock." Tr. Jeanne Tai. In Tai, ed., *Spring Bamboo: A Collection of Contemporary Chinese Short Stories*. New York: Random House, 1989, 3–18.

"Mother Lode." Tr. Jeffrey C. Kinkley. In Michael S. Duke, ed., *Worlds of Modern Chinese Fiction*. Armonk, NY: M.E. Sharpe, 1991, 319–28.

"My Light." Tr. Caroline Mason. *Renditions* 46: 7–46.

Zheng Yi

Lao jing (*Old Well*). Beijing: Zhongguo nongmin, 1994.

Shen shu (Magic Tree). Taipei: Sanmin, 1996.

* * *

Old Well. Tr. David Kwan. San Francisco: China Books and Periodicals, 1989.

Scarlet Memorial: Tales of Cannibalism in Modern China. Ed./tr. T. P. Sym. Boulder: Westview Press, 1996.

"Maple." In Perry Link, ed., *Stubborn Weeds: Popular and Controversial Chinese Literature after the Cultural Revolution.* Bloomington: Indiana University Press, 1983, 57–73.

"Morning Fog." Tr. Li Guoqing. *Chinese Literature* (Autumn 1989): 38–49.

Zheng Zhenduo

Duanjian ji (Sword). Shanghai: Wenhua shenghuo, 1936.
Haiyan (Seagulls). Shanghai: Xin Zhongguo, 1932.
Jiating de gushi (Family Stories). Shanghai: Kaiming, 1931.
Ou xing riji (Journals of My Trip to Europe). Shanghai: Liangyou, 1934.

* * *

"A Contemporary Appraisal of Lin Shu." Tr. Diana Yu. *Renditions* 5: 26–29.

Zhong Lihe

Jiazhutao (Oleander). Gaoxiong: Paise wenhua, 1997.
Lishan nongchang (Lishan Farms). Gaoxiong: Paise wenhua, 1995.
Yuanxiangren: Zhong Lihe zhong duan pian xiaoshuo xuan (The Native: Short Stories and Novellas by Zhong Lihe). Beijing: Renmin wenxue, 1983.
Zhong Lihe quanji (Complete Works of Zhong Lihe). Ed. Zhong Tiemin. Gaoxiong: Chunhui, 1997.

* * *

"Restored to Life." Tr. Timothy Ross. *The Chinese Pen* (Spring 1977): 54–77.
"The Tobacco Shed." Tr. Timothy Ross. *The Chinese Pen* (Spring 1978): 91–105.
"Together through Thick and Thin." Tr. Shiao-ling Yu. In Joseph S. M. Lau, ed., *The Unbroken Chain: An Anthology of Taiwan Fiction since 1926.* Bloomington: Indiana University Press, 1983, 57–67.

Zhong Xiaoyang

Ai ge (A Song of Sorrow). Taipei: Sansan shufang, 1987.
Ai qi (The Beloved Wife). Hong Kong: Tiandi, 1992.
Chun zai lü wu zhong (Spring in Green Wilderness). Hong Kong: Tiandi, 1993.
Gao mu si hui ji (Dead Wood and Burnt Ashes). Hong Kong: Sanren, 1996.
Liu nian (The Fleeting Time). Hong Kong: Tiandi, 1993.
Ran shao zhi hou (In the Wake of the Fire). Taipei: Maitian, 1992.
Ting che zan jie wen (Stop the Car the Ask for Directions). Hong Kong: Tiandi, 1991.

Xi shuo (In Detail). Taipei: Sansan shufang, 1993.
Yi hen chuanqi (Love in Eternal Regret). Hong Kong: Tiandi, 1996.

* * *

"Green Sleeves." Tr. Cathy Poon. *Renditions* 29/30 (1988): 132–45; also tr. Michael S. Duke. In Duke, ed., *Worlds of Modern Chinese Fiction*. Armonk, NY: M.E. Sharpe, 1991, 206–21.
"The Wedding Night." Tr. Samuel Cheung. In Hsin-Sheng C. Kao, ed., *Nativism Overseas: Contemporary Chinese Women Writers*. Albany: SUNY, 1993, 211–20.

Zhong Zhaozheng

Dadu shan fengyun (Clouds over Dadu Mountain). Taipei: Shangwu, 1966–1967.
Lubing hua (Lubing Flowers). Taipei: Mingzhi, 1962.
Taiwanren sanbuqu (Trilogy of the Taiwanese). Taipei: Yuanjing, 1980.
Zhuoliu sanbuqu (Trilogy of Muddy Current). Taipei: Yuanjing, 1979.

* * *

"Mountain Trail." Tr. Robert Hegel. *The Chinese Pen* (Summer 1973): 3–13.
"The Skull and the Faceless Clock." Tr. John Balcom. *Taiwan Literature, English Translation Series* no. 16 (2005): 83–100.

Zhou Erfu

Baiqiuen daifu (Doctor Bethune). Shanghai: Huaxia shudian, 1949.
Changcheng wan li tu (The Portrait of the Great Wall: A Historical Novel in Six Volumes [*Nanjing de xianluo* (The Fall of Nanjing); *Changjiang hai zai benteng* (The Yangtze River Flows On); *Ni liu yu an liu* (Countercurrent and Undercurrent); *Taipingyang de fuxiao* (Dawn over the Pacific); *Liming qian de ye se* (Night before Dawn); *Wu Chongqing* (Chongqing in Fog)]. Beijing: Wenhua yishu, 2004.
Shanghai de zaochen (Morning in Shanghai). Beijing: Renmin wenxue, 1958.
Yan su ya. Shanghai: Qunyi, 1950.
Ye xing ji (Poetry Collection). Shanghai: Qunyi, 1950.

* * *

Doctor Norman Bethune. Tr. Alison Bailey. Beijing: Foreign Languages Press, 1982.
Morning in Shanghai. Tr. A. C. Barnes. Beijing: Foreign Languages Press, 1962.

Zhou Libo

Bao feng zhou yu (The Storm). Beijing: Xinhua shudian, 1949.
He chang shang (On the Rice Threshing-Ground). Shanghai: Shanghai wenyi, 1960.
Shan xiang ju bian (*Great Changes in a Mountain Village*). Beijing: Zuojia, 1958.
Tie shui benliu (The Iron Rushes). Beijing: Zuojia, 1955.

* * *

Great Changes in a Mountain Village: A Novel in Two Volumes [Shan xiang ju bian]. Tr. Derek Bryan. Beijing: Foreign Languages Press, 1961.
The Hurricane [Bao feng zhou yu]. Tr. Hsu Meng-hsung, Beijing: Foreign Languages Press, 1955.
Sowing the Clouds: A Collection of Chinese Short Stories by Chou Li-po [Zhou Libo], Li Chun and Others. Beijing: Foreign Languages Press, 1961.

Zhou Lunyou

Dakai routi zhi men/Feifei zhuyi: cong lilun dao zuoping (Opening the Door of Flesh/Feifeism: From Theory to Practice). Ed. Zhou Lunyou. Lanzhou: Dunhuang wenyi, 1994.
Fan jiazhi shidai (The Era of Anti-Values). Chengdu: Sichuan renmin, 1999.
Ranshao de jingji (Burning Thorns).
Zhou Lunyou shi xuan (Poems by Zhou Lunyou). Guangzhou: Huangcheng, 2006.

Zhou Meisen

Chong e (Double Yoke). Guangzhou: Huacheng, 1990.
Juedui quanli (Absolute Power). Beijing: Zuojia, 2002.
Tianxia caifu (The Wealth of the World). Beijing: Renmin wenxue, 1997.
Yuan yu (The Original Prison). Beijing: Renmin wenxue, 1997.
Zhongguo zhizao (Made in China). Beijing: Zuojia, 1999.

Zhou Zuoren

Bing zhu tan (Chat under the Candlelight). Beijing: Beixin, 1940.
Fan hou suibi. Shijiazhuang: Hebei renmin, 1994.
Feng yu tan (Chat in a Windstorm). Beijing: Beixin, 1936.
Yu tian de shu (Books for Rainy Days). Beijing: Beixin, 1925.

* * *

Selected Essays by Zhou Zuoren. Tr. David Pollard. Hong Kong: Chinese University Press, 2005.

"Humane Literature." Tr. Ernst Wolfe. In Wolfe, ed., *Chou Tso-jen*. New York: Twayne, 1971, 97–105.

"On 'Passing the Itch'" Tr. David Pollard. In Pollard, ed., *The Chinese Essay*. New York: Columbia University Press, 2000, 139–49.

Zhu Tianwen

Huang ren shouji (*Notes of a Desolate Man*). Taipei: Shibao wenhua, 1994.

Shiji mo de huali (*Fin de Siécle Splendor*). Chengdu: Sichuan wenyi, 1999.

Wu yan (Words of the Witch). Taipei, INK, 2004.

Yan xia zhi du (*A City in a Hot Summer*). Taipei: Shibao wenhua, 1987.

Zui xiangnian de jijie (The Most Cherished Season). Taipei: Sansan shufang, 1989.

* * *

Notes of a Desolate Man. Trs. Howard Goldblatt and Sylvia Li-Chuan Lin. New York: Columbia University Press, 1999.

"Buddhisattva Incarnate." Tr. Fran Martin. In Martin, ed., *Angel Wings: Contemporary Queer Fiction from Taiwan*. Honolulu: University of Hawaii Press, 2003, 29–50.

"A City of Hot Summer." Tr. Michelle Yeh. *The Chinese Pen* (Summer 1988): 1–38.

"Fin de Siécle Splendor." Tr. Eva Hung. In Joseph S. M. Lau and Howard Goldblatt, eds., *The Columbia Anthology of Modern Chinese Literature*. New York: Columbia University Press, 1995, 444–59.

"Master Chai." Tr. Michelle Yeh. In David Der-wei Wang, ed., *Running Wild: New Chinese Writers*. New York: Columbia University Press, 1994, 89–100.

Zhu Tianxin

Fangzhou shang de rizi (Days of the Ark). Taipei: Lianhe wenxue, 2001.

Gu du (The Ancient City). Taipei: Maitian, 1997.

Ji rang ge: bei yi nü san nian ji (Times of Peace and Comfort: Three Years at the Taipei Number One Middle School for Girls). Taipei: Lianhe wenxue, 2001.

Zuori dang wo nianqing shi (Yesterday When I Was Young). Taipei: Sansan shufang, 2001.

Weiliao (Unfinished). Taipei: Lianhe wenxue, 2001.

* * *

The Old Capital: A Novel of Taipei. Tr. Howard Goldblatt. New York: Columbia University Press, 2007.

"Epilogue: In Remembrance of My Buddies from the Military Compound." Tr. Michelle Wu. In Pang-yuan Chi and David Der-wei Wang, eds., *The Last of the Whampoa Breed: Stories of the Chinese Diaspora.* New York: Columbia University Press, 2003. 242–70.

"The Last Train to Tamshui." Tr. Michelle Yeh. *The Chinese Pen* (Spring 1988): 41–71.

"Nineteen Days of the New Party." Tr. Martha Cheung. *Renditions* 35/36 (1991): 144–70.

"A Story of Spring Butterflies." Tr. Fran Martin. In Martin, ed., *Angelwings: Contemporary Queer Fiction from Taiwan.* Honolulu: University of Hawaii Press, 2003, 75–94.

Zhu Xining

Hua Tai ping jia chuan (The Hua Family Heritage). Taipei: Lianhe wenxue, 2002.

Jiangjun yu wo (The General and I). Taipei: Hongfan, 1976.

Tie jiang (Iron Oars). Taipei: INK, 2003.

Poxiao shifen (Dawn). Taipei: INK, 2003.

Han ba (Drought Spirit). Taipei: Yuanliu, 1991.

Mao (Cat). Taipei: Yuanliu, 1990.

* * *

"The General." Tr. David Steelman. *The Chinese Pen* (Summer 1976): 1–41.

"The Great Puppet Show." Tr. Hua-yuan Li Mowry. *The Chinese Pen* (Autumn 1980): 1–19.

"The Men Who Smelt Gold." Tr. Gorge Kao. *Renditions* 1 (1973): 107–121.

"Molten Iron." Tr. Madeline K. Spring. In Joseph S. M. Lau and Howard Goldblatt, eds., *The Columbia Anthology of Modern Chinese Literature.* New York: Columbia University Press, 1995, 201–220.

"The Wolf." Tr. Hou Chien. In Chi Pang-yuan et al., eds., *An Anthology of Contemporary Chinese Literature.* Taipei: National Institute for Compilation and Translation, 1975, II, 77–114.

Zhu Ziqing

Beiying (Silhouette). Shanghai: Kaiming, 1928.

Ouyou zaji (Trip to Europe). Shanghai: Kaiming, 1934.

Xinshi zahua (Commentaries on New Poetry). Shanghai: Zuojia shuwu, 1947.

Xue zhao (Snowy Morning). Shanghai: Shangwu, 1922.

Zong ji (Traces). Shanghai: Yadong, 1924.

* * *

Essays in David Pollard, ed., *The Chinese Essay.* New York: Columbia University Press, 2000, 217–24.

Essays in Martin Wiesker, ed., *Twentieth Century Chinese Essays in Translation.* Bochum: Bochum University Press, 2000, 38–68.
Poems in Kai-yu Hsu, ed., *Twentieth Century Chinese Poetry: An Anthology.* Garden City, NY: Doubleday, 1963, 9–13.

Zong Baihua

Liu yun xiao shi (Floating Clouds: Short Poems). Hefei: Anhui jiaoyu, 2006, rpt.
San ye ji (Three Leaves: Correspondences among Three Friends), coauthored with Tian Han and Guo Moruo. 3rd ed. Shanghai: Yadong tushuguan, 1923.
Meixue de sanbu (The Aesthetic Promenade). 3rd ed. Taipei: Hongfan, 1984.
Zong Baihua quan ji (Collected Works by Zong Baihua). Hefei: Anhui jiaoyu, 1993.

Zong Pu

Dong cang ji (Hiding in the East). Beijing: Renmin wenxue, 2001.
Nan du ji (Going South). Beijing: Renmin wenxue, 1988
Sansheng shi (*Everlasting Rock*). Tianjin: Baihua wenyi, 1981.
Zong Pu sanwen xuanji (Selected Prose by Zong Pu). Tianjin: Baihua wenyi, 1993.

* * *

The Everlasting Rock. Tr. Aimee Lykes. Boulder: Lynne Rienner, 1997.
"The Call of the Ruins." Tr. David Pollard. In Pollard, ed., *The Chinese Essay.* New York: Columbia University Press, 2000, 317–20.
"Melody in Dreams." Tr. Song Shouquan. *Chinese Literature* 8 (1979): 78–99.
"The Tragedy of the Walnut Tree." Tr. Zhu Hong. In Hong, ed., *The Serenity of Whiteness: Stories By and About Women in Contemporary China.* New York: Ballantine Books, 1991, 282–300.
Stories in Hugh Anderson, ed., *A Wind across the Grass.* Ascot Vale, Victoria: Red Rooster Press, 1985, 52–104.

ANTHOLOGIES

Another Kind of Nation: An Anthology of Contemporary Chinese Poetry. Eds. Zhang Er and Chen Dongdong. Jersey City, NJ: Talisman House, 2007.
Anthology of Modern Chinese Poetry. Ed. Michelle Yeh. New Haven: Yale University Press, 1992.
Best Chinese Short Stories, 1949–1989. Beijing: Chinese Literature Press, 1989.

China China: Contemporary Poetry from Taiwan. Ed. Germaine Droogenbroodt and Peter Stinson. Belgium: Point Books, 1986.

Chinese Drama after the Cultural Revolution, 1979–1989: An Anthology. Ed. Shiao-ling Yu. Lewiston, NY: Edwin Mellen Press, 1996.

The Chinese Essay. Ed./tr. David Pollard. New York: Columbia University Press, 2000.

Chinese Stories of the Twentieth Century. Ed./tr. Zhihua Fang. New York: Garland Publishing, 1995.

The Chinese Western: Short Fiction From Today's China. Ed. Zhu Hong. New York: Ballantine, 1988.

The Columbia Anthology of Modern Chinese Literature. Eds. Joseph S. M. Lau and Howard Goldblatt. 2nd ed. New York: Columbia University Press, 2007.

Contemporary Chinese Literature: An Anthology of Post-Mao Fiction and Poetry. Ed. Michael Duke. Armonk, NY: M.E. Sharpe, 1985.

Eight Contemporary Chinese Poets. Eds. Naikan Tao and Tony Prince. Sydney: Wild Peony Press, 2006.

From the Bluest Part of the Harbour: Poems from Hong Kong. Ed. Andrew Parkin. London: Oxford University Press, 1996.

From the Shelters: Modern Chinese Poetry, 1930–1950. Ed. Wai-lim Yip. New York: Garland, 1992.

Frontier Taiwan. Eds. Michelle Yeh and N. G. D. Malmgvist. New York: Columbia University Press, 2001.

Furrows, Peasants, Intellectuals, and the State: Stories and Histories from Modern China. Ed. Helen Siu. Stanford: Stanford University Press, 1990.

Hong Kong Collage: Contemporary Stories and Writing. Ed. Martha P. Y. Cheung. New York: Oxford University Press, 1998.

Indigenous Writers of Taiwan: An Anthology of Stories, Essays, and Poems. Ed. John Balcom, New York: Columbia University Press, 2005.

The Isle Full of Noises: Modern Chinese Poetry from Taiwan. Ed. Dominic Cheung. New York: Columbia University Press, 1987.

Jumping through Hoops: Autobiographical Stories by Modern Chinese Women Writers. Ed. Jing M. Wang. Hong Kong: Hong Kong University Press, 2003.

The Last of the Whampoa Breed (Modern Chinese Literature from Taiwan). Eds. Pang-yuan Chi and David Der-Wei Wang. New York: Columbia University Press, 2003.

Literature of the People's Republic of China. Ed. Hsu Kai-yu. Bloomington: Indiana University Press, 1980.

The Lost Boat: Avant-garde Fiction from China. Ed. Henry Zhao. London: Wellsweep, 1993.

Loud Sparrows: Contemporary Chinese Short-Shorts. Eds/trs. Aili Mu, Julie Chiu, and Howard Goldblatt. New York: Columbia University Press, 2006.

Lyrics from the Shelter: Modern Chinese Poetry, 1930–1950. Ed./tr. Wai-lim Yip. New York: Garland, 1992.

Lyrical Prose of China: Stories, Essay, and Reminiscences. Ed./tr. Cheng Mei. Boulder: Lynne Rienner, 1997.

Mao's Harvest: Voices from China's New Generation. Eds. Helen Siu and Zelda Stern. London: Oxford University Press, 1983.

Mercury Rising: Contemporary Poetry from Taiwan. Eds. Frank Stewart, Arthur Sze, and Michelle Yeh, Honolulu: University of Hawaii Press, 2003.

Modern Chinese Stories and Novellas, 1919–1949. Eds. C. T. Hsia et al. New York: Columbia University Press, 1981.

The Mystified Boat and Other New Stories from China. Eds. Frank Stewart and Herbert J. Batt. Special issue of *Manoa: A Pacific Journal of International Writing* 15, 2 (Winter 2003). Honolulu: University of Hawaii Press.

New Generation: Poems from China Today. Ed. Wang Ping. New York: Hanging Loose Press, 1999.

New Tide: Contemporary Chinese Poetry. Eds./trs. Chao Tang and Lee Robinson. Toronto: Mangajin Books, 1992.

One Hundred Modern Chinese Poems. Eds/trs. Bingjun Pang, John Minford, and Sean Golden. Hong Kong: Commercial Press, 1987.

Out of the Howling Storm: The New Chinese Poetry. Ed. Tony Barstone. Hanover, NH: Wesleyan University Press, 1993.

An Oxford Anthology of Contemporary Chinese Drama. Eds. Martha Cheung and Jane Lai. Hong Kong: Oxford University Press, 1997.

Recent Fiction From China, 1987–89: Selected Stories and Novellas. Ed. Long Xu. Lewiston, NY: Edwin Mellen Press, 1991.

The Red Azalea: Chinese Poetry since the Cultural Revolution. Ed. Edward Morin. Honolulu: University of Hawaii Press, 1990.

Roses and Thorns: The Second Blooming of the Hundred Flowers in Chinese Fiction, 1979–1980. Ed. Perry Link. Berkeley: University of California Press, 1984.

Running Wild: New Chinese Writers. Eds. David Der-wei Wang and Jeanne Tai. New York: Columbia University Press, 1994.

Science Fiction from China. Eds. Patrick Murphy and Wu Dingbo. New York: Praeger, 1989.

A Splintered Mirror: Chinese Poetry from the Democracy Movement. Eds./trs. Donald Finkel and Carolyn Kizer. San Francisco: North Point, 1991.

Spring Bamboo: A Collection of Contemporary Chinese Short Stories. Ed. Jeanne Tai. New York: Random House, 1989.

Spring of Bitter Waters: Short Fiction from Today's China. Ed. Zhu Hong. London: Allison & Busby, 1989.

Tales of Tibet. Ed. Herbert J. Batt. Lanham, MD: Rowman & Littlefield, 2001.

The Time Is Not Ripe Yet. Ed. Ying Bian. Beijing: Foreign Languages Press, 1991.

Theater and Society: An Anthology of Contemporary Chinese Drama. Ed. Yan Haiping. Armonk, NY: East Gate Books, 1998.

Trees on the Mountain: An Anthology of New Chinese Writing. Eds. Stephen Soong and John Minford. Hong Kong: Renditions, 1984.

Twentieth-Century Chinese Drama: An Anthology. Ed. Edward Gunn. Bloomington: Indiana University Press, 1983.

Twentieth-Century Chinese Essays in Translation. Ed. Martin Woesler. Bochum: Bochum University Press, 2000.

A Wind across the Grass: Modern Chinese Writing with Fourteen Stories. Ed. Hugh Anderson. Ascot Vale, Vic.: Red Rooster Press, 1985.

Worlds of Modern Chinese Fiction. Ed. Michael S. Duke. Armonk, NY: M.E. Sharpe, 1991.

Writing Women in Modern China: An Anthology of Women's Literature from the Early Twentieth Century. Eds. Amy D. Dooling and Kritina M. Torgeson. New York: Columbia University Press, 1998.

Writing Women in Modern China: The Revolutionary Years, 1936–1976. Ed. Amy D. Dooling. New York: Columbia University Press, 2005.

SURVEYS AND GENERAL CRITICAL WORKS

Anderson, Marston. *Limits of Realism: Chinese Fiction in the Revolutionary Period.* Berkeley: University of California Press, 1990.

Barlow, Tani E. *Gender Politics in Modern China: Writing and Feminism.* Durham, NC: Duke University Press, 1993.

———. *The Question of Women in Chinese Feminism.* Durham, NC: Duke Univeristy Press, 2004.

Barme, Geremie. *In the Red: On Contemporary Chinese Culture.* New York: Columbia University Press, 1999.

Chang, Shuei May. *Casting Off the Shackles of Family: Ibsen's Nora Figure in Modern Chinese Literature, 1918–1942 (Studies on Themes and Motifs in Literature, Vol. 31).* New York: Peter Lang Publishing, 2004.

Chang, Sung-sheng Yvonne. *Modernism and the Nativist Resistance: Contemporary Chinese Fiction from Taiwan.* Durham, NC: Duke University Press, 1993.

Chen, Peng-Hsiang and Whitney Crothers Dilley, eds. *Feminism/Femininity in Chinese Literature.* Amsterdam: Rodopi, 2002.

Chen, Xiaomei. *Occidentalism: A Theory of Counter-Discourse in Post-Mao China.* New York: Oxford University Press, 1995.

Chi, Pang-Yuan and David Der-Wei Wang. *Chinese Literature in the Second Half of a Modern Century: A Critical Survey.* Bloomington: Indiana University Press, 2000.

Chong, Woei Lian, ed. *China's Great Proletarian Cultural Revolution: Master Narratives and Post-Mao Counternarratives.* Lanham, MD: Rowman & Littlefield, 2002.

Chou, Ying-hsiung, ed. *The Chinese Text: Studies in Comparative Literature.* Hong Kong: The Chinese University Press, 1986.

Chow, Rey. *Women and Chinese Modernity: The Politics of Reading Between West and East.* Minneapolis: University of Minnesota Press, 1991.

——. *Primitive Passions: Visuality, Sexuality, Ethnography, and Contemporary Chinese Cinema.* New York: Columbia University Press, 1995.

——, ed. *Modern Chinese Literary and Cultural Studies in the Age of Theory: Reimagining a Field.* Durham, NC: Duke University Press, 2000.

Denton, Kirk A. *The Problematic of Self in Modern Chinese Literature: Hu Feng and Lu Ling.* Palo Alto: Stanford University Press, 1998.

Dooling, Amy D. *Women's Literary Feminism in Twentieth Century China.* New York: Palgrave Macmillan, 2005.

Duke, Michael S., ed. *Modern Chinese Women Writers: Critical Appraisals.* Armonk, NY: M.E. Sharpe, 1989.

Elvin, Mark. *Changing Stories in the Chinese World.* Palo Alto: Stanford University Press, 1997.

Farquhar, Mary Ann. *Children's Literature in China from Lu Xun to Mao Zedong.* Armonk, NY: M.E. Sharpe, 1999, 26–90.

Faurot, Jeannette, ed. *Chinese Fiction from Taiwan: Critical Perspectives.* Bloomington: Indiana University Press, 1980.

Feng, Jin. *The New Woman in Early Twentieth-Century Chinese Fiction.* West Lafayette, IN: Purdue University Press, 2004.

Feuerwerker, Yi-Tsi Mei. *Ideology, Power, Text: Self-Representation and the Peasant "Other" in Modern Chinese Literature.* Palo Alto: Stanford University Press, 1999.

——. *Ding Ling's Fiction: Ideology and Narrative in Modern Chinese Literature.* Boston: Harvard University Press, 1982.

Findeisen, Raoul D. and Robert H. Gassmann, eds. *Autumn Floods: Essays in Honour of Marian Galik.* Bern: Peter Lang, 1997.

Foster, Paul. *Ah Q Archaeology: Lu Xun, Ah Q, Ah Q's Progeny, and the National Character Discourse in Twentieth Century China.* Lanham, MD: Lexington Books, 2005.

Galik, Marian. *The Genesis of Modern Chinese Literary Criticism, 1917–1930.* London: Curzon Press, 1980.

——, ed. *Milestones in Sino-Western Literary Confrontation (1898–1979).* Weisbaden: Otto Harrassowitz, 1986.

———, ed. *Interliterary and Intraliterary Aspects of the May Fourth Movement 1919 in China.* Bratislava: Veda, 1990.

Goldblatt, Howard, ed. *Worlds Apart: Recent Chinese Writing and Its Audiences.* Armonk, NY: M.E. Sharpe, 1990.

Goldman, Merle. *Modern Chinese Literature in the May Fourth Era.* Boston: Harvard University Press, 1985.

Gun, Edward. *Unwelcome Muse: Chinese Literature in Shanghai and Peking (1937–1945).* New York: Columbia University Press, 1980.

Hanan, Patrick. *Chinese Fiction of the Nineteenth and Early Twentieth Centuries: Essays by Patrick Hanan.* New York: Columbia University Press, 2004.

Hay, John, ed. *Boundaries in China.* London: Reaktion Books, 1994.

Hom, Sharon K. *Chinese Women Traversing Diaspora: Memoirs, Essays, and Poetry (Gender, Culture and Global Politics, 3).* Milton Park (UK): Routledge, 1999.

Hsia, Chih-Tsing. *C. T. Hsia on Chinese Literature.* New York: Columbia University Press, 2004.

———. *A History of Modern Chinese Fiction.* 3rd. ed. Bloomington: Indiana University Press, 1999.

Hung, Chang-t'ai. *War and Popular Culture: Resistance in Modern China, 1937–1945.* Berkeley: University of California Press, 1994.

Huters, Theodore. *Reading the Modern Chinese Short Story.* Armonk, NY: M.E. Sharpe, 1990.

———. *Bringing the World Home: Appropriating the West in Late Qing and Early Republican China.* Honolulu: University of Hawaii Press, 2005.

Kam, Louise. *Between Fact and Fiction: Essays on Post-Mao Chinese Literature and Society.* Sydney: Wild Peony, 1989.

Keaveney. Christopher T. *The Subversive Self in Modern Chinese Literature: The Creation Society's Reinvention of the Japanese Shishosetsu.* New York: Palgrave Macmillan, 2004.

Kubin, Wolfgang and Rudolf G. Wagner, eds. *Essays in Modern Chinese Literature and Literary Criticism.* Bochum: Brockmeyer, 1982.

———, ed. *Symbols of Anguish: In Search of Melancholy in China.* Bern: Peter Lang, 2001.

Kuoshu, Harry. *Lightness of Being in China: Adaptation and Discursive Figuration in Cinema and Theater.* New York: Peter Lang, 1999.

———. *Symbols of Anguish: In Search of Melancholy in China.* Bern: Peter Lang, 2001.

Larson, Wendy. *Literary Authority and the Modern Chinese Writer: Ambivalence and Autobiography.* Durham, NC: Duke University Press, 1991.

———. *Women and Writing in Modern China.* Stanford: Stanford University Press, 1998.

Larson, Wendy, and Anne Wedell-Wedellsbog, eds. *Inside Out: Modernism and Postmodernism in Chinese Literary Culture.* Aarhus, Denmark: Aarhus University Press, 1993.

Laughlin, Charles. *Contested Modernities in Chinese Literature.* New York: Palgrave Macmillan, 2005.

Lee, Gregory B. *Troubadours, Trumpeters, Troubled Makers: Lyricism, Nationalism, and Hybridity in China and Its Others.* Durham, NC: Duke University Press, 1996.

Lee, Leo Ou-fan. *The Romantic Generation of Modern Chinese Writers.* Cambridge, MA: Harvard University Press, 1973.

———. *Lu Xun and His Legacy.* Berkeley: University of California Press, 1985.

———. *Shanghai Modern: The Flowering of a New Urban Culture in China, 1930–1945.* Cambridge, MA: Harvard University Press, 1999.

Lee, Mabel, and Michael Wilding, eds. *History, Literature and Society: Essays in Honour of S. N. Mukherjee.* Sydney: Sydney Association for Studies in Culture and Society, 1997.

Lin, Min, and Maria Galikowski. *The Search for Modernity: Chinese Intellectuals and Cultural Discourse in the Post-Mao Era.* New York: St. Martin's Press, 1999.

Lin, Yusheng. *The Crisis of Chinese Consciousness: Radical Anti-Traditionalism in the May Fourth Era.* Madison: University of Wisconsin Press, 1979.

Liu, Kang and Xiaobing Tang, eds. *Politics, Ideology, and Literary Discourse in Modern China: Theoretical Interventions and Cultural Critique.* Durham, NC: Duke University Press, 1994.

Lu, Sheldon Hsiao-peng. *Chinese Modernity and Global Biopolitics: Studies in Literature and Visual Culture.* Honolulu: University of Hawaii Press, 2007.

Lu, Tonglin. *Gender and Sexuality in Twentieth Century Chinese Literature and Society.* Albany: SUNY press, 1993.

———. *Misogyny, Cultural Nihilism, and Oppositional Politics.* Stanford: Stanford University Press, 1995.

Lupke, Christopher, and Rey Chow, eds. *Modern Chinese Literary and Cultural Studies in the Age of Theory: Reimagining a Field.* Durham, NC: Duke University Press, 2001.

McDougal, Bonnie S., ed. *Popular Chinese Literature and Performing Arts in the People's Republic of China.* Berkeley: University of California Press, 1984.

———. *Fictional Authors, Imaginary Audiences: Modern Chinese Literature in the Twentieth Century.* Hong Kong: Chinese University Press, 2003.

McDougal, Bonnie S., and Anders Hansson, eds. *The Chinese at Play: Festivals, Games and Leisure.* London: Kegan Paul, 2002.

Mi, Jiayan. *Self-Fashioning and Reflexive Modernity in Modern Chinese Poetry.* Lewiston, NY: Edwin Mellen Press, 2004.

Mostow, Joshua, and Kirk A. Denton, eds. *Columbia Companion to Modern East Asian Literatures*. New York: Columbia University Press, 2003.

Mostow, Joshua. *Women, War, Domesticity: Shanghai Literature and Popular Culture of the 1940s*. Leiden: Brill, 2005.

Ng, Hanet. *The Experience of Modernity: Chinese Autobiography in the Early Twentieth Century*. Ann Arbor: University of Michigan Press, 2003.

Nienhauser, William, ed. *Critical Essays on Chinese Literature*. Hong Kong: Chinese University of Hong Kong Press, 1976.

Palandri, Angela Jung, ed. *Women Writers of 20th-Century China*. Eugene: Asian Studies Publications, University of Oregon, 1982.

Prusek, Jaroslav. *Three Sketches of Chinese Literature*. Prague: Academia, 1969.

———. *The Lyrical and the Epic: Studies in Modern Chinese Literature*. Bloomington: Indiana University Press, 1980.

Shih, Shumei. *The Lure of the Modern: Writing Modernism in Semicolonial China, 1917–1937*. Berkeley: University of California Press, 2001.

Shu, Yunzhong. *Buglers on the Home Front: The Wartime Practice of the Qiyue School*. Albany: SUNY Press, 2000.

Sun, Lung-kee. *The Chinese National Character: From Nationhood to Individuality*. Armonk, NY: M.E. Sharpe, 2001.

Tang, Xiaobing. *Chinese Modernism: The Heroic and the Quotidian*. Durham, NC: Duke University Press, 2000.

Ting, Yi. *Short History of Modern Chinese Literature*. Associated Faculty Pr Inc, 1970.

Wagner, Rudolf. *The Contemporary Chinese Historical Drama*. Berkeley: University of California Press, 1990.

———. *Inside the Service Trade: Studies in Contemporary Chinese Prose*. Cambridge, MA: Council on East Asian Studies, Harvard University, 1992.

Wang, Ban. *The Sublime Figure of History*. Palo Alto: Stanford University Press, 1997.

———. *Narrative Perspective and Irony in Selected Chinese and American Fiction*. Lewiston, NY: Edwin Mellen Press, 2002.

Wang, Chaohua, ed. *One China, Many Paths*. London: Verso, 2003.

Wang, David Der-wei. *Fictional Realism in 20th-Century China: Mao Dun, Laoshe, Shen Congwen*. New York: Columbia University Press, 1992.

———. *The Monster That Is History: History, Violence, and Fictional Writing in Twentieth-Century China* (Philip E. Lilienthal Book in Asian Studies). Berkeley: University of California Press, 2004.

Wang, David Der-wei, and Joyce Liu, eds. *Writing Taiwan: Strategies of Representation*. Durham, NC: Duke University Press, 2006.

Wang, Mason Y. H., ed. *Perspectives in Contemporary Chinese Literature*. University Center, MI: Green River Press, 1983.

Widmer, Ellen, and David Der-wei Wang, eds. *From May Fourth to June Fourth: Fiction and Film in Twentieth-Century China.* Cambridge, MA: Harvard University Press, 1993.

Woeseler, Martin, ed. *The Modern Chinese Literary Essay: Defining the Chinese Self in the 20th Century.* Bochum: Bochum University Press, 2000.

Wong, Yoon Wah. *Essays on Chinese Literature.* Singapore: Singapore University Press, 1988.

Yang, Bian. *The Time Is Not Ripe: Contemporary China's Best Writers and Their Stories.* Beijing: Foreign Languages Press, 1991.

Yang, Mayfair Mei Hui, ed. *Spaces of Their Own: Women's Public Sphere in Transnational China.* Minneapolis: University of Minnesota Press, 1999.

Yang, Winston, L. Y., and Nathan K. Mao, eds. *Modern Chinese Fiction: A Guide to Its Study and Appreciation: Essays and Bibliographies.* Boston: G.K. Hall and Co., 1981.

Yang, Xiaobin, ed. *The Chinese Postmodern: Trauma and Irony in Chinese Avant-Garde Fiction.* Ann Arbor: University of Michigan Press, 2002.

Yi, Ting. *A Short History of Modern Chinese Literature.* University Press of the Pacific, 2001.

Yip, Wai-lim, ed., *Chinese Arts and Literature: A Survey of Recent Trends.* Occasional Papers/Reprint Series in Contemporary Asian Studies. Baltimore, 1977.

Yue, Gang. *The Mouth That Begs: Hunger, Cannibalism, and the Politics of Eating in Modern China.* Durham, NC: Duke University Press, 1999.

Zhang, Xudong. *Chinese Modernism in the Era of Reforms.* Durham, NC: Duke University Press, 1997.

Zhang, Yingjin. *The City in Modern Chinese Literature and Film.* Stanford: Stanford University Press, 1996.

Zhong, Xueping, ed. *Masculinity Besieged? Issues of Modernity and Male Subjectivity in Chinese Literature of the Late Twentieth Century.* Durham, NC: Duke University Press, 2000.

CRITICAL WORKS ON INDIVIDUAL AUTHORS

Ah Cheng

Duke, Michael S. "Two Chess Masters, One Chinese Way: A Comparison of Chang His-kuo's and Chung Ah-cheng's 'Chi Wang.'" *Asian Culture Quarterly* (Winter 1987): 41–63.

Huters, Theodore. "Speaking of Many Things: Food, Kings, and the National Tradition in Ah Cheng's 'The Chess King.'" *Modern China* 14, 4 (1988): 388–418.

Knapp, Bettina. "A Cheng's 'The King of the Trees': Exile and the Chinese Re-education Process." In David Bevan, ed., *Literature and Exile*. Amsterdam: Rodopi, 1990, 91–106.

Lonergan, Ross. "Tradition and Modernity in Ah Cheng's 'The Chess King.'" *B.C. Asian Review* 2 (1988).

Louie, Kam. "The Short Stories of Ah Cheng: Daoism, Confucianism and Life." *Australian Journal of Chinese Affairs* 18 (1987): 1–14.

Mair, Denis C. "Ah Cheng and His *King of Chess*." In Yang Bian, ed., *The Time Is Not Ripe: Contemporary China's Best Writers and Their Stories*. Beijing: Foreign Languages Press, 1991, 1–14.

Wang, Ban. "Citation of Discourse and Ironic Debunking in Ah Cheng's Work." In Wang, *Narrative Perspective and Irony in Selected Chinese and American Fiction*. Lewiston, NY: Edwin Mellen Press, 2002.

Wang, David. "Tai Hou-ying, Feng Chi-Ts'ai and Ah Cheng: Three Approaches to the Historical Novel." *Asian Culture Quarterly* 16, 2 (1988): 70–88.

Wong, Kin-yuen. "Between Aesthetics and Hermeneutics: A New Type of Bil-dungsroman in Ah Cheng's 'The Chess Champion.'" *MCL* 5, 1 (1989): 43–54.

Yue, Gang. "Surviving in 'The Chess King': Toward a Post-Revolutionary Na-tion-Narration." *Positions* 3, 2 (Fall 1995): 565–94.

———. "The Strange Landscape of the Ancients: Environmental Consciousness in 'The King of Trees.'" *American Journal of Chinese Studies* 5, 1 (1998): 68–88.

———. "Postrevolutionary Leftovers: Zhang Xianliang and Ah Cheng." In *The Mouth That Begs: Hunger, Cannibalism, and the Politics of Eating in Modern China*. Durham, NC: Duke University Press, 1999, 184–221.

Ai Qing

Palandri, Angela Jung. "The Poetic Theory and Practice of Ai Qing." In Mason Y. H. Wang, ed.,

Perspectives in Contemporary Chinese Literature. University Center, MI: Green River Press, 1983, 61–76.

Ts'ang, Ke-chia. "What Has Been Expressed in Ai Ch'ing's Recent Work?" In Hualing Nieh, ed., *Literature of the Hundred Flowers. Volume II: Poetry and Fiction*. New York: Columbia University Press, 1981, 278–82.

Ai Wu

Anderson, Marston. "Beyond Realism: The Eruption of the Crowd." In Anderson, *The Limits of Realism: Chinese Fiction in the Revolutionary Period*. Berkeley: University of California Press, 1990, 180–202.

Ge, Mai. "A Profile of Ai Wu." Tr. Lei Ming. *Chinese Literature* (Summer 1992): 40–43.

Ba Jin

Duke, Michael S. "Ba Jin (1904–): From Personal Liberation to Party 'Liberation.'" In Mason Y. H. Wang, ed., *Perspectives in Contemporary Chinese Literature*. University Center, MI: Green River Press, 1983, 49–60.

Feng, Jin. "En/gendering the Bildungsroman of the Radical Male: Ba Jin's Girl Students and Women Revolutionaries." In Feng, *The New Woman in Early Twentieth-Century Chinese Fiction*. West Lafayette, IN: Purdue University Press, 2004, 83–100.

Galik, Marian. "Pa Chin's *Cold Night*: The Interliterary Relations with Zola and Wilde." In Galik, ed., *Milestones in Sino-Western Literary Confrontation (1898–1979)*. Weisbaden: Otto Harrassowitz, 1986, 201–24.

Hsia, C. T. "Pa Chin." In Hsia, *A History of Modern Chinese Fiction*. 2nd ed. New Haven: Yale University Press, 1971, 237–56, 375–88.

Lang, Olga. *Pa Chin and his Writings: Chinese Youth between the Two Revolutions*. Cambridge, MA: Harvard University Press, 1967.

Mao, Nathan. *Pa Chin*. Boston: Twayne, 1978.

Ng, Mau Sang. "Ba Jin and Russian Literature." *Chinese Literature: Essays, Articles, Reviews* 3, 1 (Jan 1981): 67–92.

Shaw, Craig. "Changes in The Family: Reflections on Ba Jin's Revisions of Jia." *Journal of the Chinese Language Teachers Association* 34, 2 (1999): 21–36.

Tang, Xiaobing. "The Last Tubercular in Modern Chinese Literature: On Ba Jin's *Cold Nights*." In Tang, *Chinese Modernism: The Heroic and the Quotidian*. Durham, NC: Duke University Press, 2000, 131–60.

Bai Xianyong

Chow, Rey. "'Love Me, Master, Love Me, Son': A Cultural Other Pornographically Constructed in Time." In John Hay, ed., *Boundaries in China*. London: Reaktion Books, 1994, 243–56.

Eom, Ik-sang. "The Death of Three Men: Characters in Pai Hsien-yung's Love Stories." *Chinese Culture* 32, 1 (1991): 83–98.

Lau, Joseph S. M. "Celestials and Commoners: Exiles in Pai Hsien-yung's Stories." *Monumenta Serica* 36 (1984–85): 409–23.

——. "'Crowded Hours' Revisited: The Evocation of the Past in *Taipei jen*." *Journal of Asian Studies* 35, 1 (1975): 31–47.

Lee, Mabel. "In Lu Hsun's Footsteps. Pai Hsien-yung, A Modern Chinese Writer." *Journal of the Oriental Society of Australia* 9 (1972/3): 74–83.

Lupke, Christopher. "(En)gendering the Nation in Pai Hsien-yung's *Wandering in the Garden Waking from a Dream.*" *Modern Chinese Literature* 6, 1 /2 (1992): 157–178.

McFadden, Susan. "Tradition and Talent: Western Influence in the Works of Pai Hsien-yung." *Tamkang Review* 9, 3 (1979): 315–44.

Ou-yang, Tzu. "The Fictional World of Pai Hsien-yung." In Jeannette L. Faurot, ed., *Chinese Fiction from Taiwan: Critical Perspectives*. Bloomington: Indiana University Press, 1980, 166–78.

Yang, Winston L. Y. "Pai Hsien-yung and Other Emigre Writers." In Winston L. Y. Yang and Nathan K. Mao, eds., *Modern Chinese Fiction: A Guide to Its Study and Appreciation: Essays and Bibliographies*. Boston: G.K. Hall and Co., 1981, 67–78.

Bei Dao

Janssen, Ronald R. "What History Cannot Write: Bei Dao and Recent Chinese Poetry." *Critical Asian Studies* 34, 2 (2002): 259–77.

Li, Dian. "Ideology and Conflicts in Bei Dao's Poetry." *Modern Chinese Literature* 9, 2 (1996): 369–86.

——. "Translating Bei Dao: Translatability as Reading and Critique." *Babel, the Official Journal of the International Federation of Translators* 44, 4 (1999): 289–303.

——. *The Chinese Poetry of Bei Dao, 1978–2000: Resistance and Exile*. Lewiston, NY: Edwin Mellen Press, 2006.

Lin, Min. "The Search for the 'Unknowable' and the Quest for Modernity in Contemporary Chinese Intellectual Discourse: A Philosophical Interpretation of Bei Dao's Short Story '13 Happiness Street.'" *Journal of the Oriental Society of Australia* 22–23 (1990–91): 57–70.

Lin, Min, and Maria Galikowski. "Bei Dao's '13 Happiness Street' and the Young Generation's Quest for the 'Unknowable.'" In Lin and Galikowski, *The Search for Modernity: Chinese Intellectuals and Cultural Discourse in the Post-Mao Era*. New York: St. Martin's Press, 1999, 89–102.

McDougall, Bonnie S. "Bei Dao's Poetry: Revelation and Communication." *Modern Chinese Literature* 1, 2 (1985): 225–52.

——. "Zhao Zhenkai's Fiction: A Study in Cultural Alienation." *Modern Chinese Literature* 1, 1 (1984): 103–30.

Williams, Philip. "A New Beginning for the Modernist Chinese Novel: Zhao Zhenkai's *Bodong.*" *Modern Chinese Literature* 5, 1 (1989): 73–90.

Bian Zhilin

Fung, Mary M. Y. "Editor's Introduction." In Bian Zhilin, *The Carving of Insects*. Ed. Mary M. Y. Fung; trs. Mary M. Y. Fung and David Lunde. Hong Kong: Renditions Books, 2006, 11–34.

Haft, Lloyd. *Pien Chih-lin: A Study in Modern Chinese Poetry*. Dordrecht: Foris Publications, 1983.

Bing Xin

Bien, Gloria. "Images of Women in Ping Hsin's Fiction." In A. Palandri, ed. *Women Writers of 20th-Century China*. Eugene: Asian Studies Publications, University of Oregon, 1982, 19–40.

Bouskova, Marcela. "The Stories of Ping Hsin." In Jaroslav Prusek, *Studies in Modern Chinese Literature*. Berlin: Akademie-Verlag, 1964, 114–29.

——. "On the Origin of Modern Chinese Prosody: An Analysis of the Prosodic Components in the Works of Ping Hsin." *Archiv Orientalni* 32, 5 (1946): 619–43.

Larson, Wendy. "Female Subjectivity and Gender Relations: The Early Stories of Lu Yin and Bing Xin." In X. Tang and L. Kang, eds. *Politics, Ideology, and Literary Discourse in Modern China: Theoretical Interventions and Cultural Critique*. Durham, NC: Duke University Press, 1993, 278–99.

McDougall, Bonnie. "Disappearing Women and Disappearing Men in May Fourth Narrative: A Post-Feminist Survey of Short Stories by Mao Dun, Bing Xin, Ling Shuhua, and Shen Congwen." In McDougall, *Fictional Authors, Imaginary Audiences: Modern Chinese Literature in the Twentieth Century*. Hong Kong: Chinese University Press, 2003, 133–70.

Pao, King-li. "Ping Hsin, A Modern Chinese Poetess." *Literature East and West* 8 (1964): 58–72.

Can Xue

Cai, Rong. "In the Madding Crowd: Self and Other in Can Xue's Fiction." *China Information* 11, 4 (Spring 1997): 41–57.

Lu, Tonglin. "Can Xue: What Is So Paranoid in Her Writing?" In Lu, *Gender and Sexuality in Twentieth Century Chinese Literature and Society*. Albany: State University of New York Press, 1993, 175–204.

Posborg, Susanne. "Can Xue: Tracing Madness." In Wendy Larson and Anne Wedell-Wedellsborg, eds., *Inside Out: Modernism and Postmodernism in Chinese Literary Culture*. Aarhus, Denmark: Aarhus University Press, 1993, 91–98.

Solomon, Jon. "Taking Tiger Mountain: Can Xue's Resistance and Cultural Critique." *Modern Chinese Literature* 4, 1/2 (1988): 235–62.

Wang, Ban. *The Sublime Figure of History*. Stanford: Stanford University Press, 1997. [final chapter has readings of Can Xue's fiction]

Wedell-Wedellsborg, Anne. "Ambiguous Subjectivity: Reading Can Xue." *Modern Chinese Literature* 8, 1/2 (1994): 7–20.

Yang, Xiaobin. "Can Xue: Discursive Dystopias." In Yang, *The Chinese Postmodern: Trauma and Irony in Chinese Avant-Garde Fiction*. Ann Arbor: University of Michigan Press, 2002, 129–49.

———. "Can Xue: Ever-Haunting Nightmares." In Yang, *The Chinese Postmodern: Trauma and Irony in Chinese Avante-Garde Fiction*. Ann Arbor: University of Michigan Press, 2002, 74–92.

Zha, Peide. "Modernism Eastward: Franz Kafka and Can Xue." *B.C. Asian Review* 5 (1991).

Cao Yu

Galik, Marian. "Ts'ao Yu's *Thunderstorm*: Creative Confrontation with Euripides, Racine, Ibsen and Galsworthy." In Galik, ed., *Milestones in Sino-Western Literary Confrontation (1898–1979)*. Weisbaden: Otto Harrassowitz, 1986, 101–22.

Gunn, Edward. "Cao Yu's *Peking Man* and Literary Evocations of the Family in Republican China." *Republican China* 16, 1 (1990): 73–88.

Hu, John Y. H. *Ts'ao Yu*. New York: Twayne, 1972.

Lau, Joseph S. M. *Ts'ao Yu: The Reluctant Disciple of Chekhov and O'Neill: A Study in Literary Influence*. Hong Kong: Hong Kong University Press, 1970.

Noble, Jonathan. "Cao Yu and *Thunderstorm*." In Joshua Mostow, ed., and Kirk A. Denton, China section, ed., *Columbia Companion to Modern East Asian Literatures*. New York: Columbia University Press, 2003, 446–51.

Robinson, Lewis S. "On the Sources and Motives Behind Ts'ao Yu's *Thunderstorm*: A Qualitative Analysis." *Tamkang Review* 16 (1983): 177–92.

Wang, Aixue. *A Comparison of the Dramatic Work of Cao Yu and J. M. Synge*. Lewiston, NY: Edwin Mellen Press, 1999.

Chen Cun

Chen, Jianguo. "The Logic of the Phantasm: Haunting and Spectrality in Contemporary Chinese Literary Imagination." *Modern Chinese Literature and Culture* 14, 1 (Spring 2002): 231–65.

Chen Ran

Huot, Claire. "Chen Ran's Western Footnotes." In Huot, *China's New Cultural Scene: A Handbook of Changes*. Durham, NC: Duke University Press, 2000, 36–41.

Larson, Wendy. "Women and the Discourse of Desire in Postrevolutionary China: The Awkward Postmodernism of Chen Ran." *Boundary 2* 24, 3 (1997). In Xudong Zhang and Arif Dirlik, eds., *Postmodernism and China*. Durham, NC: Duke University Press, 2000, 337–57.

Visser, Robin. "Privacy and Its Ill Effects in Post-Mao Urban Fiction." In Bonnie S. McDougall and Anders Hansson, eds. *Chinese Concepts of Privacy*. Leiden: Brill, 2002, 171–94.

Wang, Lingzhen. "Reproducing the Self: Consumption, Imaginary, and Identity in Chinese Women's Autobiographical Practice in the 1990s." In Charles Laughlin, ed., *Contested Modernity in Chinese Literature*. New York: Palgrave Macmillan, 2005, 173–92.

Chen Ruoxi

Duke, Michael S. "Personae: Individual and Society in Three Novels by Chen Ruoxi." In Duke, ed., *Modern Chinese Women Writers: Critical Appraisals*. Armonk, NY: M.E. Sharpe, 1989, 53–77.

Hsu, Kai-yu. "A Sense of History: Reading Chen Jo-hsi's Stories." In Jeannette L. Faurot, ed., *Chinese Fiction from Taiwan: Critical Perspectives*. Bloomington: Indiana University Press, 1980, 206–33.

Kao, George, ed. *Two Writers and the Cultural Revolution: Lao She and Chen Jo-hsi*. Hong Kong: Chinese University Press, 1980.

Lau, Joseph S. M. "The Stories of Ch'en Juo-hsi." In Wai-lim Yip, ed., *Chinese Arts and Literature: A Survey of Recent Trends*. Occasional Papers/Reprint Series in Contemporary Asian Studies. Baltimore, 1977, 5–16.

Lee, Leo Ou-fan. "Dissent Literature from the Cultural Revolution." *Chinese Literature: Essays, Articles, Reviews* 1, 1 (1979): 59–79.

McCarthy, Richard M. "Chen Jo-hsi: Memoirs and Notes." *Renditions* 10 (Autumn 1978): 90–92.

Chen Yingzhen

Kinkley, Jeffrey. "From Oppression to Dependency: Two Stages in the Fiction of Chen Yingzhen." *Modern China* 16 (1990): 243–68.

Lau, Joseph S. M. "Death in the Void: Three Tales of Spiritual Atrophy in Ch'en Ying-chen's Post-Incarceration Fiction." *Modern Chinese Literature* 2 (1986): 21–28.

——. "How Much Truth Can a Blade of Grass Carry? Ch'en Ying-chen and the Emergence of Native Taiwan Writers." *Journal of Asian Studies* 32, 4 (Aug. 1973): 623–38.

——. "Ch'en Ying-chen and Other Native Writers." In Winston L. Y. Yang and Nathan K. Mao, eds., *Modern Chinese Fiction: A Guide to Its Study and Appreciation: Essays and Bibliographies*. Boston: G.K. Hall and Co., 1981, 79–94.

Miller, Lucien. "A Break in the Chain: The Short Stories of Ch'en Ying-chen." In Jeannette L. Faurot, ed., *Chinese Fiction from Taiwan: Critical Perspectives*. Bloomington: Indiana University Press, 1980, 86–109.

——. "Introduction." In Miller, ed./tr., *Exiles at Home: Short Stories By Ch'en Ying-chen*. Ann Arbor: Michigan Center for Chinese Studies, University of Michigan, 1986, 1–26.

——. "Occidentalism and Alterity: Native Self and Foreign Other in Chen Ying-zhen and Shusaku Endo." *Chinoperl Papers* 20–22 (1997–99): 197–218.

Robinson, Lewis S. "The Treatment of Christianity in the Fiction of Chen Yingchen." *Ching Feng: Quarterly Notes on Christianity and Chinese Religion and Culture* 32, 1 (Mar. 1989): 41–81.

Shieh, Wen-shan. "Ideology, Sublimation, Violence: The Transformation of Heroines in Chen Ying-chen's Suicidal Narratives." *Tamkang Review* 32, 2 (Winter 2001): 153–74.

Wang, David Der-wei. "Three Hungry Women." *Boundary 2*. Special issue edited by Rey Chow. 25, 2 (Fall 1998): 47–76.

Yang, Xiaobin. "Telling (Hi)story: Illusory Truth or True Illusion." *Tamkan Review* 21, 2 (1990): 127–47.

Chi Li

Lee, Lily Xiao-hong. "Localization and Globalization: Dichotomy and Convergence in Chi Li's Fiction." *Canadia Review of Comparative Literature* (Dec. 1997): 913–26.

Lu, Jie. "Cultural Invention and Cultural Intervention: Reading Chinese Urban Fiction of the Nineties." *Modern Chinese Literature and Culture* 13, 1 (Spring 2001): 107–39.

Dai Wangshu

Lee, Gregory. *Dai Wangshu: The Life and Poetry of a Chinese Modernist*. Hong Kong: The Chinese University Press, 1989.

——. "Western Influences in the Poetry of Dai Wangshu." *Modern Chinese Literature* 3, 1/2 (1987): 7–32.

Mi, Jiayan. *Self-Fashioning and Reflexive Modernity in Modern Chinese Poetry*. Lewiston, NY: Edwin Mellen Press, 2004.

Deng Youmei

Yang, Gladys. "Deng Youmei and His Fiction." In Yang Bian, ed., *The Time Is Not Ripe: Contemporary China's Best Writers and Their Stories*. Beijing: Foreign Languages Press, 1991, 41–47.

Ding Ling

Alber, Charles. *Enduring the Revolution: Ding Ling and the Politics of Literature in Guomindang China*. Westport, CT: Praeger, 2002.

———. *Embracing the Life: Ding Ling and the Politics of Literature in the PRC*. Westport, CT: Praeger, 2004.

Barlow, Tani. "Gender and Identity in Ding Ling's 'Mother.'" *Modern Chinese Literature* 2, 2 (1986): 123–42.

———. "Feminism and Literary Technique in Ting Ling's Early Short Stories." In A. Palandri, ed., *Women Writers of 20th-Century China*. Eugene: Asian Studies Publications, University of Oregon, 1982, 63–110.

Bjorge, Gary J. "'Sophia's Diary': An Introduction." *Tamkang Review* 5, 1 (1974): 97–110.

Chang, Jun-mei. *Ting Ling, Her Life and Her Work*. Taipei: Institute of International Relations, 1978.

Dien, Dora Shu-fang. *Ding Ling and Her Mother: A Cultural Psychological Study*. Huntington, NY: Nova Science, 2001.

Feng, Jin. *The New Woman in Early Twentieth-Century Chinese Fiction*. West Lafayette, IN: Purdue University Press, 2001, 149–96.

Feng, Xiaxiong. "Ding Ling's Reappearance on the Literary Stage." *Chinese Literature* 1 (1980): 3–16.

Feuerwerker, Yi-tsi Mei. *Ding Ling's Fiction: Ideology and Narrative in Modern Chinese Literature*. Cambridge, MA: Harvard University Press, 1982.

Huang, Xincun. "Politics, Gender and Literary Writings: A Study of Ding Ling in the Early 1940s." *Journal of Asian Culture* 14 (1990): 33–54.

Kinkley, Jeffrey. "Echoes of Maxim Gorky in the Works of Ding Ling and Shen Congwen." In Marian Galik, ed., *Interliterary and Intraliterary Aspects of the May Fourth Movement 1919 in China*. Bratislava: Veda, 1990, 179–88.

Kubin, Wolfgang. "Sexuality and Literature in the People's Republic of China, Problems of the Chinese Woman before and after 1949 as Seen in Ding Ling's 'Diary of Sophia' (1928) and Xi Rong's story 'An Unexceptional Post' (1962)." In Wolfgang Kubin and Rudolf G. Wagner, eds., *Essays in Modern Chinese Literature and Literary Criticism*. Bochum: Brockmeyer, 1982, 168–91.

Lai, Amy Tak-yee. "Liberation, Confusion, Imprisonment: The Female Self in Ding Ling's 'Diary of Miss Sophie' and Zhang Jie's 'Love Must Not Be Forgotten.'" *Comparative Literature and Culture* 3 (Sept. 1998): 88–103.

Lo, Man Wa. "Female Selfhood and Initiation in Shen Congwen's *The Border Town* and Ding Ling's *The Girl Ah Mao*." *Chinese/International Comparative Literature Bulletin* 1 (1996): 20–33.

Tang, Xiaobing. "*Shanghai Spring 1930*: Engendering the Revolutionary Body." In Tang, *Chinese Modernism: The Heroic and the Quotidian*. Durham, NC: Duke University Press, 2000, 97–130.

Yuan Liangjun. "On the Fiction of Ding Ling." Tr. Song Xianchun. *Social Sciences in China* 7, 3 (1986): 131–50.

Duo Duo

Huang, Yibing. "Duo Duo: An Impossible Farewell, or, Exile between Revolution and Modernism." *Amerasia Journal* 27, 2 (2001): 64–85.

Van Crevel, Maghiel. "Man and Nature, Man and Man: Aspects of Duoduo's Poetry." In Lloyd Haft, ed., *Words from the West: Western Texts in Chinese Literary Context: Essays to Honor Erik Zurcher on his Sixty-fifth Birthday*. Leiden: CNWS Publications, 1993, 100–15.

———. *Language Shattered: Contemporary Chinese Poetry and Duoduo*. Leiden: CNWS Research School, 1996.

Fei Ming

Gunn, Edward. *Rewriting Style and Innovation in Twentieth-Century Chinese Prose*. Stanford: Stanford University Press, 1991, 125–29, 284–86.

Li, Ningyi. "Fei Ming's Short Stories: A Poetry of Folk Elements." *Studies on Asia* Series II, 2, 2 (Fall 2005): 112–25.

Liu, Haoming. "Fei Ming's Poetics of Representation: Dream, Fantasy, Illusion, and Alayavijnana." *Modern Chinese Literature and Culture* 13, 2 (Fall 2001): 30–71.

Shih, Shu-mei. "Writing English with a Chinese Brush: The Work of Fei Ming." In Shi, *The Lure of the Modern: Writing Modernism in Semicolonial China, 1917–1937*. Berkeley: University of California Press, 2001, 190–203.

Feng Zhi

Cheung, Dominic. *Feng Chih*. Boston: Twayne, 1979.

Galik, Marian. "Feng Chih's *Sonnets*: The Interliterary Relations with German Romanticism, Rilke and van Gogh." In Galik, ed., *Milestones in Sino-Western Literary Confrontation (1898–1979)*. Weisbaden: Otto Harrassowitz, 1986, 177–200.

——. "Feng Zhi and His Goethean Sonnet." In Masayuki Akiyama and Yiu-nam Leung, eds., *Crosscurrents in the Literatures of Asia and the West: Essays in Honor of A. Owen Aldridge*. Newark: University of Delaware Press; Cranbury, NJ: Associated University Presses, 1997, 123–34.

Haft, Lloyd. "Some Rhythmic Structures in Feng Zhi's Sonnets." *Modern Chinese Literature* 9, 2 (1996): 297–326.

Fangfang

Wu, Lijuan. "Fang Fang, Reflecting Her Times." Tr. Li Ziliang. *Chinese Literature* (Summer 1997).

Fei Ming

Dang, Shengyuan, and Gao Jie. "About Fei Ming." Tr. Li Guoqing. *Chinese Literature* (Spring 1990): 123–27.

Gunn, Edward. *Rewriting Style and Innovation in Twentieth-Century Chinese Prose*. Stanford: Stanford University Press, 1991, 125–29, 284–86.

Li, Ningyi. "Fei Ming's Short Stories: A Poetry of Folk Elements." *Studies on Asia* Series II, 2, 2 (Fall 2005): 112–25.

Liu, Haoming. "Fei Ming's Poetics of Representation: Dream, Fantasy, Illusion, and Alayavijnana." *Modern Chinese Literature and Culture* 13, 2 (Fall 2001): 30–71.

Shih, Shu-mei. "Writing English with a Chinese Brush: The Work of Fei Ming." In Shih, *The Lure of the Modern: Writing Modernism in Semicolonial China, 1917–1937*. Berkeley: University of California Press, 2001, 190–203.

Feng Jicai

Braester, Yomi, and Zhang Enhua. "The Future of China's Memories: An Interview with Feng Jicai." *Journal of Modern Literature in Chinese* 5, 2 (2002): 131–48.

Gaenssbauer, Monika. "The Cultural Revolution in Feng Jicai's Fiction." In Woei Lian Chong, ed., *China's Great Proletarian Cultural Revolution: Master Narratives and Post-Mao Counternarratives*. Lanham, MD: Rowman & Littlefield, 2002, 319–44.

Li, Jun. "Feng Jicai: A Giant of a Writer in More Ways Than One." In Yang Bian, ed., *The Time Is Not Ripe: Contemporary China's Best Writers and Their Stories*. Beijing: Foreign Languages Press, 1991, 78–84.

Martin, Helmut. "What If History Has Merely Played a Trick on Us? Feng Chi-ts'ai's Writing, 1979–1984." In Yu-ming Shaw, ed., *Reform and Revolution in Twentieth Century China.* Taipei: Institute of International Relations, 1987, 277–90.

Wang, David. "Tai Hou-ying, Feng Chi-Ts'ai and Ah Cheng: Three Approaches to the Historical Novel." *Asian Culture Quarterly* 16, 2 (1988): 70–88.

Gao Xiaosheng

Decker, Margeret. "Living in Sin: From May Fourth via the Antirightist Movement to the Present." In Ellen Widmer and David Wang, eds., *From May Fourth to June Fourth: Fiction and Film in Twentiety-Century China.* Cambridge, MA: Harvard University Press, 1993, 221–46.

Faurot, Jeanette L. "Shoes That Fit—The Stories of Gao Xiaosheng." In Mason Y. H. Wang, ed., *Perspectives in Contemporary Chinese Literature.* University Center, MI: Green River Press, 1983, 77–88.

Feuerwerker, Yi-tsi Mei. "Reassesing the Past in the 'New Era': Gao Xiaosheng." In Feuerwerker, *Ideology, Power, Text: Self-Representation and the Peasant "Other" in Modern Chinese Literature.* Stanford: Stanford University Press, 1998, 146–87.

Li, Guoqing. "Roots in the Same Land: On Hwang Ch'un-ming and Kao Hsiaosheng's Stories." *Chinese Culture* 38, 3 (1997): 117–35.

Wagner, Rudolf. *Inside the Service Trade: Studies in Contemporary Chinese Prose.* Cambridge, MA: Council on East Asian Studies, Harvard University, 1992, 431–80.

Gao Xingjian

Barme, Geremie. "A Touch of the Absurd—Introducing Gao Xingjian and His Play *The Bus Stop.*" *Renditions* 19/20 (1983): 373–77.

Chan, Wai-sim. "Postscript: On Seeing the Play *Bus Stop*: He Wen's Critique in the Literary Gazette." *Renditions* 19/20 (1983): 387–92.

Chen, Xiaomei. "A *Wildman* Between the Orient and the Occident: Retro-Influence in Comparative Literary Studies." In Chen, *Occidentalism: A Theory of Counter-Discourse in Post-Mao China.* New York: Oxford University Press, 1995, 99–118.

He, Wen. "On Seeing the Play *The Bus Stop.*" Tr. Chan Sin-wai. *Renditions* 19/20 (1983): 387–92.

Kinkley, Jeffrey C. "Gao Xingjian in the 'Chinese' Perspective of Qu Yuan and Shen Congwen." *Modern Chinese Literature and Culture* 14, 2 (Fall 2002): 130–62.

Kuoshu, Harry H. "Will Godot Come by Bus or through a Trace? Discussion of a Chinese Absurdist Play." *Modern Drama* 41, 3 (Fall 1998): 461–73.

Larson, Wendy. "Realism, Modernism, and the Anti-'Spiritual Pollution' Campaign in Modern China." *Modern China* 15, 1 (Jan. 1989): 37–71.

Lee, Gregory, and Noel Dutrait. "Conversations with Gao Xingjian: The First Chinese Winner of the Nobel Prize for Literature." *China Quarterly* 167 (2001): 738–84.

Lee, Mabel. "Personal Freedom in Twentieth Century China: Reclaiming the Self in Yang Lian's *Yi* and Gao Xingjian's *Lingshan*." In Mabel Lee and Michael Wilding, eds., *History, Literature and Society: Essays in Honour of S. N. Mukherjee*. Sydney: Sydney Association for Studies in Culture and Society, 1997, 133–55.

——. "Gao Xingjian's *Lingshan*/Soul Mountain: Modernism and the Chinese Writer." *HEAT* 4 (1997): 128–43.

Lin, Sylvia Li-chun. "Between the Individual and the Collective: Gao Xingjian's Fiction." *World Literature Today* (Winter 2001): 20–30.

Lovell, Julia. "Gao Xingjian, the Nobel Prize, and Chinese Intellectuals: Notes on the Aftermath of the Nobel Prize 2000." *Modern Chinese Literature and Culture* 14, 2 (Fall 2002): 1–50.

Moran, Thomas. "Lost in the Woods: Nature in *Soul Mountain*." *Modern Chinese Literature and Culture* 14, 2 (Fall 2002): 207–36.

Quah, Sy Ren. *Gao Xingjian and Transcultural Chinese Theater*. Honolulu: University of Hawaii Press, 2004.

Riley, Josephine, and Michael Gissenwehrer. "The Myth of Gao Xingjian." In Riley and Else Unterrieder, eds., *Haishi Zou Hao: Chinese Poetry, Drama and Literature of the 1980s*. Bonn: Engelhard-Ng Verlag, 1989, 129–51.

Rojas, Carlos. "Without [Femin]ism: Femininity as Axis of Alterity and Desire in Gao Xingjian's *One Man's Bible*." *Modern Chinese Literature and Culture* 14, 2 (Fall 2002): 163–206.

Tam, Kwok-kan, ed. *Soul of Chaos: Critical Perspectives on Gao Xingjian*. Hong Kong: Chinese University Press, 2001.

Xu, Gang Gary. "My Writing, Your Pain, and Her Trauma: Pronouns and (Gendered) Subjectivity in Gao Xingjian's *Soul Mountain* and *One Man's Bible*." *Modern Chinese Literature and Culture* 14, 2 (Fall 2002): 99–129.

Zhao, Henry Y. H. *Towards a Modern Zen Theatre: Gao Xingjian and Chinese Theatre Experimentalism*. London: School of Oriental and African Studies, 2000.

Ge Fei

Kong, Shuyu. "Ge Fei on the Margins." *B.C. Asian Review* 10 (1996/97).

Wang, Jing. "The Mirage of Chinese 'Postmodernism': Ge Fei, Self-Positioning, and the Avant-garde Showcase." *Positions* 1, 2 (1993): 349–88.

Yang, Xiaobin. "Ge Fei: Indeterminate History and Memory." In Yang, *The Chinese Postmodern: Trauma and Irony in Chinese Avant-garde Fiction*. Ann Arbor: University of Michigan Press, 2002, 168–87.

Zhang, Xudong. "Fable of Self-Consciousness: Ge Fei and Some Motifs in Meta-Fiction." In Zhang, *Chinese Modernism in the Era of Reforms*. Durham, NC: Duke University Press, 1997, 163–200.

Gu Cheng

Brady, Anne-Marie. "Dead in Exile: The Life and Death of Gu Cheng and Xie Ye." *China Information* 11, 4 (Spring 1997): 126–48.

Galik, Marian. "Gu Cheng's Novel *Ying'er* and the Bible." *Asian and African Studies* 5, 1 (1996).

Kubin, Wolfgang. "Gu Cheng: Peking, Ich." In Raoul Findeison and Robert Gassmann, eds., *Autumn Floods: Essay in Honour of Marian Galik*. Bern: Peter Lang, 1997, 415–30.

Li, Xia. "'Nameless Flowers': The Role of Nature in Gu Cheng's Poetry and in His Narrative Prose *Ying'er*." In Raoul Findeison and Robert Gassmann, eds., *Autumn Floods: Essays in Honour of Marian Galik*. Bern: Peter Lang, 1997, 431–46.

——, ed. *Essays, Interviews, Recollections and Unpublished Material of Gu Cheng, Twentieth Century Chinese Poet: The Poetics of Death*. Lewiston, NY: Edwin Mellen Press, 1999.

——. "Gu Cheng's *Ying'er*: A Journey to the West." *Modern Chinese Literature* 10, 1 (1998): 135–148.

Liu, Shusen. "Gu Cheng and Walt Whitman: In Search of New Poetics." In Ed Folson, ed., *Whitman East & West: New Contexts for Reading Walt Whitman*. Iowa City: University of Iowa Press, 2002, 208–20.

Patton, Simon. "Desire and Masculinity at the Margins in Gu Cheng's *Ying'er*." In Kam Louie and Morris Low, eds., *Asian Masculinities: The Meaning and Practice of Manhood in China and Japan*. New York: Routledge Curzon, 2003.

——. "The Unbearable Heaviness of Being: Gender, Sexuality and Insanity in Gu Cheng and Xie Ye's *Ying'er*." *Modern Chinese Literature* 9 (1996): 399–415.

——. "Notes Toward a Nomad Subjectivity: The Poetics of Gu Cheng (1956–1993)." *Social Semiotics* 9, 1 (1999): 49–66.

——. "The Forces of Production: Symmetry and the Imagination in the Early Poetry of Gu Cheng." *Modern Chinese Literature and Culture* 13, 2 (Fall 2001): 134–71.

Gu Hua

Van Der Meer, Marc. "'Hibiscus,' 'The Garden of the Literati,' and Mao Zedong's Biography: A Brief Introduction to the Life and Work of Writer Gu Hua." *China Information* 7, 2 (1998): 20–29.

Guo Moruo

Chan, Wing-Ming. "Li Po and Tu Fu by Kuo Mo-jo—A Reexamination." *Chinese Literature: Essays, Articles, Reviews* 4, 1 (Jan. 1982): 75–90.

Doar, Bruce. "Images of Women in the Dramas of Guo Moruo: The Case of *Empress Wu*." In C. Tung and C. Mackerras, eds., *Drama in the People's Republic of China*. Albany: State University of New York Press, 1987, 254–92.

Dolezelova-Velingerova, Milena. "Kuo Mo-jo's Autobiographical Works." In Jaroslav Prusek, ed., *Studies in Modern Chinese Literature*. Berlin: Akademie-Verlag, 1964, 45–75.

Galik, Marian. "Kuo Mo-jo's *The Goddesses*: Creative Confrontation with Tagore, Whitman and Goethe." In Galik, ed., *Milestones in Sino-Western Literary Confrontation (1898–1979)*. Weisbaden: Otto Harrassowitz, 1986, 43–72.

———. "Kuo Mo-jo and his Development from Aesthetic-Impressionist to Proletarian Criticism." In Galik, *The Genesis of Modern Chinese Literary Criticism, 1917–1930*. London: Curzon Press, 1980, 28–62.

Lee, Haiyan. "Tears That Crumbled the Great Wall: The Archaeology of Feeling in the May Fourth Folklore Movement." *Journal of Asian Studies* 64, 1 (Feb. 2005): 35–65.

Liu, Ruoqiang. "Whitman's Soul in China: Guo Moruo's Poetry in the New Culture Movement." In Ed Folson, ed., *Whitman East & West: New Contexts for Reading Walt Whitman*. Iowa City: University of Iowa Press, 2002, 172–86.

Mi, Jiayan. *Self-Fashioning and Reflexive Modernity in Modern Chinese Poetry*. Lewiston, NY: Edwin Mellen Press, 2004.

Ou, Hong. "Pantheistic Ideas in Guo Moruo's *The Goddesses* and Whitman's *Leaves of Grass*." In Ed Folson, ed., *Whitman East & West: New Contexts for Reading Walt Whitman*. Iowa City: University of Iowa Press, 2002, 187–96.

Prusek, Jaroslav. "Kuo Mo-jo." In Prusek, *Three Sketches of Chinese Literature*. Prague: Oriental Institute in Academia, 1969, 99–140.

Roy, David T. *Kuo Mojo: The Early Years*. Cambridge, MA: Harvard University Press, 1971.

Shih, Shu-mei. "Psychoanalysis and Cosmopolitanism: The Work of Guo Moruo." In Shih, *The Lure of the Modern: Writing Modernism in Semicolonial China, 1917–1937*. Berkeley: University of California Press, 2001, 96–109.

Trappl, Richard. "'Modernism' and Foreign Influences on Chinese Poetry: Exemplified by the Early Guo Moruo and Gu Cheng." In Marian Galik, ed., *Interliterary and Intraliterary Aspects of the May Fourth Movement 1919 in China*. Bratislava: Veda, 1990, 83–92.

Tsang, Winnie. "Kuo Mojo's *The Goddesses*." *JOS* 12 (1977): 97–109.

Tsu, Jing. "Perversions of Masculinity: The Masochistic Male Subject in Yu Dafu, Guo Moruo, and Freud." *Positions* 8, 2 (Fall 2000): 269–316.

Wagner, Rudolf. *The Contemporary Chinese Historical Drama*. Berkeley: University of California Press, 1990, 246–50; 282–89.

Yip, Terry Siu-Han, and Kwok-Kan Tan. "European Influence on Modern Chinese Drama: Kuo Mo-jo's Early Historical-Problem Plays." *JOS* 24, 1 (1986): 54–65.

Han Shaogong

Feuerwerker, Yi-tsi Mei. "The Post-Modern 'Search for Roots' in Han Shaogong, Mo Yan, and Wang Anyi." In Feuerwerker, *Ideology, Power, Text: Self-Representation and the Peasant "Other" in Modern Chinese Literature.* Stanford: Stanford University Press, 1998, 188–238.
Iovene, Paola. "Authenticity, Postmodernity, and Translation: The Debates around Han Shaogong's *Dictionary of Maqiao.*" *Annali dell'Università degli Studi di Napoli L'Orientale* 62 (2002): 197–218.
Lau, Joseph S. M. "Visitation of the Past in Han Shaogong's Post-1985 Fiction." In Ellen Widmer and David Wang, eds., *From May Fourth to June Fourth: Fiction and Film in Twentiety-Century China.* Cambridge, MA: Harvard University Press, 1993, 295–326.
Lee, Vivian. "Cultural Lexicology: *Maqiao Dictionary* by Han Shaogong." *Modern Chinese Literature and Culture* 14, 1 (Spring 2002): 145–77.
Leenhouts, Mark. "Is It a Dictionary or a Novel? On Playfulness in Han Shaogong's *Dictionary of Maqiao.*" In Bonnie McDougall and Anders Hansson, eds, *The Chinese at Play: Festivals, Games and Leisure.* London: Kegan Paul, 2002.
———. *Leaving the World to Enter the World: Han Shaogong and Chinese Root-Seeking Literature.* Leiden: CNWS Publications, 2005.
Rong, Cai. "The Subject in Crisis: Han Shaogong's Cripple(s)." *The Journal of Contemporary China* 5 (Spring 1994): 64–77.

Hao Ran

Egan, Michael. "A Notable Sermon: The Subtext of Hao Ran's Fiction." In Bonnie S. McDougal, ed., *Popular Chinese Literature and Performing Arts in the People's Republic of China.* Berkeley: University of California Press, 1984, 224–43.
Elvin, Mark. "The Magic of Moral Power: Hao Ran, *The Children of the Western Sands.*" In Elvin, *Changing Stories in the Chinese World.* Stanford: Stanford University Press, 1997, 149–77.
Huang, Joe C. "Hao Ran [Hao Jan]: The Peasant Novelist." *Modern China* 2 (1976): 369–96.
Jenner, W. J. F. "Class Struggle in a Chinese Village—A Novelist's View: Hao Ran's *Yan Yang Tian* [Yen-yang t'ien]." *Modern Asian Studies* 1 (1967): 191–206.

King, Richard. "Revisionism and Transformation in the Cultural Revolution Novel." *Modern Chinese Literature* 7, 1 (Spring 1993): 105–29.

Wong, Kam-ming. "A Study of Hao Ran's Two Novels: Art and Politics in *Bright Sunny Skies* and *The Road of Golden Light*." In Wolfgang Kubin and Rudolf Wagner, eds., *Essays in Modern Chinese Literature and Literary Criticism*. Bochum: Brokmeyer, 1982, 117–49.

He Qifang

Galik, Marian. "Early Poems and Essays of Ho Ch'i-fang." *Asian and African Studies* (Bratislava) 15 (1979): 31–63.

———. "Ho Ch'i-fang's *Paths in Dreams*: The Interliterary Relations with English, French Symbolism and Greek Mythology." In Galik, ed., *Milestones in Sino-Western Literary Confrontation (1898–1979)*. Weisbaden: Otto Harrassowitz, 1986, 153–76.

McDougall, Bonnie S. "European Influences in the Poetry of Ho Ch'i-fang." *Journal of the Oriental Society of Australia* 5, 1/2 (1967): 133–51.

———. "Memories and Metamorphoses of a Thirties' Intellectual: A Study of He Qifang's 'Old Men' (Lao ren)." *Chinese Literature: Essays, Articles, Reviews* 3, 1 (Jan. 1981): 93–107.

Huang Chunming

Goldblatt, Howard. "The Rural Stories of Hwang Chun-ming." In Jeannette L. Faurot, ed., *Chinese Fiction from Taiwan: Critical Perspectives*. Bloomington: Indiana University Press, 1980, 110–33.

Kubin, Wolfgang. *Search for Identity: Huang Chunming's 'Sayonara-Zaijian.'* Honolulu: Workshop on Critical Approaches to Modern Chinese Short Stories, East-West Center, 1982.

Lai, Stanley. "The Short Stories of Huang Chun-ming." *Fu Jen Studies* 10 (1977): 25–40.

Li, Guoqing. "Roots in the Same Land: On Hwang Ch'un-ming and Kao Hsiao-sheng's Stories." *Chinese Culture* 38, 3 (1997): 117–35.

Tam, King-fai. "Beautiful Americans, Ugly Japanese, Obsequious Chinese: The Depiction of Race in Huang Chunming's Stories." In Berel Lang, ed., *Race and Racism in Theory and Practice*. Lanham, MD: Rowman & Littlefield, 2000, 165–77.

Jia Pingwa

Barme, Geremie. "Soft Porn, Packaged Dissent, and Nationalism: Notes on Chinese Culture in the 1990s." *Current History* 98, 584 (Sept. 1994): 270–76.

——. *In the Red: On Contemporary Chinese Culture.* New York: Columbia University Press, 1999, 181–85.

Louie, Kam. "The Macho Eunuch: The Politics of Masculinity in Jia Pingwa's 'Human Extremities.'" *Modern China* 17, 2 (1991): 163–87.

Lu, Sheldon Hsiao-peng. *China, Transnational Visuality, Global Postmodernity.* Stanford: Stanford University Press, 2001, 239–59.

Sun, Jianxi. "Jia Pingwa and his Fiction." In Yang Bian, ed., *The Time Is Not Ripe: Contemporary China's Best Writers and Their Stories.* Beijing: Foreign Languages Press, 1991, 99–111.

Wang, David Der-wei. "Review of *Turbulence.*" *Modern Chinese Literature* 6, 1/2 (1992): 247–250.

Wang, Yiyan. "Mr Butterfly in *Defunct Capital*: Soft Masculinity and (Mis)engendering China." In Kam Louie and Morris Low, eds., *Chinese and Japanese Masculinities.* London: Routledge, 2003.

——. *Narrating China: Jia Pingwa and His Fictional World.* London, New York: Routledge, 2006.

Zha, Jianying. "Yellow Peril." *TriQuarterly* 93 (Spring-Summer 1995): 238–64.

——. *China Pop: How Soap Operas, Tabloids, and Bestsellers Are Transforming a Culture.* New York: The New Press, 1995: 129–39, 146–64.

Lao She

Bady, Paul. "Death and the Novel—On Lao She's 'Suicide.'" *Renditions* 10 (1978): 5–20.

Bickers, Robert. "New Light on Lao She, London and the London Missionary Society." *Modern Chinese Literature* 8 (1994): 21–39.

Birch, Cyril. "Lao She: The Humourist in His Humour." *China Quarterly* 8 (1961): 45–62.

Brandauer, Frederick P. "Selected Works of Lao She and Mao Tun and Their Relevance for Christian Theology." *Ching Feng* 11, 2 (1968): 25–43.

Chan, Stephen. "Split Consciousness: The Dialectic of Desire in *Camel Xiangzi.*" *Modern Chinese Literature* 2, 2 (1986): 171–97.

Chow, Rey. "Fateful Attachments: On Collecting, Fidelity, and Lao She." In Michel Hockx and Ivo Smits, eds., *Reading East Asian Writing: The Limits of Literary Theory.* New York and London: Routledge Curzon, 2003, 1–22.

Duke, Michael. "Images of the Urban Poor in Lao She's Short Stories." *Journal of the Chinese Language Teachers Association* 13, 2 (1978): 137–49.

Faurot, Jeannette. "Lao She's Philosophy and *The Philosophy of Lao Zhang.*" *Chinoperl Papers* 20–22 (1997–99): 159–68.

Galik, Marian. "Lao She's *Looking Westward to Ch'ang-an* and Gogol's *The Inspector General.*" In Galik, ed., *Milestones in Sino-Western Literary Confrontation (1898–1979).* Weisbaden: Otto Harrassowitz, 1986, 225–42.

Grossholtforth, Petra. *Chinesen in London: Lao She's Roman "Er Ma."* Bochum: Brockmeyer, 1985.

Ho, Koon-ki Tommy. "*Cat Country*: A Dystopian Satire." *Modern Chinese Literature* 3 (1987): 71–90.

Hsia, C. T. "Lao She." In Hsia, *A History of Modern Chinese Fiction*. 2nd ed. New Haven: Yale University Press, 1971, 165–88, 366–75.

Hu, King. "Lao She in England." Tr. Cecelia Y. L. Tsim. *Renditions* 10 (1978): 46–52.

Hung, Chang-t'ai. "New Wine in Old Bottles." In Hung, *War and Popular Culture: Resistance in Modern China, 1937–1945*. Berkeley: University of California Press, 1994, 187–220.

Kao, George, ed. *Two Writers and the Cultural Revolution: Lao She and Ch'en Jo-hsi*. Hong Kong: Chinese University Press, 1980.

——. "Lao She in America—Arrival and Departure." *Renditions* 10 (1978): 68–77.

Lee, Leo Ou-fan. "Lao She's 'Black Li and White Li': A Reading in Psychological Structure." In Theodore Huters, ed., *Reading the Modern Chinese Short Story*. Armonk, NY: M.E. Sharpe, 1990, 3–21.

Leung, Yin-nan. "Lao She and the Philosophy of Food." *Asian Culture Quarterly* 21, 4 (1993): 1–10.

Li, Peter. "Lao She and Chinese Folk Literature." *Chinoperl Papers* 19 (1996): 1–20.

Louie, Kam. "Constructing Chinese Masculinity for the Modern World: with Particular Reference to Lao She's *The Two Mas*." *China Quarterly* 164 (2000): 1062–78.

Munro, S. R. *The Function of Satire in the Works of Lao She*. Singapore: Chinese Language Centre, Nanyang University, 1977.

Slupski, Zbigniew. *The Evolution of a Modern Chinese Writer: An Analysis of Lao She's Fiction with Biographical and Bibliographical Appendices*. Prague: Czechoslovak Academy of Sciences, 1966.

Towery, Britt. *Lao She: China's Master Storyteller*. Waco, TX: The Tao Foundation, 1999.

Vohra, Ranbir. *Lao She and the Chinese Revolution*. Cambridge, MA: Harvard University Press, 1974.

Wang, David. "Radical Laughter in Lao She and His Taiwan Successors." In Howard Goldblatt, ed., *Worlds Apart: Recent Chinese Writing and its Audiences*. Armonk, NY: M.E. Sharpe, 1990, 44–63.

——. *Fictional Realism in Twentieth-Century China: Mao Dun, Lao She, Shen Congwen*. New York: Columbia University Press, 1992.

Wong, Yoon Wah. "Lao She's Obsession with Joseph Conrad's *Stories of the Tropics*." In Wong, *Post-Colonial Chinese Literatures in Singapore and Malaysia*. Singapore: Dept of Chinese Studies, National University of Singapore, 2002, 127–40.

Zhao, Qiguang. "Who Is Ruan Ming? A Political Mystery in Lao She's *Camel Xiangxi*." *China Information* 12, 3 (Winter 97–98): 104–22.

Li Ang

Chien, Ying-ying. "Women Crossing the Wild Zone: Sexual/Textual Politics in the Fiction of Ding Ling and Li Ang." *Fu Jen Studies* 28 (1995): 1–17.

Goldblatt, Howard. "Sex and Society: The Fiction of Li Ang." In Goldblatt, ed. *Worlds Apart: Recent Chinese Writing and Its Audiences*. Armonk, NY: M.E. Sharpe, 150–65.

Haddon, Rosemary. "From Pulp to Politics: Aspects of Topicality in Fiction by Li Ang." *Modern Chinese Literature and Culture* 13, 1 (Spring 2001): 36–72.

Liao, Sebastion Hsien-hao. "Jekyll Is and Hyde Isn't: Negotiating the Nationalization of Identity in *The Mystery Garden* and 'Breakfast at Tiffany's.'" *Journal of Modern Literature in Chinese* 5, 1 (2001): 65–92.

Liu, Joyce C. H. "From Loo Port to Taipei: The World of Women in Lee Ang's Works." *Fu Jen Studies: Literature and Linguistics* 19 (1986): 65–88.

Martin, Helmut. "From Sexual Protest to Feminist Social Criticism: Li Ang's Works 1967–1987." In Wong Yoon Wah, ed., *Chinese Literature in Southeast Asia*. Singapore: Goethe-Institut, 1989, 127–51.

Ng, Sheung-Yuen Daisy. "Feminism in the Chinese Context: Li Ang's *The Butcher's Wife*." *Modern Chinese Literature* 4, 1/2 (1988): 177–200.

——. "Li Ang's Experiments with the Epistolary Form." *Modern Chinese Literature* 3, 1/2 (1987): 91–106.

——. "The Labyrinth of Meaning: A Reading of Li Ang's Fiction." *Tamkang Review* 18, 1–4 (1987–88): 97–123.

Yeh, Michelle. "Shapes of Darkness: Symbols in Li Ang's *Dark Night*." In Michael S. Duke, ed., *Modern Chinese Women Writers: Critical Appraisals*. Armonk, NY: M.E. Sharpe, 1989, 78–95.

Yue, Gang. "Embodied Spaces of Home: Xiao Hong, Wang Anyi, and Li Ang." In *The Mouth that Begs: Hunger, Cannibalism, and the Politics of Eating in Modern China*. Durham, NC: Duke University Press, 1999, 293–330.

Li Jinfa

Liu, David Jason. "Chinese 'Symbolist' Verse in the 1920's: Li Chin-fa and Mu Mu-t'ien." *Tamkang Review*. 12, 3 (1981): 27–53.

Mi, Jiayan. *Self-Fashioning and Reflexive Modernity in Modern Chinese Poetry*. Lewiston, NY: Edwin Mellen Press, 2004.

Tu, Kuo-Ch'ing. "Symbolist Imagery in Li Jinfa's *Weiyu*." *Journal of Oriental Studies* 25, 2 (1987): 187–96.

———. "The Introduction of French Symbolism into Modern Chinese Poetry." *Tamkang Review* 10, 3–4 (1980): 343–67.

———. "Li Chin-fa and Kamara Ariake: The First Symbolist Poets in China and Japan." In *Essays in Commemoration of the Golden Jubilee of the Fung Ping Shan Library.* University of Hong Kong, 1982.

Li Rui

Coers, Donald. "An Interview with the Chinese Writer Li Rui." *Texas Review* 11, 1/2 (Spring/Summer 1990): 18–25.

Li Yongping

Lau, Joseph, S. M. "The Tropics Mytho-poetized: The Extraterritorial Writing of Li Yung-p'ing in the Context of the *Hsiang-t'u* Movement." *Tamkang Review* 12, 1 (1981): 1–26.

Rojas, Carlos. "Of Motherlands and Maternities: Special Topographies in Li Yongping's *Haidong Qiing*." In David Wang and Joyce Liu, eds., *Writing Taiwan: Strategies of Representation*. Durham, NC: Duke University Press, 2006.

———. "Paternities and Expatriotism: Li Yongping's *Zhu Ling Manyou Xianjing* and the Politics of Rupture." *Tamkang Review* 29, 2 (Winter 1998): 22–44.

Wang, David. "Imaginary Nostalgia: Shen Congwen, Song Zelai, Mo Yan, and Li Yongping." In Ellen Widmer and David Wang, eds., *From May Fourth to June Fourth: Fiction and Film in Twentiety-Century China*. Cambridge, MA: Harvard University Press, 1993, 107–32.

Liang Xiaosheng

Lin, Min, and Maria Galikowski. "Liang Xiaosheng's Moral Critique of China's Modernization Process." In Lin and Galikowski, *The Search for Modernity: Chinese Intellectuals and Cultural Discourse in the Post-Mao Era*. New York: St. Martin's Press, 1999, 123–42.

Lin Bai

Wang, Lingzhen. "Reproducing the Self: Consumption, Imaginary, and Identity in Chinese Women's Autobiographical Practice in the 1990s." In Charles Laughlin, ed., *Contested Modernity in Chinese Literature*. New York: Palgrave Macmillan, 2005, 173–92.

Lin Huiyin

Shih, Shu-mei. "Gendered Negotiations with the Local: Lin Huiyin and Ling Shuhua." In Shih, *The Lure of the Modern: Writing Modernism in Semicolonial China, 1917–1937*. Berkeley: University of California Press, 2001, 204–30.

Lin Yutang

Anderson, A. J., ed. *Lin Yutang: The Best of an Old Friend*. New York: Mason/Charter, 1976.

Brandauer, Frederick. "Lin Yutang's Widow and the Problem of Adaptation." *Journal of the Chinese Language Teachers Association* 20, 2 (1985): 1–14.

Fu, Yi-chin. "Lin Yutang: A Bundle of Contrasts." *Fu Jen Studies* 21 (1988): 29–44.

Ling Shuhua

Chow, Rey. "Virtuous Transactions: A Reading of Three Stories by Ling Shuhua." *Modern Chinese Literature* 4 (1988).

Cuadrado, Clara. "Portraits of a Lady: The Fictional World of Ling Shuhua." In A. Palandri, ed., *Women Writers of 20th-Century China*. Eugene: Asian Studies Publications, University of Oregon, 1982, 41–62.

Lang-Tan, Goat Koei. "Women in Love: Two Short Stories of Ling Shuhua (1900–1990) Compared to Katherine Mansfield's (1888–1923) 'Psychology' (1921)." In Marian Galik, ed., *Chinese Literature And European Context*. Bratislava: Rowaco Ltd. & Institute of Asian and African Studies of the Slovak Academy of Sciences, 1994, 31–142.

Laurence, Patrica. *Lily Briscoe's Chinese Eyes: Bloomsbury, Modernism, and China*. Columbia: University of South Carolina Press, 2003.

McDougall, Bonnie. "Dominance and Disappearance in May Fourth: A Post-Feminist Review of Fiction by Mao Dun and Ling Shuhua." In Raoul Findeisen and Robert Gassmann, eds., *Autumn Floods: Essays in Honour of Marian Galik*. Bern: Peter Lang, 1997, 283–306.

———. "Disappearing Women and Disappearing Men in May Fourth Narrative: A Post-Feminist Survey of Short Stories by Mao Dun, Bing Xin, Ling Shuhua and Shen Congwen." In McDougall, *Fictional Authors, Imaginary Audiences: Modern Chinese Literature in the Twentieth Century*. Hong Kong: Chinese University Press, 2003, 133–70.

Ng, Janet. "Writing in Her Father's World: The Feminine Autobiographical Strategies of Ling Shuhua." *Prose Studies* 16, 3 (1993): 235–50.

Shih, Shu-mei. "Gendered Negotiations with the Local: Lin Huiyin and Ling Shuhua." In Shih, *The Lure of the Modern: Writing Modernism in Semicolonial China, 1917–1937*. Berkeley: University of California Press, 2001, 204–30.

Yu, Clara. "Portrait by a Lady: The Fictional World of Ling Shuhua." In Angela Jung Pallandri, ed., *Women Writers of 20th-Century China*. Eugene: University of Oregon Press, 1982, 41–62.

Liu Bannong

Hockx, Michel. "Liu Bannong and the Forms of New Poetry." *Journal of Modern Literature in Chinese* 3, 2 (Jan. 2000): 83–117.

Liu Heng

Huot, Marie-Claire. "Liu Heng's *Fuxi Fuxi*: What About Nuwa?" In Lu Tonglin, ed., *Gender and Sexuality in Twentieth-Century Chinese Literature and Society*. Albany: State University of New York Press, 1993, 85–106.

Linder, Birgit. "Alienation and the Motif of the Unlived Life in Liu Heng's Fiction." *Journal of Modern Literature in Chinese* 2, 2 (January 1999): 119–48.

Liu Na'ou

Braester, Yomi. "Shanghai's Economy of Spectacle: The Shanghai Race Club in Liu Na'ou's and Mu Shiying's Stories." *Modern Chinese Literature* 9, 1 (1995): 39–58.

Lee, Leo Ou-fan. "Face, Body, and the City: The Fiction of Liu Na'ou and Mu Shiying." In Lee, *Shanghai Modern: The Flowering of a New Urban Culture in China, 1930–1945*. Cambridge, MA: Harvard University Press, 1999, 190–231.

Liu, Jianmei. "Shanghai Variations on 'Revolution Plus Love.'" *Modern Chinese Literature and Culture* 14, 1 (Spring 2002): 51–92.

Shih, Shu-mei. "Gender, Race, and Semicolonialism: Liu Na'ou's Urban Shanghai." In Shih, *The Lure of the Modern: Writing Modernism in Semicolonial China, 1917–1937*. Berkeley: University of California Press, 2001, 276–301.

Liu Suola

Zhang, Zhen. "The World Map of Haunting Dreams: Reading Post-1989 Chinese Women's Diaspora Writings." In Mayfair Mei Hui Yang, ed., *Spaces of Their*

Own: Women's Public Sphere in Transnational China. Minneapolis: University of Minnesota Press, 1999, 308–35.

Liu Xinwu

Chao, Pien. "Liu Hsin-wu's Short Stories." *Chinese Literature* 1 (1979): 89–93.
Kam, Louie. "Youth and Education in the Short Stories of Liu Xinwu." In Louie, *Between Fact and Fiction: Essays on Post-Mao Chinese Literature and Society.* Sydney: Wild Peony, 1989, 14–20.

Liu Zhenyun

Yue, Gang. "Monument Revisited: Zheng Yi and Liu Zhenyun." In *The Mouth That Begs: Hunger, Cannibalism, and the Politics of Eating in Modern China.* Durham, NC: Duke University Press, 1999, 228–62.

Lu Ling

Denton, Kirk A. "Lu Ling's Literary Art: Myth and Symbol in *Hungry Guo Su'e.*" *Modern Chinese Literature* 2, 2 (1986): 197–209.
———. "Lu Ling's *Children of the Rich*: The Role of Mind in Social Transformation." *Modern Chinese Literature* 5, 2 (1989): 269–92.
———. *The Problematic of Self in Modern Chinese Literature: Hu Feng and Lu Ling.* Stanford: Stanford University Press, 1998.
Liu, Kang. "The Language of Desire in the Novels of Lu Ling, D. H. Lawrence, and Thomas Mann." *Comparative Literature in China,* 15, 2 (1992): 57–74.
———. "Mixed Style in Lu Ling's Novel *Children of the Rich*: Family Chronicle and Bildungsroman." *Modern Chinese Literature* 7, 1 (1993): 61–87.
———. "Revolution and Desire in Lu Ling's Fiction: Modern Chinese Literature in the 1940s." *Chinese Culture* 34, 3 (1993): 39–57.
Shu, Yunzhong. "Different Modes of Intellectual Intervention: Lu Ling's Short Stories." In Shu, *Buglers on the Home Front: The Wartime Practice of the Qiyue School.* Albany: State University of New York Press, 2000, 107–28.
———. "Manifestations of Self-Transcendence: Lu Ling's *Children of Wealth.*" In Shu, *Buglers on the Home Front: The Wartime Practice of the Qiyue School.* Albany: State University of New York Press, 2000, 1289–1352.
Wang, David Der-wei. "Three Hungry Women." *Boundary 2.* Special issue edited by Rey Chow. 25, 2 (Fall 1998): 47–76.

Lu Xun

Alber, Charles. "Wild Grass, Symmetry and Parallelism in Lu Hsun's Prose Poems." In William Nienhauser, ed., *Critical Essays on Chinese Literature*. Hong Kong: Chinese University of Hong Kong Press, 1976, 1–20.

Anderson, Marston. *The Limits of Realism: Chinese Fiction in the Revolutionary Period*. Berkeley: University of California Press, 1990.

———. "Lu Xun's Facetious Muse: The Creative Imperative in Modern Chinese Fiction." In E. Widmer and D. Wang, eds., *From May Fourth to June Fourth: Fiction and Film in Twentieth-Century China*. Cambridge, MA: Harvard University Press, 1993, 249–68.

Benton, Gregor. "Lu Xun, Leon Trotsky, and the Chinese Trotskyists." *East Asian History* 7 (1994): 93–104.

Brown, Carolyn. "The Paradigm of the Iron House: Shouting and Silence in Lu Xun's Stories." *Chinese Literature: Essays, Articles, Reviews* 6, 1–2 (1984): 101–20.

———. "Woman as Trope: Gender and Power in Lu Xun's 'Soap.'" *Modern Chinese Literature* 4, 1–2 (1988): 55–70.

Chan, Stephen. "The Language of Despair: Ideological Representations of the 'New Woman' by May Fourth Writers." In Tani E. Barlow, ed., *Gender Politics in Modern China: Writing and Feminism*. Durham, NC: Duke University Press, 1993, 13–32.

Chang, Shuei-may. "Lu Hsun's 'Regret for the Past' and the May Fourth Movement." *Tamkang Review* 31, 4/32, 1 (Summer-Autumn 2001): 173–203.

Chen, Pearl Hsia. *The Social Thought of Lu Hsun, 1881–1936*. New York: Vantage, 1976.

Cheung, Chiu-yee. "Beyond East and West: Lu Xun's Apparent 'Iconoclasm' and his Understanding of the Problem of Chinese Traditional Culture." *Journal of the Oriental Society of Australia* 20/21 (1988/89): 1–20.

———. "Lu Hsun and Nietzsche: Influence and Affinity after 1927." *Journal of the Oriental Society of Australia* 18/19 (1986/87): 21–38.

———. "The Love of a Decadent 'Superman': A Re-reading of Lu Xun's 'Regret for the Past.'" *Journal of the Oriental Society of Australia* 30 (1998): 26–46.

Davies, Gloria. "The Problematic Modernity of Ah Q." *Chinese Literature: Essays, Articles, Reviews* 13 (1991): 57–76.

Farquhar, Mary Ann. "Lu Xun and the World of Children." In Farquhar, *Children's Literature in China from Lu Xun to Mao Zedong*. Armonk, NY: M.E. Sharpe, 1999, 26–90.

Fokkema, Douwe W. "Lu Xun: The Impact of Russian Literature." In Merle Goldman, ed., *Modern Chinese Literature in the May Fourth Era*. Cambridge, MA: Harvard University Press, 1977, 89–103.

Foster, Paul. *Ah Q Archaeology: Lu Xun, Ah Q, Ah Q's Progeny, and the National Character Discourse in Twentieth Century China.* Lanham, MD: Lexington Books, 2005.

Galik, Marian. "Lu Hsun's Contribution to the History of Modern Chinese Literary Criticism and His Struggle for a United Marxist Front." In Galik, *The Genesis of Modern Chinese Literary Criticism, 1917–1930.* London: Curzon Press, 1980, 236–84.

——. "Lu Hsun's *Call to Arms*: Creative Confrontation with Garshin, Andreev and Nietzsche." In Galik, ed., *Milestones in Sino-Western Literary Confrontation (1898–1979).* Weisbaden: Otto Harrassowitz, 1986, 19–42.

——, ed. *Interliterary and Intraliterary Aspects of the May Fourth Movement 1919 in China.* Bratislava: Veda, 1990, 67–82.

Goldman, Merle. "The Political Use of Lu Xun." *China Quarterly* 91 (1982): 446–61.

Hanan, Patrick. *Chinese Fiction of the Nineteenth and Early Twentieth Centuries.* New York: Columbia University Press, 2004.

Hsia, T. A. "Aspects of the Power of Darkness in Lu Hsun." *The Gate of Darkness: Studies on the Leftist Literary Movement.* Seattle: University of Washington Press, 1968, 146–62.

Huang, Martin Weizong. "The Inescapable Predicament: The Narrator and His Discourse in 'The True Story of Ah Q.'" *Modern China* 16, 4 (October 1990): 430–49.

Huang, Sung-k'ang. *Lu Hsun and the New Culture Movement of Modern China.* Amsterdam: Djambatan, 1957.

Huters, Theodore. "Blossoms in the Snow: Lu Xun and the Dilemma of Modern Chinese Literature." *Modern China* 10, 1 (Jan. 1984): 49–77.

Kaldis, Nicholas. "The Prose Poem as Aesthetic Cognition: Lu Xun's *Yecao.*" *Journal of Modern Literature in Chinese* 3, 2 (Jan. 2000): 43–82.

Kelly, D. A. "Nietzsche in China: Influence and Affinity." *Papers on Far Eastern History* 27 (March 1983): 143–72.

Kowallis, Jon. *The Lyrical Lu Xun: A Study of His Classical Style Verse.* Honolulu: University of Hawaii Press, 1996.

Kuoshu, Harry H. "Visualizing Ah Q: An Allegory's Resistance to Representation." *Journal of Modern Literature in Chinese* 2, 2 (Jan. 1999): 1–36.

Larson, Wendy. *Literary Authority and the Modern Chinese Writer: Ambivalence and Autobiography.* Durham, NC: Duke University Press, 1991.

Lee, Haiyan. "Sympathy, Hypocrisy, and the Trauma of Chineseness." *Modern Chinese Literature and Culture* 16, 2 (Fall 2004): 76–122.

Lee, Leo Ou-fan. *Voices from the Iron House: A Study of Lu Xun.* Bloomington: Indiana University Press, 1987.

——, ed. *Lu Xun and His Legacy.* Berkeley: University of California Press, 1985.

Lin, Yu-sheng. *The Crisis of Chinese Consciousness: Radical Anti-Traditionalism in the May Fourth Era*. Madison: University of Wisconsin Press, 1979.

Liu, Ts'un-yan. "Lu Xun and Classical Studies." *Papers on Far Eastern History* 26 (Sept 1982): 119–44.

Lu, Junhua. "Ah Q's Spiritual Victory: The Philosophical and Psychological Implications." *Social Sciences in China* 3 (1981): 21–60.

Lundberg, Lennart. *Lu Xun as a Translator: Lu Xun's Translation and Introduction of Literature and Literary Theory, 1903–1936*. Stockholm: Orientaliska Studier, Stockholm University, 1989.

Lyell, William A. *Lu Hsun's Vision of Reality*. Berkeley: University of California Press, 1976.

McDougall, Bonnie S. "Lu Xun Hates China, Lu Xun Hates Lu Xun." In Wolfgang Kubin, ed., *Symbols of Anguish: In Search of Melancholy in China*. Bern: Peter Lang, 2001, 385–440.

——. *Love-Letters and Privacy in Modern China: The Intimate Lives of Lu Xun and Xu Guangping*. Oxford: Oxford University Press, 2002.

Mills, Harriet. "Lu Xun: Literature and Revolution—From Mara to Marx." In Merle Goldman, ed., *Modern Chinese Literature in the May Fourth Era*. Cambridge, MA: Harvard University Press, 1977, 189–220.

Ng, Janet. *The Experience of Modernity: Chinese Autobiography in the Early Twentieth Century*. Ann Arbor: University of Michigan Press, 2003.

Ng, Mau-sang. "Symbols of Anxiety in *Wild Grass*." *Renditions* 26 (1986): 155–64.

Park, Min-woong. "On Lu Xun's Attitude toward the Masses." *Chinese Culture* 39, 1 (1998): 93–108.

Prusek, Jaroslav. *The Lyrical and the Epic: Studies in Modern Chinese Literature*. Bloomington: Indiana University Press, 1980.

Pusey, James Reeves. *Lu Xun and Evolution*. Albany: State University of New York Press, 1998.

Schwarcz, Vera. "Writing in the Face of Necessity: Lu Xun, Brecht, and Satire." *Modern China* 7, 3 (July 1981): 289–316.

——. "A Curse on the Great Wall: The Problem of Enlightenment in Modern China." *Theory and Society* 13 (1984): 455–70.

Semanov, V. I. *Lu Hsun and His Predecessors*. Tr. Charles Alber. White Plains, NY: M.E. Sharpe, 1980.

Shih, Shu-mei. *The Lure of the Modern: Writing Modernism in Semicolonial China, 1917–1937*. Berkeley: University of California Press, 2001.

Sun, Lung-kee. "To Be or Not to Be 'Eaten': Lu Xun's Dilemma of Political Engagement." *Modern China* 14, 4 (1986): 459–85.

——. *The Chinese National Character: From Nationhood to Individuality*. Armonk, NY: M.E. Sharpe, 2001.

Wang, Ban. *Narrative Perspective and Irony in Selected Chinese and American Fiction*. Lewiston, NY: Edwin Mellen Press, 2002.
——. *The Sublime Figure of History*. Stanford: Stanford University Press, 1997.
Wang, David Der-wei. "Lu Xun, Shen Congwen, and Decapitation." In Xiaobin Tang and Liu Kang, eds., *Politics, Ideology, and Literary Discourse in Modern China: Theoretical Interventions and Cultural Critique*. Durham, NC: Duke University Press.
Xu, Jian. "The Will to the Transaethetic: The Truth Content of Lu Xun's Fiction." *Modern Chinese Literature and Culture* 11, 1 (Spring 1999): 61–92.
Yang, Shuhui. "The Fear of Moral Failure: An Intertextual Reading of Lu Hsun's Fiction." *Tamkang Review* 21, 3 (1991): 239–54.
Yin, Xiaoling. "Lu Xun's Parallel to Walter Benjamin: The Consciousness of the Tragic in 'The Loner.'" *Tamkang Review* 26, 3 (Spring 1996): 53–68.
Yue, Gang. "Lu Xun and Cannibalism." In *The Mouth That Begs: Hunger, Cannibalism, and the Politics of Eating in Modern China*. Durham, NC: Duke University Press, 1999, 67–100.
Zhou, Jianren (Chou Chien-jen). *An Age Gone By: Lu Xun's Clan in Decline*. Beijing: New World Press, 1988.

Lu Yin

Feng, Jin. "Sentimental Autobiographies: Feng Yuanjun, Lu Yin and the New Woman." In Feng, *The New Woman in Early Twentieth-Century Chinese Fiction*. West Lafayette, IN: Purdue University Press, 2004, 126–48.
Larson, Wendy. "Female Subjectivity and Gender Relations: The Early Stories of Lu Yin and Bing Xin." In X. Tang and L. Kang, eds., *Politics, Ideology, and Literary Discourse in Modern China: Theoretical Interventions and Cultural Critique*. Durham, NC: Duke University Press, 1993, 124–46.
Liu, Jianmei. "Feminizing Politics: Reading Bai Wei and Lu Yin." *Journal of Modern Literature in Chinese* 5, 2 (2002): 55–80.

Ma Yuan

Causer, Frances. "Daedalus Goes to Tibet, But What Exactly Is He Doing There? A Reading of the Chinese Avant-Garde Writer Ma Yuan's Novella *Fabrication*." *Bulletin of Seikei University* 29, 5 (July 1997): 1–57.
Yang, Xiaobin. "Narratatorial Parabasis and *Mise-en-Abyme*: Ma Yuan as a Model." In Yang, *The Chinese Postmodern: Trauma and Irony in Chinese Avant-garde Fiction*. Ann Arbor: University of Michigan Press, 2002, 153–67.

Mao Dun

Abbas, M. A., and Tak-wai Wong. "Mao Tun's 'Spring Silkworm': Rhetoric and Ideology." In Ying-hsiung Chou, ed., *The Chinese Text: Studies in Comparative Literature*. Hong Kong: The Chinese University of Hong Kong, 1986, 191–207.

Anderson, Marston. "Mao Dun, Zhang Tianyi, and the Social Impediments to Realism." In Anderson, *The Limits of Realism: Chinese Fiction in the Revolutionary Period*. Berkeley: University of California Press, 1990, 119–79.

Berninghausen, John. "The Central Contradiction in Mao Dun's Earliest Fiction." In Merle Goldman, ed., *Modern Chinese Literature in the May Fourth Era*. Cambridge, MA: Harvard University Press, 1977, 233–59.

Bichler, Lorenz. "Conjectures on Mao Dun's Silence as a Novelist after 1949." In Raoul Findeisen and Robert Gassmann, eds., *Autumn Floods: Essays in Honour of Marian Galik*. Bern: Peter Lang, 1997, 195–206.

Chan, Chingkiu Stephen. "Eros as Revolution: The Libidinal Dimension of Despair in Mao Dun's *Rainbow*." *Journal of Oriental Studies* 24, 1 (1986): 37–53.

Chen, Susan Wolf. "Mao Tun the Translator." *Harvard Journal of Asiatic Studies* 48 (1988): 71–94.

———. "The Personal Element in Mao Tun's Early Fiction." *Harvard Journal of Asiatic Studies,* 43 (1983): 187–213.

Chen, Yu-shih. "False Harmony: Mao Dun on Women and Family." *Modern Chinese Literature* 7, 1 (1993): 131–52.

———. *Realism and Allegory in the Early Fiction of Mao Dun*. Bloomington: Indiana University Press, 1986.

———. "Image of the Fallen Woman and the Making of the Chinese Proletarian Consciousness: Mao Dun's *Shuizao xing* (1936)." In Marian Galik, ed., *Interliterary and Intraliterary Aspects of the May Fourth Movement 1919 in China*. Bratislava: Veda, 1990, 155–66.

Chung, Hilary. "Questing the Goddess: Mao Dun and the New Woman." In Raoul Findeison and Robert Gassmann, eds., *Autumn Floods: Essays in Honour of Marian Galik*. Bern: Peter Lang, 1997.

Feng, Jin. "The Temptation and Salvation of the Male Intellectual: Mao Dun's Women Revolutionaries." In Feng, *The New Woman in Early Twentieth-Century Chinese Fiction*. West Lafayette, IN: Purdue University Press, 2004, 101–25.

Feuerwerker, Yi-tsi Mei. "The Dialectics of Struggle: Ideology and Realism in Mao Dun's 'Algae.'" In Theodore Huters, ed., *Reading the Modern Chinese Short Story*. Armonk, NY: M.E. Sharpe, 1990, 51–73.

Galik, Marian. *Mao Tun and Modern Chinese Literary Criticism*. Wiesbaden: Franz Steiner Verlag, 1969.

——. "Mao Tun's *Midnight*: Creative Confrontation with Zola, Tolstoy, Wertherism and Nordic Mythology." In Galik, ed., *Milestones in Sino-Western Literary Confrontation (1898–1979)*. Weisbaden: Otto Harrassowitz, 1986, 73–100.

——. "Mao Tun's Struggle for a Realistic and Marxist Theory of Literature." In Galik, *The Genesis of Modern Chinese Literary Criticism, 1917–1930*. London: Curzon Press, 1980, 191–213.

Hsia, C. T. "Mao Tun (1896–)." In C. T. Hsia, *A History of Modern Chinese Fiction*. 2nd ed. New Haven: Yale University Press, 1971, 140–64, 350–9.

Huters, Theodore. "Mao Dun's *Fushi*: The Politics of the Self." *Modern Chinese Literature* 5, 2 (1989): 242–68.

Leung, Yiu-nam. "High Finance in Emile Zola and Mao Tun." In Masayuki Akiyama and Yiu-nam Leung, eds., *Crosscurrents in the Literatures of Asia and the West: Essays in Honor of A. Owen Aldridge*. Newark, NJ: Associated University Presses, 1997, 145–62.

Lin, Sylvia Li-chun. "Unwelcome Heroines: Mao Dun and Yu Dafu's Creations of a New Chinese Woman." *Journal of Modern Literature in Chinese* 1, 2 (Jan. 1998): 71–94.

McDougall, Bonnie S. "The Search for Synthesis: T'ien Han and Mao Tun in 1920." In A. R. Davis, ed., *Search for Identity: Modern Literature and the Creative Arts in Asia*. Sydney: Angus and Robertson, 1974, 225–54.

——. "Disappearing Women and Disappearing Men in May Fourth Narrative: A Post-Feminist Survey of Short Stories by Mao Dun, Bing Xin, Ling Shuhua and Shen Congwen." In McDougall, *Fictional Authors, Imaginary Audiences: Modern Chinese Literature in the Twentieth Century*. Hong Kong: Chinese University Press, 2003, 133–70.

Prusek, Jaroslav. "Mao Tun." In *Three Sketches of Chinese Literature*. Prague: Academia, 1969. Rpt. in *The Lyrical and the Epic: Studies of Modern Chinese Literature*. Bloomington: Indiana University Press, 1980.

Shen, Gloria. "A Theoretical Approach to Naturalism and the Modern Chinese Novel: Mao Tun as Critic and Novelist." *Tamkang Review* 25, 2 (Winter 1994): 37–66.

Shih, Vincent Y. C. "Mao Tun: The Critic (Part I)." *China Quarterly* 19 (1964): 84–98.

——. "Mao Tun: The Critic (Part II)." *China Quarterly* 20 (1964): 128–62.

Wang, David Der-wei. *Fictional Realism in 20th-Century China: Mao Dun, Lao She, Shen Congwen*. New York: Columbia University Press, 1992. [chapters 2 and 3 deal with Mao Dun]

Wong, Tak-wai, and M. A. Abbas. "Mao Tun's 'Spring Silkworms': Rhetoric and Ideology." In Ying-hsiung Chou, ed., *The Chinese Text: Studies in Comparative Literature*. Hong Kong: Chinese University Press, 1986, 191–207.

Mo Yan

Braester, Yomi. "Mo Yan and *Red Sorghum*." In Joshua Mostow, ed., and Kirk A. Denton, China section, ed., *Columbia Companion to Modern East Asian Literatures*. New York: Columbia University Press, 2003, 541–45.

Cai, Rong. "Problematizing the Foreign Other: Mother, Father, and the Bastard in Mo Yan's *Large Breasts and Full Hips*." *Modern China* 29, 1 (Jan. 2003): 108–37.

Chan, Shelley W. "From Fatherland to Motherland: On Mo Yan's *Red Sorghum* and *Big Breasts and Full Hips*." *World Literature Today* 74, 3 (Summer 2000): 495–500.

Chen, Jianguo. "The Logic of the Phantasm: Haunting and Spectrality in Contemporary Chinese Literary Imagination." *Modern Chinese Literature and Culture* 14, 1 (Spring 2002): 231–65.

Chou, Ying-hsiung. "Romance of the Red Sorghum Family." *Modern Chinese Literature* 5, 1 (1989): 33–42.

Duke, Michael. "Past, Present, and Future in Mo Yan's Fiction of the 1980s." In Ellen Widmer and David Wang, eds., *From May Fourth to June Fourth: Fiction and Film in Twentieth-Century China*. Cambridge, MA: Harvard University Press, 1993, 295–326.

Feuerwerker, Yi-tsi Mei. "The Post-Modern 'Search for Roots' in Han Shaogong, Mo Yan, and Wang Anyi." In Feuerwerker, *Ideology, Power, Text: Self-Representation and the Peasant "Other" in Modern Chinese Literature*. Stanford: Stanford University Press, 1998, 188–238.

Goldblatt, Howard. "Forbidden Food: 'The Saturnicon' of Mo Yan." *World Literature Today* 74, 3 (Summer 2000): 477–86.

Inge, Thomas M. "Mo Yan through Western Eyes." *World Literature Today* 74, 3 (Summer 2000): 501–06.

Ling, Tun Ngai. "Anal Anarchy: A Reading of Mo Yan's 'The Plagues of Red Locusts.'" *Modern Chinese Literature* 10, 1/2 (1998): 7–24.

Lu, Tonglin. "*Red Sorghum*: Limits of Transgression." In X. Tang and L. Kang, eds., *Politics, Ideology, and Literary Discourse in Modern China: Theoretical Interventions and Cultural Critique*. Durham, NC: Duke University Press, 1993, 188–208.

Ng, Kenny K. K. "Critical Realism and Peasant Ideology: *The Garlic Ballads* by Mo Yan." *Chinese Culture* 39, 1 (1998): 109–46.

———. "Metafiction, Cannibalism, and Political Allegory: *Wineland* by Mo Yan." *Journal of Modern Literature in Chinese* 1, 2 (January 1998): 121–48.

Wang, David Der-wei. "Imaginary Nostalgia: Shen Congwen, Song Zelai, Mo Yan, and Li Yongping." In Ellen Widmer and David Wang, eds., *From May Fourth to June Fourth: Fiction and Film in Twentieth-Century China*. Cambridge, MA: Harvard University Press, 1993, 107–132.

——. "The Literary World of Mo Yan." *World Literature Today* 74, 3 (Summer 2000): 487–94.

Wu, Yenna. "Pitfalls of the Postcolonialist Rubric in the Study of Modern Chinese Fiction Featuring Cannibalism: From Lu Xun's 'Diary of a Madman' to Mo Yan's *Boozeland*." *Tamkang Review* 30, 3 (Spring 2000): 51–88.

Yang, Xiaobin. "*The Republic of Wine*: An Extravaganza of Decline." *Positions* 6, 1 (1998): 7–31. Rpt. in Yang, *The Chinese Postmodern: Trauma and Irony in Chinese Avant-garde Fiction.* Ann Arbor: University of Michigan Press, 2002, 207–29.

Yue, Gang. "From Cannibalism to Carnivorism: Mo Yan's Liquorland." In *The Mouth That Begs: Hunger, Cannibalism, and the Politics of Eating in Modern China.* Durham, NC: Duke University Press, 1999, 262–88.

Zhong, Xueping. "*Zazhong gaoliang* and the Male Search for Masculinity." In Zhong, ed., *Masculinity Besieged? Issues of Modernity and Male Subjectivity in Chinese Literature of the Late Twentieth Century.* Durham, NC: Duke University Press, 2000, 119–49.

Zhu, Ling. "A Brave New World? On the Construction of 'Masculinity' and 'Femininity' in *The Red Sorghum Family*." Lu Tonglin, ed., *Gender and Sexuality in Twentieth-Century Chinese Literature and Society.* Albany: State University of New York Press, 1993, 121–34.

Mu Shiying

Braester, Yomi. "Shanghai's Economy of Spectacle: The Shanghai Race Club in Liu Na'ou's and Mu Shiying's Stories." *Modern Chinese Literature* 9, 1 (1995): 39–58.

Lee, Leo Ou-fan. "Face, Body, and the City: The Fiction of Liu Na'ou and Mu Shiying." In Lee, *Shanghai Modern: The Flowering of a New Urban Culture in China, 1930–1945.* Cambridge, MA: Harvard University Press, 1999, 190–231.

Liu, Jianmei. "Shanghai Variations on 'Revolution Plus Love.'" *Modern Chinese Literature and Culture* 14, 1 (Spring 2002): 51–92.

Shih, Shu-mei. "Performing Semicolonial Subjectivity: The Work of Mu Shiying." In Shih, *The Lure of the Modern: Writing Modernism in Semicolonial China, 1917–1937.* Berkeley: University of California Press, 2001, 302–38.

Williams, Philip F. "Twentieth Century Chinese Fiction's Growing Tension between Narrator and Implied Reader: The Case of Mu Shiying." *Chinese Culture* XL, 1 (March 1999): 71–84.

Zhang, Yingjin. *The City in Modern Chinese Literature and Film.* Stanford, Stanford University Press, 1996, 154–85.

Ru Zhijuan

Hegel, Robert E. "Political Integration in Ru Zhijuan's 'Lilies.'" In Theodore Huters, ed., *Reading the Modern Chinese Short Story*. Armonk, NY: M.E. Sharpe, 1990, 92–104.

Sha Ting

Anderson, Marston. *The Limits of Realism: Chinese Fiction in the Revolutionary Period*. Berkeley: University of California Press, 1990. [final chapter treats Sha Ting]

Pin, Chih. "Sha Ting [She T'ing] the Novelist." *Chinese Literature* 10 (1964): 97–104.

Shen Congwen

Hsia, C. T. "Shen Ts'ung-wen (1902–)." In Hsia, *A History of Modern Chinese Fiction*. 2nd ed. New Haven: Yale University Press, 1971, 189–211, 359–66.

Kinkley, Jeffrey. "Shen Congwen's Legacy in Chinese Literature of the 1980s." In Ellen Widmer and David Wang, eds., *From May Fourth to June Fourth: Fiction and Film in Twentieth-Century China*. Cambridge, MA: Harvard University Press, 1993, 71–106.

———. "Echoes of Maxim Gorky in the Works of Ding Ling and Shen Congwen." In Marian Galik, ed., *Interliterary and Intraliterary Aspects of the May Fourth Movement 1919 in China*. Bratislava: Veda, 1990, 179–88.

———. *The Odyssey of Shen Congwen*. Stanford: Stanford University Press, 1987.

———. "Shen Congwen and the Uses of Regionalism in Modern Chinese Literature." *Modern Chinese Literature* 1, 2 (1985): 157–84.

Li, Rui. "Shen Congwen: A Different Commemoration." *Chinese Cross Currents* 1, 2 (2004): 8–22. [in English and Chinese]

Lo, Man Wa. "Female Selfhood and Initiation in Shen Congwen's *The Border Town* and Ding Ling's *The Girl Ah Mao*." *Chinese/International Comparative Literature Bulletin* 1 (1996): 20–33.

McDougall, Bonnie. "Disappearing Women and Disappearing Men in May Fourth Narrative: A Post-Feminist Survey of Short Stories by Mao Dun, Bing Xin, Ling Shuhua and Shen Congwen." In McDougall, *Fictional Authors, Imaginary Audiences: Modern Chinese Literature in the Twentieth Century*. Hong Kong: Chinese University Press, 2003, 133–70.

Ng, Janet. "A Moral Landscape: Reading Shen Congwen's Autobiography and Travelogues." *Chinese Literature: Essays, Articles, Reviews* 23 (2002): 81–102. Rpt. in Ng, *The Experience of Modernity: Chinese Autobiography in the Early Twentieth Century*. Ann Arbor: University of Michigan Press, 2003, 119–44.

Nieh, Hua-ling. *Shen Ts'ung-wen*. Boston: Twayne, 1972.

Oakes, Timothy S. "Shen Congwen's Literary Regionalism and the Gendered Landscape of Chinese Modernity." *Geografiska Annaler, Series B, Human Geography* 77, 2 (1995): 93–107.

Peng, Hsiao-yen. *Antithesis Overcome: Shen Congwen's Avant-Gardism and Primitivism*. Taipei: Institute of Chinese Literature and Philosophy, Academica Sinica, 1994.

Stafutti, Stefania. "Wonderful China?—On Shen Congwen's 'Travelogue of Alice in China.'" In Raoul Findeisen and Robert Gassmann, eds., *Autumn Floods: Essays in Honour of Marian Galik*. Bern: Peter Lang, 1997.

Wang, David. *Fictional Realism in Twentieth-Century China: Mao Dun, Lao She, Shen Congwen*. New York: Columbia University Press, 1992.

———. "Imaginary Nostalgia: Shen Congwen, Song Zelai, Mo Yan, and Li Yongping." In Ellen Widmer and David Wang, eds., *From May Fourth to June Fourth: Fiction and Film in Twentieth-Century China*. Cambridge, MA: Harvard University Press, 1993, 107–132.

———. "Lu Xun, Shen Congwen, and Decapitation." In X. Tang and L. Kang, eds. *Politics, Ideology, and Literary Discourse in Modern China: Theoretical Interventions and Cultural Critique*. Durham, NC: Duke University Press, 1993, 278–99.

Wong, Yoon Wah. "Structure, Symbolism and Contrast in Shen Congwen's *The Border Town*." In Wong, *Essays on Chinese Literature*. Singapore: Singapore University Press, 1988, 67–81.

Yue, Gang. "Shen Congwen's 'Modest Proposal.'" In *The Mouth That Begs: Hunger, Cannibalism, and the Politics of Eating in Modern China*. Durham, NC: Duke University Press, 1999, 101–44.

Shen Rong

Larson, Wendy. "Women, Writers, Social Reform: Three Issues in Shen Rong's Fiction." In Michael S. Duke, ed., *Modern Chinese Women Writers: Critical Appraisals*. Armonk, NY: M.E. Sharpe, 1989, 174–95.

Yang, Gladys. "Shen Rong and Her Fiction." In Yang Bian, ed., *The Time Is Not Ripe: Contemporary China's Best Writers and Their Stories*. Beijing: Foreign Languages Press, 1991, 185–92.

Shi Zhecun

Ge, Mai. "The Modern Writer Shi Zhecun." Tr. Chen Haiyan. *Chinese Literature* 4 (Winter 1991): 156–161.

Hidveghyova, Elena. "The Decadent Obsession: Eros versus Celibacy in the Work of Shi Zhecun and Anatole France." *Asian and African Studies* (Bratislava) 4, 1 (1995): 47–70.

Jones, Andrew F. "The Violence of the Text: Reading Yu Hua and Shi Zhicun." *Positions: East Asia Cultures Critique* 2, 3 (1994): 570–602.

Lee, Leo Ou-fan. "The Erotic, The Fantastic, and the Uncanny: Shi Zhecun's Experimental Stories." In Lee, *Shanghai Modern: The Flowering of a New Urban Culture in China, 1930–1945.* Cambridge, MA: Harvard University Press, 1999, 153–89.

Liu, Jianmei. "Shanghai Variations on 'Revolution Plus Love.'" *Modern Chinese Literature and Culture* 14, 1 (Spring 2002): 51–92.

McGrath, Jason, "Patching the Void: Subjectivity and Anamorphic Bewitchment in Shi Zhecun's Fiction." *Journal of Modern Literature in Chinese* 4, 2 (2001): 1–30.

Schaefer, William. "Kumarajiva's Foreign Tongue: Shi Zhecun's Modernist Historical Fiction." *Modern Chinese Literature* 10, 1/2 (1998): 25–70.

Shih, Shu-mei. "Capitalism and Interiority: Shi Zhecun's Tales of the Erotic-Grotesque." In Shih, *The Lure of the Modern: Writing Modernism in Semicolonial China, 1917–1937.* Berkeley: University of California Press, 2001, 339–70.

Zhang, Hongbing. "Writing 'the Strange' of the Chinese Modern: Sutured Body, Naturalized Beauty, and Shi Zhecun's 'Yaksha.'" *Journal of Modern Literature in Chinese* 5, 2 (2002): 29–54.

Shu Ting

Chen, Zhongyi. "Afterword: Some Thoughts on Shu Ting's Poetry." In Shu Ting, *Selected Poems.* Hong Kong: Renditions Paperbacks, 1994, 131–34.

Kubin, Wolfgang. "Writing with Your Body: Literature as a Wound—Remarks on the Poetry of Shu Ting." *Modern Chinese Literature* 4, 1/2 (1988): 149–62.

Swihart, De-an Wu. "Introduction." In *The Mist of My Heart: Selected Poems of Shu Ting.* Tr. Gordon T. Osing and De-an Wu Swihart. Ed. William O'Donnell. Beijing: Panda Books, 1995, 5–17.

Su Tong

Deppman, Hsiu-Chuang. "Body, Space, and Power: Reading the Cultral Images of Concubines in the Works of Su Tong and Zhang Yimou." *Modern Chinese Literature and Culture* 15, 2 (Fall 2003): 121–53.

Knight, Deirdre Sabina. "Decadence, Revolution and Self-Determination in Su Tong's Fiction." *Modern Chinese Literature* 10, 1/2 (1998): 91–112.

Leenhouts, Mark. "The Contented Smile of the Writer: An Interview with Su Tong." *China Information* 11, 4 (Spring 1997): 70–80.

Tang, Xiaobing. "The Mirror as History and History as Spectacle: Reflections on Hsiao Yeh and Su T'ung." *Modern Chinese Literature* 6, 1/2 (1992): 203–20.

Visser, Robin. "Displacement of the Urban-Rural Confrontation in Su Tong's Fiction." *Modern Chinese Literature* 9, 1 (1995): 113–38.

Xu, Jian. "*Blush* fom Novella to Film: The Possibility of Critical Art in Commodity Culture." *Modern Chinese Literature and Culture* 12, 1 (Spring 2000): 115–63.

Tashi Dawa

Danxhu, Angben. "Tashi Dawa and His Works." Tr. Chen Haiyan. *Chinese Literature* (Autumn, 1991): 58–62.

Tie Ning

Chen Xiaoming. "The Extrication of Memory in Tie Ning's *Woman Showering*: Privacy and the Trap of History." In Bonnie S. McDougall and Anders Hansson, eds., *Chinese Concepts of Privacy*. Leiden: Brill, 2002, 195–208.

Yip, Terry Siu-han. "Place, Gender and Identity: The Global-Local Interplay in Three Stories from China, Taiwan and Hong Kong." In Kwok-kan Tam et al., eds., *Sights of Contestation: Localism, Globalism and Cultural Production in Asia and the Pacific*. Hong Kong: The Chinese University Press, 2002, 17–34.

Wang Anyi

Chen, Helen H. "Gender, Subjectivity, Sexuality: Defining a Subversive Discourse in Wang Anyi's Four Tales of Sexual Transgression." In Yingjin Zhang, ed., *China in a Polycentric World: Essays in Chinese Comparative Literature*. Stanford: Stanford University Press, 1999, 90–109.

Feuerwerker, Yi-tsi Mei. "The Post-Modern 'Search for Roots' in Han Shaogong, Mo Yan, and Wang Anyi." In Feuerwerker, *Ideology, Power, Text: Self-Representation and the Peasant "Other" in Modern Chinese Literature*. Stanford: Stanford University Press, 1998, 188–238.

McDougall, Bonnie, S. "Self-Narrative as Group Discourse: Female Subjectivity in Wang Anyi's Fiction." *Asian Studies Review* 19, 2 (November 1995): 1–24.

Tang, Xiaobin. "Melancholy against the Grain: Approaching Postmodernity in Wang Anyi's *Tales of Sorrow*." In Xudong Zhang and Arif Dirlik, eds., *Postmodernism and China*. Durham, NC: Duke University Press, 2000, 358–78.

Wang, Ban. "Love at Last Sight: Nostalgia, Commodity, and Temporailty in Wang Anyi's *Song of Unending Sorrow*." *Positions* 10, 3 (Winter 2002): 669–94.

Wang, Lingzhen. "Wang Anyi." In Joshua Mostow, ed., and Kirk A. Denton, China section, ed., *Columbia Companion to Modern East Asian Literatures*. New York: Columbia University Press, 2003, 592–97.

Ying, Hong. "Wang Anyi and Her Fiction." In Yang Bian, ed., *The Time Is Not Ripe: Contemporary China's Best Writers and Their Stories*. Beijing: Foreign Languages Press, 1991, 217–24.

Yue, Gang. "Embodied Spaces of Home: Xiao Hong, Wang Anyi, and Li Ang." In *The Mouth That Begs: Hunger, Cannibalism, and the Politics of Eating in Modern China*. Durham, NC: Duke University Press, 1999, 293–330.

Zhang, Xudong. "Shanghai Nostalgia: Postrevolutionary Allegories in Wang Anyi's Literary Production in the 1990s." *Positions* 8, 2 (2000): 349–387.

Zhong, Xueping. "Sisterhood? Representations of Women's Relationships in Two Contemporary Chinese Texts." In Tonglin Lu, ed., *Gender and Sexuality in Twentieth Century Chinese Literature and Society*. Albany: State University of New York Press, 1993, 157–73.

Wang Meng

Arkush, R. David. "One of the Hundred Flowers: Wang Meng's 'Young Newcomer.'" *Papers on China* 18 (1964): 155–86.

Barme, Geremie. "A Storm in a Rice Bowl: Wang Meng and Fictional Chinese Politics." *China Information* 7, 2 (Autumn 1992): 12–19.

Ch'a, Ling. "Wang Meng's Rustication and Advancement." *Issues and Studies* 22, 9 (1986): 50–61.

Chang, Tze-chang. "Isolation and Self-Estrangement: Wang Meng's Alienated World." *Issues and Studies* 24, 1 (Jan. 1988): 140–54.

Feuerwerker, Yi-tsi Mei. "Text, Intertext, and the Representation of the Writing Self in Lu Xun, Yu Dafu, and Wang Meng." In Ellen Widmer and David Wang, eds., *From May Fourth to June Fourth: Fiction and Film in Twentiety-Century China*. Cambridge, MA: Harvard University Press, 1993, 167–93.

Keyser, Anne Sytske. "Wang Meng's Story 'Hard Thin Gruel': A Socio-Political Satire." *China Information* 7, 2 (Autumn 1992): 1–11.

Larson, Wendy. "Wang Meng's *Buli* (Bolshevik salute): Chinese Modernism and Negative Intellectual Identity." In *Bolshevik Salute: A Modernist Chinese Novel*. Seattle: University of Washington Press, 1989, 133–54.

Lin, Min, and Maria Galikowski. "Wang Meng's 'Hard Porridge' and the Paradox of Reform in China." In Lin and Galikowski, *The Search for Modernity: Chinese Intellectuals and Cultural Discourse in the Post-Mao Era*. New York: St. Martin's Press, 1999, 71–88.

Martin, Helmut. "Painful Encounter: Wang Meng's Novel *Hsiang chien shih nan* and the 'Foreign Theme' in Contemporary Chinese Literature." In Yu-ming

Shaw, ed., *China and Europe in the Twentieth Century.* Taipei: Institute of International Relations, National Chengchi University, 1986, 32–42.

Tay, William. "Wang Meng, Stream-of-consciousness, and the Controversy over Modernism." *Modern Chinese Literature* 1, 1 (1984): 7–24.

———. "Modernism and Socialist Realism: The Case of Wang Meng." *World Literature Today* 65, 3 (1991): 411–13.

Tung, Timothy. "Porridge and the Law: Wang Meng Sues." *Human Rights Tribune* 3, 1 (Spring 1992).

Wanger, Rudolf. *Inside the Service Trade: Studies in Contemporary Chinese Prose.* Cambridge, MA: Council on East Asian Studies, Harvard University, 1992, 193–212, 481–531.

Williams, Philip. "Stylistic Variety in a PRC Writer: Wang Meng's Fiction of the 1979–1980 Cultural Thaw." *Australian Journal of Chinese Affairs* 11 (1984): 59–80.

Yang, Gladys. "Wang Meng and His Fiction." In Yang Bian, ed., *The Time Is Not Ripe: Contemporary China's Best Writers and Their Stories.* Beijing: Foreign Languages Press, 1991, 238–45.

Zha, Peide. "Stream of Consciousness Narration in Contemporary Chinese Fiction: A Case Study of Wang Meng." *B.C. Asian Review* 3/4 (1990).

Zhang, Dening, and Jing Yi. "Open Our Hearts to the Panoramic World: An Interview with Wang Meng." *Chinese Literature* (Spring 1999): 5–24.

Wang Shuo

Barme, Geremie. "Wang Shuo and *Liumang* (Hooligan) Culture." *Australian Journal of Chinese Affairs* 28 (1992): 23–66.

———. "The Apotheosis of the *Liumang*." In Barme, *In the Red: On Contemporary Chinese Culture.* New York: Columbia University Press, 1999, 62–98.

Braester, Yomi. "Memory at a Standstill: From Mao History to Hooligan History." In Braester, *Witness against History: Literature, Film, and Public Discourse in Twentieth-Century China.* Stanford: Stanford University Press, 2003, 192–205.

Chen, Helen H. "From Sentimental Trilogy to Gangster Trilogy: Moral Dilemmas in a Cultural Crisis." *American Journal of Chinese Studies* 8, 1 (April 2001): 57–90.

Huang, Yibing. "'Vicious Animals': Wang Shuo and Negotiated Nostalgia for History." *Journal of Modern Literature in Chinese* 5, 2 (2002): 81–102.

Huot, Claire. "Away from Literature I: Words Turned On." In Huot, *China's New Cultural Scene: A Handbook of Changes.* Durham, NC: Duke University Press, 2000, 49–71.

James, Jamie. "Bad Boy: Why China's Most Popular Novelist Won't Go Away." *New Yorker* (Apr. 21, 1997): 50–53.

Kuoshu, Harry H. "Filming Marginal Youth: The 'Beyond' Syndrome in the Postsocialist City." In Kuoshu, *Lightness of Being in China: Adaptation and Discursive Figuration in Cinema and Theater.* New York: Peter Lang, 1999, 123–52.

Noble, Jonathan. "Wang Shuo and the Commercialization of Literature." In Joshua Mostow, ed., and Kirk A. Denton, China section, ed., *Columbia Companion to Modern East Asian Literatures.* New York: Columbia University Press, 2003, 598–603.

Rojas, Carlos. "Wang Shuo and the Chinese Imaginary: Visual Simulacra and the Writing of History." *Journal of Modern Literature in Chinese* 3, 1 (July 1999): 23–57.

Shu, Yunzhong. "Different Strategies of Self-Confirmation: Wang Shuo's Appeal to His Readers." *Tamkang Review* 29, 3 (Spring 1999): 111–26.

Wang, Jing. "Wang Shuo: Pop Goes the Culture." In Wang, *High Culture Fever: Politics, Aesthetics, and Ideology in Deng's China.* Berkeley: University of California Press, 1997, 261–86.

Yao, Yusheng. "The Elite Class Background of Wang Shuo and His Hooligan Characters." *Modern China* 30, 4 (Oct. 2004): 431–69.

Wang Wenxing

Chang, Han-liang. "Graphemics and Novel Interpretation: The Case of Wang Wen-hsing." *Modern Chinese Literature* 6, 1/2 (1992): 133–56.

Chang, Sung-Sheng. "Language, Narrative and Stream of Consciousness: The Two Novels of Wang Wen-hsing." *Modern Chinese Literature* 1, 1 (1984): 43–56.

Cheung, Sally J. S. Kao. "*Chia-Pien*: A 'Revolutionary' Chinese Novel of Today." *Fu Jen Studies* 11 (1978): 1–12.

Gunn, Edward. "The Process of Wang Wen-hsing's Art." *Modern Chinese Literature* 1, 1 (1984): 29–42.

Lupke, Christopher. "Wang Wenxing and the 'Loss' of China." *Boundary 2.* Special issue edited by Rey Chow. 25, 2 (Fall 1998): 97–128.

Shan, Te-hsing. "Wang Wen-hsing on Wang Wen-hsing." *Modern Chinese Literature* 1, 1 (1984): 57–66.

——. "The Stream of Consciousness Technique in Wang Wen-hsing's Fiction." *Tamkang Review* 15, 1–4 (1984–85): 523–45.

Shu, James C. T. "Iconoclasm in Wang Wen-hsing's *Chia-pien*." In Jeannette L. Faurot, ed., *Chinese Fiction from Taiwan: Critical Perspectives.* Bloomington: Indiana University Press, 1980, 179–93.

——. "Iconoclasm in Taiwan Literature: 'A Change in the Family.'" *Chinese Literature: Essays, Articles, Reviews* 2, 1 (1980): 73–85.

Wang Xiaobo

Larson, Wendy. "Okay, Whatever: Intellectuals, Sex, and Time in Wang Xiaobo's *The Golden Years*," *China Review: An Interdisciplinary Journal on Greater China* 3, 1 (Spring 2003), 29–56.

Shi, Anbin. "Body Writing and Corporeal Feminism: Reconstructing Gender Identity in Contemporary China." In Shi, *A Comparative Approach to Redefining Chinese-ness in the Era of Globalization*. Lewiston, NY: Edwin Mellen Press, 2003, 129–206.

Wang Zhenhe

Huang, I-min. "A Postmodern Reading of *Rose, Rose I Love You*." *Tamkang Review* 17, 1 (1986): 27–45.

Kinkley, Jeffrey C. "Mandarin Kitsch and Taiwanese Kitsch in the Fiction of Wang Chen-ho." *Modern Chinese Literature* 6, 1/2 (1992): 85–114.

Yang, Robert Yi. "Form and Tone in Wang Chen-ho's Satires." In Jeannette L. Faurot, ed., *Chinese Fiction from Taiwan*. Bloomington: Indiana University Press, 1980, 134–47.

Wen Yiduo

Hoffmann, Peter, ed. *Poet, Scholar, Patriot: In Honour of Wen Yiduo's 100th Anniversary*. Bochum, Freiburg: Projektverlag, 2004.

Hsu, Kai-yu. "The Life and Poetry of Wen I-to." *Harvard Journal of Asiatic Studies* 21. (Dec., 1958): 134–79.

———. *Wen I-to*. Boston: Twayne, 1980.

McClellan, T. M. "Wen Yiduo's 'Sishui' Meter: Themes, Variations and a Classic Variation." *Chinese Literature: Essays, Articles, Reviews* 21 (1999): 151–67.

Olney, Charles V. "The Chinese Poet Wen I-to." *Journal of Oriental Literature*, 7 (1966); 8–17.

Uberoi, Patricia. "Rhythmic Techniques in the Poetry of Wen I-to." *United College Journal* 6 (1967–68): 1–25.

van Crevel, Maghiel. "Who Needs Form? Wen Yiduo's Poetics and Post-Mao Poetry." In Peter Hoffmann, ed., *Poet, Scholar, Patriot: In Honour of Wen Yiduo's 100th Anniversary*. Bochum, Freiburg: Projektverlag, 2004, 81–110.

Wong, Wang-chi. "'I Am a Prisoner in Exile': Wen Yiduo in the United States." In Gregory Lee, ed., *Chinese Writing and Exile*. Chicago: Center for East Asian Studies, The University of Chicago, 1993, 19–34.

Wu Zuxiang

Campbell, Catherine. "Political Transformation in Wu Zuxiang's Wartime Novel *Shanhong*." *Modern Chinese Literature* 5, 2 (1989): 293–324.

Hsia, C. T. "Wu Tsu-hsiang." In Hsia, *A History of Modern Chinese Fiction*. 2nd ed. New Haven: Yale University Press, 1971, 281–87.

Williams, Philip. *Village Echoes: The Fiction of Wu Zuxiang*. Boulder: Westview, 1993.

———. Williams, Philip F. "20th-Century Iconoclasm in a Classical Tragedy: Wu Zuxiang's 'Fan Hamlet.'" *Republican China* 18, 1 (1993): 1–22.

Xu Dishan

Robinson, Lewis. "Yu-kuan: The Spiritual Testament of Hsu Ti-shan." *Tamkang Review* 8, 2 (1977): 147–68.

Xu Zhimo

Birch, Cyril. "English and Chinese Meters in Hsu Chih-mo." *Asia Major* 8 (1960): 258–93.

———. "Hsu Chih-mo's Debt to Thomas Hardy." *Tamkang Review* 8, 1 (1977): 1–24.

Chang, Pang-Mei Natasha. *Bound Feet and Western Dress*. New York: Doubleday, 1996.

Findeisen, Raoul David. "Xu Zhimo Dreaming in Sawston (England)—On the Sources of a Venice Poem." *Asiatica Venetiana* 1 (1996).

———. "Two Aviators: Gabriele d'Annunzio and Xu Zhimo." In Mabel Lee and Meng Hua, eds., *Cultural Dialogue and Misreadings*. Sydney: Wild Peony, 1997, 75–85.

Lee, Leo Ou-fan. *The Romantic Generation of Modern Chinese Writers*. Cambridge, MA: Harvard University Press, 1973.

Yang Lian

Cayley, John. "John Cayley with Yang Lian: Hallucination and Coherence." *Positions* 10, 3 (Winter 2002): 773–84.

Edmond, Jacob. "Locating Global Resistance: The Landscape Poetics of Arkadii Dragomoshchenko, Lyn Hejinian and Yang Lian." *AUMLA: Journal of the Australasian Universities Language & Literature Association* 101 (2004): 71–98.

———. "Beyond Binaries: Rereading Yang Lian's 'Norlang' and 'Banpo.'" *Journal of Modern Literature in Chinese* 6, 1 (2005): 152–69.

Golden, Sean, and John Minford. "Yang Lian and the Chinese Tradition." In Howard Goldblatt, ed., *Worlds Apart: Recent Chinese Writing and Its Audiences.* Armonk, NY: M.E. Sharpe, 119–37.

Holton, Brian. "Translating Yang Lian." In Yang Lian, *Where the Sea Stands Still: New Poems.*" Bloodaxe Books, 1999, 173–191.

Lee, Mabel. "Before Tradition: The Book of Changes and Yang Lian's *YI [Yi]* and the Affirmation of the Self Through Poetry." In Mabel Lee and A. D. Syrokomla-Stefanowska, eds., *Modernization of the Chinese Past.* Sydney: Wild Peony, 1993, 94–106.

———. "The Philosophy of the Self and Yang Lian." In Yang Lian, *Masks and Crocodile.* Sydney: Wild Peony, 1990.

Li, Xia. "Swings and Roundabouts: Strategies for Translating Colour Terms in Poetry." *Perspectives: Studies in Translatology* (Copenhagen). 5, 2 (1997): 257–66.

———. "Poetry, Reality and Existence in Yang Lian's 'Illusion City.'" *Journal of Asian and African Studies* (Brastislava) 4, 2 (1995): 149–65.

Yip, Wai-lim. "Crisis Poetry: An Introduction to Yang Lian, Jiang He and Misty Poetry." *Renditions* 23 (1985): 120–30.

Ye Lingfeng

Lee, Leo Ou-fan. "Decadent and Dandy: Shao Xunmei and Ye Lingfeng." In Lee, *Shanghai Modern: The Flowering of a New Urban Culture in China, 1930–1945.* Cambridge, MA: Harvard University Press, 1999, 232–66.

Liu, Jianmei. "Shanghai Variations on 'Revolution Plus Love." *Modern Chinese Literature and Culture* 14, 1 (Spring 2002): 51–92.

Ye Shengtao

Anderson, Marsten. "The Specular Self: Subjective and Mimetic Elements in the Fiction of Ye Shaojun." *Modern China* 15, 1 (Jan. 1989): 72–101.

———. "Lu Xun, Ye Shaojun, and the Moral Impediments to Realism." In Anderson, *The Limits of Realism: Chinese Fiction in the Revolutionary Period.* Berkeley: University of California Press, 1990, 76–118.

Hsia, C. T. "Yeh Shao-chun." In Hsia, *A History of Modern Chinese Fiction.* 2nd ed. New Haven: Yale University Press, 1971, 57–71.

Prusek, Jaroslav. "Yeh Shao-chun and Anton Chekhov." In Prusek, *The Lyrical and the Epic: Studies in Modern Chinese Literature.* Bloomington: Indiana University Press, 1980, 178–94.

Yu Dafu

Chan, Wing-ming. "The Self-Mocking of a Chinese Intellectual: A Study of Yu Dafu's *An Intoxicating Spring Night*." In Marian Galik, ed., *Interliterary and Intraliterary Aspects of the May Fourth Movement 1919 in China*. Bratislava: Veda, 1990, 111–18.

Denton, Kirk, A. "The Distant Shore: The Nationalist Theme in Yu Dafu's *Sinking*." *Chinese Literature: Essays, Articles, Reviews* 14 (1992): 107–23.

———. "Romantic Sentiment and the Problem of the Subject." In Joshua Mostow, ed., and Kirk A. Denton, China section, ed., *Columbia Companion to Modern East Asian Literatures*. New York: Columbia University Press, 2003, 478–84.

Dolezalova, Anna. *Yu Ta-fu: Specific Traits of His Literary Creation*. Bratislava: Publishing House of the Slovak Academy of Sciences, 1970.

Egan, Michael. "Yu Dafu and the Transition to Modern Chinese Literature." In Merle Goldman, ed., *Modern Chinese Literature in the May Fourth Era*. Cambridge, MA: Harvard University Press, 1977, 309–24.

Feng, Jin. "From Girl Student to Proletarian Woman: Yu Dafu's Victimized Hero and His Female Other." In Feng, *The New Woman in Early Twentieth-Century Chinese Fiction*. West Lafayette, IN: Purdue University Press, 2004, 60–82.

Feuerwerker, Yi-tsi Mei. "Text, Intertext, and the Representation of the Writing Self in Lu Xun, Yu Dafu, and Wang Meng." In Ellen Widmer and David Wang, eds., *From May Fourth to June Fourth: Fiction and Film in Twentieth-Century China*. Cambridge, MA: Harvard University Press, 1993, 167–93.

Galik, Marian. "Yu Dafu and His Panaesthetic Criticism." In Galik, *The Genesis of Modern Chinese Literary Criticism (1917–1930)*. London: Curzon Press, 1980, 104–28.

Keaveney, Christopher T. *The Subversive Self in Modern Chinese Literature: The Creation Society's Reinvention of the Japanese Shishosetsu*. New York: Palgrave Macmillan, 2004. [contains sections on Yu]

Lee, Leo Ou-fan. "Yu Ta-fu." In Lee, *The Romantic Generation of Modern Chinese Writers*. Cambridge, MA: Harvard University Press, 1973, 81–123.

Lin, Sylvia Li-chun. "Unwelcome Heroines: Mao Dun and Yu Dafu's Creations of a New Chinese Woman." *Journal of Modern Literature in Chinese* 1, 2 (Jan. 1998): 71–94.

Kumagaya, Hideo. "Quest for Truth: An Introductory Study of Yu Dafu's Fiction." *Journal of the Oriental Society of Australia* 24 (1992): 49–63.

Melyan, Gary. "The Enigma of Yu Ta-fu's Death." *Monumenta Serica* 24 (1970–71): 557–88.

Ng, Mau-sang. *The Russian Hero in Modern Chinese Fiction*. New York: State University of New York Press, 1988. [contains a chapter on Yu]

Prusek, Jaroslav. "Mao Tun and Yu Ta-fu." In Prusek, *The Lyrical and the Epic: Studies in Modern Chinese Literature*. Bloomington: Indiana University Press, 1980, 121–77.

Radtke, Kurt W. "Chaos and Coherence? Sato Haruo's Novel *Den'en no Yu'utsu* and Yu Dafu's trilogy *Chenlun*." In Adriana Boscaro, Franco Gatti, and Massimo Raveri, eds., *Rethinking Japan*. New York: St. Martin's Press, 1985, 86–101.

Shih, Shu-mei. "The Libidinal and the National: The Morality of Decadence in Yu Dafu, Teng Gu, and Others." In Shih, *The Lure of the Modern: Writing Modernism in Semicolonial China, 1917–1937*. Berkeley: University of California Press, 2001, 110–27.

Tsu, Jing. "Perversions of Masculinity: The Masochistic Male Subject in Yu Dafu, Guo Moruo, and Freud." *Positions* 8, 2 (Fall 2000): 269–316.

Wagner, Alexandra R. "Tradition as Construct and the Search for a Modern Identity: A Reading of Traditional Gestures in Modern Chinese Essays of Place." In Martin Woesler, ed., *The Modern Chinese Literary Essay: Defining the Chinese Self in the 20th Century*. Bochum: Bochum University Press, 2000, 133–46.

Wong Yoon Wah. "Yu Dafu in Exile: His Last Days in Sumatra." *Renditions* 23 (1985): 71–83.

Yu Hua

Braester, Yomi. "The Aesthetics and Anesthetics of Memory: PRC Avant-Garde Fiction." In Braester, *Witness Against History: Literature, Film, and Public Discourse in Twentieth-Century China*. Stanford: Stanford University Press, 2003, 177–91.

Chen, Jianguo. "Violence: The Politics and the Aesthetic—Toward a Reading of Yu Hua." *American Journal of Chinese Studies* 5, 1 (1998): 8–48.

———. "The Logic of the Phantasm: Haunting and Spectrality in Contemporary Chinese Literary Imagination." *Modern Chinese Literature and Culture* 14, 1 (Spring 2002): 231–65.

Jones, Andrew F. "The Violence of the Text: Reading Yu Hua and Shi Zhicun." *Positions* 2, 3 (1994): 570–602.

Knight, Deirdre Sabina. "Capitalist and Enlightenment Values in 1990s Chinese Fiction: The Case of Yu Hua's *Blood Seller*." *Textual Practice* 16, 3 (Nov. 2002): 1–22. Rpt. as "Capitalist and Enlightenment Values in Chinese Fiction of the 1990s: The Case of Yu Hua's *Blood Merchant*." In Charles Laughlin, ed., *Contested Modernity in Chinese Literature*. New York: Palgrave Macmillan, 2005, 217–37.

Larson, Larson. "Literary Modernism and Nationalism in Post-Mao China." In Wendy Larson and Anne Wedell-Wedellsborg, eds., *Inside Out: Modernism and Postmodernism in Chinese Literary Culture.* Aarhus: Aarhus University Press, 1993, 172–96.

Liu, Kang. "The Short-Lived Avant-Garde Literary Movement and Its Transformation: The Case of Yu Hua." In Liu, *Globalization and Cultural Trends in China.* Honolulu: University of Hawaii Press, 2004, 102–26.

Rong, Cai. "The Lonely Traveler Revisited in Yu Hua's Fiction." *Modern Chinese Literature* 10, 1/2 (1998): 173–190.

Tang, Xiaobin. "Residual Modernism: Narratives of Self in Contemporary Chinese Fiction." *Modern Chinese Literature* 7, 1 (Spring 1993): 7–31.

Wagner, Marsha. "The Subversive Fiction of Yu Hua." *Chinoperl Papers* 20–22 (1997–99): 219–44.

Wedell-Wedellsborg, Anne. "One Kind of Chinese Reality: Reading Yu Hua." *Chinese Literature: Essays, Articles, Reviews* 18 (1996): 129–45.

Yang, Xiaobin. "Yu Hua: The Past Remembered or the Present Dismembered." In Yang, *The Chinese Postmodern: Trauma and Irony in Chinese Avant-garde Fiction.* Ann Arbor: University of Michigan Press, 2002, 56–73.

——, "Yu Hua: Perplexed Narration and the Subject." In Yang, *The Chinese Postmodern: Trauma and Irony in Chinese Avant-garde Fiction.* Ann Arbor: University of Michigan Press, 2002, 188–206.

Zhao, Yiheng. "Yu Hua: Fiction as Subversion." *World Literature Today* (Summer 1991).

——. "The Rise of Metafiction in China." *Bulletin of Oriental and African Studies.* LV.1 (1992).

Yu Jian

Huot, Claire. "Here, There, Anywhere: Networking by Young Chinese Writers Today." In Michel Hockx, ed., *The Literary Field of Twentieth Century China.* Honolulu: University of Hawaii Press, 1999, 198–215.

van Crevel, Maghiel. "Fringe Poetry, But Not Prose: Works by Xi Chuan and Yu Jian." *Journal of Modern Literature in Chinese* 3, 2 (Jan. 2000).

——. "Desecrations? The Poetics of Han Dong and Yu Jian (part one)" *Studies on Asia* Series II, 2, 1 (2005): 28–48.

——. "Desecrations? The Poetics of Han Dong and Yu Jian (part two)." *Studies on Asia* Series II, 2, 2 (2005): 81–97.

Yuan Qiongqiong

Chang, Sung-sheng Yvonne. "Yuan Qiongqiong and the Rage for Eileen Chang among Taiwan's Feminine Writers." *Modern Chinese Literature* 4, 1/2 (1988): 201–24.

Zhang Ailing

Bohlmeyer, Jeanine. "Eileen Chang's Bridges to China." *Tamkang Review* 5, 1 (1974): 111–28.

Chang, Sung-sheng Yvonne. "Yuan Qiongqiong and the Rage for Eileen Zhang." *Modern Chinese Literature* 4, 1/2 (1988): 201–23.

Cheng, Stephen. "Themes and Techniques in Eileen Chang's Stories." *Tamkang Review* 8, 2 (1977): 169–200.

Chow, Rey. "Modernity and Narration—in Feminine Detail." In Chow, *Woman and Chinese Modernity: The Politics of Reading between West and East.* Minneapolis: University of Minnesota Press, 1991, 84–120.

———. "Seminal Dispersal, Fecal Retention, and Related Narrative Matters: Eileen Chang's Tale of Roses in the Problematic of Modern Writing." *differences: A Journal of Feminist Cultural Studies* 11, 2 (1999): 153–76.

Chow, Lim Chin. "Reading 'The Golden Cangue': Iron Boudoirs and Symbols of Oppressed Confucian Women." Trs. Louise Edwards and Kam Louie. *Renditions* 45 (Spring 1996): 141–49.

———. "Castration Parody and Male 'Castration': Eileen Chang's Female Writing and Her Anti-patriarchal Strategy." In Peng-hisang Chen and Whitney Crothers Dilley, eds., *Feminism/Femininity in Chinese Literature.* Amsterdam: Rodopi, 2002, 127–44.

Fu, Poshek. "Eileen Chang, Women's Film, and Domestic Culture of Modern Shanghai." *Tamkang Review* 29, 4 (Summer 1999): 9–28.

Gunn, Edward. *Unwelcome Muse: Chinese Literature in Shanghai and Peking (1937–1945).* New York: Columbia University Press, 1980, 200–31.

Hoyan Hang Fung, Carole. "On the Translation of Eileen Chang's Fiction." *Translation Quarterly* (Hong Kong), 18/19 (March, 2000): 99–136.

Hsia, C. T. "Eileen Chang." In Hsia, *A History of Modern Chinese Fiction.* 2nd ed. New Haven: Yale University Press, 1971, 389–431.

Huang, Nicole. "Eileen Chang and the Modern Essay." In Martin Woesler, ed., *The Modern Chinese Literary Essay: Defining the Chinese Self in the 20th Century.* Bochum: Bochum University Press, 2000, 67–96.

———. *Women, War, Domesticity: Shanghai Literature and Popular Culture of the 1940s.* Leiden: Brill, 2005.

Kao, Hsin-sheng C. "The Shaping of a Life: Structure and Narrative Process in Eileen Chang's *The Rouge of the North.*" In A. Palandri, ed. *Women Writers of 20th-Century China.* Eugene: Asian Studies Publications, University of Oregon, 1982, 111–37.

Lee, Leo Ou-fan. "Eileen Chang: Romances of a Fallen City." In Lee, *Shanghai Modern: The Flowering of a New Urban Culture in China, 1930–1945.* Cambridge, MA: Harvard University Press, 1999, 267–303.

———. "Eileen Chang and Cinema." *Journal of Modern Literature in Chinese* 2, 2 (Jan. 1999): 37–60.

Leung, Ping-kwan. "Two Discourses on Colonialism: Huang Guliu and Eileen Chang on Hong Kong in the Forties." *Boundary 2*. Special issue edited by Rey Chow. 25, 2 (Fall 1998): 77–96.

Lim, Chin-chown. "Reading 'The Golden Cangue': Iron Boudoirs and Symbols of Oppressed Confucian Women." Trs. Louise Edwards and Kam Louie. *Renditions* 45 (Spring 1996): 141–49.

Liu, Joyce Chi Hui. "Filmic Transposition of the Roses: Stanley Kwan's Feminine Response to Eileen Chang's Women." In Peng-hisang Chen and Whitney Crothers Dilley, eds., *Feminism/Femininity in Chinese Literature*. Amsterdam: Rodopi, 2002, 145–58.

Martin, Helmut. "'Like a Film Abruptly Torn Off': Tension and Despair in Zhang Ailing's Writing Experience." In Wolfgang Kubin, ed., *Symbols of Anguish: In Search of Melancholy in China*. Bern: Peter Lang, 2001, 353–83.

Miller, Lucien, and Hui-chuan Chang. "Fiction and Autobiography: Spatial Form in 'The Golden Cangue' and *The Woman Warrior*." In Michael S. Duke, ed., *Modern Chinese Women Writers: Critical Appraisals*. Armonk, NY: M.E. Sharpe, 1989, 24–43.

Pang, Laikwan. "Photography and Autobiography: Zhang Ailing's *Looking at Each Other*." *Modern Chinese Literature and Culture* 13, 1 (Spring 2001): 73–106.

Paolini, Shirley J., and Yen Chen-shen. "Moon, Madness and Mutilation in Eileen Chang's English Translation of *The Golden Cangue*." *Tamkang Review* 19, 1–4 (1988–89): 547–57.

Tam, Pak Shan. "Eileen Chang: A Chronology." *Renditions* 45 (Spring 1996): 6–12.

Wang, David Der-wei. "Three Hungry Women." *Boundary 2*. Special issue edited by Rey Chow. 25, 2 (Fall 1998): 47–76.

Williams, Philip F. C. "Back from Extremity: Eileen Chang's Literary Return." *Tamkang Review* 29, 3 (Spring 1999): 127–38.

Yin, Xiaoling. "Shadow of *The Dream of the Red Chamber*: An Intertextual Critique of *The Golden Cangue*." *Tamkang Review* 21, 1 (1990): 1–28.

Zhang Chengzhi

Liu, Xinmin. "Self-Making in the Wilderness: Zhang Chengzhi's Reinvention of Ethnic Identity." *American Journal of Chinese Studies* 5, 1 (1998): 89–110.

——. "Deciphering the Populist Gadfly: Cultural Polemic around Zhang Chengzhi's 'Religious Sublime.'" In Martin Woesler, ed., *The Modern Chinese Literary Essay: Defining the Chinese Self in the 20th Century*. Bochum: Bochum University Press, 2000, 227–37.

Xu, Jian. "Radical Ethnicity and Apocryphal History: Reading the Sublime Object of in Zhang Chengzhi's Late Fictions." *Positions* 10, 3 (Winter 2002): 526–46.

Zhang, Xuelian. "Muslim Identity in the Writing of Zhang Chengzhi." *Journal of the Oriental Society of Australia* 32/33 (2000/2001): 97–116.

Zhang Dachun

Yang, Xiaobin. "Telling (Hi)story: Illusory Truth or True Illusion." *Tamkang Review* 21, 2 (1990): 127–47.

Zhang Henshui

Altenburger, Roland. "Willing to Please: Zhang Henshui's Novel 'Fate in Tears and Laughter' and Mao Dun's Critique." In Raoul Findeison and Robert Gassmann, eds., *Autumn Floods: Essays in Honour of Marian Galik*. Bern: Peter Lang, 1997.

Lyell, William A. "Translator's Afterword." In *Shanghai Express*. Honolulu: University of Hawaii Press, 1997, 239–56.

McClellan, Thomas Michael. *Zhang Henshui and Popular Chinese Fiction, 1919–1949*. Lewiston, NY: Edwin Mellen Press, 2005.

Rupprecht, Hsiao-wei Wang. *Departure and Return: Chang Hen-shui and the Chinese Narrative Tradition*. Hong Kong: Joint Publishing, 1987.

Zhang Jie

Bailey, Alison. "Travelling Together: Narrative Technique in Zhang Jie's 'The Ark'" In Michael S. Duke, ed., *Modern Chinese Women Writers: Critical Appraisals*. Armonk, NY: M.E. Sharpe, 1989, 96–111.

Chan, Sylvia. "Chang Chieh's Fiction: In Search of Female Identity." *Issues and Studies* 25, 9 (1989): 85–104.

Chen, Xiaomei. "Reading Mother's Tale: Reconstructing Women's Space in Amy Tan and Zhang Jie." *CLEAR* 16 (1994): 111–32.

Lai, Amy Tak-yee. "Liberation, Confusion, Imprisonment: The Female Self in Ding Ling's 'Diary of Miss Sophie' and Zhang Jie's 'Love Must Not Be Forgotten.'" *Comparative Literature and Culture* 3 (Sept. 1998): 88–103.

Lee, Lily Xiao Hong. "Love and Marriage in Zhang Jie's Fangzhou and Zumulu: Views from Outside." *Chinese Literature and European Context: Proceedings of the 2nd International Sinological Symposium*. Bratislava: Institute of Asian and African Studies of the Slovak Academy of Sciences, 1994, 233–40.

Yang, Gladys. "Zhang Jie, a Controversial, Mainstream Writer." In Yang Bian, ed., *The Time Is Not Ripe: Contemporary China's Best Writers and Their Stories*. Beijing: Foreign Languages Press, 1991, 253–60.

Zhang Kangkang

Bryant, Daniel. "Making It Happen: Aspects of Narrative Method in Zhang Kang-kang's 'Northern Lights.'" In Michael S. Duke, ed., *Modern Chinese Women Writers: Critical Appraisals*. Armonk, NY: M.E. Sharpe, 1989, 112–34.

Zhang Tianyi

Anderson, Marsten. "Realism's Last Stand: Character and Ideology in Zhang Tianyi's *Three Sketches*." *Modern Chinese Literature* 5, 2 (1989): 179–96.
———. "Mao Dun, Zhang Tianyi, and the Social Impediments to Realism." In Anderson, *The Limits of Realism: Chinese Fiction in the Revolutionary Period*. Berkeley: University of California Press, 1990, 119–79.
Hsia, C. T. "Chang T'ien-i (1907–)." In Hsia, *A History of Modern Chinese Fiction*. 2nd ed. New Haven: Yale University Press, 1971, 212–36.
Sun, Yifeng. *Fragmentation and Dramatic Moments: Zhang Tianyi and the Narrative Discourse of Upheaval in Modern China*. New York: Peter Lang, 2002.
———. "Humour, Satire, and Parody in Zhang Tianyi's Writings." *Chinese Culture* XL, 2 (June 1999): 1–44.
Yuan, Ying. "Chang Tien-yi and His Young Readers." *Chinese Literature* 6 (1959): 137–39.

Zhang Wei

Lu, Jie. "Nostalgia without Memory: Reading Zhang Wei's Essays in the Context of *Fable of September*." In Martin Woesler, ed., *The Modern Chinese Literary Essay: Defining the Chinese Self in the 20th Century*. Bochum: Bochum University Press, 2000, 211–25.
Russell, Terrence. "Zhang Wei and the Soul of Rural China." *Tamkang Review* 35, 2 (Winter 2004): 41–56.
Xu, Jian. "Body, Earth, and Migration: The Poetics of Suffering in Zhang Wei's *September Fable*." *Modern Language Quarterly: A Journal of Literary History* 67, 2 (June 2006).

Zhang Xianliang

Fokkema, Douwe. "Modern Chinese Literature as a Result of Acculturation: The Intriguing Case of Zhang Xianliang." In Lloyd Haft, ed., *Words from the West: Western Texts in Chinese Literary Context: Essays to Honor Erik Zurcher On His Sixty-Fifth Birthday*. Leiden: CNWS Publications, 1993, 26–34.

Kinkley, Jeffrey C. "A Bettelheimian Interpretation of Chang Hsien-liang's Labor-Camp Fiction." *Asia Major* TS 4, 2 (1991): 83–114.

Li, Jun. "Zhang Xianliang and His Fiction." In Yang Bian, ed., *The Time Is Not Ripe: Contemporary China's Best Writers and Their Stories.* Beijing: Foreign Languages Press, 1991, 327–32.

Tam, Kwok-kan. "Sexuality and Power in Zhang Xianliang's Novel *Half of Man Is Woman.*" *Modern Chinese Literature* 5, 1 (1989): 55–72.

Williams, Philip F. "'Remolding' and the Chinese Labor Camp Novel." *Asia Major* TS 4, 2 (1991): 133–49.

Wu, Daming. *Zhang Xianliang: The Stories of Revelation.* Durham (UK): Durham East Asia Papers, University of Durham, 1995.

Wu, Yenna. "Women as a Source of Redemption in Chang Hsien-liang's Concentration-Camp Novels." *Asia Major* TS 4, 2 (1991): 115–32.

———. "The Interweaving of Sex and Politics in Zhang Xianliang's *Half a Man Is Woman.*" *JCLTA* 27, 1/2 (1992): 1–28.

Yue, Gang. "Postrevolutionary Leftovers: Zhang Xianliang and Ah Cheng." In Yue, *The Mouth That Begs: Hunger, Cannibalism, and the Politics of Eating in Modern China.* Durham, NC: Duke University Press, 1999, 184–221.

Zhong, Xueping. "Male Suffering and Male Desire: The Politics of Reading *Half of Man Is Woman.*" In Christina Gilmartin et al., eds., *Engendering China: Women, Culture, and the State.* Cambridge, MA: Harvard University Press, 1994, 175–91.

Zhou, Zuyan. "Animal Symbolism and Political Dissidence in *Half of Man Is Woman.*" *Modern Chinese Literature* 8 (1994): 69–95.

Zhang Xinxin

Jiang, Hong. "The Masculine-Feminine Woman: Transcending Gender Identity in Zhang Xinxin's Fiction." *China Information* 15, 1 (2001): 138–65.

Kinkley, Jeffrey C. "Modernism and Journalism in the Works of Chang Hsin-hsin." *Tamkang Review* 18, 1–4 (1987–88): 97–123.

———. "The Cultural Choices of Zhang Xinxin, A Young Writer of the 1980's." In Paul A. Cohen and Merle Goldman, eds., *Ideas across Cultures: Essays on Chinese Thought in Honor of Benjamin Schwartz.* Cambridge, MA: Council on East Asian Studies, Harvard University, 1990.

Martin, Helmut. "Social Criticism in Contemporary Chinese Literature: New Forms of *Pao-kao*—Reportage by Zhang Xinxin." *Proceedings on the Second International Conference on Sinology.* Taipei: Academia Sinica, 1989.

Roberts, Rosemary A. "Images of Women in the Fiction of Zhang Jie and Zhang Xinxin." *CQ* 120 (1989): 800–13.

Wakeman, Carolyn, and Yue Daiyun. "Fiction's End: Zhang Xinxin's New Approaches to Creativity." In Michael S. Duke, ed., *Modern Chinese Women Writers: Critical Appraisals*. Armonk, NY: M.E. Sharpe, 1989, 196–216.

Zhao Shuli

Birch, Cyril. "Chao Shu-li: Creative Writing in a Communist State." *New Mexico Quarterly* 25 (1955): 185–95.

Chung, Hilary, and Tommy McClellan, "The Command Enjoyment of Literature in China: Conferences, Controls and Excesses." In Chung, ed., *In the Party Spirit: Socialist Realism and Literary Practice in the Soviet Union, East Germany and China*. Amsterdam and Atlanta: Rodopi, 1996, 1–22.

Beyer, John. "Part Novel, Risque Film: Zhao Shuli's *Sanliwan* and the Scenario *Lovers Happy Ever After*." In Wolfgang Kubin and Rudolf Wagner, eds., *Essays in Modern Chinese Literature and Literary Criticism*. Bochum: Brokmeyer, 1982, 90–116.

Feuerwerker, Yi-tsi Mei. "Zhao Shuli: The Making of a Model Peasant Writer." In Feuerwerker, *Ideology, Power, Text: Self-Representation and the Peasant "Other" in Modern Chinese Literature*. Stanford: Stanford University Press, 1998, 100–45.

Lu Chien. "Chao Shu-li and His Writing." *Chinese Literature* 9 (1964): 21–26.

Zheng Chouyu

Kubin, Wolfgang. "The Black Knight on the Iron Horse: Cheng Ch'ou-yu's Poetical Version of the Passing Lover." In Howard Goldblatt, ed., *Worlds Apart: Recent Chinese Writing and Its Audiences*. Armonk, NY: M.E. Sharpe, 1990, 138–49.

Lin, Julia C. "Cheng Ch'ou-yu: The Keeper of the Old." In Lin, *Essays on Contemporary Chinese Poetry*. Athens, OH: Ohio University Press, 1985, 1–11.

Zheng Yi

Mi, Jiayan. "Entropic Anxiety and the Allegory of Disappearance: Hydro-Utopianism in Zheng Yi's *Old Well* and Zhang Wei's *Old Boat*." *China Information* 21 (2007): 109–40.

Yue, Gang. "Monument Revisited: Zheng Yi and Liu Zhenyun." In *The Mouth That Begs: Hunger, Cannibalism, and the Politics of Eating in Modern China*. Durham, NC: Duke University Press, 1999, 228–62.

Zhong Lihe

Ying, Fenghuang. "The Literary Development of Zhong Lihe and Postcolonial Discourse in Taiwan." In David Wang and Carlos Rojas, eds., *Writing Taiwan: A New Literary History*. Durham, NC: Duke University Press, 2006, 140–55.

Zhou Zuoren

Chow, William C. S. "Chou Tso-jen and the New Village Movement." *Chinese Studies* 10, 1 (June 1992): 105–34.

Daruvala, Susan. "Zhou Zuoren: 'At Home' in Tokyo." In Gregory Lee, ed., *Chinese Writing and Exile*. Chicago: Center for East Asian Studies, The University of Chicago, 1993, 35–54.

———. *Zhou Zuoren and an Alternative Chinese Response to Modernity*. Cambridge, MA: Harvard University Asia Center, 2000.

Galik, Marian. "Hu Shih, Chou Tso-jen, Ch'en Tu-hsiu and the Beginning of Modern Chinese Literary Criticism." In Galik, *The Genesis of Modern Chinese Liteary Criticism (1917–1930)*. London: Curzon Press, 1980, 9–27.

Liu, Haoming. "From Little Savages to *hen kai pan*: Zhou Zuoren's (1885–1968) Romanticist Impulses around 1920." *Asia Major* 15, 1 (2002): 109–60.

Lu, Yan. "Beyond Politics in Wartime: Zhou Zuoren, 1931–1945." *Sino-Japanese Studies* 11, 1 (Oct. 1998): 6–13.

Pollard, D. E. *A Chinese Look at Literature: The Literary Values of Chou Tso-jen in Relation to the Tradition*. London: C. Hurst and Co., 1973.

———. "Chou Tso-jen: A Scholar Who Withdrew." In Charlotte Furth, ed., *The Limits of Change: Essays on Conservative Alternatives in Republican China*. Cambridge, MA: Harvard University Press, 1976, 332–56.

Wang, C. H. "Chou Tso-jen's Hellenism." In Tak-Wai Wong, ed., *East West Comparative Literature: Cross-Cultural Discourse*. Hong Kong: Hong Kong Chinese University Press, 1993.

Wolff, Ernst. *Chou Tso-jen*. New York: Twayne, 1971.

Zhang, Xudong. "A Radical Hermeneutics of Chinese Literary Tradition: On Zhou Zuoren's *Zhongguo xinwenxue de yuanliu*." In Ching-i Tu, ed., *Classics and Interpretations: The Hermeneutic Traditions in Chinese Culture*. New Brunswick, NJ: Transaction Publishers, 2000, 427–55.

Zhu Tianwen

Berry, Michael. "Words and Images: A Conversation with Hou Hsiao-hsien and Chu T'ien-wen." *Positions* 11, 3 (Winter 2003): 675–716.

Chang, Sung-sheng Yvonne. "Chu T'ien-wen and Taiwan's Recent Cultural and Literary Trends." *Modern Chinese Literature* 6, 1/2 (1992): 61–84.

Chen, Ling-chei Letty. "Rising from the Ashes: Identity and Aesthetics of Hybridity in Zhu Tianwen's *Notes of a Desolate Man.*" *Journal of Modern Literature in Chinese* 4, 1 (2000): 101–38.

———. "Writing Taiwan's Fin-de-Siecle Splendor: Zhu Tianwen and Zhu Tianxin." In Joshua Mostow, ed., and Kirk A. Denton, China section, ed., *Columbia Companion to Modern East Asian Literatures.* New York: Columbia University Press, 2003, 584–91.

Chiang, Shu-chen. "Rejection of Postmodern Abandon: Zhu Tianwen's Fin-de-siecle Splendor." In Peng-hisang Chen and Whitney Crothers Dilley, eds., *Feminism/Femininity in Chinese Literature.* Amsterdam: Rodopi, 2002, 45–66.

Chiu, Kuei-fen. "Identity Politics in Contemporary Women's Novels in Taiwan." In Peng-hisang Chen and Whitney Crothers Dilley, eds., *Feminism/Femininity in Chinese Literature.* Amsterdam: Rodopi, 2002, 67–86.

Dutrait, Noel. "Four Taiwanese Writers on Themselves: Chu T'ien-wen, Su Wei Chen, Cheng Chiung-ming and Ye Lingfang Respond to Our Questionnaire." *China Perspectives* 17 (May/June 1998).

Hsiu-Chuang, Deppman. "Recipes for a New Taiwanese Identity? Food, Space, and Sex in the Works of Ang Lee, Ming-liang Tsai, and T'ien-wen Chu." *American Journal of Chinese Studies* 8, 2 (Oct. 2001): 145–68.

Zhu Xining

Birch, Cyril. "The Function of Intertextual Reference in Zhu Xining's 'Daybreak.'" In Theodore Huters, ed., *Reading the Modern Chinese Short Story.* Armonk, NY: M.E. Sharpe, 1990, 105–118.

Feng, Jin. "Narrating Suffering, Constructing Chinese Modernity: The Emergence of the Modern Subject in Chinese Literature." *East Asia* 18, 1 (Spring 2000): 82–109.

Zhu Ziqing

Fried, Daniel A. "Zhu Ziqing, Frantz Fanon, and the Fierce White Children." In Martin Woesler, ed., *The Modern Chinese Literary Essay: Defining the Chinese Self in the 20th Century.* Bochum: Bochum University Press, 2000, 99–114.

Wagner, Alexandra R. "Tradition as Construct and the Search for a Modern Identity: A Reading of Traditional Gestures in Modern Chinese Essays of Place." In Martin Woesler, ed., *The Modern Chinese Literary Essay: Defining the Chinese Self in the 20th Century.* Bochum: Bochum University Press, 2000, 133–46.

About the Author

Li-hua Ying was born and raised in southwestern China. After receiving her bachelor's degree in English from Yunnan Normal University in Kunming, she came to the United States in 1982 to pursue her graduate studies at the University of Texas in Austin. She received her master's degree in English in 1985 with a thesis on the American poet Marianne Moore. In the Comparative Literature Department, also at the University of Texas, she reacquainted herself with the Chinese literary tradition that she had grown up with and enrolled in a combined program of English and American literature and Chinese literature. She was granted her Ph.D. degree in 1991. Her dissertation examined the impact of Western modernism on Chinese literature in the 1980s, particularly the root-seeking movement.

Dr. Ying has taught at Yunnan Normal University, Southwestern University (Texas), University of Texas at Austin, and is presently at Bard College in Annandale-on-Hudson, New York, where she is director of the Chinese Program and teaches a wide range of courses on Chinese literature, both classical and modern, including Modern Chinese Fiction, Writing across the Strait: Literature from Taiwan and China, The Theme of Exile in Chinese Poetry and Fiction, Chinese Theater, and others. Along with various articles and papers, she has written the book *Cihai wenhui* (Magic of the Word: New Trends in Chinese Expressions). Her recent research interest is the representation of Tibet in literature and mass media. She has published translations of contemporary Chinese and American poetry, including poems by Zhang Zao, in *Another Kind of Nation: An Anthology of Contemporary Chinese Poetry*, edited by Zhang Er and Chen Dongdong. Dr. Ying also has an abiding interest in Chinese calligraphy and has taught and written on its history and aesthetics. As the executive director of the American Association of *Shufa* Calligraphy Education, an academic organization based in the United States with an international membership, she is actively engaged in promoting Chinese calligraphy education in the West.